Law, Marriage, and Society in the Later Middle Ages

Arguments About Marriage in Five Courts

This is a study of marriage litigation (with some reference to sexual offenses) in the archiepiscopal court of York (1300–1500) and the episcopal courts of Ely (1374–1381), Paris (1384–1387), Cambrai (1438–1453), and Brussels (1448–1459). All these courts were, for the most part, correctly applying the late medieval canon law of marriage, but statistical analysis of the cases and results confirms that there were substantial differences in both the types of cases the courts heard and the results they reached. Marriages in England in the later Middle Ages, the book argues, were more often under the control of the parties to the marriage, whereas those in northern France and the southern Netherlands were more often under the control of the parties' families and social superiors. Within this broad generalization the book brings to light patterns of late medieval men and women manipulating each other and the courts to produce extraordinarily varied results.

As explained in Notes About This Book, the section called 'Texts and Commentary', together with the Table of Cases, Index of Persons and Places, and Table of Authorities may be found on the website (www.cambridge.org/9780521877282) or in the e-book.

Charles Donahue, Jr., is the Paul A. Freund Professor of Law at Harvard Law School and immediate past president of the American Society of Legal History. Among other books, he is the coauthor or coeditor of *Select Cases of the Ecclesiastical Courts of the Province of Canterbury, c. 1200–1301*; *Year Books of Richard II: 6 Richard II, 1382–1383*; *The Records of the Medieval Ecclesiastical Courts*; and *Cases and Materials on Property: An Introduction to the Concept and the Institution.* He is also the author of more than 70 articles in the fields of ancient, medieval, and early modern legal history. Donahue teaches legal history in both the Law School and the Faculty of Arts and Sciences at Harvard and has taught at the University of Michigan, the London School of Economics, the Vrije Universiteit te Brussel, Columbia University, the University of California at Berkeley, Boston College, and Cornell University. Donahue is vice-president and literary director of the Ames Foundation and a councillor of the Selden Society (UK). He is a Fellow of the Royal Historical Society and a previous Guggenheim Fellow.

Law, Marriage, and Society in the Later Middle Ages

Arguments About Marriage in Five Courts

CHARLES DONAHUE, Jr.
Harvard Law School

CAMBRIDGE
UNIVERSITY PRESS

CAMBRIDGE
UNIVERSITY PRESS

University Printing House, Cambridge CB2 8BS, United Kingdom

One Liberty Plaza, 20th Floor, New York, NY 10006, USA

477 Williamstown Road, Port Melbourne, VIC 3207, Australia

314-321, 3rd Floor, Plot 3, Splendor Forum, Jasola District Centre, New Delhi - 110025, India

79 Anson Road, #06-04/06, Singapore 079906

Cambridge University Press is part of the University of Cambridge.

It furthers the University's mission by disseminating knowledge in the pursuit of education, learning and research at the highest international levels of excellence.

www.cambridge.org
Information on this title: www.cambridge.org/9780521877282

First published 2007

A catalogue record for this publication is available from the British Library

Library of Congress Cataloging in Publication data
Donahue, Charles, 1941–
Law, marriage, and society in the later Middle Ages / Charles Donahue, Jr.
p. cm.
Includes bibliographical references and index.
ISBN 978-0-521-87728-2 (hardback)
1. Matrimonial actions – Europe – History – To 1500. 2. Matrimonial actions (Canon law) – History – To 1500. I. Title.
KJC1100.D66 2007
346.01′660902 – dc22 2007001747

ISBN 978-0-521-87728-2 Hardback

Additional resources for this publication at www.cambridge.org/delange

Contents

Tables

Preface

This book had its origins in a remarkable seminar given by Stephan Kuttner and Peter Landau more than 40 years ago. At that time those of us in law schools were enamored of what we called 'policy', looking at legal doctrine from the point of view of the social objectives it was designed to achieve, or could be used to achieve. As we read Alexander III's decisions on the topic of the formation of marriage in the seminar, it struck me that the policy of those decisions was to enhance the power and control of the couple over their choice of marriage partners at the expense of others (parents, lords, etc.) who might seek to dictate that choice. I wanted to study how Alexander's decisions were used in actual cases in order to determine whether they had had this effect.

While I have not abandoned the notion that the classical canon law could have been used to enhance the freedom of a marrying couple and that it was, in some sense, designed to achieve this effect, I look back now on those initial thoughts as somewhat naïve. My understanding, and, I think, that of those who study law generally, of what goes into making an important legal change has deepened, but it has also become more incoherent. Rare is the important legal change that can be explained simply on the basis of 'policy considerations', as we understood them in the mid-1960s, and Alexander's decisions are not among those that can. A full study of the context in which those decisions arose must await another book. The Introduction offers a survey of the work that has been done since the mid-1960s, tracing their effect in actual cases. As this book and the work of others show, it is a complicated story, one that reveals remarkable variations, variations that seem to be based on the type of institution that applied Alexander's decisions, the types of people to whom they were applied, the period in which they were being applied, and – the factor that this book emphasizes (without, I hope, ignoring the others) – the place where the applications occurred.

Forty years is a long time, and one's attitudes change over time. When I took the seminar I was in my early twenties; I had just married; I had written my bachelor's essay on *Romeo and Juliet*, and I thought that Alexander's decisions were unqualifiedly a Good Thing. I am now in my mid-60s and have just become a grandfather. *Romeo and Juliet* is no longer my favorite Shakespeare play, though I still prefer *As You Like It* to *King Lear*. I still think that Alexander's decisions were a good thing, but the story that this book tells is, in many ways, a story about how they did not work.

Acknowledgments

Forty years is a long time, and the debts that I have accumulated over those years cannot be repaid, certainly not with this book. The first is to Sheila, who had no idea what she was getting into when her new husband started mumbling about Alexander III in the spring of 1965 and who has tried to teach me over the years what marriage is all about. Archivists in England and on the Continent have been unfailingly generous to a grouchy American with a thick accent, none more so than David Smith of the Borthwick Institute for Archives in York. It is largely due to his efforts that the Institute's splendid collection of cause papers, which were virtually unusable when I first looked at them more than 30 years ago, are now easily accessible. Research assistants who have, or can learn, the skills necessary to help with this kind of project are rare. There have been a number, but four stand out: David Dasef (who was able to make sense of my handwritten notes because he, too, had worked on the cause papers at the Borthwick), Kate Gilbert (who will recognize some of her descriptions of late fourteenth- and early fifteenth-century York cases), Diana Moses (who corrected the translations and reminded me that a translation ought, in the first place, to be in English; those that are not are the result of my stubbornness), and Kyle Young (who helped to proofread the text and to normalize the footnotes in a book written over many years). Two anonymous readers for Cambridge University Press were both encouraging and helpful, in a dark moment. Marcia Stentz and Monique Vleeschouwers-van Melkebeek shared with me unpublished work on the courts of Ely and of Tournai, respectively. I am particularly grateful to a group too numerous to mention individually: friends and colleagues who offered comments on pieces of this book given as papers. I have tried to acknowledge specific assistance that I received on particular matters in the notes. One person must be named here: Jane Bestor read a draft of this book that was so long that I was ashamed to show it to anyone, and she told me that I had two books and where to divide them.

Thanks of a different sort are owing to Dunker & Humblot, GmbH, Berlin, for permission to use portions of Donahue, "English and French Marriage

Cases," which appear in Chapters 7, 10, and 12; to the *Northern Kentucky Law Review*, for permission to use portions of Donahue, "A Legal Historian Looks at the Case Method," which appears in Chapter 2, to the University of Michigan Press for permission to use portions of Donahue, "Female Plaintiffs" (© by the University of Michigan 1993), which appear in the Introduction and in Chapter 3; and to Oxford University Press for permission to use a portion of Donahue, "Comparative Law" (© by the editors 2006), in the Epilogue. In all cases, the material has been substantially rewritten. Unpublished material from the Borthwick Institute for Archives at the University of York appears with the kind permission of C. C. Webb, the Keeper of Archives, and that from the Ely Diocesan Records with that of P. M. Meadows, Keeper of Ely Diocesan Records, Cambridge University Library. The image on the dust jacket appears with the permission of Harry S. Martin, Librarian of the Harvard Law School Library.

I would like to express particular thanks to Dean Elena Kagan of the Harvard Law School not only for encouragement over the years, including a sabbatical leave that allowed the book to be completed, but also for the generous subvention of the publication costs of the book, provided from research funds of the School. Many years ago the John Solomon Guggenheim Foundation gave me a fellowship that it thought was going to result in this book. It did, though the length of time that intervened must have led the Foundation to wonder whether it would ever happen.

Neither Charles Donahue, Sr, nor Rosemary Spang Donahue lived to see this book. It is dedicated to their memory.

Notes About This Book

The original version of this book, even after the division, was half again as long as it is now. Most of the material no longer in the book was in the footnotes: Latin quotations from the cases, discussions of alternative interpretations, references to primary sources that support the argument, and references to the literature on the cases, with discussions where I disagreed with it. All of these things are of some interest to the specialist but of limited value to the general scholarly reader. They are now to be found in the electronic version of this book under the label 'Texts and Commentary' (T&C), with a brief reference given in the footnotes here in the following forms: 'T&C no.' (followed by a number) within a case name means that a quotation from the case is to be found in the e-book under the number given; 'Ref. T&C no.' means that the item contains supporting references; 'Lit. T&C no.' means that the item contains references to the literature (and, normally, discussion of it); 'Disc. T&C no.' means that the item contains further discussion of the matter. I thought of eliminating all such material from the footnotes, but enough of it remains in the shorter notes that the reader will get some idea of what types of material can be found in the e-book. For the reader of the paper version of the book the material that is only in the e-book is available on a website: www.cambridge.org/9780521877282.

The e-book also contains the following tables and appendices to the chapters, which are referred to in the footnotes by their table and appendix number, rather than their T&C number:

Appendix e3.1. The Business of the Court of York, 1300–1500 in Detail (T&C no. 95)

Table e3.App.1. York Cause Papers by Decade and Type of Case (Fourteenth Century) (T&C no. 95)

Table e3.App.2. York Cause Papers by Decade and Type of Case (Fifteenth century) (T&C no. 95)

Appendix e3.2. The Chronological Imbalance in the Surviving York Cause Papers (T&C no. 149)

The name and style of the parties given in the record is frequently telling. *Marjorie daughter of Simon Tailour and servant of William de Burton leather-dresser of York c John Beek saddler of York*[1] obviously tells us more about the parties (and perhaps what the case was about) than does the standard 'short form' *Tailour c Beek*. There are, however, more than a thousand cases cited in this book, and giving the full form of the name of every case, particularly where no use is made of it, would considerably increase its length. I have therefore used the short form in all the references except in those cases where I have used in the discussion information provided by the long form. Similarly, cross-references are given to other places where the case is discussed only where it is relevant to the topic under discussion at the time. Dates and manuscript references (or references to the edition) are normally given only once, with cross-references in the other places where the case is cited. Where the references are unusually long, that fact is indicated by the note 'refs. in TCas', indicating that the references will be found in the the full Table of Cases in the e-book, which gives the long form of the name of the case and all the references to it. The key to the table (and to the cross-references in the book) is the short form of the case name. The short form omits all prefixes (*de*, *le*, *vander*, etc.) whether the clerk has separated them in his rendition of the name or not (e.g., 'Deplatea' has a short form, 'Platea').

Because of the nature of the surviving records, only the year of grace is given in the dates appended to the York case names, and even these must be regarded as only approximate. Beginning in Chapter 6, where we are relying on registers, the dating can be more precise. Here, I have used the form '1.i.85' or '1.i.1385' (for 1 January 1385), which has the advantage of being concise and unambiguous across dating conventions.

Unpublished material at the Borthwick Institute for Archives in York is cited by the archive reference number (in most cases, 'CP', followed by a letter and a number).[2] Unpublished material in the Cambridge University Library (Ely) is cited by the folio number of the Ely Act Book (Ely Diocesan Records D2/1). Paris material edited in Petit, *Registre* is cited by column number. Material from Cambrai diocese is cited to the two editions of the Vleeschouwers by document number, the two works being distinguished, as indicated in the next paragraph, by the language of the name of the case.[3]

In descriptions of cases I refer to parties by their Christian names, as the records normally do, except in cases where that would create an ambiguity (a case, for example, that has two Johns or two Joans). I have also named the parties and the cases in the language that is now spoken in the area. That created some problems in the case of Cambrai, and here I followed the practice of the editors of the *Liber sentenciarum* and the *Registres de sentences* of using French for the court at Cambrai and Dutch for that at Brussels. I have translated

[1] (1372), CP. E.121.

[2] The number refers to a file containing from as few as 1 to more than 50 documents (see Ch 3, n. 5). The individual documents are, for the most part, not numbered, but the researcher familiar with the diplomatic of medieval court records should be able to find the particular document to which I am referring on the basis of my description of it.

[3] The Table of Cases gives both page number and document number.

pars actrix and *pars rea* as 'plaintiff' and 'defendant', but have kept the Latin *actor*, *actrix*, *reus*, *rea* (which is found in the records, though less often in the academic procedural writing) where it was necessary to distinguish the parties' genders.

Cross-references are given by footnote number rather than page number. Where they are preceded by 'at', the reference is to the text, as well as, or in lieu of, the note. Where there is no chapter number given before the reference, the reference is internal to the chapter. Cross-references to footnotes also include the T&C cited in the note.

In translations, *dictus*, *antedictus*, and so on, are left out, and the definite article substituted where appropriate. With one exception in Chapter 2, I have not tried to translate direct quotations in the Latin of the depositions into the vernacular of the time. I have, however, kept the distinction between 'thou/thee' and 'ye/you' that the English clerks preserve with various forms of 'tu' and 'vos'. As is well known, English preserved the distinction between the familiar and polite forms of the second person singular well into the seventeenth century, and the usage tells us something about the relations between the people speaking, most notably where a man exchanges words of marital consent with a woman using the 'thou' form, and she replies using the 'ye' form.

Translation of technical legal terms is always problematical. I would prefer not to translate them at all, but I hoped for a book that would be comprehensible to those who are not familiar with the terminology of the *ius commune*, the law taught in the medieval universities, and, for the most part, applied in the ecclesiastical courts that are featured in this book. Most of the technical terminology of the law discussed in this book is defined in Chapter 1, and that used or implied in the registers of the courts is discussed at the beginning of Chapter 6 (at nn. 4–6), where we introduce our first register.

In transcriptions (now mostly in the e-book), extension of standard abbreviations and correction of obvious errors are done silently. Editorial additions are marked in square brackets ([]). Ellipses in square brackets ([. . .]) mean that something is missing or illegible in the manuscript; without square brackets, they simply mean that I did not reproduce the full document. Diamond brackets (<>) indicate something that is in the text that should be omitted. Carats (^^) mean that what is within the carats is interlined; 'x-[word]-x' means that a word or words are crossed out or deleted. Doubtful readings are preceded by a question mark (?). Where necessary, the end of a line in the manuscript is indicated by a slash (/). In quotations from modern and early modern editions I have normalized spelling (e.g., substituting 'i' for 'j') and punctuation.

References in the footnotes are radically abbreviated. Except in the case of the Bible (cited by standard short forms) and English statutes (cited by regnal year and chapter), full references are given in the Bibliography. I have tried to provide in the margin (as noted, the 'margin' is for the most part in the T&C section of the e-book) the original of everything that I have quoted in translation in the text. In the case of Paris and the two courts of Cambrai diocese, I have been considerably fuller in providing the original Latin text. I have done so both because there are more inferences that need to be drawn from these cryptic records and because the amount of editing that would have been required to provide comparable quotations from the unpublished records of York and Ely would have delayed the production of this book considerably. In the case of York and Ely, a number of previous works have contained transcriptions of the material, and where they have I have normally referred to, but not reproduced, those transcriptions. By contrast, the Paris and Cambrai editions are not easily available to English-speaking readers, and that fact is another reason why more from them is included here.

Introduction

The law of marriage of Western Europe in the Middle Ages was canon law, and it was complicated. The basic principles, however, of that law from the late twelfth century into the sixteenth were deceptively simple: (1) Present consent freely exchanged between a man and a woman capable of marriage makes a marriage that is indissoluble so long as both of them live, unless, prior to the consummation of the marriage, one of them chooses to enter the religious life. (2) Future consent freely exchanged between a man and a woman capable of marriage makes an absolutely indissoluble marriage so long as both of them live, if, subsequent to the exchange of future consent and prior to the formation of another marriage, the couple who have exchanged future consent have sexual intercourse with each other. (3) Any Christian man is capable of marrying any Christian woman so long as: (a) both are over the age of puberty and capable of sexual intercourse; (b) neither was previously married to someone who is still alive; (c) neither has taken a solemn vow of chastity, and the man is not in major orders (subdeacon, deacon, priest, or bishop), and (d) they are not too closely related to each other.[1] This last requirement was, indeed, complicated, but I will argue in this book that it was not so important socially as it used to be – and to some extent still is – thought to be.

These rules, and particularly the first two, can first be seen clearly in a series of decisions, known as decretals, rendered by Pope Alexander III (1159–81). The story of their origin and development is the topic for another book. Suffice it to say here that while research over the last 30 years points to academic and papal predecessors of Alexander who anticipated, to some extent, his decisions and to the importance of both academics and popes who followed Alexander in ensuring the acceptance of these rules, it has, at least in my view, confirmed

[1] See Ch 1, at nn. 13–72, for further details.

the pivotal role that Alexander played. I therefore feel comfortable calling the first two of them 'Alexander's rules'.[2]

The striking thing about Alexander's rules on the formation of marriage is not what they require but what they do not require. Although, as we shall see, the church strongly encouraged couples to solemnize their marriages, no solemnity or ceremony of any sort was necessary to contract a valid marriage.[3] There did not even have to be witnesses to the exchange of consent if both parties admitted that it took place and if the rights of third parties were not involved. Further, in an age characterized by arranged marriages and elaborate provisions in the secular law for feudal consents to be given to marriages, it is striking to find that Alexander required the consent of no one other than the parties themselves for the validity of the marriage.[4] Finally, in an age also characterized by class consciousness, it is surprising to discover that the only significant restrictions on the capacity of persons to choose marriage partners were the rules prohibiting the marriage of close relatives.[5]

In marked contrast to what seems to be reflected in Alexander's rules, marriage in the twelfth and in the three subsequent centuries, not only as a matter of secular law but also as a matter of social fact, was not the exclusive concern of the parties to the marriage. Family, financial, and feudal concerns at all levels of society and also political and military concerns at the upper levels of society dictated, in many instances, marriage choice.[6] There is evidence that the choice of the parties, particularly of the woman, was hardly considered in many marriage dealings.[7] Legal and literary evidence and that of diplomatic history combine to attest to these facts. For example, in many parts of England the daughter (and in some cases the son) of a man who held land by unfree tenure could not be married unless the tenant made a payment, known as *merchet*, to his lord.[8] Much of the land held by free tenure was subject to the lord's right of wardship and marriage, which, at the very least, meant that he could give in marriage (or sell the right to give in marriage) an infant heir or heiress, and may at times have meant that he had to consent to the marriage of any female tenant and the female child or close female relative of a male tenant.[9] The extensive records concerning dower and *maritagium* attest to the importance of the financial elements in marriages.[10] This impression is confirmed by literary

[2] The formulation of the first rule was not completely clear until the pontificate of Innocent III (1198–1215). See Ch 1, at nn. 5–6.
[3] Donahue, "Policy," 259–60.
[4] *Id.*, 256–7, and sources cited.
[5] Disc. T&C no. 1.
[6] Lit. T&C no. 2.
[7] Duby, "Les 'Jeunes'," 839, quoted T&C no. 3.
[8] Lit. T&C no. 4.
[9] See Holdsworth, *History of English Law*, 3:61–6, and sources cited; Pollock and Maitland, *History of English Law*, 1:318–29.
[10] See *id.*, 2:15–16, 420–8; Milsom, *Historical Foundations*, 167–72, and sources cited in both.

evidence, a striking example of which may be found in the *Paston Letters*.[11] The importance of marriage as a device for securing political and military alliances in the upper levels of society is too well known to need documentation.[12]

The preceding paragraphs were drawn from an article written more than 30 years ago, as the age of the references (a fact now buried in the Bibliography) shows.[13] That article also complained that social historians had to do better than Howard's *History of Matrimonial Institutions* if legal historians were properly to do their jobs. The last thirty years have seen an explosion of studies of medieval marriage and the family. There is so much that one can hardly keep up with it. The late Georges Duby, whose work in this area was just beginning 30 years ago, produced two books and a number of articles on the topic.[14] In his view, two 'models' of marriage were competing in the period from roughly 1050 to 1300: a secular one that was built on the lineage, sought tightly to control marriage choice, and had a tendency to marry in; and an ecclesiastical one that was unconcerned with lineage, emphasized the choice of the marrying couple rather than that of their families or lords, and insisted on exogamy. A recent work carries Duby's idea into the fourteenth and fifteenth centuries and argues that at least among the nobility, the tension between these two models of marriage persisted.[15] Having announced in a pioneering article on marriage cases in the Ely act book of the late fourteenth century that the attitudes toward marriage revealed in the book were "astonishingly individualistic," the late Michael Sheehan proceeded subtly to outline all of the factors that were likely to go into marriage choices in later medieval England.[16] He came to the conclusion that families, and in some places and for some people, lords, played an important role and that runaway marriages, though possible, were perhaps not that common. Others have emphasized the theme of a uniquely English individualism, but the tendency in the literature, which seems, for the most part, to deal with a slightly later period, is to emphasize a similarity if not a sameness between England and at least the northwestern parts the Continent with regard to family structure and marriage choice.[17] While the recent literature quite rightly emphasizes differences across class, temporal, and geographical lines, the basic point of the previous paragraph has been confirmed. Marriage in the twelfth and in the three subsequent centuries was not the exclusive concern of the marriage parties, and this was true at every level of society for which we have records.[18]

[11] See, e.g., *Paston Letters* 2:347–9 (no. 607), 363–6 (no. 617).

[12] See literature cited in n. 6; cf. Duby, "Lignage, noblesse, et chevalerie."

[13] Donahue, "Policy," 256–7.

[14] Duby, *Chevalier*; Duby, *Medieval Marriage*; Duby, *Mâle Moyen Age* (a collection of essays).

[15] Ribordy, *Faire les nopces*.

[16] Compare Sheehan, "Formation," 76, with Sheehan, "Choice of Marriage Partner."

[17] Lit. T&C no. 5.

[18] See Hanawalt, *Ties That Bound*, esp. 197–204; Bennett, *Women in the Medieval English Countryside*.

The article then asked what the effect of Alexander's rules was on this social pattern. It noted that until recently the only way in which we could study the effect of Alexander's rules was by drawing inferences from theological and legal commentary and conciliar legislation. The chief evil the rules led to, at least as perceived by commentators throughout the Middle Ages and into the sixteenth century, was clandestine marriages. 'Clandestine marriage' is a troublesome term because it can mean a number of things: a marriage that cannot be proved for a lack of witnesses or other evidence, a marriage that can be proved but lacks any ceremony *in facie ecclesie*, or a marriage celebrated *in facie* but lacking some element of the prescribed ceremony, for example, banns. These are distinctions to which we will have to return, but that clandestine marriages were of concern can be seen by the outpouring of legislation against such marriages in both general and local councils from before the time of Alexander until the council of Trent.[19]

A whole complex of pastoral, governmental, and jurisprudential reasons combined to stimulate the concern with clandestine marriages. For the secular law it was important that who was married to whom be a matter of public knowledge so that the complex of property rights and duties that arose out of the married state might be determined with reasonable certainty.[20] For a church that was prepared to punish fornication and adultery through a system of public criminal law, the same knowledge was also desirable. Further, since marriage was a sacrament, the church had an interest in seeing to it that the parties were in fact capable of matrimony, that they did not enter into it lightly, and that their entry into the state of matrimony be accompanied by ceremonies, such as the blessing and the nuptial mass, which befitted the sacrament.[21] Further, 'occult' clandestine marriages led to two highly undesirable results: They permitted an unscrupulous man to have sexual relations with a woman after an exchange of words of marital consent and later free himself from the consequences of the relationship by perjuring himself and denying that the words were ever exchanged.[22] Further, those who entered into an occult marriage relationship, even in good faith, and later publicly married others would be compelled by the church to live a state of adultery; the public marriage would be enforced when the previous union could not be proven. Both of these consequences were the result of the insistence of the external forum on independent witnesses to prove the exchange of present consent, a rule that created an undesirable tension between the external and internal fora.[23] This tension could also occur where the clandestine union was not occult but where the words exchanged were ambiguous or imperfectly remembered by the witnesses.[24]

[19] See Ch 1, at nn. 73–88.

[20] See Pollock and Maitland, *History of English Law*, 2:374–84.

[21] Howard, *History of Matrimonial Institutions*, 1:291–314.

[22] *Id.* at 350, citing Whitford, *Werke for Householders*.

[23] Ref. T&C no. 6.

[24] See Howard, *History of Matrimonial Institutions*, 1:340–4; Luther, *Von Ehesachen*, 102–3, in *Werke* 23.

All of these objections to clandestine marriages were serious ones. The desire to ensure that the parties were capable of matrimony, that is, that there were no impediments, was the most frequently cited reason for legislation against clandestine marriages, but each of the other reasons probably provided some motivating force for these legislative efforts. There is one further objection, however, which may have been critical: The availability of clandestine marriage permitted persons, if they were sufficiently desperate, to escape from the complex of family, financial, and feudal concerns that surrounded marriage and to enter into a valid marriage without the consent of their families or their lords, and even without their families or lords knowing about it.[25] The most familiar evidence of this phenomenon is literary, the legend of Romeo and Juliet, which originates in pre-Tridentine Italy.[26] But the most striking evidence that this particular effect of Alexander's rules on the formation of marriage was among the chief objections to these rules may be seen in the history of the Tridentine decree *Tametsi*.[27] The delegates of the king of France to the council were instructed to press for a rule that would make the consent of the parents of the marriage parties (if the parties were under parental power) a necessary element for a valid marriage. The earlier drafts of the decree contain this requirement. Only in the final draft of *Tametsi* did the council omit this requirement and return to what we might suggest is the spirit of Alexander's rules by providing that promulgation of the banns might be dispensed with where there was reason to fear force.[28]

This evidence is well known and was well known 30 years ago. What the earlier article sought to do was to begin to explore another body of material, the records of the ecclesiastical courts themselves, to determine whether they provided evidence that Alexander's rules had the effect that we suspected on *a priori* grounds they might have had and that at least some contemporaries thought that they had. At the time, relatively little work had been done on the records of those courts. R. H. Helmholz had written a dissertation on marriage litigation in the English ecclesiastical courts, which was to appear as a monograph; Michael Sheehan had written an article on marriage litigation in the only surviving medieval register of the Ely consistory court; I had begun some work on the cause papers of the York consistory.[29] On the basis of this evidence, I concluded, somewhat rashly I now confess, that Alexander's rules did have the effect of breaking down, at least in some instances, the control that families had over marriage choice and, even more rashly, that Alexander had intended them to have this effect.

There was more pioneering work contemporaneous with the article. Anne Lefebvre had written, and by the time the article was published, had published,

[25] Disc. T&C no. 7.

[26] Disc. T&C no. 8.

[27] See Epilogue and Conclusion, at nn. 1–5.

[28] Council of Trent, sess. 24, *Canones super reformatione matrimonii*, c. 1 (*Tametsi*), in *Decrees of the Ecumenical Councils*, 2:756.

[29] Helmholz, *Marriage Litigation*; Sheehan, "Formation"; Donahue, "Policy," 261–6.

a dissertation on the French ecclesiastical courts in the later Middle Ages, and Beatrice Gottlieb was writing, and by the time the article was published, had finished, a dissertation on marriage litigation in two northern French dioceses.[30] Gottlieb argued that the objection to clandestine marriage in the sixteenth century was political rather than social. The cases did not reveal many runaway marriages. There had been one in the Montmorency family that may have accounted for the edict of Henry II on the topic in 1557, but ordinary people were getting married in the ordinary way, normally with the advice and consent of their families and friends. Lefebvre had not concentrated on the issue of clandestine marriage, but what she reported about the French cases in her period looked very different from what those of us who had been working in England saw.

Clearly, a systematic comparison of the English and French material was called for. At first, I attempted a survey of all the surviving French medieval records and published the preliminary results of that survey, including some comparisons with England.[31] I became dissatisfied with the approach of that article, however, because the more that I got into the records, the more I realized that a very large variety of situations was revealed in them. The issue of control of marriage choice was there, sometimes on the face of the record, sometimes so close behind it that it could, without too much speculation, be inferred. There were, however, many other social situations in which medieval men and women invoked Alexander's rules or had them invoked against them. Again, sometimes these situations were obvious on the face of the record, and sometimes, again without too much speculation, they could be inferred. In short, medieval marriage cases illustrate a wide variety of legal problems and social situations. If one looks for it, one can find evidence to support almost any proposition about the effect of Alexander's rules, particularly if one is satisfied with the evidence of one or a few cases.

Perhaps one should be satisfied with the particular.[32] Human experience is extraordinarily varied, and the relationship between the law and that experience is anything but simple. But the mind seeks to impose patterns on the variety, to understand the experience by grouping like cases to see if larger patterns can be discerned. Fortunately, the litigation experience in medieval marriage cases can be organized into distinct categories; perhaps the underlying social experience can be so organized as well. Unfortunately, in order to do so, we are going to have to make use of numbers – 'statistics' is probably too grand a term for it.

The reasons for the need to use numbers are simple. While the surviving records of the later medieval ecclesiastical courts are not so extensive as those of the English secular royal courts or even the French secular courts, there are, when added up, records of thousands of medieval ecclesiastical marriage

[30] Lefebvre-Teillard, *Officialités*; Gottlieb, *Getting Married.*

[31] Donahue, "Canon Law and Social Practice."

[32] The next four paragraphs are derived from Donahue, "Female Plaintiffs."

cases.[33] A lifetime is too short for one person to read all of them, and the laborers are few. The only hope for getting some idea of the whole is to sample them and to describe them numerically. Skimming over the material and picking out what seem to be the most interesting records may yield an answer to certain kinds of questions, such as when a form or an idea first appeared, or when a form or an idea became part of the regular practice of a court. But the answers to these questions may benefit from the greater precision that numbers can give: When the form or idea first appeared, did it begin slowly or did it spread rapidly? What do we mean when we say that a form or idea was the 'regular' practice of a court? Underlying both questions is an implicit quantitative statement, a percentage of total cases, or of total surviving cases. Words such as 'slowly', 'rapidly', and 'regular' are proxies for a judgment about what underlying numerical measures indicate.

When we come to ask the question, moreover, of what effect the activities of the court had on society and of what effect society, as opposed to, or in addition to, the academic law, had on the behavior of the courts, the question 'how much' becomes even more critical. In a legal system, such as medieval canon law, where decisions in individual cases were not meant to set precedents for the decisions of other cases, the range of possible cases and possible solutions was wide indeed. One can find in the records of the medieval ecclesiastical courts disputes involving a great variety of social situations and support for a wide range of propositions about the law. Unless one is simply to list all the possibilities, one must generalize, and generalization ought to involve a commitment to what was normal and what was abnormal. We should also try to discern how what was normal changed over time, how what was normal became abnormal, and vice versa.

Finally, use of quantitative methods helps us to avoid the fascination of the 'interesting' case. There are many interesting cases in the records of the medieval ecclesiastical courts. They are made more interesting by the fact that in many of them, particularly in England, the depositions have survived. We can thus hear ordinary men and women of the Middle Ages speaking about their ordinary experiences. The dangers of relying on such evidence are substantial. Witnesses frequently told lies, and the process of redacting the testimony into a legal record involved considerable distortions. For historians who cannot resist the temptation to use deposition evidence, quantitative analysis is the penance for succumbing to that temptation. Quantitative evidence allows us to control the deposition evidence, to see which witnesses were telling normal lies and which abnormal, and to see whether the way in which the witness tells his or her story is more likely to be a product of the witness or of the clerk who recorded the testimony.

Because we cannot examine all the cases in all the courts, we must sample, and since the samples are unlikely to be random, we must be careful of the biases built into the samples. After a brief chapter in which we outline the

[33] See Donahue, ed., *Records 1, 2*; disc. T&C no. 9.

underlying rules and institutions (Chapter 1) and another in which we discuss in depth four English cases that have left unusually full records (Chapter 2), we begin with marriage cases in the consistory court of York in the fourteenth and fifteenth centuries. Our earliest record dates from 120 years after Alexander's death, our latest from 320 years after his death. Since our purpose is to try to determine the social effect of Alexander's rules, starting so late calls for some explanation. There are earlier records, but all the runs of records earlier than this date have some factor about them that leads us to doubt whether we are getting a typical run of marriage cases, much less of marriages. In England, the earliest runs of ecclesiastical court records come from the court of Canterbury in the thirteenth century (and this may be the earliest extensive documentation that exists anywhere). The Canterbury records are not, however, a good group of records to use for numerical analysis. They were probably preselected by the monks of Canterbury to serve as a muniment of their title to exercise vacancy jurisdiction;[34] they cover a wide range of cases, and rarely does the same type of case appear more than once. Further, the court of Canterbury was an appellate court, the most prestigious ecclesiastical court in England. We would expect, and indeed we find, a disproportionately large number of people of wealth and status litigating in that court.

By contrast, the court of York was both the appellate court for the northern province and the first instance court for the diocese of York. There is thus in the York records a much wider sample of types of litigants. Further, so far as we can tell, the survival of the records of the court was not determined by a desire to illustrate anything other than the records of the court. Finally, the records survive in loose papers rather than solely in the act books or registers that are the sole surviving records for so many other medieval ecclesiastical courts. We thus have for this court what the parties, their proctors and, to some extent, their witnesses chose to present to the court, rather than what some clerk of the court decided to write down. Experience with other medieval ecclesiastical court archives in the British Isles and in continental Europe suggests that this is the best set of such records yet to be discovered.

The three chapters on York (Chapters 3, 4, and 5) establish a pattern for the rest of the book. We begin with numbers (Chapter 3): What kinds of cases did the court hear? What kinds of marriage cases did it hear? What was the nature of the claims and defenses made? What was the gender ratio of the litigants, and what was their success ratio? We then try to burrow more deeply into the cases. We look at those from the fourteenth century (Chapter 4) to see if we can combine the legal arguments that were made with what the depositions are saying into what we call 'story-patterns'. While no two stories are exactly alike, definite patterns do emerge. We will not argue that these patterns tell us the 'true story' of any given case, but we will argue that they represent, to some extent, the social expression of medieval people when they came to dispute about marriage. We will also argue that the stories being told are not so far away

[34] *Select Canterbury Cases*, introd., 35–7.

from the experience of the judges that they would regard them as implausible or impossible. The final chapter on York (Chapter 5) looks at the fifteenth-century cases to determine what was different about the story-patterns in that century.

Chapter 6 deals with the court of Ely from 1374 to 1381. The reasons for the choice of Ely are fairly straightforward. The register that records the cases is remarkably full and well kept. It has already been analyzed in a way that allows us to control the large amount of data it contains.[35] The diocese was small and, for the most part, rural, and in marked contrast to York, the court heard quite a few marriage cases *ex officio* (i.e., roughly corresponding to our criminal procedure). We hear less of the stories that the litigants were telling than we do at York, but we hear something. We also get a very good idea, perhaps better than we do at York, of the course of the litigation. Because of the nature of the record, the story that we tell for Ely is more a story of the litigants' reactions to what the court did and to what they did to each other in court, but there is some evidence of extrajudicial behavior.

The work with Ely prepares us for our work with Paris (Chapter 7). Here, too, all we have is a register and, unfortunately, not one as well kept as that at Ely. The Paris register is close to contemporary with the Ely register (November of 1384 to September of 1387), and it reveals a very different kind of court from that of Ely. While it is difficult to penetrate behind this register to the social realm, a few dramatic cases emerge, and, probably more important, a pattern of litigation that suggests quite different marriage practices from those that prevailed at both York and Ely. To what extent those practices are only the practices of those who litigated or are those of the wider society, a court register cannot tell, but there are enough cases in the register to suggest that the difference in practice probably extended beyond the court into the wider society.

Our last courts are those of the diocese of Cambrai, which has left a series of registers from the mid-fifteenth-century court at Cambrai (1438–53) and one very large one from the separate court at Brussels in an overlapping and slightly later period (1448–59) (Chapters 8 and 9). These are registers of sentences only. There are so many sentences that we had to sample them. It takes quite a bit of effort to figure out what is going on at the legal level in these sentences, but it seems to be worth the effort. It takes even more effort to figure out what may be going on socially, because we hear only the voice of the judge, not that of the parties, nor even, as in the Ely and Paris registers, the voice of the parties as reported by the registrar. The sentences were, however, rendered by four different judges, each of whom had a distinctive style. We learn less about what the parties to the cases in Cambrai diocese were arguing, but we learn as much or more about the judges' attitudes toward the facts that they found. What seems to lie behind the Cambrai cases is not the same as what seems to

[35] Stentz, *Calendar*.

lie behind the Paris cases, but it is closer to Paris than it is to York and Ely in most important respects.

While all five courts were courts of the official (chief judge) of a bishop (archbishop in the case of York), there are some institutional differences among them that it is well to flag at the beginning, because we will have to explore the extent to which the institutional differences account for the differences that we see in the records. The official was not the only judge of the court at York, Ely, and Paris. At York and Ely there were commissaries general of the official and occasional appointments of special commissaries to hear particular cases; at Paris there was an auditor (perhaps two), though we know little about his activities in this period. At Cambrai, and eventually Brussels, the official is the only judge of the court of whom we hear. In all four dioceses there were lesser ecclesiastical courts that had some jurisdiction over marriage matters, at least such matters as broadly conceived. Once more, it is at Cambrai and Brussels where we hear the least of such jurisdictions. Professional lawyers, proctors and advocates, were available to assist the parties, at least in instance (civil) litigation, at York, Ely, and Paris. There were probably proctors and advocates at Cambrai and Brussels, though we hear nothing of them in our records.[36] The courts of Paris, Cambrai, and Brussels had promotors, professional prosecutors of office (criminal) cases. York and Ely had no promotors.

After the chapters on the diocese of Cambrai, we deal with two substantive issues largely excluded from consideration in the chapters that deal with the individual courts: separation issues (Chapter 10), where we find a marked difference between the practice of the English courts and those on the Continent, and issues about consanguinity and affinity (Chapter 11). These latter do not play a very large role at York and Paris, but they do play a large role in one court not in the group, and they play a somewhat significant role at Ely and in Cambrai diocese. We conclude with an attempt to put all our findings together and to suggest some lines for further research (Chapter 12).

There is a methodological problem with the approach taken by this book, one to which we will return in a number of places but which it is well to confront at the beginning. Disputed marriages are, in most times and most places, a rather small subset of the number of marriages; certainly that is what most married couples or couples contemplating marriage have hoped would be the case. In addition, the number of disputed marriages that find their way into a court sufficiently sophisticated to leave a record is, in many times and places (and there are good reasons for thinking that the Middle Ages in Western Europe, even the late Middle Ages was one such time and place), a rather small subset of the number of disputed marriages. The problem is well known to social historians and students of the relationship of contemporary law and society. It is the danger of generalizing from 'trouble cases' or of 'writing social history from

[36] They certainly existed by the seventeenth century. See *Ancienne procédure ecclésiastique*, 37–8, 42–3.

a police blotter'.[37] Marriage was a fundamental institution in the society of the medieval West. But this is a book about disputes. Any society in which the workings of a fundamental institution generate more than a small proportion of disputed cases is approaching the pathological. That may have been happening in the diocese of Cambrai in the mid-fifteenth century; that is an issue to which we will have to return (Chapters 8, 9, and 12). There is no evidence that it was happening at York, Ely, or Paris in the periods with which we are dealing.

The fact is, however, that except for the very top of the society, court records are the best evidence that we have about how marriage worked for ordinary people in the Middle Ages, even the later Middle Ages. Court cases, however, are not normally evidence about how an institution works but about how it does not work. There are two ways around the problem. The first is to check what we find in the court cases against what we know from other types of evidence. The sermons, liturgy, literature, and art of the later Middle Ages have quite a bit to say about marriage. We will not examine them systematically in this book, but we will occasionally refer to them and to the works of others who have examined them more closely.[38] Routine administrative records, which become more abundant for the later Middle Ages, frequently allow us to draw some inferences.[39] Again, we will not examine such material systematically in this book, but we will refer to the works of others who have. Sermons, liturgy, literature, art, and routine administrative records, of course, have their own biases. This is notorious in the case of the first four, less well known in the case of the last. The fundamental problem with the last may be summed up in the fact that the maker of a bureaucratic record frequently assumes, and hence does not describe, the very things that the modern historian is investigating.

The second approach to the problem is the one on which we will focus in this book. It is constantly to be aware of the problem, and carefully to focus on the nature of the question that we are trying to answer. At the very basic level we must ask whether the record is likely accurately to reflect what happened in court. Sometimes there are reasons to suspect that it does not, but in most cases we will be able to say that it probably does, though, of course, the clerk or judge has selected what he reports. The next question is whether what happened in court is likely accurately to reflect what happened before the parties got to court. Here, there are substantial problems of distortion, ranging all the way from outright lying by the parties and the witnesses to the more subtle process of recasting the story in such a way that fits the categories with which the court was dealing, and in such a way as was likely to be persuasive. This is a book about arguments, and arguments are, by definition, tendentious. Lies and arguments are, however, also a product of the society in which they are

[37] See further, Ch 2, between nn. 21 and 22, and at nn. 35–7.
[38] Lit. T&C no. 10.
[39] Lit. T&C no. 11.

made, and so all is not lost once we conclude that the story is not literally true. Finally, there is the question of extrapolating from what happened in court and the stories that were told there to the larger world of marriage disputes that did not come to court or to the much larger world of marriages that were not disputed. This is obviously the most speculative question, one about which reasonable people can differ. The nature of the argument in this book is that in some areas and in some places, the sheer quantity of certain kinds of disputes and stories about them makes it likely that we are looking at a pattern that was also found in disputes that did not come to court and, perhaps, allows us to infer the kind of behavior that was expected in undisputed marriages.

The bad news is that this approach has resulted in a long book. Each level of question requires discussion. Is this record likely to be an accurate record of what happened in court? Is what is recorded likely to reflect what in some sense actually happened before the parties got to court? On the basis of the answers to those questions, what conclusions can we draw about disputes that never came to court and about marriages that were never disputed? Hence, the method of the book requires not only that all the cases in the samples be reflected in the numbers, but also that a large number of them be discussed individually.[40] The process, however, does produce what, at least to me, are fascinating results.

Another reason for the length of the book has to do with the complexity of the legal institutions with which we are dealing. The substantive canon law of marriage was, as we shall see in the first chapter, quite complicated. The procedural law was equally so. There was also local law, both ecclesiastical and secular, that added to, and we shall argue, changed the practical import of, some of the general law of the church. All these bodies of law, which are quite evident in the cases, were being filtered through the medium of five sophisticated institutions operated by a group of men, some of whose personalities we can see in the records. To call these cases examples of an interaction of law and society is, to some extent, misleading. The formal law was itself a product of medieval society, as were the men who administered it. The social, in short, is reflected in the rules and institutions, just as it is reflected in the stories, reactions, and maneuverings of the lay people who came before the courts. It is tempting to contrast the attitudes of clerical professionals, who in many cases seem to have been quite learned in a law that the lay people only partially understood, with those of the lay people, and we will certainly see areas in which the contrast was

[40] Which cases get discussed individually and which more generally is very much a judgment call. I have tried to say something, either in the text or in the margin, about all the fourteenth-century York marriage cases (Ch 4), but have dealt with those from the fifteenth century only selectively (Ch 5). The cases involving male plaintiffs at Ely, because they seemed to be unusual, are dealt with quite exhaustively, those involving female plaintiffs only selectively (Ch 6). With Paris we attempted to say something about every marriage case in the register that said something different from the routine (Ch 7). In the case of Cambrai and Brussels, particularly the former, we tended to say something about all of the sentences, because we had sampled them to begin with and because we were tracing differences in the attitudes of the four judges and changes in those attitudes over time (Ch 9).

stark. But it is also striking that there seems to be a substantial overlap between the two groups. Figuring out what rules lie behind the cases (which, for the most part, do not cite specific rules) requires considerable discussion. Getting the balance right between the areas of agreement and the areas of disagreement requires more. Once again, however, at least to me, the results of the process are quite fascinating.

1

The Background Rules and Institutions

As we have said, the law of marriage of Western Europe of the Middle Ages was canon law, and it was complicated. By the beginning of the thirteenth century, the period in which we first have records of runs of cases, it was the product of a continuous development of more than seven hundred years, with roots going back into Roman law, Judaism, and early Christianity, and the customs of the non-Roman peoples of the West. A particularly notable feature of this development was the extraordinary efflorescence of learning, teaching, and promulgating law that occurred in the twelfth century. As we have also said, the story of this development is the topic for another book. Here we must briefly outline the rules as they existed, or were thought to exist, in the early years of the thirteenth century. While the next three centuries saw some development of these rules, perhaps more than is normally thought to have occurred,[1] the changes were subtle and, with the notable exception of developments in the law of separation with which we have occasion to deal in Chapter 10, they do not seem to have had much effect on marriage litigation in ecclesiastical courts, the focus of this book. Hence, the outline that we give here may be taken as the outline of the rules that the proctors, advocates, and judges of the courts with which we are dealing assumed, or should have assumed, as they presented and decided the cases that were brought to them.[2] It will not outline all the doctrine that is at stake in this book. Some points are better left to the specific cases in which they arose.

Uncontroversial as the statements in the preceding paragraph might seem, we should pause for a moment before we undertake our outline. There are few statements of legal rules that cannot be made the subject of argument. Even if the statement of the rule is more or less agreed upon, its application to the facts of any given case will frequently, perhaps always, be the subject of argument. Once the rule has been applied, either actually in a court or

[1] See Donahue, "Was There a Change."

[2] Lit. T&C no. 12.

hypothetically in a classroom, the lawyer's or judge's, student's or teacher's, plaintiff's or defendant's understanding of the rule will change. He or she will now know that the general statement of the rule applies to this set of specifics, and that knowledge changes that person's understanding of the rule. Since no given lawyer, judge, student, teacher, plaintiff or defendant will have dealt with the same set of real or hypothetical cases, no two persons' understanding of the rule will be quite the same. Shared experience, such as that produced by a common educational pattern or knowledge of the practice of a given court, can produce overlapping fields of understanding, but the potential for different understandings is always there.

The phenomenon just described is not limited to legal systems that have a doctrine of precedent. In such systems, the process by which decisions in individual cases changes the understanding of the rule is brought up to the conscious level and is allowed to change the formal statement of the rule. In systems like medieval canon law, those that do not have a doctrine of precedent, the phenomenon operates below the level of the formal rule, perhaps below the conscious level, but it is certainly there, granted the fact that no two human beings have the same experience of the rule. The phenomenon is perhaps even more notable in systems like medieval canon law (and the Anglo-American common law) where the rules are not formally codified. There are, of course, in both systems, authoritative documents that state the rules (and a hierarchy of authorities for resolving the more obvious conflicts), but in no place in medieval canon law was there a formal, systematic, authoritative, and exclusive statement of the law of marriage such as that found in the modern Code of Canon Law or in a modern European civil code.

These facts should make us uncomfortable about stating the rules of the law of marriage in the later Middle Ages, even if we confined ourselves to canon law. We would be even more uncomfortable if we broadened our scope to include other potentially applicable bodies of law, such as Roman law, as it was taught, and to some extent practiced, in the later Middle Ages, or the various customary and/or statutory systems of law that were in some areas expanding their scope of geographical coverage to correspond to that of the highest secular political authority. This latter we will not undertake here, though we will have occasion in later chapters to refer to other bodies of law as we seek to explain variations in practice in the different ecclesiastical courts. We could avoid many of the difficulties that we just stated if we confined ourselves to the canon law as described in a single work, such as the influential *Summa de matrimonio*, composed by Tancred of Bologona, for the most part, shortly before 1215, and revised by Raymond of Peñafort, probably around 1235, but even this relatively compact work is too long for our purposes, and although it was highly influential, it is in some ways an idiosyncratic work.[3] We will, therefore, adopt the organizational scheme of the Tancredian-Raymondian *Summa*, but the statement of the rules is our own, supported, in most instances, by the *Summa* and, in all

[3] Disc. T&C no. 13.

instances, by authoritative texts found in the *Liber extra*, an official collection of decretals promulgated by Pope Gregory IX (1227–41) in 1234, or Gratian's *Decreta*, the vulgate edition of which was probably completed around 1150. We believe that most late medieval canonical professionals would have agreed with this statement of the rules (if they were translated back into Latin), though in some instances they would not have phrased them in the way that we have.

Four characteristics of Christian marriage law are assumed in the Tancredian-Raymondian *Summa*, and it is well to specify them in advance: First, marriage is between a man and a woman and is monogamous. Monogamy was, so far as we can tell, Jewish practice in the time of Jesus and was also the practice, and, to a large extent, the law of the Greco-Roman world. Second, a Christian marriage once fully formed was indissoluble while both of the parties were living. This characteristic was thought, not without justification, to have been the teaching of Jesus as found in the New Testament, and it received a powerful reinforcement in the reform movement of the eleventh century. Third, close relatives could not validly marry. While this prohibition had its origins in both Jewish and Roman law, it had been greatly expanded in the early Middle Ages. The extent of the prohibition had been debated in the eleventh and twelfth centuries, and traces of these debates, and their resolution, can be found in the Tancredian-Raymondian *Summa*. Fourth, marriage between Christians once fully formed was a sacrament of the church. This idea was not fully articulated until the twelfth century, but it is accepted without comment in the Tancredian-Raymondian *Summa*.

FORMATION OF MARRIAGE

Sacramental Christian marriage is formed in either of two ways: (1) Present consent freely exchanged between a Christian man and a Christian woman capable of marriage makes a marriage that is indissoluble so long as both of them live, unless, prior to the consummation of the marriage, one of them chooses to enter the religious life. (2) Future consent exchanged between a Christian man and a Christian woman capable of marriage makes an absolutely indissoluble marriage so long as both of them live, if subsequent to the exchange of future consent and prior to the formation of another marriage, the couple who has exchanged future consent has sexual intercourse with each other.[4]

This scheme of rules is first seen clearly in the decretals of Pope Alexander III (1159–81) in the context of cases in which he was called upon to determine the priority between two attempted marriages.[5] Pope Innocent III (1198–1216) limited the grounds for dissolution of an unconsummated present-consent marriage to the one stated in the previous paragraph. Alexander and his immediate successors had contemplated other such grounds – supervenient affinity, supervenient impotence, supervenient leprosy, and possibly others – but Innocent III closed the door. A respectable body of canonical and theological opinion

[4] See Donahue, "Canon Law and Social Practice," at 144–5, and sources cited.
[5] See Donahue, "Dating."

maintained that the pope had the power to dissolve any unconsummated marriage, but from Innocent III to the beginning of the fifteenth century, no pope, so far as we are aware, did so. When the popes did begin to dissolve such marriages in the fifteenth century, they did not publicize the fact that they were doing so. Knowledge of the possibility of papal dissolution of such marriages seems to have been widespread, at least in certain circles in Italy, in the mid-fifteenth century (perhaps a bit later); it does not seem to have been generally known (or the practice common) until the sixteenth century.[6]

Innocent III also changed the statement of the second rule. For Innocent (as it had been for the canonist Huguccio), engaging in sexual intercourse after the exchange of future consent created a presumption that the parties had presently consented. This was, at least in the public forum of the courts, a *de iure* presumption; no evidence could be introduced to rebut it. Hence, for Innocent, all marriages were formed by present consent, either actual or presumed. We have stated the rule as we have, however, because this is way that at least English lawyers drafted libels in which they claimed a marriage had taken place.[7]

An exchange of future consent, if not followed by sexual intercourse, did not form a marriage. The parties could be relieved of any obligations that they had thereby contracted for cause, perhaps even by mutual consent. Whether the obligations of future consent were enforceable when one of the parties was willing and the other was not was debatable. It was clear that penalties inserted in marriage contracts were unenforceable,[8] and that a contract of marriage would not be specifically enforced against someone who had married another by either of the two methods previously described.

Hence, in the absence of subsequent sexual intercourse (and we might add, speaking of the external forum, provable subsequent sexual intercourse), it made a large difference whether the consent was characterized as present or future. There were relatively well-defined formulae for expressing each kind of consent: "I take you as wife/husband," for present consent; "I promise to take you as wife/husband," for future consent. But there was a large gray area in between. Many, perhaps most, canonists regarded "I will have you from henceforth as wife/husband" and "I will that you be my wife/husband" as expressions of present consent, while "I will have you next Easter as my wife/husband" or "I will that you be my wife/husband next Easter" were expressions of future consent. But what if a couple said to each other "I will take you as wife/husband" without specifying when? The Latin for this (*volo te accipere*) is somewhat less ambiguous than the English because Latin does not need a copulative verb to express futurity and hence the use of *volo* is clearly intended to express volition, but even though volition is clearly expressed, it is ambiguous as to the time at which the taking is to occur. The problem becomes even more complicated if we remember that few ordinary people in medieval Europe expressed themselves in

[6] See Donahue, "Policy," 252 and n. 2; Donahue, "Was There a Change," 74–7; disc. T&C no. 14.
[7] Disc. T&C no. 15.
[8] X 4.1.29 (Gregory IX, *Gemma*).

Latin. Circumstances might clarify the ambiguity, as, for example, where a couple exchanged these words at the church door after they had been engaged for some time, but where circumstances did not clarify the ambiguity and there was no other proof of their intention, it was not even clear that such an exchange created an obligatory future consent, since no words of promise were used.[9]

Returning to our definition of the rules, we will treat what modern authors call 'vices of consent' (error, insanity, etc.) and capacity under 'impediments' in the next section. One thing in the definitions remains to be explained: what of non-sacramental marriages? By the beginning of the thirteenth century it was clear that a marriage between Christians was sacramental, if it was a marriage at all. There was no such thing as a non-sacramental marriage between Christians. It was also clear that there could be no marriage between a Christian and a non-Christian.[10] Marriages between non-Christians were recognized, but they were not sacramental. We prescind from discussing such marriages here, and from discussing the related issue of what happens if one of the non-Christians becomes a Christian, because these issues do not figure in any of our cases.

IMPEDIMENTS

By the beginning of the thirteenth century the impediments to marriage were neatly divided into two kinds, diriment and impedient. The former, as the name implies, invalidated any attempted marriage; the latter did not invalidate the marriage but rendered it unlawful. Those who married in the face of an impedient impediment could be penalized (whether they were penalized is an issue to which we shall return), but their marriage was valid and could not be dissolved. By the beginning of the thirteenth century it was also clear that for an impediment to be diriment, it had to exist at the time that the marriage was contracted. The one possible exception to this rule, supervenient entry into religion following an unconsummated present-consent marriage, is probably better thought of as a voluntary dissolution of a marriage that exists but is not yet absolutely indissoluble.

The canonists and popes of the twelfth and early thirteenth centuries made considerable progress in trimming the luxurious growth of impediments that was their heritage from the past. They also made considerable progress in rationalizing and classifying the impediments. They had not yet achieved a complete rationalization and classification, however, because of the power of a mnemonic verse that they taught to their students:

> Error, condition, vow and relation,
> Crime and diff'rence of cult,
> Force, order, and bond,
> Hon'sty, affinity,

[9] See the discussion in Raymond, *De matrimonio*, 4.2, p. 511 (gloss), and Helmholz, *Marriage Litigation*, 34–40, with references.

[10] Disc. T&C no. 16.

And impotence also forbid
Marriage to be and if joined you see
What was done, by the court, undid.
Church prohibition and times of devotion
Also forbid 'em, you see,
But if they're done, they won't be undone;
The court will just let 'em be.[11]

In his discussion of the impediments, Tancred makes clear that he saw how many of the impediments were, in fact, vices of consent. The tradition had, however, already committed itself to a list of impediments. Bernard of Pavia had hit on 14; Tancred followed him; Raymond followed Tancred, and the system got stuck. This meant that madness, nonage, and unfulfilled condition, all of which were diriment impediments (the latter two, only under certain circumstances), never got incorporated into the list and were discussed, if at all, in general discussions of consent. The fixing of the number of impediments at 14 meant not only that the more sophisticated understanding of consent that had developed over the course of the late twelfth century was only partially integrated into the system, but also that further exploration of the problem of consent happened only occasionally. Another consequence of the fixing of the categories was that a rather large number of impedient impediments were never fully considered. There are far more than two: simple vow, prior *de futuro* bond, lack of the solemnities required by the Fourth Lateran Council or by local synodal legislation, and various crimes other than those encompassed in the diriment impediment of crime being the most obvious. Finally, since the list of impediments was dictated by the scansion, such as it is, of the doggerel hexameters, the *summae* treat the impediments in an order that impedes rather than aids understanding. Let us reorganize them.

Vices of Consent

These may be divided into two categories: those who lack the mental or physical capacity to consent and those who are capable of consent but whose formal consent is impeded, whether they are aware of it or not.

Insanity. Those who are insane are incapable of consent, at least while they are insane. This impediment is recognized by all the canonists, but little is said about it. It is also not prominent in the cases.[12]

Impotence and Frigidity. More is said about physical incapacity for sexual intercourse. "Impossibility of intercourse has the highest place among the other impediments," Tancred tells us, "because it impedes matrimony out of its very

[11] The Latin is not much better, T&C no. 17.
[12] Ref. T&C no. 18.

nature rather than by constitution of the church."[13] The reason for this is that it removes both primary causes of marriages, the procreation of offspring and the avoidance of fornication. It was, however, only after some hesitancy that the classical canon law recognized impotence or frigidity as a ground for dissolving a present-consent marriage, and it did so only if it existed at the time of the exchange of present consent and only if the party who was capable of intercourse did not know of the other's inability.[14] The classical law also reintroduced a three-year period during which the couple must remain together and attempt to consummate the marriage, unless the impotence or frigidity was obvious.[15]

But what if it is not obvious? The ancient rule set out in Gratian's *Decreta* was that if a man asserts that he has had intercourse with a woman and she denies it, the judge is to defer to the oath of the man.[16] Alexander III followed this rule on the one occasion that he had to deal with the issue.[17] Gregory VIII (1187) substantially modified this rule by allowing the wife's oath and the testimony of seven women, who examined the wife and declared her to be a virgin, to overcome the man's oath.[18] Hence, in the classical law the only situation in which recourse to conflicting oaths was necessary was the one in which the woman was not a virgin at the time of the marriage.

Nonage. Nonage combined notions of mental and physical incapacity. In the classical canon law, the 'espousals' (*sponsalia*) of those below the age of seven were a nullity.[19] They lacked the mental capacity to consent. Those between the age of seven and the age of puberty (notionally fixed at 12 for girls and 14 for boys) were binding in the same way that future consent was binding: They could become indissoluble marriages if the parties had intercourse or if they exchanged present consent after reaching the age of puberty, but before either of those events happened they created an obligation but no marriage. The obligation could be dissolved for cause, and it would not prevail over a subsequent marriage entered into after the parties had reached the age of puberty. If one of the parties was over the age of puberty and the other under, the party above the age of puberty was held to the contract while the party below the age of puberty was held until he or she reached the age of puberty at which time he or she had the option to rescind.[20] The focus here seems to be on physical rather than mental incapacity. Contractual consent is possible above the age of seven, but it cannot be present consent until the age of puberty is reached.

[13] Tancred, *Summa de matrimonio* 30, p. 60–1; T&C no. 19.

[14] X 4.15.6 (Innocent III, *Fraternitatis tuae*); X 4.15.4 (Lucius III, *Consultationi tuae*).

[15] See X 4.15.5 (Celestine III, *Laudabilem. Requisisti*); X 4.15.7 (Honorius III, *Litterae vestrae*).

[16] C.33 q.1 c.3 (from the capitulary of Compiègne [757]).

[17] X 4.2.6 (*Continebatur in litteris*, WH 204[a]), disc. T&C no. 20.

[18] X 2.19.4 (*Proposuisti*).

[19] Ref. T&C no. 21.

[20] X 4.2.8, 7 (Alexander III, *A nobis. De illis*, WH 4[a]–[b]).

There is a tension in the classical canon law between measuring puberty on the basis of objective criteria or fixed rules (12 for girls, 14 for boys) and measuring it on the basis of subjective criteria, the physical capacity of the individual. Alexander III's decretals on this topic, for example, seem to have moved in the direction of subjectivity. In one decretal, Alexander requires the girl to have been "near to the age" of puberty and to have had intercourse in order for the marriage to be binding.[21] In another, we hear nothing of the age of the parties, but the addressee is to inquire whether in fact they have had intercourse.[22] In yet another decretal, Alexander denies separation on the ground of nonage to those who are "near to the age that they could be joined by intercourse."[23] While the exact import (and indeed the grammar) of the last decretal is not clear, it clearly seems to be based on the possibility rather than the actuality of intercourse and thus goes the furthest in the direction of subjectivity. (Some of the classical commentators turned this into an objective measure, but the summary that appears at the head of the decretal in most printed editions of the *Liber extra* does not.)

Force or Fear. Since the canon law based its notion of marriage on the free consent of the parties, one would expect it to be open to argument that the consent was forced or prompted by fear. It was, but the authoritative statements on this topic are quite cautious. For example, Alexander III has four decretals on the topic: In one, he refuses to lay down an abstract rule: "Concerning the woman who was handed over to a man against her will and kept by him, since there are different kinds of force and you did not tell us for certain whether afterwards she consented, we cannot tell you anything for certain."[24] Similarly, Alexander rules that a young woman who took the veil with the consent of her husband and afterwards left the convent when her husband was dead and married another should be compelled to return to the convent unless she took the veil because of mortal fear of her husband.[25] Even then, she should be compelled to return if she consented after the fear had passed. Two later decretals on the topic of force, while they are not inconsistent with the earlier ones, reveal more openness to the argument that the marriage was forced. In a complicated case from Pavia, Alexander orders that the woman who has claimed that her consent was forced be placed in a safe place, away from the pressures of the contending families:[26] "Since consent has no place where there are fear and compulsion, it is necessary that when the consent of someone is at stake the occasion of compulsion be removed. Marriage is contracted by consent alone, and where that is at stake, she whose intent is being examined ought to enjoy

[21] X 4.2.6 (*n.* 17), T&C no 22.
[22] X 4.2.8, 7 (n. 20).
[23] X 4.2.9 (*Tua fraternitas. De illis*, WH 1033[b]), T&C no. 23.
[24] X 4.1.6 (*Sollicitudini. De muliere*, WH 991[b]), T&C no. 24.
[25] X 1.40.1 (*Relatum est ad audientiam*, WH 862).
[26] X 4.1.14 (*Cum locum non habeat*, WH 270), text and disc. T&C no. 25.

full security, lest out of fear she say that someone whom she hates pleases her and there follow the results that usually come about from forced marriages." In yet another case, Alexander was willing to express the matter as a general principle. A man is to be compelled to adhere to the woman with whom he had gone through a 'shotgun marriage', unless he had been compelled to consent "by a fear that could turn a constant man."[27]

While all four decretals recognize that marriage (or entry into religion) is not binding if it is forced, they seem to reflect a change in attitude toward the impediment. The first two decretals state that even if the consent is forced it may subsequently be ratified. The latter two do not. The first decretal distinguishes between types of force, and the second (admittedly in a somewhat different context) seems to suggest that only mortal fear will vitiate the consent. The third decretal suggests no standard but offers a strong statement that forced marriages are a bad idea, and the fourth, while it adopts an objective standard, adopts one considerably more relaxed than the second: "the fear that could turn a constant man."

Since all four of these decretals appeared in the *Liber extra*, it was open to the canonists to make of them what they would. They tried to find bright-line rules in the decretals:

> What sorts of fears excuse? Ask him who knows:
> Violation, slavery, death, and also hard blows.[28]

But ultimately they had to admit: "The judge will judge according to the diversity of persons and places what sort of fear it is, and will pronounce in favor of some marriages and for the nullity of others."[29]

Error. If marriages are to be based on consent, one would expect that that consent could be vitiated by mistake, just as contractual consent may be vitiated by mistake. The classical canon law resisted this conclusion, ultimately holding that only mistake of person (I marry Joan thinking that I am marrying Alice) and mistake of status (I marry a slave thinking that I am marrying a free woman) would vitiate the consent. The assumption of this latter doctrine is that a marriage between a free person and one of servile condition could be a valid marriage. This assumption is in marked contrast to Roman law, where slaves could not validly marry each other or a free person.[30] A remarkable decretal of Hadrian IV (1151–9) held that such was not the case in canon law:[31]

> Clearly, just as in Christ Jesus, according to the word of the Apostle,[32] there is no free nor slave who is to be removed from the sacraments of the church, so too, marriages

[27] X 4.1.15 (*Veniens ad nos Wi.*, WH 1071), T&C no. 26.
[28] Tancred, *Summa de matrimonio* 25, p. 47: *Excusare metus hos posse puta, quia nescis / Stupri sive status verberis atque necis.*
[29] Raymond, *De matrimonio* 4.11, pp. 551b–552a, T&C 27.
[30] See Donahue, "Case of the Man Who Fell into the Tiber," 10–11, with references.
[31] X 4.9.1 (*Dignum est*), T&C no. 28, with lit.
[32] Cf. Gal 3:28.

between slaves are not in any way to be prohibited. And if they are contracted in the face of the prohibition and unwillingness of their lords (*domini*), by no reason are they to be dissolved by the judgment of the church on this ground. They [the *servi*] ought, nonetheless, to render to their lords the customary services that they owe.

Condition. In the classical canon law the impediment of condition referred to two quite separate types of conditions. The first is the type involved in the previous paragraph, where one of the parties married in ignorance of the other's servile condition. The second is the situation where the parties made their consent conditional on the happening of some event: "I take thee to wife if my parents consent," or "I take thee to wife if your father will give me so much in dowry." The classical canon law ultimately came to the conclusion that such conditions did serve to suspend the binding effect of the marriage. If the condition was fulfilled, the parties were married automatically. They also were married automatically if they subsequently exchanged the words of present consent unconditionally or if they had intercourse. Further complexities were introduced if the condition was contrary to the nature of marriage or if it was shameful or disgraceful. The former type of condition voided the marriage; the latter did not void the marriage but was simply ignored.

Considerable academic attention was devoted to the problem of conditional marriage, and such discussion does help to explain how the academics regarded marriage.[33] In the practical realm of the decretals, however, particularly decretals in real cases, conditions were of less importance. For example, Alexander III's one decretal on conditional marriages involves a quite normal condition and one that was regarded as 'honest': "I will take you to wife if you give me so much as dowry." And Alexander's resolution of the problem anticipates, if it does not quite completely cover, the solution that the later law was to reach: "If someone takes an oath to a woman in this form of words: 'I will take you to wife if you give me so much money', he will not be regarded as guilty of perjury if he does not take her when she refuses to pay what he asked be given to him, unless present consent or sexual intercourse has followed subsequently."[34]

The classical law followed the ruling of this decretal. Gregory IX completed the classical law in a ruling that was probably made at the instance of Raymond of Peñafort:

> If conditions contrary to the substance of matrimony are inserted, for example, if one says to the other 'I contract with you if you will avoid the generation of offspring', or 'until I find another woman more worthy in honor or wealth', or 'if you will hand yourself over to adultery for the sake of gain', the contract of matrimony, though it is favored [in the law], lacks effect. If, however, other conditions are imposed on a marriage, if they are disgraceful or impossible, they ought to taken, because of the favor [of matrimony], as if they had not been added.[35]

[33] See, most fully, Weigand, *Bedingte Eheschliessung*.
[34] X 4.5.3 (*Quia nos duxit. De illis. Si vero*, WH 808[b1, b2]), T&C no. 29.
[35] X 4.5.7 (*Si conditiones*), T&C no. 30.

Religious Impediments

Disparity of Cult. The impediments of disparity of cult, orders, and vow all had as their focus the maintenance of marriage as a secular relationship between Christians. As noted earlier, the classical law was firmly committed to the notion that a Christian could not marry a non-Christian. On heretics there was some hesitancy, but the ultimate resolution was that such marriages were valid, though illegitimate.[36]

Orders. Priests and deacons could not marry, and if they married, they must dismiss their wives, who were not their wives but concubines, do penance, and return to their clerical service.[37] So far as subdeacons were concerned, there was some hesitancy. Alexander III made various pronouncements on the topic. In one decretal he says quite plainly that they may not marry.[38] In another, he praises the bishop of Le Mans for having made a subdeacon abjure his wife, and says that if the subdeacon enters religion and behaves himself, he may be promoted to higher orders. If he does not wish to enter religion, he cannot function as a subdeacon or be promoted to higher orders, but he may function in minor orders.[39] In other decretals Alexander is more qualified about subdeacons.[40] The classical law suppressed Alexander's hesitancy about whether the order of the subdiaconate was a diriment impediment to marriage. It was, and the only issue was how to punish those clerics who did so marry. In this regard, the second decretal described here became the model, just as the first was taken for the statement of the basic rules.[41]

Vows. The classical canon law distinguished between simple vows and solemn vows. Only the latter were a diriment impediment to marriage. The converse of the proposition that one who has taken a solemn vow of chastity cannot marry is that one who is married cannot take a solemn vow of chastity, at least not without the consent of his or her spouse. The foundation of this proposition is the saying of St Paul, "the husband has no mastery over his body but the wife, and the wife has no mastery over her body but the husband."[42] Husband and wife are mutual debtors; each must perform the act of sexual intercourse when asked by the other. A vow of chastity taken without the consent of one's spouse is a unilateral repudiation of that obligation. This much was clear by the time that Alexander III wrote, but precisely what was to happen if one spouse, with the consent of the other, wished to espouse the religious life was not clear. Alexander did much to clarify it.

36 Esmein, *Mariage*, 1:245. For the development of the impedient impediment of mixed religion, we must wait until the council of Trent. *Id.* 2:253–68.
37 E.g., X 4.6.1 (Alexander III, *Consuluit. De diacono*, WH 188[cd]).
38 *Ibid.*
39 X 4.6.2 (*Ex literarum tuarum*, WH 416).
40 Ref. T&C no. 31.
41 X 4.6.2 (n. 39); X 4.6.1 (n. 37).
42 1 Cor 7:4.

In a decretal that may be part of, or connected with, the bull by which he established the Italian branch of the order of Crucifers, Alexander lays out rules on the topic:[43]

> You are in no way to receive a married man among you without the permission of his wife, who if she is of such honest *fama* and opinion that no suspicion may worthily be had that she wants to transfer to another husband or that she will not live continently, such woman, when her husband is received in your group, can, having publicly professed continence in the sight of the church, remain in her own house with her children and *familia*. If, however, she is such a person about whom suspicion is not lacking, she, having celebrated a vow of continence, should separate herself from the company of secular men and remain forever in a religious place where she may serve God.

Failure to follow these rules would invalidate the entry into religion, as a recently published decretal to the prior and brothers of Dunstable shows.[44] Walter of Odell had entered the priory when his life was despaired of. His wife consented, albeit reluctantly, but she thought he was about to die. She herself, however, did not enter religion, nor did she promise to do so. Walter did not die, and now his wife wants him back. The canons are to let him go, and if they refuse to do so, papal delegates will force them to do so.

Suppose that Walter's wife, having extracted him from the priory, now dies. Is Walter obliged to go back to the priory, or may he remarry? Such questions have been asked in law schools from the twelfth century to this day, but the situation actually arose in the diocese of Pisa, and the archbishop asked Alexander what to do about it. Alexander's reply is curious:[45]

> The vow [that the man took in the monastery] is not binding; hence by reason of the vow he is not obliged to return to the monastery. Further, however, he cannot take a wife. For he promised not to require the debt.[46] That was in his power, and therefore the vow binds thus far. Not to render the debt, however, was not in his power but in that of the woman. Whence, the Apostle says, 'The man does not have mastery over his body; likewise the woman', etc. [1 Cor. 7:4]

The logic of this decretal is not perfect. On the one hand, the vow that the man took in the monastery was not only a vow of continence; it almost certainly also involved a vow of obedience or 'conversion of manners'. That vow was suspended by the higher obligation that the man owed to his wife, but now that she is dead there is no reason why he cannot perform it. On the other hand, taking another wife is not necessarily inconsistent with a vow not to require the debt. Just as the man could be said to be unable to require the debt while his former wife was alive, so too he could be said to be permitted to marry but not to require the debt. The result, then, that Alexander reaches is more like a

[43] X 3.32.8 (*Ad petitionem. Uxoratus*, WH 84), T&C no. 32.
[44] *Decretales ineditae*, no. 63, p. 109 (*Ex parte S. mulieris*, WH 466).
[45] X 3.32.3 (*Quidam intravit*, WH 814), T&C no. 33.
[46] I.e., sexual intercourse. The canonists derived from 1 Cor 7:3 an obligation of spouses to have sexual intercourse with each other when asked.

compromise than one required by the strict logic either of the vows in question or the sayings of the Apostle.

Alexander's basic resolutions of the problem of what the canonists called 'conversion of married persons' were accepted by the classical law. Both the reasoning and the result in the Pisa case caused much debate,[47] and Urban III (1185–7) attempted to overrule it, requiring, in cases in which the man had remarried, that he be separated from his new wife and forced to return to the monastery.[48] This holding, however, simply provoked more discussion, and both decretals were included in the *Liber extra*.

Crime

The classical canon law recognized that crime was a diriment impediment to marriage in two situations: (1) Where a couple had committed adultery and one or both of them then conspired in the death or participated in the killing of the spouse of either or both of them, they could not marry after the death of the spouse. (2) Where a couple had committed adultery and had pledged faith to each other that they would marry, they could not marry after the death of the spouse or spouses of either or both of them. This latter impediment also applied to those who went through a form of marriage while spouses of one or both of them were alive, since such a form of marriage would almost invariably involve a pledge of faith.

To these basic rules, Alexander III added an important qualification, which was received in the classical law. In a decretal addressed to the abbot of St Albans,[49] Alexander dealt with the case of one O. who had gone through a form of marriage with an unnamed woman, who was unaware of the fact that O. was married to another woman and had had many children by her. Now his wife was dead, and O. wanted to leave the woman with whom he was living on the ground of the impediment of crime. Alexander did not hesitate:[50]

> Although we have it in the canons that no one should couple in marriage with a woman whom he previously polluted in adultery, and particularly with her to whom he pledged faith while his wife was alive or if she has conspired in the death of the wife (*vel quae machinata est in mortem uxoris*), because, nonetheless, the woman was ignorant that he had another living wife, and it is not fitting (*dignum*) that the man, who knowingly contravened the canons, should profit from his fraud, we respond thus to your consultation, that unless the woman asks for a divorce, they are not to be separated.[51]

Clement III (1187–91) may have entertained the idea of extending the impediment to any situation in which the couple knowingly committed adultery (without regard to whether there was machination in the death of the innocent spouse

[47] See glosses *ad* X 3.32.3, 3.32.9 (Venice 1572), pp. 745a–b, 747b–748a.
[48] X 3.32.9 (*Ex parte abbatis*).
[49] Lit. T&C no. 34.
[50] X 4.7.1 (*Singulorum. Propositum*, WH 989), T&C no. 35.
[51] Disc. T&C no. 36.

or a pledge of faith),[52] but Innocent III firmly held that simple adultery without pledge of faith was not enough to impede the subsequent marriage.[53] Gregory IX, at the request of Raymond of Peñafort, completed the classical law by holding that a married man's pledge of faith to another woman, unaccompanied by adultery, did not give rise to the impediment.[54]

The Problem of Incest

Medieval canon law on the topic of incest was extensive. It applied to those who were related by blood (consanguinity), by marriage (affinity), and by spiritual bonds, usually arising out of baptism (spiritual affinity). The tendency of the preclassical canon law was to expand the number of people who were forbidden to marry because of one kind of relationship or another. The causes of this tendency are still imperfectly understood, and the literature on the topic is large.[55] The tendency in the classical canon law was to reduce the number of such people by reducing the degrees of relationships within which marriages were forbidden, by reducing the kinds of relationships that gave rise to an impediment to marriage, by tightening the procedures by which such relationships could be proved, and by authorizing the pope to dispense from all but the closest degrees of relationship.[56]

Prior to Alexander III, the twelfth-century canonists had been largely engaged in collecting the sources and trying to determine precisely what the rules reflected in the mainstream sources were. This process did result in pruning from the authoritative materials some of the more extreme statements of the rules and in fixing a limit on the expansion. This process had resulted in the fixing of the limits of the prohibition at the sixth or seventh degree of consanguinity and the same degree for those who married into a consanguineous line (affinity). The computation of the degrees was by the canonic method, that is, by tracing the number of acts of generation back to a common ancestor (where the number was unequal, the longer was used for purposes of determining the prohibition). Hence, if the seventh degree was taken, the limit was reached with sixth cousins (fifth cousins once removed, fourth cousins twice removed, etc.).

Consanguinity. Alexander III's decretals on the topic of consanguinity can be regarded as having begun the trend to cut back on the reach of the impediment. These decretals may be laid out on a series of spectra: whether and how long the marriage had existed, how remote the degrees were, and how reliable the evidence of the consanguinity was. The longer that the marriage has gone

52 X 4.7.5 (*Cum haberet*) (dictum).

53 X 4.7.6 (*Significasti nobis*).

54 X 4.7.8 (*Si quis uxore vivente*) (since the decretal is in the *Liber extra*, it dates from 1234 or before).

55 See Ch 11.

56 See Brundage, *Law, Sex*, 355–6.

unchallenged, the more remote the degrees, the less reliable the evidence, the more Alexander was likely to sustain the marriage.[57] Innocent III continued Alexander's practice.

The problem with this approach from a juridical point of view is that it makes decisions quite unpredictable. It all depends on the facts of the particular case. In the Fourth Lateran Council, Innocent III took a different approach. He reduced the prohibited degrees of consanguinity and affinity from six or seven to four, but insisted on strict observance of the rules as modified:

> We wish the prohibition to be perpetual, notwithstanding earlier decrees on this subject issued either by others or by us. If any persons dare to marry contrary to this prohibition, they shall not be protected by length of years, since the passage of time does not diminish sin but increases it, and the longer that faults hold the unfortunate soul in bondage the graver they are.[58]

This ruling made obsolete whatever had previously been said about consanguinity in the fifth degree and beyond. It also made obsolete Alexander's (and to some extent, Innocent's) carefully constructed spectrum of the length in which the marriage had gone unchallenged. It did not make obsolete what Alexander had said about separating *pendente lite* couples who had married in defiance of an interdict, nor what he had said about dispensing with the *ordo* in cases of notoriety, with the qualification that notoriety could hardly be had in cases not of the first or second degrees, and these are the only decretals of Alexander's on the topic of consanguinity that appear in the *Liber extra*.[59] Alexander's rulings in this area were more influential than their survival rate would suggest, however. The principle that Alexander established that the prohibition of intermarriage in the more remote degrees of consanguinity was a matter of human, not divine, law meant that parties could be dispensed to marry within these degrees. Popes continued to employ the dispensing power in the more remote degrees of consanguinity (fourth and third). Alexander had been the first to do so, at least extensively. Alexander's cautions about accepting the evidence of those who had an opportunity to object to a marriage and did not do so also found resonance in the later law, though here it was a decretal of Innocent III's on the topic that appeared in the *Liber extra*.[60] Finally, another decree of the Fourth Lateran Council set firm rules (which had been anticipated by both Alexander III and Innocent III) about who could be witnesses in cases of consanguinity (and affinity) and how they were to testify, with the effect of making proof in such cases more certain, but also more difficult.[61]

57 Ref. T&C no. 37.
58 4 Lateran (1215), c. 50, in *Decrees of the Ecumenical Councils*, 1:257–8, T&C no. 38.
59 X 4.16.3; X 4.19.3 (n. 57).
60 X 4.18.6 (*Cum in tua. Si vero*).
61 4 Lateran (1215), c. 52, in *Decrees of the Ecumenical Councils*, 1:259, T&C no. 39.

Affinity. After the Fourth Lateran Council, the impediment of affinity applied only to those who were related within the fourth degree of consanguinity to the spouse of the affine. It also only applied to the person who had sexual relations with someone within the consanguineous line. The baroque variations of affinity that went under the names of affinity of the second type and affinity of the third type were abolished by the council.[62]

Alexander III faced early and often the problem that would later be called *affinitas per copulam illicitam*. A man and a woman have illicit sexual relations and one or the other or both of them later seek to marry a relative of the person with whom they have had sexual relations.[63] The problem was even more serious where the subsequent marriage had already taken place when the matter came to the attention of the church authorities and especially where the illicit intercourse occurred after the marriage had taken place. In these situations the ancient canons could be read to impose a penalty of perpetual continence on the affines who had sexual relations with each other ('the ancient incest penalty').

Of a number of conclusions that we might derive from Alexander's decretals on the topic, one seems relatively obvious and does not seem to have been noted before. Where he is dealing with an affinity that arises out of a legitimate marriage, Alexander requires that the impediment be observed up to the fourth degree (third cousins), to the extent that if a marriage has been formed within those degrees, it must be dissolved.[64] Beyond the fourth degree, he does not require dissolution, but he does not forbid it either. In the case, however, of affinity *per copulam illicitam*, he is reluctant to dissolve an already-existing marriage at all, and when he speaks of degrees, he speaks of the first, second, and, occasionally, the third. In cases of affinity *per copulam illicitam*, Alexander distinguishes between public and occult affinity. Dissolution is to take place only in the former case.[65] It is possible that Alexander, like some later theologians and canonists,[66] had doubts about whether an affinity by illicit intercourse really impeded the marriage or, at least, whether it did so *iure divino*.

If this is the path of Alexander's decretals on *affinitas per copulam illicitam*, then the canonists suppressed it. None of Alexander's decretals on the topic appear in the *Liber extra*, and very few of them appear in the *Compilatio prima*. The solution of the classical law went in a different direction. In the first place, the same canon of the Fourth Lateran Council that reduced the degrees of consanguinity to four also reduced the degrees of affinity. No distinction was drawn between *affinitas per copulam illicitam* and that arising out of a lawful marriage. Hence, so far as the degrees were concerned, the council's ruling

[62] Disc. T&C no. 40.
[63] Disc. T&C no. 41.
[64] Disc. T&C no. 42.
[65] Ref. T&C no. 43.
[66] See Thomas Aquinas, *Summa Theologiae* Supp. q. 65 art. 4; disc. T&C no. 44.

was consistent with those of Alexander in the case of affinity arising out of lawful marriage and considerably broadened the degrees in the case of *affinitas per copulam illicitam*. In the second place, Innocent III expressly overruled Alexander's holding that an unconsummated *de presenti* marriage could be dissolved by reason of supervenient affinity. In the classical law, only *sponsalia de futuro* could be dissolved by supervenient affinity, and here the dissolution was mandatory. Preexisting affinity, whether by licit or illicit intercourse, was a diriment impediment to marriage. Affinity that arose by illicit intercourse after the marriage subjected the guilty party to the ancient incest penalty, but for purposes of separation the incest was treated as an aggravated case of adultery. The innocent spouse had to ask for the separation, and if he or she did, he or she could not remarry while the guilty spouse lived.[67]

All of this would suggest that Alexander's distinction between public and occult incest was totally suppressed. Such is not the case, however. The classical canon law dealt only with the external forum. Dissolution of marriages because of preexisting affinity and the imposition of the ancient incest penalty for cases of subsequent affinity only occurred in situations in which both the illicit intercourse and the degree of relationship could be proved in open court. What was to be done in the case of secret incest revealed in the privacy of the confessional was a topic for writers of manuals for confessors. It is here that we see the greatest use of the distinction that Alexander had drawn between asking for the marital debt and rendering it when asked.

Spiritual Affinity. The problem of spiritual relationship had spawned a law that we suspect was out of all proportion to its practical import.[68] The problem was that the past had left a singularly obscure set of canons, and the popes were continually asked to resolve the issue. Although there was debate about what gave rise to a spiritual relationship, the first two 'species' of prohibition were clear enough: A spiritual parent (godfather, godmother) could not marry his or her spiritual child ('spiritual paternity'), and a spiritual parent could not marry the natural parent of his or her spiritual child (*compaternitas*, what we will call 'co-paternity'). The third species, 'spiritual fraternity', was the subject of considerably more controversy. "And it should be known," Tancred writes in his *Summa de matrimonio*:

> that at one time there were varying opinions, and divers laws came forth which said that the children of two co-parents could not marry each other, whether they were born before or after the co-paternity. Other laws said that only those born after the co-paternity could not marry. Passing over all of these, it is firmly and without any doubt to be held that all children of two co-parents, whether born before or after the co-paternity can lawfully join in marriage, except that person who gives rise to the co-paternity.[69]

[67] Ref. T&C no. 45.

[68] Lynch, *Godparents*, however, does point out how important spiritual relationship was in a somewhat earlier period.

[69] Tancred, *Summa de matrimonio* 21, p. 34, T&C no. 46.

Nor are co-parents forbidden from marrying the children of their co-parents, except for the child who gave rise to the co-paternity. There were further elaborations, but since none of our cases gives rise to them, we confine the discussion to the margin.[70]

Public Honesty. Affinity could not arise unless one of the potential marriage partners had had sexual intercourse (lawfully or unlawfully) with a blood relative of the other. But if one of the parties had contracted to marry a relative of the other, either as adults or before they had reached the age of puberty, the classical canon law recognized an impediment to their marrying each other, even though no true marriage had ever existed with the relative and even if there had never been sexual intercourse between them. It was thought scandalous, for example, for a man to marry the mother of his former fiancée. And because of this focus on scandal, the impediment was called the impediment of 'public honesty'.

The doctrine of the impediment of public honestly was somewhat modified by the Fourth Lateran Council, in that the degrees of the prohibition were reduced to four. Boniface VIII (1294–1303) determined that the impediment would arise even if the contract of marriage was null (for example, because the person with whom it was formed was impotent or in orders), so long as there was proper consent by someone of appropriate age, and so long as the contract was not subject to an unfulfilled condition.[71] The impediment remained throughout the classical period and beyond, although the degrees were radically reduced by the council of Trent.[72]

Impedient Impediments – The Problem of Clandestinity and Solemnity

The only impedient impediment that regularly came before the ecclesiastical courts was lack of solemnity, which the canonists treated as a branch of the impedient impediment of marriage against the interdict of the church.[73] Only two contemporary decretals appear in the *Liber extra* under the title "Concerning clandestine espousals."

The first is a reply of Alexander III to the bishop of Beauvais concerning whether "we [i.e., the pope] ought to issue a dispensation concerning clandestine marriages."[74] Alexander replies that no dispensation is necessary. If the parties to the occult marriage do not publish it, there is nothing that the church can do about it (*non sunt aliquatenus compellendi*). The church does not judge about things that are hidden.[75] Further, if the parties do publish the marriage

[70] Disc. T&C no. 47.

[71] IV 4.1.1 (*Ex sponsalibus*). This is one of the few advances in marriage doctrine that we find in the later books of the *Corpus Iuris Canonici*.

[72] See Esmein, *Mariage*, 1:159–64 and 2:95–8 (on Trent).

[73] Disc. T&C no. 48.

[74] X 4.3.2 (*Quod nobis ex tua parte*, WH 819[a]), T&C no. 49.

[75] *Ecclesia de occultis non iudicat*, disc. T&C no. 50.

(and no impediment appears), the marriage is valid *nunc pro tunc*. Alexander then spells out the obvious implications of this ruling for the legitimacy of the children of the marriage – that they are legitimate.[76]

The second, a canon of the Fourth Lateran Council, takes a considerably less relaxed attitude toward clandestine marriages.[77] The proper way to get married, the council declared, is publicly after the proclamation of banns. Any priest who participates in a marriage where banns have not been proclaimed is to be suspended from office.[78] The council did not prescribe the 'suitable penance' (*condigna penitentia*) for the parties to such a marriage (other than the loss of the benefits of putative marriage,[79] not technically a penance), nor did it invalidate such marriages. They were illegitimate, but they were still marriages. The importance of this last qualification for our understanding of the classical law of marriage cannot be overstated. Marriages are made by the consent of the parties, or, in the case of future consent, their consent plus intercourse. The church could, and did, strongly encourage parties to publicize their marriages in advance of the event. This way the church could ensure that the parties were truly capable of marriage, and difficult problems of proof might be avoided. But neither Alexander nor any of his successors until the council of Trent took the step of invalidating such marriages.

It was left to the local churches to deal with the problem of clandestinity. For example, the prohibition of clandestine marriage and the concomitant requirement of the publication of banns was repeated, sometimes in the form of the canon of the council of Westminster of 1200,[80] sometimes in the form of the canon of the Lateran Council, and sometimes in a locally composed form, in more than 30 pieces of English conciliar legislation and episcopal decrees between 1200 and 1342.[81] None, however, excommunicated automatically the parties to such a marriage.[82] The only *ipso facto* excommunications in the English canons are for those who knowing of an impediment have their marriages solemnized nonetheless, and for clergymen who participated in marriages of persons who were not their parishioners without obtaining the requisite license or who participated in marriages not in a parish church.[83] Simply getting married at home, however, was not an offense for which the parties incurred *ipso facto* excommunication, whatever other sanctions might have been imposed for engaging in such behavior.[84]

76 Disc. T&C no. 51.

77 4 Lateran (1215), c. 51, in *Decrees of the Ecumenical Councils*, 1:258, T&C no. 52.

78 Lit. T&C no. 53.

79 See at n. 113.

80 Ref. in T&C no. 52.

81 See Sheehan, "Marriage and Family in Legislation"; *id.*, "Marriage Theory and Practice in Legislation."

82 Disc. T&C no. 54.

83 London (1342), c. 11, in Wilkins, *Concilia*, 2:707; cf. Lyndwood, *Provinciale*, 4.3.[2], p. 275–7.

84 See Donahue, "Canon Law and Social Practice," at 154 and sources cited. We will return to the English legislation in Ch 6.

Modern analysis of local French ecclesiastical legislation is just beginning, but enough has been done that we can see that in at least some dioceses, the French went further. Beginning with the synodal statutes ascribed to Eudes de Sully, bishop of Paris from 1196 to 1208,[85] French bishops not only required the promulgation of banns and the contracting of marriage publicly in the face of the church in the presence of the parish priest and witnesses, but also automatically excommunicated those who contracted marriage otherwise. A provision imposing the same sanction for the same offense is found in the synodal statutes of Guillaume de Seignelay, bishop of Paris from 1219 to 1224.[86] The sanction was being repeated in Parisian diocesan statutes as late as 1515.[87] Other French dioceses had similar legislation.[88]

DIVORCE

As we have already in part intimated, the classical canon law allowed divorce with permission to remarry (*divortium quoad vinculum*) of a consummated marriage only in the situation were there was a diriment impediment to the marriage. This divorce corresponded to what today we call 'annulment'. Divorce without permission to remarry so long as both partners were alive (*divortium quoad thorum*), what we today call 'separation', was allowed in the case of the adultery of one of the parties, and, perhaps, in other cases as well. At the beginning of the thirteenth century, the law was not clear about what other grounds for separation there might be.[89] The case of the unconsummated present-consent marriage was more complicated, as we have already seen, but the classical law allowed its dissolution, at least officially, only in the case where one of the parties entered the religious life. The basic principles of indissolubility and separation in the case of adultery were well established by the beginning of the thirteenth century, as was the proposition that no divorce, of either type, could take place without the judgment of the church. This meant, at a minimum in the case of a marriage that was public, that the public forum of the church had to be petitioned, and it is to the process in that forum that we must now turn.

PROCEDURE IN MARRIAGE CASES

Before we consider the rules of procedure, a word is in order about the courts themselves. By the middle of the thirteenth century virtually every bishop had a regularly sitting court, normally presided over by an officer called an official. These courts had their own clerks and records, and they normally had a group

[85] Statutes of Eudes de Sully, bishop of Paris (1196–1208), c. [98], in *Statuts synodaux français I*, p. 89; cf. *id.*, c. [85], in *id.*, p. 85.
[86] c. [13], *id.*, 101.
[87] Pommeray, *L'officialité archidiaconale de Paris*, 320.
[88] Ref. T&C no. 55.
[89] We outline the later developments in Ch 10, at nn. 11–20.

of lawyers attached to them, who functioned as proctors and advocates for the parties in instance cases, and as promotors (prosecutors) and defense lawyers in office cases. Below the level of the episcopal courts, there were, in many if not all dioceses, courts of lesser ecclesiastical officers; archdeacons were among the most common. Archidiaconal courts were, at least notionally, courts of limited jurisdiction, and appeal lay from them to the court of the bishop. Appeal lay from the court of the bishop to that of the metropolitan (archbishop) and from there to the pope. At the beginning of the thirteenth century, this structure was far less formal. Episcopal courts tended to be *ad hoc* bodies. Officials, though they existed, were not full-time, or almost full-time, judges of the courts, and the courts of papal judges delegate played a more important role than they did in the latter half of the thirteenth century, and certainly than they did in the later medieval centuries.

This development of a court structure had considerable implications for the practical effect of the canon law on the lives of ordinary medieval men and women, the concern of later chapters in this book. Ecclesiastical justice was available in the late twelfth and early thirteenth centuries, but it was less regularly available than it was in the second half of the thirteenth century and beyond. The procedure, however, by which these informal courts operated and by which the more formal courts of the later period operated was largely the same, the creation of the twelfth and early thirteenth centuries. We may therefore outline the procedural rules given in the Tancredian-Raymondian *Summa* and still be stating the rules that were in effect, with some variations in local practice, in the fourteenth and fifteenth centuries.[90]

Tancred was a specialist in procedure; he also had a genius for clear presentation of procedural law. We would expect much of his treatment of marriage processes, and we will not be disappointed. This part of the *Summa de matrimonio*, however, posed considerable problems of organization and presentation. Marriage process followed the Romano-canonical 'course of judicial process' (*ordo iudiciarius*), normally adopting those special rules, where they existed, that applied to 'spiritual' as opposed to civil or criminal cases.[91] To summarize, then, what one needed to know about marriage processes would involve summarizing the whole *ordo*, and Tancred had another book that did that. On the other hand, if Tancred simply listed those procedural rules that were peculiar to marriage processes, he would have ended up with a grab bag of miscellaneous rules that would have been quite unintelligible to someone who was not deeply familiar with the contents of the *ordo*. Tancred's compromise was to assume some familiarity with the overall contents of the *ordo*. He offers a brief summary of the *ordo* as it applies to marriage cases (tit. 33), an outline of the rules special to marriage cases about who may bring a case and who may be

[90] For a fuller, but eminently readable, introduction to the topic of this section, see Brundage, *Canon Law*, 120–53.

[91] Tancred uses these terms, so I will, but when we come to the procedures actually followed by the courts, 'instance' and 'office' describe them better.

a witness (tit. 34), a special section on procedure in cases of separation from bed and board on the ground of adultery (tit. 35), and more than an outline of the process of receiving, examining, publishing, and reproving witnesses, with special references to marriage cases (tit. 36–7).

We begin (tit. 33) with a division of marriage cases based on what the plaintiff (*actor*) is trying to achieve.[92] Some cases seek the joining of parties; some seek their disjunction or separation. The latter type of cases may be divided into those that seek full divorce, such that the parties may both marry others, as in the case of claimed frigidity, and those that seek a partial divorce, insofar as the mutual servitude of the carnal debt or cohabitation is concerned, but in such a way that neither party may marry another, as in the case of adultery or entry into religion (after consummation). The distinction between cases of matrimony and cases of divorce was to become fundamental in classifying cases in the ecclesiastical courts, though, as we shall see, an intermediate category developed, at least in some courts, that of cases of matrimony and divorce, in which the plaintiff sued a supposedly married couple seeking their divorce and marriage to one of them. Tancred's distinction between 'full' and 'partial' divorce came to be reflected in the terms 'divorce as to the bond' and 'divorce as to board and bed' (*divortium quoad vinculum* and *divortium quoad mensam et thorum*). Again as we shall see, some courts developed a lesser category of separation, separation of goods, which technically left the 'mutual debt of carnal servitude' intact.

If a woman claims a man, or vice versa, Tancred tells us (tit. 33), she ought to offer a libel, even though the custom of some churches is to the contrary. The practice of presenting the libel is, however, "better and more honest" because the defendant ought to be certain what is being asked of him or her.[93] Further, as we have just seen, there is an important legal difference (*obtinet de iure*) whether someone is claiming a woman as a *sponsa de futuro*, a *sponsa de presenti*, or a wife already known (*uxor iam cognita*), and so the libel ought to specify this.[94]

The libel also should specify, Tancred continues, whether the plaintiff is bringing a petitory or a possessory action. This importation from the law of property is at first glance startling (though Tancred does say that the petitory action is brought "as if she were making a claim about ownership" [*quasi agat de proprietate*]). Tancred insists upon the distinction, however, and it is fundamental to his understanding of procedure in marriage cases. Either the woman is claiming that the man "has contracted with her and asks that he should be adjudged her husband" (the petitory action) or "she asks that he be restored to her, as one who has been unjustly cast out by him whom she says is her husband" (the possessory action).[95]

92 Tancred, *Summa de matrimonio* 33, pp. 71–8.
93 *Id.*, pp. 71–2; text and disc. T&C no. 56.
94 *Id.*, p. 72, T&C no. 57.
95 *Ibid.*, text and disc. T&C no. 58.

The distinctions between the two types of actions were substantial. If the action is a petitory action, Tancred tells us, and the defendant objects ('excepts') that the marriage cannot proceed because they are consanguine, the exception should be heard before the petition, because if the exception prevails that is the end of the case. In the possessory action, however, the exception will not be heard until restitution (of conjugal rights) has been made. Among other authorities, we are told, Innocent III expressly made this distinction.[96] All the plaintiff has to do is prove that she was "in possession" (*in possessione*) (of her husband? of the marriage?) and that she was deprived of possession by her husband without the process of law (*sine iuris ordine*).[97] If she does this, she is entitled to restitution forthwith, unless she can be shown to have deprived herself of her right. (Tancred is here thinking of a case of a wife who lived in open adultery with another man.)[98]

Restoration without the exception being heard (*sine aliqua exceptione*) is not granted if (1) the exception is that the woman has engaged in public and manifest fornication; (2) the exception is one of consanguinity "prohibited by divine law,"[99] and for which proof is readily at hand;[100] (3) the exception is one of *res iudicata*, or (4) the man is seeking restoration, and there are reasonable grounds for fearing for the safety of the woman. (Even here, we later learn, restitution should be made if suitable arrangements can be made for the woman's safety, which is to be done, at least in some cases, by the man's taking an oath, or offering a pledge, or a surety.) Finally, as in the case of all possessory actions, failure in the possessory action does not preclude bringing a petitory action, but failure in a petitory action precludes a possessory action.

The distinction between petitory and possessory actions, though it had a somewhat checkered history in practice, as we shall see, is an important one here. The papal decretals (particularly Alexander's decretals) show considerable reluctance to dissolve long-term marriages and to overturn previous judgments upholding the validity of a marriage. The validity or invalidity of a marriage, however, was an absolute concept. An invalid marriage could not be made valid by having existed for a long time. Hence, the reluctance to upset the existing order had to be expressed in procedural rather than substantive terms. One could not say that a marriage became valid by prescription, but the system could, and did, give procedural advantages to the person asserting the validity of the existing order. One way of achieving this was to put the burden of proof on the person asserting the invalidity of the existing order. If, for example, a husband asserting the invalidity of his existing marriage took the law into his own hands and simply dismissed his wife, the wife could, at least under normal

96 Citing X 2.13.13 (*Literas tuas*).

97 Tancred, *Summa de matrimonio* 33, pp. 74–5.

98 Citing C.32 q.1 c.5.

99 *in divina lege prohibita*. In this context this may mean consanguinity in the fourth and lower degrees. See X 2.13.13 (n. 96).

100 In this case all other things are restored except (the right) to sexual intercourse.

circumstances, be restored to him simply by showing the fact of the existing marriage, and thus force her husband to undertake the burden of proving its invalidity.

Tancred is disappointingly vague about when a person becomes 'possessed' of his or her marriage, but simply 'contracting' the marriage (here probably meant in the sense of exchanging words *de presenti*) was not enough. Such a person must bring the petitory action and discharge the burden of proof. In all probability Tancred would have regarded a couple that lived together and had had intercourse as being 'possessed' of their marriage. Whether one element but not the other would suffice he does not say. Nonetheless, it is hard not to see here a procedural reflection of the older notion, found for example in Gratian's *Decreta*, that marriages are not 'perfected' simply by the exchange of consent.

The remainder of title 33 deals with the steps of the procedure up to the examination of the witnesses. The offer of the libel, Tancred tells us, is followed by a delay for deliberation.[101] The parties then return and take the oath to tell the truth. (Tancred insists on this, though he admits that the oath against calumny is not taken in spiritual cases.) The oath either precedes or follows the *litis contestatio*, the formal joinder of issue. This is followed by the interrogation of the parties. The process, as Tancred conceives of it, should take place in the presence of the judge and both of the parties. (He concedes that the church of Bologna follows the practice of examining the parties separately, as if they were witnesses, but he regards the practice as improper, a violation of the principle that all judgments require three persons, the plaintiff, the defendant, and the judge.) Each party, or his advocate, or the judge is to pose questions of the other party relevant to establishing the case. The party is to answer on his own, without the counsel of his advocate, though he may seek a delay if he is not sure how to answer it. The process of the parties' putting questions to each other, known in later practice as 'making positions', will be found in the documents that we will examine in later chapters.

Sometimes at this point one or both parties will confess, and these confessions will be determinative of the case unless they prejudice the marriage at stake in the case or that of some third party. This statement of the rule neatly combines the principles of the law that marriages are to be favored and that the confession of two parties cannot prejudice the rights of a third. Hence, parties could confess themselves into a marriage if the rights of third parties were not at stake, but they could not confess themselves out of a marriage. To dissolve a marriage or to obtain a judgment affecting a third party, they needed proof independent of their confessions.

The law about accusers of matrimony (tit. 34), that is, those who could bring an action to dissolve a marriage, was complicated.[102] A canon of dubious origins but ascribed to the early Roman pope Fabian held that only relatives could accuse a marriage of invalidity. Only if there were no relatives could others

101 Tancred, *Summa de matrimonio* 33, pp. 76–8.
102 *Id.* 34, pp. 78–85.

be admitted to the accusation.[103] The context of the canon strongly suggests that the only accusation of which it was speaking was the accusation that the marriage was invalid because of consanguinity or affinity. The justification later developed for the rule was that relatives know best what the degree of relationship is,[104] and the canon continued to be recited for the proposition that, unlike the situation in other cases, in consanguinity cases relatives were not only admissible witnesses but also the preferred witnesses. Tancred recites the rule excluding non-relatives from testifying when relatives were available, but then admits that perhaps as a matter of custom, in many places extraneous persons could be admitted, even if there were relatives who could accuse. After Tancred, we hear little of this rule of exclusion.

There were a number of rules disqualifying accusations on the ground of what might broadly be called estoppel. Someone who knew of an impediment and when questioned about it said nothing would not later be heard to raise the objection. Further, someone who was present in the diocese when the banns were proclaimed and who did not object to the marriage would not later be admitted as an accuser. This rule became particularly important after the Fourth Lateran Council generalized the custom of proclaiming the banns, and an elaborate body of law developed that attempted to define what would be an appropriate excuse for failing to object to the banns. Finally, an accuser should not be admitted who was shown to be bringing the accusation for nefarious motives, such as private hatred or financial gain.

Tancred continues by describing how an accusation of matrimony is to proceed. His effort is one of integrating something that had developed as a separate type of proceeding into the mainstream of Romano-canonical procedure. In the first place, he tells us, the word *accusatio* is improper; it should be called a denunciation (*denunciatio*) of a marriage, placing it, apparently, in the category of 'evangelical denunciations', a procedure ultimately derived from Matthew's gospel (18:15–18). Tancred argues that the denunciation should be in writing, like a libel, though he concedes that sometimes it is not. It should precisely specify the impediment complained of and a copy should be provided to the couple accused so that they could prepare their defense. The case is then to proceed along the lines of a standard procedure outlined previously.

Finally, Tancred tells us that the formal procedure that he has just outlined only applies to a marriage that has already been contracted, the same phrase that he uses to distinguish petitory from possessory cases. Before the marriage has been contracted, the denunciation can proceed without full proof. For this proposition he cites decretals of Alexander III and Urban III, both of which deal with the difficult-to-prove impediment of affinity by illicit intercourse.[105]

Proceedings to separate a marriage on the ground of adultery (tit. 35), Tancred tells us, are properly called 'accusations', because a crime is being

[103] C.35 q.6 c.1.
[104] See X 4.18.3 (Clement III, *Videtur nobis*).
[105] Ref. T&C no. 59.

alleged.[106] Nonetheless, the proceeding differs from the normal criminal proceeding in that if separation is sought, only the husband or wife can bring the case. Some people had argued that no libel of accusation should be offered in such cases, because in the ecclesiastical court, unlike the secular court, the plaintiff in a case of separation for adultery was not bound to commit him- or herself to the penalty of the talion if he or she failed in the proceeding. That the talion does not apply in ecclesiastical separation cases is obvious enough to Tancred; if it did, the accuser would get what he or she wanted, separation, whether the case was won or lost. But Tancred insists on the formal libel, and he lays out a form, designed for use by the provost of Gurk, the person to whom the treatise is addressed and dedicated.[107]

The right to dismiss a spouse for adultery was strictly limited. Tancred tells us that it does not apply if (1) the accuser has also committed adultery; (2) the husband has prostituted his wife; (3) she believed him dead and married another (though she must return to him if he returns); (4) she was known secretly by a man whom she believed to be her husband; (5) she was raped; (6) they were reconciled after the adultery, and (7) there have been divorces and remarriages while the couple were infidels, and both are converted. In this last situation, Tancred says, they must return to the original marriage, adding that the situation rarely occurs.

Finally, Tancred notes that once a separation has been granted, if the person to whom the separation has been granted does not live continently, he or she is to be compelled to return to the original spouse. The support for this is a decretal, probably of Clement III, which the summary tells us "can be cited all the time" (*multum allegabilis*).[108]

Tancred's two titles on witnesses (tits. 36–7) are largely derived from small treatises that he wrote on parts of the *ordo* and which were later combined in his well-known *Ordo iudiciarius*.[109] The rules are important for understanding medieval marriage litigation, though they are, for the most part, not peculiar to marriage cases.[110]

The form Tancred gives for the admission, examination, and reprover of witnesses is part of the standard overall form for the course of judgment in Romano-canonic civil procedure. After the joinder of issue (*litis contestatio*), the plaintiff is assigned a number of terms (three was standard; a fourth was given as an exceptional matter) to produce witnesses to discharge his burden of proof on his case in chief.

Once produced, the witnesses are to take an oath to tell the whole truth and to tell the truth for both parties. They are also to swear that they do not come

[106] Tancred, *Summa de matrimonio* 35, pp. 85–90.

[107] *Id.*, pp. 86–7. The date is given as 17 November 1210, giving us a *terminus a quo* for the treatise.

[108] X 4.19.5 (*Ex literis tuis*); disc. T&C no. 60.

[109] Tancred, *Summa de matrimonio* 36–7, pp. 91–104; cf. *id.*, *Ordo iudiciarius* 3.6–13, pp. 222–48.

[110] Ref. T&C no. 61.

to bear testimony for a price or out of friendship, or for private hate, or for any benefit they might receive. After they have taken the oath, the witnesses are to be examined separately and in secret, after the manner of Daniel's questioning of the elders.

When all the witnesses have been examined, the parties are to renounce further production of witnesses. The witnesses' depositions will then be published by the notary who has written them down. The defendant now has an opportunity to except to the testimony of the witnesses. He may except to their persons, if he has reserved the right to do so when they are produced, or he may seek to demonstrate that their testimony is false in some respect.

The proceduralists like Tancred not only outlined the form by which witnesses were to be admitted, examined, and reproved; they also elaborated some basic principles of their system of proof by witnesses. At the core of that system are three propositions: (1) The character of each witness is to be examined; certain witnesses are not to be heard because of their status, and the testimony of others is to be regarded as suspicious because of their status or mores or their relationship to one or the other of the parties. (2) Witnesses are to be examined carefully to determine if they are telling the truth about events they saw and heard themselves. (3) On the basis of the written depositions and what has been demonstrated about the character of the witnesses, the judge is to determine whether the standard of proof fixed by law has been met.

As a general matter, Tancred tells us, two witnesses make a full proof.[111] But not everyone may be a witness. Slaves, women (in certain circumstances), those below the age of 14, the insane, the infamous, paupers (though Tancred has some doubts about this), and infidels may not be witnesses. Criminals may not be witnesses. No one may be a witness in his own cause. Judges, advocates, and executors may not be witnesses in cases in which they have performed their official duties. Children may not testify on behalf of their parents or parents on behalf of their children, with certain exceptions. Familiars and domestics of the producing party and those who are enemies of the party against whom they are produced may not be witnesses. This is all summed up in another set of mnemonic verses:[112]

> Condition and gender, age and discretion
> Fame and fortune and troth
> If these aren't found in the *testes*
> You should, to admit 'em, be loath.

Witnesses are to be questioned, Tancred continues, about all the details of what they have seen and heard, for only then can it be determined whether they are consistent. They are to be asked about the matter, the people, the place, the

[111] What was required for full proof (*probatio plena*) was complicated and somewhat controversial. It is best dealt with where it arises, e.g., Ch 5, at n. 48; Ch 9, at nn. 50–2.

[112] *Conditio, sexus, aetas, discretio, fama / Et fortuna, fides, in testibus ista requires.* Tancred, *Summa de matrimonio* 37, p. 99.

time, perhaps even what the weather was like, what the people were wearing, who was consul, and so on. In only a few instances, such as computing the degrees in incest cases, is hearsay testimony to be accepted.

If a witness contradicts himself, Tancred concludes, then his testimony should be rejected. If the witnesses agree, and their *dicta* seem to conform to the nature of the case, then their *dicta* are to be followed. If the witnesses on one side disagree among themselves, then the judge must believe those statements that best fit the nature of the matter at hand and that are least suspicious. If the witnesses on one side conflict with those on the other, then the judge ought to attempt to reconcile their statements if he can. If he cannot, then he ought to follow those more trustworthy – the freeborn rather than the freedman, the older rather than the younger, the man of more honorable estate rather than the inferior, the noble rather than the ignoble, the man rather than the woman. Further, the truth-teller is to be believed rather than the liar, the man of pure life rather than the man who lives in vice, the rich man rather than the poor, anyone rather than he who is a great friend of the person for whom he testifies or an enemy of him against whom he testifies. If the witnesses are all of the same dignity, then the judge should stand with the side that has the greatest number of witnesses. If they are of the same number and dignity, then absolve the defendant. The basic principle, then, is that the burden of proof rests on the one who is asserting the proposition (*onus probandi incumbit ei qui dicit*).

SECULAR CONSEQUENCES OF MARRIAGE

Legitimacy

Tancred's section on legitimacy is short but important.[113] The basic proposition about legitimacy in canon law and in civil (Roman) law was that legitimate children were those who were born of a valid marriage. Granted the rules about what made a valid marriage, this meant that a marriage lacking solemnities could, nonetheless, produce legitimate children. The church had also added, as Roman law had not, the notion of what was called, although Tancred does not use the term, 'putative marriage'. If a couple married publicly and believed their marriage to be valid, their children would be legitimate, even if it later turned out that the marriage was invalid. As we have seen, an important provision of canon 51 of the Fourth Lateran Council denied the benefit of putative marriage to those who did not follow the formal requirements of the statute (basically, public proclamation of the banns).

The rules of putative marriage required that at least one of the couple believe in good faith in the validity of the marriage. If both of them had guilty consciences (*laesam conscientiam*) and knowingly married against the canons, their children were bastards. Much decretal law was devoted to this topic.

[113] *Id.* 38, pp. 104–7.

Tancred offers a fourfold division among children, derived in part from Roman law, and elaborated by the glossators. Children are either (1) natural and legitimate (those procreated in lawful marriage), (2) natural and not legitimate (those born of a concubine or fornication between two unmarried persons), (3) legitimate and not natural (adopted), and (4) not legitimate and not natural, that is 'spurious' (those born of [knowing] incest or adultery). The distinction was important because in canon law (secular law had more doubts), natural children could be legitimated by the subsequent marriage of their parents, but spurious children could not. Innocent III's famous decretal *Per venerabilem* had asserted that the papacy had the power to legitimate even spurious children.[114] Tancred proceeds to elaborate on the various methods of legitimating children in the civil law, but closes with the note that the civil law does not have a method for legitimating spurious children.

Marital Property

Tancred's treatment of marital property is skimpy.[115] He apologizes for this at the end, though he says enough about it that we can get some idea of what his concepts were. He asserts at the beginning of the section that matters concerning marital property belong to the ecclesiastical judge as accessory to marriage cases. He seems to be thinking principally of the proposition that when an ecclesiastical judge grants a divorce, he should also make a decree about the restoration of marital property. He mentions a custom in Bologna that judges will not deal with a divorce case unless the man posts security that he will restore the woman's dowry if the divorce is granted.[116]

On this relatively narrow base, the classical canon law built quite a bit. Urban III authorized the dean and chapter of Lisieux both to order the restoration of *dos* and to supervise the division of community property incident to a divorce.[117] Clement III chastised a papal judge delegate for not ordering restoration of the *dos* when he pronounced a divorce for consanguinity between a couple. The return of the *dos* is 'incident' to the main cause, and jurisdiction over it is 'accessory' to the jurisdiction over the main cause.[118] The same pope also pronounced that a woman separated from her husband for adultery lost her dowry (the Roman-law rule).[119] Innocent III ordered the restoration of a husband's *donatio propter nuptias* when the wife's retention of it was impeding the dissolution of a marriage that Innocent regarded as incestuous.[120] Both Innocent and Gregory IX made rulings that tended to equate canonical marital property with that of the *ius commune* and hence of Roman law.[121]

114 X 4.17.13.
115 Tancred, *Summa de matrimonio* 39, pp. 107–11.
116 Disc. T&C no. 62.
117 X 4.20.2 (*Significavit P.*). Granted where we are, the *dos* here may be dower rather than dowry.
118 X 4.20.3 (*De prudentia vestra*).
119 X 4.20.4 (*Plerumque*).
120 X 4.20.5 (*Etsi necesse sit*).
121 Ref. T&C no. 63.

CONCLUSION

We have just sketched what seems to be a complicated body of law, and indeed it is. Before we look at how it was used, we should ask the question whether on an *a priori* basis it is possible to make some guesses as to which portions of it are likely to have been socially significant and which not. In order to do so we will have to make some broad assumptions about the nature of medieval marriage as a social institution, assumptions that we will later have to question but that find support in the current literature. We will also anticipate some of the findings that are supported more fully later.

It took far more space to describe the basic rules about impediments than it did to describe the basic rules about marriage formation (and in the former case, we, in many cases, only skimmed the surface), so one's first reaction might be that it would be the rules about impediments that gave rise to the most controversy and confusion. Simply explaining these rules to a population, the vast majority of whom could not read, would have been a formidable task, and unless this population had already absorbed these rules and made them customary by the beginning of the thirteenth century (and all the evidence suggests that it had not), we might imagine that enforcement of the rules about impediments would be difficult and disputes about them common.

We are going to discover that this last, by and large, was not the case. True, instances of violation of the rules about impediments and disputes about all but the most arcane of them can be found, but those were not the issues to which most ecclesiastical courts that heard a large number of marriage cases (and we will see that not all did) devoted most of their time.

Knowing that fact we can go back to the rules to try to discern if there is anything about the rules themselves and about the institutional structures that were designed to apply them that makes this fundamental finding less surprising than it might at first seem. In the case of the impediments that we broadly described as 'vices of consent', a group of rules dealing both with physical and mental capacity to consent and with defective or incomplete (conditional) consent, there is something about the rules themselves that suggests why disputes about them might be uncommon – they were all waivable. In some cases the waivability was built into the statement of the rule. A person who claimed to have been forced into a marriage could not obtain dissolution of that marriage if he or she later freely consented to it, and consent would be presumed, at least in some statements of the rule, after a year's cohabitation. Subsequent consent without defect would also waive the impediments of insanity, error, expressed condition, and nonage, and sexual intercourse had by the couple after the impediment was removed gave rise to a *de iure* presumption of consent.

In some cases, the waivability, even if not normally stated as part of the rule or only partially stated, lay in the nature of the impediment itself. If a couple who could not have sexual intercourse continued to cohabit and neither complained about the inability of the other, no one would be the wiser for it. (While it is hard to imagine this happening with a younger couple, it is quite possible to imagine it with an older couple.) The practical waivability of this impediment was reinforced by the rule that stated that if a person who was capable of having sexual intercourse knowingly married someone who was not, the marriage could not be dissolved. It was further reinforced by the doctrine, of uncertain scope, but which certainly applied to this impediment, that the only person who could 'accuse' a marriage of certain kinds of invalidity was one of the marriage partners. (Limitation of the accusers to the marriage partners was probably also the rule in the case of the other impediments that we labeled as 'vices of consent'.)

The impediment of crime was also waivable by the innocent spouse, if there was one. In this case, the accusers were probably not limited to the marriage partners themselves,[122] but the innocent spouse could block dissolution of the marriage (though he or she could not block the imposition of penalties on the guilty spouse).

That leaves the religious impediments, those that were formed around the incest taboo, and prior bond (*ligamen*), all of which were emphatically not waivable and all of which could be the subject of public accusation. Prior bond did give rise to a considerable amount of litigation, both office and instance. That litigation, as we might expect, frequently raised fundamental issues about marriage formation. We will have occasion in Chapter 11 to ask why it is that the elaborate set of rules about incest did not, so far as we can tell in the present state of our knowledge, give rise to many disputes. So far as the religious impediments are concerned, we can only offer some speculation here as to why we do not find more disputes about them.

In the case of the impediment of disparity of cult, our surviving records are from areas in which there were not many non-Christians, except, in some areas and in some periods, for Jews. Jews, like Christians, were endogamous by law, and Jewish communities in the West tended to be endogamous in practice. Canon law demanded the conversion to Christianity of the proposed Jewish marriage partner of a Christian; Jewish law, as I understand it, demanded the reverse. Each community regarded conversion to the other as apostasy. Intermarriage certainly did occur, both legally according to one or another set of laws, and illegally, and the problems to which it gave rise were discussed academically. It did not, however, leave any records that we have been able to find in the church courts.[123]

The impediments of vows and of orders did give rise to some cases and disputes. That they did not give rise to many is probably the product of both the fact that the vows had to be solemn (and hence relatively easy to prove, though there were disputes about the nature of them) and the fact that the conferral of orders was normally, from the thirteenth century on, recorded (and, hence again, relatively easy to prove). The insistence on the celibacy of those in major orders cannot be firmly dated before the eleventh century. There is evidence that it was not totally accepted in the twelfth century. By the thirteenth century,

[122] Disc. T&C no. 64.
[123] Disc. T&C no. 65.

it does seem to have been accepted at least as a matter of principle. Hence, the rather large number of prosecutions of those in major orders that we find in the thirteenth and later centuries are prosecutions for what is described as clerical concubinage. Whether all the clerics and their partners regarded their relationship as no better than concubinage is hard to know, but so far as the church courts were concerned, the issue was one of prosecuting a form of aggravated fornication, not one of dealing with a potential marriage.

That brings us back then to the basic rules about marriage formation. We have already seen that there was considerable ambiguity in the formulation of the rules about what constituted present and what future consent, an ambiguity heightened by the difficulties of translation from the vernaculars in which the words of consent were normally spoken into Latin. Further, in the Introduction we suggested that perhaps the most striking thing about the rules about marriage formation was not what they required but what they did not require. How did people behave under a body of rules that said that a couple could get married by an informal exchange of present consent without solemnity or ceremony of any sort and without obtaining the consent of anyone else or by an equally informal exchange of future consent followed by sexual intercourse? It is to that question that much of the rest of this book will be devoted.

In closing this chapter, we should emphasize another point that has not been featured in the chapter because its origins and most of its development lie before the period to which this chapter has been devoted. From the point of view of comparative law, perhaps the most striking feature of the medieval canon law of marriage is not the fact that it allowed the formation of marriage with relatively little formality; it is the fact that marriages, whether formed formally or informally, were indissoluble so long as both parties lived. Jewish law, Roman law, and Greek law, to take three possible antecedents of the Christian law of the Middle Ages, all allowed divorce relatively freely. That some marriages simply do not work out seems to be a virtually universal phenomenon, even in societies like those of the Middle Ages where there were strong economic and social pressures holding couples together and where shorter life spans ensured that in many cases 'so long as both parties lived' might not be very long. We would expect, and we will find, that there was a curious interplay between the rules about marriage formation and those about marriage dissolution. To put the matter more bluntly, the formal unavailability of a mechanism to dissolve a properly formed marriage put pressure on those seeking to dissolve a marriage to find in its formation reasons why it was not validly formed. It also put pressure on the courts to find a way to separate, if they could not dissolve, couples whose marriages had proved hopeless.

2

Lying Witnesses and Social Reality

Four English Marriage Cases in the High Middle Ages

Let us depart from the law as stated and ask about the law as applied. Our sources for this are annoyingly incomplete, nothing like what they are, for example, for the English central royal courts, but we do have substantial pieces of the picture, runs of records from various courts in various places at various times. The four cases I have chosen as examples are all typical of English marriage-formation cases. They differ from those on the Continent in ways that we will come to in later chapters. They differ from most of the other English cases only in that these examples have left particularly full records.

DOLLING C SMITH

In our first case, Alice Dolling appeared in the consistory court of Salisbury on 10 July 1271, claiming that William Smith was her husband.[1] William denied the charge, and Alice was told to produce her witnesses before the rural dean of Amesbury (Wilts). In September, the depositions of her three witnesses were published in open court. In October, William confessed that he had had intercourse with Alice but denied that he had married her. He claimed that he had been in another town on the St Stephen's day (26 December), almost three years previously, the day on which Alice alleged that they exchanged the words of marital consent in Winterbourne Stoke (Wilts). The dean of Amesbury was to examine William's 10 witnesses. In December, Alice answered William's claim with four witnesses who alleged that William had indeed been in Winterbourne Stoke on that St Stephen's day. After William's depositions had been published, the official asked him to produce his witnesses again, but he said that he could not, citing what seem to be formulaic excuses. In May of 1272, the official rendered sentence for Alice declaring that William was her lawful husband. William appealed to the court of Canterbury, the metropolitical court.

[1] *Dolling c Smith* (10.vii.1271 to 31.x.1272), *Select Canterbury Cases*, 127–37, discussed in Donahue, "Proof by Witnesses," 147–8, 151–2, 153–5.

The three sets of depositions are included in the record (*processus*) made up for the appeal: Alice first produces three witnesses, all women. The first testifies that on 26 December two years previously, she was present in the house of one John le Ankere in Winterbourne Stoke at nightfall, in front of the bed that she and Alice shared. William and Alice were sitting, probably on a bench in front of the bed. He was dressed in a black tunic of Irish homespun with an overtunic and hood of russet; she was dressed in a white tunic with a blue hood and wore shoes with laces. William took her by the hand and said: "I William shall have thee (*habebo te*) Alice as wife so long as we both shall live and to this I pledge thee my troth." Alice replied: "And I Alice shall have thee as husband and to this I pledge thee my troth."[2] Asked why William had come there, she says to have carnal knowledge of Alice if he could. Asked if she had ever seen them having intercourse, she says no, but she did see them naked in the same bed. The second witness, calling herself the sister of the first, basically agrees with the first's testimony, though she says that William's tunic, overtunic, and hood were all gray. She never saw them lying together. The third witness has a slightly different version of the words exchanged: William said: "I William take thee (*accipio te*) Alice as my wife if holy church allow it, and to this I pledge thee my troth." She said: "I Alice shall have thee (*habebo te*) as husband and shall hold thee (*tenebo te*) as my husband."[3]

William's 10 witnesses, all men, tell a different story. William was in Bulford, four miles away, on St Stephen's day two years previously. They give a vivid description of an all-day ale feast, held by the parish guild. William was serving at the feast and could not possibly have been in Winterbourne Stoke that day.

Alice's four replication witnesses, all women, say that they saw William in Winterbourne Stoke that day, where he is described as leading around a crowd of women or going hand in hand with a woman.

What are we to make of all this? In the first place, someone was clearly lying.[4] William could not have been at Winterbourne Stoke exchanging consent with Alice and continuously attending an all-day guild feast at Bulford, four miles away, at the same time. Two of Alice's witnesses on the principal case and one of her replication witnesses seem to have been related to her: They were probably her half sisters. The witnesses on the principal case are not completely clear about what words were exchanged: Two of them seem to testify to *verba de futuro*, one of them to *verba de presenti*, at least on William's part – but the tense of the verbs should make no difference when intercourse is conceded. The three sets of witnesses are not completely certain about their dates, though this may be the result of scribal error rather than any confusion on the witnesses' part.

Now none of the observations made in the preceding paragraph is new. In fact, they are all made in a remarkable document that survives from the

2 *Select Canterbury Cases*, 129, T&C no. 66.
3 *Id.*, 130, T&C no. 67.
4 As Helmholz, *Marriage Litigation*, 157, points out with regard to exceptions of absence generally, citing a number of other examples.

case on appeal.[5] The judge of the provincial court of Canterbury asked the examiners of the court to look at the *processus* transmitted by the Salisbury court and evaluate it for him. They committed their evaluation to parchment, and this has survived. In the end the examiners suggest that there are too many inconsistencies in Alice's story, and failing all else, 10 witnesses are better than 7. The judge of the provincial court seems to have agreed; he reversed the decision of the official of Salisbury.

There are many cases like this from all levels of the English ecclesiastical courts that have left records and from all periods in the Middle Ages.[6] Indeed, such cases continue after the Reformation. It was not until 1753 that the English finally came to invalidate clandestine marriages.[7] Can we draw any social conclusions from such cases?

I think we can. Even though we will never know what William Smith was doing on 26 December 1268, we do know that most liars do not make things up out of nothing. William may not have been at a guild feast in Bulford that day, but feasts like that took place. The witnesses would not have been able to describe it so vividly if it was not within their experience. Similarly, William and Alice may never have exchanged words of matrimonial consent before the bed in the house in which she was probably a servant, but people did such things. If they did not, the testimony would not have convinced the official of Salisbury.

Further, a hundred years after Alexander III's decisions on the topic of the formation of marriage, news of them had reached Winterbourne Stoke. The women seem to have had a good idea of what it is that Alice and William should have been saying in order for Alice to have a case. Whether they knew that in Alice's case it made no difference whether the words were of present or future tense is harder to know. If any exchange took place, I suspect it was a future one. William's confession of intercourse comes after the publication of the depositions. Before the confession the witnesses could not have known that Alice did not need to prove intercourse in order to make out her case. It is probably not by chance that the one witness who testifies, admittedly somewhat ambiguously, to words of the present tense is also the one who says nothing about intercourse.

As soon as we realize, however, that the witnesses know what it is that they have to say – and this knowledge, not surprisingly, seems to increase as the Middle Ages go on – we are faced with a problem: Can we ever be sure that the witnesses are telling anything like what really happened? To put the problem more bluntly, it seems highly likely that William's witnesses were lying. The official of Salisbury asked him to produce them again. It seems inconceivable that all 10 of them were either dead or had left the province on a pilgrimage or for some other necessity, and this is what William claims. It seems far more likely that having gotten them to lie before the dean, he could not

[5] *Select Canterbury Cases*, 134–6.
[6] See Helmholz, *Marriage Litigation*, passim.
[7] Lord Hardwicke's Marriage Act, 26 Geo. 2, c. 33 (1753).

persuade them to come to Salisbury and lie before the bishop's official. But what we have said here suggests that William's witnesses may not be the only ones who were lying. We can have no confidence in the veracity of Alice's witnesses either. What we have, then, may be a charade, and the historical record, dramatic as it is, is not completely credible evidence of the veracity of either the claim or the defense.

Can we say anything about what happened in Winterbourne Stoke? Not much with certainty, but we can offer some speculation. William seems to have been something of a local Don Juan. The women all suggest this, and William himself admits that he had intercourse with Alice. Now Don Juan was a member of the nobility. William was certainly no nobleman, but he had enough money to go to Canterbury to get his case reversed. Alice never appeared at Canterbury, and the testimony does not suggest that she was of particularly high station. The details will always escape us, but the whole affair has an aura of sexual politics about it. It looks as if the women of Winterbourne decided that William ought to marry Alice. There may have been more than just sexual relations between them; there was probably less than what her witnesses say. By contrast, William's alibi seems to be a lie, pure and simple. I suspect that the official of Salisbury knew all this, too. There was no third party involved, no reason why William could not marry Alice, and he had had intercourse with her. What the official could not do was put together a record that was proof against appeal, at least when Alice did not appear to defend herself at Canterbury.

MERTON C MIDELTON

The second case comes from about a century later.[8] On 15 April 1365, Marjorie (Margery) de Merton appeared before the official of York seeking that Thomas de Midelton, chapman of Beverley, be adjudged her husband. The official interrogated Thomas, who confessed that he had had intercourse with Marjorie, but he denied that they had ever exchanged words of consent. The official then delegated the hearing of the case to Mr Adam of York, who was the precentor of York cathedral and official of the archdeacon of Richmond.[9] Marjorie's case before Adam rested essentially on two allegations: (1) that in his brother Richard's house in Beverley on the afternoon of 5 January 1364, Thomas had promised to marry Marjorie and that they had had sexual intercourse that night, and (2) that Thomas had confessed in the decanal chapter of Beverley around Michaelmas in the same year that he had promised to marry Marjorie and that sexual intercourse had followed. Witnesses were heard on both these allegations at the end of May; a further deposition of Mr Ralph Waleys, the vicar of the dean of Beverley who had heard the case in the decanal chapter, was received in July. At the end of July, Thomas excepted to the persons

[8] *Merton c Midelton* (1365–7), CP.E.102. For the absence of references to particular documents within the file, see Notes About This Book, n. 2.

[9] Ref. T&C no. 68.

of Marjorie's witnesses; after the summer holiday at the end of September, he excepted that he was absent from Beverley on 5 January 1364; at the end of October, he excepted again, this time that the confession that he had made before Mr Ralph was not made with the intent of contracting marriage. Depositions on Thomas's exceptions were not taken until the middle of November, and they focused on the characters of Marjorie's witnesses and on the events in the decanal chapter of Beverley. In January of 1366, Adam of York interrogated Marjorie, and she stuck by her story. In March, Adam rendered sentence for Marjorie.

In April of 1366, Thomas appealed from Adam's sentence to the official of York. In his appeal he renewed all the substantive exceptions that he had made before Mr Adam. At this point the chronology becomes obscure. It would seem that almost a year passed. In March of 1367, testimony was finally received from Thomas's witnesses. They testified to his absence from Beverley and his presence in Middleton on 5 January three years previously. One deposition on behalf of Marjorie followed in the beginning of April. At the end of July, the official rendered a confirmatory sentence on behalf of Marjorie. Thomas appealed to the Apostolic See, an appeal that he may have pursued, because a *processus* seems to have been made up for purposes of the appeal, but no further record in the case has been found.

All the depositions have survived, and once more they are of some interest. Two women testify on Marjorie's articles in the principal case. They both describe events in Richard of Middleton's house, and their testimony is quite consistent: Thomas asked Marjorie why she was pursuing him before the court of the dean of Beverley; he promised to marry her after Easter; he offered her money in recompense for the litigation expenses that she had already incurred, and they spent the night together: "a man alone with a woman alone, a naked man with a naked woman, in one bed."[10] In the same depositions, three men testify about the events before Mr Ralph in the decanal chapter. The first, Thomas de Raventhorp, the apparitor of the court, states that he had cited Thomas and Marjorie for fornication. They both confessed the intercourse, and, under oath, Marjorie confessed a *de futuro* contract. Thomas had refused to take an oath but confessed that he had promised to marry Marjorie and that he had had intercourse with her after the promise. Later, privately, Thomas confessed the promise again, and banns were proclaimed between them. The other two men are more circumspect. According to them, Thomas had confessed that he promised to marry Marjorie if she behaved herself properly, and intercourse had followed. Following this confession, Mr Ralph declared them married and that banns should be proclaimed. These witnesses say nothing about any private confession of Thomas's.

Thomas's five witnesses before Mr Adam, all men, tell a quite different story. Two of them suggest that Marjorie's female witnesses were of bad reputation, both of them having been guilty of sexual offenses. All five men testify about

[10] *solus cum sola, nudus cum nuda in uno lecto*. Ref. T&C no. 69.

the events in the decanal chapter. In their view, Thomas de Raventhorp and Mr Ralph were trying to get both Marjorie and Thomas to confess that a marriage had taken place. After some hesitancy Marjorie confessed that it had, but all that Thomas said was that he had once told her in bed that she could behave herself in such a way that he would marry her.

Thomas's witnesses on appeal are even more striking. They tell a vivid story of Thomas's presence in Middleton on 5 January 1364. One witness had been with him most of the day. They went to mass together in the morning and spent most of the day drinking in various public houses where Thomas was trying to collect debts owed him and to make more sales. The witness remembers the events because he and Thomas had quarreled that day about the price of three ells of cloth that Thomas had sold him. Coming from the mill the next morning, the witness saw Thomas heading off for Beverley. Thomas's servant was riding a horse and carrying a sack of merchandise; Thomas was driving before him another horse loaded with merchandise. Altogether, six witnesses confirm various parts of Thomas's story.

Marjorie produces only one witness on appeal, Richard of Middleton's wife, and she testifies against Marjorie. According to Richard's wife, Thomas was not present at her house in Beverley on 5 January 1364.

Again, the question is whether we can make anything at all out of this. As in the case of *Dolling c Smith*, someone is clearly lying. Thomas could not have been at Beverley and in Middleton on the same day in 1364. Also, as in the case of *Dolling c Smith*, neither set of witnesses inspires much confidence. The two women who testify on Marjorie's behalf are of lower station, are clearly Marjorie's supporters, and could even have been bribed. The men of Middleton who testify on Thomas's behalf are his fellow townsmen, and there are not so many of them that they too could not have been corrupted. It is especially suspicious that it takes Thomas almost two years to produce them, enough time carefully to fabricate a story.

As in the case of *Dolling c Smith*, too, while the precise events of 5 January 1364 may never be known, the witnesses are testifying to things that are close to their experience. Thomas may not have spent 5 January 1364 visiting the pubs of Middleton, but chapmen did spend January days doing just that, and the witness's description of Thomas, his servant, and the horses conjures up a picture out of a fourteenth-century miniature. Similarly, the events at the house of Richard of Middleton may never have happened, but things like this did happen. Marjorie was Thomas's mistress; everyone concedes this. She probably hoped that he would marry her someday. Men in Thomas's position worried about prosecution before the lower-level church courts. They made vague promises of marriage, and some of them, like Thomas, got caught.

What distinguishes this case from *Dolling c Smith* is the role of the decanal court and its personnel. In *Dolling*, it is the women of Winterbourne Stoke who get together, if our speculations are correct, and decide that William should marry Alice. Here, there is a strong suggestion that the apparitor and commissary of the decanal court of Beverley made the decision and sought to shape the events to ensure that it happened. Again, we may never know precisely what Thomas said in the decanal chapter (just as we may never know what his real objections to marrying Marjorie were), but the fact that even Marjorie's witnesses, with the exception of the apparitor and the commissary, testify to a considerably more ambiguous confession than do the apparitor and the commissary suggests that Thomas's version of the story may be at least as accurate as Marjorie's. The truth may lie someplace in between.

INGOLY C MIDELTON, ESYNGWALD AND WRIGHT

The third case, the simplest in terms of the surviving documentation, also comes from the consistory of York, about 60 years after *Merton c Midelton*.[11] In March of 1430, Joan Ingoly of Bishopthorpe, wife of John Midelton, sued her husband, Robert Esyngwald of Poppleton, and his wife Ellen Wright, alleging that neither her marriage to John nor Robert's to Ellen could stand because she and Robert had exchanged words of present consent before either her marriage to John or Robert's to Ellen. Witnesses on her articles were heard in April. At the beginning of July, the commissary general rendered sentence declaring both *de facto* marriages null and that Robert and Joan were husband and wife. John's proctor appealed to the Apostolic See, but a week later the official formally refused to grant dimissory letters (*apostoli*),[12] and the case disappears from view.

The depositions have survived, and they are of some interest. Two witnesses testify solely to the marriage of John and Joan, which took place in the presence of a priest in the parish of St Margaret's Walmgate, York, on 25 November 1414. Three witnesses testify to the marriage of Robert and Ellen, which took place in the presence of a priest in Poppleton chapel, on 25 May 1410. The two witnesses to Robert and Joan's informal marriage, Robert and Alice Dalton, are husband and wife; Alice is Joan's sister. They testify that on 22 July 1408, or perhaps it was 1409, Robert Esyngwald and Joan had contracted marriage in the high street of Upper Poppleton, at the end of the garden of one Thomas del Leys. Robert Dalton testifies that they both used the same form of words: "I will have you as wife/husband and to this I give you my troth." Alice has a slightly different version of Robert's words, "I will have thee and take (*conducere*) thee as wife and to this I pledge thee my troth."[13] Both agree that Robert held Joan by the right hand; after the words were exchanged they joined hands and kissed. Both Robert Dalton and Alice were in service when the marriage of Robert Esyngwald and Ellen took place, and both denied knowing anything about it until after it happened. Although Alice was present at Joan and John's wedding in St Margaret's Walmgate, she said nothing because she believed that Robert's earlier marriage to Ellen had been authorized by letters from the

[11] *Ingoly c Midelton, Esyngwald and Wright* (1430), CP.F.201; lit. T&C no. 70.
[12] See disc., n. 18.
[13] *Ibid.*, T&C no. 71.

archbishop. Robert Dalton alleges the same belief and adds that he believed that reclaiming against the banns of Joan and John would have had no effect because the marriage of Robert and Ellen had been solemnized "many years" previously.[14]

Unlike *Dolling c Smith* and *Merton c Midelton*, there is no necessary reason why any of the witnesses in this case needs be lying. The two solemnized marriages almost certainly happened much as described, and the informal marriage could have happened as well. Certainly there is no reason to doubt the main outlines of the witnesses' stories of their lives. Their terms of service in York are with identifiable people, and the story of their lives is typical of the 'middling sort' of people in this period and well beyond.[15] Young people in service, required by the custom of their society to postpone marriage, frequently slept together and sometimes – often enough to produce a number of surviving cases – exchanged words importing some form of marital consent.[16] It is thus possible that Robert and Joan had some sort of relationship during their period of service, a relationship that led them to exchange words that might be regarded as words of marital consent.

What I find hard to believe, however, is that this story was anything like as straightforward as the record makes it out to be. In the first place, the Daltons' alibis for failing to come forward when Robert and Ellen were married look highly suspicious. Robert Dalton says that he spent the six or seven weeks preceding and following the marriage on his master's service in Lincoln diocese; Alice simply alleges that she was in service in York and so knew nothing about a marriage in Poppleton. Poppleton is only three miles northwest of York, and Alice came from there. It is hard to believe that she did not hear of the impending marriage, and if she really thought that Robert Esyngwald had married her sister, one wonders why she did not do anything about it when he married someone else. One possible explanation is that Joan may have decided that she was well enough rid of Robert Esyngwald, in which case one wonders why 21 years later she changed her mind. It seems more likely that nothing had occurred between Robert and Joan, or that what had occurred was not so clear as the witnesses make it out to be. The story of the rumors about letters from the archbishop is also hard to believe. Not that rumors like this did not circulate, but once it was clear that the letters did not exist, the failure of Robert and Alice to take any action calls for more of an explanation than the examiner demanded of them. Indeed, the examiner's questioning is remarkably lax. Other than asking why Robert and Alice had allowed the other two marriages to go ahead, he does little cross-examining. He does not inquire into the circumstances of the events in Upper Poppleton, the clothes the parties wore, the weather, and so on. Nor does he ask what the two witnesses did when they finally did find out about the conflicting marriages. He fails to ask the most obvious question: Granted

14 Text and disc. T&C no. 72.

15 Ref. T&C no. 73.

16 See Goldberg, "Marriage, Migration, Servanthood and Life-Cycle"; *id.*, *Women, Work.*

that you did not know about the other marriage at the time it took place, why have you remained silent for 19 years?

If this case raises so many doubts, why does it leave such a simple record? Even taking the record on its face, there are difficulties. As R. H. Helmholz has pointed out,[17] Alice's version of the words that Robert spoke go right to the edge of what the canonists and the courts would take as words of the present tense, and no one testifies to sexual intercourse. Yet the judge does not interrogate the parties; no exceptions are filed to the witnesses; the case goes forward without a hitch; it is so straightforward that *apostoli* are denied.

Perhaps a different explanation fits the evidence better: If we assume that this is not a contested case, much of what seems to be incomprehensible becomes comprehensible. Three defendants, represented by the best proctors of the day in the York court, present no defense to a weak case. Could it be that they presented no defense because this was the result that all of them wanted? This is certainly the case with Robert Esyngwald, because the *acta* in the case indicate that he admitted the facts in Joan's libel from the very beginning.[18]

But what of the personnel of the court? If the parties to the case were in some sense abusing the process of the court in order to obtain a consent judgment, why did the proctors and the judge allow this to happen, particularly when it involved the dissolution of two marriages of long standing? Surely, they knew, or suspected, that the defendants were not pursuing the case very vigorously. Even if all the parties to the case had consented to the judgment, the court personnel should have been concerned about the bond of the sacrament of marriage and about the potential scandal that the case might cause. My explanation for why the court allowed this to happen so easily is simple, if somewhat shocking: One of the defendants in the case, the reader will recall, was named Robert Esyngwald; his proctor was also named Robert Esyngwald, and the judge in the case was named Roger Esyngwald. My suggestion is, then, that the court personnel were complicitous in what was happening.

The name Esyngwald derives from the small town, now spelled 'Easingwold', 12 miles northwest of York. At least 13 men named Easingwold (with various spellings) appear in the court and city records of York in the first decades of the fifteenth century.[19] The cluster of men with this name in the York records in this period, coupled with their relative absence from earlier and later periods, suggests that many or most of our Easingwolds are connected. Blood relationship is demonstrable or probable in a number of cases. In other cases the connection is more likely to be geographical. Not that all of them came from Easingwold (Robert, the defendant in our case, may well have been born in Poppleton), but the fact that they bore the same toponym suggests relatively recent origins in Easingwold. This in turn would probably have led men named Easingwold

17 *Marriage Litigation*, 32; cf. *id.*, 64–5.

18 Cons.AB 3, fol 60v; disc. T&C no. 74.

19 The proctor and the judge in this case are well known. The defendant may be Robert, a tailor, who obtained the freedom of the city in 1423. Ref. T&C no. 75.

to patronize younger men with the same origin. It is certainly not pure chance that the commissary general and one of the proctors in our case both bore the same name. Nicholas Easingwold in the previous generation of proctors almost certainly passed on his practice to Robert, although he does not seem to have been his father, and he may have been the father of Roger, the commissary general.[20] John Easingwold, a moneymaker at the archbishop's mint, benefited from the patronage of Roger Easingwold, the commissary general.[21] Similarly, it is probably not by chance that Robert Easingwold the tailor, and perhaps the defendant in our case, was enrolled as a freeman of the city in the same year that Thomas Easingwold was the mayor. Hence, it is also probably not pure chance that Robert Easingwold, the putative tailor, is able to discard his wife of 19 years and marry another who has been another man's wife for 16 in a case in which another Robert Easingwold serves as his proctor and a Roger Easingwold is the judge. It is more plausible that something like this could have happened when we learn that the archbishop (John Kempe, who had been in office for only four years) was the chancellor of England and probably not paying much attention to what was going on in his court at York. We might even speculate that there is a connection between this case, and the scandal that it may have caused, and the fact that shortly after this time, Easingwolds disappear not only from positions of prominence in the court of York but also from positions of prominence in the city.

Now what does all this have to do with Alexander III and with the principles and policies that seem to have guided his decisions? Clearly, the connection is not simple and direct. On the one hand, we probably should avoid the conclusion that Alexander's decisions had no social effect at all. They clearly affected the parties in all three cases, and there are dozens of cases like them. On the other hand, there is the obvious problem of writing social history from a police blotter. We have hundreds of medieval marriage cases in various states of preservation, but there were millions of medieval marriages, and the litigated ones are not only a small sample but also a highly biased sample of the whole group. A skeptic would say that all we can know from these cases is that when people got to court, Alexander's rules were applied to whatever facts the parties chose to present. What went on outside of court cannot be known from the court records.

The cases do, however, give us some evidence that we can use to tell a story that might otherwise not be told: First, people did seem to know what the rules were. Informal marriages were valid, if not approved; no one's consent other than that of the parties was necessary for a valid marriage. Quite clearly, some of the people in some of the cases are making use of Alexander's rules to escape from the pressure of families and lords. It does not seem too far-fetched to suggest that others did the same, even though they produced no cases that left a record.

[20] See T&C no. 75.

[21] He calls him *magister meus* in his will and leaves him a small legacy. *Testamenta Eboracensia II*, 16.

Second, because people knew what the rules were, they knew what they had to say in order to achieve the desired result in court. In some cases we may suspect lying, pure and simple. In many cases – and the marriages described in all three of our cases may be examples – what the witnesses testify to may represent more shading of what happened than outright lies. That the witnesses did this, and that they seem to have done it quite frequently, may suggest not so much corruption, though there is some evidence of that, as it does that the witnesses shaded their testimony in order to produce a result that they believed to be a just one. This, in turn, could not have happened regularly without the tacit approval of the court personnel. Such approval was forthcoming in the case of the official of Salisbury in *Dolling c Smith* and of the York consistory in *Ingoly c Midelton*. It was not in *Merton c Midelton*, where the personnel of the decanal court take a much more active role in shaping the proceedings, using the ambiguities of the law and the facts to force what they seemed to have believed to be a proper result. The judgment of the personnel of the decanal court in this case was apparently shared by those of the York consistory. Nor was approval forthcoming from the appellate court in *Dolling c Smith*, where the personnel of the appellate court, divorced from the situation of the parties and the underlying facts, behaved much more like academic lawyers.

What causes the courts sometimes to accept the results that the parties and witnesses are urging them to accept and sometimes to reject them is a complicated question, the answer to which is highly problematical. Suffice it to say here that the result in the Salisbury court in *Dolling* and in the York consistory in *Ingoly* is more typical of the results in English medieval marriage cases than is that on appeal in *Dolling* or, with qualifications, that in both courts in *Merton*.

Third, as Michael Sheehan has noted, the attitudes toward marriage reflected in these court records are extraordinarily individualistic. Though there are cases in which people are clearly escaping from the pressure of families and lords, they pale in comparison with the number of cases in which families and lords are no place to be found. This is surprising only if one reads other types of sources about medieval marriage where the role of the choice of others than the parties seems to tell the whole story. There are two possible conclusions: Either all the cases that we are looking at are cases of runaway marriages, Romeo and Juliet run rampant, which seems unlikely, or the model of marriage that we get from other sources, manor records, charters, and literary evidence needs modification in the light of what the church court records seem to suggest was a wider practice than that prevailing among the people who ended up litigating.

This individualism, however, has limits. Where the couple are agreed and will stick to their story, the larger society is, by and large, forced to accept their judgment. Even here, however, the couple need some support, at least two witnesses, if the rights of third parties are at stake. Where the couple cannot agree, however (and not surprisingly most litigated cases are of this type), then the wider society has a role to play. The wider society may be a social group, like the women of Winterbourne Stoke, who chose to support Alice against William, or it may be an official group, like the personnel of the decanal court of Beverley, who seem to have played a considerable role in encouraging Marjorie to bring her case, and perhaps even in telling her what she ought to say.

TIRYNGTON C MORYZ

Our last case is laden with ambiguity. It will serve in some ways to confirm the conclusions at which we tentatively arrived with the first three, but it will also expose us, in a way more dramatic than the others, to the difficulties of drawing even tentative social conclusions from legal records.

In June of 1367, Walter de Tiryngton (Terrington) of Tadcaster in the West Riding of Yorkshire sued Agnes daughter of William Moryz (Morice), his *de facto* wife, before the official of the archdeacon of York.[22] He claimed that their marriage of 15 (or perhaps it was 13) years should be dissolved on the ground that Agnes had precontracted marriage with one Henry Littester 16 years previously.[23] Agnes conceded each element in the complaint. The official appointed a special commissary before whom testimony was taken.[24]

Walter offers two witnesses to the precontract, Agnes's maternal aunt and her husband, Matilda and William Sturgis, who testify that around Michaelmas "two years after the first pestilence," they were present in the house of Richard Hare in Wilstrop where Henry and Agnes contracted marriage "at the procuration" of the two witnesses.[25] Henry says (I translate here from the Latin into the probable Middle English): "Ik taa thee her Agnes til wife if haaly kirk it suffer and to that ik plight thee my trauth."[26] And he took her by the right hand, and she said the same. William says that he remembers the time because around that time he and Matilda had moved into the house in which they now live. He and his wife toted up the years, and it will be 16 years next Michaelmas. Henry is still living in Wetherby, and William knows this because he saw him many times in the last quarter.[27] William cannot testify whether the couple had sexual intercourse but says that they confessed it.

Matilda agrees with William in all things, with the following additions: She had spoken with Henry in Tadcaster on the previous feast of John the Baptist (24 June). On the question of intercourse, she says that on the day of the contract, she saw Henry and Agnes lie together *nudus cum nuda, solus cum sola, in uno lecto*.[28]

The third witness, Agnes Payge, does not testify directly about the contract between Agnes and Henry. Rather, she testifies to the solemnization of the marriage between Agnes and Walter in the parish church of Tadcaster around

[22] *Tiryngton c Moryz* (1367–8), CP.E.95, disc. T&C no. 76.
[23] Disc. T&C no. 77.
[24] Disc. T&C no. 78.
[25] T&C no. 79. Wilstrop, Yorks, North Riding, is 2 mi. northwest of Long Marston.
[26] T&C no. 80. I am grateful to Nicholas Watson for help with the dialect.
[27] Reading *et hoc bene scit quia vidit dictum Henricum pluries infra quarterium anni ultimo preteriti*. Wetherby, Yorks, West Riding, is 14 mi. west of York.
[28] See text and n. 10.

24 June, 15 years previously. She recalls the time because her daughter Joan was 2 at the time, and Joan is now 17, and because around that time Joan's father went to Berwick where he was captured and imprisoned for two and a half years. The witness, too, had seen Henry in Tadcaster the previous 24 June, and she had heard Agnes say many times before the present litigation that she had precontracted with Henry and that he knew her before the solemnization with Walter, to which she was "craftily induced" (*contumeliose inducta*) by her aunt, Matilda Sturgis.[29] In addition, "[the witness] believes that the articles are true because there was never a good life between Walter and Agnes from the time the marriage was solemnized between them, but they were always quarrelling with each other, and she frequently took off and separated herself from his company (*consortium*) and had children by another man, as was said."[30]

On the basis of this testimony and Agnes's confession, the special commissary of the archdeacon rendered sentence for Walter.[31]

In the following autumn, Agnes sued Walter in the consistory court of the archbishop of York, alleging that Walter had abandoned her without cause.[32] Walter excepted to these proceedings on the basis of the judgment of the commissary of the archdeacon's official and introduced the documents from the lower court.[33] In May of the following year, Walter was back in the consistory court, petitioning again for divorce. At this point the documentation in the case ceases, with a notice on the back of the last petition that the case is pending.

We are dealing here with three propositions of law: First, if Agnes exchanged words of present consent with Henry before she married Walter, then her marriage to Walter was bigamous and void. It makes no difference whether Henry was still alive at the time of the suit, so long as he was alive at the time of the marriage between Walter and Agnes, though the fact that he is still alive now means that Agnes and Walter cannot set things right by marrying now.[34] It also makes no difference whether Agnes and Henry had intercourse or that they did not solemnize their marriage. If the marriage between Agnes and Henry was one of the present tense and can be proved by two independent witnesses, the marriage of Walter and Agnes is void.

Second, the words that Agnes and Henry are alleged to have exchanged are words of the present tense. Indeed, the formula that they use is so common in cases involving informal marriages that we might imagine that many men and women in late medieval Yorkshire had it memorized. There is, however, one potential ambiguity in the formula "if haaly kirk it suffer," *si sancta ecclesia hoc permittat*. This might be taken as making the marriage conditional on the permission of the church, one that would come about, for example, with the

[29] Text and disc. T&C no. 81.
[30] T&C no. 82.
[31] Disc. T&C no. 83.
[32] Disc. and lit. T&C no. 84.
[33] See at n. 47.
[34] Disc. T&C no. 85.

proclamation of the banns. That is not the only way of taking the phrase, but if it be so taken, then the fact that Agnes and Henry had intercourse would be deemed to have waived the condition. Hence, testimony is introduced about intercourse.

Third, there is another reason for the testimony about intercourse: As we have already noted, what counted as words of the present tense and what of the future was a matter of some controversy. If, however, the words of consent, be they present or future, were followed by sexual intercourse, then an indissoluble marriage had occurred without regard to the tense of the verbs. The standard allegation of a marriage in the pleadings in the York court in this period, as it was in this case, was to allege that X and Y "by words expressing their mutual present consent and/or by espousals by words of the future tense followed by sexual intercourse between them contracted marriage lawfully."[35] Whatever testimony came in, then, all the bases were covered.

These facts, however, pose a problem for the historian trying to reconstruct events from litigation records. They pose a particular problem for the historian trying to see in depositions medieval people telling stories about their lives. It is not only that the narrative is being reported by a clerk who is interested only in what is legally relevant and who is writing in a language that is normally not the language that the witnesses are speaking; it is also that most of the witnesses in the church courts of late medieval York have a very good idea what it is that they have to say in order for the party who produced them to have a case. If the law requires, or recommends, *hic accipio te in uxorem meam* or *maritum meum* as words to create a *de presenti* marriage, then the witness will say that what the parties said was "ik taa thee her Agnes *or* Harry til wife *or* husbonde." And if the witness cannot quite say that she saw them having intercourse, she will say "ik saw them bare-ersed in bedde, and ye wit what cam after," and the clerk will solemnly write down that the witness saw them *solus cum sola, nudus cum nuda, in eodem lecto*.

So in this case as in the preceding cases, if we are to use depositions as sources of narrative about medieval people's lives, the first thing that we should look to are the details that are not legally relevant, to the details that will not affect the outcome of the case. Witnesses were normally required to support their statements about when a particular event happened. They do so, quite frequently, by tying it into an event in their lives. I have little doubt that William and Matilda did indeed move into a new house in the autumn of 1351, and this move may well be connected to the disruption caused by the 'first pestilence' of 1348–9, to which William refers at the beginning of his deposition. More mysterious, but more intriguing, is Agnes Payge's reference to her daughter Joan, born at the end of the first pestilence in 1350, whose father, who does not seem to have been Agnes's husband, took off for Berwick on the Scottish border,[36] where he proceeded to spend two and a half years in jail. Captured by

[35] T&C no. 86.
[36] Disc. T&C no. 87.

the Scots? Perhaps, but Agnes's description suggests a more regular and perhaps well-deserved captivity.

But what of the main narrative, the story of the other Agnes, of Henry and of Walter? Here we must be cautious. A valid marriage once formed was *de iure* indissoluble. As we will see in later chapters, some ecclesiastical courts in this period – certain continental courts were notable – were experimenting with ways in which they could at least separate, if they could not divorce, in the modern sense, couples whose marriages had proved hopeless. The York court was not among them. It would seem that only adultery, and by the end of the fourteenth century perhaps extreme physical cruelty, would suffice to ground an action for separation, and, of course, this was without permission to remarry.[37] We would expect that couples involved in hopeless marriages would seek a way out, and it would seem that the conveniently remembered precontract was one, perhaps the most common, way to do it. All it required was the cooperation of the couple, two obliging witnesses, and a court that was not too skeptical.

Hence, the only thing that I find completely credible about this case is Agnes Payge's testimony that "Walter and Agnes did not have a good life together." It is also clear that Agnes Morice consented to the divorce, at least while the case was before the archdeacon's court. We may have considerably more doubt that the precontract with Henry happened, or at least that it happened with quite the clarity that the witnesses recall after 16 years. The subsequent proceedings in the court of York are something of a puzzle. It may be no more than a question of jurisdiction; the parties were advised to sue there again because of doubt over whether the special commissary had authority to render a divorce decree.[38] It may be, however, that Agnes had second thoughts. As we will see in Chapter 4, there is at least one case in the York archives in which the woman sues to have a divorce judgment before an archdeacon's court set aside, confessing that she had suborned perjury to a precontract in the previous action.[39]

If we put all the cases involving precontract together, it is clear that in litigation before the court of York in the later Middle Ages, the allegation and defense of precontract gave rise to a substantial amount of perjury, or shading of the truth. This is not to say that all the witnesses in such cases were lying, simply that in any case where we have evidence that the current marriage has broken down and where the divorce action is confessed, we have reason to suspect that the witnesses to the precontract are coloring their story.

It is hard to believe that the court was deceived by such cases. In *Ingoly c Midelton*, it would seem that the court was conniving in the false judgment.[40] In other cases, its attitude seems to have been more passive. In one case brought before the archbishop, the archbishop simply dropped the case when, we suspect, he came to realize that the plaintiff was not simply the innocent victim of

[37] See Ch 10, at nn. 27–32.
[38] Ref. and disc. T&C no. 88.
[39] *Palmere c Brunne and Suthburn* (1333), CP.E.25.
[40] See at nn. 18–19.

a runaway wife.[41] If the parties to a hopeless marriage were willing to agree to a consent judgment, the court was not going to press too firmly. The judgment had to be by consent, and the parties had to have witnesses to support them, but if those two conditions were fulfilled, it would seem that the court would leave them to their consciences.

But what of the parties' consciences? Obviously, we do not know what went on in their minds or what they told their confessors. We do have cases that suggest quite strongly that having agreed to a false judgment, some of these parties had qualms of conscience about what they had done.[42] In the other cases, *Ingoly c Midelton* may be an example, they may not have cared, brazenly manipulating the processes of the court to get what they wanted. There is also some suggestion of a third possibility. As we have said, the York court was strict about separations. On the other hand, we know that a number of these parties were stuck in what seem to have been hopeless marriages. It is possible that in such circumstances they were able to convince themselves that they really had never been married to the person with whom they were now living so badly. Hints of such an attitude may be found in the deposition of Agnes Payge, who testifies that Walter and Agnes Morice had not had a "good life." That fact is, of course, legally irrelevant to the question whether Agnes Morice had precontracted with Henry. But it is clearly not irrelevant in the witness's mind. The fact that Walter and Agnes did not have a good life seems to have convinced the witness that they were not married; their bad life was a punishment for the fact that they married each other when Agnes should have married Henry. Not only does the witness believe this but she also seems to think that Agnes Morice believes it as well.

This cast of mind is hard for us to grasp. It requires a belief in divine providence that borders on superstition and a total ignorance of what we believe to be the causes of marital breakdown. Under this cast of mind, if Agnes and Walter's marriage did not work out, that must have been because there was something wrong with it in the first place. There are other cases where witnesses testify to the same effect in cases involving consanguinity or affinity.[43] If the parties are related, the marriage cannot prosper. God will see to it that it does not. Similarly, if Agnes and Walter's marriage is not prospering, that must be because they are not really married. Thinking along these lines leads Agnes, and eventually her witnesses, to thinking about Henry. Over the course of 15 miserable years, the thinking can change subtly from "I/She would have been better off if I/she had married Harry" to "I/She did marry Harry, and that is why she is having so much trouble with Walter; she isn't married to him." Eventually, they come to the point where they can testify, perhaps even with a clean conscience, that Henry and Agnes exchanged words of present consent 16 years previously.

41 *Huntyngton c Munkton* (1345–6).
42 *Palmere c Brunne and Suthburn* (1333) is probably an example.
43 Example T&C no. 89.

But if we are going to engage in this kind of reconstruction – and I must confess that I find it irresistible – we cannot ignore other possibilities. If we are to imagine that Agnes Morice and Agnes Payge were engaged in self-deception, what of Matilda Sturgis and her husband? And what of the special commissary? The latter, of course, may have taken a bribe or simply not have cared. His questioning is certainly lax. He fails to ask the obvious question of the Sturgises: "Where were you when the banns were proclaimed between Walter and Agnes, and where have you been for the past fifteen years when you knew they were living in sin?"[44] Perhaps even more to the point: "Where's Harry? Why don't you have him come in and testify?" Is there something about the way in which William and Matilda tell their story that would have made it sound plausible to an experienced cleric? The clue may lie in William's statement that the marriage with Henry was done "at the procuration" of his wife and himself.[45] Agnes Morice's parents are never mentioned; her maternal aunt and her husband may have been her guardians. She could have been as young as 12 at the time of the marriage with Henry. The guardians arrange the marriage with Henry; consent is exchanged; then, for some reason, perhaps financial, the negotiations break down. Agnes is allowed to marry Walter (perhaps the Sturgises arrange that marriage, too), and Henry is conveniently forgotten. Now, 16 years later and faced with the disaster of Agnes's marriage to Walter, the Sturgises have qualms of conscience, and they tell Walter about the precontract. This scenario would fit well with Agnes Payge's statement that Agnes Morice told her that she was "craftily induced" into the marriage with Walter by her aunt.[46]

This scenario is, of course, not completely inconsistent with the scenario of self-deception that we outlined previously. We cannot, however, ignore any scrap of evidence, including negative evidence. Agnes Payge may have thought that Agnes Morice's bad life was punishment for her not having married Walter validly, but there is no evidence that Agnes Morice thought so. Indeed, other than her confession before the archdeacon's court, which could have been the product of considerable pressure, we hear nothing of Agnes Morice's version of the story. We do know, however, that two months after the special commissary had rendered judgment against her, she petitioned the archbishop's court to restore her husband to her, and that despite the impressive documentation of the previous case that Walter was able to present before that court,[47] he was advised to bring his suit all over again the following spring. Then he fails to pursue the case, and more than six hundred years later, it is still pending.

[44] As was required by X 4.18.6 (Innocent III, *Cum in tua. Si vero*).

[45] See at n. 25.

[46] See at n. 29.

[47] Disc. T&C no. 90.

3

Statistics

The Court of York, 1300–1500

The approach that we have taken to these cases so far is the traditional historian's one of trying to tell a story. We found that it may be possible to tell stories from this type of case material, but it is difficult. The litigation context distorts the story, particularly if one is trying to tell a story of what happened, as opposed to the story of what happened in the litigation. There is a further difficulty for the historian who is seeking to discover the social context of Alexander's rules: Frequently the particular makes us lose sight of the general. We suggested that there were many cases like *Dolling c Smith* and like *Merton c Midelton*, but there are not many cases like *Ingoly c Midelton*. Indeed, it is the only York case I have found in which *two* formal marriages are dissolved on the basis of an informal precontract prior to either one of them,[1] and it is one of only a handful in which there is such strong evidence that considerations far different from those that are found in Alexander's decisions played a dominant role in the decision. *Tiryngton c Moryz* may be such a case as well, but in the end, we had doubts. We were able to construct a plausible version of a story in which the precontract did happen, and of course the couple, so far as we can tell, never obtained a final judgment.

We turn then, for reasons described in the Introduction, to the court of York and to numbers.[2] Before we do that, however, a brief description of the court is in order. As we have already noted, the consistory court of York in the later Middle Ages served both as a first-instance court for the diocese and as an appellate court for the province, which included, in addition to York, the dioceses of Durham and Carlisle.[3] The diocese of York was large, and there

[1] There are other cases that involve three marriages, or two marriages and a claimed third; disc. T&C no. 91.

[2] An earlier version of this chapter appeared as Donahue, "Female Plaintiffs." Further analysis, particularly of the fifteenth-century cases, has led to a revision of the figures and some recasting of the argument.

[3] Disc. T&C no. 92.

were five active archdeacons who on occasion heard marriage cases, some of which were appealed to the court of York. The archbishop of York was the second most important prelate in England after the archbishop of Canterbury. As such, he was frequently absent from York. Three of the archbishops during our period also served as chancellors of England.[4]

In addition to being an important ecclesiastical center in this period, the city of York was also a governmental center. It served as the county town for the three large ridings of Yorkshire; Edward III moved his government to York when he wanted to be nearer to Scotland. It was also an important trading center. Along with those of London and Bristol, its mayor provided a registry for statutes merchant under the statutes of Acton Burnell (1283) and of Merchants (1285) and for statutes staple under that statute (1353). The York cycle of mystery plays dates from our period. In addition to York, our records mention other trading centers in the diocese, Kingston upon Hull probably being the most important.

YORK CAUSE PAPERS OVER TWO CENTURIES: THE BUSINESS OF THE COURT AND CLAIMS AND DEFENSES IN MARRIAGE CASES

There survive at the Borthwick Institute for Archives in York case files (cause papers) from 570 different cases that were heard before the archbishop's consistory court in the period from 1301 through 1499.[5] Their subject matter may be divided as shown in Table 3.1.[6]

As can be seen from the table, 215 of these cases are matrimonial cases (a case involving the validity, dissolution, or separation of a marriage or of the marriages of connected parties),[7] approximately 38 percent of the total.[8] The records, as we have already noted, are unusually full, and in marked contrast to most records of medieval ecclesiastical courts, they are spread over a relatively long period of time. They would seem, then, to be a good base of data to use for asking questions about the nature of medieval marriage litigation and about how it may have changed over the course of the later Middle Ages. In order to do this, we will deal first with the records as a whole and then subdivide the 86 marriage cases that date from the fourteenth century and the 129 such cases that date from the fifteenth century.

It is well to sound a note of caution at the start: The York records are good, but they are not a random sample of medieval English marriage litigation, and certainly not of marriage litigation in the Latin West. To focus on the differences

[4] Details T&C no. 93.
[5] Lit. and disc. T&C no. 94.
[6] Tables dividing the cases by decade, refining the subject matter, and explaining the differences from previous counts may be found App. e3.1, "The Business of the Court of York, 1300–1500 in Detail" (see T&C no. 95).
[7] Disc. with examples T&C no. 96.
[8] Disc. T&C no. 97.

TABLE 3.1. *York Cause Papers by Type of Case (1300–1499)*

Type of Case	Total	% of Total
Unknown	26	4.6
Breach of faith	35	6.1
Defamation	55	9.6
Ecclesiastical		
Benefice	44	7.7
Tithes	70	12.3
Other	73	12.8
SUBTOTAL	184	32.3
Matrimonial	215	37.7
Miscellaneous	6	1.1
Testamentary	46	8.1
TOTAL	570	100.0

Source: York, Borthwick Institute, CP.E; CP.F.

between the records of the court of York and those in other medieval ecclesiastical jurisdictions, the consistory court of York seems not to have exercised much office jurisdiction as a matter of first instance. There are a few office cases found in the cause papers, but most of them are cases that were being appealed from other courts or where the court was enforcing one of its own orders (and there are relatively few of either of these).[9] Clearly the criminal enforcement of the church's marriage law was socially important throughout the Middle Ages (as *Merton c Midelton* shows), and to the extent that it is only tangentially illustrated in the York records, these records are a biased sample of the whole picture. Second, the York court was both the consistory court for a diocese that had many active archdeacons and the appellate court for the province. We would thus expect to find, and we do find, a disproportionate number of the wealthy, the powerful, and the persistent among the litigants.[10] There is also a geographical bias in the first-instance cases, many of them being brought by parties who lived in or close to the city of York.[11] The two biases are probably related. Within a radius of about 40 miles from the city (and we might expand that number where the parties lived along the routes of the old Roman roads), the litigants in the court of York were quite ordinary people, ranging from citizens of York to village tradesmen and the wealthier peasants. Such people probably make up at least two-thirds of the litigants; it may be as high as four-fifths. As the distance from the city of York increases, so does the wealth of the litigants. The remaining one-fifth to one-third is heavily biased

[9] Listed with disc. T&C no. 98.
[10] E.g., *Hagarston c Hilton* (1467), CP.F.314; disc. T&C no. 99.
[11] Pedersen, *Marriage Disputes*, 184–5 and nn. 22–3.

in the direction of the wealthy, though normally not rising above the class of simple knights.[12] The very poor are almost, but not entirely, absent.

We will be able to correct for the first bias in Chapter 6 in which we will examine a consistory court from a small diocese (Ely) that did a substantial amount of office business. We will be able to correct, to some extent, for the second bias as well, because the Ely court did relatively little appellate business (though it did do some); its jurisdictional reach, as a practical matter, extended throughout the diocese at least so far as matrimonial litigation was concerned, and it seems to have dealt with more quite ordinary people. Here too, however, we may doubt whether the court often reached the very poor. We will be dealing throughout this book with litigation in ecclesiastical courts that left surviving records. As such we are dealing with an activity in which the very poor probably did not often engage, and any social conclusions that we attempt to draw from these records must bear that fact in mind. It is hard to imagine that the very poor did not, at least occasionally, have disputes about marriage, but when they did, they were probably most often resolved informally, perhaps occasionally in manorial or archidiaconal courts, courts that for the most part have left such cryptic records that we normally cannot tell more than that parties appeared before them and were fined.[13]

If the York records are not a random sample of all English medieval marriage litigation (and certainly not a random sample of all English medieval marriages), they may be a random, or at least an unbiased, sample of all such litigation that came to the court of York over the course of two hundred years. The arguments supporting this proposition are sufficiently complicated that they must be left to an appendix to this chapter.[14] Suffice it to say here that I am sufficiently convinced of the validity of those arguments that we will employ some kinds of simple statistical tests with this data (confidence intervals and z tests). Two apparent biases in the surviving records deserve attention here:

First, there is a chronological bias in these records. Although there are records of marriage cases (and of other types of cases) from every decade over the two hundred years, the decades from 1380 to 1440 produced a disproportionate number of the surviving files.[15] (This is not a bias peculiar to marriage cases; there is a similar bias in the records of non-marriage cases.) There is, however, no reason to believe that this bias in the sample does not reflect an actual bias in the underlying population. Appendix e3.1 to this chapter suggests that the decline in the later fifteenth century may well reflect York's economic decline in the same period, and the increase over the fourteenth century may well reflect a steady growth in the court's business over the course of that century, slowed, but not halted, by the plague years in the middle of the century.

12 Lit. T&C no. 100.

13 Example T&C no. 101.

14 App. e3.3, "The Surviving York Cause Papers as an Unbiased Sample" (see T&C no. 150).

15 See App. e3.2, "The Chronological Imbalance in the Surviving York Cause Papers" (see T&C no. 149).

Second, there is a chronological imbalance in the number of matrimonial cases appealed from lower courts in the fourteenth century.[16] The first three decades of the century produced only 7 percent of the cases (6/86), but they accounted for 16 percent of the appeals (4/25). The phenomenon continued if we add the next decade: The first four decades produced 16 percent of the cases (14/86), but 28 percent of the appeals (7/25). Were it not for the fact that the last decade of the century produced appeals in almost the same proportion as it did cases (32% of appeals [8/25], 33% of cases [28/86]), the imbalance of appeals toward the earlier part of the century would be even greater. The fifteenth century saw a dramatic decline in the proportion of appeals from lower courts in marriage cases: 10 percent (13/129) as opposed to 29 percent (25/86), and these appeals are clustered in the first half of the century: 11 of them (85%) before 1442, even though the second half of the century saw 38 percent of the cases (49/129).

Clearly, there is something happening here that needs explaining, but once again, there is no reason to believe that the sample is not reflecting something that was happening in the underlying population. The overall trend in the data is clear. Appeals from lower courts in marriage cases steadily declined over the course of the two centuries. At the same time, the proportion of first-instance marriage cases in the court increased quite steadily, at least until the middle decades of the fifteenth century. The two phenomena could be related, at least to the extent that people who were likely to appeal from the results that they got in archidiaconal courts tended, as time went on, to begin in the diocesan court to start off with. This explanation does not explain the aberrant decade of the 1390s, but then again, there is much about that decade that is unusual. It has, for example, the highest number of marriage cases of all the decades in the two centuries. It is possible that a particularly litigious decade also brought with it an unusually large number of appeals in marriage cases from lower courts.

A final note of caution: Good as they are (and this is a remarkably good set of records, as medieval church court records go), there are annoying gaps. We frequently do not know how a case ended. (Sometimes we suspect that it was compromised or abandoned, but sometimes we have reasonably good evidence that it was not, and we still do not know what the result was.) Sometimes we have the claim but not the defense; sometimes we have the defense but not the claim; sometimes we have the result but neither the defense nor the claim. In what follows, we have read the record as a whole and drawn what we believe to be reasonable inferences from it about matters that are not directly stated. Where both pleadings and depositions have survived, we have taken the depositions as indicating the 'true' nature of the legal claim or defense in preference to the pleadings, but where the depositions have not survived, we have used what can be gleaned from the pleadings. We have, on occasion, reconstructed the nature of a claim from the defense, sometimes even from the sentence. We have frequently reconstructed the result of a case in a lower court

[16] Disc. T&C no. 102.

on the basis of what is claimed on appeal. Someone else might classify some of these cases differently; perhaps one more cautious would leave more gaps in the base of evidence. Numbers imply a precision that the nature of medieval records does not always warrant. We do not believe, however, that the overall thrust of the numerical evidence would be greatly affected by a different or more cautious approach.

A particular warning is in order about the cause papers from the second half of the fifteenth century. The record-keeping practices of the court changed in this period with the result that cause papers from this period are not so helpful as those from the earlier ones.[17] The hope that I expressed earlier that a more thorough analysis of the surviving fifteenth-century act books would reveal more cases from that century and also provide more information about cases that are only skimpily recorded in the fifteenth-century cause papers has proved, for the most part, to be unfounded.[18] Thanks to a recent analysis of those books, we have been able to fill in a few details when we discuss individual cases in later chapters, but for the most part, the act books do not coincide with the dates of the cause papers, and what they tell us about the cases that do not have surviving cause papers is usually not enough even for the relatively simple statistical purposes of this chapter.[19]

The subject matter of the fourteenth- and fifteenth-century York marriage cases may be divided according to the type of claim that is being brought, employing a classification of types of claims that is found in the records themselves: There are two-party actions to enforce a marriage, what the records call *cause matrimoniales*, like *Dolling c Smith* or *Merton c Midelton*. We may further divide these (though the name of the action is the same) into those cases in which the record taken as a whole indicates that what is sought to be enforced is an informal *de presenti* marriage, those in which the record indicates that what is sought to be enforced is a *de futuro* promise normally followed by intercourse, those in which what is sought to be enforced is an 'abjuration under penalty of marriage' (*abiuratio sub pena nubendi*)[20] followed by intercourse (or, occasionally, appearance in suspicious places), and those in which it is unclear what type of marriage is at stake.

There are also three-party actions to enforce a marriage. These may be divided into cases that the records call *cause matrimoniales et divorcii*, in which the plaintiff sues a husband and wife seeking a divorce of their marriage and the enforcement of his or her own prior marriage to one of the couple, and cases involving what the records frequently call *competitores*, where two women sue a man or two men sue a woman each claiming that the defendant is his or her lawful spouse.[21]

[17] Details T&C no. 103.
[18] See Donahue, "Female Plaintiffs," 185–6. Details about the act books T&C no. 104.
[19] See App. e3.4, "What Can We Learn from the York Act Books?" (see T&C no. 151).
[20] A conditional marriage entered into before a judge hearing, normally a fornication case: "I take thee to wife/husband if I have carnal knowledge of thee." See n. 49.
[21] Disc. T&C no. 105.

TABLE 3.2. *York Marriage Cases – Claims (1300–1499)*

Type of Claim	14th c No.	14th c %	15th c No.	15th c %	Total No.	Total %
Two-party – *causa matrimonialis*						
De presenti	24	28	37	29	61	28
De futuro	9	10	7	5	16	7
Abjuration *sub pena nubendi*	9	10	2	2	11	5
Uncertain form of marriage	3	3	19	15	22	10
SUBTOTAL	45	52	65	50	110	51
Three-party actions						
Competitores	10	12	24	19	34	16
Causa matrimonialis et divorcii	10	12	14	11	24	11
SUBTOTAL	20	23	38	29	58	27
Causa divorcii a vinculo						
Precontract	5	6	5	4	10	5
Other[a]	11	13	10	8	21	10
SUBTOTAL	16	19	15	12	31	14
Other[b]	5	6	11	9	16	7
GRAND TOTAL	86	100	129	100	215	100

Notes: See T&C no. 106.
Source: York, Borthwick Institute, CP.E; CP.F.

Closely related to the three-party enforcement cases in the issues that they raise are actions for divorce from the bond of marriage (*cause divorcii a vinculo*) brought on the ground of precontract. These differ from *cause matrimoniales et divorcii* only in that the person with whom the precontract was made is not a party to the action. (*Tiryngton c Moryz* was such a case.) Hence, a judgment for the plaintiff, who is one of the parties to the alleged subsequent marriage, will result only in a declaration of the nullity of the present marriage and not in a declaration of the validity of the prior one. (Joan Ingoly avoided this feature in *Ingoly c Midelton* by bringing both an annulment action against her husband and a *causa matrimonialis et divorcii* against Robert Esyngwald and Ellen Wright.) There are also actions for divorce from the bond of marriage brought on grounds other than precontract: affinity, force or nonage, impotence, crime, and servile condition. There are cases of separation from bed and board (*divorcium quoad mensam et thorum*), including cases that began as marriage-enforcement actions, and the separation issue is raised as a defense.[22] The grounds on which such a separation is sought are normally both adultery and physical cruelty, sometimes just one or the other. Finally, there are miscellaneous cases, such as an action to recover payment for registration of marriage sentence or an action to obtain a letter certifying freedom from marriage. Table 3.2 lays out the number and percentage of each type of case.

What we might make of the differences in types of claims in the two centuries will be discussed later in this chapter, but one difference calls for comment here.

[22] One certainly so, one probably so.

The number of cases that deal with a claim of marriage of an uncertain form increases substantially in the fifteenth century (3% vs 15%). The reason why this is so has to do with the nature of the fifteenth-century records.[23] There is no reason to believe that this difference in record keeping reflects any difference between the two centuries in the nature of the underlying litigation.[24]

Table 3.2 shows that the great majority of actions concerning marriage brought in the York court in the two centuries were actions to enforce a marriage (168/215, 78%), while only 14 percent (31/215) were actions to dissolve a marriage (excluding in both cases the 16 actions classified as 'other').[25] Even if we exclude the marriage-and-divorce cases, the percentage of 'straight' marriage-enforcement actions is still high (144/215, 67%). But looking at the cases totally from the point of view of what was sought to be enforced does not tell us what was the crux of the case from a legal point of view, much less from a social point of view. To do this we need to know how the cases were defended (Table 3.3), and what the results were (to be shown in Tables 3.5 and 3.6).

When we combine the claims and the defenses, we see that classifying the actions according to the claim frequently obscures what the core legal issue was in the case. For example, the core legal issue in a divorce case brought on the ground of precontract is identical to the core legal issue in a marriage-and-divorce case.[26] The remedy sought was different because the person with whom the precontract was made was not made a party to the action, but the core legal issue was the same.[27] The issue in such cases was also identical to that in all the cases involving *competitores*, and in the 13 two-party marriage-enforcement actions that were defended on the ground of precontract. While it is logically possible that cases involving *competitores* could have involved defenses to both marriages – and one case in each century did, though in somewhat unusual ways[28] – the fact-pattern that normally emerges is the same in all four types of cases: A marriage had concededly occurred. The concession might be *sub silentio*, but there was rarely much argument about it. Frequently, though not always, the conceded marriage was a formal one.[29] The issue was whether another marriage claimed or defended as precontract had also occurred, and if it had occurred whether it had antedated the conceded one. Normally the claimed precontract was an informal *de presenti* marriage, although this was not always the case.[30]

[23] It is the same reason why there are more cases of an unknown type in Table e3.App.2 (T&C no. 95) than there are in Table e3.App.1 (T&C no. 95): There are more partial records from the fifteenth century than there are from the fourteenth.

[24] See App. e3.3.

[25] Disc. T&C no. 107.

[26] Disc. T&C no. 109.

[27] Disc. T&C no. 110.

[28] Disc. T&C no. 111.

[29] I use the terms 'formal' and 'informal' in order to avoid that most difficult of terms, 'clandestine' marriage. Definition T&C no. 112. In later chapters, however, when the court uses the term 'clandestine', we will use it.

[30] Disc. T&C no. 113.

TABLE 3.3. *York Marriage Cases – Defenses (1300–1499)*

	14th c		15th c		Total	
Type of defense[a]	No.	%	No.	%[b]	No.	%
Precontract						
Divorce for precontract	5	6	5	5	10	6
Marriage and divorce	11	14	15	15	26	15
Competitors	9	12	24	24	33	19
Two-party enforcement[c]	8	10	5	5	13	7
SUBTOTAL[d]	33	42	49	49	82	46
Denial						
'Straight' denial[e]	12	15	10	10	22	12
Exceptions to witnesses	16	21	19	19	35	20
Absence	9	12	16	16	25	14
Disparity of wealth	5	6	6	6	11	6
SUBTOTAL[d]	33	42	43	43	76	43
Force and/or nonage						
Force[f]	10	13	14	14	24	13
Nonage[g]	6	8	4	4	10	6
SUBTOTAL[d]	10	13	17	17	27	15
Other						
Consanguinity/affinity[h]	9	12	7	7	16	9
Unfulfilled condition[i]	4	5	4	4	8	4
Crime[j]	4	5	0	0	4	2
Procedural objections[k]	4	5	0	0	4	2
Servile condition[l]	2	3	1	1	3	2
Impotence[m]	2	3	4	4	6	3
Vow	0	0	1	1	1	1
Orders	0	0	1	1	1	1
Mental incapacity[n]	0	0	1	1	1	1
SUBTOTAL	25	32	19	19	44	25
GRAND TOTAL[o]	78	100	100	100	178	100

Notes (including a reconciliation with Table 3.2): See T&C no. 108.
Source: York, Borthwick Institute, CP.E; CP.F.

Cases raising the issue of precontract occurred more frequently in the York medieval marriage cases than in cases raising any other type of issue (46%, Table 3.3),[31] although straight-out denial of the factual validity of the claim occurred in a comparable number of cases (43%). This latter type of defense produced a second cluster of legal issues, sometimes found in combination with issues involving precontract. We may have a simple denial of the factual validity of the claim, with no further defense being offered or surviving (12%). More often we have an attack on the witnesses for the other side, alleging that they were unreliable because of their personal characteristics or because they were

[31] The percentages in Table 3.3 are calculated on the basis of those cases in which the defense (or, in the case of divorce, the claim) is known.

corrupted or, simply, because they got the story wrong (20%).[32] Frequently, an attack on the witnesses was accompanied by an exception of absence, an 'alibi' defense: The marriage alleged could not have taken place because one of the parties was someplace else at the time.[33] Exceptions of absence are found in 14 percent of the York medieval marriage cases. Finally, an unusual defense is found in 11 of our cases (6%), the exception of disparity of wealth. Disparity of wealth was legally irrelevant to the question of whether a marriage had been formed. The defense was raised in order to attack the credibility of the claimant's story. The defendant, so the argument ran, could not possibly have married someone whose status was so much below his or hers. The defense was also offered in order to attack the plaintiff's witnesses: The claimant and his or her witnesses were alleged to have fabricated the story in an effort to get the defendant's wealth.

All other issues pale in comparison with the defense or claim of precontract and the attack on the factual validity of the claim of the marriage sought to be enforced. The next most common defense was force or nonage (15%). Altogether, 83 percent of the cases raise one or a combination of these three types of defenses.[34] We occasionally see one of the numerous other issues to which the medieval canon law of marriage could give rise. Sixteen cases (9%), including 6 of the 31 divorce cases, raise issues of affinity or consanguinity. Seven of the marriage-enforcement actions and one of the cases of divorce on the ground of precontract (4%) argue that the marriage in question was conditional and that the condition was not fulfilled. Six cases (3%), all divorce cases, claim the impediment of impotence. Four cases (2%), including one divorce case, suggest issues involving the impediment of crime.[35] Four (2%), including three of the abjuration cases, focus on procedural objections to the proceedings in the lower court. (*Merton c Midelton* is one of these.) Three, including two divorce cases, raise the issue of the impediment of servile condition.[36] One claims the impediment of prior bond (*ligamen*) not in the way that is typical of precontract cases, for here it is clear that a prior marriage did take place, and the issue is whether the former spouse was still living at the time of the subsequent marriage (not tabulated). The fifteenth century sees one each of claims of the impediment of orders, vow, and mental incapacity (drunkenness). Altogether, 25 percent of the cases (9% being divorce cases) raised one or more of these issues that we have classified as 'other'. (The reason that 83% of the actions involved precontract, denial, and/or force/nonage, but nonetheless 25% of the actions raised an 'other' defense, is that in 8% of the cases that have defenses, one or more of the 'core' defenses was raised and one or more of the 'other' defenses.)

[32] For a summary of the types of issues that could be raised in such exceptions with references to York cases, see Donahue, "Proof by Witnesses."

[33] On exceptions of absence, see Donahue, "Roman Canon Law," at 693–5; Donahue, "Proof by Witnesses," at 144, and sources cited.

[34] Disc. T&C no. 114.

[35] See Ch 1, at nn. 49–54.

[36] See Ch 1, at nn. 30–2.

Before we get to the results and before we even begin to ask what the social significance of all this might be, one thing is quite clear from what we have already shown. What was *legally* significant about marriage litigation in the court of York in the fourteenth century was the principle that present consent freely given between parties capable of marriage, even without solemnity or ceremony, makes an indissoluble marriage. The type of marriage sought to be enforced or claimed as precontract was most often a *de presenti* informal marriage (Table 3.4).[37] Of the 260 marriages at stake in the York medieval marriage cases, 194 (75%) were *de presenti* marriages, 18 (7%) were *de futuro*, and the type of the remaining 48 (18%) cannot be determined.[38] Of the 123 *de presenti* marriages claimed in the first instance, 115 were informal and only 8 formal.[39] The proportion of formal marriages raised by way of defense was higher, 28 out of 60 (47%). All told, of the 183 *de presenti* marriages raised by way of claim or defense,[40] 147 (80%) were informal. When this fact is coupled with the fact noted previously[41] that 83% of the cases in which the defense is known involved one or a combination of a defense on the facts, precontract, or force or nonage, the legal significance of the core principle becomes apparent.

RESULTS IN THE FOURTEENTH CENTURY

How did the court react to these claims and defenses? To discuss this question, it is better to divide the two centuries because there were some differences between them. Marriage cases in fourteenth-century York produced a high proportion of judgments,[42] much higher than in any other type of case. Sixty-seven of our 86 fourteenth-century cases (78%, see Table 3.5) have judgments from at least one level of court. Although in many cases we lack the results on appeal, confirmations were more common than reversals in those cases where we do have a result on appeal. Thus, any judgment may be taken as some indication of what the result on appeal is going to be. The first and perhaps the most striking characteristic of judgments in marriage cases in fourteenth-century York is the number that are favorable to the plaintiff (56/67, 84%). We should discount this number for the possibilities that some of them would have been reversed on appeal and that plaintiffs abandoned or settled unfavorably some of the cases that have no judgments when it became apparent that judgment would probably go against them. Even if we do discount the number in this way, the court of York in the fourteenth century was still a decidedly pro-plaintiff court in marriage litigation.[43]

[37] There are some differences between the two centuries, which are discussed in the text following n. 70.

[38] Disc. T&C no. 115.

[39] Disc. T&C no. 116.

[40] Again, excluding the abjuration cases and the cases of divorce on grounds other than precontract.

[41] Text and n. 34.

[42] Disc. T&C no. 118.

[43] Disc. T&C no. 119.

TABLE 3.4. *York Marriage Cases – Types of Marriages (1300–1499)*

	Claimed First						Defense						
Type of Case	Inf Dp	For Dp	TOT Dp	TOT Df	Unc	Total	TOT Dp	Inf Dp	For Dp	TOT Df	Unc	Total	Total
Two-party enforcement													
De presenti	61	2	63	0	0	63	7	3	4	0	2	9	72
De futuro	0	0	0	14	1	15	1	1	0	0	0	1	16
Abjuration[a]	0	0	11	0	0	11	2	2	0	0	0	2	13
Uncertain	0	0	0	0	22	22	1	0	1	0	0	1	23
Three-party actions													
Competitors[b]	31	0	31	2	0	33	23	22	1	1	10	34	67
Marriage and divorce[c]	15	5	20	1	3	24	18	4	14	0	9	27	51
Annulment													
Precontract[d]	8	1	9	0	0	9	8	0	8	0	1	9	18
Other[e]	2	13	15	0	7	22	0	0	0	0	0	0	22
Other	1	4	5	0	11	16	0	0	0	0	0	0	16
TOTAL	118	25	154	17	44	215	60	32	28	1	22	83	298
% of TOTAL	55	12	72	8	20	100	72	39	34	1	27	100	
TOTAL less divorce[f]	115	8	134	17	26	177	60	32	28	1	22	83	
% of TOTAL less divorce	65	5	76	10	15	100	72	39	34	1	27	100	
TOTAL 'spousals' cases[g]	147	36	194	18	48	260							
% of TOTAL 'spousals' cases	57	14	75	7	18	100							
TOTAL determinable solemnity[h]	147	36	183	18	0	201							
% of previous TOTAL	73	18	91	9	0	100							

Notes: Inf Dp = informal *de presenti* marriage; For Dp = formal *de presenti* marriage; TOT Dp = total *de presenti* marriage; TOT Df = Total *de futuro* marriages; Unc = uncertain formality of marriage. The summary totals at the bottom begin by totaling all the columns and then proceed to exclude certain kinds of cases. 'Spousals' cases exclude divorce, separation, and abjuration cases, and the total includes both claims and defenses. The final total excludes 'uncertain' marriages from the 'spousals' cases.

For notes *a–h*, see T&C no. 117.

Source: York, Borthwick Institute, CP.E; CP.F.

TABLE 3.5. *York Marriage Cases – Gender Ratios and Judgments (Fourteenth Century)*

Type of Case[a]	FP	MP	Total Cases	%F	SFP	SMP	TOT	SFD	SMD	TOT	GTOT
Two-party *de presenti*	16	8	24	67	14	3	17	1	0	1	18
Two-party *de futuro*	9	0	9	100	5	0	5	0	2	2	7
Abjuration	9	0	9	100	6	0	6	0	3	3	9
Two-party marriage (other)	3	0	3	100	1	0	1	0	0	0	1
Three-party competitors[b]	4	6	10	40	4	6	10	0	0	0	10
Three-party marriage & div[c]	9	1	10	90	5	0	5	0	3	3	8
Divorce precontract	1	4	5	20	0	4	4	0	0	0	4
Divorce other	6	5	11	55	3	3	6	0	1	1	7
Other	4	1	5	80	1	1	2	0	1	1	3
TOTAL	61	25	86	71	39	17	56	1	10	11	67

Notes: FP = female plaintiff; MP = male plaintiff; %F = ratio of female plaintiffs to total plaintiffs; SFP = sentence for female plaintiff; SMP = sentence for male plaintiff; TOT = total judgments for plaintiffs (or defendants); SFD = sentence for female defendant; SMD = sentence for male defendant; GTOT = grand total of judgments.

Ratio of judgments to cases: 78% (67/86).
Ratio of FPs to total Ps: 71% (61/86).
Ratio of successful female Ps to total successful Ps: 70% (37/58).
Female plaintiff success rate: 80% (39 won, 10 lost).
Female plaintiff success rate: 64% (39 won, 61 cases).
Male plaintiff success rate:[d] 94% (17 won, 1 lost).
Male plaintiff success rate:[d] 68% (17 won, 25 cases).
Male plaintiff drop rate: 28% (7 no judgment, 25 cases).
Female plaintiff drop rate: 20% (12 no judgment, 61 cases)[e].
Overall female success rate: 60% (40 won, 27 lost).
Overall male success rate: 40% (27 won, 40 lost).
For notes *a–e*, see T&C no. 120.

Source: York, Borthwick Institute, CP.E.

Plaintiffs were successful in almost all types of actions. Seventeen of the 18 (94%) two-party actions to enforce a *de presenti* informal marriage that have judgments resulted in judgments for the plaintiff, as did the one two-party action to enforce a marriage where the type of marriage cannot be determined. All 10 of the three-party competitor actions have judgments for one plaintiff or the other. Plaintiffs won six of the seven judgments (86%) in actions for divorce on grounds other than precontract, and four of the four judgments

(100%) in actions for divorce on the ground of precontract. Plaintiffs were, however, comparatively less successful in actions to enforce a *de futuro* contract of marriage (5 won, 2 lost, 67%), in abjuration actions (6 won, 3 lost, 67%), and in marriage and divorce actions (5 won, 3 lost, 63%).[44] They were even less successful in separation actions, losing the only one in which a judgment survives.[45]

Obviously the judgment in each case depends on the how successful each of the parties and their witnesses were in persuading the judge, but the pattern of successes and failures suggests some places where we might look for clues to what the judges found to be persuasive. One principle that will explain many of the results is that the York court (and many of the lower courts in the province) indulged in a broad presumption in favor of marriage.[46] If the great majority of the cases are marriage-enforcement actions, the great majority of plaintiffs will be successful if the court indulges in that presumption. This principle also explains some of the exceptions to the general rule that plaintiffs usually win. The two-party *de presenti* enforcement action that the plaintiff did not win involved a defense of precontract.[47] A presumption in favor of marriage will not help in this type of case; the question must be to which marriage the presumption will attach. Similarly the relatively low success rate of plaintiffs in marriage-and-divorce actions may be explained by the fact that these were hard cases. However the judge ruled, a marriage, or at least a claimed marriage, was going to be upset. The same is true of the cases involving competitors. All 10 of them were won by plaintiffs, but the nature of the action means that in 10 such cases plaintiffs lost.[48] The presumption in favor of marriage will also explain the singular lack of success of those seeking a separation.

The presumption in favor of marriage will not, however, explain the relative lack of success of plaintiffs in abjuration actions. Although plaintiffs ultimately won two-thirds of these actions (6/9), it took some doing to get there. Two plaintiffs had to appeal to the official from adverse decisions of the commissary general before prevailing. It is hard to escape the sense that the institution of abjuration *sub pena nubendi* was not favored by the York court, particularly at the end of the fourteenth century.[49]

The presumption in favor of marriage will also not explain the success rate of plaintiffs in cases of divorce other than those based on precontract. Here again we must look more deeply at the cases themselves. Suffice it to say here that in four of the cases, the plaintiff puts in a straightforward and compelling

[44] For possible exceptions, see T&C no. 121.
[45] Disc. T&C no. 122.
[46] Such a presumption has support in the academic law. See de Naurois, "Matrimonium gaudet favore iuris."
[47] Ref. and disc. T&C no. 123.
[48] Disc. T&C no. 124.
[49] Lit. T&C no. 125.

case; one does not give the nature of the ground for the divorce, and the final one is a complicated case involving affinity in the fourth degree.[50]

On the face of it, then, the results all seem quite close to what we have called the core principle of the medieval canon law of marriage: Present consent, even if informally given, will prevail over all else, so long as it is freely given. In almost all the cases where an alleged marriage did not prevail, another prior in time was asserted and proven, or it was shown that the consent was not given or that the consent was not free. Occasionally the numerous other issues to which the canon law of marriage could give rise were raised, and occasionally they prevailed, but only occasionally. Take away the core principle, and one cannot explain the bulk of the marriage cases that were litigated in fourteenth-century York.

But what is the social significance of this core legal principle? To put the question another way, why do so many cases raise issues about informal *de presenti* marriage? This is not the type of question for which litigation records give us an easy answer, particularly if we are confining ourselves to what can be learned from numbers. It is possible to organize the fact-patterns of the cases into groups and to draw some numerical conclusions from the proportions and changes of proportions in the types of stories that the witnesses told. That procedure, however, involves a substantial amount of interpretation of the records.[51] For our purposes here, let us rather look at a number that requires no interpretation to derive, the gender ratio of the litigants.

Marriage litigation in the court of York in the fourteenth century was an activity that women initiated. Sixty-one of our 86 fourteenth-century marriage cases (71%) have female plaintiffs (Table 3.5).[52] Since a high percentage of the judgments were in favor of the plaintiffs, marriage litigation in the York court in the fourteenth century was not only an activity that women initiated but also an activity at which women were successful. The ratio, moreover, of successful female plaintiffs to all successful plaintiffs approximates the ratio of female plaintiffs to all plaintiffs (70% vs 71%).

Female plaintiffs did not, however, have as high a success rate as did male plaintiffs (80% vs 94%).[53] Thus, despite the fact that women win a large number of cases, the success rate of male plaintiffs is higher. (If the female plaintiffs had been as successful as the male, they would have lost 2.9 cases rather than 10, and if the male plaintiffs had been as unsuccessful as the female, they would have lost 5.3 cases rather than 1.)[54] The reason that the success rate of male plaintiffs is higher despite the fact that women win cases in proportion to their proportion in bringing them is that 49 of the 61 female plaintiffs (80%), so far

[50] Listed T&C no. 126.
[51] We will undertake it in the next chapters.
[52] Lit. T&C no. 127.
[53] Statistical disc. T&C no. 128.
[54] Statistical disc. T&C no. 129.

as we can tell, pursued their cases to judgment, whereas only 18 of the 25 male plaintiffs did (72%).[55] The women had to lose more cases than did the men in order to get a number of favorable judgments equal to their proportion in the population.[56]

Why did the female plaintiffs lose more cases proportionally than did male plaintiffs? One possible reason is that women litigants pursued cases that they ought not to have pursued because they misestimated their chances of success. This could have been because, despite the high number of successes, the court was biased against women. Even more of them should have won than did win. The fact, however, that women as both plaintiffs and defendants had a 60 percent success rate, while men had only a 40 percent success rate, does not suggest bias on the part of the court.[57] Or it could have been because women did not have access to the advice that men had, and so pursued cases that men knew were better not brought. Finally, it could have been that women pursued more cases because they had more to gain by winning or less to lose by losing. Classically 'rational' behavior would suggest that someone will pursue a course of conduct even if her perception of the odds is the same as another's if the benefits to be gained from success are greater or the costs of losing are less.[58]

There is some evidence for this last suggestion in the final numerical analysis that we shall undertake of this group of cases. Although women, overall, brought almost three out of four of the marriage cases brought in the York court over the course of the fourteenth century, this ratio was by no means constant over the different types of cases (Table 3.5).

We suggested earlier that the legal issues in three-party cases of either type and in cases of divorce on the ground of precontract were identical. But the gender ratios were not. Men hardly ever brought a marriage-and-divorce action, women hardly ever brought an action for divorce on the ground of precontract, and the competitor actions were evenly divided between the genders. This is hard to explain, but some hint at an explanation may be given by the other types of cases in which there is an imbalance. Except for the competitor actions, the cases in which men were dominant as plaintiffs were all cases in which the result of the action, if successful, would be that the man would get out of a marriage and not get into another one. Women, on the other hand, were dominant in cases in which the result, if the case was successful, would be that the plaintiff would be declared the wife of the defendant.

In four of the eight two-party *de presenti* enforcement actions in which a man was the plaintiff, the defendant was a widow.[59] That suggests that financial considerations were important. In three of the other such cases, the defendant

[55] Statistical disc. T&C no. 130.
[56] Statistical disc. T&C no. 131.
[57] See Table 3.5.
[58] Lit. T&C no. 132.
[59] Listed T&C no. 133.

raises a defense of nonage or force.[60] That suggests an arranged marriage and, again, that financial considerations played an important role. In two of the six competitor cases in which men were the plaintiffs, the defendant was also a widow.[61]

The evidence, then, suggests the following: Men sued to enforce a marriage when the financial stakes were high. They did not bring cases when the chances of success did not look good. They sued to get out of a marriage more frequently than did women. Women, on the other hand, sued in cases in which the financial advantages to them are less obvious. They sued to enforce a marriage far more often than did men; they sued to dissolve one much less often. They were the only plaintiffs in cases alleging a *de futuro* promise followed by intercourse and in cases of abjuration *sub pena nubendi*. They were more persistent in their suits and, as a result, lost more cases than did the men.

So summarized, the evidence suggests a tentative hypothesis: Female litigants seem to have valued marriage *qua* marriage more than did male litigants. This was particularly true in cases in which they had been compromised (an allegation that is rarely denied), but it was also true in cases in which it was not alleged, or even suggested, that intercourse had taken place. If we hypothesize that the female litigants valued marriage more than the male did, that would explain why they sued when the financial considerations are not obvious, why they sued more often to enforce a marriage, less often to dissolve one, and why they were more persistent.

Why women should have valued marriage more than men did is only hinted at in our records, and yet the question is fundamental. Marriage in the Middle Ages, as in many societies, seems to have given women more in the way of security and status than it did men. As is well known, the economic opportunities outside of marriage and family were far more limited for most medieval women than they were for most medieval men, even when they were quite limited for most medieval men. This fact meant that gender relations were imbalanced. A man could give a woman more by marrying her than she could give him. That in turn meant that the balance of power in gender relations lay with the men. The York court in the fourteenth century, with its plaintiff-friendly pattern of judgments, served, to some extent, to redress this imbalance of power.

So far all we have is an hypothesis, one that we suggested was at least plausible. To prove that hypothesis, or at least to put it on a firmer footing, we must do more: We must burrow into the depositions and see if there is a difference in the types of stories that women tell and those that men tell that gives credence to the hypothesis suggested by the numbers. That is a large undertaking, and we will attempt it in the next chapters. The numbers will not

[60] *Thomeson c Belamy* (1362), CP.E.85; *Marrays c Rouclif* (1365), CP.E.89; *Whitheved c Crescy* (1368), CP.E.97.

[61] *Dowson and Roger c Brathwell* (1391), CP.E.188; *Garthe and Neuton c Waghen* (1391), CP.E.245.

help us with this inquiry. What the numbers have done is help us considerably in framing the question.

RESULTS IN THE FIFTEENTH CENTURY

The numbers also help us considerably in tracing changes across time. To illustrate this point, let us look at the York marriage cause papers from the fifteenth century. Some commentators have suggested that there were gradual and subtle changes in marriage litigation in England in the fifteenth century.[62] These are just the types of changes that ought to be capturable with numerical indicators.

Table 3.2 suggests that the pattern of claims brought in the fifteenth century was similar to that in the fourteenth, with one major difference: There were 6 percent more three-party actions (29% vs 23%),[63] an increase that was made up for by a corresponding reduction in the number of annulment actions (12% vs 19%).[64] This means that it is even truer of the fifteenth century than it was of the fourteenth that the overwhelming majority of actions (79%) were actions to enforce a marriage, while only 12% were actions to dissolve a marriage. (In the remainder, the basic claim is miscellaneous or uncertain.)[65]

As it was with the fourteenth-century cases, if we seek to discover the crux of the matter from a legal point of view and to begin to explore its social implications, we need to know how the fifteenth-century cases were defended and what the results were. Table 3.3 shows that a somewhat greater percentage of fifteenth-century cases involved a defense that sought to establish another marriage (49% vs 42%),[66] while approximately the same number involved a factual denial of the claim (43% vs 42%),[67] and somewhat more a claim of force or nonage (17% vs 13%).[68] There are fewer cases defended on the grounds of consanguinity and/or affinity (7% vs 12%) or the impediment of crime (0% vs 5%). By contrast, the fifteenth-century gives us one example each of defenses that we do not see in the fourteenth century: vow, orders, and drunkenness (indicating mental incapacity to consent).[69] While some of these differences may be statistically significant, none is very great.[70] Overall, we may say that marriage cases were defended in approximately the same way in fifteenth-century York as they were in fourteenth-century York.

Similarly, what was *legally* significant about the rules of the medieval canon law of marriage in the York cases of the fifteenth century, as it was in the

62 Helmholz, *Marriage Litigation*, 165–83.
63 $z = .99$; significant at .68.
64 $z = 1.37$; significant at .83.
65 Disc. T&C no. 134.
66 $z = .94$, significant at .65.
67 $z = .134$, significant at .10, i.e., not statistically significant.
68 $z = .748$, significant at .55.
69 We also find, as we do not in the fourteenth century, one instance each of condonation and ratification as defenses in divorce cases.
70 Statistical disc. T&C no. 135.

fourteenth century, is what we have called the core principle: present consent freely given between parties capable of marriage, even without solemnity or ceremony, makes an indissoluble marriage. We broke down the data in Table 3.4 by century in order to explore possible differences. Most of the differences that we found (principally having to do with more marriages of uncertain type) are more likely to be the product of the different types of records that survive from the two centuries than they are of differences in the underlying population. There are two differences that may reflect a difference in the underlying population. The first we have already noted: the decline of litigation concerning abjuration *sub pena nubendi*.[71] The second is a possible decline in litigation concerning marriages formed by a promise of marriage followed by intercourse, which by one measure went down from 8 percent of the marriages at stake in the litigation to 5 percent.[72] Even if this decline is real, we should hesitate to draw any social conclusions from it. While it might reflect an increasing awareness that the *de presenti* form of marriage was more certain of enforcement, it might also reflect a difference in the way that litigants chose to frame their cases.

Despite these differences in the types of marriages being litigated in the two centuries, the overall results are quite similar. In both centuries, they confirm the legal significance of the core principle.

As was the case with the fourteenth century, marriage cases in fifteenth-century York produced a high proportion of judgments (59%) (Table 3.6, compared to Table 3.5). The percentage, however, was not so high as it was in the fourteenth century (78%). As a descriptive matter, the reason for this difference is that the decades from 1460 to 1490 produced relatively few cases with judgments, but it is not clear why there should have been fewer judgments in these decades. A combination of different types of record keeping and a general decline of the court probably produced this phenomenon.[73] For our purposes, what it means is that when we speak of judgments in fifteenth-century York cases, we are speaking for the most part about judgments in the first six decades of the century.

The court of York remained a decidedly pro-plaintiff court in the fifteenth century. Fifty-six out of the 73 judgments that survive (77%) are favorable to the plaintiff (vs. 84% [56/67] in the fourteenth century). As it was in fourteenth century, plaintiffs dominated all types of actions with a couple of exceptions. Plaintiffs won 12 of the 19 (63%) judgments in the two-party actions to enforce *de presenti* marriages, although this rate is markedly lower than the 94 percent success rate in the fourteenth century. The success rate in two-party actions of uncertain type is similar (67%, 4/6). Nineteen of the 24 (79%) competitor actions resulted in a judgment for one plaintiff or the other (the remainder have

[71] Fourteenth: 9/110 (8%); fifteenth: 2/150 (1%); difference yields $z = 2.47$, significant at .99. N. 65 compares the number of cases to the same effect.

[72] Fourteenth: 9/110 (8%); fifteenth: 8/150 (5%); difference yields $z = .813$, significant at .63.

[73] Statistical disc. T&C no. 136.

TABLE 3.6. *York Marriage Cases – Gender Ratios and Judgments (Fifteenth Century)*

Type of Case[a]	FP	MP	Total Cases	%F	SFP	SMP	TOT	SFD	SMD	TOT	GTOT
Two-party *de presenti*	19	18	37	51	7	5	12	4	3	7	19
Two-party *de futuro*	7	0	7	100	1	0	1	0	2	2	3
Abjuration	1	1	2	50	1	1	2	0	0	0	2
Two-party marriage (other)	11	6	17	65	2	2	4	0	2	2	6
Three-party competitors[b]	15	9	24	63	11	8	19	0	0	0	19
Three-party marriage & div[c]	8	6	14	57	5	2	7	0	3	3	10
Divorce precontract	3	2	5	60	2	1	3	1	0	1	4
Divorce other	7	3	10	70	4	3	7	0	0	0	7
Other	5	2	7	71	1	0	1	0	2	2	3
TOTAL	76	47	123	62	34	22	56	5	12	17	73

Notes: Abbreviations as in Table 3.5.
Ratio of judgments to cases: 59% (73/123).
Plaintiff success rate:[d] 77% (56/73).
Ratio of FPs to total Ps: 62% (76/123).
Ratio of successful female Ps to total successful Ps: 61% (34/55).
Female plaintiff success rate: 74% (34 won, 12 lost).
Female plaintiff success rate: 45% (34 won, 76 cases).
Male plaintiff success rate:[e] 81% (22 won, 5 lost).
Male plaintiff success rate: 47% (22 won, 47 cases).
Male plaintiff drop rate: 43% (20 no judgment, 47 cases).
Female plaintiff drop rate: 39% (30 no judgment, 76 cases).
Overall female success rate: 53% (39 won, 35 lost).
Overall male success rate: 47% (35 won, 39 lost).
For notes *a–e*, see T&C no. 137.
Source: York, Borthwick Institute, CP.F.

no recorded judgment). Marriage and divorce actions produced seven wins and three losses (70% vs 78% in the fourteenth century). Plaintiffs won three of the four judgments in actions for divorce brought on the ground of precontract and all seven of the judgments in actions for divorce on grounds other than precontract.

As in the fourteenth century, plaintiffs had some difficulty with other types of actions: Separation actions produced one win and one loss (50%),[74] and

[74] Listed T&C no. 138.

actions to enforce a *de futuro* contract, one win and two losses (33%), the only type of action in which plaintiffs lost fewer than half of the recorded judgments.

By contrast with the results in the fourteenth century, plaintiffs in fifteenth-century York won both the abjuration actions they brought. In both, the plaintiffs had compelling cases.[75] We may speculate that the relative lack of success of fourteenth-century plaintiffs in such actions led to their being disfavored by plaintiffs. Only plaintiffs who had particularly strong cases would bring them. That could account both for plaintiffs' success in such actions in the fifteenth century and for the quite small number of such actions. The same phenomenon could also account for the one success that a plaintiff had in a separation action – she had a powerful case[76] – and for the fact that relatively few plaintiffs brought such actions, which, as we have already seen, were probably disfavored at York.[77]

As in the fourteenth century, the presumption in favor of marriage will explain why plaintiffs remained generally successful in two-party enforcement actions in fifteenth-century York. It will not explain, however, the larger proportion of two-party actions that they lost. There are 11 of these. Five of the *de presenti* cases are defended on the ground of absence (with one adding a defense of disparity of wealth and another a more general attack on the witnesses), and two defended on the ground of force.[78] One of the *de futuro* cases is defended on the ground that no intercourse followed after the promise, and the other, it would seem, on the ground that what was said was not sufficient to constitute a promise of marriage (intercourse is conceded).[79] The defenses in the two cases of uncertain type are less clear.[80] In order to understand what is happening in these cases, we will need to examine their records more closely in Chapter 5, but we have said enough here to suggest that the York court was open to accepting a wider range of defenses in two-party marriage-enforement cases in the fifteenth century than it was in the fourteenth.

As in the fourteenth century, the presumption in favor of marriage also, somewhat paradoxically, explains the mixed results in the three-party cases in the fifteenth century. All the competitor cases that have judgments were won by one competitor and lost by another, and plaintiffs won seven but lost three marriage-and-divorce cases. The presumption, as we have previously noted, makes all of these difficult cases: To which claimed marriage should the presumption attach?

The presumption will not, of course, explain plaintiffs' success in divorce cases brought on grounds other than precontract. The absolute number of such

[75] *Frothyngham c Bedale* (1418), CP.F.78; *Office c Gregory and Tapton* (1434–8), CP.F.123.

[76] *Wyvell c Venables* (1410), CP.F.56 (adultery).

[77] See at n. 49.

[78] Listed T&C no. 139.

[79] *Carvour c Burgh* (1421), CP.F.129 (also unfulfilled condition); *Kichyn c Thomson* (1411–12), CP.F.42.

[80] *Wakfeld c Fox* (1402), CP.F.22; *Kurkeby c Holme* (c. 1419), CP.F.32/12 (probably factual denial in both cases).

cases is small, although plaintiffs' success rate is high, and in each case the result may be explained by the fact that the plaintiff put in a convincing case, and all but one of them, so far as we can tell, went undefended.[81] Again, the disfavored action is brought only by those who have a strong case.

When we come, however, to the gender ratios of the parties, marriage litigation in fifteenth-century York witnessed some changes from the fourteenth century. In the first place, although women still brought more actions than men (62%), the disproportion was considerably less than it was in the fourteenth century (71%).[82] As in the fourteenth century, however, the ratio of successful women plaintiffs to total successful plaintiffs was approximately the same as their ratio to total plaintiffs (61% vs 62%). As in the fourteenth century, moreover, female plaintiffs' success rate in the fifteenth century was lower than that of the men (74% vs 81%, 60% vs 63%, 65% vs 71%, 66% vs 74%, depending on how you calculate the rate; see Table 3.6). In many cases, however, particularly if we ignore the problems caused by the competitor cases, the difference in the rates was smaller, sometimes quite a bit smaller, than it was in the fourteenth century (79% vs 94%, 72% vs 74%, 76% vs 81%, 77% vs 92%).[83]

It remained true in the fifteenth century as it was in the fourteenth that women won cases in proportion approximately equal to their proportion in the population as plaintiffs, and that their success rate was lower than that of the men. We attributed this seemingly paradoxical result in the fourteenth century to the fact that women plaintiffs in that century pursued more cases to judgment than did the men. This characteristic remained in the fifteenth century, but once more it narrowed. Women pursued, so far as we can tell, 61% of their cases to judgment, while men pursued 57% (fourteenth century: 80% vs 72%).[84] One more difference between the two centuries is quite dramatic. Women in the fourteenth century, whether as plaintiffs or defendants, won 60% of the cases for which we have judgments (and men won only 40%). Once more, in the fifteenth century the gap narrowed, and the figures become 53% and 47%.

We thus have two changes to explain: Why does the percentage of female plaintiffs go down in fifteenth-century York, and why do their results in litigation become more like those of male plaintiffs? We cannot offer definitive answers to these questions, but we close this chapter by offering some suggested answers to them.

We suggested that fourteenth-century women plaintiffs valued marriage more than did men. We supported this by evidence that suggested that women plaintiffs sued to enforce a marriage more often than men did, less often to dissolve one, and that they did so in situations where financial considerations

[81] Listed T&C no. 140.
[82] $z = 1.37$, significant at .83.
[83] See n. 53.
[84] Disc. T&C no. 141.

were not obvious. Neither of these characteristics seems as true of the fifteenth century. Both men and women sue in cases in which financial considerations seem to be important, and both men and women sue in cases in which such considerations are not obvious.[85] Further, and perhaps more reliably, the dominance of women in actions to enforce a marriage (as opposed to actions to dissolve one) simply disappears. Only in the relatively few actions to enforce a *de futuro* promise do women maintain the dominance that they had in the fourteenth century. In two-party marriage actions of uncertain type, competitor actions, and marriage-and-divorce actions, their proportion as plaintiffs approximately equals their overall proportion as plaintiffs. In two-party actions to enforce a *de presenti* marriage and abjuration actions, their proportion as plaintiffs is less than their overall proportion as plaintiffs.[86] The converse of this proposition is that men no longer dominate certain types of actions. Their proportion in actions for divorce on the ground of precontract and in competitor actions equals their overall proportion as plaintiffs. It exceeds that proportion by quite a bit (11 percentage points) in two-party actions to enforce a *de presenti* marriage. Women dominate the fifteenth-century actions brought for divorce on grounds other than precontract, whereas in the fourteenth century, the percentage of male and female plaintiffs in such actions equaled approximately their overall proportion as plaintiffs.[87]

This is not to say that the cases do not provide some evidence for the proposition that fifteenth-century women valued marriage more than did men. The overwhelming proportion of fifteenth-century actions are actions to enforce a marriage, and women bring 62 percent of all actions. Women do seem to have been more persistent than men in pursuing their cases in the fifteenth century, as they were in the fourteenth century. But we cannot confirm our suspicion that women valued marriage more than did men by looking at the different types of actions brought in the fifteenth century.

We are dealing with proportions, not with absolutes. If it is plausible that women in the fourteenth century valued marriage more than did men, the fact that their litigation rate in the fifteenth century goes down when compared to men's suggests that the relative valuation of the two genders of marriage changed over the course of the centuries. This could have happened either because women valued marriage in the fifteenth century less than they did in the fourteenth, and so brought fewer cases, with the men moving in to fill up the slack, or because men valued marriage more in the fifteenth century than they did in the fourteenth, and so brought more cases, thus reducing the percentage of women. The two explanations are not logically inconsistent, and the data are consistent with either or both explanations.[88]

[85] Support for these propositions must await Ch 5.

[86] See Table 3.6.

[87] See Tables 3.5 and 3.6.

[88] Disc. T&C no. 142.

Further, and perhaps most troubling, is the fact that some of the changes in proportions may be the result not of changes in the values that plaintiffs placed on winning, but in their perception of their chances of winning. If male plaintiffs were successful in certain kinds of actions in the fourteenth century, female plaintiffs in the fifteenth century may have learned from their experience and brought more of these types of action. Conversely, male plaintiffs could have learned from the success of female plaintiffs in the types of actions in which women tended to dominate and could have brought more of these types of actions.

While I suspect that some such transfer of knowledge between the two groups of plaintiffs was occurring, such transfer will probably not fully explain the differences that we see between the two centuries. It probably, for example, does not fully explain the decline in the proportion of female plaintiffs, nor does it explain the larger proportion of women seeking to dissolve an existing marriage or get out of a proposed one rather than enforce one.[89] We are forced to ask, therefore, if there is any ground for believing that there was either a relative increase in men's valuation of marriage in the fifteenth century over the fourteenth or a relative decrease in women's valuation of marriage over the same two centuries. I suggested that women in the fourteenth century valued marriage more than men did because marriage gave women more security and status than it gave men. It would be foolish to suggest that the resulting imbalance of power in gender relations was eliminated in the fifteenth century, and the fact that women continued to bring more cases than men suggests that it was not. On the other hand, if we focus on the last decades of the fourteenth century (from which most of our fourteenth-century cases come) and the early decades of the fifteenth century (from which most of our fifteenth-century cases come), there are suggestions, and I must emphasize 'suggestions', in the social, and particularly in the economic, history of the two periods that make the notion that women were less dependent on marriage in the latter period at least plausible.

As is well known, the decades following the Black Death saw a sharp increase in prices and also an increase in the value of labor. At the same time, population fluctuated radically, as new outbreaks of plague defeated the natural tendency of a population to replenish itself after a disaster. These decades would also seem to be – this is more controversial – a period in which many traditional social networks broke down, as laborers migrated in search of high wages and geographical areas adjusted to the differential impact of plague on the population.[90] This combination of circumstances might have been peculiarly unfavorable to single women. Obviously, there would be substantial differences among such women depending on their class, wealth, and skills, but as a general matter, a single adult woman in a society where prices were fluctuating radically but generally rising, and where wages were rising as well, would be worse off

[89] Disc. T&C no. 143.
[90] Lit. T&C no. 144.

than a single adult woman in a society where prices were steady and labor cheap. Unable to be self-sustaining, both because of her physical inability to do certain kinds of work (ploughing, for example) and because of the social barriers that prevented her from doing other kinds of work (many trades, for example), the single woman with some capital (be it land, goods, or skills) would be better off in a society in which she need not expend much of her capital to obtain basic necessities and where she could easily hire men to do what she could not do herself.[91] When prices and wages went up, particularly when they fluctuated on an upward trend, single women had more need of the economic potential of a husband to give them some measure of economic security. This would be all the more important if social networks were breaking down, since that could have meant that there were fewer stable households where single women could work as servants or live as 'paying guests' or as members of an extended family.

In the fifteenth century, prices stabilized at a level higher than they were before the plague but lower than they had been in the fourteenth-century peaks. Wage rates also stabilized at a relatively high level, sufficiently high that many students of the subject believe that there was a substantial transfer of wealth from the upper economic classes to the working population. Population, on the other hand, took a sharp drop, and then began a slow process of increasing. Social networks may well have become more stable. This combination of circumstances might have been less unfavorable to single women than the circumstances at the end of the fourteenth century. The greater stability of the economic circumstances of the early decades of the fifteenth century would have allowed a greater amount of wealth to be stored and transferred to women by way of inheritance or dowry and, thus, would have made women less dependent on the earnings of their husbands. There may have been more stable households in which single women could have lived. Particularly among lower-level merchants and tradesmen and the upper levels of the peasantry (classes that seem to have formed the bulk of the litigating population at York), greater wealth and greater stability could have meant that women would have had an easier time living as single. If they were wealthier, they could have brought more into a marriage than they could have in the later decades of the fourteenth century. The economic contribution that each partner made to a marriage would thus have tended to equalize. In these circumstances, we would expect to find more men and fewer women seeking to enforce marriages in the fifteenth century than in the fourteenth. And that is just what we find.

Pursuit of this argument would take us far afield.[92] We offer only one analysis here, a comparison of male and female behavior in marriage litigation in the last three decades of the fourteenth century and the first four of the fifteenth (Table 3.7). If we break these numbers down by type of case, the sample sizes in each cell are too small for statistical purposes. Indeed, even the aggregate numbers are sufficiently small that they can only be suggestive, not conclusive.

[91] Disc. T&C no. 145.

[92] Lit. and disc. T&C no. 146.

TABLE 3.7. *York Marriage Cases – Gender Ratios and Judgments (1370–1439)*

Decade[a]	FP	MP	Total Cases	%F	SFP	SMP	TOT	SFD	SMD	TOT	GTOT
1370–1399	34	13	47	72	21	10	31	1	7	8	39
1400–1439	47	22	69	68	27	11	38	3	9	12	50
TOTAL	81	35	116	70	48	21	69	4	16	20	89

Notes: Abbreviations as in Table 3.5.
Ratios 1370–1399:
Ratio of judgments to cases: 83% (39/47).
Plaintiff success rate: 79% (31/39).
Ratio of FPs to total Ps: 72% (34/47).
Ratio of successful female Ps to total successful Ps: 68% (21/31).
Female plaintiff success rate: 75% (21 won, 7 lost).
Male plaintiff success rate: 91% (10 won, 1 lost).
Male plaintiff drop rate: 15% (2 no judgment, 13 cases).
Female plaintiff drop rate: 18% (6 no judgment, 34 cases).
Overall female success rate: 56% (22 won, 17 lost).
Overall male success rate: 44% (17 won, 22 lost).
Ratios 1400–1439:
Ratio of judgments to cases: 72% (50/69).
Plaintiff success rate: 76% (38/50).
Ratio of FPs to total Ps: 68% (47/69).
Ratio of successful female Ps to total successful Ps: 71% (27/38).
Female plaintiff success rate: 75% (27 won, 9 lost).
Male plaintiff success rate: 79% (11 won, 3 lost).
Male plaintiff drop rate: 36% (8 no judgment, 22 cases).
Female plaintiff drop rate: 23% (11 no judgment, 47 cases).
Overall female success rate: 59% (30 won, 21 lost).
Overall male success rate: 41% (21 won, 30 lost).
For note *a*, see T&C no. 147.
Source: Tables 3.5, 3.6.

The ratio of female plaintiffs to total plaintiffs went down in the first decades of the fifteenth century from what it had been in the last decades of the fourteenth (72% vs 68%),[93] but it was not so low as it was for the whole century (62%). This means, of course, that there was a rather steep decline in the proportion of female plaintiffs in the last 60 years of the century. As was the case in the aggregate numbers for both centuries, the ratio of successful female plaintiffs approximated their proportion in the plaintiff population (it was slightly lower in the last decades of the fourteenth century and slightly higher in the first decades of the fifteenth). As was also the case in the aggregate numbers for both centuries, the female plaintiffs' success rate was lower than that of male plaintiffs in both periods, but the gap had narrowed substantially in the first decades of the fifteenth century.[94] In the case of the overall statistics, I suggested

[93] $z = .464$, significant at .65.

[94] Fourteenth: 75% vs 91%, $z = 1.35$, significant at .82; fifteenth: 75% vs 79%, $z = .306$, significant at .75.

that that gap might be accounted for by the fact that female plaintiffs pursued more cases to judgment than did male. That will not explain the gap in the last decades of the fourteenth century. In these decades, male plaintiffs actually pursued proportionally more cases to judgment than did female (85% vs 82%). Here, the only explanation that I can think of is that male plaintiffs were more cautious in selecting the cases that they chose to litigate. A gap in the 'drop rate' does reemerge in the first decades of the fifteenth century. Male plaintiffs pursued, proportionally, fewer cases to judgment than did female (64% vs 77%).

Though, once more, the evidence is not conclusive, it does seem to suggest that certain trends had begun to emerge in marriage litigation in York in the early decades of the fifteenth century, well before the economic decline that occurred in the area in the second half of the century. The proportion of female plaintiffs was going down; the gap between their success rate and that of the men was lessening. The men seem to be almost as willing as the women to take a chance on losing a case, though the women remain more persistent once the case has begun. If our suggested economic explanation of why these changes might have occurred in the early years of the fifteenth century is correct, however, it means that the high proportion of female plaintiffs that we see in the York court in the fourteenth century is not an indication of a high status for women in the society at large but quite the reverse, and that their relative absence as plaintiffs as the fifteenth century wears on suggests some improvement in that status.

Finally, what of the court and its reaction to, and effect on, these social patterns? I suggested earlier that the pro-plaintiff pattern of judgments of the court served, to some extent, to redress the imbalance of power between the genders in late fourteenth-century York. With the appearance of more male plaintiffs and more female defendants in the fifteenth century, the court's pattern of sentencing did change, though not dramatically. As we have seen, the proportion of judgments favorable to plaintiffs across the century went down from 84 percent to 76 percent, but this decline was shared approximately equally by both female and male plaintiffs.[95] We will suggest in Chapter 5 that the reason for the decline may well have been that the court became skeptical of arguments that were perhaps too easily successful in the fourteenth century. The court, however, remained a decidedly pro-plaintiff court. In individual cases, one can detect a particular sympathy of the court with the story that a woman is telling or particular skepticism about the one that a man is telling. We will attempt to do so in the next two chapters. In the statistics, however, the exclusive focus of this chapter, the York court appears as a pro-plaintiff court, whether the plaintiff is a man or woman.[96]

[95] See Table 3.6.

[96] Indeed, in the penultimate three decades of the fifteenth century, which have the lowest proportion of female plaintiffs, the recorded judgments are only in favor of male plaintiffs. Statistical disc. T&C no. 148.

4

Story-Patterns in the Court of York in the Fourteenth Century

At the end of Chapter 3, we suggested, tentatively, that the York court in the later fourteenth century played a role that allowed it to redress, at least to some extent, the imbalance in power between women and men that prevailed in the period. Assuming that this is correct, two questions immediately come to mind: First, if the court's role had this effect in the cases that were litigated, did it have any effect on people who did not litigate? Obviously our records do not give us any direct evidence to answer this question, and the picture that we get from other types of records, both of medieval marriage and of gender relations, is very different from what we see in the court records. Nonetheless, perhaps with more courage than wisdom, we will eventually suggest that what this court and others like it were doing did have an effect beyond the effect on the parties to the cases, albeit over a very long term and with considerable crosscurrents that make it seem at times as if the effect were not there at all.

Second, once again assuming that the York court was having this effect, was the court aware of it? Certainly no one connected with the court would have put it in these terms, but then no one in the fourteenth-century court of York was familiar with the terms of historical sociology. Men and women of the fourteenth century were, however, familiar with paradigms and parables, and we will see that the patterns of the stories that they told suggest an awareness of a problem for which we have no better term than 'imbalance of power'.

We will also see that the willingness of the court to accept stories that fell within certain patterns exposed it to being manipulated into serving what seem, with the advantage of hindsight, to be quite different purposes from those which the stories suggest. The results of the four cases that we described in Chapter 2 all suggest that the underlying thrust of the story got lost. If we take Alice Dolling's story at face value, she was ultimately wronged by a bounder who had enough money to go to Canterbury and get the case reversed. Marjorie Merton won, but she won in a situation so loaded with ambiguity that we wondered if justice was done. Joan Ingoly won too, but by brazenly manipulating the processes of the court to obtain what we suspect everyone knew was a false judgment. Agnes Morice did not win, although ultimately she did not lose either, and her story we never hear.

TWO-PARTY *DE PRESENTI* ENFORCEMENT ACTIONS

Chapter 2, however, contains only four stories, and Chapter 3 shows that there are a lot more cases. Let us attempt the difficult task of integrating the stories with the statistics. We must now ask if it is possible to see patterns in the stories that can be told from these cases and what relationship, if any, these patterns have to the patterns of litigation that we have previously outlined numerically. Let us begin with a basic story, the story of Alice and Bill, *Dolling c Smith*: The core of the story is that Alice sues Bill, seeking that she be declared his wife. (Sometimes Bill sues Alice, but as we have seen, that happens far less frequently.) She introduces witnesses who testify to an informal exchange of marital consent. He excepts to the witnesses, challenging the factual validity of their story, or he could admit their story and allege some impediment between them. Of our 86 fourteenth-century York cases, 27 tell variants on this core story.[1] Let us call the variant of *Dolling c Smith*, which can only exist if a woman is suing a man, 'the case of the woman wronged'.

The earliest two-party *de presenti* enforcement action, *Joan daughter of Walter Chapelayn c Andrew Cragge of Whitby*, consists principally of a long *processus* held for the most part before the official of the archdeacon of Cleveland, and ultimately appealed to the consistory court.[2] The outline of the case bears a strong resemblance to *Dolling c Smith*. In July of 1301, Joan and Andrew appeared personally before a commissary of the archbishop, who may have been conducting a visitation, at Whitby. Joan claimed Andrew as her husband. Andrew denied all, and Joan immediately produced two witnesses. The case was committed to the official of the archdeacon, and the testimony of Joan's witnesses was published in October.

Joan's witnesses, both women, testify to an exchange of present consent in Joan's parents' bedroom in May four years previously. According to both witnesses, the couple were standing in front of Joan's bed at nightfall. There is some variation between the witnesses as to the words exchanged. The first witness testifies that Andrew said, "Joan, I take thee here as my lawful wife to have and to hold all the days of my life if holy church allow it, and to this I pledge thee my troth."[3] Joan replied, "Andrew, I take thee here as my lawful husband, for better, for worse, for fouler, for fairer, and to this I pledge thee my troth."[4] The second witness testifies more simply: "Joan/Andrew, I take thee here as my lawful wife/husband, to have and to hold all the days of my life and

[1] See Table 3.2, disc. T&C no. 152.
[2] *Chapelayn c Cragge* (1301), CP.E.1.
[3] *Ibid.*, T&C no. 153, with lit.
[4] *Ibid.*, T&C no. 154.

to this I pledge thee my troth."[5] Neither witness says anything about sexual intercourse. Both deny that they received anything or were promised anything for giving testimony.

In November, Andrew, now appearing by a proctor, excepted to Joan's witnesses on the ground that they were corrupted. After a number of delays, Andrew produced three witnesses, all women, whose testimony was finally published in June of 1302.

They tell a remarkable story.[6] All three testify that they were in the house of one of them. This house happened to adjoin Joan's house, separated by a thin wall, through which there was a hole for a chimney. Looking through this hole on a May day, they saw Joan talking with her two witnesses. Joan gave each of them three shillings and a hood of green cloth. On the basis of this, all the witnesses agree that Joan had "hired" (*dicit pro firmo quod bene scit ipsas ... esse conductas*) her witnesses, though they cannot testify that these witnesses were "suborned" (*quoad subornationem ... dicit ... se nichil scire*).[7] Andrew's witnesses' testimony is consistent, except about the date of the event. The first witness testifies that it was on the feast of the finding of the Holy Cross (3 May) in 1301, that is, two months before Joan appeared before the archbishop's commissary. The second witness testifies that it was on the same feast "last past, four years ago," that is, in 1297, when the exchange of consent between Andrew and Joan was alleged to have taken place. The third witness testifies that it was on the same feast "now two years past." Considering that the testimony was given in March in 1302, this probably refers to May of 1300, possibly May of 1299.

It is possible, as it was in *Dolling c Smith*, that we are dealing here with a scribal error and not with any inconsistency in the underlying testimony. Even if we ignore this inconsistency, however, there is much about the testimony that provokes suspicion. The story that a witness saw something through a hole in the wall or through a window occurs relatively frequently in medieval marriage depositions.[8] Medieval houses were not so tight as ours, and medieval villagers do seem to have spent quite a bit of time spying on their neighbors. If the story were not at least vaguely plausible, it would not have been worth telling. Nonetheless, when the story is told, it tends to have an element of a deus ex machina about it, and I cannot recall any case in which such a story alone is accepted.[9]

Even if we accept the story of the exception witnesses, it is not completely clear that it should lead, as a matter of law, to the rejection of the testimony of the principal witnesses. The mere acceptance of payment was not sufficient to reject a witness's testimony out of hand. A witness could legitimately be paid

[5] *Ibid.*, T&C no. 155.
[6] These depositions are printed in Helmholz, *Marriage Litigation*, 230–2.
[7] *Id.*, 230; cf. *id.* 231.
[8] Ref. T&C no. 156.
[9] *Walker c Kydde* (1418–19), CP.F.79, may be an exception.

expenses for testifying. Indeed, some canonists argued that even the acceptance of payment offered as a bribe should not automatically lead to the rejection of the witness's testimony.[10] The judge had to determine whether the witness had in fact been corrupted by the bribe. Now in this case, the principal witnesses both testified that they had received nothing for giving their testimony. If the payment was in fact a payment for expenses, one might argue that the testimony was true, that they could testify that they had received no payment for giving testimony if they had only been paid expenses.[11] On balance, however, it seems unlikely that the payment could be regarded as a payment of expenses. The examination of the allegedly corrupted witnesses seems to have taken place in Whitby. One of the witnesses was from Whitby and the other may have been.[12] Three shillings and a green hood seems a high price to pay for expenses for a morning's testimony in one's own town.[13] Hence, the payment, if proven, would at least have meant that the witnesses lied when they said that they had received nothing "for giving testimony," and the judge could have rejected their testimony without getting into the question of whether the witnesses were in fact corrupted.

We cannot tell which, if any, of these considerations would have moved the judge if he had been called upon to decide the case on the basis of this exchange alone. Andrew's defense is best attacked from the legal point of view on the basis of the inconsistency of his witnesses' testimony, and this is probably the reason that he seems to have abandoned this line of defense. At the end of June he proposed another exception: He could not marry Joan because he had precontracted with one Margaret de Botolstan.

The rest of the year was taken up with procedural maneuvering. Andrew finally asked for and received a three-month delay to produce witnesses who were outside the province, witnesses whom he alleged were resident in the dioceses of Lincoln and Ely. The witnesses finally arrived in Whitby in January of 1303 and were examined by two chaplains on 25 January. More procedural maneuvering occupied the months of February and March, and the testimony was finally published at the end of March. On 6 May, Joan's proctor, who seems to have been her father, Walter Chapelayn, excepted to the publication of the witnesses on the grounds: (1) that she was not adequately notified of their production and examination, (2) that it took place on a feast day, and (3) that they did not prove that Margaret was still living at the time the exception of precontract was made.[14] A "great argument" (*magna altercatio*) about these exceptions took place on 20 May.[15] On 17 June, the official rendered sentence for Joan.

[10] See Helmholz, *Marriage Litigation*, 230 (with references to the formal law).
[11] Disc. T&C no. 157.
[12] Though her toponymic (*de Allenmouth*) suggests Alnmouth in Northumberland.
[13] Lit. T&C no. 158.
[14] Disc. T&C no. 159.
[15] Lit. T&C no. 160.

The depositions of the witnesses to the precontract are included in the *processus*. Four witnesses, all men, testify to Andrew's exchange of *de presenti* consent with Margaret in the house of Robert de Wylebet in Boston (Lincs) late in the afternoon on the Sunday after the feast of St Martin in winter, nine years previously (15 November 1293).[16] The depositions are terse but consistent. All the witnesses testify to the words exchanged: "I take thee here, Margaret/Andrew, as my wife/husband, to have and to hold all the days of my life and to this I pledge thee my troth."[17] They also all testify that they saw Margaret alive in Boston at various dates in the previous year.

Skimpy as these depositions are, the story they tell is at least as plausible as that of Joan's witnesses. Why did the official reject them, almost out of hand? Certainly, the exceptions made to Andrew's witnesses do not seem very convincing. True, the exception witnesses do not prove that Margaret was alive when the exception was made, but she does not have to have been alive for the exception of precontract to be valid. All she has to have been was alive when Joan's contract with Andrew was alleged to have been made, and all the witnesses testify that she was.[18] The two procedural objections, if they are true (and the second certainly seems to have been), might be grounds for requiring that Andrew produce his witnesses again, but they are hardly grounds for simply discarding the testimony of his witnesses. The sentence of the archdeacon's official, then, must be based on the fact that he simply did not believe Andrew's witnesses.

I do not believe them either. If forced to choose between Joan's two women and Andrew's four men, I would side with the two women. They come from the community and must go back and face their neighbors, including three who are firmly convinced that they took a bribe to testify. The four men from Linconshire, on the other hand, even though they braved travel in the middle of January, come in from the outside simply for the purpose of testifying to a marriage nine years earlier, and the woman involved in the marriage does not herself appear.[19] But, of course, we do not have to believe either set of witnesses. The whole thing may have been a charade, like *Dolling c Smith*.

Certainly, we can construct motivations for the sentence of the archdeacon's official in this case, similar to those we constructed for that of the official of Salisbury in *Dolling c Smith*. If Andrew is not married to Margaret, then there is no reason why he cannot marry Joan. He may not have exchanged words of present consent with her in quite the form that the witnesses state, but there was probably something between them. Assuming that the archdeacon's official was not himself corrupted, as I think we ought to, absent evidence to the contrary,

16 Robert's house was a public house or an inn, to judge by one witness's reference to him as *hospes*.

17 CP.E.1, T&C no. 161.

18 But see n. 14.

19 As Helmholz, *Marriage Litigation*, 76 n. 7, points out, she did not have to appear, but normally she did, if only nominally.

these are probably the reasons that motivated him to find for Joan, despite the testimony concerning the corruption of her witnesses and despite the witnesses to the precontract.

If we look at the *processus* further, however, the similarity to *Dolling c Smith* begins to fall apart. True, as in *Dolling c Smith*, the man seems to have been of slightly higher station than the woman. Andrew in this case has enough money to hire a proctor to represent him at most of the stages of the proceeding, to pay for witnesses to come from quite a distance, and to appeal the case to the court of York. Joan, on the other hand, appears personally at most of the hearings. She does use two proctors, one who seems to appear only once, and the other, her father, who represents her in the final stages. This does not mean that she lacked professional advice.[20] The exceptions that her father introduces to the witnesses to the precontract have all the hallmarks of professional drafting, and Joan's personal appearance may be as much a device to earn the sympathy of the judge as testimony to her relative poverty.

More to the point is the fact that there is no evidence in this case, as there was in *Dolling c Smith*, that Andrew had had sexual relations with Joan, nor that he was a local ladies' man. In *Dolling c Smith*, seven women of Winterbourne Stoke are willing to put their souls on the line to testify in favor of Alice. In *Chapelayn c Cragge*, only two women are willing to put their souls on the line for Joan, and three women from the same area are willing to put theirs on the line that these two were corrupted.[21] Nor is Joan nearly so alone as Alice in *Dolling c Smith* seems to have been. Joan lives in her parents' house; her father is alive and serves as her proctor. Finally, one of the witnesses on appeal gives us a fact that we might have suspected from the rest of the story. The witness tells us that he has known Andrew for about 40 years, Joan for 20. These are probably round numbers, but when they are coupled with the fact that the precontract with Margaret is alleged to have taken place nine years earlier, while the contract with Joan is alleged to have taken place four years earlier, and that no one testifies to having known Joan for more than 20 years, we get the impression that there was a substantial gap in age between Joan and Andrew.

If the story, then, of *Dolling c Smith* is the story of a young woman in service wronged by a local bounder, the story that may ultimately emerge from *Chapelayn c Cragge* is that of an ambitious and unscrupulous young woman seeking, with the help of her father, to get her hands on a middle-aged local bachelor who was somewhat better off than she. Desperate to escape from her clutches, he obtains the support of some local women, who, unfortunately, cannot get their story of the bribery of Joan's witnesses straight. He therefore tries to get out of it by concocting a story of a precontract in Lincolnshire. This fails to convince the local judge. We do not know the result on appeal, but perhaps like the appellate court in *Dolling c Smith*, the appellate court here

20 This advice could have come from Hugh de Seton, the first proctor, or the clerk of the court.
21 Disc. T&C no. 162.

had the sense to focus not on the weakness of the defendant's story but on the weakness of the plaintiff's. If *Dolling* is a case of a woman wronged, we might call this one a case of a 'woman wronging'. At a minimum, we can see that this is the story that Andrew is trying to tell, until he panics and brings in the men from Boston.

In October of 1326, Elizabeth, daughter of Sir Simon Lovell of 'Drokton' in Ryedale, claimed Thomas son of Robert Marton as her husband before the official of the court of York.[22] In November, Thomas, sworn to tell the truth, admitted that while the litigation was pending, he had solemnized a marriage with one Ellen daughter of Jordan of 'Aneport' at 'Ryngoy' in the diocese of Chester (i.e., Lichfield),[23] but he asserted that there was a precontract between Ellen and him. Elizabeth introduced nine witnesses, two of them her sisters. The first sister testifies to an exchange of consent in Sir Simon's brewhouse on the previous 30 January in this form: "Behold, this is my troth that I shall not take another as wife except thee." And Elizabeth said: "Behold this is my troth that I shall at no time have another as husband unless I have thee."[24] On Tuesday in Easter week (5 April) of the same year, she was present with her sister in the room above the gate in Sir Simon's house where Thomas was lying naked in his bed. Thomas said that he had been to the friars, his confessors, who told him that the prior contract was not valid, and that they were both free to marry someone else. Immediately, they exchanged further words, each saying to the other: "I take thee here Elizabeth/Thomas as my faithful wedded wife/husband, to have and to hold to the end of my life and to this I pledge thee my troth."[25] The other sister testifies to the second exchange but not to the first.

The remaining seven witnesses testify to a meeting held in Hovingham church between Sir Simon and Robert Marton and some of their friends. The upshot of the meeting, according to most of the witnesses, was that Thomas confessed that he had exchanged words of present consent with Elizabeth, but that he had done so conditionally, with a mental reservation that his relatives would approve of what he had done. Robert Marton and the man whom Thomas is alleged to have consulted before he made his confession both assert that Thomas said that the condition was expressed.

Whether the first exchange sufficed for consent in law is a difficult question about which authority can be cited on both sides.[26] There is no question, however, that the second exchange, if it happened, constituted a valid marriage. Thomas's mental reservation, even if we believe it, would not have sufficed. If, on the other hand, the condition had been expressed, it could have sufficed to turn the marriage from a present one into a future one (absent intercourse,

22 *Lovell c Marton* (1326–9), CP.E.18, disc. T&C no. 163.

23 Neither name is easy to identify. There is an Allport in Bromborough in Cheshire (*Place-names of Cheshire*, 4:240) and an Alport in Derbyshire (Ekwall, *English Place-names*, s.n).

24 Latin in Helmholz, *Marriage Litigation*, 193.

25 *Id.*, 194.

26 See Helmholz, *Marriage Litigation*, 40–5, though on balance, the friars' advice seems sound.

which was neither alleged nor proven).[27] That Thomas's defense was dependent on demonstrating this condition is clear from his answers to Elizabeth's positions (interrogatories). He introduces no further testimony, however, and it is not surprising that he loses the case.[28]

In some ways this case is similar to *Dolling c Smith* and *Chapelayn c Cragge*. The woman alleges the exchange of present consent. She has few witnesses, and those she has are close to her. The man attempts to defend on one of the grounds that the law allowed. And yet, socially, this seems like a very different case. Robert Marton, though he may have been of quite respectable status, was not a knight, and Simon Lovell was. Thomas was apparently in service in Sir Simon's house. Both the parties seem to have been quite young. There is no suggestion of seduction, on either side. They knew what they were doing. The story of the friars is plausible (one is reminded of the friar in *Romeo and Juliet*), but after it was all over, Thomas changed his mind. Why? We will never know. The fact, however, that Thomas alleges that the marriage was conditional on his relatives' consent and the fact that the case was contested suggest that the relatives did not consent. Despite the fact that Sir Simon was a knight and Robert Marton was not, Robert did not want his son to marry the knight's daughter.[29] He had someone else in mind for him. Thomas does not come across as a young man of strong will. He marries Ellen, as we suspect that his father wanted him to do, but he also does not resist Elizabeth's case very strongly. We cannot imagine that Sir Simon was pleased with the whole affair, but he supports his daughter.[30] She presents the case, and Thomas is honest enough not to attempt to obtain perjured witnesses, for example, to the precontract that he alleged having had with Ellen before the contract with Elizabeth.

In short, unlike *Dolling c Smith* and, particularly, *Chapelayn c Cragge*, the record in this case seems reliable. If there is any lying, it is lying by both the parties. Possibly, they got the result that they wanted all along. Thomas could not resist his father absent a judgment of the official of York, but he was willing to concoct a case with Elizabeth that ensured the result they wanted.[31] While this reading of the record is possible, I am more inclined to take it more straightforwardly. Thomas was weak. His father talked him out of the marriage, but did not – perhaps he did not even suggest it – talk him into suborning perjury.

We now have three stories to tell out of basically the same type of legal record. We have the woman wronged, Alice Dolling, the woman wronging, Joan Chapelayn, and the young couple, one of whom tries to back out after he realizes what he has done, Elizabeth Lovell and Thomas Marton. Two more cases will serve to show significant variations on these basic types of stories.

[27] Disc. T&C no. 164.

[28] Though it is not until 18 months after the depositions that the official finally renders judgment for Elizabeth.

[29] Politics may have been involved; see disc. T&C no. 165.

[30] Lit. T&C no. 166.

[31] Lit. T&C no. 167.

In the autumn of 1393, Alice de Foston of York, widow of Thomas Walshe, jeweler, late of Ireland, sued Robert Lofthouse, draper of York, before the dean of Christianity of York claiming Robert as her husband.[32] Alice produced four witnesses. They testify to a long-term relationship between Alice and Robert. She had had two children by him, and one of the witnesses testifies to exchanges of present consent two and six years previously. The key events had taken place, however, the previous Lent in the cell of Lady Margaret Elys, a nun of Clementhorpe Priory.[33] The fullest account of the exchange is given by Alice's 20-year-old son, who says that in answer to Lady Margaret's questioning, Robert said: "The troth that I promised her, I will keep, and I shall make of her a good woman, as I am a man, and I will have her as my wife."[34] Alice replied: "I keep me well content, and have always kept me well content, and so thou promised me long before this time."[35] Lady Margaret and another nun confirm this testimony but with somewhat less specificity.

It is by no means clear that this exchange is enough to make a canonically valid marriage, particularly since no one is prepared to testify that intercourse followed. Robert, however, does not defend on the ground of the inadequacy of the consent. Rather, he defends on the ground that Alice cannot prove that Thomas Walshe is dead. This defense is ultimately defeated by a document from the dean of Bristol testifying to Thomas's death.[36] The dean of Christianity of York finds for Alice in July of 1394. The last document in the case is Robert's proposition before the commissary general of the consistory court, attacking Alice's witnesses on the ground that they are his enemies (he is careful not to mention the nuns), that Alice is after his money, and that the dean of Bristol has no jurisdiction in the case.[37] The document is endorsed with the names of six witnesses, but if their depositions were ever taken, they have not survived.

The story told here is obviously a variant on the theme of the woman wronged, but the variations are significant. There is no doubt that the parties in this case had had intercourse. There is not really any suggestion that Alice was seduced by promises of marriage. Both of the parties to the case were obviously mature. Alice's relationship with Thomas Walshe had clearly broken up before she knew he was dead. She may even have formed her liaison with Robert when she knew that Thomas was not dead.[38] There are thus three elements that distinguish this case from cases like *Dolling c Smith*: the fact that the parties had been living in what they knew was concubinage and which they may have known was adulterous, a relationship that the woman is now seeking to turn into a marriage; the fact that they are mature, and the fact that the woman

[32] *Foston c Lofthouse* (1393–4), CP.E.198.

[33] Lit. T&C no. 168.

[34] Latin in Pedersen, *Marriage Disputes*, 115 n. 16.

[35] *Ibid.*

[36] Disc. T&C no. 169.

[37] This may be an attempt to set up an argument that the dean's certificate of Thomas's death is not to be believed.

[38] For the suggestion that the impediment of crime was involved in this case, see lit. T&C no. 170.

had previously been uncontrovertibly married. As we will see, many variations on the three initial types of story will have one or more of these elements.

On 13 May 1332, Alice de Brantice, daughter of Richard de Draycote of Cropwell Butler, claimed William Crane of Bingham as her husband before the official of the archdeacon of Nottingham.[39] She produced three witnesses to a contract that took place in the house of one Henry Kyketon in Cropwell Butler, eight years previously. The words of consent that they describe are the standard ones: "I take thee here Alice/William as my lawful wife/husband, to have and to hold all the days of my life, if holy church allow it, and to this I pledge thee my troth."[40] From the beginning it is clear that the issue in the case is not whether the exchange of consent took place but what the age of the parties was when it happened, and whether, assuming that William was under age when it happened, he dissented from the contract when he reached the age of puberty. Alice's witnesses are not completely consistent about the parties' ages, testifying variously that Alice was 14 or 13 and that William was 13 or 14. Four witnesses, all men, testify on William's behalf. They assert that he was 11 at the time of the contract, that he was forced into the contract by his godmother (*commater*), Elizabeth Crane,[41] one of Alice's witnesses, and that he dissented from the contract consistently thereafter. Despite this testimony, the archdeacon's official found for Alice.

The legal issue presented by this case is not easy. As we have seen, Alexander's rules, rather than fixing a 'bright line' at age 14 for the man and 12 for the woman, leave considerable ambiguity. Marriages may be valid if the parties are "near puberty" (*pubertati proximi*) or if "*malitia* makes up for age" (*malitia suppleat aetatem*). Further, though Alexander is clear that if one of the parties marries below the age of puberty and dissents upon reaching puberty, the marriage is not valid, what the party must do to dissent and when he must do it are not clear either in Alexander's rules or in the canonists' commentary.[42] The piece of testimony in this case that we find the most striking is the statement by William's witnesses that his godmother told him that if he did not come along and marry Alice, she would cut off his ear. That is not the sort of threat that a woman makes to a grown man or even a hulking teenage boy; it is the sort of threat that one makes to a little boy. On the other hand, eight years passed after the events described, and one is left to wonder why William, who was now a minimum of 19, did not do something to clarify his marital status.[43]

The interest of this case, however, lies not so much in the ambiguity of the legal issues, which certainly could have gone either way, but in the story that is told. William was apparently an orphan; his parents are nowhere mentioned, and his godmother, Elizabeth, seems to have been taking care of him. Elizabeth's

[39] *Brantice c Crane* (1332–3), CP.E.23.
[40] Lit. T&C no. 171.
[41] The fact that they share a surname suggests that she was also his paternal aunt.
[42] See Ch 1, at nn. 19–23; Helmholz, *Marriage Litigation*, 199–200.
[43] Lit. T&C no. 172.

husband was a servant in Henry de Kyketon's house. Another of the witnesses is the son of Felicia, Henry de Kyketon's wife. The third is a servant in the house. Alice's mother is called Alice de Kyketon; she may have been related to Henry. In short, what we have here is probably a family alliance of the type that we are used to seeing in accounts of the upper classes in the Middle Ages, but which we know happened in other classes as well. Why this particular arrangement came undone, we do not know. Both Henry de Kyketon and his wife died in the interim, and it may be that the financial arrangements upon which the match depended died with them. But it seems more likely, especially considering that Elizabeth Crane is still supporting the match, that William, when he grew up, simply changed his mind.

In all of these cases we have relatively full records, claim and defense, witnesses on both sides, and a judgment at some level of court. Even here, we cannot always be sure what story is being told and what the counter-story is. It is even more difficult when we have an incomplete record. The question, then, is whether the legal claim or defense gives us at least some clue as to which type of case we have, so that we may make at least tentative classifications of cases where the record is not so full.

It is difficult, but clues there are. In the first place, the claim of force or nonage usually indicates an arranged marriage that has for some reason gone awry. It is not necessary that the claimed defense be true (it may well not have been true in *Brantice c Crane*), but for the claim to be plausible, the witnesses normally have to testify to something that looks like an arranged marriage. In the second place, the claim of intercourse, much less of cohabitation and children, is sufficiently rare that we can suspect that the story being told is either one of a woman wronged or of an ongoing relationship. We cannot always be sure which story is being told, and perhaps that is because the stories are sufficiently similar that the plaintiff can afford to let them blend into each other. Third, the claim of precontract, by itself, tells us virtually nothing. The reason is that this is such a powerful claim legally (it is the only defense that wins in a two-party *de presenti* marriage case) that the temptation to raise it speciously is strong. Sometimes, as in *Lovell c Marton*, it indicates, at a minimum, that the person raising the claim has changed his or her mind. Sometimes, as in *Chapelayn c Cragge*, it indicates desperation, the last refuge of a defendant who has no place else to turn. But that in turn forces us to look at the claimed marriage. The reason for the desperation may be that the defendant is finally caught in his duplicity, or it may mean, as we suspected in *Chapelayn*, that he has been caught in a web of false testimony.

Let us look at the rest of our 24 two-party *de presenti* marriage-enforcement actions to see if this typology holds up.[44] For convenience, we will refer to the types of stories as follows: Type one cases tell the basic story of the woman wronged, *Dolling c Smith*; type two, the case of the woman (it will turn out that it can be a man, too) wronging, *Chapelayn c Cragge*; type three, the young

44 Disc. T&C no. 173.

couple who may have gone too far, *Lovell c Marton*; type four, types one through three with the variants of long-term relationship and/or mature parties, *Foston c Lofthouse*; type five, the arranged marriage gone awry, *Brantice c Crane*. Because they are the easiest to identify, we will begin with the fifth type.

Margaret de Tofte c William de Maynwaryng of Peover[45] seems to be a case of an arranged marriage gone wrong. No depositions survive, but we know that the defense was the nonage of the defendant and force (also precontract). The *reus* in the case appealed from a sentence for the *actrix* to the court of Canterbury and thence to the Apostolic See whence it was delegated to the archbishop of York, facts that suggest that the parties were of some wealth.[46]

William son of Adam de Hopton c Constance daughter of Walter del Brome of Skelmanthorpe[47] has elements in it that suggest a type four case, but what we have puts it more clearly in the arranged-marriage category. The defendant, a widow, was in the wardship of the plaintiff's father. That suggests that either she or her husband held land by military tenure. Constance defends on the grounds that her former husband was related to the plaintiff, that the former husband was alive at the time of the contract, that the plaintiff was underage, that she was forced into the arrangement, and that she (perhaps subsequently) married another man. No result is recorded.

In three other cases from mid-century, a woman defendant resists a claim of *de presenti* marriage on the ground that she was forced into the arrangement, and in two of them on the additional ground that she was underage. In the first case, the witnesses say that the defendant's great-uncle threatened to pick her up by the ears and put her in a fountain or a well if she did not go through with the marriage. The fear is said not to have been enough to move a constant woman, at least where there were others present who could have prevented it, and the case goes against her.[48] In the second, according to the witnesses, if the defendant was not underage, she was certainly very close, and both her relatives and the man's are promoting the match.[49] This case, too, goes against the defendant.[50]

The third case, *William Whitheved of Brayton c Alice daughter of John Crescy*, had originally been in the court of the keeper of the spirituality of Selby in which, the then-defendant now alleges, she falsely confessed to having exchanged consent and having had intercourse with the then-plaintiff.[51] She also alleges that she is underage and a virgin. The one witness whose testimony survives, a chaplain, confirms her story. According to him, Alice was underage at the time of the confession, though she is now 12. He believes that she would

[45] *Tofte c Maynwaryng* (1324), CP.E.15.
[46] Lit. T&C no. 174.
[47] *Hopton c Brome* (1348), CP.E.62; lit. T&C no. 175.
[48] *Thomeson c Belamy* (1362), CP.E.85; lit. T&C no. 176.
[49] *Marrays c Rouclif* (1365), CP.E.89, discussed with lit. T&C no. 177.
[50] Lit. T&C no. 178.
[51] *Whitheved c Crescy* (1368), CP.E.97.

not have consented to marry William without her parents' consent,[52] and that she confessed because William threatened to kill her if she did not confess. Unfortunately, the chaplain is not asked the grounds of his belief, and no other depositions and no sentence survive. The story here, or at least what we have of it, is quite different from the others in which the defenses of force and nonage are raised. Here we do not have a defendant trying to get out of an arranged marriage, but a defendant who seems to be seeking to upset what was clearly not an arranged marriage, on the ground that she was underage and forced into it.[53]

With the possible exception of the last, these cases are evidence for the proposition that marriage in fourteenth-century Yorkshire was not always the sole concern of the marriage partners. Whatever Alexander's rules might state, arranged marriages did exist, and many of them probably went ahead without the difficulties experienced by the parties who litigated. But if 5 (*Brantice* and all those described, except the last) of our 24 cases tell stories of arranged marriages, 18 do not.[54] In an additional 9 cases, parents or relatives of the parties seem to be trying to enforce the marriage or to break it up, or, as in the *Lovell* case, both.[55] That still means that in close to half of our cases, parents or relatives are no place to be found, and we will see that the percentage gets higher when we add the other types of marriage-formation cases. Comment on the possible significance of this must be saved for the end of Chapter 5.

Type four cases are the next easiest to identify, if only because the descriptions of the parties normally tell us when we are dealing with a widow.

In *Alice de Wetherby c John Page leather-dresser of York*, all that survives is John's defense.[56] Alice was the wife of William Cave of York. Five witnesses agree that their marriage was solemnized 14 years previously. There seems to be no doubt that they lived together following the marriage and that it considerably antedated the marriage of Alice and John. The only real ambiguity in the testimony is whether William Cave is still alive, and on this point the witnesses testify variously. None testifies that he is alive at the time of the depositions, only that he was said to be alive at the time of the contract between Alice and John, or, in one case, that he was alive within the previous two years.[57]

Lacking much information on the alleged marriage of Alice and John, we can only speculate as to why their relationship fell apart.[58] What we have is consistent with the notion that John left Alice because he came to believe that his relationship with her was bigamous. It is also, however, consistent with the notion that the prior marriage is an excuse, concocted after John had left Alice

52 *Id.*, T&C no. 179.

53 Compare the abduction cases in the fifteenth century in Ch 5, at nn. 70–97.

54 For the composition of the 24, see n. 44.

55 Listed T&C no. 180.

56 *Wetherby c Page* (1338), CP.E.36; lit. T&C no. 181.

57 Disc. T&C no. 182.

58 Only the fifth witness testifies to the marriage of Alice and John, and his testimony is hard to read, even under ultraviolet light.

for quite different reasons and because he thought that she could not prove that William was dead. No result is recorded.

In one other case, the record suggests that a widow has engaged in a long-term relationship with a man, but in this case it is the widow who is seeking to avoid a marriage.[59] All that survives is the *rea*'s exception that she did not exchange the words of present consent with the *actor* after her husband's death. This is not much to go on, but it is enough to suggest that the case is one of parties of some maturity, and the defense, in addition to denial of the contract, suggests the impediment of crime. (If she did not exchange consent with him after her husband's death, did she do so before his death? If so, and if they had committed adultery, the impediment of crime would have been made out.)

John de Carnaby esquire c Joan Mounceaux lady of Barmston in Holderness[60] is another case of a man suing a widow, and this case has left us considerably more, enough to suggest not a long-term relationship but a case more akin to type two (*Chapelayn c Cragge*), with the genders reversed. Clearly the defendant was a rich widow, and she defends on the ground of disparity of wealth. Her witnesses testify, without contradiction, that she has been lady of Barmston for 40 years and is worth 300 marks a year. The plaintiff's status was more problematical. He calls himself *armiger*, a status which Joan's witnesses never grant him. He is, they say, a bastard, living on £10 a year that his uncle gives him. His witnesses allege that he is his father's heir, worth £100 a year. Neither set of witnesses inspires much confidence. John's are alleged to be servants, and if they are not, they seem pretty clearly to be 'his men'. Prominent among Joan's witnesses is her son, who quite clearly does not want to acquire a stepfather. As in so many of these cases, there was probably more between the parties than the defendant's witnesses allege and less than the plaintiff's witnesses allege. Unfortunately, there is no sentence.[61]

There is considerably less of a record in *John Trayleweng of Yokefleet c Agnes widow of Richard son of John alias Jackson of Swinefleet*.[62] All we know is that John is seeking to enforce a *de presenti* informal marriage with Agnes who is a widow, but, absent more, that is enough to assign the case tentatively to the category of 'mature parties', if not 'long-term relationship'.

Our final type four cases do not involve widows but do involve what seem to have been long-term relationships between parties of some maturity. In *Joan de Barneby of York c John Fertlyng alias Wartre of York*, all that survives is the case for the plaintiff.[63] Her witnesses, including the local vicar, tell a story of an exchange of present consent (there is some variation in words) eight years previously in a house in Howden. A child followed, perhaps two children. The record gives no indication of what had happened in the interim. The only

[59] *Clifton c [. . .]* (?1345), CP.E.241I.
[60] *Carnaby c Mounceaux* (1390), CP.E.179.
[61] Lit. T&C no. 183.
[62] *Trayleweng c Jackson* (1348), CP.E.61.
[63] *Barneby c Fertlyng* (1398), CP.E.239.

clue as to what may have been at stake is the rather striking description of the defendant's costume at the time of the alleged exchange of consent. He was wearing a fur-lined cloak and high boots and spurs as if for riding, and, according to one witness, he was carrying a bow and arrows. This may suggest a man of somewhat higher station, and the absence of a defense certainly suggests the story-type of the wronged woman, coupled with the long-term relationship. In the event, the commissary general holds for the plaintiff, and the defendant appeals to the Apostolic See.

Alice daughter of Robert Wright of Brayton c William de Ricall of Brayton is an interesting variation on the theme of the long-term relationship.[64] Alice's witnesses, whose depositions are the only ones that survive and perhaps the only ones that there ever were, seem clear that William was a substantial farmer, worth a mark a year. Alice worked for him, not, apparently, as a servant but more as a bailiff.[65] They married, according to the witnesses in Alice's father's house, informally and *de presenti*. William confesses that he had intercourse with Alice. Alice's father and her sister are the sole witnesses to the exchange of present consent. There is no defense other than that implied in the interrogatories concerning the defendant's greater wealth. The commissary general finds for Alice, and though the case was appealed to the official, there is no evidence that the appeal was pursued.

Financial arrangements are clearly important in this case. Alice's position makes her, in the eyes of the witnesses, working for William "as for her husband."[66] Presumably, a fourteenth-century Yorkshire farmer would not have hired a single woman to work with him on the financial affairs of the farm. It is also probably significant that William sold his farm, and only after that did Alice sue him. In William's eyes it would seem that his relationship with Alice and the farm went together. He may even have sold the farm in order to terminate his relationship with Alice. (There is no suggestion that he sold it because he had fallen on hard times.) When sued, he seeks to turn the story into one of the wronging woman, only after his wealth. Alice, on the other hand, sees the relationship as lasting beyond the sale of the farm, and so do her kin. She sues on the ground of the woman wronged, a story that does not quite fit because she seems so competent.[67] As in many of these cases, it is hard to know just what swayed the judge. We may doubt that he accepted the testimony of clearly biased witnesses totally on its face. On the other hand, William had had intercourse with Alice and there seemed to be no reason why he couldn't marry her; hence, judgment for Alice.

In examining the cases involving mature parties or long-term relationships, we discovered that the lack of a complete record frequently makes it hard to know whether we are dealing with a variant on type one (*Dolling*), or type

64 *Wright c Ricall* (1361), CP.E.84.
65 Lit. T&C no. 184.
66 Text T&C no. 184.
67 Lit. T&C no. 185.

two (*Chapelayn*), or even type three (*Lovell*). The same difficulty is present in cases where the parties are young and there is no suggestion of a long-term relationship. For example, all that survives in *Agnes Romundeby of York c William Fischelake mercer of York* are William's depositions on his defense of absence and on the corruption of Agnes's witnesses.[68] The witnesses to absence, all William's brothers, are not very convincing, and the testimony to corruption is all hearsay. What we cannot tell from the record, however, is whether it is more likely that William concocted this story because, having seduced Agnes, he wanted to get out of the consequences of his acts, or that Agnes was pursuing him for his money (he is a freeman of York). The nature of the defense, however, suggests that the case in not a variation of type three.

The claim and defense of another case of 1372, *Marjorie daughter of Simon Tailour and servant of William de Burton leather-dresser of York c John Beek saddler of York* also suggests that it could be a type one or a type two but not a type three case.[69] The case was brought by Marjorie before the archbishop personally, perhaps as a result of her reclamation of John's banns with another woman. The archbishop heard the libel and the oaths of the parties in his audience before delegating the case to the official, who ultimately delegated it to a special commissary. Marjorie's witnesses on the principal are all women, one age 15 and a fellow servant of hers, another a 16-year-old and not otherwise described, and the third a married woman in her late 20s from the suburbs. With a few variations in detail, they describe a handfasting in the house of William Burton (variously described as a cordwainer or tanner), in which Marjorie and John exchanged words of present consent, and then John made a garland of field flowers (one witness describes some of the flowers as "coufloppis," i.e., foxglove),[70] placed it over Marjorie's head, and kissed her through the garland. This clearly impressed the 15-year-old, who says that she remembered the event because of the garland.[71]

John defends on the inconsistent grounds of absence and that it was all a joke.[72] He did produce witnesses, but their depositions are now missing. Marjorie produced replication witnesses, including a married couple who lived nearby and who provided some beer for the party, and another servant who arrived at Burton's house a bit later and saw both John and Marjorie there. Absent John's defense one cannot be sure, but what we have gives us a strong impression that Marjorie was a woman wronged. One of the first group of witnesses says that John asked them not to say anything to anyone about the handfasting, and that suggests either that his commitment to Marjorie was not

[68] *Romundeby c Fischelake* (1395), CP.E.216.

[69] *Tailour c Beek* (1372), CP.E.121.

[70] See OED s.v. *cow*, n1, meaning 8.

[71] The testimony of the second witness is printed in Helmholz, *Marriage Litigation*, 28–9. She is a bit less gushy but to the same effect.

[72] Lit. T&C no. 186.

so strong as it seemed or that he knew that there were those who would oppose the match. It is not surprising that judgment is rendered for Marjorie.[73]

Emma daughter of John de Drifeld of North Dalton c John son of John of North Dalton[74] presents even more clearly a conflict between type one and type two, with little possibility that type three is involved. Emma's two witnesses tell a straight story of a *de presenti* marriage in an upper chamber in her father's house on a bench before her bed. The story is not particularly convincing; the details do not quite match, and there are only two witnesses to the contract (only one, Emma's sister, to a second contract). A third female witness testifies to *fama*. John's witnesses, five men in all, are also not very convincing. They suggest that Emma's male witness is also related to her, that John is richer than Emma and she is after his money, and that there is no *fama*. They do not completely support John's allegations, however. Some say that the women are honest, though all of them seem to agree that the sister is promoting her sister's cause because John is richer than Emma. It would seem that this is either a case of a wronged woman or of a woman wronging; the record does not give us enough information to allow us to tell which. The auditor of causes of the chapter of Beverley rendered sentence for Emma, and John appealed to the York consistory, at which point the record in the case ends.

Cases raising the defense of affinity by illicit intercourse, like cases raising the defense of precontract, frequently look suspicious. Certainly, the raising of this defense tells us little about which of our basic types of stories is involved. Fortunately, the three cases in our group that raise this defense have full enough records to allow us to draw tentative conclusions about the underlying stories.

In *Joan daughter of Peter de Acclum of Newton c John son of John de Carthorp*,[75] we lack the depositions on the claim, although we know that Joan alleged a *de presenti* marriage. The witnesses for the defense of affinity by illicit intercourse with a first cousin once removed of the plaintiff 16 years previously are interesting. Their testimony to the affinity is routine, but some also testify that John impregnated Joan and was forced into marrying her. Unlike many cases where the defense of force is raised, this does not seem to have been an arranged marriage that went awry; rather, it seems to have been a case in which an older man took advantage of a younger woman (the wronged-woman pattern).[76] Her relatives, we might speculate, then took matters into their own hands and put considerable pressure on him to marry her. Unfortunately we have no sentence.[77]

In *Agnes Godewyn daughter of Beatrice sub monte of Clifton c Nigel le Roser of Clifton*, like *Brantice c Crane* an appeal from the official of the archdeacon of

[73] Lit. T&C no. 187.
[74] *Drifeld c Dalton* (1335), CP.E.28.
[75] *Acclum c Carthorp* (1337), CP.E.33.
[76] Disc. T&C no. 188.
[77] Lit. T&C no. 189.

Nottingham,[78] the defendant confesses the exchange of present consent with the plaintiff, and immediately raises the defense of affinity by illicit intercourse – he had previously had intercourse with a relative of Agnes's, Alice Godwin. Examination of the record suggests that this case is really a variant that combines type three (*Lovell*) and type one (*Dolling*). The witnesses testify that the first they knew of the relationship between Nigel and Alice was when Alice's mother objected to the banns of Agnes and Nigel, on the ground of the affinity. They also say that the mother hated Nigel because he had made Alice pregnant. The archdeacon's official ultimately decides for Agnes, not, it would seem, because he doubted that the intercourse had ever taken place but because none of the witnesses seems able to demonstrate the relationship between Alice and Agnes, despite the similarity in their surnames. (There is no result on the appeal.) As in the *Dolling* case, the man in this case does not look very good. He impregnated Alice and then abandoned her. But like the *Lovell* case, he really does not seem to know his own mind. Having married Agnes informally and having brought the matter to the point that banns were proclaimed between them, he then seemed to have had qualms of conscience when Alice's mother objected to the banns. More the record does not allow us to say, but it is clear here, as in *Lovell*, that we are dealing with two relationships that actually happened, rather than, as in *Chapelayn*, with a second one made up for purposes of defeating the claim.[79]

Emmota servant of Henry Rayner of Beal c Robert son of John Willyamson of Kellington and Thomas son of John Willyamson of Kellington[80] is interesting because the objection to the marriage does not come from the parties themselves. Emmota's action against Robert is straightforward. She alleges a *de presenti* informal marriage, which he confesses. Her action against Robert's brother, Thomas, is for defamation: Thomas has said that he had sexual intercourse with her. The action proceeds largely on the basis of the confessions of the parties. It is clear that Thomas did say that he had had intercourse with Emmota; indeed, he says he said it in order to impede the marriage. The special commissary decides for Emmota in her suit against Robert; no judgment is recorded in the suit against Thomas. It is unclear whether the ground of the judgment is that the commissary did not believe Thomas's claim or whether he believed it but thought that there was insufficient evidence that it had happened before the marriage with Robert (in which case the impediment of affinity by illicit intercourse would not arise).[81] On the basis of this record, we might suggest that the case is a variant of type three, where the young couple decide to go ahead with the marriage and their kin try to break it up.

For a male defendant to raise the defense of affinity by illicit intercourse in which he was involved automatically puts him the position of a type one

[78] *Godewyn c Roser* (1306), CP.E.241B.
[79] Lit. T&C no. 190.
[80] *Rayner c Willyamson and Willyamson* (1389), CP.E.181.
[81] Lit. T&C no. 191.

defendant. John de Carthorp never succeeded in extricating himself. His witnesses, if anything, made him look worse. Nigel le Roser did partially extricate himself, but when the case is all over, it is hard to escape the impression that the man is at best weak, and at worst a cad. In another case, the defendant automatically put himself in the type one category by raising the defense that the consent that the plaintiff alleged he exchanged with her was conditional on her having intercourse with him, intercourse that did not follow.[82] This is not quite the defendant charged with parricide throwing himself on the mercy of the court because he is an orphan, but it is close. The legal issue has some ambiguity,[83] but since the defendant offered no testimony, it is not surprising that the case went against him and was confirmed on appeal.

Our final cases involve the defense of precontract, and one has elements that suggest type three:

Alice Bernard daughter of Peter Huetson of Walkerith [?Lincs] c Peter le Walker of Tadcaster[84] involves an allegation of a *de presenti* precontract made five years previously. The allegation is made for the first time on an appeal to the official from the sentence for the plaintiff by the commissary general. Again, lacking the depositions on the basic claim, we cannot be sure what is really involved, but the witnesses to the precontract are strikingly young (20, 22), a fact suggesting that the parties to the precontract were very young at the time (midteens). The fact that the defense is not raised until the appeal casts some doubt on its validity, but not much. It seems to have been a fairly regular practice in the York court for the defendant to save his main defense for the appeal.[85] Considering the fact that the man came from Walkerith and is now living in Tadcaster and also the age of the parties, this case would seem to hang in the balance between a type one (he married her and then left town) and a type three (they were young; he really didn't know his mind). Unfortunately, we have no sentence on appeal.

John de Topclyf of Ripon c Emmota Erle of Wakefield involves an ambiguity in the initial exchange of consent, as well as a defense of precontract.[86] The witnesses on the principal claim describe an exchange of consent of considerable ambiguity. (Not all witnesses lie.)[87] The case is defended on the ground of precontract, and the depositions to the precontract are solid.[88] The commissary general renders sentence for the defendant, the only such sentence in a two-party *de presenti* marriage case from the entire group.

In *Topclyf*, there is room for considerable doubt whether the parties had said enough to contract a canonically valid marriage. In both *Bernard* and *Topclyf*,

82 *Scherwode c Lambe* (1379), CP.E.116.

83 See discussion in Helmholz, *Marriage Litigation*, 51–3, with reference to this case.

84 *Bernard c Walker* (1341), CP.E.40.

85 See, e.g., *Scargill and Robinson c Park* (at n. 212).

86 *Topclyf c Erle* (1381), CP.E.124; cf *Topclyf c Grenehode* (1381), CP.E.241T, printed in *Select Cases on Defamation*, no. 2, pp. 4–5; disc. T&C no. 192.

87 Details and lit. T&C no. 193.

88 These witnesses may have been introduced on appeal because they seem to be dated after the commissary general's sentence.

the defendant may have genuinely believed that he or she was not married to the plaintiff. What it takes, however, to get a favorable sentence is an allegation and proof of precontract. We need not assert that the testimony to the precontracts in these cases was false, though that in *Topclyf* is certainly slick. What must be asserted is that what is obvious to us after more than six hundred years must have been painfully obvious to the proctors who represented defendants, particularly male defendants, before the York court. There are many defenses that can be raised to a claim of *de presenti* marriage, but the only one that stands much chance of winning is the defense of precontract. This will become relevant when we consider the competitor cases.

We are on shakier ground when we assert that what was obvious to the proctors was also known by those people who were not yet in litigation. Much depends on their access to rather sophisticated types of information. Suffice it to say here that if a man or woman, particularly a man, in fourteenth-century York sought my advice about what to do about the fact that he had engaged in an ambiguous matrimonial transaction with a woman and he now wanted to get out of it, I would advise him to marry someone else as quickly as possible. However much he might believe in his own conscience that he was not married to the first woman, he would stand the best chance of success if he could show that success for *her* in the case would cause the upsetting of an otherwise valid marriage. This will become relevant when we consider the marriage-and-divorce cases.

What does all this add up to? In the first place, our typology has held up reasonably well. Not that all of the cases are 'pure' types; indeed relatively few of them are. Nor can we be sure in the majority of the cases what story *we* should tell from the record. The records are too spotty and the possibility of lying witnesses too great for us to have much confidence about what happened in all but a few of the cases. What has held up, however, are the elements of types. Whatever the legal claim or defense they may have been raising, few, if any, of our parties and their witnesses seem to be telling stories that depart too far from our typical patterns. Where both claim and defense and the depositions about them have survived (or a claim without any indication that the case was defended), we can construct the stories on both sides with reasonable confidence. We can sometimes do it even where we have only half of the case. We can almost always construct the story on one side of the case. We are, of course, here constructing only the stories that the parties or their proctors chose to tell, but that is the reality that a court record presents. Where we have both sides of the case, we can frequently go a bit further: We can construct a composite story that may in some sense be 'the' story of the case. Not that we can completely capture the underlying social reality of the case, but we can combine, like a judge, the stories presented and suggest what seems to be persuasive within the context of what seem to be the underlying values of the culture. I suggested that this was possible in the five cases used for developing the types. I will now suggest that it is possible in several more. But first let us return to numbers for a moment and count the types of stories and story-elements that we have already seen.

As already noted, five cases involve arranged marriages gone awry, four of them quite clearly so, one probably.[89] In none of these cases do we have a clear idea why the arranged marriage went awry. The reason we do not is that it is legally irrelevant to the defense of force or of nonage, and none of the witnesses in this group gives us the legally irrelevant but socially significant element of the motivation.[90] Our storytellers, then, are taking for granted Alexander's principle that marital consent must be freely given. If one of the parties was forced, and does not now want to go through with the marriage, the reasons for the dissent are irrelevant. The party's will in this case is sovereign.

Seven of our cases involve mature parties or long-term relationships.[91] These cases are difficult to classify beyond that fact, and the fact that they are difficult to classify may tell us something. The Western church has always been uncomfortable with second marriages, even when the prior spouse was dead.[92] In addition, medieval culture was ambivalent about widows. They were regarded as desirable, both because they were often wealthy and because of their sexual experience. At the same time, they were frequently thought to be domineering and of uncontrollable sexuality. To confuse the picture even more, another strand in the culture regarded widows as *miserabiles personae*, fitting objects of charity.[93] It is not surprising, therefore, that no clear story emerges from the cases involving widows or long-term relationships. In two of the cases, the pattern is one of the woman wronged,[94] and that may be the story in one other case.[95] In one case, brought by a man against a widow, the defense asks us to focus on the man as a fortune hunter, and the man does not seem to have any counter-story to resist this one.[96] That may well be the story in two other cases.[97] The final case, involving not a widow but a long-term relationship, is the most complex of the whole group.[98] The woman seems to be telling the story of the woman wronged, the man that of the woman wronging. The witnesses tell us enough, however, to allow us to see that she is far from innocent, but that what she is seeking is not access to his wealth but more like what she has come, with some justification, to regard as an entitlement. The fact that her father is involved in supporting her case from the beginning, if we are to believe his testimony, introduces the final element. This case, therefore, involves a combination of four of our five story-elements.

The largest group, 12 cases in all, involve variants on or versions of the initial three types of stories without any suggestion of an arranged marriage or the

[89] Listed T&C no. 194.

[90] They may have given it, and the clerk may not have taken it down.

[91] Listed T&C no. 195.

[92] Brundage, *Law, Sex*, 97–8.

[93] See, e.g., Brundage, "Widows and Remarriage," and Rosenthal, "Fifteenth-Century Widows," both with ample references.

[94] *Foston c Lofthouse* (at nn. 32–38); *Barneby c Fertlyng* (at n. 63).

[95] *Wetherby c Page* (at nn. 56–7).

[96] *Carnaby c Mounceaux* (at nn. 60–1).

[97] *Clifton c [. . .]* (n. 59); *Trayleweng c Jackson* (at n. 62).

[98] *Wright c Ricall* (at n. 64).

additional complexity of mature parties or long-term relationships. Two cases clearly tell the story of the woman wronged, and there is little to counter it.[99] Four tell the story of the woman wronged or of the woman wronging, depending on whose version of the story one believes.[100] (I have already suggested in one of these, *Chapelayn c Cragge*, that the story of the woman wronging is more plausible.) Two tell the story either of a woman wronged or of a relationship that may have gone too far, depending on whose version of the story one believes.[101] To this group we should probably add *Whitheved c Crescy*, the case of the young woman seeking to escape from the marriage that was not arranged, on the ground that she was forced into consenting publicly with the man.[102] One involves either a man wronging or a relationship that may have gone too far.[103] Two, including the base story out of which type three was created, squarely pose the issue of whether the relationship had actually become a marriage.[104]

How did the court react to these stories? The number of examples in each category is so small that we should not, of course, expect anything like statistically significant differences. There are, nonetheless, some interesting numbers that emerge from these cases. The number of sentences is quite high; 16 of the 24 cases have sentences at least at one level of court. Defendants who tried to get out of what seem to be arranged marriages do not appear to have found particular favor with the courts. We have sentences in four of the five cases, and all favor the plaintiff (two female plaintiffs and two male).[105] The only one, however, that indicates any real lack of sympathy with the claim of force or nonage is *Thomeson*, the case of the woman whose great-uncle is alleged to have threatened to put her in a well if she did not marry the plaintiff. The only other case that has given us a record with depositions, *Marrays*, is full of charges and countercharges about the witnesses. One has the distinct impression in this case that what is at stake is not so much the will of the young woman in question but that of competing sets of her relatives. The final case involving force, *Whitheved*, in which the young woman alleges that the man forced her into falsely confessing to having married him, does have a sentence for the man, but this is from the lower court, before the defense of force is raised.

In cases involving mature parties or long-term relationships, three of the four female plaintiffs obtained a favorable sentence (one case has no judgment); none of the male plaintiffs obtained a favorable sentence (three cases without judgments).[106] All of the latter cases involve widows. Since none of them has an adverse sentence, we cannot be sure what might have happened (or perhaps even did happen in a lost record), but, as suggested, many of the cases that have

[99] *Acclum c Carthorp* (at n. 75); *Scherwode c Lambe* (at nn. 82–3).
[100] Listed T&C no. 196.
[101] *Godewyn c Roser* (at nn. 78–9); *Bernard c Walker* (at nn. 84–5).
[102] *Whitheved c Crescy* (at nn. 51–3).
[103] *Topclyf c Erle* (at nn. 86–8).
[104] *Lovell c Marton* (at nn. 22–31); *Rayner c Willyamson* (at nn. 80–1).
[105] Listed T&C no. 197.
[106] Listed T&C no. 198.

no judgments were probably abandoned or compromised unfavorably to the plaintiff.[107]

Case types one, two, and three produce the most interesting pattern of judgments. In six of eight cases (two having no sentence) in which there is a suggestion of the woman wronged (i.e., cases classified as type one, or type one or two, or type one or three), the *actrix* obtains a favorable judgment.[108] If a female plaintiff could tell a plausible story of a man marrying her and then abandoning her, it certainly looks as if the man was going to lose whatever counter-story he proposed.

Even if an *actrix* did not tell the story of a woman wronged, but both parties told a story of a relationship that may or may not have gone too far, the *actrix* won (two cases out of two).[109] Where, on the other hand, an *actor* tried to argue that a relationship had actually resulted in a marriage, and the *rea* argued that it had not, the *actor* incurred an adverse judgment.[110] (We should note, however, that in this case, the *rea* also raised the defense of precontract.)

Any firm conclusions from this evidence should await our analysis of the other case types, but enough has already been said to cast some doubt on the suggestion that the pattern of sentencing can be explained solely by the fact that the courts indulged in a broad presumption in favor of marriage. Such a presumption may be at work in the arranged-marriage cases, but it cannot explain the notable lack of success of men pursuing widows or of men pursuing women in circumstances other than arranged marriages. Much, however, can be explained if we couple what may well have been a strong presumption in favor of marriage with an additional element: the power of the story of the woman wronged. The story of the wronged woman, of course, is a story only a woman can tell. That fact may explain not only why men are relatively less successful in two-party *de presenti* marriage cases but also why they bring relatively few of them.

DE FUTURO AND ABJURATION CASES

Eight cases raise a claim of *de futuro* consent followed by intercourse. One of them, *Merton c Midelton*, has already been dealt with extensively in Chapter 2. Although *Merton* offers us an unusually full record and some additional story-elements, its basic outlines are typical of this type of case. All the cases are brought by women. The man rarely denies that the intercourse took place. He almost always challenges the factual validity of the woman's claim that he had promised to marry her, frequently by excepting to her witnesses or by alleging his absence.

[107] Disc. T&C no. 199.
[108] Listed T&C no. 200.
[109] *Lovell c Marton* (at nn. 22–31); *Rayner c Willyamson* (at nn. 80–1).
[110] *Topclyf c Erle* (at nn. 86–8).

Matilda de Bradley of York c John de Walkyngton barker of York[111] is the most like *Merton*. It does not, however, involve a long-term relationship between the parties, but rather what seems to have been a 'one-night stand' in which John is alleged to have promised to marry Matilda in order to persuade her to come to bed with him – which she did. John admits the intercourse and denies the contract. Two of Matilda's witnesses confirm her story. Though there is some ambiguity in the words alleged to have been said in Matilda's house seven months previously, it is probably enough for *de futuro* consent. A third witness testifies to *publica fama*.

John's defense both before the dean of Christianity of York and before the official of York is to attack Matilda's witnesses on the grounds that they were hired, that they are his enemies, and that their word is unreliable.[112] Matilda produces character witnesses for her witnesses on appeal, including the husband of the woman to whom one of her witnesses is alleged to have broken her oath. Matilda's case, though based essentially on only two witnesses, a mother and her 15-year-old son, convinces both the dean of Christianity and the official of York.

Two other cases[113] probably involve variants of the same story. In the first case, the plaintiff alleges a promise followed by intercourse and a child. Her witnesses, again, testify to an ambiguous exchange, but probably enough for *de futuro* consent, and the intercourse seems to be conceded. No depositions on the defendant's exception of absence have survived. The plaintiff wins both before the official of Durham and before a special commissary of the York court. (A woman's name on the dorse of the Durham *processus* suggests that a third party may have been involved.) In the second case, the *processus* from the Carlisle consistory tells an interesting story of what the parties thought was a deathbed promise of marriage, followed by intercourse when the woman recovered. The Carlisle official finds for the plaintiff (we lack a sentence on appeal), and the only defense recorded is the procedural one, on appeal, that the Carlisle official rendered sentence in the defendant's absence.

In *Alice Redyng of Scampston c John Boton of Scampston chapman*, the intercourse, ultimately, is conceded.[114] The initial exchange of future consent is proven by two witnesses, one of whom is concededly a beggar, the other of whom is Alice's second cousin. There is also proof of *publica fama*. Most of John's case is concerned with his exceptions to the witnesses' persons. He also offers an affirmative defense: Alice is of servile status, and he dissented from her as soon as he learned of this. There is little doubt that Alice's stepfather, who is one of her chief witnesses in this aspect of the case, is of servile status. Alice claims, however, that her mother was free and that she (Alice) was manumitted. The testimony on this topic is by no means clear (nor do Alice's witnesses on

111 *Bradley c Walkyngton* (1355), CP.E.82.
112 Lit. T&C no. 201.
113 Listed T&C no. 202.
114 *Redyng c Boton* (1366), CP.E.92.

the principal inspire much confidence), but the commissary general finds for Alice.[115]

If *Redyng* suggests that the defense of servile condition will not succeed, at least in the absence of clearer proof than John was able to produce, *Anabella Blakden of Kilburn c William Butre of Rievaulx*, though it has no sentence, does not suggest that the defense of consanguinity will fare any better.[116] Anabella's witnesses do not survive, but William's admit that he and Anabella had intercourse and that he fathered a child by her. He resists the claim of marriage, not on the ground that he did not consent but on the ground of consanguinity. His witnesses, however, do not prove the consanguinity, testifying variously that they are within the fourth or fifth degree of relationship, without the usual careful tracing of the relationship that we find in the few cases where such a defense is successful.[117] It is hard to imagine that this case could have resulted in anything but a judgment for Anabella.

Cecily de Wywell of York c John Chilwell of Nottingham, on the other hand, shows that simply claiming *de futuro* consent and intercourse is not enough.[118] Two witnesses testify that John promised Cecily, "I will marry thee if thou grantest me what I have sought."[119] Both witnesses took him to refer to having intercourse. Neither of them, however, can testify to the intercourse, the first stating that she believes that it happened, the second saying that she does not know whether it did or not. John excepts to the witnesses but introduces no testimony. Here, the combination of the ambiguity of the alleged exchange and the fact that the parties are not clearly shown to have had intercourse probably accounts for the unusual sentence in favor of the defendant.[120]

It is a shame that no sentence survives in *Matilda Schipin of Steeton c Robert Smith of Bolton Percy*, because this case has the weakest proof of consent to marriage in any in which the intercourse is conceded.[121] The plaintiff's witnesses testify to a most casual relationship eight weeks previously. There are only two witnesses, a husband and wife, and the husband testifies basically *ex relatu* of his wife. She tells a remarkable story of lying sick in a cowshed where she saw the defendant take the plaintiff from his house to the cowshed in an attempt to have intercourse with her. The plaintiff said, "May God forbid that thou shouldst have power to know me in the flesh unless thou willst take me to wife." He replied, "This is my troth: if I take any woman as wife, I shall take thee."[122] She said, "This is my faith: I will be at your [*sic*] will." And the defendant took her in his arms and knew her on the floor of the cowshed.

115 Disc. and lit. T&C no. 203.

116 *Blakden c Butre* (1394), CP.E.210.

117 See Ch 11.

118 *Wywell c Chilwell* (1392), CP.E.157.

119 *Ibid.*, T&C no. 204.

120 Disc. T&C no. 205.

121 *Schipin c Smith* (1355–6), CP.E.70.

122 Latin in Pedersen, *Marriage Disputes*, 63 n. 17. For whether these words constitute a binding contract, see Helmholz, *Marriage Litigation*, 40–5.

Robert defends on the ground of the absence of the key witness and excepts to the witnesses' persons. His witnesses are not completely legible, but they seem to confirm that the key witness spent the day in question helping her husband thatch a roof in the next village. The witnesses are not particularly convincing. One of them apparently thinks that the feast of St Luke (18 October) comes before Michaelmas (29 September). Overall, we have the impression that neither set of witnesses is reliable and that what we have here is a variation on *Dolling c Smith*, without the element of the strong support from the women of the community that Alice Dolling was able to obtain. If we disbelieve the witness's story of having heard the exchange in the cowshed, however, we are left to wonder why she did not testify to a more formulaic, and more clearly legally binding, contract. We may doubt that the witness was there, but it is possible that she was testifying to a real exchange that she learned of from the plaintiff.[123]

All the plaintiffs in these cases begin with a type one story: He promised to marry me, had intercourse with me, and is now seeking to get out of it. The fact that in all but one case (*Wywell*) there is no doubt about the intercourse lends initial plausibility to the story. But Alexander's rules required consent, at least *de futuro* consent, in addition to the intercourse. Faced with uncontroverted evidence of intercourse, the York court required some evidence of consent, and most of the cases involved proof of a somewhat longer-term relationship.[124] *Bradley c Walkyngton* is probably the weakest of the cases that have a sentence for the plaintiff, for in this case there are only two witnesses to an ambiguous exchange, but the very ambiguity of the exchange suggests that the witnesses are telling the truth. All the other cases offer something in addition to evidence of consent and intercourse. *Merton c Midelton* clearly involves a long-term relationship and also official intervention by the lower court. The Durham case and *Blakden* involve not only intercourse but a child. The Carlisle case involves what has clearly been a long-term relationship. In *Redyng*, however much we may disbelieve the specific story of the exchange of consent, it is relatively clear that marriage negotiations had been going on between John and Alice. Hence, the case is at least type three, if not type one. By contrast, the one case that has an adverse sentence for the plaintiff has no clear proof of intercourse (*Wywell*), and the case that has the most implausible story of exchange of consent (*Schipin*) has no sentence at all.

We may conclude, therefore, that the behavior of the court in *de futuro* cases was consistent with its behavior in *de presenti* cases. No doubt, the court was prepared to resolve doubts in favor of a marriage. No doubt, too, the story of the woman wronged had considerable persuasive force. Frequently, the judge seems to have been tempted to order the parties to do what they ought to have done, rather than what they may have been strictly required by law to do. This

[123] Lit. T&C no. 206.

[124] The weaker form of this proposition is that most of the cases involve an attempt to prove something more than a single act of intercourse.

is most evident in *Merton c Midelton*, where the exception of absence has some plausibility and where the lower court seems pretty clearly to have been trying to encourage the defendant to do right by the plaintiff. There are, however, limits to the presumption and to the court's willingness to be persuaded by the story of the woman wronged. Where there is no evidence of intercourse and, hence, the possibility that the woman has not been wronged at all, the sentence goes against the plaintiff (*Wywell*). Where the woman may well have been wronged but the story of the witnesses stretches our credulity to the extreme (*Schipin*), there is no sentence.

The conclusions about the parties and their witnesses must be more tentative. As in the *de presenti* cases, clearly some or both of the parties and their witnesses were prepared to color what actually happened in order to convince the court of what they believed was right. There are, however, a striking number of ambiguous exchanges evidenced in these cases (*Bradley*, *Wywell*, *Schipin*). This may be because there was no set formula for exchanging *de futuro* consent, but it also may be that these witnesses are, in fact, more honest than those in the *de presenti* cases. Curiously, the defendants in these cases never seem to have lied about the intercourse. Whenever they are questioned about it, they admit it (*Redyng*, *Bradley*, etc.). This is odd because intercourse is not easy to prove, even in a world that had less privacy than does ours, and by admitting intercourse the defendants conceded a large part of the story of the wronged woman. We may speculate that most defendants could not reconcile an outright denial about intercourse with their consciences. Words are ambiguous; sexual intercourse, normally, is not. Compelled by their consciences to confess, however, these defendants put themselves in a position where their chances of success in court were slim.[125]

As already noted, the cases involving allegations of abjuration *sub pena nubendi* followed by intercourse do not show the same rate of success of plaintiffs as do the cases alleging simply a *de futuro* espousal followed by intercourse.[126] The earliest of these cases, *Matilda Nunne daughter of William Shepherd of Bugthorpe c Walter Cobbe of North Grimston*,[127] illustrates the problems that plaintiffs had with proof in these cases and also the caution with which the York court proceeded. The case begins with Matilda's appearance before the official of the archdeacon of East Riding in March of 1312. She alleges abjuration *sub pena nubendi* followed by intercourse, which Walter denies. In June Matilda produces four witnesses whose depositions are singularly unhelpful. The first testifies *ex relatu* that there were two abjurations, one about 16 years earlier, the other at a time not specified, and that the *fama* was that Walter knew Matilda after the abjuration. The second two testify that they know nothing about the matter. The fourth testifies not only that she knows

[125] See Ch 9, at n. 239.
[126] See Ch 3, n. 20; lit. T&C no. 207.
[127] *Nunne c Cobbe* (1312), CP.E.6.

nothing about the matter but also that she believes that Walter did not know Matilda after the abjuration.

Matilda produces a fifth witness in July, who testifies to an abjuration in the prebendal court of Bugthorp followed by intercourse. In November, the same witness is examined again by the keeper of the spirituality of Bugthorp. This time she says that she cannot remember the date of the abjuration, but that for a week afterwards she saw them through the window of Matilda's house, *solus cum sola, et nudus cum nuda*. In December the official of the archdeacon asks the keeper to examine this witness for a third time. Again, she cannot recall the date of the abjuration, but she repeats the testimony about Walter's week-long visit to Matilda's chamber and her seeing them through the window, adding, this time, that she also had free access to the chamber and saw them there. In the meantime, Walter confesses that he did abjure Matilda at an unnamed place three years previously.

Almost a year passed with only one inconclusive entry in the *processus*, and in December of 1313, Walter appealed to the court of York. In February a special commissary of the official rendered sentence for Walter.

There may have been testimony on appeal that is now missing,[128] but assuming that what we have is representative of what there was, we can reconstruct grounds on which the special commissary could have found for Matilda. One witness testified to the intercourse; two testified to the *fama* of the area. Under standard rules of proof, one witness plus *fama* can make up a full proof.[129] It is, however, quite understandable why the sentence went the other way. Matilda's 'star witness' is not very convincing in any of her three appearances. The story of seeing something through the window is, as previously suggested, always suspicious. Matilda's other witnesses seem to have had second thoughts about what they were going to testify to when they came before the archdeacon's official,[130] and one of them testifies against her. The special commissary's decision, then, is not surprising. It is simply that he could have gone the other way. In this case, however, the power of the story of the woman wronged does not overcome the obvious weakness of her case. The wronged woman becomes a woman wronging.

Our next case bears a remarkable resemblance to *Merton c Midelton*. In December 1372 (or the beginning of January 1373), Hugh Strie of Tickton appealed from an order of the court of the chapter of Beverley that he solemnize his marriage with Cecily daughter of William de Routh *alias* Beton of Tickton.[131] A somewhat scrappy record returned from the court of Beverley records that Hugh had abjured Cecily *sub pena nubendi* in the chapter of Beverley, that he had then confessed to having had intercourse with her, and that the auditor of the court had ordered them to solemnize their marriage.

[128] Disc. T&C no. 208.
[129] See Ch 5, at n. 48.
[130] Including one who was supposed to testify directly to the intercourse.
[131] *Routh c Strie* (1372–3), CP.E.114.

Hugh excepted to the record on the grounds that he did not abjure Cecily *sub pena nubendi* but under the penalty that if they had intercourse thereafter he would be whipped six times around Beverley church and six times around the square, and that he was not in Beverley on the day when he was supposed to have confessed that he had subsequently had intercourse with Cecily. In April, Hugh produced six witnesses, all men, four of whom were of servile condition, who confirmed his story. Their testimony is lively and credible. At the first appearance in the Beverley court, they say, the presiding officer, the dean of Beverley, was trying to get Hugh to abjure Cecily *sub pena nubendi*, but this he refused to do. Fewer of the witnesses testify to the absence, but those who do say that he was weeding a field of grain all day. Hugh also obtained a commission to the auditor of causes of Beverley, who examined two women witnesses who confirm Hugh's story of absence.

Cecily replied that the record from the lower court was good. She introduced five witnesses, two of them priests who confirm her story that the abjuration was *sub pena nubendi*, and she also introduced a notarial instrument of the abjuration. Despite the fact that none of her witnesses can testify to Hugh's presence when he is alleged to have confessed the intercourse, her case looks solid, at least as solid as that of Marjorie Merton; yet she loses before the commissary general, and the dorse of her depositions suggests that she renounced her appeal to the audience of the official.

It seems unlikely that the commissary general disbelieved the official witnesses of the abjuration. A notary public, two priests, and three seemingly respectable men of Beverley would probably not have put their professional reputations, much less their souls, on the line for a marriage case involving a farm laborer with a number of friends who were serfs. On the other hand, as in *Merton c Midelton*, there is probably something to Hugh's witnesses' account of what happened before the dean.[132] Hugh may ultimately have abjured Cecily *sub pena nubendi*, but we suspect, and the commissary general may well have suspected too, that he did so under considerable pressure from the dean. We can have less confidence in the terse account of the proceedings before the dean when Hugh is alleged to have confessed. No witness testifies to having seen them; the record of them is not a public instrument, and Hugh's witnesses to his absence are solid. Absent the confession, there is no solid proof that Hugh had intercourse with Cecily after the abjuration.

But how could the dean possibly have ordered the solemnization of the marriage? Here we may suspect that much the same thing happened as happened in *Merton c Midelton*. The court of Beverley made up its mind that Hugh ought to get married and tried to manipulate the process to ensure that it happened. The ploy worked in *Merton*, though ultimately we had doubts that justice was done. Seven years later, it did not work; the appellate court intervened as it did not in *Merton*. While we cannot be sure what caused this difference, we can offer the following speculations: (1) The issue in *Merton* was

[132] Lit. T&C no. 209.

whether the parties had said enough to each other to constitute *de futuro* consent. Intercourse had concededly taken place between them. In this case, however, the only time that Hugh consented was under pressure from the dean. The court of York was not prepared to invalidate all abjurations, but the institution itself was far from the free choice that seems to have been the core principle of Alexander's rules, and the court of York may well have been uncomfortable with the institution. (2) The court of York was prepared to go quite far in upholding the discipline of lower church courts. After all, the system was dependent on respect for their judgments. But lower ecclesiastical courts, like lower courts in many times and many cultures, could get sloppy about their procedures. They did a high-volume routine business largely involved with sexual offenses. It was moderately lucrative, hardly very interesting, rarely subject to review by a higher court, and not the sort of legal work that encourages the highest standards of due process. Judges of such courts were in a position that encouraged paternalism, and in some instances, high-handedness. In some cases, such judges were suspected of corruption. Here we have no reason to suspect financial corruption, but we have some reason to suspect a different kind of corruption, the same kind in which many of the witnesses seem to have been involved: manipulating the process to achieve what they believed to be the proper result, in this case helping out a young woman who seemed to be in trouble without considering what the man's side of the story might be.

In many cases, as in *Merton*, the appellate court would have to let such behavior pass. Perhaps in some cases, the appellate court even agreed with what the lower court was trying to do. But the law was that marriage was the choice of the parties, not of their parents, their lords, the local community, or even the judge of a lower ecclesiastical court.[133] The very institution of abjuration *sub pena nubendi* seems inconsistent with Alexander's principle, however much it might be made to conform to the letter of his rules. In this case, moreover, the dean had gone too far. The appellate court insisted on evidence independent of the dean's unsupported record that intercourse had followed the abjuration.

Obviously, much of what we have just said is speculation, but there is one piece of evidence supporting this account of the motivation for the commissary general's sentence. The last document introduced by Hugh's proctor into evidence in the case, just prior to the commissary general's sentence, is a letter of the auditor of causes of the chapter of Beverley to the chantry chaplain of Hull Bridge, ordering him, in the name of the dean of Beverley, to proclaim the banns between Hugh and one Sissota daughter of Beatrice of Tickton and to solemnize their marriage if no impediment appeared. The grounds of the order stated in the letter are that Hugh had abjured Sissota *sub pena nubendi* and had afterwards confessed intercourse with her. The letter is dated three weeks before the dean's alleged order to Hugh to solemnize his marriage with Cecily.

[133] See the suggestive remarks on this topic in Helmholz, *Marriage Litigation*, 177.

Since no pleadings were submitted or depositions taken about this document, and whatever arguments were made about it were not recorded, we must try to reconstruct why Hugh's proctor introduced it. It is possible that Sissota daughter of Beatrice and Cecily are the same person. If so, the letter would be firm evidence that the dean had decided a full three weeks before Hugh's alleged confession that he was going to order Hugh to marry Cecily. It is more likely, however, that they are not the same person ('Sissota' is a possible alternative to or confusion of 'Cecily', but Cecily is never called *filia Beatricis* in the rest of the documents). It thus seems more likely that Hugh's proctor introduced the letter as evidence that the dean was 'out to get' Hugh, ordering him to marry anyone he could think of. From the point of view of the commissary general, however, it was unnecessary to decide which was involved. Either the dean ordered Hugh to marry Cecily three weeks before he said that he obtained proof of the intercourse, or he ordered Hugh to marry two different women within three weeks without considering which woman had the better claim. In either event, the dean's judgment cannot be allowed to stand. The fact that Cecily renounced her appeal to the audience of the official suggests that she was advised that she had little or no chance of persuading the official to reinstate the dean's judgment.

It was suggested earlier that the court of York was uncomfortable with the institution of abjuration *sub pena nubendi*, although it was not prepared to abolish the institution entirely. Certainly, defendants attempted to attack the institution facially, and although no direct attack succeeds, the fact that such attacks were made suggests that the argument was not totally implausible, at least when combined with other arguments. In one case in 1372, the defendant, a widower who had employed the plaintiff as a servant, admitted both the abjuration and the intercourse, but said that he was compelled by fear of excommunication and that he had no intention of ever taking the defendant as wife.[134] He then proceeded to raise a substantive defense of the impediment of crime. There is little doubt that he committed adultery with the plaintiff before his wife died. This seems to have been well known by many, including the now-deceased wife. Whether the couple exchanged promises to marry while the wife was alive is more problematical. The witnesses seem clear that the defendant so promised, but all they will testify to on behalf of the plaintiff is the statement (in English) "I hald thar to." This may not be enough for proof of mutual promises, which the law required, but the result for the plaintiff in this case can also be explained on the ground that the York court did not look favorably on the defense of the impediment of crime, and perhaps more important, that the story told by the defendant's own testimony is one of a long-term sexual relationship in which the defendant had certainly made promises of marriage. Now that the plaintiff wants to hold the defendant to those promises, the court will not look sympathetically either at his defense of crime or at his defense that his will was forced by the abjuration procedure.[135]

134 *Suardby c Walde* (1372), CP.E.111.

135 Lit. T&C no. 210.

Six of our nine abjuration cases come from the years 1387 to 1394, and in these cases we can most clearly see the interplay of the various considerations just outlined. The first case is defended by a traditional attack on the witnesses' persons, but no testimony seems to have been offered on the defense.[136] The plaintiff's witnesses describe an exchange between the plaintiff and defendant after the abjuration in which they seem consciously to have chosen to have intercourse in order to be married. Not surprisingly, the sentence goes for the plaintiff.[137]

In the second case, the intercourse following the abjuration is conceded.[138] The abjuration is proven from the record of the special commissary of the archbishop for hearing correctional cases (who also was the receiver of the archbishop's exchequer) and by official witnesses.[139] The defense offered by the defendant who appears *pro se* (a proctor is assigned to be of counsel to him) is the purely legal one that he consented to the abjuration out of fear and that the abjuration procedure is illegal.[140] As just suggested, the court was not prepared to accept such a direct challenge to abjuration procedure, and the sentence goes against him, although the defendant does appeal to the Apostolic See.[141]

In the third case, the surviving documentation principally concerns the propriety of the appeal from the sentence of the official of the archdeacon of Richmond for the plaintiff, and it is only interstitially that we learn that abjuration was in some way involved.[142] Since there seems also to have been further claims, the court's dismissal of the appeal probably is based on the validity of the procedural defense, coupled with a conviction that there was more between this couple than just abjuration and intercourse.

The fourth case is also largely taken up with procedural objections, this time to the *processus* held before the official of the archdeacon of Cleveland.[143] The abjuration before the official is conceded; the issue is whether intercourse followed. Although the commissary general renders sentence for the defendant, which is then appealed to the official of York, not much can be gleaned from this fact because the plaintiff had not even had the *processus* transmitted from the official of Cleveland before she asked for the commissary's sentence. We do not know for sure whether the official or his special commissary ever rendered sentence for the plaintiff, but the case ends with an appeal by the defendant to the Apostolic See and the issuance of refutatory *apostoli*, and this suggests that the case ultimately went against the defendant.

136 *Holm c Chaumberleyn* (1387), CP.E.135.
137 Lit. T&C no. 211.
138 *Appleton c Hothwayt* (1389), CP.E.150.
139 Lit. T&C no. 212.
140 Lit. T&C no. 213.
141 Lit. T&C no. 214.
142 *Grene c Tuppe* (1390), CP.E.178.
143 *Thyrne c Abbot* (1392), CP.E.191; lit. T&C no. 215.

In another case in 1392, the commissary general also rendered sentence for the defendant.[144] The proceedings are hard to reconstruct because many of the dates are missing or unclear. It would seem, however, that the plaintiff claimed abjuration followed by intercourse, and that the defendant admitted the abjuration and denied the intercourse. As in the previous case, this may be all of the proceedings before the commissary general, and he rendered sentence for the defendant. On appeal, the plaintiff produced witnesses who testify that the parties had lived together and had had children, that they abjured each other *sub pena nubendi* before the dean of Holderness on the usual condition of intercourse in future, and that they lived together following the abjuration. The witnesses had no proof, however, of intercourse following the abjuration. The plaintiff also produced a *processus* before the official of the archdeacon of East Riding in which the defendant abjured her not only on the condition they have intercourse but also on the condition that they be found together in suspicious places. This *processus* was confirmed by the testimony of both the official and of his registrar. The official of York reversed the sentence of the commissary general.

Both of these cases ultimately go for the plaintiff, but both have an initial sentence for the defendant. Both the sentences for the defendants are explicable, granted the fact that so little of the case in chief was presented to the commissary general. The question is why the parties chose to defer their main arguments for the appeal from the commissary general. While we cannot be sure, it is possible that the commissary general, Robert de Oxton, was known to be unsympathetic to claims of abjuration *sub pena nubendi*.

He certainly was not sympathetic to the claim of Alice Partrick of Thirsk against John Mariot of Sowerby, our last case in this group.[145] John had abjured Alice before the dean of Bulmer. The record on this is quite clear, and John concedes it. It is also clear that he had intercourse with Alice before the abjuration and that he had a child by her. As to intercourse after the abjuration, Alice produced two witnesses who saw Alice go into John's bedroom at night and stay there a half hour or an hour. Their testimony on *publica fama* is mixed, but there is probably enough to establish its existence. Whether this testimony is enough to make a full canonical proof of intercourse is open to question.[146] Certainly John had hit upon the weak spot in the case when he conceded all except the intercourse. The commissary general found for John; Alice appealed to the official. The official examined John using interrogatories supplied by Alice's proctor.[147] John makes a good witness for himself. Alice, he says, came to him in his father's house at night and entered. "What are you doing here?" he said. "I want to be here," she said. "Get out," he said, "for surely, thou willst not be here." Then she asked him to close the door so that the neighbors in the

[144] *Hobbesdoghter c Beverage* (1392), CP.E.202; disc. and lit. T&C no. 216.
[145] *Partrick c Mariot* (1394), CP.E.211.
[146] Disc. T&C no. 217.
[147] No dates; this may have occurred before the commissary general, but I doubt it.

street did not see them. At which point, he says, he took her by the shoulders and put her out of the house and shut the door behind her.[148] The official, too, finds for John.

Our account of the abjuration cases has emphasized the importance of the fact that in such cases, the defendant's consent was granted under circumstances that suggest that his will was not his own. The difference, however, between this type of case and the basic case of the woman wronged is not great. The plaintiff, always a woman, adds to the story of a woman wronged that this is not just her version of the story but one approved by some church official: the defendant was to marry her if he wronged her again. He did wrong her again and now is refusing to solemnize the marriage with her, and so she is doubly wronged. This is a powerful story, made more so by the fact that some of the key elements of it have already been approved by some church official. The fact that some defendants manage to escape the power of this story gives rise to our speculation that the inconsistency of the abjuration procedure with Alexander's basic principle of free choice probably accounts for some of the sentencing pattern.

But the fact is that the defendants who win have something else going for them other than the questionable legality of abjuration procedure. Walter Cobbe is able to convince the court, and us as well, that Matilda de Bugthorpe is a woman wronging, not a woman wronged, that her 'star witness' is lying. Similarly, Alice Partrick's proof of intercourse was none too solid, and John Mariot made a credible witness for himself. The story of the woman wronged again became the story of the woman wronging. Hugh Strie is able to show from the dean of Beverley's own documents that the dean was at best careless and perhaps engaged in a campaign against him. While a number of defendants raise defenses that depend on the peculiarly official nature of the abjuration procedure, Hugh is the only defendant who ultimately is successful in attacking the procedure used by the lower court.

THREE- AND FOUR-PARTY ENFORCEMENT ACTIONS

As noted earlier, the cases involving three parties divide neatly into 10 'marriage and divorce' actions, in which, typically, a single female plaintiff is seeking to upset a current marriage between two defendants and to obtain a declaration that she is the lawful wife of the *reus*, and 10 'competitor' actions, in which two plaintiffs sue a single man or woman, each claiming that he or she is his or her lawful spouse. The underlying legal issues in such cases are similar; they all involve the question of the priority of one exchange of consent over another, and thus normally involve what would be in a two-party case an exception of precontract. The stories that these cases tell are also similar. Most, though not all, involve a claim of a woman wronged. We will therefore deal with them together. There are, however, three differences between the two types

[148] *Id.*, Latin text and lit. T&C no. 218.

of cases. (1) Marriage-and-divorce cases are spread out over the century with representatives from every decade from the 1330s on, except for the 1340s and 1360s. Competitor cases, on the other hand, are clustered in the latter portion of the century. The earliest is from 1368; there is one in the 1370s, two in the 1380s, and six in the 1390s. (2) All of the marriage-and-divorce cases but one are brought by women; five of the competitor cases are brought by men. (3) In most, though not quite all, of the marriage-and-divorce cases the marriage sought to be divorced is solemn and well established. A divorce decree must be rendered in this type of case; whereas in the competitor cases, a simple judgment in favor of one marriage and against the other will suffice.

The following recital will suggest that the core story in a marriage-and-divorce case is that of a woman who, for one reason or another, did not object at the time that the second marriage took place and is suing now. Some of the competitor cases involve the same story, with the suit brought somewhat earlier, a fact that suggests increasing sophistication among the litigants. Others of the competitor cases suggest a somewhat different pattern, a third party brought in to add weight to the defendant's story in what is basically a two-party case. Again, the chronological pattern suggests increasing sophistication among the litigants.

The story told by the plaintiff in *Cecily de Portyngton of York c John de Grenbergh of Craven Bower and Alice daughter of William Cristendom his de facto wife* is typical of marriage-and-divorce cases and of some of the competitor cases as well.[149] Three women witnesses describe the exchange of present consent between Cecily and John in the house of one of the women in York around Michaelmas the previous year. The words are standard: John gave Cecily a silver ring; intercourse followed. The following Corpus Christi, John and Alice were married solemnly in St Michael Ousebridge, York, banns having been proclaimed. We have no indication why John abandoned Cecily and married Alice; indeed he offers, so far as we can tell, no defense. The special commissary finds for Cecily – on these facts she is clearly a woman wronged – and the official confirms on appeal.

Few of the other women who tell a similar story in a marriage-and-divorce case are successful. *Alice de Wellewyk of Beverley c Robert de Midelton son of Henry de Midelton deceased of Bishop Burton and Elizabeth de Frothyngham his wife* is typical.[150] Alice has but two witnesses. The first, Alice de Harpham, Alice de Wellewyk's former servant, says that while she was working in Alice's house nine years earlier, Robert used to come there frequently, and he and Alice had intercourse. Eventually, she had a child by him. One day around Palm Sunday (probably 21 March 1350), they called the servant into their presence, and Robert said: "Look thee here, Alice de Harpham, it is decided between me and this Alice de Wellewyk.... And this Alice de Wellewyk, your mistress,

[149] *Portyngton c Grenbergh and Cristendom* (1370), CP.E.106.
[150] *Wellewyk c Midelton and Frothyngham* (1358–60), CP.E.79.

wants me to make thee surety of these things in her name, and thus I want thee, Alice de Harpham, to bear witness to this my troth: I shall take this Alice de Wellewyk as my wife if it happens that she conceive and bear a child of me."[151] The witness says that they had intercourse that night and many others, and she knows this because she saw them lying in bed together.

The other witness, a canon of Warter Priory and the keeper of St Giles hospital Beverley, testifies that Alice and Robert came to him before Robert solemnized his marriage with Elizabeth. The witness told them that if what he has heard is true (and he recited what the previous witness testified), they ought to get married. Robert said that he could not deny what had been said, and he promised to pay Alice ten marks, a promise that the canon believed was made in order to ensure that Alice not object to the solemnization of the marriage between Robert and Elizabeth.

Robert and Elizabeth's witnesses are much more straightforward. They testify to the solemnization of their marriage after Easter eight years previously. They emphasize that no one objected to their banns. They also testify to an informal marriage between them during the previous Lent.

After the testimony was in, the official interrogated Robert *ex officio*.[152] He swore that he was free from any contract with Elizabeth when he promised that he would marry Alice if he knew her and had a child by her, that he did know her and have a child by her before, as he firmly believes, he contracted marriage with Elizabeth. He cannot, however, recall the words of his contract with Alice.

The commissary general rendered sentence for Robert and Elizabeth. Three months later, the official confirmed this sentence on appeal.

The question, of course, is how we are to explain these sentences. In the first place, as a matter of law, the condition that Alice have a child is irrelevant (though there is testimony that the condition was fulfilled). Once the parties had had intercourse following a conditional marriage contract, the condition was deemed waived and the marriage valid.[153] There is no difficulty with the dates. Alice's witness, in December of 1358, testifies to a contract made on "the Monday next after Palm Sunday to come, there will be nine years passed," that is, 1350.[154] Robert's and Elizabeth's, in April of 1359, testify to a contract in Lent, eight years previously, that is, 1352 (possibly 1351), followed by a solemnization after Easter of the same year. It is possible, of course, that the judges simply did not believe Alice's witnesses.

We are dealing here with parties of some wealth. Elizabeth's father had a chapel in which the first exchange of consent took place, and more than a

151 *Ibid.*, T&C no. 219.

152 Note that the official does the questioning even though the case is still before the commissary general. Lit. T&C no. 220.

153 Lit. T&C no. 221.

154 Latin in Pedersen, *Marriage Disputes*, 78 n. 41.

hundred people are said to have been at the subsequent solemnization of their marriage.[155] But Alice is also a woman of some stature, if not wealth: Her kinsman is the prior of Warter and her closest friend a canon of the same place. This does not look like a case of a woman wronging, or a woman attempting to get a man's wealth. Robert's confession in court, however, may have provoked suspicion. The judges may not have believed Alice and her witnesses because they suspected that the whole story was made up in order to allow Robert to divorce his current wife. That is possible, but if that is what is happening, then one wonders why they told such a complicated story, a story of a *de futuro* conditional marriage, with the promise made to a servant and not to the woman herself, when a *de presenti* marriage, as in *Ingoly c Midelton*, would have done the job much more neatly. Indeed, the very messiness of the story makes it plausible. I think that Robert did contract with Alice pretty much as he and she said he did, and then he paid her not to object to the banns. Whether this litigation nine years later is the result of qualms of conscience that they both had, or whether Robert conveniently remembered it because he wanted to get out of his current marriage, we will never know.

Should their consciences have bothered them? Did Robert have grounds for voiding his marriage with Elizabeth, assuming that we accept the testimony? The question is not easy to answer. Had Robert made his promise directly to Alice de Wellewyk, there would have been no doubt. They would have been married as soon as they had intercourse. But Robert did not make his promise to Alice de Wellewyk; he made it to Alice de Harpham, deliberately, it would seem, in order to avoid the result that would have followed had he promised Alice de Wellewyk and then had intercourse with her.[156] That they were married even when the condition was fulfilled was clearly not the view of the canon of Warter. What he tells Robert is that he is obliged to marry her, not that he is married to her.[157] While he suspected that the payment to Alice was in consideration of her not objecting to the solemnization, he does not seem to have regarded himself as being obliged to reclaim against the banns, which he almost certainly would have felt obliged to do had he thought that they were married. In short, the payment could be open to the interpretation that it was compensation for a release from a contractual obligation, not a bribe not to raise the issue of an existing marriage.

There is no evidence, however, that the canon of Warter was a canonist, and what he thought was the law may not, in fact, have been the law. I have been unable to find a discussion of this particular problem in the canonists (though one is almost certainly there to be found), but the following pieces of doctrine suggest that the canon of Warter was wrong.[158] While the early Roman law of *sponsalia* required an exchange of consent in question-and-answer form, like

155 *Id.*, at 79 and n. 43.
156 See n. 153.
157 Latin in Pedersen, *Marriage Disputes*, 80–1 n. 45.
158 Ref. T&C no. 222.

that of the formal verbal contract of *stipulatio*, the canon law of *sponsalia* did not. What the canonists were looking for was an expression of consent, be it present or future, to which both parties agreed. An agent could express the consent. That the consent was expressed in the form of a contractual obligation made to a third party does not make it any less consent to the other party, who, herself, knew of it and clearly consented. Hence, if this is correct, Robert is not Elizabeth's husband, and the result in this case forces him to live in adultery with her. Clearly, moreover, if we are to take Robert's confession in court seriously, he regards himself as married to Alice and not to Elizabeth, and, hence, the judgment in this case puts him in a most difficult moral position.

We may, I think, assume that the judges were as aware of this as we are. The judges, nonetheless, found for Elizabeth because the case is a three-party case. The only innocent party in this case is Elizabeth. She married Robert, so far as the record shows, not knowing of the prior relationship with Alice, and she was prevented from knowing about it because Robert paid, and Alice took, a bribe so that Elizabeth would not know about it. As a matter of law – and this can be found in Alexander's decretals – a public, solemnized marriage could not be upset on the basis of a prior clandestine one, even if both parties to the clandestine marriage admitted it.[159] Now, Robert's marriage to Alice was not clandestine in the sense that there were no witnesses to it, but it was not proven by two unbiased eyewitnesses. The only direct witness is Alice de Harpham, and she could be regarded as biased; the other witness, the canon of Warter who testifies to Robert's confession, is clearly biased, and the confession that he reports has some ambiguity. (Robert seems to have said that he would not or could not deny the contract that the canon had just described.)[160] None of this is to suggest that the court could not have found that the prior marriage was proven; it is simply to suggest that the court did not have to find that the prior marriage was proven. Granted that the court had discretion, it chose to side with the most innocent of the three parties.[161]

Why does this case come out differently from the *Portyngton* case? In *Portyngton*, we have a full and undeniable canonical proof of a *de presenti* precontract. No defense is offered. Faced with such a record, the judge had no discretion. He had to find for Cecily. Also, in the *Portyngton* case, the action was brought soon after the events rather than nine years later. Cecily Portyngton and John exchanged words of the present tense, according to the witnesses, around Michaelmas; the solemn marriage with Alice took place around the following Corpus Christi; by November Cecily was in court.

Isabella Rolle of Richmond c John Bullok of Richmond and Margaret de Massham his wife is another case in which a woman who was clearly a former mistress of the *reus* loses because her proof gives the judges room in which to

[159] See Ch 1, text between nn. 101 and 102.

[160] Unfortunately, the main verb is hard to read in the deposition. What he seems to have said is *nolo contradicere quin ita fuit nec possum*.

[161] Lit. T&C no. 223.

maneuver.[162] The problem in Isabella's case is not that she lacks a full proof of the exchange; she has three witnesses, at least to the expression: "If I take any woman as wife, I shall take thee."[163] All testify that intercourse followed. The legal problem that such words presented is not an easy one.[164] Suffice it to say here that a respectable argument can be made for the proposition that this is sufficient to make a conditional future contract of marriage. There is at least one two-party case in the fourteenth century in which the court seems to have enforced such an expression of consent.[165] The archdeacon of Richmond's official in this case was also prepared to enforce it. He was reversed, however, by the commissary general of York, and the commissary general's decision was confirmed by the official. While a respectable argument can be made for the proposition that there was a valid contract here, a respectable argument can also be made that there was not. It would seem that where a seemingly innocent third party was involved, the court would resolve legal as well as factual doubts in favor of that party and hence, in this case, against the precontract.

Alice Colton of Ryedale c Robert Whithand of Scackleton and Agnes daughter of John Lowe of Barton le Street his wife is another case in which a former mistress of the man sues to dissolve his current marriage on the ground of precontract.[166] The witnesses testify that three years previously, John had cohabited with Alice and had had two children by her, but they cannot testify to any contract between them except by hearsay. Not surprisingly, Alice loses before both the commissary general and a special commissary of the official. This is, of course, a woman wronged, but the law required at least some proof of marital consent, certainly if a seemingly valid and solemnized marriage was to be dissolved because of it.[167]

In *Joan Fossard c Master William de Calthorne and Katherine daughter of Roger de Wele his wife*, the plaintiff also apparently tries to tell the story of a woman wronged.[168] The depositions of her witnesses have not survived, but he excepts on the grounds of absence, of disparity of wealth, and of prejudice of her witnesses against him. The disparity of wealth claim seems to have some bite. Joan seems to be a pauper, and William is a York proctor.[169] His exception of absence is supported by 13 witnesses who describe William doing business in Calthorne on the two days in question, settling his father's estate. They are as plausible as such witnesses can be. Two more witnesses testify that they heard Joan and her witnesses making up the story of the precontract with William. Although no sentence survives, it is hard to imagine that this case could have been decided favorably for the plaintiff. What we cannot tell from the record is

[162] *Rolle c Bullok and Massham* (1351–5), CP.E.71; lit. T&C no. 224.
[163] T&C no. 225.
[164] Lit. T&C no. 226.
[165] Lit. T&C no. 227.
[166] *Colton c Whithand and Lowe* (1398), CP.E.236.
[167] Lit. T&C no. 228.
[168] *Fossard c Calthorne and Wele* (1390), CP.E.175.
[169] Lit. T&C no. 229.

whether Joan is totally a woman wronging, as William would have us believe, or whether there really was something between them before he married Katherine.

The earliest of the competitor cases, *Cecily daughter of Adam de Wright and Joan wife of John Birkys c John Birkys*,[170] tells essentially the same story as in the *Portyngton* case. Cecily's sister and her brother-in-law testify that Cecily and John were having intercourse regularly in their house four or five years earlier. On a number of occasions, John promised to marry Cecily, and intercourse followed. One occasion, described by the brother-in-law, is particularly poignant: Cecily said, "John, I fear me, that thou willst deceive me and never contract marriage with me nor take me to wife."[171] "Certainly, I will," John replied, "and see thee well that I will not take me to any other woman, and fear thee not that I will have thee as wife and no other woman."[172] The sister testifies that he said "I will take thee as wife as soon as I can on account of my mother."[173] The matter apparently led to an abjuration *sub pena nubendi*. During the summer four years previously, John cooled. The previous Lent he confessed on the high road in the presence of his mother and the witnesses that he had had intercourse with Cecily (but not, apparently, after the abjuration), but said that he never wished to espouse Cecily. And she replied bitterly, "Thou still dost not know."[174] John, the witnesses say, is richer than Cecily, but of servile status, being a serf of the duke of Lancaster. John's witnesses confirm the disparity in wealth, but say that both parties are free. Cecily's brother-in-law, however, they say, is a serf of the duke of Lancaster.[175]

Though neither of the witnesses testifies to precisely the same contract, this is enough for a typical two-party *de futuro* case, and it is not surprising that the special commissary of the commissary general finds for Cecily.[176] On appeal to the audience of the official, Joan intervenes. Her witnesses testify to a solemn marriage a year previously.[177] The dorse of these depositions records an examination of John by the official in which John confesses to having had intercourse with Cecily in the summer four years previously and to having subsequently abjured her before the vicar of Leeds. The case then disappears from view.[178]

One of the latest cases involving female competitors has a similar fact-pattern.[179] The parties to the original case are clearly of disparate wealth. There is no direct testimony about intercourse; there is one witness who clearly, and with considerable detail, testifies to present consent, and another who testifies

[170] *Wright and Birkys c Birkys* (1368), CP.E.103.
[171] *Ibid.*, T&C no. 230.
[172] *Ibid.*, T&C no. 231.
[173] *Ibid.*, Latin text and lit. T&C no. 232.
[174] *Ibid.*, T&C no. 233.
[175] Lit. T&C no. 234.
[176] The sentence does not actually say that he was a special commissary (it is a draft), but it seems quite clear that that is what he was.
[177] Lit. T&C no. 235.
[178] Lit. T&C no. 236.
[179] *Graystanes and Barraycastell c Dale* (1394), CP.E.215.

to *fama*. While one can imagine that the case could have come out the other way, the sentence by the official of Durham in favor of the first competitor is not surprising. The second competitor does not appear until the appeal to York. Her marriage is clearly later, and probably took place after the Durham sentence. The testimony to the preliminary negotiations leading to the marriage (including a promised dowry of 20 marks) is clear enough, as is the testimony about the banns, but the testimony about the exchange of present consent is curious. It took place at the doors of a church that the witnesses refuse to name, at dawn, before a priest whom the witnesses refuse to name. Again, we lack a sentence on appeal, but it is hard to imagine that the second competitor's appearance made any difference.[180]

Shortly after the *Birkys* case we begin to see the competitor action used in a somewhat different way. On 5 October 1373, Alice Malman of Raskelf sued John Belamy of Raskelf in a *de presenti* marriage action.[181] Three days later he was sued in the same action by Matilda daughter of Richard de Raskelf.[182] The depositions in both cases are hard to read, but it would seem that the exchange with Alice took place the day before that with Matilda, but that the exchange with Alice may not have amounted to words of the present tense, whereas that with Matilda did.[183] Matilda's action goes without a defense, whereas John enters a vigorous exception to Alice's action, excepting to the persons of her witnesses, alleging his absence, and raising the issue of disparity of wealth. The cases proceed in tandem, and in March of 1374 a special commissary renders judgment against Alice and orders John to solemnize his marriage with Matilda. The ground of the sentence may be the ambiguity of the exchange with Alice, but it certainly looks as if John was seeking to get the advantage of the presumption in favor of an existing marriage in a situation in which the marriage had not been solemnized. Unlike the *Birkys* case, where the existence of the third party did not become apparent until the appeal, Matilda's action in this case forced the court to compare her claim to that of the allegedly wronged Alice from the beginning.

Another case of female competitors, *Ellen de Layremouth and Isabella de Holm c William de Stokton of York*, involves a fact-pattern similar to that of *Birkys*.[184] According to witnesses for Ellen, she and the defendant were lying naked in bed in her brother's house in Newcastle three years previously. They exchanged vows in the form "I take thee/you here," and intercourse followed.[185] One of the witnesses knows that they had intercourse because she shared a bed with them when it happened. A third witness was present somewhat more than a year previously when Ellen accused William of planning to

[180] Lit. T&C no. 237.

[181] *Malman and Raskelf c Belamy* (1373–4), CP.E.113, *ex* CP.E.131.

[182] *Ibid.*

[183] Text and lit. T&C no. 238.

[184] *Layremouth and Holm c Stokton* (1382), CP.E.126.

[185] *Ibid.*, T&C no. 239.

take another woman as wife, and William swore on a roll (*rotulus*) that he never intended to take another but Ellen.

Isabella sued only a day after Ellen. Her witnesses, one a notary public, testify to an exchange of present consent in the house of William's master, Roger de Moreton, a merchant of York, about a year previously. Although the words that they describe are those of the present tense, one of them says that Isabella told William that she would wait until he obtained Roger's consent (*beneplacitum*). They are less clear than Ellen's witnesses about intercourse, but they say that the parties confessed it.

The commissary general, a special commissary of the official, and the official himself found against Isabella and in favor of Ellen. Since neither case was defended, it is hard to know what William's views of the matter were. What the case shows, however, is that simply suing at the same time as the wronged woman will not be sufficient for a judgment, if the wronged woman tells a good story.[186]

That getting in early can make a difference is suggested by the final case involving female competitors, *Marjorie Spuret of York and Beatrice de Gillyn of York c Thomas de Hornby saddler of York*.[187] Early in November of 1394, Marjorie appeared before the dean of Christianity of York claiming Thomas as her husband. She admitted that she had no proof of her claim, and the dean dismissed them to their consciences. In January of 1394, she sued again before the dean, and this time she produced witnesses whose depositions have not survived but whose testimony can be reconstructed from what follows. They included Marjorie's mother and a kinswoman named Juliana, and they testified that Marjorie and Thomas exchanged vows in the form "I will have thee" in Roger Green's house in York in September of 1389.[188] Immediately thereafter, Beatrice de Gillyn made her appearance before the dean and introduced evidence to prove that she and Thomas exchanged vows in the same form the previous November, shortly after Marjorie's first appearance before the dean.

Thomas vigorously contested Marjorie's case. He produced four witnesses, all saddlers, who testify that five years earlier, Thomas was an apprentice saddler in his uncle Roger Green's house while Marjorie was a servant there. Two witnesses say that Marjorie was absent from York on the day on which they are alleged to have exchanged vows. The other two say that Thomas was at Crayke, 12 miles from York, on the same day. Marjorie's replication witnesses respond more to Thomas's allegations that Marjorie and her mother were promoting the match because of his superior wealth. They allege that it was Thomas who was poor, not Marjorie, that her mother was a kempster[189] and an honest woman, and Juliana, one of her witnesses, was a saddler with her husband. Marjorie

186 Lit. T&C no. 240.
187 *Spuret and Gillyn c Hornby* (1394–5), CP.E.159.
188 *Ibid.*, T&C no. 241, with disc.
189 A comber of wool, normally female, OED. s.v.

also introduced witnesses to the marriage negotiations between her kinsmen and Thomas.

Marjorie appealed to the consistory of York before the dean was able to render sentence. There were more charges and countercharges about the witnesses, but what seems to have been the key move in this process was the reappearance of Beatrice. Her petition to intervene alleges that Marjorie and Thomas are colluding, but this seems to be common form. After Beatrice was admitted, her lawyer introduced what seems to be the key piece of evidence, a deed poll of the original proceedings before the dean in which Marjorie admitted that she had no proof of the marriage. The commissary general found in favor of Beatrice and against Marjorie. Marjorie appealed to the official who confirmed the commissary general's sentence.

Clearly, this is a case that could have gone either way. Marjorie's initial admission before the dean is the most powerful piece of evidence against her, and I suspect that the testimony of her subsequent witnesses was fabricated. On the other hand, we can imagine a court saying that all she meant when she confessed before the dean was that she had no proof to hand, that she had not talked to her witnesses, perhaps that she did not know that "I will have thee" (as opposed to "I shall have thee") was generally taken as words of the present tense. After all, the dean before whom she made the confession allowed her to litigate the matter over again, just a couple of months after the confession. Certainly the case that she ultimately presented, despite the exceptions taken to it, could have led to a sentence in her favor if it had only been a two-party case. But it was not a two-party case. Beatrice, though her contract was later and just as informal as Marjorie's, presented herself as the innocent party. Her contract clearly happened; no one denied it. Admittedly, it was subsequent to Marjorie's, but Marjorie's was doubtful, or at least her proof was doubtful. In these circumstances, the court will decide for Beatrice.[190]

The stories told in the next four of the marriage-and-divorce cases are quite different from those told in the five marriage-and-divorce cases and the five competitor cases that we have just discussed, although the legal issues overlap. If the first 10 cases ask us to focus on the precontract and the possibility that a woman was wronged, these 4 tell quite plainly why the second marriage has gone awry. The claim of precontract, then, in all of these cases is facially suspicious. We know that the second marriage has broken up or that one of the parties to it is seeking to break it up.

The clearest case in which this has happened is *Alice daughter of Gilbert Palmere of Flixton c Geoffrey de Brunne of Scalby and Joan de Suthburn his wife*.[191] Alice and Geoffrey had been married, apparently solemnly; they had a child. The marriage, however, was a hopeless one, according to her witnesses. Geoffrey had violent and ungovernable temper and beat Alice regularly. In order to escape from this marriage, again according to Alice's witnesses, Alice and

[190] Lit. T&C no. 242.

[191] *Palmere c Brunne and Suthburn* (1333), CP.E.25.

her father, perhaps with Geoffrey's consent, concocted a story of a precontract with Joan and suborned perjured witnesses before the official of the archdeacon of East Riding, who rendered a decree of divorce. Alice apparently had qualms of conscience, for she confessed this to the archbishop who delegated the case, ultimately, to the official. Alice's witnesses look plausible, and no defense survives, though Geoffrey's answers to her positions indicate that he resisted her suit.

The legal issue posed by the case is difficult. Alexander III himself had at one time decided that where a divorce had been decreed on the basis of perjured testimony, the sentence should not be revoked if the parties had married others, and at another time he seems to have decided that the marriage sentence can never completely be *res iudicata*; it may always be reopened on the ground that the "church has been deceived."[192] By the fourteenth century, the greater weight of canonic opinion held with the second decision, but the first was in the *Liber extra*, leaving the matter open for argument in any court. It is perhaps not by chance that no sentence is recorded in this case.[193]

The fact is, however, that the York court was willing to break up marriages on the ground of precontract, even where we strongly suspect that the problem lay with the second marriage and not with the first. In *Eva daughter of Thomas le Forester of Staynford (?Stainforth) c John de Staynford of Rawcliffe near Snaith and Alice daughter of Thomas Cissor his wife*, two witnesses testify that four or five years before the defendant contracted solemnly with Alice, he contracted informally with Eva and had children by her (the couple seem to have been very young at the time).[194] The story is plausible if not totally compelling. What makes this case more like the preceding one, however, is the account of the marriage with Alice. It was a formal marriage, but it had been done under the compulsion of the official of the archdeacon of York. The parties did not cohabit. What we have here, then, is more like an abjuration where we suspect, as the court probably did, high-handedness on the part of the archdeacon's official. The commissary general renders sentence for the plaintiff.

Alice de Normanby c William de Fentrice of Tollesby and Lucy widow of William Broun of Newby is a strange case that has been rather badly handled in the literature.[195] We first see the case in the depositions of two witnesses taken in July of 1357. They both testify that Lucy had been married to William for seven years, that she had left him in the previous autumn, and that on the previous Monday (17 July 1357, if we have the date of the depositions right), in a dramatic scene in the main street of Tollesby, she asked that he take her back until it was determined whether he had a greater right to her or to Alice.

[192] Compare *Sicut nobis*, X 2.20.9, with *Lator praesentium*, X 2.27.7, T&C no. 243.

[193] Lit. T&C no. 244.

[194] *Forester c Staynford and Cissor* (1337), CP.E.37.

[195] *Normanby c Fentrice and Broun* (1357–61), CP.E.77. See Pedersen, *Marriage Disputes*, 166, 169–70; Goldberg, *Women, Work*, 256 and nn. 176, 263.

This William refused to do. She then asked that he pay her litigation expenses and support payments. This William also refused to do unless a court ordered him to do it. The witnesses also testify that William has a minimum of 100s of their common goods and that he is supporting Alice with those goods.[196] The witnesses will not say that William is paying Alice's litigation expenses with those goods, though apparently that was charged. They are also reluctant to testify that Alice and William are committing adultery, but they say that it is commonly thought that they are. The witnesses know that Alice is working for William, and one of them saw her driving a plough team while William guided the plough.

When it comes to the question of why Lucy left William, the witnesses differ (and in both cases they are testifying from common, not personal, knowledge). One witness says that after seven years of normal marital life, Lucy left without William's license and that he refused to take her back because she had left him "deprived of her aid in the time of autumn in his great necessity."[197] A farm wife should not walk out on her husband at harvest time. The other says "that the same William during the time that they were together often beat Lucy, and on account of the great cruelty and beatings of this William, as the neighbors said, Lucy finally left William and his *consortium* at the beginning of last autumn and from that to today she was separated from his *consortium*, and still is."[198]

Clearly, these witnesses have quite different attitudes toward what happened between Lucy and William, and in neither case are the witnesses speaking of their personal knowledge. Whether the local rumor mill was divided on the question of whether Lucy was justified in leaving her husband or whether the witnesses came to different conclusions on the basis of a consistent set of rumors, we cannot tell. We certainly cannot state unqualifiedly that Lucy left her husband because he beat her, though that is certainly possible.

Lucy apparently obtained at least some of the support that she was seeking in order to defend the litigation, because the case continued for another four years. Actually, two cases continued, one brought against Lucy by William for divorce and another brought against both of them by Alice for marriage and divorce. In both cases, the argument was that Alice and William had precontracted before William married Lucy. Unfortunately, we lack the depositions on behalf of William and Alice, but they must have been quite convincing because three experienced canonical judges who had no particular reason to defer to Cleveland peasants decided that Alice and William were married and that Lucy and William were not. The judgments are even more remarkable because we do have the depositions of two witnesses who testified just before the final appellate sentence was rendered. Both had testified previously. One simply confirms his previous testimony. The other, William's brother, dramatically reverses his

[196] Disc. T&C no. 245.
[197] CP.E.77, T&C no. 246.
[198] *Id.*, T&C no. 247.

previous testimony. He says that he has confessed his perjury publicly and that he has received and done penance for it:

Lucy is the true wife of William ... and the marriage between [Lucy and William] was celebrated in the church, banns having first been proclaimed, no one reclaiming so far as this witness knows or ever heard until the time that the present litigation was brought, at which time he first heard that William de Fentrice precontracted with a certain Alice ... and he well dares to say on his oath that this precontract is made up and fabricated in a false manner by the malice of William, though the same witness otherwise asserted the contrary to this in this case, and he says that he is very sorry about this.[199]

Other documents in the case suggest that Lucy may have received some financial settlement. She clearly, however, wanted to get William back, and in this she did not succeed.

Having gotten what we can from our record, we may be entitled to speculate: Neither Lucy nor William was young. She had been married before and seems to have been an experienced farmwife. She lost her husband, perhaps in the plague, and remarried another farmer in a nearby town. Whether the marriage was a seven-year disaster or whether it somehow blew up in the summer of 1356 we do not know. What we do know is that Lucy left William at harvesttime in the early autumn of 1356. Farm workers were hard to find in England in 1356, particularly at harvesttime. Granted her experience, Lucy was probably able to make good money during that harvest. William, however, was in a bind. He engaged as a servant a woman with whom he had had a relationship before he married Lucy. Now Lucy was in trouble, because William did not need her for the farm work. She ran out of money and asked William to take her back. In the meantime, however, William and perhaps Alice (her action may be later) brought actions in the court of York seeking to have William's marriage to Lucy set aside and Alice's precontract with William declared valid. All of this makes Lucy seem less competent; she left William for a short-term advantage, and did not think about the long term. (Perhaps she was desperate, but we probably should not assume that on the basis of the testimony of one contradicted witness.) We might describe her as feckless. None of this, however, puts William in a good light. Totally apart from his treatment of Lucy, about which we cannot be sure, he left Alice, a woman whom three experienced canonical judges ultimately declared was his wife, in order to take up with Lucy. That makes him, in Victorian terminology, a cad.

Joan Brerelay of Skinningrove c Thomas Bakester (alias Littester) of Seamer begins as a simple two-party case alleging *de futuro* consent followed by intercourse and a child.[200] Two witnesses testify to ambiguous words, probably sufficient for future consent. In the words of one of them, Thomas said, "Joan, if you wish to wait to the end of my apprenticeship, I wish to take you as wife."[201]

199 *Id.*, T&C no. 248.
200 *Brerelay and Sandeshend c Bakester and Brerelay* (1383–4, 1389), CP.E.255, 256.
201 *Id.*, T&C no. 249.

This case apparently resulted in a judgment for Joan because six years, later we find one Margaret de Sandeshend, supported by Thomas, suing Thomas and Joan in a divorce action on the basis of precontract. Lacking any depositions or a sentence, we cannot know for sure what was involved in this latter case, but it certainly looks as if Thomas's desire to get out of a marriage forced by the court is a key element in the story of this case.

In the final marriage-and-divorce case, all that survives is a *processus* made into a deed poll by the official.[202] Nothing is clear from the record, other than that a man is apparently suing a woman and, perhaps, her *de facto* husband.

The competitor cases involving male plaintiffs tell very different stories from those involving female plaintiffs or from the marriage-and-divorce cases, all but one of which involve female plaintiffs. This is due partly to the fact that men cannot tell the story of a woman wronged. The cases, however, go further than that. They seem to be a different type of action. I suspected in some of the cases involving female competitors that some of the plaintiffs were 'friendly', plaintiffs who sued at the connivance of the defendants, or whose action was at the least not unwelcome. This is even clearer in the case of the male plaintiffs. In four of the cases, the *rea* confesses the action of one of them.

John Dewe of Nunnington and Laurence Scarth of Whorlton c Joan daughter of William Mirdew of Swainby is typical.[203] John sues first, alleging a *de presenti* marriage, and Laurence sues a few days later alleging a prior *de presenti* marriage. Joan confesses John's action and denies Laurence's. John introduces two witnesses to an informal marriage in a garden a year previously, apparently followed by banns.[204] Laurence introduces no testimony. Not surprisingly, John wins. While the record does not state it, it is quite likely that John's action is a 'strike suit'. Laurence may have objected to the banns, or someone may have objected to them on his behalf. John's suit, then, represents an attempt, successful in this case, to get a judgment as to the validity of his marriage before Laurence has the opportunity to fabricate a case against him (perhaps, also, in order to still rumors that Joan had married Laurence). Perhaps Laurence was perfectly willing to let this happen. He certainly does not prosecute his case with any vigor, and judgment goes against him in six weeks' time.

Thomas del Garthe citizen and apothecary of York and John de Neuton esquire c Agnes widow of Richard de Waghen of York is similar.[205] Thomas's action is confessed; John's is denied. Thomas produces three witnesses, two of them well-connected churchmen, who testify to a *de presenti* contract in Agnes's father's house two months previously.[206] Apparently, Agnes's relations with John were of concern at the time because she was asked about and denied

[202] *Newporte c Thwayte* (1387–8), CP.E.148.
[203] *Dewe and Scarth c Mirdew* (1392), CP.E.186.
[204] Lit. T&C no. 250.
[205] *Garthe and Neuton c Waghen* (1391), CP.E.245.
[206] Lit. T&C no. 251.

that she had contracted marriage with him. The only document that survives for John is a standard set of exceptions to Thomas's witnesses, though the sentence suggests that there may have been more documentation on his behalf. In the event, the official finds for Thomas, a month after the action is brought.

William Dowson of North Cave and William Roger of Pontefract c Alice Brathwell of Doncaster tells us more and may give a hint of the kind of thing that was going on in the other two cases.[207] Roger's action is confessed, and we hear nothing of his story until the sentence. Dowson's was denied, and he produces two witnesses to a standard *de presenti* contract with Alice in her house a couple of months previously. Alice excepts to these witnesses on the grounds that one is Dowson's servant and that they got the story wrong: The discussion in question was of a future contract, not a present one. Her witnesses describe a dinner at Alice's house in which John Bukton, one of Dowson's witnesses, extolled Dowson's virtues and told her that she would do well to marry him. She replied that she did not want to marry anyone until a year after the death of her late husband. Apparently there was another meeting the next week in which Alice, in response to Bukton's insistence on the match, said that the matrons of Doncaster would speak ill of her if she married, without deliberation, an outsider whom she had not known previously. Alice agreed on a date six weeks thence for giving her final answer. Bukton and Dowson subsequently got the interval shortened to a month. Dowson subsequently confessed before the townsmen of Doncaster, including the witnesses, that he had not contracted with Alice but that they had fixed a day for contracting. (Even that is an exaggeration if the previous testimony is true.) "To avoid scandal," the townsmen insisted that Dowson move out of Alice's house and put him up in another part of town.[208] The witnesses are all quite clear that John Clerk, the other witness, was Dowson's servant: he carried Dowson's sword, rode the horse that carried the baggage, took off Dowson's boots at night, and so on. The replication witnesses, all from Dowson's area, testify that Bukton and Clerk are honorable men. A special commissary finds for William Roger and against William Dowson.

Clearly, there was something between Alice and Dowson, and his presence in her house suggests that the relationship was more than platonic. Her witnesses, however, though clearly biased against the outsiders, tell a plausible story of a marriage negotiation that never quite became a marriage. All that Dowson has is a formulaic recital of the words of the marriage ceremony by men who were clearly his intimates, if not in his employ. The lesson of the case seems to be that a well-off widow will be given her choice of marriage partner, and she clearly now wants Roger, not Dowson.[209]

William Lemyng of York and John Dyk servant of Walter Bakster c Joan Markham servant of Thomas Couper of York involves people at a different stage

207 *Dowson and Roger c Brathwell* (1391), CP.E.188.
208 *Ibid.*, T&C no. 252.
209 Lit. T&C no. 253.

of life and probably of less wealth, but the result is similar.[210] The depositions are skimpy and not completely legible even under ultraviolet light, but William's witnesses testify to an exchange of present consent in the "I take thee here" form in a garden sometime between the preceding Easter and Pentecost. John's witnesses testify to events on a street just before the preceding Lent. One testifies to an exchange in the "I will have thee" form, which, as we have seen, is normally taken at York as words of the present tense. What is legible in the other's testimony suggests that this witness did not testify to the same exchange, and he may have testified only to words of the future tense.[211] Joan confessed William's action and denied John's, and William obtains the favorable sentence.

William Scargill of York and William Robinson servant of Adam Brynnand wright of Cattal c Alice daughter of Roger del Park of Moor Monkton began as a two-party case with Scargill suing on the ground of an informal exchange of *de presenti* consent.[212] Alice first alleged that the exchange of consent was conditional on her parents' consent, a consent that was not forthcoming. She introduced no testimony on this defense, but Scargill's witnesses on the principal suggest considerable ambiguity in the two exchanges of consent to which they testify. Nonetheless, the commissary general found for Scargill. Alice appealed, alleging precontract with Robinson, who was admitted to the defense. Alice introduced three witnesses to an exchange of consent in a manor hall, previous to that with Scargill. The official reversed.

The last case involving competitors, *William de Myton cordwainer of York and Richard del Ostell mason of York c Alice de Lutryngton of York*, is the most unusual.[213] Myton wins the case on the basis of an informal *de presenti* marriage, the only male competitor who wins when the defendant does not confess the action. Then again, Richard does not seem to have put in a case. Eighteen months later, Alice is back in court, suing as plaintiff in a marriage-and-divorce action against William Dryghouse of Doncaster and Isabel his wife and joining her now-husband, William de Myton.[214] She claims a precontract with Drynghouse, antedating both his contract with Isabel and hers with Myton. There is no sentence in this later action, but it clearly belongs to the type of marriage-and-divorce action described earlier in this section, where the problem seems to lie more with the second marriage, the one forced by the court, than with the first.

DIVORCE FROM THE BOND

As we noted, the cases seeking a divorce on the basis of precontract have a strong factual and legal resemblance to the marriage-and-divorce actions and

210 *Lemyng and Dyk c Markham* (1396), CP.E.242.
211 *Ibid.*, T&C no. 254.
212 *Scargill and Robinson c Park* (1398), CP.E.238, disc. T&C no. 255.
213 *Myton and Ostell c Lutryngton* (1386–7), CP.E.138.
214 *Lutryngton c Drynghouse, Drynghouse and Myton* (1389), CP.E.161.

to some of the competitor cases. Two of them are among the most spectacular cases in the cause papers.

Agnes daughter of the late Richard de Huntyngton of York c Simon son of Roger de Munkton and goldsmith of York began, apparently, as an action before the official in late July of 1345.[215] Whether Agnes sought an annulment of her marriage at this time or simply a separation we cannot be sure, because her libel has not survived, but a document describing the action suggests that it was the former.[216] During the summer recess of the court, Simon went to the archbishop and alleged that his wife had left him without cause; he sought to have her restored to him. In September, the archbishop intervened, bringing the case before his audience court. This stage of the proceedings produces extensive documentation, some of which cannot be precisely dated. We know that the archbishop issued an article *ex officio* against Agnes, charging her with having left her husband without cause. Agnes appointed a proctor but resisted appearing before the archbishop personally on the ground that she feared for her safety at the hands of Simon. She also alleged that Simon had beaten her, and that this was the reason that she had left him. She further alleged that she had precontracted with one John de Bristoll, and so was not Simon's wife.

Simon introduced some routine witnesses to his solemn marriage with Agnes five years previously. Agnes introduced witnesses supporting her allegation that she feared for her safety at Simon's hands, and Simon introduced some witnesses who deny that he had treated her cruelly or, at least, say that she had returned to him after the incident. Nothing further was said in the archbishop's court about the exception of precontract.[217]

At the end of February 1346, on the day on which Simon's witnesses had been heard, the archbishop committed the case to the official and his commissary general. While the motives of this action are not stated, it would seem from the depositions that Agnes had made enough of a case (and that Simon had not made enough of a case) for the archbishop to decide that the matter should proceed as an instance action and not as a correctional matter.

Apparently no new libel was introduced before the consistory court, at least none has been found among the 62 documents that have survived from this case. The charges and countercharges about cruelty were renewed, and the case proceeded for a couple of months as if it were an action by Agnes for separation on the ground of cruelty. Apparently sometime in May, Agnes renewed her allegations about John de Bristoll, and from here on the case proceeded as an action for divorce *a vinculo* on the ground of precontract. (Simon renewed his petition for restitution in July, but nothing came of it.)

The witnesses on both sides tell plausible stories. Clearly, there had been some relationship between Agnes and John, seven years previously, and equally

[215] *Huntyngton c Munkton* (1345–6), CP.E.248. See Pedersen, "*Romeo and Juliet* of Stonegate"; *id.*, *Marriage Disputes*, 25–58 and passim.

[216] *Id.*, 37–8 and n. 27.

[217] Detailed account in *id.*, 39–44.

clearly, it was a relationship about which her family had not known and of which, when they found out about it, they did not approve. Agnes's witnesses describe a strong-willed young woman eager to go ahead with the relationship with John despite her family's opposition, and, so they allege, she exchanged words of present consent with him. Ultimately, the matter became public. The dean of Christianity of York convened a court to inquire into the matter. John admitted that they had exchanged consent but alleged that Agnes's consent was conditional on her relatives approval. The dean dismissed them to their consciences.[218]

Simon's witnesses tell an equally romantic story. One has an account of an exchange of present consent while Simon was standing in a garden and Agnes standing on a balcony – Romeo and Juliet 250 years earlier. Precisely when Agnes and Simon exchanged consent was a matter of some debate, with Simon's own witnesses, it would seem, contradicting themselves. It is clear, however, that Agnes's marriage to Simon was ultimately solemnized with the approval of Agnes's relatives.[219]

The case ends with a bitter series of charges and countercharges about the witnesses on either side, including an apparent attempt by Simon's witnesses to backdate his informal exchange of consent with Agnes, and no sentence is recorded.[220]

In a previous paper, I used this case as evidence that runaway marriages could happen in the Middle Ages, and that the parties to such a marriage could use Alexander's rules to support marriages of love over those of convenience.[221] I still think that this case is evidence for both of those propositions, but the reality that the record presents suggests that the point may be exaggerated. In the first place, it is not at all clear that the relationship with Simon was a runaway marriage any more than that with John. Simon has the story of the balcony on his side, but the story of John's relationship with Agnes suggests parental opposition even more strongly. Clearly, this is not a case of a woman involved in an arranged marriage avoiding it by marrying someone else clandestinely. Neither marriage was arranged, and the man with whom Agnes ultimately solemnized was the man of whom Agnes's relatives ultimately approved.

Second, there can be little doubt that Agnes's marriage to Simon turned out badly. He may not have treated her as badly as she alleges, but he admits enough that we can tell that he did not treat her gently. There are also documents in the file suggesting that he was in bad financial straits, and that in turn suggests that however romantically the marriage may have begun, it fell apart when its financial basis fell apart.[222]

218 Details in *id.*, 29–33.
219 Details in *id.*, 33–6, 54–5.
220 Details in *id.*, 52–5.
221 Donahue, "Policy," 265, 268.
222 Lit. T&C no. 256.

Finally, the role of both the archbishop and the consistory is ambiguous. The case does not end, as I have elsewhere suggested, in a sentence by the archbishop for Simon.[223] The archbishop washes his hands of the whole affair, and so far as we can tell, so did the consistory court. Perhaps the parties were exhausted by over a year of intense litigation, but perhaps they were advised that neither of them was likely to get a favorable judgment. Agnes's witnesses to her precontract with John look suspicious. Not that we should disbelieve that there was a relationship between them, simply that we should doubt that it ever went as far as the witnesses say it did. That means that Agnes is married to Simon, but he is not a good husband, and he will not be granted his petition for restitution. Agnes will live apart from him, though without the sanction of the church and without permission to remarry. Not a very happy result, perhaps, but the romantic couple of the garden have turned into a singularly unattractive pair.[224]

If the story of Simon de Munkton and Agnes de Huntyngton bears some resemblance to *Romeo and Juliet*, that told by the witnesses in *Edmund de Dronesfeld c Agnes (Margaret) de Donbarre alias 'White Annays'* is straight out of Sir Walter Scott.[225] According the witnesses, Agnes had married one William de Brigham at "Lauthean" in Scotland in 1342.[226] The witnesses disagree as to how long the marriage lasted – one of them testifies that they had three or four children – but it seems clear that Agnes left William and went off with one Robert Corbet; perhaps Robert abducted her. In June of 1352, Agnes, now calling herself Margaret, married Edmund de Dronesfeld at a private ceremony in the church at Bedale (Yorks, North Riding).[227] The doors were closed; no banns were proclaimed, and no one was there except the chaplain who officiated and another man who became a witness. At Christmas in 1363, the king of Scotland visited York, and in his company was William de Brigham, now serving as a knight in the Scottish royal household.[228] William learned that Agnes was living there and commissioned some acquaintances to make a search for her. When Edmund learned of William's existence, he quit Agnes's company and shortly thereafter brought this suit.

The witnesses' stories of their own lives lends plausibility to the story they tell of Agnes's. One is a Scot (Thomas Scott) who had been in England ever since the battle of Neville's Cross (1346), where he was captured. Another (John de Sadbery) is a native of the diocese of Durham, who witnessed Agnes's first marriage while he was being held captive by the Scots. He was released after the battle of Neville's Cross.[229] A third, Agnes's first cousin, does not explain

223 Donahue, "Policy," 268.

224 Lit. T&C no. 257.

225 *Dronesfeld c Donbarre* (1364), CP.E.87. See Owen, "White Annays and Others," for a full discussion and transcriptions.

226 Lit. T&C no. 258.

227 Lit. T&C no. 259.

228 Lit. T&C no. 260.

229 Disc. T&C no. 261.

his presence in England, but he, too, may have come to England after Neville's Cross. He says that he had not seen William from the time of the wedding until he appeared in York in 1363.

Agnes's case goes virtually undefended. She asks for alimony *pendente lite*, and she tries to argue that the matter is *res iudicata*, a bad argument in any event, as we have seen, and a particularly bad argument when no testimony is introduced as to the previous proceedings. Not surprisingly, the dean of Christianity of York, acting as special commissary of the official, declares the marriage null.

We have already dealt at length in Chapter 2 with another of the cases of divorce on the ground of precontract, *Tiryngton c Moryz*. I suggested that in that case, there may have been an agreement to obtain a collusive divorce that fell apart.

Where the deal does not come apart, we can have only our suspicions to go on. In *John de Thetilthorp c Joan daughter of Peter atte Enges of Patrington his wife*,[230] John alleges that he and Joan contracted marriage and solemnized it five years previously. The marriage cannot stand, however, because 13 years previously, Joan had contracted marriage with Richard son of Thomas Carter. Joan confesses the action. Two witnesses describe a *de presenti* contract between Richard and Joan 13 years earlier when Joan had been a servant in one deponent's house in York and Richard a servant in the other's. Two others describe the solemn marriage between John and Joan. In a fifth deposition, taken a few months later, Richard's brother testifies that he had seen Richard three years before but has not seen him since.[231] He does not know whether he is alive or dead. In the event, the commissary general renders sentence for John, about five months after the case has begun. A similar case in 1389 also results in a quite rapid sentence for the plaintiff.[232]

If we put these cases together with *Ingoly c Midelton*, it is clear that the allegation and defense of precontract gave rise to a substantial amount of perjury, or shading of the truth, in litigation before the court of York in the later Middle Ages. In only one case, *Dronesfeld c Donbarre*, can we have any confidence in the veracity of the witnesses, and that is because Agnes's deception is so plausible in the context of the intermittent border wars between England and Scotland and of the plague in the mid-fourteenth century. This is not to say that all the witnesses in the other cases were lying (some of the testimony in *Huntyngton c Munkton* has a ring of truth), simply that in any case where we have evidence that the current marriage has broken down and where the divorce action is confessed, we have reason to suspect that the witnesses to the precontract are coloring their story.

230 *Thetilthorp c Enges* (1374), CP.E.155; lit. T&C no. 262.

231 Disc. and lit. T&C no. 263.

232 *Elme c Elme*, CP.E.153; lit. T&C no. 264.

As to the parties' consciences, we can add little to what has already been said about this topic in Chapter 2.[233] It is even conceivable that thoughts like those of Agnes Payge were going through the minds of Agnes de Huntyngton and her witnesses, but Agnes did not get a judgment because Simon would not consent. And we should, perhaps, recall that lying under oath, in support of what they seemed to have believed was a higher cause, was something that Englishmen of the class with which we are dealing in most of these cases appeared to have done quite frequently while serving on criminal juries.[234]

The cases of divorce *a vinculo* that do not raise issues of precontract present varied grounds for the divorce. There are two cases of divorce on the ground of the impediments of force or nonage. In two-party marriage-enforcement actions, we discovered that this defense frequently indicated a story of an arranged marriage that had gone awry. In one of the divorce cases, that is clearly the case.[235] The proof shows clearly that the parties were underage (8 and 12) when the marriage took place. Relatively little is said about force, though one witness does testify that the relatives of the defendant girl forced the boy to stay with her for a week when he was 14. The real issue, however, seems to be whether the couple consented or had intercourse after they reached the age of puberty. The defendant insists that they did, but the plaintiff's witnesses suggest both that the plaintiff was impotent and that the defendant was unfaithful. The commissary general decides for the plaintiff, and we may wonder why the case is successful when the similar marriage-enforcement action defended on the same grounds was not.[236] Here the evidence that this marriage had no place to go was particularly strong.

What we have in *John son of Ralph de Penesthorp c Elizabeth daughter of Walter de Waltegrave* was clearly not an arranged marriage, at least not in the normal sense of the term.[237] The second of the first two witnesses, a servant of John's father Ralph, was sent by his master to find his son who had disappeared on the night of 1 August 1333 and whom he suspected of being at Walter's house. The witness describes how by starlight he saw five or six men enter Walter's bakehouse with swords and daggers drawn. Elizabeth entered the bakehouse and the witness heard Richard, Elizabeth's brother, tell John to take Elizabeth by the hand and contract marriage with her; otherwise he would kill him. John and Elizabeth did contract. John was greatly wounded and barely escaped with his life. As soon as he did, he reclaimed and never went in Elizabeth's company again. Although the first witness's testimony is illegible, we know that he was a fellow servant of the second, and he probably testified as the second witness did.

233 Text and nn. 40–3.
234 See Green, *Verdicts According to Conscience*, 28–102.
235 *Aungier c Malcake* (1357), CP.E.76; lit. T&C no. 265.
236 *Brantice c Crane* (at nn. 39–43), lit. T&C no. 266.
237 *Penesthorp c Waltegrave* (1334), CP.E.26.

About two months later, Richard and his 18-year-old servant testify. Richard had heard it said that John had common access to his sister, and he had heard from a certain woman that John was going to be in the bakehouse that night. He found John there and confronted him. He drew his sword so that John would not leave the bakehouse and sent his servant to get Elizabeth. When Elizabeth and her sister Alice appeared, he told John to contract with her. John did so, and Elizabeth replied with the same words. Although Richard is unwilling to testify that John suffered "the fear that could fall upon a constant man," he does say that he believes that John would not have done what he did had he, Richard, not been there and done what he did. The servant basically confirms the story, adding that he does believe that John was compelled, because he saw Richard draw his sword and threaten John and order him to take Elizabeth by the hand and contract. Both men testify that the only people present were John, the two witnesses, and the two women. Neither says anything about a wound, but they do say that John has not had contact with Elizabeth after that night.

There are substantial discrepancies between the testimony of the two sets of witnesses. I think it highly unlikely that the first and second witnesses were telling the truth. Indeed, I think it highly unlikely that they were in the bushes by the bakehouse on that August night.[238] What they told was what John told them, perhaps elaborated by what a lawyer told them would clearly be sufficient to make out a case of force. There is more reason to accept the testimony of the brother and his servant. They are presumably on Elizabeth's side, but what they said almost certainly caused her to lose the case, as she did. We might wonder why this case came out in favor of the plaintiff, while the woman who alleged that her great-uncle threatened to put her down a well if she did not marry the plaintiff did not prevail.[239] There are many possible explanations, but the fact that the threat in this case came from someone on the other party's side may be an important difference.

But why did Elizabeth's brother and his servant give testimony so damaging to her case? Perhaps the answer lies in the fact that all three witnesses testify that John had not come near Elizabeth since the events in the bakehouse. From Elizabeth's point of view, this was not ideal. From a moral point of view, an honest woman with no husband may be better off than a dishonest one with a lover, but after that wild August night, Elizabeth may have had second thoughts. It is quite remarkable that John was able to get Richard and his servant to testify, essentially, on his behalf. Elizabeth, and perhaps also the senior members of the Waltegrave family, may have thought that everyone would be better off without John as an absent son-in-law. Richard may have thought on that August night that he was 'doing the right thing'. By the time he testified, he may have changed his mind (or had it changed for him). If this is so, then even he may have exaggerated the amount of force that was applied.

[238] Lit. T&C no. 267.

[239] *Thomeson c Belamy* (n. 48), disc. T&C no. 268.

There are two cases in which women successfully sue for divorce on the ground of their husband's impotence. In one, the defendant is contumacious when ordered to submit to inspection by matrons. The plaintiff's witnesses tell a chilling story of how she was forced by her husband, a member of the knightly class, not to raise the issue of his inability to have intercourse.[240] In the other case, the man does submit to the inspection by the matrons, which he fails, resulting in the usual embarrassing depositions.[241]

There are three cases in which divorce is sought on the ground of affinity.[242] The first case begins quite unusually as an office action brought by the vicar general of the bishop of Durham, seeking to divorce the parties on the ground of affinity by illicit intercourse. (The record is difficult to read, but the charge seems to be that the man had intercourse with his wife's half sister.) The parties appeal from the vicar general apparently before he is able to render sentence, and no result on appeal is recorded.[243] The second is a complicated case of affinity in the fourth degree. The issue seems to be whether the plaintiff ever consented to the marriage after the parties had obtained a papal dispensation. The commissary apparently concludes that she did not, because he renders sentence for her.[244] In the final case, all that survives is the testimony of two witnesses to the effect that the defendant had intercourse with the plaintiff's first cousin more than 12 years earlier.[245] This is the only case in which we may suspect that the rules about consanguinity or affinity were being used by the parties to get out of a marriage for reasons quite different from those alleged in the documents.

There is one case in which divorce is sought on the ground of the servile status of the defendant.[246] The argument meets with no more favorable conclusion than it did in the one marriage-enforcement action in which it was raised.[247] Here, the defense of manumission is particularly powerful, supported as it is by testimony of the son of the lord who is alleged to have done the manumitting and by a deed of manumission.[248]

One case, on appeal from the consistory court of Carlisle, raises the impediment of crime.[249] There seems little doubt that the plaintiff committed adultery with the defendant while her husband was still alive; the only issue is whether they agreed to marry before he died. No sentence is recorded.[250]

[240] *Paynell c Cantilupe* (1368–9), CP.E.259; lit. T&C no. 269.
[241] *Lambhird c Sundirson* (1370), CP.E.105; lit. T&C no. 270.
[242] There is further discussion of these cases in Ch 11.
[243] *Office c Baker and Barker* (1339), CP.E.82/8d; disc. T&C no. 271.
[244] *Nutle c Wode* (1372), CP.E.140; lit. T&C no. 272.
[245] *Helay c Evotson* (1394), CP.E.212; lit. T&C no. 273.
[246] *Sturmy c Tuly* (1396), CP.E.235.
[247] *Redyng c Boton* (at nn. 114–15).
[248] Lit. T&C no. 274.
[249] *Kyrkebryde c Lengleys* (1340), CP.E.46.
[250] Lit. T&C no. 275.

Two divorce cases do not give us the grounds on which the divorce was claimed. In the first, all that survives is an article and depositions in support of the plaintiff's claim that he paid the defendant alimony and court costs incurred by her brother in defending the action.[251] In the other, we have a sentence granting a female plaintiff license to remarry, but nothing else.[252]

OTHER TYPES OF ACTIONS

Three actions originally brought by a woman to enforce a marriage become so involved in extraneous legal issues that the underlying story is lost.

In *Joan daughter of Robert son of Stephen of Doncaster c John son of Gilbert of Doncaster*,[253] we lack any documentation of Joan's initial claim, and so we do not know whether she claimed words *de presenti* or words *de futuro* followed by intercourse. We know, however, that her action was successful and that the official ordered John to solemnize his marriage with Joan. From this we may surmise that the relationship was an informal one. Banns were proclaimed, and John objected to them on the ground of consanguinity. The commissary general apparently rejected John's objections and excommunicated him for failure to obey the official's order.[254] When we see the case, it is on appeal from the commissary general to the official. Depositions of four witnesses for John survive. There are some discrepancies in the details, but they testify consistently that the couple are third cousins. Though there is no sentence, we have no reason to disbelieve the story. The only thing that is slightly suspicious is the fact that it took John so long to demonstrate the relationship. That fact, at least, casts doubt on the witnesses' testimony that everyone in Doncaster knows about the relationship. But the witnesses look respectable; they have no obvious connection with John, and the story is sufficiently complicated that it is hard to believe that they made it up out of whole cloth.

In *Juliana daughter of John Gudefelawe of Kenton c William Chappeman de Jeddeworth of Newcastle upon Tyne*, the record is taken up solely with objections to the official of the archdeacon of Northumberland, who had originally heard the case.[255] Juliana originally brought an action to enforce a marriage before the archdeacon's official. Her positions and articles before him are in what had become the standard form by this time: She alleges both words *de presenti* and words *de futuro* followed by intercourse. No other documents from this stage of the case survive, but later Juliana was to allege that the archdeacon's official refused to admit and examine her witnesses. Fifteen months later, Juliana appealed to the consistory court of Durham, alleging as her ground

[251] *Colvyle c Darell* (1324), CP.E.14, disc. T&C no. 276.
[252] *Talkan c Bryge* (1395), CP.E.158 (recto).
[253] *Doncaster c Doncaster* (1351), CP.E.69.
[254] The case is then, technically, *ex officio*.
[255] *Gudefelawe c Chappeman* (1387–90), CP.E.137.

for the appeal that the archdeacon's official was a bigamist.[256] The Durham court apparently accepted her appeal and was ready to hear her witnesses when William appealed to the court of York. Here, the only documentation is Juliana's defense of her appeal to the Durham consistory. In the court of York she argues that in addition to being a bigamist, the archdeacon's official had taken a bribe from William. The record closes with the depositions of two priests from the Newcastle area who confirm Juliana's allegations, though mostly on the basis of hearsay.[257]

In *Katherine daughter of John Pynton of York c John Thurkilby spicer of York*, all that survives is an appeal by Thurkilby from the commissary general of York to the Apostolic See.[258] The mention of papal judges delegate in the appeal suggests that this is not the first time that this case has been brought to the Roman court.

There are three cases in the fourteenth-century York cause papers, in addition to those already discussed, in which women raise issues that might have led to a divorce *a mensa et thoro* (separation).[259] In none of them is the woman successful; two have sentences for the man. One, *John Hadilsay c Elizabeth daughter of John Smalwod of Cowick*, is an action for restoration of conjugal rights brought by the husband.[260] We do not know the grounds on which the woman defended the action, but the sentence tells us that she made a proposition; it probably alleged grounds for separation.[261] She loses. In another, *Marjorie wife of Thomas Nesfeld of York c the same Thomas*, the woman sues for separation on the ground of cruelty (beating).[262] She loses the action when her husband offers security for his good behavior in the future. The third case, *Richard Scot of Newcastle-upon-Tyne c Marjorie de Devoine*, has no judgment.[263] It was probably an action for restoration of conjugal rights that the woman defended on the ground of both the cruelty and the adultery of her husband.

Two cases are actions brought about marital property, rather than about the marriage itself. One of them, however, *Katherine widow of John Hiliard of [Long] Riston c Peter son of John Hiliard*,[264] rapidly raises issues familiar from marriage-enforcement actions. Katherine brought an action in the central royal courts to obtain an assignment of dower from her late husband's heir, Peter. Peter challenged the marriage in the king's courts on the grounds that the marriage was not solemnized and that it was invalid on the ground of consanguinity. The case was referred to the audience of the archbishop who, in

256 Disc. T&C no. 277.
257 Lit. T&C no. 278.
258 *Pynton c Thurkilby* CP.E.241V (?1395 X ?1398); lit. T&C no. 279.
259 Listed T&C no. 281.
260 *Hadilsay c Smalwod* (1395), CP.E.274.
261 Text and disc. T&C no. 280.
262 *Nesfeld c Nesfeld* (1396), CP.E.221.
263 *Scot c Devoine* (1349), CP.E.257. We return to these cases in Ch 10.
264 *Hiliard c Hiliard* (1370), CP.E.108.

turn, delegated it to his consistory court. Katherine's witnesses to the solemnity do not describe much of a solemnity. The marriage, they say, took place seven years previously at dawn in Riston chapel. The chaplain went to the door of the chancel and proclaimed the banns, but, of course, no one objected because the only people there were the parties and their witnesses (Katherine's mother and half sister and John's brother). The witnesses are not even sure that the doors of the church were open. They also seem to be trying to establish that even if there was consanguinity between them, Katherine did not know about it. To this end, Katherine introduces a number of what might be called 'character witnesses', who testify that Katherine would never have married John if she had known he was her kinsman. One of them, a neighbor, testifies to John's death. Katherine told the dying John, "I have been too often a widow and have ungrateful children." John, raising his hands from the bed, replied, "If any of my children does thee any wrong, I curse them as fully as I begot them."[265]

Peter's witnesses, by contrast, are devastating to Katherine's cause. Eight witnesses solidly describe the relationship between Katherine and John (they were second cousins once removed).[266] Two years previously, they had been cited before the archbishop's audience court for consanguinity, and the court deferred making a judgment in order to allow them time to petition the pope for a dispensation. One John de Esthorp, a priest, was commissioned to go to the papal court to get the dispensation, but he returned empty-handed. He testifies that he was told in the papal court that he could not get such a dispensation for a hundred pounds.[267]

There is no sentence. There needs be no sentence because Katherine has clearly lost her case. In the absence of a sentence, perhaps Peter will remember his father's curse and see to it that Katherine gets something, but she will not get the substantial dower that she claims.[268]

The other case is about marital property, pure and simple. Two knights, Alexander Percy and Robert Colvyle, arranged a marriage of their heirs, Alexander's son John and Robert's daughter Elizabeth.[269] Their age is not mentioned anywhere, but the depositions suggest that they were quite young. The negotiations resulted in a contract that was confessed before the official of York. It is probably this fact, rather than the fact that the contract concerned a marriage, that gave the court its unquestioned jurisdiction for the later action for breach of contract. The contract called for Alexander to give the couple 25 marks worth of land and rents, perhaps in lieu of any dower claim by Elizabeth, and for Robert to give Alexander 180 marks as *maritagium*. All proceeded according to plan. The couple seem to have been married and to have gone

[265] Lit. T&C no. 282.
[266] Disc. and lit. T&C no. 283.
[267] Disc. and lit. T&C no. 284.
[268] For how substantial the dower was, see Pedersen, *Marriage Disputes*, 166–9, 190.
[269] *Percy c Colvyle* (1323), CP.E.12, disc. T&C no. 285.

to live in Alexander's house; Alexander gave them the land. Then Elizabeth died, and Robert never paid Alexander the 180 marks, for which Alexander is now suing. All that survives from the case are Alexander's libel, positions, articles, and depositions, but the positions have answers on them, and so we know that Robert conceded that the contract had been made. The fact that the witnesses testify about the cohabitation of Elizabeth and John suggests that Robert's defense was going to be that his obligation to pay was dependent on something that did not happen: cohabitation, consummation of the relationship, perhaps even having a child. Nothing more survives of the case, and it was almost certainly compromised.[270]

What is interesting about these miscellaneous cases is how many of them support generalizations that are made about medieval marriage on the basis of other sources, and how few of them there are. We are told, for example, that the canonic prohibitions on marriages of relatives were so extensive that no marriage in the Middle Ages was stable. One could always find an unsuspected relationship that would allow the couple to break up. This seems to have been the situation of the couple in the *Doncaster* case.[271] It looks as if John is going to get out of having to marry Joan because of a relationship between them that neither knew anything about at the time of their courting. The *Doncaster* case, however, is the only one like it in the 86 cases that survive from this century at York, with the possible exception of the *Hiliard* case.

Whether we classify the *Hiliard* case as one of the same type depends on whether we believe the testimony of Katherine's witnesses that she knew nothing of the consanguinity at the time she married John. She has a reason to allege that she was unaware of the relationship. In the first place, it makes her case a sympathetic one. If she was unaware of the relationship, she has lived as a man's faithful wife for seven years (no one denies that the relationship was a stable one), and now is being denied her dower by her stepson. Further, if she was unaware of the relationship, she may be able to claim the advantages of a putative marriage. This is a complicated topic. It is not at all clear that the king's courts would accept the doctrine of putative marriage, but the church courts did.[272] The question, then, is how the archbishop would report the matter to the king's courts if he found that there had been a putative marriage. Even if Katherine had been unaware of the relationship, she would not have been able to claim a putative marriage unless she had been married solemnly. There was some flexibility as to the requirements of solemnity, but no canonist of whom I am aware would regard the hasty, dawn ceremony that the witnesses describe as proper solemnity. Finally, if Katherine was unaware of the relationship between John and herself, she would at least escape the automatic excommunication that fell upon those who, knowing of an impediment, nonetheless got married

[270] Lit. T&C no. 286.
[271] See at n. 253.
[272] Disc. T&C no. 287.

clandestinely.[273] That clandestinity is an issue in this case is indicated by the fact that one of Peter's witnesses testifies that the chaplain who officiated at the marriage had been suspended from office for having done so.[274]

On balance, it seems to be better to regard the *Hiliard* case as one in which the parties were aware that they were consanguine, and in which they failed to get a dispensation before they married. That obtaining such a dispensation took time and was expensive is, of course, probably the reason why they failed to do so, and as the chaplain testifies, it was by no means automatic. A cynic might suggest that though John and Katherine clearly had the money to get a dispensation, they didn't have the clout. Although they were fairly wealthy, there is nothing to suggest that they had much influence.[275] Thus, although this case illustrates the fact that the rules about consanguinity could affect the lives of medieval people in ways that are quite unusual to modern eyes, the case neither supports the proposition that all medieval marriages were automatically voidable on the grounds of consanguinity nor that the rules were used by parties to marriages only for purposes of manipulation.[276]

Two cases, *Gudefelawe* and *Thurkilby*, illustrate the oft-made claim that appeals in canon law were so frequent that the main point of the case was lost sight of. Certainly *Gudefelawe* involves much procedural wrangling. It probably also illustrates the fact that low-level justice could be pretty rough-and-ready. That is, of course, why appeal was possible, and again, the case is alone. All that *Thurkilby* illustrates is that appeals to the Apostolic See did occur even in the later Middle Ages. To balance against these cases, we have a large number that were resolved, apparently quite satisfactorily, at the local level, and a number in which appeal to the Apostolic See is threatened but nothing seems to come of it.

Two cases, *Nesfeld* and *Scot*, involve allegations of wife beating, and one, *Hadilsay*, certainly involves a marriage in which the woman was unhappy. In the *Scot* case, there is no sentence, and the story the witnesses tell may be exaggerated. In *Nesfeld*, where a beating is conceded, the woman fails to obtain her judgment of separation. We do not know, however, whether she will be compelled to live with her husband. In the one case where a woman is compelled to return to a husband, *Hadilsay*, she could prove no justification at all for her behavior, and so we have no idea what the standard is.[277] Nor do we know whether the court accepted Nesfeld's justification of the beating or whether it simply thought the incident was not serious enough to warrant granting a separation. The paucity of separation cases and the results of those

[273] See Ch 1, at n. 83.

[274] Pedersen, *Marriage Disputes*, 22 n. 55, notes that a drawing of a hand points to this statement in the record.

[275] The other possibility, suggested in n. 267, was that they were unfortunate in their choice of an agent to get the dispensation.

[276] We return to this issue in a broader context in Ch 11.

[277] But see *Huntyngton c Munkton* (n. 215), where the court does not order Agnes to return to Simon after she introduces her evidence about cruelty.

that we do have, however, suggest that the court was reluctant to grant them. The implications of this for the power relationships between men and women in fourteenth-century York are obvious, and they provide a counter to the positive effect that the court seems to have had in its judgments in marriage-formation cases.[278]

The last case, *Percy*, provides some support for the notion that medieval marriages were usually arranged and that the parties had little to say about them. Again, *Percy* is the only case like it in the whole group. It is perhaps significant that it involves parties of the highest social level that appear before the consistory court. Even when we combine this case with other cases that seem to involve arranged marriages, the number pales in comparison with those where the parties seem to be doing the arranging themselves.

CONCLUSION

The conclusions with which we closed the previous section were negative: There are relatively few cases in the York cause papers of the fourteenth century that support the stereotypes of medieval marriage. Positive conclusions are harder to come by. Many, if not most, of the two-party cases can be organized into what we called 'story-types'. There was considerable variety in what the parties and their witnesses said when they came to court, but the five patterns proposed – the woman wronged, the woman (or man) wronging, the young couple who went too far, the mature couple, the arranged marriage gone awry – held up reasonably well. The three-party cases introduced additional complexities, if only because there were, at least potentially, three stories to be told. The longer a marriage had been existence, the more we had reason to suspect that the stories involved considerable shading of the truth, if not outright lies. This was true whether the form of the action was a three-party marriage-and-divorce action or a two-party action based on precontract.

Eighty-six cases are quite a few, particularly when many are quite well documented. There are, however, more marriage cases in the York cause papers of the fifteenth century (129), some of which are similar to those of the fourteenth century and some of which are not. Let us focus in the next chapter on those that are different. We can then return at the end of the chapter to a conclusion that will emphasize the common elements on the basis of considerably more evidence.

[278] We attempt to place these separation cases in a larger context in Ch 10.

5

Story-Patterns in the Court of York in the Fifteenth Century

The focus of this chapter is twofold, on the differences in the fifteenth-century court's reaction to story-patterns that were well established in the fourteenth century and on story-patterns that emerged in the fifteenth century that were different from those of the fourteenth. This focus on difference can lead to the impression that radical changes occurred in litigation about marriage in the court of York in the fifteenth century. That was not the case, and a final section in the chapter will briefly sketch the large elements of continuity between the two centuries. It will, however, not be necessary to go into detail about the cases that were basically the same as those in the fourteenth century.

DIFFERENT REACTIONS TO OLD STORY-PATTERNS

The statistics have already showed us that plaintiffs' success rate went down in the fifteenth century, though the York court remained decidedly plaintiff-friendly.[1] The decline is particularly noticeable in two-party actions, where defendants received favorable judgments in 37 percent of the cases that have judgments (11/30), while the comparable figure for the fourteenth century is 18 percent (6/34). If we exclude the abjuration cases, which, as we have seen, produced an unusually high number of judgments for defendants in fourteenth-century York and are virtually, though not entirely, missing in the fifteenth century, the contrast becomes even more dramatic: 39 percent (11/28) versus 12 percent (3/25). Just on the basis of the numbers, one cannot determine which (or which combination) of the possible explanations for this phenomenon is likely to be the correct one. It is possible that fifteenth-century plaintiffs, encouraged by the success of fourteenth-century plaintiffs in such cases, brought increasingly weaker cases until the court finally drew the line, or the court could have changed its attitude toward certain kinds of claims or certain kinds of defenses, or the court could have been listening to somewhat different stories,

[1] See Table 3.6, and the accompanying discussion.

to which it reacted in a new way. Let us, then, take a more careful look, focusing particularly on those cases that defendants won.

The Exception of Absence

In 1423, Beatrice Pulayn of (Church) Fenton brought an action against Thomas Neuby (Newby) of the same, alleging that she had contracted an informal marriage with him.[2] She produced two witnesses, Thomas and John Studdard, father and son. They both testify that between vespers and nightfall on Sunday, 4 July 1423, in a house in Little "Brokylhurst" between Little Fenton and Biggin, Thomas Studdard asked Beatrice and Thomas Neuby if either of them had the right (*ius habendi*) to have someone else as husband or wife.[3] They both replied that they did not. Then he asked each of them if it was their will to have each other, and both replied that it was. He then proceeded to dictate the full formula of words of marital consent, which they repeated after him. Whether or not these events happened as described, Thomas Studdard clearly knew how to conduct a marriage ceremony and had probably done so on other occasions.

Thomas Neuby excepted to the testimony that he was absent. He was, he said, in Barkston, eight miles away, on 4 July 1423 from dinner to nightfall. Further, John Studdard had lied when he said he was not an affine of Beatrice; he is, in fact, her brother-in-law, having married her sister. Four witnesses testify to Neuby's presence in Barkston. He was at a football match (*pilam pedalem*), and then the witnesses and he went out drinking. Two of the witnesses also say that they do not believe the Studdards because of John's relationship to Beatrice.

There is much to be skeptical about in this testimony. Not only is it a story that had been told since at the least the thirteenth century, but it also contains within it a palpable exaggeration that we can detect more than 580 years after it was told. Barkston is not eight miles from Biggin; it is more like three miles, and Little Fenton is even closer to Barkston. There was also much time for which to account; it stays light for a long time in early July in Yorkshire.

Nonetheless, the commissary general *sede vacante*, Richard Arnall, an experienced judge who was to become the official of the court, rendered sentence for Neuby.[4] Why he may have done so can be inferred from an unusual move that he made in this case.[5] He ordered John Studdard to undergo purgation (that is, produce oath-helpers) for his role in the case.[6] I think it unlikely that the reason for the purgation was that John had denied being an affine of Beatrice's, because

[2] *Pulayn c Neuby* (1423–4), CP.F.137.

[3] A striking use of the word *ius* in the objective sense. We would probably call this a duty. See Donahue, "*Ius* in the Subjective Sense."

[4] Beatrice appealed to the Apostolic See, though we may doubt whether the appeal was pursued.

[5] I know of no other case in which this was done, although, of course, we have nothing like a full set of act books for this period.

[6] Cons.AB.2, fol. 39v.

John had admitted in his deposition that he had married Beatrice's sister. I suspect that John did not know what an affine is and that Arnall probably knew that. I think it is far more likely that Arnall was convinced that the Studdards were lying, and he wanted to make John come up with oath-helpers, if he could, to make sure that the lies he told were not a cause of scandal. It would seem, then, that like the appellate court in *Dolling c Smith*, Arnall focused not on the weakness of the defendant's case but on the weakness of the plaintiff's.[7]

In the autumn of 1427, Robert Thomson of Scawton brought an action before Roger Esyngwald, the commissary general of York, against Marjorie Wylson of Osgoodby (Grange), alleging that he had informally contracted marriage with her.[8] He produced two men of Scawton, ages 33 and 40, respectively, who say that on the Sunday, 27 July 1427, Robert approached them before mass and asked them to come with him after dinner to witness the matrimonial words he hoped to exchange with Marjorie. They went with him to Osgoodby Wood near Osgoodby Grange and hid among the thorns and brambles under the bank of a ditch near a hedge.[9] Robert went off to Osgoodby Grange and returned with Marjorie. They sat under an ash tree, exchanged words of present consent, handfasted, and kissed.[10] Robert gave her two silver rings and a jewel called an "Agnus dei." Both witnesses give a reasonably consistent description of the clothes the couple wore. They say that Marjorie did not know that they were there, but they were no more than 12 feet away.

The details of this story are vivid and consistent. One can have little doubt that the place described did exist in Osgoodby Wood. Whether Marjorie and Robert were there and did what they are said to have done is a matter about which we may have more doubt. So far as we can tell, however, Marjorie offered no defense before the commissary general, and he rendered sentence for Robert.

Marjorie appealed to the official, who delegated the case to Robert Alne, the examiner general of the court. As happened frequently, particularly in the fifteenth century, Marjorie had saved her defense for the appeal. She introduced five male witnesses, ranging in age from over 40 to 17, who account for her presence, first at a wedding in Kilburn and then at her father's house in Osgoodby Grange. Apparently, Marjorie and her brother had been invited to the wedding but not to the reception (*convivium*), and so they came home, had dinner with the witnesses, and awaited the return of their parents. One of the witnesses also outlines a relationship between Robert and one of his witnesses on the principal case (he had married Robert's second cousin).

The story is plausible. It is made more so by the fact that the couple who married in Kilburn that day were probably somewhat older than Marjorie, her brother, and their friends. (The woman of the couple was a widow; a witness

[7] Disc. T&C 288.

[8] *Thomson c Wylson* (1427–8), CP.F.169, 170.

[9] *Id.*, T&C no. 289.

[10] Helmholz, *Marriage Litigation*, 29 and n. 24 has it as an oak tree.

in a later deposition describes her as the man's *uxor moderna*, suggesting that he, too, was previously married.) Perhaps the couple invited only the people who were closer to them in age to the *convivium*. If we look at the witnesses more closely, however, we begin to have doubts. There are three young men, ages 17, 18, and 20, who are described as of the *familia* of Marjorie's father, Robert Wylson. They also seem to be friends of Marjorie and her brother. Two of them say that they all (including Marjorie) went out and played handball (*pilam manualem*) after dinner that Sunday. Two of the witnesses are older, one 30 and the other more than 40, and they both say that they just happened to come to Robert Wylson's house that day to do unspecified business with him and waited around for him to come back from the *convivium* (and presumably watched the young people play handball).

It is these two witnesses whom Robert attacks in replication. He offers six witnesses, all seemingly respectable men in their 30s and 40s who variously testify that they saw one of the two a mile away from Osgoodby Grange that afternoon and that the other had previously admitted that he had not seen Marjorie that day. Take away these two witnesses and what we have is three teenagers sticking up for a young woman whose father is their master and whose brother is their friend.[11]

Robert Alne decides for Marjorie, reversing the sentence of the commissary general (though he is careful to say that the commissary general decided correctly on the basis of the record he had before him). As in the case of Richard Arnall's judgment in the *Pulayn* case, we may suspect that the reason why he decided as he did was not so much the strength of Marjorie's case as the weakness of Robert's. That two witnesses were hiding in the thorn bushes when Robert and Marjorie exchanged words of the present tense stretches credulity almost to the breaking point. That they told the rector of their church about what they had seen, as they testify, and that he told them to keep quiet about it, is also hard to believe. Their testimony is, perhaps, enough if there were no defense to the case, but one can certainly see how a judge could come out the other way when the case was vigorously defended. Even if we believe, as I am inclined to believe, that the two unrelated witnesses to Marjorie's presence in her father's house that afternoon were suborned (one can well imagine how Robert Wylson talked two of his friends into committing perjury when he was told that the three teenagers would not make a strong case), we still have to wonder how plausible it is that Marjorie would have sneaked off into the woods that afternoon to engage in what she assumed to be an unwitnessed handfasting. What little evidence we have does not suggest that Marjorie was a shy or demure young woman. She plays handball with the boys. Hence, I would suggest that she might have been quite capable of handfasting while her parents were away at a wedding reception. What we might doubt is whether

[11] One of the witnesses in replication calls them *garciones*, a word that captures both 'boy' and 'servant'.

she would have done it without witnesses and whether she would have done it with Robert Thomson, whose relationship with her is testified to only by his statements to his otherwise suspect witnesses, and who may have been quite a bit older than she.[12]

In three other cases in the fifteenth century, a defendant who raises an exception of absence prevails. Agnes Brignall of St Michael le Belfrey, York, has two female witnesses, one of them her sister, to her informal present-consent marriage, followed by handfasting and kissing, to John Herford of St Olave in the suburbs of York. The marriage took place in Agnes's house in Bootham, on the Wednesday before Palm Sunday (9 April), 1432.[13] Both witnesses are quite strong on the proposition that John had intercourse with Agnes that night, and many times thereafter. The witnesses' testimony is consistent and detailed. One even mentions that they had fish for dinner after the handfasting, it being Lent. Another witness, a male servant of a seemingly unrelated man, testifies to another occasion on which they contracted, but his testimony is not supported by any other witness. John replies with seven male witnesses who testify that on that day, John had dinner at the sign of the Lion in Pontefract and then rode off to Doncaster with Robert Herford, a monk of St Mary's York and probably a relative of John. John did not come back to York until the following Friday. The witnesses are remarkably detailed about the dinner, and include the hostler at the inn. No one mentions how far Pontefract is from York; they do not have to. It is about 15 miles to the south, as the crow flies, and Doncaster is another 13 miles to the south of it.[14] Roger Esyngwald, the commissary general, decides the case for John, and no appeal is taken.

Thirty-two years later Margaret Barley was equally unsuccessful.[15] Her two witnesses to her informal present-consent marriage to Nicholas Danby, chandler of York, in the house of William Raburn in Micklegate at dinnertime are met with four witnesses who say that they were having dinner with Danby in his house at the same time on the same day.[16] John Worseley, the commissary general, renders judgment for Nicholas.

The same thing happens in a rural setting with the genders reversed. William Wikley of Carlton in Snaith offers three male witnesses (including his brother) to his informal exchange of present consent, handfasting, kissing, and exchange of gifts with Alice Roger in her house in Adwalton in Birstall.[17] She counters with six witnesses, four of whom are members of her *familia* but two unrelated, who testify that Alice and her *familia* were haying in their fields and were not in the house all day. Robert Thornton, commissary of the commissary general, renders judgment for Alice.[18]

[12] Disc. T&C no. 290.
[13] *Brignall c Herford* (1432–3), CP.F.104.
[14] Lit. T&C no. 291.
[15] *Barley c Danby* (1464), CP.F.203.
[16] Lit. T&C no. 292.
[17] *Wikley c Roger* (1450), CP.F.186.
[18] An appeal to the Apostolic See is met with refutatory *apostoli*.

In fact, there is only one two-party matrimonial case in the fifteenth-century cause papers where the plaintiff is able to prevail against a defense of absence.[19] (Five cases in which it was raised or seems to have been raised have no recorded judgment.)[20] That case is one of the most bizarre in the York records. In 1418, Alice Walker of Kirkby Overblow sued John Kydde of the same to establish a present-consent marriage followed by intercourse and the birth of a child. Two women in their 40s from the suburbs of York testify that two years previously, they had been sharing a bed in the house of Roger Remyngton in Sicklinghall when they heard through the wall Alice say to John in bed, "You are trying to deceive me." John then said to Alice, "Alice, I take thee here as my wife, and I give you my faith to marry you and no other but you." Alice said: "I take thee here, John, as my husband and to this I pledge thee my troth." She then shouted next door, "It's as sure as if it were sealed."[21] They then proceeded to have sexual relations noisily throughout the night. Both witnesses say that they do not know John; one of them quite frankly says that she would not recognize him if she ran into him in the street, but both are willing to swear that it was John, both because Alice told them and because everyone (apparently including John) agreed that Alice's child is also his. John's mother, it is said, prevented the solemnization of the marriage.

On the strength of this questionable testimony, Richard Burgh, as special commissary of the commissary general, rendered sentence for Alice. John appealed to the commissary general and raised an exception of absence. Four young men (now ages 23, 22, 22, and 20) say that they decided to go fishing with John that day but changed their minds and went to John's house, staying up half the night drinking and fooling around (*ludentes*, *iocantes*, *et bibentes*). John's father eventually threw them out, but by that time John had his shoes and socks off and was ready for bed. The father locked the door behind them. The next morning they saw him at mass. They also testify that the two buildings in the Remyngtons' complex are far enough apart that no one could hear through the walls. The buildings have stone foundations up to a man's height, and the beds in the two chambers are 15 feet apart.

Alice's witnesses in replication are five respectable-looking men and women of middle age. Two are the godparents of Alice's child, who testify that the child's other godmother is John's mother. All testify that the Kyddes recognize the child as John's and that John and his parents support the child. The Remyngtons, husband and wife, both testify. They explain that Alice's original witnesses were women whom they had known for some time, who used to come to stay with them when they lived in Kirkby Overblow (the parish within which Sicklinghall is located). They cannot testify that the women were there that night because both of them were away, Roger Remyngton in Harfleur and Alice Remyngton apparently in the service of Nicholas Middleton, knight. Alice was like a servant

[19] *Walker c Kydde* (1418–19), CP.F.79.
[20] Listed T&C no. 293.
[21] *Id.*, T&C no. 294.

to them (*quasi serviens*), and she had the governance of the house while they were away. All five witnesses are quite clear about the arrangement of the complex of their buildings, Roger particularly so. Roger brought to court a cord and rod that he used to measure the distance between the buildings, about eight feet. The foundations are stone, but only about a foot in height. The rest is wattle and daub. The heads of the beds adjoin the adjacent walls, and so one in the bed of one building could hear someone in the bed of the other building if they spoke in a loud voice. On the basis of this testimony, Richard Arnall, the commissary general, confirms Burgh's judgment for Alice.

In many ways this case resembles *Thomson c Wylson*, with the genders reversed. I don't believe that Alice's witnesses heard the exchange of marital consent through the walls any more than I believe that Robert Thomson's witnesses heard a similar exchange when they were hiding in the thorn bushes. Also, neither set of witnesses to the defendant's absence inspires confidence. In the case of *Thomson c Wylson*, I suggested that it was not the strength of the witnesses to absence but the weakness of the witnesses to the principal case that led to the judgment for Marjorie. Why does an equally weak case for the plaintiff not lead to the same result here?

The answer may well be that Alice is obviously a woman wronged. She has a child and no husband, and there is no reason why the father of her child cannot marry her. Two seemingly respectable women are willing to put their souls on the line in support of the proposition that John did marry her,[22] and his defense fails spectacularly. John's alibi witnesses are no more convincing than such witnesses had been for centuries, and their attempt to demonstrate that her witnesses could not have heard what they said they heard fails in the face of a graphic demonstration by respectable people that they could have.

That does not mean that they did. If the women were in the other building, and they may have been, I suspect that all they heard was John and Alice having sexual intercourse. The rest they probably learned from Alice.

This is the earliest case in this group. Richard Arnall was later to decide the *Pulayn* case against the plaintiff, and from then on, fifteenth-century judges consistently decide for a defendant who raises a credible, even if barely credible, claim of absence. None of the unsuccessful plaintiffs, however, puts in a claim to have been a woman wronged as powerful as that of Alice. Agnes Brignall comes close, but she is not responsible for an illegitimate child; she has her own house, and if we can judge from the age of her sister, she was old enough to know what she was doing when she repeatedly had intercourse with John Herford. Then, too, in many of the cases that defendants win, there are more than hints that the defendant is of higher station or wealthier than the plaintiff, although that defense is raised specifically in only one case.

In the case in which the defense is raised, it does seem to have some validity. Alice Roger seems to have been running an inn in Adwalton.[23] She also owns

[22] John's attempt to impugn their characters does not succeed.

[23] Disc. and lit. T&C no. 295.

a hayfield and has two male and two female servants to help her with the haying. Nothing would suggest that William Wikeley was of similar status. His pleadings emphasize how much he gave Alice by way of gifts before the alleged marriage, allegations that his own witnesses do not completely support.[24]

For the rest we have to go on hints. Nicholas Danby's witnesses seem to be trying to emphasize what an important person he is. He is described as a chandler of York. Margaret Barley, the plaintiff in the case, lives in another man's house. She may have been a servant, though she is not so described. John Herford, as we have seen, has what seems to be a relative who is a monk of St Mary's York, and his witnesses are trying to impress us with the guest list at the dinner at the Lion in Pontefract. Agnes Brignall, though she has her own house, seems to be a cut below. Robert Wylson, Marjorie's father, has three servants and local men waiting for him to come home from a big wedding feast in a neighboring parish so that they may do business with him. There are no indications of the status of Robert Thomson. In all of these cases, the judge may have suspected that the plaintiff was trying to improve his or her status by marrying up.

In one three-party case in the fifteenth century, the defense of absence fails. Early in 1431, John Thorp of (South) Stainley sued Agnes Shilbotill of Scarborough, claiming a *de presenti* informal contract of marriage.[25] He introduced five witnesses, two to an exchange of present consent in the house of one Northeby in Kingston upon Hull on 1 January 1431, and two others to an exchange of present consent in the house of one Menthorp in Scarborough on 29 November 1430. The fifth speaks of events about two weeks before Christmas. It is unclear whether he is describing the 29 November or 1 January event (and is confused about the dates) or whether he is describing yet a third exchange. It is probably the latter. Whichever is the case, his testimony is thereafter ignored.

Over the course of the spring of 1431, Agnes introduced 20 witnesses to her absence from both events, the depositions of 12 of which have survived. The testimony with regard to the events on 1 January is particularly problematical. The witnesses say that at the time about which the previous witnesses testified, Agnes was not in the parlor of Northeby's house; rather she was in the hall, drinking with the other guests. Those about her absence on 29 November have a better story: Agnes was not in Menthorp's house that day but someplace else in Scarborough.[26]

We know from the judgment in the case that John filed a replication to these exceptions. Testimony may have been taken on this replication, but if it was, it has not survived. Sentence was not rendered until 12 May 1432, when Robert Alne as special commissary of Roger Esyngwald, the commissary general, found for John, and Agnes appealed to the Apostolic See.

[24] Disc. T&C no. 296.
[25] *Thorp and Sereby c Shilbotill* (1431–4), CP.F.113, 324.
[26] Lit. T&C no. 297.

In April of 1433, the court issued a letter patent saying that the appeal to Rome had failed for non-prosecution and sent a copy to John. In May of the same year, Richard Sereby, late of Scarborough (Agnes is now also so described), filed a proposition against the process in the previous case on the grounds that John's witnesses had lied and that he and Agnes had contracted marriage and solemnized it. He introduced five witnesses to his exchange of present consent with Agnes in his house in Scarborough in June of 1430.

John intervened in the case. (So far as we can tell, Agnes did not defend this case.) He introduced nine witnesses to support the proposition that all of Richard's witnesses were out of the diocese when they said that they were in Scarborough; they were in Lincoln, in Barton on Humber, in Carlisle diocese. Richard replicated against John's exception witnesses and introduced 10 witnesses attacking those of John. One of the witnesses had the rector go through the tithe books where they discovered that a witness who said he lived in a particular town did not. Another was said to be a relative of John's.

On 4 November 1434, Roger Esyngwald as special commissary of the official rendered judgment against Richard. Both Richard and Agnes appealed to the Apostolic See, and *apostoli* were granted. Nothing more survives of the case at York.

Shilbotill is not a common name, and it is probable that Agnes was related to John Shilbotill, a York proctor who practiced for a brief period in the early 1400s.[27] She is almost certainly connected with Robert Shilbotill, senior, whose will was probated in 1409 and who also came from Scarborough.[28] She does not seem, however, to have been the daughter of either man, because she is described in the case as the daughter of William Northeby,[29] one of the few facts given in the case that we have no reason to disbelieve. The fact that she is called Shilbotill throughout the case, rather than by her father's surname, suggests that her connection, whatever it was, with the Shilbotills was socially more important than that with the Northebys. It is possible that she was the widow of one of the Shilbotills, perhaps even of John or of his son, though she is never so called. In the depositions about her alleged marriage on 1 January 1431, she is said to be wearing black, an odd color for a medieval woman to be wearing to a party unless she were a widow. Her probable relationship to the proctor also suggests that the York court and its personnel might have been sympathetic to her case. There is some evidence of this. The documentation in the case is elaborate. The depositions of the 20 witnesses whom she produces in the first instance could well have been transcribed at 'cut rates'. Ultimately, however, the court is unable to decide for her at first instance, and matters go

27 He disappears before 1410. Dasef, *Lawyers*, 90. Dasef was not able to develop a biography of Shilbotill, though he mentions him in *id.* passim.

28 See *Carthorp and Shilbotill c Bautre* (1415–17), CP.F.69.

29 Perhaps the man, or a relative of the man, in whose house the New Year's party was held in Kingston in 1431.

from bad to worse. Her initial appeal to the Apostolic See goes nowhere. This could well have been because she did not have the money to pursue it. (The alternative, that William Driffield, her proctor, simply neglected to pursue it, is possible, but if he had failed in this regard, one suspects that Agnes would have hired another proctor for the second instance.)[30]

The court was obviously skeptical of Richard's entire case. It has all the hallmarks of an afterthought, designed to defeat Thorp's claim after the first appeal to Rome failed. I must confess, however, some skepticism about Thorp's claim as well. The two men, one of whom was Thorp's father's servant, hanging around in the door of the parlor do not make very powerful witnesses to the supposed marriage on 1 January, and while there is less on its face to warrant skepticism about the earlier claim (29 November), the fact that Thorp thought it necessary to make up what he claims about 1 January casts doubts on what he claims about 29 November. It is striking how in all this documentation, Agnes's voice is simply not heard. We must puzzle why the court did not question Agnes about the whole affair. Some well-put questions in the manner of those we will see shortly that the court put to Agnes Kichyn might have clarified the matter and certainly could not have made it any more confused.[31] As it is, at the distance of almost six hundred years, we may question whether justice was done, and we may hope that this time the appeal to the Apostolic See got off the ground.

What needs to be explained, however, is why the York court behaved as it did in this case. If we discount Richard Sereby's story entirely, as we may be entitled to do, what distinguishes this case from the others that plaintiffs lost in the same period when faced with exceptions of absence? It may be the cumulative effect of John Thorp's stories, coupled with the fact that there is no indication that he was of lower status than Agnes. The cumulative effect of John's initial witnesses is that something was going on between Agnes and him around Advent and Christmastime in 1430. They were probably together in Menthorp's house in Scarborough on 29 November. They certainly were at the party in Kingston on 1 January. Something probably happened a couple of weeks before Christmas, though only one witness testifies to it. What distinguishes this case, then, from the ones that plaintiffs lost is that we have evidence of a continuous relationship over a period of more than a month. For some reason, Agnes changed her mind. By February, she was determined not to marry John, but by that time she may have said too much. The court was not going to upset more than a century of plaintiff-friendly judgments in her case.[32]

Another way of testing whether there is really a difference between the two centuries with regard to two-party cases is to ask what fourteenth-century cases might have come out differently if the court in that century had behaved more like the court in the fifteenth century. *Merton c Midelton* certainly might have

[30] Disc. T&C no. 298.

[31] See text following n. 52.

[32] Disc. T&C no. 299.

come out differently.[33] While we had our usual doubts about the exception of absence in that case, the testimony about the *de futuro* contract was weak, and one of the witnesses to the contract dramatically reversed her testimony in the court of York. We can be less sure about the two other two-party cases with judgments for plaintiffs in which the exception of absence is raised.[34] In both cases, we lack the depositions on the exception of absence. In one case, the plaintiff tells a powerful story of a woman wronged, but the fifteenth-century court might have focused more on the ambiguity of the exchange of future consent that preceded the intercourse that led to the birth of a child.[35] (We should recall, however, that the one fifteenth-century two-party case in which the exception of absence does not prevail is a story of a woman wronged.)[36] In the other case, the plaintiff introduced reasonably convincing witnesses to the defendant's presence at a time quite close to the contract, a feature that is not present in any of our fifteenth-century cases, with the possible exception of the *Shilbotill* case, and in *Shilbotill*, too, the exception of absence fails.[37]

A Slight Tilt in the Direction of Defendants?

We deal here with four cases that are not covered in previous or subsequent discussions. They are all fifteenth-century marriage-enforcement actions that resulted in judgments for defendants. The question that we ask about them is whether they collectively or individually provide any evidence that the fifteenth-century court was slightly more favorable to defendants than it had been in the fourteenth.

Berwick c Frankiss is the least amenable to such an inference.[38] In a marriage-enforcement action brought by Thomas Berwick *alias* Taverner of Pontefract against Agnes Frankiss of the same, the plaintiff introduces two witnesses who describe matrimonial negotiations between Thomas's father and Agnes's. John Taverner, Thomas's father, agreed to give to Thomas and Agnes and the heirs of their bodies lawfully begotten his entire tenement in the town of Pontefract where he lived; Agnes's parents agreed to give them £10. Then the couple exchanged *de presenti* consent. Clearly, Thomas's witnesses already know what the defense is going to be, for one says that the couple exchanged consent "purely and freely and without any compulsion or coercion whatsoever so far as the witness in any way knew or perceived."[39]

It is this last point that Agnes's nine witnesses seek to refute. They all agree that Agnes's parents forced her to consent, and a number of them testify that they beat her with a stick (*baculus*) in order to get her to consent. After this

33 Ch 2, at nn. 8–10.
34 Listed T&C no. 300.
35 *Waller c Kyrkeby* (n. 34).
36 *Walker c Kydde* (n. 19).
37 *Tailour c Beek* (n. 34); on *Carthorp and Shilbotill c Bautre*, see n. 32.
38 *Berwick c Frankiss* (1441–2), CP.F.223.
39 *Id.*, T&C no. 301.

testimony, it is not surprising that Robert Dobbes, the commissary general, renders judgment for Agnes.

It is hard to imagine that the fourteenth-century court would not have decided this case the same way. It is true that there is one case in the fourteenth century decided for the plaintiff where the defendant's great-uncle is said to have threatened to throw the defendant down a well if she did not consent, but the witnesses in that case are at pains to point out that the threat was not credible, because others were present who would have seen to it that the threat was not carried out.[40] Here, if we believe the witnesses, we have more than threats of physical force; we have the force itself.[41]

All that survives in *Joan Kurkeby of York c William Holme of Cawood* is the sentence for the defendant.[42] From it we learn that Joan had produced only one witness who was not even examined. The fact that the court was unwilling to examine the singular witness may indicate some lack of sympathy with Joan's case. ("Joan, you need two witnesses; we're not going to bother to examine your first witness until we can be sure that you have another.") But it hardly indicates a departure from fourteenth-century practice. The two-witness requirement was well established in the fourteenth century, and none of the judgments for plaintiffs in the fourteenth century is based on the testimony of one witness alone.

In *Wakfeld c Fox*, there were more than two witnesses, but they did not testify to the same event.[43] The depositions have been in print for some time and may briefly be summarized here:[44] Christina de Knaresburgh testifies that Thomas Fox brought Isabella de Wakfeld to him almost four years previously to have her work as an apprentice seamstress. She questioned them about their relationship, and, rather coyly, they said that they were engaged to be married.[45] She also testifies that the couple regularly had intercourse around this time, "as she believes." Another witness was present at the confession, but Christina knew only her Christian name, and she does not appear. Joan Bever testifies that at approximately the same time of which Christina spoke, Isabella and Thomas appeared at her house asking for lodging. Her husband said that he would not give it to them unless they exchanged words of present consent in his presence, and they did. They stayed in her house for six days, lying in the same bed naked. Joan is required to repeat her testimony. She confirms what she previously said and adds that what she had said is a matter of *publica fama* in York and particularly in the parishes from which she and Christina came. A third witness says that at approximately the same time, though he is the most vague about the date, he was present with one John Ward in the chambers of the dean of Christianity of York when Thomas and Isabella were cited before

[40] *Thomeson c Belamy* (Ch 4, at n. 48).

[41] Lit. T&C no. 302.

[42] *Kurkeby c Holme* (c. 1420), CP.F.32/12 recto (i)

[43] *Wakfeld c Fox* (1402), CP.F.22.

[44] Helmholz, *Marriage Litigation*, 228–9.

[45] *Ibid.*, T&C no. 303.

the dean for fornication. They confessed the fornication but said that they were engaged to be married (*ad matrimonium contrahendum affidati*). Because of this, the dean gave them a lighter penance. John Ward also testifies, but all that he remembers is that the dean told him that two people whose names he cannot remember were affianced.

On the basis of this testimony, Robert de Ascheburn, the commissary general, rendered sentence for Thomas. Isabella appealed to the official, but no result on appeal is recorded.

The case has been used to illustrate the legal rule that there must be two witnesses to the same event.[46] That some canonists announce such a rule is undeniable,[47] but the law about what made a 'full proof' was complicated. Suffice it to say here that at least in some circumstances, some authors would allow a 'half-full' proof (such as that provided by one unimpeachable witness) to be converted into a full proof by other *indicia*, such as circumstantial evidence or solid evidence of *publica fama*.[48] This is not to say that Ascheburn's judgment was wrong, but that it might have gone the other way. Indeed, there is evidence that Ascheburn was thinking along these lines, because he ordered the repetition of Joan Bever's testimony, a repetition that added what could have been the crucial element of *publica fama*.

We may have some sympathy for Isabella. An apprentice seamstress was fairly far down on the social ladder, and she may have lacked both the resources and the clout to put on a more convincing case. It probably would have taken very little more to change the result in this case. Thinking along these lines, however, might lead us to question whether Ascheburn may not have done the right thing, totally apart from the rules about what made up a full proof. Christina was Isabella's mistress; she may be still. She tells a charming story, but she can't even remember the surname of the other woman who is supposed to have been there. Joan Bever has every reason to testify to what she said; otherwise, she and her husband would be running a house for assignations between the young people of York. The story she tells is basically a story of what her husband did, but where is her husband? There is no suggestion that he is dead or out of the province; why did he not come with her to testify? The same questions may be raised about the events that are supposed to have taken place before the dean of Christianity. We can have little doubt that deans did mitigate penances for couples who said they were affianced, but did this dean do it for this couple? John Ward, who is supposed to have been there, cannot remember a thing about it.[49]

Kichyn c Thomson provides the clearest indication of a slight tilt in favor of defendants in the fifteenth century.[50] In February of 1411, Agnes Kichyn of

[46] *Id.*, 228.
[47] *Id.* at n. 31 has a quotation from Hostiensis that is squarely on point.
[48] Disc. and lit. T&C no. 304.
[49] Disc. T&C no. 305.
[50] *Kichyn c Thomson* (1411–12), CP.F.42.

Redmire sued William Thomson of the same before the commissary general of the official of the archdeacon of Richmond. William conceded that he had had intercourse with Agnes but denied that he had contracted with her. Two witnesses, one of them Agnes's brother, testify that a year ago in a field in Redmire, they heard Agnes and William contract. The first witness says that Alice said "I will have thee," and William said "I will espouse thee and take thee to wife." The brother says that both of them said "I will have thee." The first witness is recalled and asked again about just what was said. This time he gives his testimony in English and settles on "I will wede the."[51]

At this point William appealed to the court of York. The grounds of the appeal are a bit unclear. They seem to include both that the judge should not have reexamined the witnesses and that he should not take *desponsare* to mean the same thing as *habere*.[52] The Richmond judge declared the appeal frivolous and set the case down for sentencing. William was contumacious, and the judge found for Agnes. William then entered his appeal in the court of York, alleging for his grounds that the Richmond judge refused to allow his appeal before sentencing and rendered an unjust sentence.

The record in the court of York consists of judicial examinations of both Agnes and William, and a sentence by Richard Arnall for William, reversing the Richmond judgment. Agnes gives the most circumstantial account that we have of the events in the field. Her brother said to William, "The reason for my coming here is to find out how it stands between thee and Agnes my sister, and whether you have contracted marriage with each other." Agnes then said, "William, you know well that on various occasions when you urged me on to have intercourse, you promised that if I would allow you to know me carnally, you would take me as your wife." William said, "I confess this well, and whatever I promised you before this time, I will perform with a good heart."[53] That is all he said. After that they had intercourse many times. William, whose examination is much shorter, once more confesses that he had intercourse with Agnes and denies having contracted with her.

Each of the formulae that the parties are alleged to have used raises legal problems.[54] "I will have thee (*volo habere te*)," as we have seen, was normally taken as words of the present tense, although there was an argument that it should be regarded as words of the future tense. If that is what the parties said, however, it should make no difference in this case because intercourse was conceded (though it is not entirely clear that subsequent intercourse was conceded). "I will espouse thee (*volo desponsare te*)" has the same problem as *volo habere te* (should the expression of will be taken as implying a present will or a future intention?), with the additional problem that it suggests that an

[51] *Ibid.*, T&C no. 306.

[52] The quotation in Helmholz, *Marriage Litigation*, 39 and n. 51, would seem to have been drawn from this aborted appeal.

[53] CP.F.42, T&C no. 307.

[54] See Helmholz, *Marriage Litigation*, at 38–9.

espousal, even one of the future tense, has not yet taken place. There is even more ambiguity in the Middle English "I will wede the." Does it refer to a future wedding in the modern sense? Or does it refer to an intention or promise to make a pledge sometime in the future, that is, not a contract but a promise to contract?[55] It is possible, then, to understand these words as not constituting future consent to marry, and hence the subsequent intercourse did not create a marriage. "I will do what I promised before" raises the obvious question of what was promised before. There were no witnesses to the previous promise, but William confessed the promise, at least according to Agnes, and what he confessed is hard not to take as a seduction with a promise of marriage.

We should remember, however, that William was denying that he contracted at all. He did so once in his *litis contestatio* in Richmond; he did so again under oath before Arnall. On Agnes's side, we have three, possibly four, versions of what was said, only one of which is clearly sufficient to constitute marital consent. If we incline toward Agnes, as the commissary general of Richmond clearly did, one can certainly see how one could decide in her favor. Totally apart from the legal issues that each of these phrases raises, however, one can certainly see how Arnall came out the other way. Agnes did not have a full canonical proof of any of the statements. Her brother is a suspect witness because of the relationship. The independent witness did not testify to the same words, and Agnes, when questioned, had yet a third version of what was said.[56] When we couple these facts with the decided impression given by the *processus* from Richmond that the lower court judge was being high-handed, the result at York is quite understandable.

It is, however, a quite different result from that in *Merton c Midelton*. In that case, too, there was evidence of high-handedness in the lower court, and the proof of what the parties had said was none too clear. In that case, however, the fourteenth-century court decided for the plaintiff; the fifteenth-century court, faced with a similar case, did not.

Force

Fourteen cases in the fifteenth century raise a defense of force to a marriage-enforcement action or seek a dissolution of one on the grounds of force (Table 3.3). Most of them tell stories and have results indistinguishable from those in the fourteenth century;[57] three tell quite different stories and will be dealt with in the next section. Two tell a story with which we should be familiar from the fourteenth century but which have quite different results.

In 1443, Christine widow of Robert Haryngton, knight, of Bishophill, York, sued her husband Thomas Sayvell, knight, of Thornhill, York, for divorce on the ground that her marriage had been forced.[58] Six witnesses testify to the solemn

55 Disc. T&C no. 308.
56 Disc. T&C no. 309.
57 E.g., *Berwick c Frankiss* (at nn. 38–41).
58 *Haryngton c Sayvell* (1443), CP.F.263.

marriage between the couple, celebrated in the church of St Mary, Bishopthorpe, by the vicar of Silkstone. They also testify that Christine was weeping at the time and that she married Thomas because she feared her former husband's brother, Thomas Haryngton of Hornby, and that she slept with Sayvell only two nights, in her shift, and did not have intercourse with him. Five further witnesses, led by Thomas Haryngton, are examined on commission by the archdeacon of Richmond.[59] Thomas testifies that he threatened to deprive Christine of her dower lands if she did not marry Sayvell. He had power over the lands, he said, because his brother had left no charters to testify to them. The other witnesses confirm the story. There is no record of any defense by Sayvell, and considering the rapidity with which the case proceeded, it is unlikely that he put one in. Richard Langton, as special commissary of the commissary general, rendered sentence for Christine less than three months after she had put in her libel.[60]

From the point of view of the common law, the background of this case is relatively easy to decipher. Thomas Haryngton was almost certainly his brother's heir. As such, he was obliged to assign Christine her dower. His threat was, therefore, legally an empty one. Thomas had the obligation whether there were charters or not, and Christine could have brought an action for dower *unde nihil habet* against him if he did not assign her "reasonable dower."[61] But the threat may not have been an idle one in the real world. Christine might not have known what a strong case she had; process in the central royal courts where the action would have had to be brought was expensive and slow, and Westminster was a long way from Yorkshire. Hence, I have no doubt that the threats, which everyone, including Thomas, concedes took place, could have led Christine to marry a man whom she would not otherwise have married.

From the point of view of the canon law and of the practice of the York court, the case is considerably more troubling. Although the law itself had some ambiguities, the standard usually proposed (derived from a decretal of Alexander III) was "the fear that could turn a constant woman." This was normally taken to mean that there had to be physical force, or at least threats of it. All of the fourteenth-century cases in which force was successfully alleged (and, indeed, all of the fifteenth-century cases except this one and one other to be discussed right after this one) involve physical force or threats of it, and many seem to require a quite high degree of physical force or real credibility of the threat.[62] The one possible exception in the fourteenth century is probably best seen as a case involving nonage, rather than force.[63]

Now it must be confessed that in most of the other cases, the defense or claim of force was quite vigorously resisted, and most do not involve parties of as high a social status as this one,[64] but annulments were not normally given

[59] Thomas Kempe, BDiv, ref. T&C no. 310.
[60] The libel is dated 3 May, the sentence 23 July.
[61] Lit. T&C no. 311.
[62] Listed and disc. T&C no. 312.
[63] *Aungier c Malcake* (Ch 4, n. 235).
[64] Ref. and disc. T&C no. 313.

just because the parties wanted them, and not everyone who called himself a knight or a lady got what he or she wanted. There are two factors that might explain why the court seems so lenient in this case. First, the marriage was not consummated. We may be skeptical, but the witnesses firmly support this proposition. There was a respectable body of canonic literature that held that an unconsummated *de presenti* marriage could be dissolved; it was not indissoluble in the eyes of God. The law of the church was that the only ground for such a dissolution was the entry of one of the parties into religion, but this was human law. We have also seen that in the beginning of the fifteenth century, the popes, quite quietly, began to issue dispensations in such cases.[65] That this was happening was not widely known until later in the century, but the personnel of the York court could have known that it was happening. If they did, it might account for the court's quite relaxed attitude toward granting the divorce in this case.

Second, if we focus, once more, on the fact that the marriage was not consummated, it is at least possible that there is a fact in this case that does not appear in the record. Perhaps the marriage was not consummated because Sayvell could not consummate it; he was impotent. This would have given Christine an unimpeachable ground for divorce, but bringing such a case would have been embarrassing for Sayvell. We have already seen how one fourteenth-century knight used force to try to prevent his wife from raising such a claim (which was almost certainly valid), and the 'inspection by matrons' that we see in other such cases could hardly have been pleasant for men far below the social status of a knight.[66] If this situation were known to the court, that might explain why the parties were allowed to proceed to obtain a divorce on grounds legally more dubious but socially far less embarrassing.

Thirty years later, the court may have been prepared to go further. Witnesses for Margaret daughter of Stephen Dalling of Easingwold, who is defending a matrimonial enforcement action brought against her by William son of Robert Smyth of the same,[67] testify that her father told her "thou shall never have penyworth of goodes of myne and thou shall have goddis malisoun and mynn" if she did not marry Robert. They also say that she had dissented from the arrangement before the contract and that they had never seen the couple "speaking amicably or favorably as husband and wife" since the time of the contract.[68] They do not testify about any physical force or threats of it. It is perhaps significant that Margaret alleges that the couple never had intercourse and that William does not deny this allegation, much less introduce testimony to counter it.

On the basis of these two cases it has been argued that a credible threat of loss of inheritance, absent physical force, could, under some circumstances, lead to

[65] See Ch 1, at n. 6.

[66] *Paynell c Cantilupe* (Ch 4, n. 240); cf. *Lambhird c Sundirson* (Ch 4, n. 241).

[67] *Smyth c Dalling* (1484–5), CP.F.268.

[68] Lit. T&C no. 314.

the invalidation of a marriage on the ground of force.[69] Without denying the truth of that statement, it might perhaps be better to say that in the fifteenth century, the York court was willing to dissolve an unconsummated present-consent marriage where it seems clear that the only reason why the woman consented was that she feared the loss of money that she reasonably expected or to which she was entitled. It is probably also important that in both cases, the woman consented only once and was known to have dissented both before and immediately thereafter. It probably also helped in the development of this practice that the first case in which we know that it happened may have been a case in which there was another diriment impediment, although it was one that would have been awkward to prove.

NEW STORY-PATTERNS

Abduction

There are four cases in the fifteenth-century cause papers in which a woman alleges that she has been abducted. There are none in the fourteenth century, although the circumstances described by the witnesses in one case may indicate that something like an abduction lay behind it.[70]

We begin with the case where the facts seem the clearest (and even here they are not really clear).[71] In 1414, Thomas Peron of Crayke sued Alice Newby of Skipton on Swale, alleging that they had contracted marriage. The case was heard by summary procedure. We know that Alice put in a *factum contrarium* that she was forced to consent, and Thomas replied that no force was applied. Only one set of depositions survives, and that may have been all there were, because the witnesses testify both to the contract and to the question of force.

They tell quite a story. According to the testimony, Thomas Peron, his two brothers, and 11 other men,[72] descended on the fields of Skipton on Swale on horseback in the beginning of August a year earlier and picked up Alice who was haying in the fields with her mother and brothers. They carried her off to the wood and park of Crayke, where they encountered William de Berkesworth, donzel, who was accompanied by 12 men, also on horseback. Thomas and William's group agreed to leave the park because it was a part of the domain of John, the king's brother.[73] They rode into the fields of Crayke, where William said to Alice: "Alice, what are you doing here? Do you want to have Thomas Peron as your husband?" She answered, "If it is my parents' will."[74] William questioned her again, at least according to some versions of the story,

[69] Helmholz, *Marriage Litigation*, 94.

[70] *Whitheved c Crescy* (Ch 4, n. 51).

[71] *Peron c Newby* (1414–15), CP.F.68.

[72] Details T&C no. 315.

[73] This would be Henry V's brother John, shortly to become duke of Bedford and earl of Richmond.

[74] CP.F.68, T&C no. 316.

insisting that she say yes or no, unconditionally. He also swore that as he would be answerable on judgment day, no one wanted to do her any harm. Alice then said, "By my faith, I want to have this Thomas as my husband, not requiring or having the consent of my parents or anyone else."[75] Then, William told her to take Thomas's hand. (They were both on horseback, she on the back of Thomas's brother's horse.) William once more gave her an opportunity to back out, and once more she declared her will. She and Thomas then exchanged words of present consent.

What happened after that is a bit unclear. Thomas's brother testifies that William insisted that he bring Alice back to Topcliffe because of the capture in the king's brother's jurisdiction, but William promised to hand her over there to Thomas, who is described as her husband, and his party. As they were riding off, Alice (now apparently on the back of William's horse) cried out that William was going to bring her back to her relatives. She asked Thomas's brother to take her to Crayke to his parents' house. In the end, however, she rode off with William, who immediately delivered her to her parents, who kept her from Thomas ever since.

This story is told by three witnesses, all of whom were members of Thomas's party. Different witnesses provide different details. According to two of them, the abduction had been arranged by Alice and Thomas, making use of a go-between, whom one witness calls Emma. Another is particularly clear that William broke his promise when he took Alice away. Yet another says that Alice was crying when the party swooped down and picked her up, but as soon as she was out of sight of her relatives, she ceased to cry. Still another, however, makes the potentially damaging concession that when she contracted, Alice was "in the power and governance" of Thomas and his party.[76]

William Berkesworth also testifies. His deposition is damaged in places, including at the critical spot where he testifies as to whether Alice's consent was ultimately conditional on that of her parents. His testimony is less detailed and, perhaps understandably, he says less about his own role in shaping the exchange of consent between Alice and Thomas, and his own subsequent perfidy. What he does say, however, generally confirms what the members of Thomas's party had said.

Richard Burgh, special commissary of the commissary general, Richard Arnall, rendered judgment for Alice. Thomas appealed to the audience of the commissary general, who once more delegated the case to a special commissary, John Selawe, inceptor in canon law, who affirmed Burgh's decision, approximately a year after the depositions were taken. Thomas appealed again to the audience of the commissary general, and here the documentation ceases.

A few things may be said about this case with a reasonable amount of certainty. In the first place, if anything like what the witnesses described happened, Thomas Peron, and probably his friends, could have been prosecuted for rape

[75] *Ibid.*, T&C no. 317.

[76] *Ibid.*, T&C no. 318.

before the king's justices by Alice's parents (or by indictment). What they did was a felony under the 'statute of Rapes' of 1382,[77] and for these purposes, Alice's consent was irrelevant, so long as her parents did not consent, which they clearly did not. Secondly, it seems to have been the rule in the central royal courts that a deed made or an obligation incurred while the grantor or obligor was 'imprisoned' by the grantee or obligee was void. The word 'imprisoned' seems to have been taken broadly and might well include Alice's circumstances in this case.[78]

We are dealing here with the canon law, however, and not the common law. In addition to the general rules about force and fear, as previously outlined, the canon law had a set of specific rules that dealt with *raptus*, a term that can mean forcible rape in the modern sense but also abduction and, at least in some circumstances, abduction that was consented to by the person abducted but not by her parents. Out of a confused body of law from the past, some statements of which suggested that *raptus* created a diriment impediment to marriage, Gratian had created what seems to us to be a reasonable compromise. The *rapta* could validly marry her *raptor*, but only after he had released her and she and her father consented to the marriage.[79] Decretals both of Lucius and Innocent made it clear that it was the choice of the woman and not of her father that was the relevant choice.[80] They did not make clear whether the *rapta* had to be released before she could validly consent, and the standard canonical commentaries are also unclear on the point, but one might argue that that piece of Gratian's resolution was still in effect.[81]

If we assume that the testimony we have is all the testimony that there was, this is not an easy case. Under the general law on force and fear, it is not clear that a sufficient amount of force was applied to Alice to invalidate her consent. William's presence, and the fact that Thomas and his friends were following his directions, might have led the court to hold that she did not at that point have a reasonable fear that serious harm would come to her if she did not consent. (And, of course, we have to discount entirely the testimony that the abduction had been arranged by Thomas and Alice.) If we have recourse to the law on *raptus*, however, we can see a line that the court might have taken, even if we take the testimony as valid: A woman who is abducted must be released by her abductors before she can validly consent to marriage.

As in the case of Agnes Shilbotill, we have to wonder why the court did not, so far as we can tell, question Alice. Perhaps it did, and perhaps she told a quite different story. The record we have before us, however, suggests that the court was more concerned about Alice's parents than it was about Alice. It also

[77] 5 Ric. 2, stat. 1, c. 6; see Post, "Sir Thomas West and the Statute of Rapes."

[78] See Donahue, in *Year Books 6 Richard II*, introd. 99, and sources cited in n. 93.

[79] Ref. T&C no. 319.

[80] X 5.17.6 (Lucius III, *Cum causam*); X 5.17.7 (Innocent III, *Accedens*). See also Köstler, *Väterliche Ehebewilligung*, 132–6, and sources cited.

[81] Ref. and disc. T&C no. 320.

suggests that the commissary general, Richard Arnall, was reluctant to come to a final decision about the matter. He delegated the case twice, knowing full well that it was the practice of the court to allow appeals from special commissaries to the judge who had commissioned them. Even if he had rendered a decision, another appeal to the official would have been possible.

Thomas seems to have abandoned the case after the second adverse judgment. It is possible, however, that the case was compromised. Thomas did not bring his case until almost a year after the events occurred. If Alice's parents were simply refusing to speak to him, we would suspect that he would have sued sooner. Perhaps negotiations were going on, and the issue was not whether but how much.

One must imagine that the court was relieved to see the last of Thomas. The gap between the secular law and the canon law on this topic was wide indeed. The canonists note this gap (referring to Roman law, not English common law) and are insistent that the canon law prevails.[82] If the court had ultimately held for Thomas, which is to say, if it ultimately held that Thomas and Alice were of one mind on the topic and only parental opposition stood in the way, the potential for conflict with the secular authorities would have been great. To hold that a valid marriage could be formed in the course of a potentially capital felony would be strange indeed.

The only other abduction case in which a judgment is recorded is a competitor case.[83] The documentation is complicated, and not all of it has survived, but enough has that we can reconstruct the course of the litigation with reasonable certainty. At the end of July in 1410, both John de Thornton, citizen and merchant of York, and John Dale (no place of residence given) sued Agnes widow of Hugh Grantham of York,[84] each claiming that she had married him. Agnes confessed Thornton's suit, and it rapidly became apparent that they had contracted a *de presenti* marriage in the arbor of the garden of John Laxton's house in the parish of St Michael le Belfrey in York on the preceding 19 July. There are six solid witnesses to this marriage, and no one thereafter challenges it. Agnes had also precontracted marriage with Dale on 3 July; that, too, is undenied. The question is whether she was forced to do so.

Agnes was a brewer and a tavern-keeper; she was probably about 60. Thornton is described as a bailiff of York and one of the 24 *seniores* of the city; he was probably in his 40s. Dale is variously described as being 24 or 30; he was a *famulus* of William Ferriby, the master of St Leonard's hospital.

Agnes's story emerges from a remarkable set of positions and articles (with answers by Dale) and from the testimony of a number of witnesses.[85] On 3 July,

[82] E.g., X 5.17.7 v° *Accedens* (Venice, 1572), p. 1014b–1015a.

[83] *Thornton and Dale c Grantham* (1410–11), CP.F.38.

[84] Agnes may have been the widow of the York apparitor of the same name (personal communication from David Dasef).

[85] Details T&C no. 321.

Agnes set out with Thomas, her son, and Alice, her servant, for Acomb to eat with William Ferriby at his grange there. For a long time, Alice had supplied William and his *familia* with beer, but the main reason for this particular visit was that Dale had told her that if she dined with William the next day, she might get a benefice that was in William's gift for her son (who is described in some of the depositions as a deacon). On the king's highway en route to Acomb, the party was met by Dale and two accomplices, one of them the forester of Healaugh Park. They seized Agnes and threw her like a sack athwart one of their horses and offered violence to Alice and Thomas, warning them not to follow. They took Agnes to the forester's lodge in Healaugh Park, where they threatened her with physical injury and said that they would take her deep into Knaresborough Forest if she did not exchange matrimonial words with Dale. Dale also threatened to rape her. Eventually, after trying to resist, she gave in and said the matrimonial words. After one of the accomplices went to the grange to ask William's advice, they then took Agnes to the village of Healaugh and made her repeat the vows before bystanders.

Meanwhile, Alice and Thomas were off getting help. Alice had tried first at the grange, and when William had been unhelpful, she returned to York and aroused several of Agnes's neighbors. Thomas got a horse and some recruits near where the abduction had taken place. They all (or at least the York party) caught up with Agnes in Healaugh, apparently after Agnes had confessed her vows before witnesses. She had been flattering her captors in an attempt to get free. They must have thought she was reconciled to the marriage, because after she informally confessed it to her friends, Dale let her go. Immediately she went to the grange, renounced the vows, and upbraided William. Then, when she got back to York, she gathered more witnesses and renounced again. Witnesses testify that during the whole day, she was trembling too much to get a glass to her lips, and so drank nothing. She seems to have stayed in her house for about another fortnight, but after the contract with Thornton, she moved in with William Pomfret, Thornton's business partner in the parish of All Saints' Pavement.

Dale's version of the story can be derived from his answers to the positions and articles.[86] According to him, Agnes went out riding with him that day. She contracted voluntarily and confessed voluntarily, and there is at least a suggestion that she voluntarily had intercourse with him. The only surviving depositions on behalf of Dale are those of his witnesses to his exceptions against the witnesses of Agnes and Thornton. From Dale's point of view, these witnesses could not have been worse. Yes, they say, Thomas and Alice are Agnes's son and servant, respectively, but they are sound and independent people. Alice is not Agnes's apprentice or of servile status. She was the barmaid in Alice's tavern and also sold beer on her behalf outside the pub. Agnes did indeed move in with Pomfret after her marriage to Thornton, although she continued to return to

[86] Disc. T&C no. 322.

her house to finish up her business. (Dale had accused Agnes's witnesses of lying when they said that she had moved in July.) The testimony in the case closes with more depositions about Agnes's activities between July and October, apparently designed to show that Agnes had genuinely moved and was not evading the process server in Dale's case. (The depositions contain some telling detail about how one went about closing up a brewing business in early fifteenth-century York.)

Summary procedure does help. Despite all this activity, the cases were ready for judgment less than year after they were filed. On July 9, Richard Arnall rendered sentence for Thornton and Agnes and against Dale. Dale appealed to the Apostolic See, and *apostoli* were granted.

This last fact indicates that Arnall did not regard the appeal as frivolous. Since the documentation that we have in the case is overwhelmingly on Agnes's side, we must try to reconstruct what can be said for Dale's case. In the first place, other than Agnes's say-so, there are no witnesses to the threats of force that were applied to her in the forester's lodge. She obviously told her story to her friends and neighbors when she got back, and she was able to generate *publica fama* that this had happened to her. The testimony about her trembling hand is telling. She was clearly very upset, but that could have been because she had just done something really stupid, like exchanging words of consent with a man 30 years her junior and, perhaps, having sexual intercourse with him. Secondly, there are the events in Healaugh. If Agnes really had been captured by Dale and his companions, why did she not ask the villagers of Healaugh to free her as soon as she got there, rather than confessing to having done something that she now says she did under duress?

While we do not know what Dale's witnesses said, we do know who they were. One of them was the vicar of Healaugh; another was a man from Healaugh. These men probably testified to the confession at Healaugh and may have said that Agnes did not look like a woman who'd just been carried around on a horse like a sack of potatoes and forced to consent under threats of rape. Another is a man from Wighill, where the forester's lodge is said to have been. It is possible that he was the forester, or that he saw the party riding along the road with no evidence of distress.

If we look at the weaknesses in the case as Agnes and Thornton presented it, and speculate just a bit about what may have been said on the other side, the case becomes a lot closer than it looked at first blush. Hence, two bits of testimony become crucial: Alice's and Thomas's that Agnes was abducted, and that of the neighbors that she renounced the arrangement as soon as she got back to York and was among friends. Hence, too, the testimony about the reliability of Alice and Thomas given by Dale's own witnesses becomes crucial and truly devastating to his case. We need not believe all the details about the violence; all we need believe is that Agnes was taken away against her will by a group of men on horseback.[87] The law about abduction, as previously outlined, was not a law that was developed for women of Agnes's age or station, but it

[87] Disc. T&C no. 323.

could be applied to her. The consent given by a *rapta* is not valid while she is in the power of her *raptor*. She must consent after she has been released and returned to friends. That, most emphatically, Agnes did not do.[88]

The other two abduction cases tell us less, but they tell us something. Probably early in 1477, Alice Townley defended a marriage-enforcement action by Roger Talbot on the grounds both of force and consanguinity and probably counterclaimed for divorce.[89] All that survives from the case are the depositions of six witnesses on Alice's behalf, whose testimony was taken between March and May of 1477. If we put the testimony of the witnesses together, they tell a chilling story. Sometime in Epiphany week the previous year,[90] Roger had come to Alice by night and had taken her away by force. There are no witnesses to this event, and the testimony about it is obviously dependent on the story that Alice herself subsequently told. Perhaps the next day, perhaps a couple of days later, Roger and his men took her to a 'barkhouse'[91] near the banks of the Ribble and also near Roger's manor of Salesbury.[92] There they threatened to drown her in the river or strangle her with a towel if she did not consent to marry to Roger, but she refused. A week or so later (probably 20 January), Roger and a party of his followers woke up the chaplain of Stidd first thing in the morning and asked him to solemnize a marriage between Roger and Alice, who was with them. The chaplain refused to do this because the couple were "within the degrees." So, a friar who was accompanying the party performed the ceremony. At first Alice refused,[93] but she eventually consented when Roger pulled out his dagger and threatened to stab her.

Shortly thereafter, Alice's first cousin attempted to go see her in the manor of Salesbury but was told that none of her relatives would be allowed access to her. Sometime in the autumn (the dating is particularly expansive here), Alice appeared in the house of Agnes Hoghton in Pendleton, saying that she had escaped from Roger and asking to be taken to the manor of Sir John Pudsay in Bolton.[94] She showed her cousins wounds that she said had been inflicted on her by Roger. Two or three of her cousins did as she asked and subsequently brought her to York.

Testimony about the consanguinity is more straightforward. There seems to be little doubt that Alice and Roger were second cousins once removed.

This last is important. There is much in this story about which one might be skeptical. The witnesses who testify in March to Alice's escape are her cousins. All the rest of the story they know by hearsay, almost certainly hearsay from

[88] Did the archbishop bring criminal proceedings against Ferriby? He certainly should have.

[89] *Talbot c Townley* (1477), CP.F.257, disc. T&C no. 324.

[90] Disc. T&C no. 325.

[91] A house for storing tanners' bark. OED, s.v. *bark*, *tan-house*.

[92] This area was at this time within the deanery of Amound, archdeaconry of Richmond, in York diocese.

[93] Saying: "Trewly to dy prefere, I will never consent to you for we er over mere sybbe." Helmholz, *Marriage Litigation*, 79 n. 16.

[94] Details T&C no. 326.

Alice. The witnesses who testify to the events in the barkhouse and to the unusual wedding in the chapel of Stidd do not appear until May. They are two young men, in their early 20s, who have trouble getting the details straight.[95] Our usual skepticism about such witnesses might lead us to discard their testimony entirely. It seems particularly hard to believe that these young men just happened to be near the barkhouse and at the chapel of Stidd 10 days later, both at the crucial moments. The strength of Alice's case on the consanguinity issue, however, might lead us to be less skeptical. Although we lack Roger's version of the story, it looks as if she had solid grounds to resist his suit, totally apart from the issue of force. I am inclined to believe that something quite grim happened to Alice at the hands of Roger during the first months of 1476, and that like many victims of violence before and since, her healing process required that as much of the story as possible be told on a public record. We can be less sure whether the force was applied in order to get Alice to marry Roger or whether it began only after she had married him. Only in the former case would it have been relevant in an action for a divorce *a vinculo*, though both would be relevant in an action for restoration of conjugal rights.

The last case tells us less. In 1472, William Oddy of Givendale brought a two-party action to enforce a *de presenti* marriage against Esota Donwell of Kirkby Overblow.[96] Esota defends the case on the ground of force. The surviving depositions do not support this claim (they may not be the depositions of Esota's witnesses but of William's),[97] but the witnesses say enough to suggest that something strange is going on. One witness describes arriving at Esota's house with a group of men including William. Finding Esota upstairs, he called to her: "Come down, Esota, for surely you will go with us." She came down before the arrival of her brother, took up her outer garments and put them on, and went out with them. A female servant of Esota's said to the witness, "Allas, John, what mene ye that ye er of consell to take away our deme?" He replied, "I lat you with that it is for her wele."[98]

Richard Redehode of Mulwith (parish of Ripon) says that a group of men on horseback, including William, but also including two men who are described as blood relatives (*consanguinei*) of Esota, arrived at his house one day in the autumn and asked for a place near the fire to warm Esota and the baby that she was carrying with her. The witness complied, and then they asked him if Esota could stay there for a couple of days. For the two days following, the two relatives of Esota and two women, one the wife of a local *armiger*, negotiated a marriage between Esota and William in the witness's house. On the following Sunday, they all went to a close in Givendale (also parish of Ripon), where a man with the same surname as the *armiger* conducted the marriage ceremony.[99]

[95] Details T&C no. 327.
[96] *Oddy c Donwell* (1472), CP.F.250.
[97] Disc. T&C no. 328.
[98] Transcription in Helmholz, *Marriage Litigation*, 90 n. 56.
[99] Lit. T&C no. 329.

One can imagine how a story of force could have been constructed out of this narrative. Esota's claim may well have been that she had been abducted by the riding party and that she was not free to leave the house in Mulwith. Richard, of course, would have had to be complicitous in all of this, but if so, that would account for his otherwise hard-to-explain willingness to allow Esota to stay in his house for several days while her relatives and the women representing William were conducting marriage negotiations. Of course, we also have to believe that the relatives themselves were part of the conspiracy. What makes the charge of force at least vaguely plausible is that after the negotiations were all over, the parties, rather than going out to find a priest, chose instead to celebrate the marriage in a close with men strongly associated with Givendale and with no one from Kirkby Overblow mentioned. No judgment is recorded.

I cannot fit the baby into this narrative. It could have been William's child, though that is no place stated. What is striking about this case is that a woman who appears to be a single mother is strongly resisting marriage. There would seem to be no other case in the cause papers where a woman in Esota's situation defends a marriage-enforcement action.

Unusual Defenses

In 1418, John Frothyngham, parish clerk of St Helen on the Walls, York, sued Matilda Bedale of the same parish, alleging that they had formed a marriage by sexual intercourse following an abjuration *sub pena nubendi*. The case is unusual for a number of reasons. First, it is the only case in the medieval cause papers where a man brings an action to enforce a marriage formed by intercourse following an abjuration *sub pena nubendi*. Second, the case is passed among various York institutions in a way that, if not unique, is certainly not common. Third, the woman defends the case on the ground that she was drunk when the intercourse took place.[100]

The abjuration took place before the dean of Christianity of York, but the marriage-enforcement action seems to have been brought as a matter of first instance in the consistory court. Richard Arnall, the commissary general, had to be out of York on the day assigned for the hearing of the case, and he commissioned Richard Burgh to take his place. (Burgh frequently served as Arnall's special commissary.) Neither John nor Matilda seemed to have been pleased with having Richard as judge, but he finally persuaded them to proceed with the case.

Richard questions both of them under oath. John describes a standard-form abjuration before the dean of Christianity and alleges that he had had sexual intercourse with Matilda shortly thereafter, on which occasion Matilda was sober. This is the first hint that we get of what her defense is going to be. Matilda's version of the abjuration is different from John's. She says that she abjured under the form "if I have intercourse with you hereafter, I marry you if

[100] *Frothyngham c Bedale* (1418), CP.F.78.

I ever marry any man."[101] She also says that she cannot remember subsequently having intercourse with John because she was drunk. Richard then takes testimony from both the dean and his clerk. The dean remembers the abjuration, though he cannot recall when it took place, but he says that it was in the standard form. He also says that subsequently, Matilda appeared before him and confessed to having intercourse with John, but that she said she was drunk at the time. The clerk is even less helpful. He knows that Matilda and John did penance for fornication, but he does not recall any abjuration. Matilda subsequently confessed fornication again (and received a penance for it), but the clerk, at least in parts of the document that are legible, says nothing about the claim of drunkenness.[102]

Matilda asks that a proctor and an advocate be assigned to her. This suggests that she is claiming poverty, though the dean of Christianity's clerk testified that she had commuted one of her penances for a money payment, from which we might infer that she was not destitute. She gets her proctor; she may have gotten an advocate, though one of the advocates of the court apparently refused to take the case because he thought it "unjust."[103] The proctor immediately asks Burgh to recuse himself, and when he refuses, he appeals to the audience of the archbishop. This is itself an unusual move. The normal appeal route was from a special commissary to the commissary general and then to the official. Perhaps this is necessitated by the interlocutory nature of the appeal or by the unusual nature of the defense.

The appeal was allowed and a *processus* was made up (its survival is the reason why we know so much about the procedural maneuverings in this case).[104] If, however, the purpose of the appeal was to get the case heard before a higher-level court, it failed. The archbishop redelegated the case to the commissary general, who rendered sentence for John, and Matilda appealed to the Apostolic See.

We are not impressed with Matilda's case. It seems highly unlikely that the dean would have allowed her to abjure in the unusual form that she alleges, and the dean's own testimony here must be taken as probably the more accurate. Also, if the dean is to be believed, Matilda had already conceded that she subsequently had intercourse with John (and the clerk confirms this). She should not now be heard to say that she does not remember whether she did. That, however, leaves the drunkenness defense, one that is legally quite interesting.[105] The institution of abjuration *sub pena nubendi*, already a problematical one, as we have seen, was legally dependent on the notion that when the couple had

[101] T&C no. 330.

[102] Disc. T&C no. 331.

[103] Text and disc. T&C no. 332.

[104] The *processus* that we have was probably made up for the subsequent appeal to the Apostolic See because it continues beyond the appeal.

[105] Lit. T&C no. 333.

intercourse, they willed to marry. Even that is not completely clear, because a couple could make a conditional marriage dependent on a condition that was out of their control: "I marry you, if your father pays me £100." It seems more likely, however, that the institution was thought of as being dependent on the same argument that made a marriage by an exchange of future consent plus intercourse (by having intercourse, the argument went, the couple turned future consent into present) or that made a conditional marriage an unconditional one by intercourse (by having intercourse, the argument went, the couple had waived the condition). It is hard to imagine, for example, that if John had disguised himself, and Matilda had intercourse with him thinking she was having intercourse with another man, a valid marriage would have been formed.

How much the court was aware of these arguments we do not know. One of the annoying features of the York records is that the legal arguments of the advocates were made orally and not recorded. Matilda does not seem to have presented any evidence of her drunkenness, and John denied it. Arnall's judgment may have been predicated on the proposition that however interesting the legal issues that Matilda raised, she failed to prove an essential element necessary to get to those issues. The fact that the case was appealed to the Apostolic See, that *apostoli* were granted, and, it would seem, a *processus* made up for the appeal suggest that these arguments may have been raised in a higher court.[106]

But what is going on at York? I have already said that we may doubt that Matilda was destitute. The steps that she takes to appeal to the Apostolic See also suggest that this expensive proceeding was not out of the question for her. If that is right, then her request for an assignment of a proctor and an advocate was not grounded on her poverty but on the fact that she could not persuade any of the personnel of the court to take her case unless they were assigned. Frothyngham, the parish clerk of a local church, was the type of man whom the court personnel would have known socially. It is possible that Matilda thought, perhaps justifiably, that the court and its personnel were biased against her. In the case of Richard Burgh, we will suggest in the next subsection a reason why Matilda might have been particularly mistrustful of him.[107] If she thought that the men of the court were out to get her for Frothyngham, that may mean that there was something about her that was worth it for Frothyngham to get. That, in turn, confirms our earlier suggestion that she may have been quite well-off. Unfortunately for her, her behavior put her in a position where her only defense involved a considerable stretch of the law, a stretch that a court, possibly biased against her anyway, was not prepared to make.

In January of 1439, Joan Wright of North Street, York, sued John Dunsforth of York, clerk, to enforce a *de presenti* contract of marriage.[108] She has two witnesses to the contract, one of them her mother, who testify that in November,

[106] See n. 104.
[107] See at n. 132.
[108] *Wryght c Dunsforth* (1439), CP.F.181.

five years previously, in the parlor of her parents' house, John said to her "Here I take thee Johannet to my wedded wife, thee for to take afore all other for to life, and thare to plight I thee my trouth."[109] Joan replied in similar language.

I have listed this case as one defended on the ground of the impediment of orders, the only such case in the medieval York cause papers. In fact, there is little evidence that the case was defended at all. Joan filed her libel on 15 January; her witnesses were examined on 19 January; on 4 February, her proctor filed with the court a letter patent in which Richard Arnall, who, in his capacity as vicar general of the archbishop, declared that John was ordained a subdeacon on 20 September 1438. The sentence is undated, but it seems to have followed shortly thereafter. Robert Dobbes, now the commissary general, ordered John to solemnize his marriage with Joan, "notwithstanding the fact that he had rashly taken the order of subdeacon."[110]

We might regard this case as administrative. John had indeed "rashly taken the order of subdeacon," but that was a public act. In order to solemnize his marriage with Joan, something that he apparently wanted to do or was at least willing to do, they both needed a court order, supported by a public record that established the fact that he had married her before he became a subdeacon. This the court provided them in short order.

On balance, however, I am inclined to think that there may be more to this case than that. There is no testimony about intercourse. If John and Joan had presently consented but had not had intercourse, John, if he had wanted to, could have espoused the religious life.[111] Joan's pleadings are damaged and not completely legible, but they do contain an interesting allegation: that John took orders without her consent. The implication is that had she consented he might have been able to do so. That proposition is wrong as a matter of law, at least as the law was normally stated,[112] but when we couple the pleading with the fact that there is no allegation or proof of intercourse, the situation becomes more complicated than it at first appears.

Had John chosen to defend the case, there is much that he could have said. One of only two witnesses to the contract more than five years earlier was Joan's mother, and he did not know that she was witnessing it. As the other witness describes it, she was standing in the cellar looking through a window into the parlor. I have previously expressed skepticism about the testimony of purportedly hidden witnesses, and there is no reason not to be skeptical here.

So the question then becomes what happened between 20 September 1438, when John took orders, and 15 January 1439, when Joan filed her libel, for there can be little doubt that by that time the result in the case was a foregone conclusion. In order to suggest an answer to that question, we have to speculate as to the state of the relationship between John and Joan in September. What had

[109] Disc. T&C no. 334.

[110] *Wryght c Dunsforth* (n. 108): *ordine subdiaconatus temere ?suffecto non obstante.*

[111] Disc. T&C no. 335.

[112] Disc. T&C no. 336.

happened between them since that November evening in 1433? There are two broad possibilities. The first is that John had forgotten about the relationship – he had, as we say today, 'moved on' – but Joan had not. When she found out that he had taken orders, she was furious and went to court essentially to get the orders upset.[113] That is possible, but had that been the case, I suspect that John would have defended it more vigorously. The other possibility is that a great deal had gone on between them since that November evening and that John had taken orders on the assumption that a great deal would continue to go on between them. In this expectation, he was surprised. Joan had no desire to be a subdeacon's concubine. Forced to choose between Joan and his orders, John chose Joan. But then the problem became what to do about the orders. They had exchanged consent five years previously, but, in fact, only one of the witnesses had been there. The law insisted on two witnesses. Joan's mother was only too happy to supply the deficiency.

In 1403, Thomas Poleyn of Knaresborough brought what was apparently a marriage-enforcement action against Margaret widow of William de Slyngesby of Knaresborough before the court of the official of the archdeacon of Richmond.[114] Margaret defended on the ground that she had taken a vow of perpetual continence. That she had done so was apparently conceded because the commissary general of Richmond ordered Margaret to solemnize with Thomas and to do penance for having violated her vow. Most of the documents in the case are concerned with an appeal that Margaret took from this judgment to the Apostolic See; on the way she sought the protection (tuition) of the court of York. Because so little of the documentation concerns the substance of the case, we are not in a position to tell whether the judgment of the Richmond court was correct, but it certainly could have been. As we have seen, vows of continence constituted a diriment impediment to marriage only if they were solemn; simple vows constituted an impediment but not a diriment impediment.[115]

Margaret is called a noblewoman (*nobilis mulier*) several times in the documents. While we must allow for some exaggeration in the rhetoric, it is quite possible that her deceased husband held land by knights' service. If he did, his lord had the right to dictate whom his widow would marry. We have considerable evidence that many upper-class widows in the later Middle Ages sought to evade this right. Some bought the right to marry whom they chose; some bought the right not to marry at all.[116] Margaret was probably trying another route to reach the same result. Fearful that she could not resist her lord to his face (particularly if he were the king), she took a vow of continence in the hope that she could then defend a marriage-enforcement action in the church

113 The orders actually would not be upset, but John could not function as a subdeacon if he were married.

114 *Poleyn c Slyngesby* (1404–5), CP.F.13.

115 See Ch 1, at nn. 42–8.

116 See Walker, "Feudal Constraint and Free Consent."

court. If this is what she was trying to do, the law was against her for reasons that had nothing to do with her situation. The insistence that the vow be solemn to constitute a diriment impediment meant that she was unlikely to be able to take it without her lord finding out about it, and, perhaps, preventing it.

Scandal in the Courtroom

Medieval courts were used extensively by their officers. The officers of the three central royal courts in Westminster enjoyed the privilege of suing and being sued exclusively in their own courts and without regard to the normal jurisdictional limits of those courts. It is therefore not at all surprising to find the court officers at York making use of the court, and those connected with court officers making use of the connection. In the fourteenth century, as we have already seen, William Cawod, an advocate of the court who was to become the official in the early fifteenth century, saw to it that his widowed daughter exchanged consent *de presenti* in front of three well-connected churchmen, and then probably arranged for his future son-in-law, Thomas del Garthe, citizen and apothecary of York, to bring a 'strike-suit' in which the competitor for her hand, John de Neuton, esq, was unable to come up with any proof of his claim.[117] Robert Esyngwald, to put it as tactfully as possible, probably benefited from the fact that he shared a surname with both his proctor and the judge in his case.[118] Agnes Shilbotill probably got more help from the court than would someone who was not related to a deceased proctor of the court, although ultimately, the court was not able to find in favor of the man whom she pretty clearly preferred.[119]

Apart from these quite ordinary uses of the court by insiders and uses of insiders by those outside the court, two quite extraordinary cases were heard in the fifteenth century, both matrimonial cases against officers of the court.[120] I will argue that both cases were, so far as we can tell from the record, decided correctly, and that this is a considerable tribute to the integrity of the court. I will also argue that they reveal a decidedly seamy side of the lives of these two officers.

Early in 1414, Agnes Horsley of Ampleforth sued Mr Thomas Cleveland, clerk and advocate of the court of York, to enforce a marriage.[121] Agnes put in a set of positions and articles, to which Thomas gave the usual evasive answers. This was quite standard practice in the court, and Thomas's answers are no more evasive than most and probably less evasive than some. He ultimately admits that he had had intercourse with Agnes, though not on as many occasions as

117 *Garthe and Neuton c Waghen* (Ch 4, at nn. 205–6).
118 *Ingoly c Midelton, Esyngwald and Wright* (Ch 2, at nn. 11–21).
119 See at n. 25–37.
120 Disc. T&C no. 337.
121 *Horsley c Cleveland* (1414), CP.F.63.

she alleges, but he denies that he ever contracted with her. Agnes produces five witnesses, only two of whom testify to the same event, a hermit over 60 years of age, who normally resided near a chapel in Helmsley parish, and another, a woman in her 30s, who says that she is the godmother of Agnes's daughter. They both testify that one night the preceding autumn outside York Minster, Agnes and Thomas exchanged matrimonial words, she saying "I take you," and he saying "I will have you," or "I shall have you," depending on whose version of the story we accept.[122] The singular witnesses all testify to occasions on which Thomas said something that sounded like matrimonial consent, at least consent in the future tense, or on which he indicated that he regarded himself as being married to Agnes. On one occasion, he asked a friend not to let Agnes alienate any of her goods because he wanted to take charge of them as her husband. On another occasion, he said that he would give Agnes the title and honor that all her friends freely gave him, by making her his wife. (Modesty does not seem to have been Thomas's long suit.) On yet another occasion, Agnes said that she was going to visit Thomas's father, who seems to have been living in a monastery, and ask if there were any impediment to their marrying. Thomas is said to have replied that that was not necessary: "This is my faith, I will have you as wife (*volo habere te in uxorem*)." The judge interrogates Thomas about all these occasions. Unfortunately, the record of the interrogation is messy and difficult to read. Thomas clearly knew that he could not confess even to words of the future tense, granted his concession of intercourse. Ultimately, he confesses that when Agnes was sad or unwell, he would try to cheer her up by saying things like "If I will not have you, I will have no other woman as wife," or "If I should happen to take any woman as wife, I will take you."[123]

Thomas files exceptions against Agnes's witnesses, particularly against the two who testify to the events outside the Minster. The hermit, he says, is a thief, the woman an adulteress who was told what to testify. The former exception gets to the stage of positions and articles. The charge of theft is based on the fact that the hermit was said to collect oblations at a chapel in Helmsley that ought to belong to the parish church. No testimony is introduced on the exceptions against the witnesses.

At the end of July, Richard Arnall renders sentence for Agnes against Thomas. Thomas appeals to the Apostolic See and is granted *apostoli*.

Thomas was clearly trying to wriggle out of an awkward situation. The words to which he ultimately confessed could be regarded as matrimonial words, though the weight of opinion seemed to be against it.[124] His argument was a clever one, for he was making use of the fact that he knew the law, and that Arnall knew that he knew it. His effort, then, was to blunt the testimony of seemingly respectable people who might have thought that what he said were

[122] *Ibid.*, T&C no. 338.
[123] *Ibid.*, T&C no. 339.
[124] Ch 4, at n. 165.

matrimonial words but which in fact were not. Equally clearly, Arnall did not buy the argument. We may wonder whether the witnesses to the exchange outside the Minster got it quite right, but the cumulative effect of the half-proofs about the other occasions was substantial. This man had been saying a great deal to this woman, and then he had intercourse with her.[125] She was a woman wronged, and the practice of this court was to decide in favor of such people. Thomas Cleveland, advocate of the court of York, was not entitled to special treatment in this regard.

Seven years later, Katherine Carvour of York sued Mr Richard Burgh, clerk, with basically the same claim as Agnes's.[126] (Indeed, Agnes's success may have prompted her to bring the case.) We have seen Mr Richard Burgh several times before. He was an advocate of the court of York in the early years of the fifteenth century, and he served on numerous occasions as special commissary of the commissary general. By the time Katherine sued him, he had become official of the court of Durham.

Katherine puts in a standard set of matrimonial positions and articles, to which Richard replies with the standard "He does not believe [it]," or "He does not believe [it], as it is put." On the article that there was *publica vox et fama* to this effect, he puts in the somewhat less standard "He does not believe [it], except by the false confession of the woman."[127] Katherine then puts in another set of positions, which are not standard: (1) When Katherine's parents had worked out another marriage for her, Richard promised to marry her, and for this reason she refused the other man. (2) Richard negotiated with Katherine's brother about a marriage. (3) Katherine's brother paid Richard to solemnize the marriage. (4) Richard sent Katherine love letters.[128] To all of these Richard replies: "He does not believe [it]," except for the last which he denies as it is put.

Katherine's four witnesses are not very convincing. Two testify to *publica fama* that Richard had had intercourse with Katherine and had children by her. Three, including her brother, who was a priest and vicar choral of York, describe the matrimonial negotiations. It seems reasonably clear that £40 had been fixed as the figure. It also seems clear that Richard was reluctant to accept the offer because he would have to give up his benefice if he married. It is not clear that he did accept the offer. In all this vagueness, there is one telling moment. The rector of a moiety of the church of St Helen's on the Walls had dinner with Katherine and Richard in Katherine's house just before Richard went to Durham. Richard said that in a short while he was going to Durham and he would have to wear a cowl and a scapula lined with fur (a reference to the costume of the

[125] Disc. T&C no. 340.

[126] *Carvour c Burgh* (1421), CP.F.129.

[127] *Ibid., non credit nisi ex falsa confessione mulieris.*

[128] *Ibid.*, [*Ricardus Katerine*] *litteras satis placabiles ut vir uxori sue plures affectus maritales* [?*vo*]*ventes destinavit.*

monastic chapter of Durham). Katherine looked sadly at Richard's face, and he responded quickly, "A married man can wear a cowl and a scapula lined with fur."[129]

From these scraps of material, we can reconstruct Katherine's probable argument. She was trying to establish either one of two things. The first alternative was a promise of marriage followed by sexual intercourse. She failed to establish the promise, and she had no evidence, other than *publica fama*, that the intercourse followed after it. Alternatively, she was trying to establish a *de presenti* marriage conditional on her brother's paying the £40. She failed, however, to prove the contract or that the condition was fulfilled. It is not surprising that less than a month after she brings her case, the commissary general decides against her and issues refutatory *apostoli* to her appeal to the Apostolic See.[130]

It seems probable that Katherine was Richard's mistress. That was the *publica fama* in York, and Richard never denied it. Her relatives, particularly her brother the priest, were trying to turn this relationship into a respectable one, but they failed. Perhaps they might have succeeded had Richard not gotten the promotion to Durham. One can hardly form a good impression of Richard. His remarks to Katherine at the dinner, which we have no reason to doubt that he made, were cruel. Ultimately, however, there is no real evidence that he married her, and that was what the court of York was called upon to decide.

Advocates are shadowy figures in the York records. One normally sees them only as witnesses to judgments. Thomas Cleveland does not seem to have been adversely affected by his loss of the case (but maybe he did the right thing and married Agnes).[131] We have already noted that three years before the case against Richard Burgh, Matilda Bedale had a particularly strong objection to having Richard Burgh as her judge.[132] She may have known the *publica vox et fama* about him. It may not be too much to suggest that his promotion to Durham was not the only reason for Richard Burgh's departure from York.

MORE ARRANGED MARRIAGES

The last difference that we notice in the fifteenth-century cases as compared to the fourteenth-century ones is that there is more evidence in the fifteenth century of the involvement of people other than the couple themselves in marital choice. The difference is a subtle one. We have already noted that there are a number of cases in the fourteenth century in which we have evidence of the parents, relatives, or social superiors of the couple being involved in their marriage choices, whether arranging the marriage or supporting or opposing

129 *Ibid.*, T&C no. 341.
130 Probably Roger Esyngwald; Richard Arnall was made official in 1420.
131 See Dasef, *Lawyers*, 85.
132 See at n. 107.

the couple's choice, but that what was striking about the cases in this century was the fact that in so many of them – we estimated that it was more than half – such third parties were no place to be found.[133] This negative evidence must be viewed cautiously. What was legally relevant was whether the parties had consented, and it is quite possible that in some of the cases in which the testimony focuses solely on the consent of the parties, there were, in fact, third parties in the background who were also supporting or opposing or even dictating that consent. It seemed unlikely, however, that all the cases that show no evidence of the choice of people other than the couple themselves had such unrecorded background parties.

The proposition here is that there are fewer such cases in the fifteenth century, and the converse of that proposition is that there are more cases in which third parties are quite obviously in the background. Since there is no evidence that clerks in the fifteenth century were more likely to include matters that were legally irrelevant than were those in the fourteenth century, we conclude that marriages litigated in the fifteenth century were more likely than those in the fourteenth century to involve parties other than the couple themselves. Whether this proposition can be generalized to those marriages that were not litigated is a question best left to the conclusion of this chapter.

The evidence for the basic proposition is both numerical and impressionistic. Neither bit of evidence is overwhelming, but both bits point in the same direction. Perhaps in this case we can say that two *probationes semiplenae* add up to a *probatio plena*.

First, the numerical evidence: I suggested that in the fourteenth century, most of the cases that involved the defenses of force or nonage were also cases in which persons other than the couple were involved in the formation of the alleged marriage. The same is true in the fifteenth century, and the proportion of cases that raise such defenses is approximately the same (17% vs 13%; see Table 3.3).[134] By their very nature, what we called 'type five' cases in the fourteenth century (arranged marriages gone awry) involve persons other than the couple. Of the 36 two-party marriage-enforcement actions in that century,[135] 5 (14%) fell into that category, and an additional 9 (25%) involved parents, relatives, or superiors who were trying to enforce a marriage or break it up.[136] The equivalent figures for the fifteenth century are 13 (21%) and 10 (16%) out of 63.[137]

So far there is no reason to believe that anything very different is happening between the two centuries. If we try to get a total, however, there is some suggestion of a difference, one that we expand upon later in the chapter.[138]

133 See Ch 4, at nn. 54–5.
134 Disc. T&C no. 342.
135 Disc. T&C no. 343.
136 See Ch IV, at nn. 54–5.
137 Listed T&C no. 344.
138 We will have occasion later (Table 5.1) to expand this number for both centuries by adding cases in which outside involvement is likely.

Coding conservatively, and eliminating the duplicates, we identified 14 marriage-enforcement cases in the fourteenth century in which third parties, normally parents or relatives, are definitely involved in arranging, enforcing, or breaking up a marriage. None of the three-party cases had to be included in that category, though we had our suspicions about some of them. If we include three-party cases, the equivalent figure for the fifteenth century is 39. The difference in proportions is not large (fourteenth: 14/86, 16%; fifteenth: 39/129, 30%), though it is statistically significant.[139] What convinces us that we are looking at a somewhat different world is the detail that appears in some of these cases about the matrimonial negotiations.

The case that gives us the most detail is *Elizabeth daughter of John Suthell (Sothell) junior of Lazencroft c Thomas Gascoigne gentleman* (1477).[140] Elizabeth's proctor filed an elaborate set of positions, which Thomas (or his proctor) answered:[141]

> [1] In the first place the said proctor [not previously named][142] poses and intends to prove by way of his proxy that some days before the marriage contract entered into between Thomas Gascoigne, gentleman, and Elizabeth Suthell, natural and legitimate daughter of John Sothell junior of Lasyngcroft, the same John came to Thomas Gascoigne all the way to the town of Cawthorn, desiring him to grant him certain lands and tenements then specified between the same John and Thomas in farm[143] for as many years as he had obtained from the father of Thomas along with the fee that the father had granted him for collecting certain farms. Reply: He [i.e., Thomas] confesses the arrival of John Sothell at the town of Cawthorn and his desire concerning the farm of the lands. His desire, however, for the fee, he denies.
>
> [2] Again he poses that Thomas firmly promised that he would lease and demise in farm to John the same lands and tenements for as many years after his father's death as he [John] had of the grant of the father in the lands and tenements that were then specified by John and also the fee that [the father] had granted to John to be paid after the death of the father as it had been paid annually in his life. Reply: He does not believe [it] as it is posed.
>
> [3] Immediately after the promises and grants, John handed over to Thomas 20 pence by way of earnest money.[144] Reply: He confesses the receipt of 20 pence but he does not believe [what is said] about the promise and grant made by way of earnest.

139 $z = 2.48$, significant at .99.

140 *Suthell c Gascoigne* (1477), CP.F.345.

141 Latin text in App. e5.1, *Elizabeth daughter of John Suthell (Sothell) junior of Lazencroft c Thomas Gascoigne, gentleman* (see T&C no. 387).

142 See T&C 387 n. 1.

143 In the medieval sense, 'lease'.

144 The Latin of this and most of the subsequent positions begins *Item quod* for *Item ponit quod*.

[4] Immediately after the handing over of such earnest, Thomas and John spoke about a marriage to be contracted between Thomas and Elizabeth the daughter of John Sothell. Reply: He does not believe [it] as it is posed.

[5] At that time Thomas asserted that he loved Elizabeth so much that he aspired to be married to her more than to any other woman.[145] Reply: He does not believe [it].

[6] Soon after speaking the last of these words, Thomas and John agreed to meet at the house of Agnes Tonge, widow of Birstal, to have a conference between them about the marriage to be contracted between Thomas and Elizabeth. Reply: He does not believe [it].

[7] On that occasion, John asked Thomas whether he was at that time, as he was previously, of a mind to contract marriage with Elizabeth. Reply: He does not believe [it] as it is posed.

[8] After Thomas had been so questioned, he immediately replied that he wished to contract marriage with Elizabeth and with no other woman. Reply: He does not believe [it].

[9] Again he poses that John immediately after the proffering of these words gave Thomas 20 pence of English money on the condition that Thomas take Elizabeth to wife. Reply: He believes the receipt of the pennies but he does not believe the condition.

[10] Between the feasts of St Martin in Winter [11 November] last past and the purification of the Blessed Mary [2 February] then next following, Thomas, with 'marital affection',[146] frequently [and] continuously had access to the dwelling house of John called 'Lasyngcroft' [Lazencroft in Barwick in Elmet, Yorks, West Riding] spending the night in this house at his pleasure many times. Reply: He believes the access but not the marital affection, and he does not believe that [there was] any [such] overnight [there] during this time.

[11] Alice, the natural and legitimate mother of Elizabeth, during the time of his access addressed Thomas in this way: "Cousin Thomas, my husband has told to me that he made motion unto you for matrimony to be had between you and Elizabeth my daughter and I beseech you plainly tell me how my said daughter pleaseth you in that behalf and whether ye intend to her to your wife or no."[147] Reply: He does not believe [it].

[12] Thomas immediately after the question replied to Alice in this form of words: "I like her well and by the troth in my body I shall wed her if ever I wed any woman." Reply: He does not believe [it].

[145] An awkward but significant phrase: *quod pocius cum ipsa quam cum aliqua alia muliere maritari affectabat.*

[146] *affectione maritali*, a phrase of wide semantic range. See Pederson, *Marriage Disputes* 153–75. Here it could mean 'with a mind toward marriage'.

[147] I have somewhat modernized the spelling of the English quotations of the original but have not 'translated'.

[13] Immediately after proffering the last of these words, Alice gave Thomas 20 pence under the condition that he take Elizabeth to wife. Reply: He believes the gift of the pennies without the condition.

[14] Thomas received the pennies from Alice under this condition willingly. Reply: He believes the receipt without the condition.

[15] A certain day around the feast of the exaltation of the Holy Cross [14 September] last past, Thomas, simply of his own motion and not at the request or asking of John and Alice his wife came to the manor commonly called 'Sothelhall' [Soothill, Yorks, WR], where at that time John Sothall, grandfather of Elizabeth, was staying, with whom Thomas then dined. Reply: He believes [it] as it is posed.

[16] When the dinner was over, John Sothell, grandfather of Elizabeth, proffered the following words to Thomas: "Cousin Thomas, I understand by relation of my son John that he and ye have had said communication for matrimony to be had between you and my cousin his daughter Elizabeth, and if it so please you and her father it shall cost me 100 marks of mine own purse rather or your purpose and pleasure therein be broken." Reply: He believes [it] as it is posed.

[17] To these words Thomas replied as follows: "I trow we shall agree." Reply: He does not believe [it].

[18] Tuesday next before Michaelmas last past [24 September 1476], Thomas came to the house of John father of Elizabeth and there promised to meet John at Wakefield on the Friday next before Michaelmas [27 September], to conclude the marriage contract. In fact, the two met there with other gentlemen, to wit, John Nevill of 'Lewerseth' [Liversedge, Yorks, WR], John Woodroff of 'Wolley' [Woolley, Yorks, WR], [and] Thomas Lacy of 'Caiwaiwell Bothom' [probably Cromwell Bottom, Yorks, WR] with certain other gentlemen, where they promised to meet again on the Thursday next following [3 October] at the manor called 'Sothelhall' finally to conclude that marriage and all things concerning that marriage. Reply: He believes the meeting there, but he does not believe the cause of the meeting as it is posed, and he believes the promise to have a meeting on the Thursday as it is posed.

[19] After this meeting had at Wakefield and the assignment of the Thursday next following (on which day they came together at Sothelhall), John Sothell sent a certain servant of his called Robert Wylson to Thomas to tell Thomas in the name of John that he ought not come unless he wanted to fulfill his promise finally to conclude the marriage. Reply: He does not believe [it].

[20] On the same Thursday Thomas came to Sothelhall and there made promises with John Sothell sr, John Sotelhall his son, with John Woodroof, Thomas Lacy, Henry Rokley of 'Ledes' [Leeds, Yorks, WR], Thomas Popely of 'Wesbery' [?Westby, Yorks, WR] and many other gentlemen who after dinner was over on that day took counsel under a certain oak outside the gates of the manor of Sothelhall where they then

had discourse and dealing with one another concerning a marriage to be contracted between Thomas and Elizabeth. Reply: He believes [it] as it is posed.

[21] When the discourse and dealing were finished, Thomas Gascoigne and John Sothell jr promised, pledging faith in the hands of John Woodroff to stand firmly by the ordinance and arbitration of eight gentlemen concerning the feoffment of Elizabeth and a sum of money to be given to Thomas along with her, to wit, Sir John Pilkyngton kt, John Woodroff, Thomas Lacy, and Sir John Kent vicar of Birstal, on the side of John Sothell jr, and Sir William Stapleton kt, Nicholas Mare gent, Richard Gascoigne and Sir William Waven chaplain, on behalf of Thomas Gascoigne. Reply: He believes that these persons concerning whom it is posed were chosen not about the feoffment but about the marriage to be contracted so that as soon as he had effectively escaped from their hands he would not have further dealings with them alone.[148]

[22] When the promises were completed the gentlemen returned to the manor of Sothelhall to a certain parlor and standing in the south part of the parlor at a 'copburd' they ate upon it a pasty of flour and a capon and then they drank wine there together. Reply: He believes [it] as it is posed.

[23] When these things had been done as previously described, John Sothell, the grandfather of Elizabeth, standing in the same parlor said to Thomas Gascoigne: "Stand near, cousin Thomas." And immediately he said to Elizabeth: "Stand near, cousin Elizabeth." When Thomas and Elizabeth came to him side by side (*pariter*), John the grandfather said to Thomas: "Cousin Thomas, are ye in will to have this gentlewoman Elizabeth to your wife?" To whom Thomas thus replied: "Yea, by the faith of my body, I will." Reply: He does not believe [it] as it is put, but he does believe other words, to wit, John Sothell said: "Thomas Gascoigne may ye find in your heart to have Elizabeth Sothell to your wife?" To whom Thomas: "I may find in my heart to have her with counsel and advice of my friends." And John Sothell asserted to Elizabeth: "Elizabeth may ye find in your heart to have Thomas here to your husband?" And he believes that she said "yes" in a low voice.

[24] Immediately after this response, John Sothell sr said to Elizabeth in this form: "Elizabeth will you have this gentilman Thomas Gascoigne to your husband?" To whom she replied: "Yea, sir." And then John said to her: "if you wilt [*sic*] have him to your husband say by the faith of your body thou wilt have him to your husband." And then she replied: "Yea, by the faith of my body will I." And then John Woodroff said to Thomas Gascoigne: "Take her, sir, and kiss her and I pray God it be in the best time of the year." And he did so, and then they drank together. Reply: He does not believe the words as it is posed, but he believes the kiss.

148 Text is probably corrupt here.

[25] When these things were accomplished, Thomas Gascoigne mounted his horse and rode from the manor of Sothellhall to the place where he intended to spend the night. Someone riding with him delivered to him a silk ribbon sent to him by Elizabeth before this contract was made and finished (as previously described) and which had been offered to him but not received by him, he saying at that time that he did not wish to receive it. But after the contract was finished (as previously described) he received it willingly, saying to the bearer of the ribbon while he was riding: "Yea, now I will take it with a good will and wear it for his [i.e., my] love." Reply: He believes the offering but does not believe the receipt.

[26] These things are true, public, notorious and manifest in the towns and places aforesaid and other surrounding places, and about these things before the present suit was brought, there was and is at work *publica vox et fama*. Reply: He believes about those things that he believes and does not believe about those things he denies.

Despite the wide variations in the spelling of John and Elizabeth's surname and that of John's father, there can be little doubt that the name is 'Soothill', derived from the placename in the West Riding. The manor at which the grandfather lives is in the modern place. All the other placenames that we have been able to identify make sense in this context. Birstall, Wakefield, Liversedge, Leeds, Cromwell Bottom, and Woolley are within a few miles of Soothill.[149]

A number of the third parties who are mentioned in the case are easy to identify. The two knights who were to head the arbitration panel, Sir John Pilkyngton and Sir William Stapleton, appear frequently in the Chancery rolls.[150] John Woodroff of Woolley, who plays a key role in the negotiations and was to serve on the arbitration panel, and John Nevill of Liversedge, who participated in the negotiations at Wakefield, were also quite prominent.[151]

The principal parties are harder to identify. A John Suthill, esq, of Everingham, whose Yorkshire inquisition *post mortem* is dated 15 January 1495, is probably not our John Suthell. His holdings are all in the East Riding (and in Wiltshire and Lincolnshire).[152] Our John Suthell may be the same as the John Sotehill, esq, who on 7 November 1476 gets an exemplification of two fines dealing with the lands in Yorkshire and Nottinghamshire of his wife Elizabeth, the heiress of Sir William Plompton, but it seems equally, if not more likely, that this John is the same John who died in 1494.[153] Our John and the John who died in 1494 may be related. All people named Soothill ultimately derive their name from the West Riding placename.[154] The East Riding Soothills may

149 Disc. T&C no. 346.
150 Ref. T&C no. 347.
151 Ref. T&C no. 348.
152 *CIPM* (*1485–97*), no. 1145, pp. 498–500.
153 *CPR* (*1467–77*), 601.
154 Reaney, *Surnames*.

be a cadet branch of the family, who ultimately fared better than did the senior branch.

Thomas Gascoigne is equally difficult to identify. The surname is fairly common, but with one exception who does not seem to be our Thomas,[155] no Yorkshire Thomas Gascoigne appears on the Chancery rolls for our period. There is, however, a quite prominent Gascoigne family in the West Riding. A William Gascoigne served as justice of the peace in the West Riding in 1472 and 1473, and as commissioner of array in the West Riding in 1470, 1472, and 1473.[156] In none of these entries is he called a knight.[157] After a gap of eight years, a Sir William Gascoigne appears as JP for the West Riding, and he continues to serve through 1485; he also serves on various commissions, always styled as a knight.[158] On 14 July 1480, this William obtains license for himself and his heirs to crenellate his manor of Gawthorpe and to impark 1,200 acres of land, 410 acres of meadow, 260 acres of pasture, and 640 acres of wood in various places, one of which cannot be identified, but all the rest of which lie in the West Riding.[159] This man could be the William Gascoigne who appears eight years previously, having raised his status, perhaps by a fortunate marriage. It is more likely, however, that it is his son (who may well have done the same).

It would make sense if our Thomas were the younger brother of this Sir William. Thomas has lands that he has acquired as the result of his father's death, but this could have been because his father provided for him by a feoffment to the use of his will, while giving his elder brother the lion's share of the inheritance. A marriage between the younger son of a knightly family that seems to be on the make and the daughter (we don't know whether she was an heiress but she may have been) of a gentle family that holds the ancient manor of Soothill but seems to be in somewhat reduced circumstances would be the kind that delighted matchmakers in the Middle Ages and well into the early modern period.

Somehow, however, it seems to have fallen apart. Why, we do not know. We do not even know whether it ultimately did fall apart, because the documentation ceases after depositions are taken on Elizabeth's articles. It is possible that the arbitrators worked something out and that Thomas ultimately did marry Elizabeth. What the positions and their accompanying answers tell us, however (with some help from the depositions), is what everyone agreed had happened and where the disagreements lay.

From the point of view of the law, the key events are those that took place at the second meeting at Soothill (positions 20–4). If Thomas said what Elizabeth's proctor says he said (position 23: "by the faith of my body I will [have this

[155] Disc. T&C no. 349.
[156] *CPR* (*1467–77*), 638 (JP), 190, 349, 408 (commissioner).
[157] Disc. T&C no. 350.
[158] *CPR* (*1476–85*), 580 (JP), 214, 345, 399, 492 (commissions).
[159] Details T&C no. 351.

gentlewoman Elizabeth to my wife]"), and she *mutatis mutandis* said the same thing, then there was at least a contract by words of the future tense between them and, perhaps, *de presenti* consent.[160] Thomas's version of what was said, on the other hand, (*ibid*.: "I may find it in my heart to have her with the advice and counsel of my friends") constitutes, at best, a conditional future contract, and probably does not constitute a contract at all. It is not at all surprising that Elizabeth's witnesses focus on what was said, and it is also not surprising that they support Elizabeth's version of what was said.

The rest of Elizabeth's positions are legally irrelevant, though they clearly were not irrelevant to her proctor. The reason that they were not irrelevant to her proctor, we might suggest, was that if matters had proceeded as the positions describe, then we would be expecting Thomas to have consented, at least by making a binding future contract, by the second time that he came to Soothill. Thomas's answers suggest that his position was that matters had not proceeded that far. This can be seen most clearly in his disagreement about what the arbitrators were to arbitrate. Elizabeth's version is that what they were to arbitrate is what was to be paid by whom for a marriage that was concededly going to take place; Thomas's version is that they were to arbitrate whether a marriage was going to take place.[161]

But Thomas's disagreement with the positions goes further back than that. He denies that he agreed to grant John the leases of the lands that his father had granted John, though he admits that they discussed the matter on the occasion the positions mention.[162] He denies that he took earnest money for the grant of the leases and that he twice took it to contract marriage with Elizabeth. He admits that he had access to Elizabeth but denies that he ever spent the night at Lasyngcroft. He admits that he met with Elizabeth's grandfather, but denies that he said there that he wanted to marry her. He denies that he took the ribbon. In short, his version of the story is that Elizabeth and her kin were proposing the marriage to him, but that he had never responded to the proposals in such a way that he might have been expected to confirm his intentions at the second meeting at Soothill (see, particularly, position 19).

While we cannot tell whether the negotiations went through all the stages described in the positions, we can assume that such stages were expected. The issue of the marriage arises in the context of a lease of lands that John had held from Thomas's father and which now belong to Thomas. In addition to the lease of lands, John is also negotiating for what we would call a commission for collecting certain rents, a commission that John had also received from Thomas's father. John's version of the story is that Thomas at this time promised to lease the lands for the same term as his father had leased them and that he

[160] Disc. T&C no. 352.

[161] It is not at all clear that the determination of whether marital consent was to be given could be handed over to arbitrators.

[162] 'Admit' and 'deny' are a bit strong for *credit* and *non credit* (*ut ponitur*), but probably accurately reflect what he thought.

had granted John the commission. Thomas's position is that the commission was not discussed and that he did not promise to grant the leases on the same terms – an answer that leaves open the possibility that he could have agreed to the lease of the lands under different terms. Following this, according to John, he gave Thomas 20 pence in earnest of the bargain. Thomas admits the receipt of the money but says that it was not in earnest of the bargain.

This is the first of three alleged payments of 20 pence in earnest, the subsequent ones being from John and from Alice in earnest of the contract of marriage. Thomas answers all three positions the same way. I find it hard to believe Thomas here. Twenty pence is not a large enough sum that people of this class would be giving it to each other as anything other than as earnest. Perhaps Thomas was going to argue that it was in earnest of something else, but the fact that he admits he received it, either because his conscience would not allow him to deny it or because it was sufficiently public that he could not deny it, undercuts his argument that there was no agreement at these three points.

The leases and the fee are, of course, legally irrelevant to the question of whether Thomas contracted marriage with Elizabeth, but they are clearly not socially irrelevant. If John was going to be a substantial tenant of Thomas's and was going to perform a function like that of a steward with regard to certain rents, that would make a marriage between John's daughter and Thomas more plausible than if he was not. Thomas may even have seen the land deal and the deal for Elizabeth as being interconnected. If one fails, so does the other. As it is, having denied that there was a land deal, at least having denied that there was a deal in quite the way that John put it, Thomas then proceeds to deny that there was a discussion between them about "a marriage to be contracted between Thomas and Elizabeth," but he is careful to say that he does not believe that there was a discussion in the way that John says there was (position 4: *non credit ut ponitur*). To the position that Thomas said the "he aspired to be married to her more than to any other woman," he simply says that he does not believe it (position 5: *non credit*), which we may take to mean that he does not think that he said this or anything like it.

Thomas's answers to the positions about subsequent exchanges in the negotiations follow a similar pattern. He denies that the meetings proceeded in quite the way that is posed (*non credit ut ponitur*), but whenever he is alleged to have said something that might be taken as contractual words, he denies it outright (*non credit*). Hence, with regard to the discussion in the house of Agnes Tonge (?a matchmaker), he denies that John asked him whether he was, as he was previously, proposing to contract marriage with Elizabeth in quite the way that John describes (position 7: *non credit ut ponitur*), and he flatly denies that he said that he wished to contract marriage with Elizabeth and with no other woman (position 8: *non credit*). He flatly denies (*non credit*) that he exchanged the words described with Elizabeth's mother (positions 11–12), but he admits that he received 20 pence from her, but not as earnest for fulfilling the contract. He admits that he met with Elizabeth's grandfather at Soothill and that the grandfather, in effect, promised him 100 marks if he married Elizabeth (position 16: *credit ut ponitur*), but denies (position 17: *non credit*) that he said "I trow we shall agree."

Elizabeth's proctor is attempting to establish the converse of what Thomas is denying. In his version of the story, the matter was first discussed in the context of the successful negotiations about John's and Thomas's relationship, in which it was agreed that John would have the same relationship with Thomas as he did with Thomas's father. At this point, Thomas asserted that he so loved Elizabeth that "he aspired to be married to her more than to any other woman" (position 5), a phrase that, as we have seen, could be taken as a promise to marry. They next met in the presence of a witness, and a female one at that, where Thomas said "that he wished to contract marriage with Elizabeth and with no other woman" (position 8). After earnest was given, Thomas then had "access" to Lazencroft (and presumably to Elizabeth) and spent the night there (positions 9–10). This last Thomas denied, presumably because he wanted to counter any possible argument that he had sexual intercourse with Elizabeth. It was on one of these occasions that Elizabeth's mother elicited the statement from Thomas, "I like [Elizabeth] well and by the troth in my body I shall wed her if ever I wed any woman" (position 12), the first time that any of his statements can be described as an oath. According to Elizabeth's proctor, the third exchange of earnest took place at this time (positions 13–14), thus making Thomas bound in earnest to both of Elizabeth's parents. There followed the exchange with the grandfather at Soothill (positions 16–17), and then the elaborate series of meetings, first at Lazencroft, then at Wakefield with other 'gentlemen' (both position 18), and finally once again at Soothill where the agreement to arbitrate and the exchange of consent are alleged to have taken place (positions 20–4).

This is the most elaborate description of matrimonial negotiations that I have found in the York records, but other fifteenth-century cases give us glimpses into what seem to be similar exchanges.

If Elizabeth Suthell had, so far as we can tell, virtually nothing to say about the matrimonial negotiations involving her, the same cannot be said of Agnes Ruke.[163] Agnes seems to have been an orphan. Her uncle, a canon of Nostell Priory, is the person who conducts the negotiations for her, and she lives in Thorne where her godfather, Reginald, is the chaplain, but in what is described as her house. Her suitor, both in the matrimonial sense and in the sense of one who ultimately brings suit, is John Porter of Carlton in Snaith, just to the north of Thorne.

John's four witnesses do not tell a completely consistent story. Two young men, ages 30 and 24 respectively, the younger of whom had previously acted as a go-between for John and Agnes, describe events that occurred on a Friday in the previous Lent (we are now in October). One seems to testify that it was Good Friday; the other that it was Friday in mid-Lent. One was present when Agnes and John exchanged vows in the "I take ye here" form; the other was out

163 *Porter c Ruke* (1418–20), CP.F.84.

getting beer when this happened. Both were, however, present when John gave Agnes a pair of gloves. One witness reports that Agnes placed the gloves in her bosom and sighed. John said, "Don't sigh, for this agreement [*pactum*] is one of the best that you have ever made." Agnes replied, "May God so grant."[164] One of the witnesses was also present around the following Pentecost when Agnes had said in reply to John's statement that he wanted to marry her, "I want willingly to have you as my husband, so long you want to marry me and lead (*ducere*) me to my very own house here in the village of Thorne."[165]

The special commissary examined Agnes *ex officio*. She denied that she had ever contracted with John, saying that when he had asked her to marry him on a Friday in Lent, she said that she was a little girl (*infantula*) and wanted to rely on her friends' guidance. She never discussed the matter with John after that, although her uncle and John's father had continued to negotiate. She did admit taking the gloves, though she did not want to do so, because she was not capable of making a counter-gift. She gave the gloves to her uncle and does not know what he did with them.

We might be inclined to believe Agnes were it not for the fact that there are two more witnesses on John's side, both seemingly respectable men of Carlton, ages 40 and 30. The former describes in some detail negotiations during the preceding summer between Agnes's uncle and John's father, Richard, in the latter's house in the presence of the witness, one John Draper of Pontefract, and a couple named Mergrave from Thorne. Richard told the canon that he would give John 20 marks worth of goods to have Agnes as his wife and that John was his (Richard's) heir with respect to a tenement of land in Thorne. The canon said that he was well pleased. Agnes was not there; she was in Snaith at the time, but previously she had come to Carlton and had examined John's *facultates et bona* in his father's house. The other witness confirms these stories and adds that Agnes had said that she was well content.

We probably would not have had all this detail had it not been for the fact that John's case on the basic exchange of matrimonial consent was weak. There was only one witness to the exchange on the Friday in Lent and one to a later statement that also suggests consent. Frequently, as we have noted, the York court required two witnesses to the same event. It is also hard to believe that Agnes contracted as unconditionally on the Friday in Lent as the witness says that she did. Both witnesses mention the necessity of getting the consent of her uncle (which they both allege was obtained). We cannot, however, take Agnes's version of the story at face value either. Two unrelated witnesses saw her in Carlton with John checking out his goods. That she had not spoken to him after that Friday in Lent is hard to believe. It is plausible to imagine that the initial contract in Lent was subject to confirmation by the uncle, but that there was probably some sort of contract. Once the uncle had consented, there remained the question of whether Agnes was happy with the arrangement, and what the unrelated witnesses say suggests that she was. Richard Burgh was

164 *Ibid.*, T&C no. 353.
165 *Ibid.*, T&C no. 354.

certainly stretching the two-witness requirement when he held for John, but one can see why he did so. Agnes appealed to the commissary general, but no result on appeal is recorded, the last document in the case being an inhibition to her not to marry another *pendente lite*.

What is interesting about this case is the elements that it has in common with the *Suthell* case. We are obviously dealing here with people of lower status than those in *Suthell* (20 marks versus 100, to put it crudely). Agnes as an orphan cannot have a father negotiate for her, and the initial steps are taken by the man dealing first through a go-between and then directly with Agnes herself. But the property details must be worked out, and ultimately, it would seem, it is the elders who do it. This is far less formal than the arbitration contemplated in *Suthell*, but the purpose is the same: A marriage is going to take place, unless the property details cannot be worked out. While the details are being worked out, the parties hold themselves to the contract by various tokens. In *Suthell* it is the earnest money; in this case it is the gloves. When the deal falls apart (again for reasons that we cannot tell, but may have to do with the living arrangements that one of the witnesses mentions and that seem to have been made a condition of Agnes's initial consent), the question is whether the parties have said too much to back out now. Richard Burgh thought that they had; we may have our doubts.

In other cases, we can infer that the marriage was, in some sense, arranged because of who was present at the exchange of consent and, sometimes, because of the casual mention of the property arrangements. *Joan daughter of William Webster of Hambleton c Nicholas Tupe of Cawood* is typical.[166] Here, there are three solid witnesses to the exchange of consent, two being a middle-aged butcher and his wife from York. They remember the date, what the parties wore, and what the weather was like. They describe an exchange of present consent in the "I take ye here" form, followed by handfasting and a kiss. That this was probably arranged, or at least done with the full consent of Joan's parents, is clear because it takes place in William's house, in his presence and in that of Joan his wife, their son John (who is not only Joan, the daughter's, brother but also the husband of Nicholas's sister), and one John Moselay of Bubwith, who does not testify but probably came with Nicholas. After the contract, Nicholas asked his brother-in-law to go to the chaplain of Brayton to have the banns proclaimed the following Sunday.

This is more than enough for a case, particularly when there is no defense, and it is not surprising that Roger Esyngwald renders sentence for Joan quite quickly.[167] What is odd, however, is that Joan's proctor thought it necessary to add an unusual article to the standard set of marriage articles: "Nicholas, after these things [the marriage contract], handed over and delivered to Joan a noble of gold as to his wife, which noble Joan received from the said Nicholas as from her husband and had it to her uses and converted it to her will."[168]

166 *Webster c Tupe* (1425–6), CP.F.159.
167 Nicholas appeals, but no result on appeal is recorded.
168 CP.F.159, T&C no. 355.

There is only one witness to this exchange, the brother/brother-in-law John. He testifies that after everyone else had left the room, "Nicholas handed over and delivered to Joan in the sight and notice of this witness a noble, telling the same Joan, who was reluctant to take this noble, in this form of words, 'Joan, I give this noble to you as to my wife, because whatever is mine is yours, and if I live you will have a hundred more'."[169]

Similar details about the property settlements are fairly rare, but we do find them. The witnesses in *Robert Inkersale of Greasbrough in Rotherham c Agnes daughter of William Beleby of Anston* describe negotiations in which the father of the bride ended up by promising to give 25 marks *in maritagium*.[170] In *William Gell of Kirk Hammerton and Thomas Smyth of Wistow c Joan daughter of Roger Serill of Cawood*, William's father agreed to give his son an animal for every animal that Roger gave his daughter as dowry (*pro dote*).[171] In *Berwick c Frankiss*, the force case discussed earlier, Thomas Taverner's father agreed to give Thomas and Agnes Frankiss and the heirs of their bodies lawfully begotten his entire tenement in the town of Pontefract, and Agnes's parents agreed to give the couple £10.[172]

The marriage of Katherine Blayke, servant of John Dene, citizen and merchant of York, and Roger Nebb, servant of Peter Kayn, tailor of York, was clearly entered into with the consent of the masters of both parties and, perhaps, was arranged by them.[173] The witnesses, John Dene and Joan his wife, and Peter Kayn describe events in the house of the former in November two years previously. John asked Roger, "By the faith of your body could you find it in your heart to have this Katherine here present as your wife?"[174] And Roger replied that he could. John asked the same question of Katherine and got the same response. (According to Peter, Katherine's consent was conditional on his and his wife's consent, but both of them consented.) John then asked each of them "Wilt thou (*vis*) have Katherine/Roger as wife/ husband?" and received an affirmative response from both. Then the couple had a drink "in sign of this contract." Two witnesses mention that banns were proclaimed, one specifically saying that this was done "by the common consent of the parties and their chief friends."[175]

Joan Dene also testifies that in the summer prior to this contact, Roger and Katherine had contracted (again the *volo te habere* form) in the house of Alice wife of John Roby, citizen and weaver of York. Alice confirms this testimony.

Legally, the issue in this case is whether the formula *volo te habere* is to be taken as words of the present or of the future tense. That Roger may have

169 *Ibid.*, T&C no. 356.

170 *Inkerslae c Beleby* (1466), CP.F.242.

171 *Gell and Smyth c Serill* (1427–8), CP.F.168; lit. T&C no. 357.

172 See at nn. 38–9. The gift of real property was almost certainly intended as a jointure in lieu of dower.

173 *Garforth and Blayke c Nebb* (1449–50), CP.F.184, 185.

174 *Ibid.*, T&C no. 358.

175 *Ibid.*, T&C no. 359.

been defending on the ground that they constitute, at best, words of the future tense is suggested by the fact that his interrogatories ask whether the parties at the time handfasted (*manus suas dexteras simul plicatas habuerunt* or *manus traxerunt*) and kissed. None of the witnesses can testify to this except for Alice Roby, who says that the couple handfasted and kissed during the exchange in her house. We do not know how the court reacted to this argument. The case quickly becomes involved in a parallel suit against Roger by one Margaret Garforth, and no sentence survives.[176]

A number of other cases show us parents or social superiors playing an active role in marriages. For example, in *Elizabeth Pereson of Cawood c Adam Pryngill of Cawood*, Elizabeth's father is said to have invited the witnesses to come and be present at the marriage contract.[177] Her mother then stands up and calls them to witness, and the father conducts the ceremony. The depositions in *Robert Chew of Eastburn c Agnes daughter of William Cosyn of Eastburn* contain, among other things, a quite elaborate description of the negotiations that led to the couple's marriage.[178]

In addition to those cases in which third parties are mentioned as being involved in the marriage choice of the couple, there are a number of cases where we cannot explain the behavior of the parties unless we assume that they were under considerable pressure to marry. The most dramatic of these cases is *John Thorp mercer of Pontefract and John Kent minstrel c Agnes widow of John Nakirer of York*.[179] The case begins as a routine marriage-formation case brought by Thorp against Agnes. She denies that she married him, and Kent intervenes. Agnes confesses Kent's libel. Thorp's depositions describe, in the standard fashion, a marriage in the house of Robert and Joan Gowsell in Walmgate on Thursday in Easter Week (31 March 1407). Robert and Joan both testify, as does Robert Chesterfield, a mercer of Pontefract. The only hint that we get of anything untoward is that Joan specifically testifies that Agnes was not forced (this is not usually mentioned unless it is an issue), and all three witnesses say that a week after the marriage, John and Agnes confessed it before the chaplain of St Peter le Willows. This, again, is an indication that they knew that something might be wrong.

Something was indeed wrong. Two minstrels testify that the week before the marriage with Thorp, on Holy Thursday, Agnes had married John Kent in the house of Thomas Kerby above Walmgate Bar. The depositions are standard, perhaps a bit less detailed than those for Thorp, but not so skimpy as to raise doubts about the veracity of the witnesses.

Thorp files an exception to the witnesses for Kent in which he alleges that they are "infamous by the infamy of law and fact, and such as cannot testify according to law and are stained by the mark of infamy because they were and

[176] See at n. 189.
[177] *Pereson c Pryngill* (1474), CP.F.354.
[178] *Chew c Cosyn* (1453–4), CP.F.189.
[179] *Thorp and Kent c Nakirer* (1407), CP.F.33.

are public minstrels and public jesters (*ioculatores*) and they exercised and exercise the job (*officium*) of minstrels and jesters for pay and dishonestly."[180] The exception, of course, reflects medieval middle-class prejudices, but we should recall that in Roman law, actors were legally infamous. There is support for this exception in the learning of the medieval *ius commune*.[181] No depositions are taken on this exception, but perhaps none needs to have been taken. Kent's witnesses had admitted that they were minstrels and had even sought to blunt the force of the exception in their depositions. One says that he is retained by the lord Mauley, the other that he spends his time with the king's son John.[182]

The exception did not impress the commissary general. The case having been brought in late April and the witnesses having been heard in late May, the commissary general renders judgment for Kent in early July. An appeal is mentioned, but none seems to have been taken.[183]

No parents or relatives are mentioned in the case, but third parties are clearly in the background. Whether they found out about the marriage to Kent and hastily attempted to put a stop to it by having Agnes marry John Thorp, or whether the marriage to John Thorp was already in the wind and Agnes frustrated their plans by marrying Kent first, we cannot tell.[184] Whoever was putting pressure on Agnes, she apparently could not resist them to their faces. She did go through with the marriage to Thorp and confessed it before the priest, but two weeks later, Thorp took her to court. Granted the facts, and the court's unwillingness to allow the exception against the witnesses, it was just a matter of time, and not very much time at that, before Kent would win. The respectable mercer went back to Pontefract, and Agnes went "off with the raggle-taggle gypsies, O."

The question remains whether we can extrapolate from this spotty evidence in the cases to the society at large. If the fifteenth-century cases suggest that there were more arranged marriages, more marriages in which third parties were involved than was the case in the fourteenth century, can we suggest that the same thing was likely to have been happening in marriages that never went to court? I think that we can, at least as a matter of probabilities. Self-arranged marriages, particularly those involving young people, were probably more likely to end up in the consistory court than those that were arranged by parents or other third parties. The number of such marriages in the fourteenth-century records may well be out of proportion to their actual numbers in the population at large. The fact, however, that the proportion of such marriages to

[180] *Ibid.*, T&C no. 360.

[181] Ref. T&C no. 361.

[182] The king's son John would be John, later duke of Bedford, who was 18 in 1407, a year younger than the witness.

[183] Thorp's proctor protests an appeal but says that he wants to consult with an advocate. That is the last we hear of the case.

[184] Lit. T&C no. 362.

the total number of litigated cases declines in the fifteenth century does suggest that the proportion of such marriages in the overall population, whatever it was, was going down. This argument assumes that the factors that caused a marriage to end up in the consistory court remained constant over the two centuries, but that seems to be a fair assumption.

RURAL VERSUS URBAN CASES

The suggestion that there were more arranged marriages in the fifteenth century than there were in the fourteenth fits quite well with some recent work on the history of the medieval English family. Lawrence Stone posits a shift from open-lineage families in the Middle Ages to restricted patriarchal families in the Renaissance.[185] One need not fully accept Stone's models in order to suggest that greater social control over marriage in the fifteenth century than in the fourteenth is consistent with those models.

What we have found, however, does not fit particularly well with Jeremy Goldberg's suggestion that the most important variable in determining how much control the couple, as opposed to a wider circle, had over marriage choice is whether the couple, or rather the woman, was resident in a rural area or in an urban one.[186] We should remember, to start off with, that nothing in late medieval Yorkshire corresponds to what we would call 'urban' today. Except for York, which may have had as many as twelve thousand people, the largest towns probably had populations considerably less than ten thousand. Then too, the cases show that the division between urban and rural was permeable. William Gell, who is variously described as coming from Kirk Hammerton and Bilton, would probably have to be classed as a resident of a rural area, as would Joan daughter of Roger Serill of Cawood. That animals are to be exchanged as part of their marriage settlement confirms what the location of the places suggests. Their alleged marriage, however, took place in a house in Micklegate in York.[187] Even more problematical is a case like *Ingoly c Midelton, Esyngwald and Wright*.[188] At the time the action was brought, Joan Ingoly and John Midelton lived in Bishopthorpe, and Robert Esyngwald and Ellen Wright lived in Poppleton, both places that would qualify as rural. But John and Joan had been married in St Margaret's Walmgate in York; the witnesses in the case were in service in York at the time of the key events; Robert Esyngwald may have obtained the freedom of the city. Poppleton is about three miles northwest of York, and Bishopthorpe is about three miles south of the city. In the fifteenth century, this is not quite the suburbs of York, but these peoples' lives clearly centered around York.

185 Stone, *Family, Sex and Marriage*, 4–9.
186 See Goldberg, *Women, Work*, particularly at 217–66.
187 See at n. 171; disc. T&C no. 363.
188 *Ingoly c Midelton, Esyngwald and Wright* (Ch 2, at nn. 11–21).

An even more striking example of the porousness of the rural/urban distinction is found in *Garforth and Blayke c Nebb*.[189] Roger Nebb was, at the time of the litigation, a tailor of York and had been a servant of Peter Kayn, also a tailor of York. Katherine was a servant of John Dene, citizen and merchant of York. Roger's marriage to Katherine, I have argued, was arranged by their respective masters. So far we have what seems to be a typically urban case. But Roger's marriage to Margaret Garforth, on the first of January three years previously, was alleged to have happened in a field called "Bouresflatt" in Bracewell, high up in the Pennines, and three of his witnesses to his absence in Marton in Craven (which is close to Bracewell) are named Kayn, all described as "of York," the last of whom, one Peter, turns out to be Roger's first cousin once removed. One of the Kayns says that his parents still live in Marton in Craven; another says that the rector of Marton in Craven is a relative of his. It seems likely that the Kayns had relatively recent origins in Marton in Craven, and that a number of young men of the clan went back there for the Christmas holidays. Curiously, the marriage, if such it was, in the rural area was not arranged, it would seem, whereas that in York was – just the opposite of the pattern that Goldberg posits.

Women who were working independently in urban areas may have been able, as a general matter, to have more say about whom they would marry, but not all of them seem to have exercised this capacity. As we have just seen, the marriage of Katherine servant of John Dene citizen and merchant of York and John servant of Peter Kayn tailor of York seems to have been arranged by their masters.[190] Nor are cases lacking in which rural couples seem to have done the arranging by themselves. We have seen that Agnes Ruke was considerably more involved in arranging her marriage than she was willing to admit. If that is not regarded as a good example because she was an orphan, then consider *John Wistow of Welton c Elena Cowper of Welton*. The couple 'handfasted' (the English word is used a number of times, both in the positions and in the depositions) without her parents' knowledge.[191] When her father found out about it, he said to her, "Thow harlot why hast thow doon' this with Johis Wistow and I know it not? For ther is noe man I like nearre and that thow knowest wille ynoughe."[192] The case was defended on the ground of spiritual affinity (Elena's mother was John's godmother), but the defense collapsed when John produced a papal dispensation.[193]

Perhaps the best evidence for the proposition that country couples could arrange their own marriages comes not from the relatively few cases in which there was obvious parental opposition but from the considerably larger number of cases where such opposition is not mentioned, indeed, where the parents are

189 See at nn. 173–5.
190 *Ibid.*
191 *Wistow c Cowper* (1491), CP.F.280.
192 Disc. T&C no. 364.
193 Lit. T&C no. 365.

no place to be found. *William Northefolk of Millington c Richard Swyer of North Burton and Joan Thornton his wife* is typical.[194] William brought a marriage-and-divorce action against Richard and Joan. Two witnesses, including one who was related to Joan, though he cannot say quite how, testify to an exchange of present consent in an upper room (*orio*) in the house of Thomas, Joan's father's, in Meltonby a year earlier. The witnesses both describe themselves as of 20 years of age. One says he was a servant of another man in Meltonby, while the other says that he was staying with another man in Meltonby. Both agree that William was the servant of Thomas. After exchanging consent, the couple handfasted and kissed. They told no one, other than the two witnesses.

Shortly thereafter, Thomas moved his family to Burton Fleming, which the witnesses describe as 18 miles away (that's about right). It was for this reason that they did not hear about the proposed marriage between Joan and Richard, which they now know took place the following summer. (That is confirmed by two other witnesses who were present at the solemnization.) One of the witnesses also says that he was in Lincolnshire when it happened. Thomas Appilton LLB, special commissary of the commissary general, renders judgment for William, a judgment that is affirmed on appeal by Roger Esyngwald, the commissary general, all within approximately six months of the case's being brought.

It is possible that this is a case like *Ingoly*, a charade in which Joan rids herself of her new husband (for whatever reason) by procuring perjured or exaggerated testimony of her previous exchange with William.[195] The cases are roughly contemporary. Richard's defense is not particularly vigorous. All that his proctor does on appeal is introduce the *acta* from the case before Appilton and argue about them. He does not try, for example, the quite standard device of raising exceptions against the witnesses (one was probably available against John Thornton, who admits that he was a blood relative of Joan's). The fact that he makes a substantive attempt to get the case reversed, however, does suggest that Richard did not consent to the judgment. Further, the excuses of the witnesses for not having objected to the banns seem far more plausible than do the similar excuses offered by the witnesses in *Ingoly*, and William has a far more plausible claim that he was surprised by what happened in Burton Fleming, since he brings the case within a few months after the marriage occurred, rather than years after, as was the case in *Ingoly*.

Since it seems plausible to believe that in this case things happened pretty much as the witnesses say that they did, one must ask why they happened. Here, of course, it is possible that Thomas, like Elena Cowper's father, found out about the marriage between Joan and William and moved the family 18 miles away and married her to another man in an attempt to end her relationship with

194 *Northefolk c Swyer and Thornton* (1433), CP.F.177.
195 Ch 2, at nn. 11–21.

William. In other cases where there is parental opposition, however, we find out about it, and while we must assume that Joan's parents were involved in the marriage to Richard, we have no evidence that they knew anything about her relationship with William.

The witnesses to the marriage with William both say that the couple kept it secret. Perhaps we should believe them. Both the couple and their witnesses were probably in their late teens or very early 20s at the time of the marriage. William was still a servant, though we can well imagine that he hoped to achieve a higher status as he grew older. Joan may have kept her story to herself for a while in the hopes of raising the issue with her family at a more opportune moment, a moment at which William would be well enough established to make him a plausible candidate. If this was the plan, it was frustrated by the move. We do not know whether Joan changed her mind when she met Richard or whether her family swept her into a marriage with him, only that William knew that he had enough to take his case to the consistory of York and get her back.

We return to two basic propositions: First, marriage choice in the later Middle Ages in Yorkshire involved the choice of third parties far more often than it does in our society, and, second, the law as applied in the consistory court focused exclusively on the choice of the parties to the marriage and not on that of third parties. If we read behind the lines in the cases, we see a great deal of variation in what we can estimate was the amount of real freedom the couple (and particularly the women) had in making their marital choices. Age, gender, social class, economic independence (or potential for economic independence), and the personalities of the parties (this last being perhaps the most important and least easy to detect) all played a role. I am prepared to believe that young women were likely to have more economic independence or potential for economic independence in the larger towns, and hence, that the rural/urban distinction played some role in the amount of freedom of choice that urban as opposed to rural young women had. The other factors, however, were at least as important, and in combination they could, and did, overcome this one.

Elizabeth Suthell was from the highest social class that we regularly see in the records; she was female, and probably quite young; her personality, at least so far as we can tell from the record, was passive.[196] The fact that we would probably classify her as 'rural' would have to come quite far down on the list of reasons why she seems to have had nothing to say about her marital choice. Elena Cowper was equally rural; she seems to have come from a slightly lower social class than Elizabeth Suthell, but she was certainly not poor.[197] She may have been a bit older than Elizabeth Suthell, but there is no evidence that she was economically independent. (The friend with whom she stayed after she left her house to escape her parents' wrath was 24.) The depositions tell us that she organized the handfasting that took place in the house of a middle-age couple

[196] At n. 163, and preceding text.
[197] At nn. 191–3.

(both of whom testify). The litigation was probably necessitated by the fact that her husband, John Wistow, could not provide them with a place to live at the time that they handfasted. A year later, however, he sued and had in the meantime gotten the necessary papal dispensation. He won his suit quite quickly, and there was no appeal. The law was on Elena's side, and she and John knew how to use it.

While what I have just said suffices to summarize my disagreement with Goldberg, it fails to do justice to his argument, which is developed over the course of a long book and the core of which, for our purposes, takes up a full 36 pages.[198] It also violates a core principal of this book: Granted the great variety of cases to be found in the cause papers, we must report not only on what could happen but what was normal. Let us, then, look at Goldberg's argument a bit more closely.

There is much in it with which we can agree. Had the whole been argued with the caution that is displayed in the conclusion, we would not have cause to complain.[199] On the basis of the evidence that we have before us (which does not move into the sixteenth century), we cannot confirm that there is a decline in the freedom of choice of women in the late fifteenth and early sixteenth centuries, but we cannot deny it either.[200] Like Goldberg, we see more evidence of arranged marriages among the landed of relatively high social rank and among the wealthier peasants than we do among people living in urban areas and the less well-off in the country. Like Goldberg, we see considerable evidence of young people of all social ranks and geographical locations arranging their own marriages and marrying, it would seem, for love. My disagreement does not lie with this final summary; it lies rather with earlier sections in the chapter where it seems that Goldberg exaggerates the differences between urban and rural.

The argument begins with evidence that more rural adolescents, particularly girls, tended to live at home than did those in urban areas. To the extent that this is true (and there are some interesting variations, depending on whether or not the household was devoted to agricultural employment and whether that agriculture was pastoral or grain-based), Goldberg argues, parents were in a better position to supervise their children's marriage choice than if their children were in service in a town.[201] That statement can hardly be denied, but the fact that parents were in a better position to supervise their children's marriage choice does not mean that they did so. The fourteenth- and fifteenth-century cases that Goldberg cites to illustrate rural young women living at home show the difficulty of proceeding from the opportunity to the fact. *Penesthorp c Waltegrave* involves a marriage that neither set of parents was 'supervising'. The woman's brother brought matters to a head at sword's point, and the

[198] Goldberg, *Women, Work*, 243–79.
[199] *Id.*, 272–9.
[200] See App. e3.2.
[201] Goldberg, *Women, Work*, 243–4.

marriage was dissolved for force.[202] *Malman and Raskelf c Belamy* involves an older woman who is said to have sought her brother's consent to a marriage and a woman who may have been younger and who exchanges consent in her father's house. That her father arranged this marriage is possible, but the witnesses do not say that.[203] *Northefolk c Swyer and Thornton* also involves two marriages, one of which was emphatically not supervised by the woman's parents and the other of which may have been. It is the first that prevails.[204] *Chew c Cosyn*, however, is clearly a case in which the woman's parents were deeply involved in arranging the marriage (and then, perhaps, in trying to break it up).[205]

Goldberg then states: "It is evident that the consent of a parent or guardian was an expected requirement for any woman contemplating matrimony."[206] That seems an extreme statement in the light of the evidence that we have before us. The fact that one woman told a man's brother "I will have hym in to my Husband if my Fadir will assent" is some evidence of social attitudes, but certainly not enough on which to posit a societal expectation across all individuals and groups within the society. Perhaps more telling are the cases where the consent of a parent, relative, or employer is alleged to have been made a condition of the contract.[207] Against these should be balanced the very large number of cases in which such conditions were not present. Certainly, there is nothing like the number of contracts conditional on parental consent that we find at Paris in the late fourteenth century.[208]

Goldberg then offers a number of examples of rural arranged marriages, cases where the parents played a significant role or where parents took "the initiative in bringing young people together."[209] Two of the cases cited are from the sixteenth century. Of the remaining three cases (one of which is cited twice), the description of the negotiations in *Inkersale c Beleby* is substantially accurate. The only difficulty is that the depositions describing these negotiations is the only document that survives from the case. We do not know what the dispute was about and why the *actor* had to sue to enforce what seems from the depositions to have been a 'done deal'.[210] *Graystanes and Barraycastell c Dale* is much more problematical. Goldberg's description of the negotiations that led to the second marriage in the case is substantially accurate, but he fails to note that they are alleged to have taken place after the exchange with the first *actrix* and that the solemnization of the second marriage, such as it was, took place after the official of Durham had ordered the *reus* to solemnize with

202 Ch 4, at nn. 237–9.
203 Ch 4, at nn. 182–3.
204 See at nn. 194–5.
205 See at n. 178; Ch 11, at n. 64; Goldberg, *Women, Work*, 240, 258.
206 *Id.*, 244.
207 Examples and lit. T&C no. 366.
208 See Ch 7, esp. at nn. 27–73.
209 Goldberg, *Women, Work*, 245–6.
210 See at n. 170; Goldberg, *Women, Work*, 245, 246.

the first *actrix*.[211] It is possible that what was involved here was a marriage of convenience, in preference to one of love, but it also possible that the story of the marriage of convenience is partially, or entirely, fabricated. That the family was of two minds about these marriages is suggested by the fact that the *actor*'s aunt testifies on behalf of the first *actrix*. The problematical nature of *John Sell of Bagby c Margaret Mawer of Pickhill and John Mawer her husband* is indicated by Goldberg himself. The issue in the case is whether Margaret was forced into the marriage with Sell by her grandfather (she seems to have been only 14 at the time). Whether Margaret's parents were involved is, in fact, one of the issues in the case; there is testimony on both sides of that issue. The case comes from the end of the fifteenth century, a period in which, we have argued, arranged marriages were more common. The case seems, however, to fit fairly nicely into the pattern of type five, the arranged marriage gone awry. Such cases had existed since the fourteenth century; the question is how common they were.[212]

Goldberg next concedes that "young people in the countryside sometimes [took] the initiative in much the same way as their urban cousins," subject only to the consent of their parents.[213] He cites *Wright c Ricall* as an example. As discussed earlier, I think it better fits the evidence to see that case as one of somewhat more mature parties who had been engaged in a long-term relationship.[214] *William Haynes of Methley and Richard Northcroft of Darfield c Margaret Atkynson of Billingley* does, however, fit the pattern; only there is no indication here that Richard and Margaret obtained the consent of her parents. In fact, the depositions suggest quite strongly that she married William not only under parental pressure but lordly. The marriage took place in the manor hall of a local knight. Eight months previously, however, she had exchanged consent with Richard with only two witnesses present, both of whom had been brought by Richard and who had been sworn to secrecy by Richard for fear "that it would come to the ears of certain relatives and friends of Margaret who wanted to work against it."[215] Richard won his case, and I think we must imagine that that result was not unwelcome to Margaret. Goldberg then goes on to describe *Wistow c Cowper* and argues, I think correctly, that Elena's courage was rare in the cause papers and probably also in reality.[216] Perhaps we might add that what Margaret and Richard did was probably more common, but no less effective.

The question, of course, is whether these cases, all of which are concededly rural, are typically 'rural' in that they show regular involvement of parents and relatives in marriage choice, except for the occasional rebellious couple whose

211 Ch 4, at nn. 179–180.

212 *Sell c Mawer and Mawer* (1499–1500), CP.F.308; Goldberg, *Women, Work*, 246.

213 *Ibid.*

214 Ch 4, at nn. 64–7.

215 *Haynes and Northcroft c Atkynson* (1455), CP.F.194, T&C no. 367. See Goldberg, *Women, Work*, 246–7, 255.

216 See at nn. 191–3.

rebelliousness is shown by the obvious opposition that their choice provokes. This is contrasted with the urban situation, where, Goldberg asserts, relatively few daughters remained living with their parents until marriage, and there is only one case, and this late, of parental opposition to a daughter's marriage.[217] The problem with this argument is that it takes two pieces of evidence – the residence pattern of adolescents, particularly young women, which, as we have already seen, need not inevitably lead to parental control over marriage; and an example of open conflict over marriage choice between parents and children, which seems to have been rare – and uses them to make an argument about the normal pattern of marriage in rural versus urban areas.

Goldberg seeks to reinforce his argument on subsequent pages, and we will not follow him there. Let us look instead at the evidence in a different way. Table 5.1 lists all of the cases, both urban and rural, in both centuries in which there is some evidence of parental involvement. 'Parental involvement' is here defined broadly, as Goldberg seems to define it. It includes any case in which relatives or social superiors of the couple, such as masters or lords, seem to have played a role in the marriage, be it in arranging it or supporting it or in attempting to thwart it. The table lists first those cases in Goldberg's data set (JG) and then those that are not in Goldberg's data set (CD).

The proportion of cases with parental involvement is higher in the JG data set than it is in the CD. This is what we would expect, granted that the JG data set is better documented than is the CD. There is no reason, however, to think that the proportion of cases with parental involvement in urban as opposed to rural cases should be any different in the JG data set from what is in the CD. Hence, the numbers for the JG data set probably better reflect the underlying reality if the question is what proportion of cases has parental involvement, while the total numbers probably better reflect the underlying reality (because the sample is larger) if the question is what is the difference between urban and rural cases.

What the numbers show is quite interesting. Whether we look at the overall numbers or any subset of them, the proportion of cases with parental involvement is always higher for the rural samples than it is for the urban. Goldberg's instinct that there was more parental involvement in his rural sample than in his urban was quite correct. The urban sample, however, is not devoid of parental involvement. Except in a couple of subsamples where the number of cases is small, the proportion of cases with parental involvement in the urban samples ranges from 24 percent to 34 percent. (The equivalent proportions in the rural samples range from 24% to 50%.) There is also a definite chronological trend. The proportion of cases with parental involvement is higher in every fifteenth-century cell from what it is in the corresponding fourteenth-century cell. This is, of course, consistent with our earlier finding that the proportion of cases involving arranged marriages goes up in the fifteenth century. Finally, in our focus on what is there, we should also emphasize what is not there. Even the

[217] Goldberg, *Women, Work*, 247; disc. T&C no. 368.

TABLE 5.1. *'Parental Involvement' in York Marriage Cases (1300–1499)*

Set	Rural/Urban	No. Cases	No. w/ Parental Involvement	% w/ Parental Involvement
JG – 14th	Rural	39	16	41
	Urban	24	7	29
SUBTOTAL		63	23	37
CD – 14th	?Rural	3	1	
	Rural	14	3	
	SUBTOTAL	17	4	24
	Urban	5	0	0
SUBTOTAL		22	4	18
JG & CD – 14th	Rural	56	20	36
	Urban	29	7	24
TOTAL		85	27	32
JG – 15th	Rural	50	24	48
	Urban	38	13	34
SUBTOTAL		88	37	42
CD – 15th	?Rural	1	1	
	Rural	17	8	
	SUBTOTAL	18	9	50
	Urban	8	1	13
SUBTOTAL		26	10	38
JG & CD – 15th	Rural	68	33	49
	Urban	46	14	30
TOTAL		114	47	41
All JG & CD	Rural	124	53	43
	Urban	75	21	28
GRAND TOTAL		199	74	37

Notes: Set = data set; No. Cases = number of cases; No. w/ Parental Involvement = number of cases with 'parental involvement' as defined in the text following n. 217; % w/ Parental Involvement = the proportion of cases with 'parental involvement'; JG = numbers derived from Goldberg, *Women, Work*, and CD = numbers that of derived from the records for cases not in JG's data set. The total number of cases is 16 smaller than the total number of marriage cases in the cause papers because I have excluded 1 fourteenth-century case and 15 fifteenth-century cases in which the surviving documentation would not have indicated whether there was parental involvement. The 4 cases marked '?Rural' do not have a place of residence of the parties, but from the nature of the record, it seemed more likely that they were rural than urban.

Source: Goldberg, *Women, Work*; York, Borthwick Institute, CP.E; CP.F.

rural samples of the fifteenth century never show parental involvement in more than half the cases. That means that in half the cases, parents, relatives, lords, and masters are no place to be found.[218]

So what is the nature of this 'parental involvement' in the urban cases? It varies, as it does in the rural cases. In the fourteenth-century cases in the JG data set, the involvement includes brothers of the *reus* who supported his story

[218] Disc. T&C no. 369.

of absence, a father who represented his daughter as a proctor in a marriage case (and who clearly was involved in supporting her marriage choice, if not arranging it), a master in whose house the exchange of consent took place and whose consent to the arrangement must be obtained, a mother who witnessed her daughter's informal contract with an apprentice saddler and whose kin are said to have been negotiating with him about the marriage, a woman who alleged that her exchange of consent was conditional on her parents' consent, an advocate of the court of York who arranged his widowed daughter's remarriage in such a way as to preclude the claim of another suitor, and the mother and stepfather of a strong-willed young woman who vigorously and, it would seem, successfully opposed her choice of a marriage partner.[219]

We have already discussed some of the fifteenth-century cases in the JG data set in this chapter. There are two urban cases of forced marriages, one in which the force was applied by the woman's parents and one in which the force was applied by her lord.[220] There is one case in which a (probably) young widow thwarted the designs of others for her marriage by marrying a minstrel a week earlier.[221] There is another case in which the masters of a servant couple clearly consented to their marriage, and perhaps they arranged it.[222] In yet another case, the brother, who was a priest, of a woman engaged in a meretricious relationship with an officer of the court of York attempted to turn the relationship into marriage by straightening out the financial arrangements.[223]

The references in the more routine cases are less dramatic and in some cases more problematical, but they point in the same direction. The depositions in *Katherine Thorp of St Sampson York c Thomas Horton of St Mary Castlegate York* describe in some detail a ceremony of handfasting in the house of the witnesses, a married couple described as "forty or more." At a minimum, this suggests a younger couple bringing their intentions formally to the attention of older married people in the community. It may be more than that. Though the witnesses both describe themselves as unrelated to either of the couple, they both are asked, quite unusually, if the male witness ever had sexual intercourse with Katherine. While there are a number of reasons why this question might be asked, the most obvious one would be that the defense (which does not survive) will be that the male witness is, in fact, related to Thomas and, hence, the marriage is impeded by affinity by illicit intercourse.[224]

The only surviving set of depositions in *Joan Lawrens of York and Agnes Seton of York c Thomas Karlell cardmaker of York* are to the marriage that Thomas concedes.[225] They describe a handfasting in the house of a seemingly unrelated couple in the presence of the couple, an outside witness, and

219 Listed T&C no. 370.
220 Listed T&C no. 371.
221 *Thorp and Kent c Nakirer* (at nn. 179–84).
222 *Garforth and Blayke c Nebb* (at nn. 173–5).
223 *Carvour c Burgh* (at nn. 126–30).
224 *Thorp c Horton* (1465), CP.F.208.
225 *Lawrens and Seton c Karlell* (1413), CP.F.65.

(apparently) Joan's mother. One of the witnesses testifies that Joan lives with her mother.

In *Alice Williamson of Methley c William Haggar of York*, three witnesses testify to an exchange of consent in a garden after the couple had had two children.[226] Alice's father, who also testifies, seems to be involved in trying to regularize this relationship.

The parental involvement is more obvious in *John Astlott c Agnes Louth of Kingston upon Hull*.[227] Two witnesses, John's mother and his stepfather, describe the exchange of present consent between the couple about a year previously. They had dined with John in Kingston on a Sunday and were walking back with him to their house in Ella when they encountered Agnes, who was milking a cow near the town gate called 'Beverlaygate'.[228] The meeting had apparently been prearranged, at least by John and Agnes, because they then and there exchanged words of present consent in the presence of his parents. John, they testify, was at the time worth £40 and could have had a much richer woman, but Agnes's father was a substantial *textor*.[229] He owned a house that Agnes stood to inherit. There was some talk as to how Agnes's parents were to be told of the contract, but ultimately Agnes told her sister who told her parents, and within a week the contract was common knowledge.[230] Various gifts were exchanged. Two other witnesses testify to an occasion, probably a month later, on which Agnes asked John to solemnize their marriage, because her father was unhappy (as was she) about leaving matters as they were. John, however, said that he could not do so until he returned from a trip abroad. While John was away, Agnes dealt in John's goods, carried the keys to his house and shop, and otherwise behaved as his wife.[231] On that trip, however, John lost a good part of his fortune, and now Agnes and her parents did not want go through with the marriage. No result is reported, but it is clear enough that both sets of parents were very much involved.[232]

The documentation in *Walter Lematon c William Shirwod of York father of Joan* is skimpy and damaged, and only one deposition survives. The cause of action is an unusual one, an action by a would-be son-in-law against his would-be father-in-law for impeding the marriage. If the deposition is reliable, there can be little doubt that that was what William was doing.[233]

Margaret Foghler of York and Margaret Barker dwelling with John Marsshall of York tailor c John Werynton of York servant of John Baune of York cordwainer is clearly a case in which the master of Werynton, who at the time was also the master of Barker, played a key and controversial role.[234] According to

226 *Williamson c Haggar* (1465), CP.F.336.
227 *Astlott c Louth* (1422), CP.F.46.
228 Disc. T&C no. 372.
229 Disc. T&C no. 373.
230 Disc. and lit. T&C no. 374.
231 Disc. T&C no. 375.
232 Lit. and disc. T&C no. 376.
233 *Lematon c Shirwod* (1467), CP.F.244; lit. T&C no. 377.
234 *Foghler and Barker c Werynton* (1416–17), CP.F.74; lit. T&C no. 378.

the testimony of three witnesses, including Baune's wife, Baune forced Werynton into contracting with Barker because he had caught them more than once having intercourse. It was assize week early in Lent, and Baune threatened to have Werynton put in jail if he did not contract with Barker. One of Werynton's objections to contracting, we might note, is that he would not do so if his father and relatives were there. I think there can be relatively little doubt that something along these lines happened, though whether this constitutes sufficient grounds for invalidating the contract is perhaps another matter. Whether the contract with Foghler also happened is a matter about which we may have more doubt, though Werynton confesses it. Foghler and Werynton are alleged to have contracted twice, once in Baune's house (though he is not said to have been present), in the autumn before the contract with Barker. There is one reasonably solid witness to that contract, but the second, a young man who was playing ball in the street and who was called in to witness to their contracting again, says simply that they confessed to him that they had contracted. Even more suspiciously, the same witnesses happened to be present in the cemetery of York Minster around Easter (following the contract with Barker) when Foghler and Werynton contracted again. While the witnesses are not sure whether the couple had intercourse after the first contract, they are convinced (for reasons they do not state) that they did so many times after the second contract.

Sentence is rendered for Foghler and against Barker. The wording of the sentence for Foghler is unusual. She proved her case, it says, "sufficiently for the purposes of this our sentence."[235] That is not a standard phrase in the diplomatic of sentences, and it may indicate that what she had shown was sufficient, when combined with Werynton's confession, to allow her to win her case. That probably means that the judge had doubts about whether she had proven her precontract, but it made no difference because he was going to hold the subsequent contract with Barker invalid for force.[236]

A considerable documentation survives in *Robert Lede tailor of York c John Skirpenbek cordwainer of York and Agnes Miton his wife*, but we do not have all the testimony, and some of what we have is confused as to the critical dates.[237] What follows resolves the ambiguities in the dates in such a way as to make sense of the story. According to John Duraunt, a baker of York in his forties, Robert and Agnes contracted marriage with the usual words of the present tense in his house in Ousegate on 15 October 1433. Duraunt's wife, Agnes, and Richard Claybank, another baker, also witnessed the handfasting, and although their testimony does not survive, they almost certainly did testify because Skirpenbek's exceptions to their testimony do survive.

On the same day that Duraunt testifies, Hugh Killom, a capmaker of Micklegate, who describes himself as the former master of Agnes and the godfather of

[235] *Ibid.*: *quia invenimus . . . [Margaretam] intencionem suam coram nobis in iudicio deductam quoad hanc nostram sententiam sufficienter probasse.*

[236] Lit. T&C no. 379.

[237] *Lede c Skirpenbek and Miton* (1435), CP.F.115.

her child, testifies that sometime between 1 August and 11 November of 1433, Robert came to him and said that he and Agnes had contracted marriage but that Agnes "at the instance of certain enemies of this Robert had withdrawn her heart from this Robert and did not wish to observe the pact between them."[238] Hugh consulted Agnes about this, and she said that she never had matrimonial words with him. Somewhat later, he and John were in Agnes's house speaking of the matter. They told her that Robert was threatening to bring suit in the court of York, and she told them to tell Robert that "he was laboring in vain if he hoped to take her to wife because she was the wife of John Skirpenbek, cordwainer, and she wished to have him as her husband, and by way of earnest of the marriage contract between them she had received and had by gift of this John half a quarter of wheat."[239] Hugh then describes a meeting held in the chapter house of the Dominicans at which he and Duraunt delivered this answer to Robert in the presence of witnesses, including Richard Claybank, and they all agreed that they would go the following Sunday (3 January 1434) to the cathedral at the time of the high mass and declare the matter to Mr John Marchall the receiver of the archbishop.[240] This they did, and on that occasion, Robert said that "since Agnes said and affirmed that she was the wife of John Skirpenbek it was not, nor is it, his intention to desire the wife of another man." He therefore said that he did not wish to proceed further in the matter but to rid himself completely of it.[241] The same day after dinner, Agnes and John handfasted and exchanged words of the present tense in Hugh's house in his presence and that of his wife and two other men. Hugh also testifies by hearsay that the marriage was solemnized the following autumn in All Saints' Pavement.

William Barton, a York bower, aged fifty, testifies to the handfasting at Hugh's house and to the solemnization of the marriage the following 12 September.[242] He also testifies that before the contract in January, there was *fama* in York that Agnes had contracted with Robert. His most interesting testimony, however, concerns an exchange that occurred in the shop of one John Haggas (or Haggard), who later also testifies and describes himself as a baker and the godfather of two of Agnes's children. Hugh, John Haggas, Agnes, and the witness were all in the shop when Hugh told them that he had "been at the minster of St Peter's, York, and there it was found and declared that Agnes was a free woman absolved of any pretended matrimonial contract had with Robert Lede, so that she could contract marriage elsewhere as she wished."[243] This is, of course, considerably different from Hugh's description of the same events in the minster. Even more interestingly, William goes on to say: "When this

[238] *Ibid.*, T&C no. 380.
[239] *Ibid.*, T&C no. 381.
[240] Lit. T&C no. 382.
[241] *Ibid.*, T&C no. 383.
[242] This date proves particularly difficult to tie down, though there seems to be no reason to doubt that the event actually happened.
[243] *Ibid.*, T&C no. 384.

was said, this witness and John Haggas, executors of the testament of William Miton, deceased, the former husband of Agnes, spoke to Agnes and warned [the word can also mean 'threatened'] her that unless she took John Skirpenbek as her husband, these executors would make her suffer a penalty of 20 marks."[244]

William is the only witness to add this telling detail. John Haggas's testimony is consistent with William's, but he does not mention his role as executor of William Miton's testament. John also tries to establish the proposition that Agnes had contracted with John Skirpenbek before she had any words with Robert, but of this precontract there is clearly no firm evidence.

The remainder of the testimony, 11 witnesses in all, is devoted to establishing the proposition that John Duraunt and his wife were at Agnes's wedding and that they had perjured themselves when they testified that they were not. This is important not only because of the perjury charge but also because, had they been there, they should have reclaimed the banns.[245] Whether the informal ruling of John Marchall, if such it was, would have sufficed to excuse them from so reclaiming is a question that we cannot answer, because no sentence survives.

As is frequently the case in these records, we cannot be sure that we are hearing Agnes's voice. If she spoke as Hugh alleges her to have spoken, then she wanted to marry John Skirpenbek, and John Duraunt's testimony (and that of his co-witnesses, which does not survive) is fabricated. Duraunt was almost certainly not telling the truth when he said that he was not at Agnes's wedding, but that may have been because he was not aware that he had what was probably a good excuse for not having reclaimed the banns. One does wonder, however, whether we are getting the full story from Agnes's witnesses. If she had firmly made up her mind to marry John before she had any dealings with Robert, why was it necessary to threaten her with the loss of what was probably a legacy in her deceased husband's testament? I have no doubt that Agnes did "at length" (*tandem*) consent to marrying John, as William Barton says. What we cannot tell is whether she did so because the men who were running the operation told her that Robert had given up.

Joan Kirkby of York c Henry Helwys of York and Alice daughter of John Newton of York glover is a marriage-and-divorce case in which Joan prevailed.[246] Henry was ordered to solemnize with Joan; he refused, and by a process that cannot quite be recovered, this seems to have lead to an *ex officio* inquiry into whether Joan's witnesses were suborned. The witnesses are quite divided on the basic question, but one of them, the rector of Goldsborough and Joan's parish priest at the time, tells a story that has a ring of truth. He says that Joan came to him with the story of her precontract prior to Henry's marriage to Alice, and he told her to reclaim, which she did, but the marriage was solemnized anyway. Then Henry taunted Alice with the precontract, telling her that

244 *Ibid.*, T&C no. 385.

245 See Ch 1, text following n. 104.

246 *Kirkby c Helwys and Newton* (1430), CP.F.99.

she was only his whore because of the precontract. Word of this got to John Newton, who went to see the rector; Joan repeated her story, and the rector advised legal action.[247] The Newton family may have been deeply divided over the matter. John seems to have gotten the action going and firmly testifies that there was no subornation. Alice's brother, however, equally firmly testifies that there was. Of Alice's view of the matter we hear nothing, but the fact that she did not bring a divorce action on the ground of the precontract suggests that she preferred to remain with Henry.[248]

Further pursuit of this issue would take us into more detail than the matter warrants. Suffice it to say here that there are differences between the urban and rural cases in the York cause papers. When, however, one carefully compares similar types of actions or phenomena, as we did in cases that show parental involvement, the differences turn out to be less stark than Goldberg in some places argues.

CONCLUSION

This chapter has tended to emphasize differences, differences between fourteenth- and fifteenth-century cases, in the first sections, and differences between rural and urban across both centuries, in the most recent section. We concluded the last section by warning against exaggerating the rural/urban distinction. We conclude, for now, our discussion of York by emphasizing the substantial elements of continuity across the two centuries.

First, the modal case at York concerns a *de presenti* informal marriage. Where three parties are involved (a minority but a substantial minority of the marriage-formation cases), one of the marriages may be formal, or at least more formal than the other. Cases involving promises to marry, unaccompanied by intercourse, are very rare. There are a number of cases in which sexual intercourse has taken place, and so the tense of the verbs is irrelevant.

Second, the court is decidedly friendly to plaintiffs' claims, whether those plaintiffs are women, as they are in the majority of cases in the fourteenth and first half of the fifteenth century, or men, as they are in the majority of cases in the second half of the fifteenth century.

Third, the court of York provides a forum for dispute resolution. It is not, for the most part, in the business of law enforcement. Other courts within the diocese were involved in law-enforcement, but of those courts we know relatively little. What we see in the cause papers of the court of York are cases that at least one and sometimes both of the parties wanted to bring before the court.

Fourth, cases of separation *a mensa et thoro* are rare, and the court does not seem to have been particularly favorable toward them. Cases of divorce are

[247] At this point the deposition breaks off and is clearly unfinished.

[248] Granted the conflicting testimony here, I would hesitate to draw any firm conclusions as to what happened. Lit. T&C no. 386.

more common, though not common when compared to cases about marriage formation. In a number of divorce cases and in a number of marriage-formation cases, we suspected that the claim of precontract was being made mendaciously.

Fifth, the cases involve people at a number of different stages of life. The majority of cases concern people who are marrying, or attempting to marry, for the first time, but a number involve widows and widowers, and others involve people who have been living together without the benefit of a formal marriage.

Sixth, there is evidence of arranged marriages and evidence of third parties being involved in marriage choice. There is, however, less such evidence than we would expect on the basis of what we know about medieval marriage from other sources.

Seventh, going from the evidence of the patterns of the cases to conclusions about marriages that were not disputed is, of course, highly risky. It is made more risky by the fact that we do not seem to have a single marriage pattern revealed in the cases but, rather, a number of marriage patterns, patterns that correspond, at least in some sense, to the five story-patterns outlined at the beginning of Chapter 4. Focusing, however, on the story-element that seems to be the most common, the story of the woman wronged, one might wonder whether the reason why it plays such an important role is that many times, behavior that led to the woman being wronged in the litigated cases had a happy ending in cases that were not litigated. While it is difficult to determine the age of the litigants, most of the women seem to have been, at a minimum, in their late teens or early 20s. They were old enough to know what they were doing. Some may have been swept away by passion and did something that they later regretted, but their behavior is more explicable if we posit that one marriage pattern that was prevalent in the diocese of York in the later Middle Ages was for a couple to handfast before friends, and perhaps before older people not necessarily their parents; then, in all probability, to have sexual intercourse and, eventually, have the banns proclaimed and begin formal coresidence. If this was a marriage pattern that they had seen their sisters, in some cases quite literally, follow successfully, then we have a better explanation why those young women who were ultimately betrayed did what they did.

Eighth, if going from litigated cases to marriage patterns in cases that were not litigated is difficult, assessing reactions to the role of the court in the overall society is even harder. Suffice it to say here that there seem to be storm clouds on the horizon, at least by the fifteenth century. Litigants seem to have been aware of the possibility of corrupt allegations, and allegations of precontract that could lead to the breakup of adequately formed marriages, allegations in marriage-formation cases of contracts that did not exist with anything like the clarity that the witnesses say that they did. Those that lost such cases could hardly have been pleased. The potential for wrong judgments of church courts to lead to morally intolerable situations had concerned churchmen from at least the twelfth century. If the increasing evidence that we see of arranged marriages corresponds to an increasing number of arranged marriages in the society at large, then the ability of young people to make use of the canon-law rules to thwart what their elders had planned for them could have led to an increasing distaste among the elders for what the court was doing. All of these reactions are possible. None, so far as I am aware, can be proved for the diocese of York, even at the end of the fifteenth century. The fact that the court becomes somewhat more cautious in the fifteenth century, however, lends some plausibility to the notion that there was increasing concern at least about the first of the problems outlined here.

6

Ely

THE BUSINESS OF THE COURT OF ELY

The diocese of Ely was the second smallest in geographical area in England, covering only the county of Cambridgeshire and the Isle of Ely. From August of 1373 to June of 1388, its bishop was Thomas Arundel, a well-connected prelate who was later translated to York and who ultimately became archbishop of Canterbury.[1] Close to the beginning of Arundel's tenure, Robert Foxton, a notary public and registrar of the court, began what he called "a register of causes of the consistory of Ely."[2] This is a chronological record of all the business that came before the court of the bishop's official between the years 1374 and 1381. The period in question covers the tenure of three different officials and a number of commissaries. There are 3,215 entries of judicial business in the book (excluding the entries that indicate the court session and its adjournment). The quality and care with which Foxton composed the 142 folios of this book make it one the most informative of the surviving English medieval church court act books. It is also one of the earliest.

The first question we must ask when we are confronted with such a huge amount of data is how to organize it. Much of what we see in the Ely act book is easily translatable into modern legal categories, and there is some evidence that Foxton was thinking in these categories. Hence, it is all too easy to make the leap and to use modern categories. To do so, however, runs considerable risk of anachronism. It may be well, therefore, to proceed more slowly and to ask what the evidence is for the existence of these, or other, categories in the mind of our fourteenth-century notary. We can be reasonably sure that what was in his mind was also in the minds of the other professionals of the court.

[1] See Aston, *Arundel.*

[2] CUL, DMA, D2/1; lit. and disc. T&C no. 388.

We can, of course, be far less sure that what was in their minds was also in the minds of the litigants or of the society at large.

Two large overlapping sets of categories seem to have been dominant in Foxton's mind as he sought to impose order on his massive collection of material, one set that we would call procedural and one that we would call substantive, though there is no evidence that he would have used these terms, and considerable evidence that the distinction between procedure and substance did not play the dominant role in his thinking that it does in the thinking of modern lawyers. The substantive categories are more in evidence in the book, since Foxton uses them in the headings of the cases that he writes to keep track of the cases from court session to court session. The entry for the first appearance of a case will read "X was cited at the instance of Y in a cause of Z."[3] The marginal tag line for the case in the next entry will then, almost invariably, be some shortened form of 'Y', and the opening line of the case will begin "In a cause of Z, between X and Y."[4]

The substantive categories represented by 'Z' in the preceding paragraph are relatively few: 'Matrimonial' (*matrimonialis*), 'of divorce' (*divorcii*), 'of defamation' (*diffamationis*), 'of tithes' (*decimarum*), 'of breach of faith or perjury' (*fidei lesionis seu periurii*), 'of violence' (*violencie*), and 'testamentary' (*testamentaria*) are by far the most common.

The procedural categories are less well attested in the book; some, but not all, appear in the captions. Cases will migrate from one procedural category to another without that fact being explicitly noted. The major procedural categories are dependent on how a case is begun. If someone other than a court officer, acting in his capacity as a court officer, asks that a person with whom he or she has a quarrel be cited before the court to answer to a complaint and to do right by him or her, this is described as a 'cause' (*causa*, alternatively 'case') brought at the instance (*ad instanciam*) of the *actor* (approximately 'plaintiff'). Such cases roughly correspond to what modern Western lawyers would call 'civil', though so far as I am aware, that term is not used in the book; we call them 'instance cases'.

The next largest group of cases are begun with a citation, frequently though not invariably called *ex officio* ('out of the office [of the judge]'). These are sometimes called '*matters*' (*negotia*, alternatively 'businesses'), sometimes with the additional phrase 'of correction' (*correctionis*). The object of the citation is to have the person or persons who are called explain, if they can, why they should not be subjected to a penalty for, or at least an order to desist from, behavior that appears on its face to be illegal. While some of these cases involve offenses that modern Western lawyers would call 'criminal' (e.g., adultery, assault) or that could be understood to be criminal in the context of the law of the time (e.g., clerical concubinage), others would be called criminal only in the most extended sense of the term. Hence, we find in this category cases involving contempt, or

[3] Disc. T&C no. 389.

[4] Text, citation form, and lit. T&C no. 390.

seeming contempt, of court orders; failure to attend a synod (which may be excused but needs to be explained); failure of a chaplain who has no other job to serve in a parish when asked, and so on.

A few of these office cases are specifically said to be 'promoted' by someone other than a court officer. After the initial citation, the promotor has the responsibility to conduct the case, producing the necessary witnesses, and so on. If successful, the promotor will see the *reus* (roughly, 'defendant') punished, or ordered to desist from his behavior, and will not receive money damages, but that last feature does not distinguish office cases from instance, since many of the latter also do not result in money damages (notably, marriage and defamation cases).

The Ely act book also recognizes a third category of cases, appeal cases. Underlying these appeals is normally the judgment or action of some subordinate court or subordinate of the official in an instance or office case. Formally, the appeal cases in the Ely consistory are instance cases: They begin with a citation at the instance of the appellant.[5] Many of them do not say what the substance of the underlying case was because the appeal focuses on an alleged procedural defect in the proceedings in the court below. It is possible, however, to surmise whether the underlying case was one of instance or office (with a possible ambiguity if the underlying case was a promoted office case), because in the former, the appeal is brought against the successful party in the court below, while in the latter, the appeal is brought against (and defended by) the inferior judge personally.

In a final category of cases, there is no citation and, so far as we can tell, no dispute. The court is asked to perform some act within its competence. Approving the appointment of a proctor, roughly equivalent to a modern attorney or solicitor, is the most common such entry, followed by the probate of the testament of a deceased person. Various acts of ecclesiastical administration fall into this category as well: appointing a *curator* or assistant for an old or infirm priest; sequestering the revenues of a benefice, the incumbent of which has died; and accepting professions of obedience from holders of benefices. We have called such entries 'administrative' (though there is no warrant in the book for that term).[6]

A final matter of definition before we try to get some sense of the business of the Ely consistory court recorded in our book. There are, as we have said, 3,215 entries of judicial business in the book. These entries are divided into an as-yet-to-be-defined number of cases. Robert Foxton had a rather narrow view of what constituted a 'case', and as result, the number of his cases is large. If, for example, the abbot and convent of Thorney had had cited nine different parishioners of their appropriated church of St Mary, Whittlesey, in a case about tithes, mortuary, oblations, and the office of holy water clerk, Foxton made seven different entries, corresponding, it would seem, to the number of

[5] Disc. T&C no. 391.
[6] Disc. T&C no. 392.

mandates of citation that were issued.[7] In the next session of the court, the case was compromised and peace was restored between the abbot and convent and all nine parishioners.[8] Classifying these entries as representing seven (or nine) different cases would exaggerate the number of disputes about these topics in the book. Our initial count of cases, therefore, combines into one the cases brought by the same *actor* against the same or multiple *rei* or by multiple *actores* against the same *reus*, where the issues are the same or similar and the cases proceed in tandem, even if Foxton made separate entries for them.

We first organized the material by dividing it into cases organized by procedural categories and then further subdivided it into substantive categories. For reasons that will become apparent, this did not prove to be a particularly helpful way of organizing the material, and we do not reproduce the table here. What it did show was that under our definition of a 'case', there were 566 cases in the book divided among the procedural categories as follows: administrative 96 (17%), appeal 72 (13%), instance 266 (47%), office 120 (21%), and office promoted 12 (2%).

The exercise also showed that it was necessary to expand and fill out the substantive categories used by Foxton in the instance cases in the following ways: We created a category 'court' that includes 'housekeeping' entries that relate to the court or its officers (under 'administrative'), orders by the court and penalties imposed in aid of its jurisdiction (under 'office'), and cases in which proctors, advocates, and registrars seek to recover their fees (called 'salaries', *salaria*) against private parties (under 'instance'). By far the most common entries on the administrative side are records of proxies (202, all classified as one 'case'), substitutions of proctors (20), and one revocation of a proxy without an appointment of a substitute.[9] There are also other housekeeping items of the court: records of appointments of apparitors, admission of advocates and proctors, commissions of the official, a commission of temporary commissaries, and an ordinance concerning cases in which a court officer is claiming his fee (no libel needs be filed). The 'court' cases in the 'office' category are mostly cases of contempt, proceedings, frequently against an ecclesiastic, for refusing to follow a court order. Some seem to be related to the ongoing dispute in the diocese between the official and the archdeacon.[10] The fee cases (under 'instance') could be treated as breach of faith cases, but they are never so called, and there does not seem to have been the necessity (as there was in the case of breach of faith) that the agreement to pay be supported by an oath.

We also created another substantive category, 'ecclesiastical', which is found in all four procedural categories. This includes cases of tithes and other ecclesiastical revenues (mortuaries, pensions, oblations, etc.), but it also includes a wide variety of matters pertaining to the administration of the church: appointment

[7] *Thorney (abbey) c Whitheved et al.* (17.i.82 to 7.ii.82), fol. 160v.
[8] *Id.*, fol. 161r.
[9] Disc. T&C no. 393.
[10] Extensively discussed in Aston, *Arundel*, 83–132.

of administrators and curators for sick priests, sequestration of vacant benefices, professions of obedience, and so on. The office version of this category includes cases of defalcation in office, tithes (2 cases), proceedings against a chaplain for engaging in magic, deprivation of rector for defect of birth, and so on. The instance version is mostly cases about ecclesiastical revenues, tithes litigation being the dominant form (22 cases and one instance appeal), but it also includes cases about the repair of churches, finding a chaplain for a chapel, rent owing to a church, the salary of a chaplain, and so on. We have attempted to group these cases together, even where Foxton did not do so. Thus, for example, where the rector of a given church is given an administrator and then dies and his church is sequestered and then the sequestrator renders his account, we have treated it all as one case. Similarly, if the court then probates the testament of the rector and/or approves the inventory of the executors, we have classified the case as 'ecclesiastical/testamentary'.

We similarly expanded the category of 'matrimonial'. It includes not only what Foxton characterizes as *cause matrimoniales* (basically, actions to establish a marriage), but also cases of divorce and the prosecution of sexual offenses (adultery and fornication). Matrimonial cases, so defined, are found in three of the four procedural categories (all except 'administrative'). We will further subdivide this category later.

Testamentary cases are found in all four categories. Where the court simply probates a will or approves executors' accounts, the matter is 'administrative'. Where it hears litigation brought by or against executors, it is 'instance' or 'appeal'. Where it proceeds on its own motion against executors, it is 'office'.

Cases of breach of faith, defamation, and violence were left as Foxton classified them. (In later chapters, we will group them under the general category 'obligation'.) The first named is found only in the 'instance' and 'appeal' categories; the latter two are also found in the 'office' category.

What this exercise in classification demonstrated is that the procedural categories are not particularly helpful in understanding the business of the court. Similar substantive matters are spread out into two, three, or even four procedural categories. Classifying the cases by procedural type also exaggerates the number of cases. This is nowhere more apparent than in the matrimonial category. A case involving one couple may have an instance aspect, but also involve office proceedings for illegal solemnization. A case that is basically a matrimonial case may also cross over substantive lines and appear in the court category, where, for example, the court proceeds *ex officio* to hold an ecclesiastical officer in contempt for failing to serve process, or to hold the couple in contempt for failing to obey its order.

In Table 6.1, we have ignored the procedural categories and classified the case by the substantive issue involved. We have also combined cases across substantive lines where the same issue or cluster of issues seems to be involved. Obviously, some judgment is called for here. Hence, for example, where a woman's husband promoted an office case against a priest for adultery with the man's wife and the priest immediately sued the husband for defaming

TABLE 6.1. *The Business of the Court of Ely by Type of Case (1374–1381)*

Type of Case	Case Def. 1	Reduction	Case Def. 2	% Def. 2	Max. No. Entries	Avg. Entries	Total Entries	% Total
Unknown[a]	46	−4	42	8	17	4.9	222	7
Breach of faith	30	0	30	6	15	3.2	93	3
Court	40	−4	36	7	202	6.8	270	8
Defamation	90	−9	81	16	59	5.4	490	15
Ecclesiastical[b]	120	−4	116	23	29	3.2	381	12
Ecclesiastical/ testamentary	13	−2	11	2	3	2.1	27	1
Miscellaneous[c]	4	0	4	1	38	10.8	43	1
Matrimonial[d]	156	−39	117	23	89	9.1	1422	44
Testamentary	56	−2	54	11	37	3.2	179	6
Violence	11	0	11	2	38	8.0	88	3
TOTAL	566	−64	502	100			3215	100

Notes: Case Def. 1 = the definition of a 'case' for the first analysis; Case Def. 2 = the definition of a 'case' for this analysis; Reduction = the difference between the two definitions; Max. No. Entries = the maximum number of entries of any one case in the group ('Court' is misleading here because all constitutions of proctors are combined as one 'Case'). The minimum number of entries in all cases is 1.

For notes *a–d*, see T&C no. 395.

Source: CUL, DMA, D2/1; Stentz, *Calendar*.

him by accusing him of adultery, we treated the case as one 'matrimonial' case.[11]

Table 6.1 shows that consolidating cases produces a reduction of 64 in the number of cases.[12] This reduction works across all the categories (except 'breach of faith', 'miscellaneous', and 'violence'), but it is most noticeable in the 'matrimonial' cases, which experience a reduction of 39, more than four times the number in any other category ('defamation' has nine).[13] This heightens a phenomenon that was already noticeable when the cases were arranged by procedural categories: matrimonial cases tend to produce more entries than do other types of cases. Indeed, in Table 6.1 matrimonial cases account for approximately a quarter of the total number of cases but for approximately 45 percent of the entries. We should be careful not to ascribe too much significance to this fact. Many of these entries are routine continuations of cases from session to session (but such entries also occur in other types of cases). It does suggest, however, that matrimonial cases occupied an amount of the court's time out of proportion to their numbers.

The differences between the substantive jurisdiction of York court and that of Ely are about what we would expect, granted the differences in the two places, the nature of the courts, and the nature of the surviving records. As we noted earlier, the Ely court did everything. It entertained instance, office, appellate, and 'administrative' business (though we suspect that it did less office business than did the archdeacon). By contrast, the York consistory court seems to have heard very few office cases as a matter of first instance, except in aid of its own jurisdiction.[14] Any routine administrative business that it did is not recorded in the cause papers. (There are some recognizances and routine proxies that survive in the fourteenth- and fifteenth-century act books. There are no probates of testaments; these were handled elsewhere.)

The proportions of the types of cases at Ely are different from what they were at York in the fourteenth century. This is true whether we compare the York proportions to the overall proportions at Ely (as in Table 6.2) or simply to the proportions of instance cases. In order to make the comparison, the York 'miscellaneous' cases have been classified as 'violence' (because that is what they are), while the Ely 'ecclesiastical/testamentary' cases have been merged with 'ecclesiastical', because that is clearly their basic concern.

What Table 6.2 shows is the dominance of ecclesiastical litigation at York, in contrast to Ely. There is virtually no benefice litigation at Ely, in marked contrast with York. There is some tithes litigation and litigation concerning other ecclesiastical matters, but not so much of it as there is at York. The difference is made up in various ways. There is far more defamation litigation at Ely than at York (though most of it is compromised relatively quickly). Nothing

[11] *Office and Adekyn c Bassingbourn* (*vicar*); *Bassingbourn* (*vicar*) *c Adekyn* (29.v.77 to 22.x.77), fol. 74v–79v; cf. T&C no. 394, for a similar case.

[12] Lit. T&C no. 396.

[13] Disc. T&C no. 397.

[14] See Ch 3, n. 9.

TABLE 6.2. *York Cause Papers (Fourteenth Century) and Ely Act Book (1374–1381): Comparison of Proportions of Types of Cases*

Type of Case	Ely No.	Ely %	York 14th c No.	York 14th c %
Unknown	42	8	5	2
Breach of faith	30	6	15	6
Court	36	7	0	0
Defamation	81	16	21	8
Ecclesiastical	127	25	101	39
Matrimonial	117	23	86	33
Miscellaneous	4	1	0	0
Testamentary	54	11	24	9
Violence	11	2	2	1
TOTAL	502	100	257	100

Source: Tables e3.App.1, 6.1.

that corresponds to the court category at Ely is found in the York cause papers. There are also more breach of faith cases at Ely, if we look solely to the instance litigation at Ely.[15] (This may be related to the date of the Ely book; at York breach of faith litigation increases as the century progresses.) Most important for our purposes, the York court has proportionally 33 percent more marriage litigation than does Ely. Ely marriage litigation, however, does not suffer nearly so great a reduction in its proportion when we move from the instance figure to the total, as, for example, does defamation and breach of faith.[16] Ely office cases involving marriage were an important part of the court's jurisdiction, as they were not at York.

Despite these differences, the Ely court and the York court are clearly operating in closely related legal worlds. The categories that they employ are similar where they are not the same. The proportions of types of litigation are roughly similar. When we come to look at the Paris consistory court in approximately the same period, we will discover a quite different legal world.

COUNTING MARRIAGE CASES IN THE COURT OF ELY

Let us now see if the patterns of marriage litigation that we established for the York court in Chapter 3 can be applied to marriage litigation in the Ely court. Here, we are somewhat hampered by the Ely records. Usually, we can tell the nature of the claim; sometimes, but not always, we can tell the nature of the defense. Because we lack the depositions of the witnesses, we can rarely tell what the 'core issue' in the case was, though we sometimes can guess. We certainly cannot construct detailed stories out of most of these records in the

[15] 11% of the instance cases (29/277).

[16] Matrimonial cases are 26% of the instance cases at Ely (69/266); defamation 30% (81/266).

way that we were able to do so for many of the York records. Nonetheless, some patterns do emerge.

The type of Ely case that is most comparable to those in the York cause papers is the 'straight' instance action, begun, as we noted, in the Ely consistory with the formula "X was cited at the instance Y in a matrimonial cause." While a number of these cases also have office aspects, such as proceedings for illegal solemnization, or appellate aspects, we have classified as 'straight' instance cases all those that began in the consistory as instance actions, whatever other proceedings may have been involved as well.

The Ely consistory also entertained a number of cases of appeal in marriage cases, principally, though not exclusively, from the official of the archdeacon. Most of these are also quite comparable with the marriage cases in the York cause papers. Where the appeal was one from an underlying instance case, the action normally began in the Ely consistory with a citation of the appellee to answer to the appellant in an appeal case, the fact that it was a matrimonial case frequently being added to the formula. Where, by contrast, the archdeacon's official had proceeded *ex officio*, the official himself was the appellee, and it was he who was cited. Adding these instance appeals to the table does no violence to the basic scheme, except that it greatly increases the number of claims of marriage of "uncertain form," because the appellate record normally does not give the nature of the underlying claim except to say that it was "matrimonial."

There are also a rather large number of cases that are begun in the Ely consistory with an *ex officio* citation and then turn into instance cases ('office/instance'). Four cases of reclamation of banns begin with the *ex officio* citation of the person who had reclaimed the banns to appear and explain why he or she had reclaimed.[17] They then turn into three-party instance marriage cases, except that the distinction between 'competitor' cases and 'marriage and divorce' cases becomes even more problematical in such situations. We have classified them all as 'competitor' cases (there is, after all, no certain marriage to divorce), but the line is not a sharp one. Two more reclamation cases fit more problematically into the scheme that we developed for the York cause papers. The reclaimer does not appear in either case, but the couple seem to dispute between themselves about the validity of their proposed marriage.[18] With some hesitation, we have added these to the two-party cases.

Similarly without doing violence to the overall scheme, we may add to these cases others that are begun with an office citation but then proceed as regular instance cases.[19] While cases begun in this fashion fit the scheme quite nicely, they seem to produce a disproportionate number of cases of future consent followed by *copula* and of divorce (Table 6.3). The numbers in the cells, however, are sufficiently small that we should be careful not to infer much from this observation.

[17] Disc. and lit. T&C no. 398.
[18] Both cases involve affinity by illicit intercourse; disc. T&C no. 399.
[19] The types of citation are laid out in Table 6.7.

TABLE 6.3. *York (Fourteenth Century) and Ely (1374–1381) – Types of Marriage Cases Compared*

Type of Claim[a]	Straight Instance	Appellate[b]	Office/ Instance	Straight Office	Total	% Total	York 14th c No.	%York 14th c
Causa Matrimonialis								
Two-party								
De presenti only	3	0	4	0	7	6	24	28
De presenti plus *copula*	2	0	6	3	11	10		
De futuro	0	0	0	2	2	2	9	10
De futuro plus *copula*	0	0	3	2	5	5		
Contract plus *copula* (?*de futuro*)	2	0	1	2	5	5	0	0
'Formula'[c]	6	0	3	0	9	8	0	0
Abjuration *sub pena nubendi*	2	0	0	1	3	3	9	10
Uncertain form of marriage	2	10	2	2	16	15	3	3
SUBTOTAL	17	10	19	12	58	54	45	52
Three-party								
Causa matrimonii et divorcii	9	3	3	0	15	14	10	12
Competitores	8	1	11	0	20	19	10	12
SUBTOTAL	18	3	14	0	35	33	20	23
Causa divorcii a vinculo								
Precontract[d]	2	1	1	2	6	6	5	6
Other	1	0	2	3	6	6	11	13
Uncertain ground	0	0	0	1	1	1	0	0
SUBTOTAL	3	1	3	6	13	12	16	19
Causa divorcii quoad mensam et thorum[e]	0	0	0	0	0	0	3	3
Other	0	0	0	0	0	0	2	2
Uncertain claim	0	1	0	0	1	1	0	0
TOTAL Comparable	37	16	36	18	107	100	86	100
Adultery	0	1	0	6	7			
Fornication	0	0	0	2	2			
Wife beating	0	0	0	1	1			
GRAND TOTAL	38	17	36	27	117			

Notes: 'Office/instance' = cases begun in office mode but which shift to instance mode or cases specifically said to be *ex officio promoto*; both columns of proportions take into account only those cases at Ely that are comparable to those in the York cause papers.

For notes *a–e*, see T&C no. 400.

Source: CUL, DMA, D2/1; Stentz, *Calendar*; Table 3.2.

The cases that begin with an office citation and never turn into instance cases ('straight office') are the most difficult to fit into the scheme based on the York cause papers. Obviously, there is nothing comparable in the York cause papers to a case brought against a priest for adultery because, so far as we know from the cause papers, the York court did not hear such cases. There are, however, 'straight' office cases in the Ely act book that do have parallels in the York cause papers. If John and Joan are cited about informal marriage followed by intercourse but not solemnized, we are obviously dealing with a fact-pattern that is familiar from the York cause papers. If they then concede the contract and the intercourse, we have no dispute; they are simply ordered to solemnize their marriage. They could, however, have disputed the matter between themselves, and we would have had a case indistinguishable from a York two-party enforcement action. Similarly, an office citation to a couple that raises the issue whether there is an impediment to their marriage could have given rise to a case in the York cause papers. It is simply that some third party (and we will have occasion to ask who this third party might be) is raising the issue, rather than the couple themselves. The fact is that most of the marriage cases in the Ely act book do lend themselves to comparison with the cases in the York cause papers, and Table 6.3 seeks to do so (though the different types of proceedings are first broken out before they are combined).

The comparison with the York cause papers shows, again, that the two courts were clearly operating in closely related legal worlds. Two-party actions to enforce a marriage account, in both courts, for somewhat more than a half of all marriage cases. Three-party enforcement actions account for about a quarter more (one-third at Ely). Divorce actions are relatively rare in both courts. There is a somewhat greater proportion of enforcement actions in the Ely court than there is in the York cause papers, the difference being made up by the smaller proportion of actions for divorce *a vinculo*. The Ely act book records no actions for divorce *quoad mensam et thorum* and no actions dealing with marital property.

The Ely court heard relatively few actions for adultery, fornication, or wife beating. (We suspect that the archdeacon's court heard far more.) Most of the straight-office cases in the Ely records are connected with enforcement actions of one sort or another (including a large number of illegal solemnization actions, which will be discussed separately).

Most of the differences between the two courts can be explained by the different types of records that survive. There are libels at York that allege a 'formula' marriage, but in all cases, the record allows us to go behind the formula and make the claim more precise. Similarly, the greater number of claims of marriages of uncertain form in the Ely records is accounted for, as noted, by the fact that appeal cases in the Ely records rarely tell us the precise nature of the claim in the court below. One difference does survive these observations: The York cause papers do contain a significantly larger number of cases of abjuration *sub pena nubendi*.[20] The institution clearly existed in Ely

[20] $z = 1.17$, significant at .91.

diocese, but it does not seem to have generated so much litigation as it did in York.[21]

As in the case of York, so too in the case of Ely, we must look at how the cases were defended before we can get some sense of what was legally, much less what was socially, significant about marriage disputes that were brought before the court. We cannot do as good a job as we did in the case of York, where we could learn something about the defense of virtually all the fourteenth-century cases. We do, however, know how many of the Ely cases were defended, and in a few cases we can speculate about what the 'core issue' was.

Our initial impression that we knew less about the defenses in Ely cases than we knew about the York cases is, to some extent, belied by the last row of Table 6.4, which gives the number of cases for which a defense is known as a percentage of total cases in the group. We, in fact, know more of the defenses in the Ely instance cases than we do in the York cases and almost as many in the office cases that turn into instance cases. We do, however, know about far fewer defenses in both the appeal cases and in the office cases that never turn into instance cases. This is at least partially the result of the fact that many of these cases never proceed to the defense stage. As we shall see in more detail, a large number of these cases are either conceded (and disposed of in one or two sittings) or never get going because the parties fail to appear.

Where we do have much more information about the York cases than we do about the Ely cases is those that have defenses based on the facts. Foxton recorded that exceptions to witnesses were offered in only a couple of cases. There probably were more defenses that would have been styled as exceptions to witnesses at York (defenses, for example, that basically challenge the witnesses' version of the facts) that Foxton did not record as exceptions to witnesses. The presence of the articles, and in many cases the depositions, in the York cases allows us to see more clearly the nature of the factual argument. The overall impression, moreover, is that marriage litigation in the Ely consistory was somewhat less sophisticated legally than was that at York. This is, of course, just what we would expect, considering the different nature of the two courts.

As in the case of the claims, however, so too in the case of the defenses, the overall impression is that the York and Ely courts were operating in the same legal world. Somewhat more cases at Ely raise the issue of precontract or competing contract; somewhat fewer are known to have been defended on the facts (though as many may have been). Precontract and denial of the charge produce the overwhelming majority of the defenses in both courts. In the category of 'other' types of defenses (or objections to a marriage), one appears to a somewhat greater extent at Ely than it does at York: the cluster of claims that can arise out of the complicated medieval law of consanguinity and affinity.[22] These claims are more noticeable in the cases that begin as office cases. Their presence suggests, though it certainly does not prove, that the Ely court was more concerned with these issues than were the parties themselves.

[21] Further examples T&C no. 401.

[22] These are discussed at some length in Ch 11.

TABLE 6.4. *York (Fourteenth Century) and Ely (1374–1381) – Defenses in Marriage Cases Compared*

		Ely				
Type of Defense[a]	York 14th c	Straight Instance	Appellate	Office/ Instance	Straight Office	Total
Precontract						
Divorce for precontract	5	2	1	1	2	6
Marriage and divorce	11	10	2	3	0	15
Competitors	9	8	1	11	0	20
Two-party enforcement	8	2	1	2	0	5
SUBTOTAL	33	22	5	17	2	46
Denial						
'Straight' denial	12	8	4	13	4	29
Exceptions to witnesses	16	4	1	1	0	6
Absence	9	0	0	0	0	0
Disparity of wealth	5	0	0	0	0	0
SUBTOTAL	42	12	5	14	4	35
Force and/or nonage						
Force	10	1	0	2	0	3
Nonage	6	0	0	0	0	0
SUBTOTAL	16	1	0	2	0	3
Other						
Consanguinity/affinity	9	5	0	4	6	15
Unfulfilled condition	4	3	0	4	0	7
Crime	4	0	0	0	2	2
Procedural objections	4	1	4	1	1	7
Servile condition	2	0	0	1	0	1
Impotence	2	0	0	2	0	2
Vow/orders	0	1	0	1	0	2
Other[b]	0	2	0	0	1	3
SUBTOTAL	25	12	4	13	9	38
GRAND TOTAL Defenses	116	47	14	46	15	122
Duplicates	−37	−12	−6	−15	−3	−34
GRAND TOTAL Cases	79	35	8	31	13	88
% Defense/case	90%	92%	57%	86%	68%	81%

Notes: See T&C no. 402.

Source: CUL, DMA, D2/1; Stentz, *Calendar*; Table 3.3.

At this point in Chapter 3, we analyzed the types of marriages claimed and defended in the York court in the fourteenth and fifteenth centuries (Table 3.4). We will not do that here for Ely. We rely instead on Michael Sheehan's count that of 122 marriages at stake in the Ely cases, 89 "involved a union, real or alleged, that was clandestine."[23] In 70 of these cases, the first publication of the

[23] Lit. T&C no. 404.

marriage was, so far as we know, the appearance of the couple before the court. In 13 cases, the couple had proceeded some of the way toward solemnization of a marriage that turned out to be valid. In 6 cases, the couple had illegally solemnized a marriage.[24]

Table 6.5 shows the gender of the parties in the Ely marriage cases and the judgments that were recorded in them. It combines the instance cases begun in the Ely consistory with the appeals in instance cases but separates the instance cases from those that were begun as office cases but then proceeded as instance cases.

The table shows that there is relatively little difference in the two types of cases. In both, female plaintiffs dominate; in both, there is a high percentage of judgments, and in both, the plaintiffs tend to be successful. There are fewer female plaintiffs in the cases begun as office cases (69% vs 58%). We will return to this difference at the end of this section to offer some speculations as to why this might be so.

Table 6.6 calculates the ratios for the two groups of Ely cases and for the combined totals from Ely and compares those ratios to those that we have already calculated for York. The table shows some remarkable elements both of consistency and inconsistency. The high percentage of judgments in Ely marriage cases is comparable to that of York in the fourteenth century. (The fact that it does not track that of York in the fifteenth century is probably, as we noted in Chapter 3, the result of poor record keeping.) The ratio of total female plaintiffs to total plaintiffs at Ely is lower than that at York in the fourteenth century (64% vs 71%) and slightly higher than that at York in the fifteenth century (64% vs 62%).[25] The figures are closer to the York fourteenth-century figures if we compare just the Ely instance cases (69% vs 71%). Clearly, the office citations are bringing in a higher proportion of male plaintiffs than is found in the almost entirely instance litigation at York.

The total plaintiffs' success rate at Ely was quite a bit less than it was at York in either century (59% vs 85% and 77%).[26] Here, too, the presence of the office citations does seem to have been a factor, but in the opposite direction from what we might expect. The total plaintiffs' success rate was lower in instance cases than it was in office/instance cases (56% vs 63%), but the difference is neither large nor significant.[27]

At York there was a considerable discrepancy between the male and female plaintiffs' success rates, and we sought, in part, to explain that discrepancy by looking to greater persistence of female plaintiffs in litigation. There is no, or virtually no, discrepancy between male and female success rates at Ely, but female plaintiffs were, nonetheless, more persistent.[28] The overall percentage

[24] Lit. T&C no. 405.
[25] Statistical disc. T&C no. 406.
[26] Fourteen: $z = 3.56$, significant beyond .99; fifteenth: $z = 2.36$, significant at .98.
[27] $z = .60$, significant at .45.
[28] Disc. T&C no. 407.

TABLE 6.5. *Gender Ratios and Judgments in Marriage Cases at Ely (1374–1381)*

	Instance											Office/Instance										
Type of Claim[a]	FP	MP	Total Cases	%F	SFP	SMP	Total Cases	SFD	SMD	Total Cases	GTOT	FP	MP	Total Cases	%F	SFP	SMP	Total Cases	SFD	SMD	Total Cases	GTOT
Spousals																						
Two-party																						
De presenti only	0	2	3	33	0	0	0	1	1	2	2	1	4	4	0	0	2	2	2	0	2	4
De presenti plus *copula*	5	0	2	100	1	0	1	0	1	1	2	2	1	6	83	3	0	3	1	2	3	6
De futuro plus *copula*	3												0	3	100	2	0	2	0	1	1	3
Contract plus *copula* (? *de futuro*)	1	0	2	100	0	0	0	0	2	2	2	2	0	1	100	1	0	1	0	0	0	1
'Formula'	0	4	6	33	0	2	2	2	1	3	5	2	3	3	0	0	1	1	0	0	0	1
Abjuration	0	0	2	100	1	0	1	0	1	1	2	2	0	0	0	0	0	0	0	0	0	0
Uncertain	2	3	12	75	4	1	5	1	3	4	9	9	0	2	100	1	0	1	0	1	1	2
SUBTOTAL	11	9	27	67	6	3	9	4	9	13	22	18	8	19	58	7	3	10	3	4	7	17
Three-party																						
Marriage & divorce	2	3	12	75	4	2	6	1	4	5	11	9	1	3	67	1	0	1	1	1	2	3
Competitors	7	2	9	78	6	1	7	0	0	0	7	7	4	11	64	5	2	7	0	2	2	9
SUBTOTAL[b]	9	5	21	76	10	3	13	1	4	5	18	16	5	14	64	6	2	8	1	3	4	12
Divorce																						
Precontract	0	1	2	50	0	0	0	0	0	0	0	1	1	1	0	0	0	0	0	0	0	0
Other	1	1	1	0	0	1	1	0	0	0	1	0	1	2	50	1	0	1	0	0	0	1
SUBTOTAL	1	2	3	33	0	1	1	0	0	0	1	1	2	3	33	1	0	1	0	0	0	1
TOTAL	21	16	51	69	16	7	23	5	13	18	41	35	15	36	58	14	5	19	4	7	11	30

Notes: Abbreviations as in Table 3.5.

For notes *a–b*, see T&C no. 403.

Source: CUL, DMA, D2/1; Stentz, *Calendar*.

TABLE 6.6. *Ely (1374–1381) and York (1300–1499) – Gender Ratios and Judgments in Marriage Cases Compared*

	Ely Instance			Ely Office/Instance			Ely Total			York 14th c			York 15th c		
	No.	Total	%	No.	Total	%	No.	Total	%	No.	Total	%	No.	Total	%
Ratio judgments/cases	41	51	80	30	36	83	71	87	82	67	86	78	73	123	59
Ratio FPs/total Ps	35	51	69	21	36	58	56	87	64	61	86	71	76	123	62
Ratio SFPs/total SPs	16	23	70	14	19	74	30	42	71	39	56	70	34	56	61
Total P success rate	23	41	56	19	30	63	42	71	59	56	67	84	56	73	77
FP success rate	16	29	55	13	20	65	30	50	60	39	49	80	34	46	74
MP success rate	7	12	58	5	9	56	12	21	57	17	18	94	22	27	81
FP drop rate	6	35	17	0	21	0	6	56	11	12	61	20	30	76	39
MP drop rate	4	16	25	6	15	40	10	31	32	7	25	28	20	47	43

Source: Tables 6.5, 3.5, 3.6.

of male plaintiffs who pursued their cases to judgment is considerably lower than that of the female plaintiffs (68% vs 89% [the converse of the "drop rate" given in the table]). Not only that, there were some notable differences in the different types of cases. Female plaintiffs pursued 83 percent of the Ely instance cases to judgment, as opposed to 75 percent of the males; they pursued a remarkable 100 percent of the office/instance cases to judgment, as opposed to just 60 percent for the males. Female persistence was higher than that of their sisters at York in both classes of cases at Ely and for both centuries at York (83% and 100% vs 80% and 61%), but males at Ely were also more persistent than their brothers at York in instance litigation (75% vs 72% and 57%), although they pursued proportionally fewer office/instance cases to judgment (60%) than they did instance cases at York in the fourteenth century (72%), but slightly more than in the fifteenth century (57%).[29]

Obviously, we will have to look more closely at the Ely litigation to see if we can discern why there are these differences, but we can make a few suggestions here on the basis of the numbers and on what we already know about the two courts as institutions. In the first place, we must discount our observations by the fact that it is likelier at York than it is at Ely that there were judgments for which we have no surviving record, particularly in the fifteenth century. There is also a reason other than better record keeping why we might expect that there would be a higher percentage of judgments at Ely than there were at York. At York, there was little danger that the court would pursue a case if the parties did not. The Ely court took a more proactive role. Not only did it conduct office litigation on its own and bring parties into court by office citations in order to pursue what was essentially instance litigation, but it also, at least occasionally, stepped in where the parties failed to do so. In one case, where the party failed of proof, the court brought in an *ex officio* witness.[30] In a number of cases, the court insisted on the presence of one or both of the parties at each session because, as the record in one case says, "the court feared that the man would flee."[31] None of these efforts was particularly successful, but the fact that they happened suggests that it was more difficult to walk away from the Ely court than from the York court.

What this general observation does not tell us is why there is such a difference between the rates at which men and women pursued the different kinds of cases. Here, we shall offer some hypotheses that we will then seek to reinforce by looking at the skimpy information given us by the records. I suggested that at York, women valued marriage more than did men, particularly in the later years of the fourteenth century (just the period of our Ely records). Hence, they sued more often than men did to establish a marriage. Hence, too, they seem to have been somewhat more persistent in pursuing cases. The greater proportion

[29] Statistical disc. T&C no. 408.
[30] See at n. 61.
[31] E.g., *Malyn c Malyn* (2.v.81), fol. 150r: *quia timemus de viri fuga.*

of female plaintiffs in the Ely act book suggests the same conclusion. What this overall observation cannot explain is the greater persistence of male plaintiffs in instance litigation (but not in office/instance litigation) and why female plaintiffs were more persistent in office/instance litigation than they were in ordinary instance litigation.

That women were more persistent in office/instance litigation may be explained by the fact that they saw the court as being on their side. The official, after all, had issued a citation of his own motion. Female plaintiffs in office/instance cases may also have perceived that the community was on their side. (The citations are sometimes said to have been issued as a result of *publica fama*, and even where they do not say this, they probably were the result of some sort of community reporting to the court.)[32] Now the fact is that the persistence of female plaintiffs in office/instance litigation did not pay off. Female plaintiffs had only a slightly higher success rate in such litigation than they did in ordinary instance litigation (65% vs 62%). We may doubt, however, that anyone until now noticed this fact; the perception may be more important here than the reality.

That leaves the persistence of male plaintiffs in ordinary instance litigation as the hard observation to explain. Their success rate is only slightly higher in instance litigation than it is in office/instance litigation (58% vs 56%), but they walked away from two-fifths of the office/instance cases and only a quarter of the instance cases. Let us look more closely at the four groups of cases (instance and office/instance litigation with female and male plaintiffs) to see if we can explain these different rates of persistence. In the process, we will be able to describe marriage litigation at Ely quite fully; we will have less success in explaining the differences in rates of persistence.

CASES INVOLVING MALE PLAINTIFFS

Before we look at the cases involving male plaintiffs individually, we should note some general characteristics about such cases. In the first place, our characterization of male plaintiffs as persistent requires some qualification. True, our 31 male plaintiffs collectively pursued 21 cases to judgment, but in many instances, it did not take much pursuit. The average length of time from the first entry to the sentence in such cases was less than a year (325 days). If we exclude from the count two monstrous cases that took a week short of six years and four years and three months, respectively,[33] the average length of time from first entry to last is a modest 163 days, or less than six months. One of our sentences in cases involving male plaintiffs was rendered in just one session of the court, another three in fewer than 20 days, and another four in fewer than 45 days. Whether the York court also heard such relatively easy cases we cannot say in

[32] Disc. T&C no. 409.

[33] *Anegold and Schanbery c Grantesden* (n. 95); *Fisschere c Frost and Brid* (n. 91).

the present state of our knowledge; what we can say is that such cases tended not to leave survivals in the cause papers.[34]

As we noted, male plaintiffs pursued to judgment more cases begun as instance cases than they did those begun with an office citation. It also took them longer to get a judgment in the straight-instance cases than it did in the office/instance cases. The average length from first entry to sentence in the former is 450 days, that of cases begun by office citation 159 days. This discrepancy is caused almost entirely by the two 'monster' instance cases. Take them out and the average length of the two groups of cases is almost the same (166 vs 159 days). This comparison, however, understates the speed at which office cases were normally heard. Two of the four office/instance cases that last longer than 45 days were office cases only in a manner of speaking. One is a case of marriage and divorce that proceeds for 445 days as an ordinary instance case in all respects, except for the fact that it was begun by a citation by the bishop. Apparently, the plaintiff asked the bishop's audience court to hear the case; this it refused to do, but it helped him out by providing the initial citation and then delegated the case to three officers of the consistory.[35] The other case, which lasted 238 days, began with an instance citation by the commissary of the bishop in the deanery of Ely. We put it over on the 'office' side because the commissary mentions that he had been informed by members of the community about the existence of the marriage contract between the couple.[36] In a third case, it is the instance element of 'office/instance' that seems to be lacking. The couple both appear to want to get married, but a reclamation of their banns had raised the issue of whether their marriage was impeded by affinity by illicit intercourse.[37] The parties confess the illicit intercourse and say that they do not know whether the woman with whom the man committed fornication is related to the female marriage partner or not. Witnesses are produced – it is not said by whom – and the court ultimately rules against the marriage. It takes 323 days to reach this result, but it is not at all clear that the persistence is that of the man (of whose suit, it is ultimately said, the woman is absolved) or that of the court. Take out these three cases and the average length of the six remaining office/instance cases with male plaintiffs and judgments is 70 days.[38]

Is there anything about the straight-instance cases (and the two that we have reclassified as instance for all practical purposes) that distinguishes them from the office cases in which the man ultimately played the role of plaintiff? Admittedly there is not much; the two types of cases are quite similar in the issues they raise. When we look at who the defendants were, however, there is

34 Further analysis of the fifteenth-century act books will help in this regard.
35 *Wedone c Cobbe and Franceys* (10.ix.77 to 29.xi.78), fol. 79v–104v.
36 *Bradenho c Taillor* (21.vii.79 to 15.iii.80), fol. 119v–134r; lit. T&C no. 410.
37 *Office c Symond and Page* (26.vii.75 to 28.vii.75), fol. 28.
38 For the fourth case that lasts longer than 45 days, see at n. 82.

this difference: There are five cases in the straight-instance cases in which the defendant is described as a widow; there are none in the cases begun with office citations. There are also three cases begun with office citations in which either the plaintiff or the defendant is described as a servant or a former servant; there are none in the straight-instance cases. We noted in the York cases that male plaintiffs tended to pursue widows and that servants had a tendency to get into matrimonial trouble. The evidence would suggest, though it certainly does not prove, that the Ely court was paternalistic about the young people who were engaged in terms of service. With more mature couples, it left them to their own devices to pursue the case.

There is other evidence that male plaintiffs in instance cases were pursuing women whom they deemed to be desirable marriage partners because of their status or wealth. This evidence is best considered as we try to combine the claims, defenses, and sentences into a coherent story.

Seventeen of the 31 cases involving male plaintiffs are two-party marriage-enforcement actions (9 straight-instance and 8 office/instance, one of which we might well reclassify as instance). Six (4 instance,[39] 2 office/instance) result in sentences for the male plaintiff, seven (4 instance, 3 office/instance) in sentences for the *rea*. Two of the cases are against widows, one of which results in a sentence for the defendant, despite the fact that the plaintiff is able to produce three witnesses to the contract,[40] and one of which results in what I have treated as a sentence for the plaintiff, because the couple marry voluntarily after the male plaintiff appeals from an adverse sentence of the archdeacon.[41] One other instance case suggests that the woman is of a relatively high status in that she claims that the contract, which she concedes, was dependent on a gift to her of lands and tenements. A commission is issued to examine the witnesses to the contract, and the plaintiff fails to appear thereafter.[42] Two others give some hint of higher status, or at least of some legal sophistication, in that a woman defends on the ground that her consent was conditional on parental consent. In one, the woman prevails, though it is unclear whether this is because the man's witnesses proved her exception or because they did not prove that there was a contract at all.[43] In the other, the man prevails, though it is unclear whether this is because his witnesses proved an unconditional contract or because they showed that the condition had been fulfilled.[44]

For the rest, the instance cases are a decidedly mixed bag. One case is hardly a case at all. The woman affirmatively contests the suit, and one wonders why it is that the man is forced to produce witnesses to the contract (which he does)

[39] Including the reclassified *Bradenho c Taillor* (n. 36).

[40] *Band c Pryme* (13.ii.76 to 3.vii.76), fol. 39r–50v (instance).

[41] *Furblisshor c Gosselyn* (17.iii.79 to 22.ix.79), fol. 112r–120r (instance). For the only other appeal case in this group, see T&C no. 411.

[42] *Stenkyn c Bond* (26.iv.80 to 23.vii.80), fol. 141r–143r.

[43] *Lewyne c Aleyn* (12.vii.80 to 28.vii.80), fol. 141v–143r.

[44] *Bradenho c Taillor* (n. 36).

before obtaining a favorable sentence.[45] It may be that a third party, or parental or community opposition to the marriage, was lurking in the background.

The most uninformative records are the ones where we suspect that the result of the case was dependent on the proof of the facts of the marriage. In one, the man produces four witnesses over the course of four months and obtains a favorable judgment.[46] In another, the man has five witnesses but loses his case in six days.[47]

Two office cases with male plaintiffs involve substantive objections to the marriage. In one, the woman apparently had objected that the man was of villein status, but she admits that she knew of his status at the time when she informally contracted with him.[48] The court orders them to solemnize the marriage. The other case, which arose on reclamation of banns, involves the impediment of affinity by illicit intercourse. It is not at all clear that the man is pursuing the case, but it does end with an order dismissing the *rea* from the man's suit.[49]

Just as in the instance cases, so too in the office cases, there are those that are hardly cases at all. In one, the couple is cited *ex officio* for a marriage contract known by *publica fama*. The man, a servant, swears that he has no proof (suggesting that he might have wished that he had).[50] Sentence is given for the *rea*, and the matter is explicitly said to be left to their consciences.

There is considerable evidence in some of both the instance and the office cases that one or both of the parties was not fully engaged in the dispute. Thirty-one entries in an instance case, beginning with the first session of the book, tell us that "[s]ince John [Killok of Ely, the plaintiff] is out of the country, it is not known where, but he is said to be dead, the case is pending."[51] John Weston of Sutton, who is described as a leech, had Agnes daughter of Nicholas Attehull of Stretham cited in a marriage case.[52] Fearing that he would flee, the court assigned him all terms (i.e., required his personal presence at every session). He in fact appears at none of them, and the court's attempt to supply his absence with an *ex officio* witness fails to prove the marriage. Agnes obtains a judgment in her favor. In an office/instance case, a Cambridge cordwainer obtains a sentence in favor of his marriage with a servant girl. He has only two witnesses, but the defendant never appears.[53] In another such case, another Cambridge cordwainer fails to appear after introducing some testimony about his principal claim.[54]

45 *Bretenham c Attehull* (29.v.77 to 9.vii.77), fol. 73r–76v.
46 *Curteys c Polay* (15.vii.77 to 12.xi.77), fol. 77v–81v.
47 *Mille c Cordel* (18.xii.76 to 24.xii.76), fol. 59v.
48 *Everard c Beneyt* (3.xi.76 to 17.xii.76), fol. 55Bv–58v (at nn. 67–74).
49 *Page c Chapman* (17.iii.79 to 3.ii.80), fol. 113r–128r; lit. T&C no. 412.
50 *Boyton c Andren* (16.x.76 to 3.xi.76), fol. 55Bv.
51 *Killok c Pulton* (24.iii.74 to 3.vii.76), fol. 5v–50r; text and disc. T&C no. 413.
52 *Weston c Attehull* (29.v.77 to 9.vii.77), fol. 73r–76v; disc. T&C no. 414.
53 *Schrovesbury c Curtyes* (10.vi.79 to 21.vii.79), fol. 117r–119r.
54 *Arneys c Salman* (10.vi.79 to 25.x.80), fol. 117r–144v; lit. T&C no. 415.

In this group of cases, the most blatant example of noncooperation with the court occurs in *John Saffrey of Wimpole c Alice daughter of Richard Molt of Wendy*.[55] Cited *ex officio* for clandestine contract of marriage and intercourse, the couple never appear together. John admits something that looks like a *de futuro* contract. Alice appears by an uninformed proctor, is suspended, requests absolution, promises to obey, and then goes out and marries another man. She is cited, along with her new husband, Warren Martyn of Royston, and her father, Richard, who is said to have arranged the marriage. They appear and claim that the archdeacon has cognizance of the case, a claim that the court seems to accept so far as proceedings for illegal solemnization are concerned. The case ends with several entries stating that Alice is to be cited, and then it disappears from view.[56]

I have suggested that the line between instance and office cases at Ely was not a sharp one. This group illustrates that proposition well. If the nine straight-instance cases seem to fit the model of civil litigation, with two private parties disputing and the court serving as a neutral arbiter, there are fissures in this picture. Was Robert Mille's case determined in six days (18–24 December 1376) because, despite his five witnesses, he decided to give up?[57] Or was it determined in six days because the court told him: "We're not impressed with your witnesses, Robert, why don't you let Annabel go home free for Christmas?" Why does John Bretenham need to produce witnesses to his marriage contract when Agnes Attehull conceded that it had taken place?[58] The two cases in this subgroup that do not have sentences show how extraordinarily reluctant the court was to give a default judgment.[59] There are no authorized compromises of marriage cases in the Ely act book. There are many such compromises (indicated by *pax*) in cases of breach of faith or defamation.

Cases that we have characterized as office/instance do not form a single group. Some of these cases are virtually indistinguishable from instance cases, except, for example, that the commissary hearing the case mentions that in addition to the plaintiff's request for an instance citation, he had heard about the case through *publica fama*, or that the bishop heard the case initially and commissioned his consistory officials to hear it, after citing the defendant.[60] In other cases, the court takes a much more active role. In one case, begun as an instance case and already noted, the court makes considerable effort to get the plaintiff to pursue it, and when he fails to do so, tries to introduce evidence of the marriage *ex officio*.[61] In another, also already noted, it would seem that the court insisted on investigating whether the marriage was impeded by affinity

[55] *Saffrey c Molt* (3.vii.75 to 28.ii.76), fol. 27r–40v; lit. T&C no. 416.

[56] Lit. T&C no. 417.

[57] *Mille c Cordel* (n. 47).

[58] *Bretenham c Attehull* (n. 45). For a possible answer, see *Weston c Attehull* (n. 52), which almost certainly involves the same defendant.

[59] *Killok c Pulton* (n. 51); *Arneys c Salman* (n. 54).

[60] *Bradenho c Taillor* (n. 36); *Wedone c Cobbe and Franceys* (n. 35).

[61] *Weston c Attehull* (n. 52).

by illicit intercourse, and came to the conclusion, apparently contrary to the wishes of both of the parties, that it was.[62]

Why the court was more active in some cases than in others we do not know. That the court in many instances knew or suspected things about the parties that do not appear in the record seems virtually certain. That the different judges whose activity is recorded in the Ely act book differed among themselves in their personalities and legal outlooks is at least possible.[63]

One thing does seem relatively clear from the evidence of these cases, though it is admittedly circumstantial. Cordwainers who were thought to have contracted marriage with servant girls – to take the case that gives us the greatest indications of class and status of the parties – were more likely to receive an *ex officio* citation in a marriage case than were male residents of the environs of Cambridge who claimed that they had contracted with a widow in a village six miles to the south of Cambridge, particularly when both of them could afford proctors.[64]

If, however, we are asking questions (even though we may not be able to answer them) about the knowledge and attitudes of the judges, we should ask similar questions about the parties. Here, there seems to have been a wide range of attitudes. Some of the parties seem to have accepted the intervention of the court or, at least, to have tolerated it. Others, like Alice Molt and her father, did their best to evade it.[65] Not surprisingly, there is more evidence of evasion and resistance in cases begun with *ex officio* citations than there is in cases begun with instance citations, though John Weston's behavior suggests that the correlation is far from perfect.[66]

Weston's case also leads to another point: Unlike many continental ecclesiastical courts, the Ely court (like all English ecclesiastical courts of which I am aware) had no promotors, court officials who were responsible for presenting evidence in office cases. As Weston's case shows, and as we will discover when we look at the straight-office cases, the court could bring forward *ex officio* witnesses. How they found them we do not know, but one suspects the activity of the local clergy and perhaps also of the apparitors. But as Weston's case also shows, such witnesses did not always present a very powerful case. The court in that case had to admit that its own witness did not prove it. Hence, even in office cases, the court was frequently dependent on the cooperation of the parties.

The necessity for the cooperation of the parties leads immediately to another question that has been the subject of some discussion in the literature. How sophisticated were the parties? How much did they know about what they needed to show in order to have a case or to defeat one? The evidence of this

62 *Office c Symond and Page* (n. 37).
63 Disc. T&C no. 418.
64 Compare, e.g., *Schrovesbury c Curtyes* (n. 53), with *Band c Pryme* (n. 40).
65 *Saffrey c Molt* (n. 55).
66 *Weston c Attehull* (n. 52).

group of cases (and this will be confirmed in other groups), is that by the time they got to court, they certainly knew the basics. The Cambridgeshire residents, many of whom do not seem to have been of very high status, who could present an oral libel stating that they had contracted marriage "by words of the present tense or by words of the future tense followed by sexual intercourse" (what we have called the 'formula' libel) clearly knew, again by the time they got to court, the basic rules of the canon law on the formation of marriage.

Similarly, as we have seen, the parties present defenses of unfulfilled condition (three cases), servile condition, and affinity by illicit intercourse (two cases). This, too, suggests some sophistication, but here we must be cautious. Knowing the defense (or learning about it) and knowing how to present it effectively are not the same thing. The case involving servile condition is particularly interesting because the record is unusually vivid:[67]

John Everard of Ely and Joan residing with Robert Beneyt of the same [were] cited before us, the official of Ely [Richard Scrope], for the Monday after the feast of All Saints' [3.xi.76] in the church of Holy Trinity of the city of Ely, concerning a contract of marriage that *publica fama* reports was entered into or made between them. They both appeared[68] personally before us and were sworn to tell the truth and questioned about the contract. John confessed, and proposed and alleged that he and Joan contracted marriage with each other in words of the present tense expressing their mutual consent. Both of them then confessed and acknowledged this contract in the presence of each other and of other trustworthy persons, and *publica fama* is known to be at work about these things. Wherefore John asked that Joan be adjudged by definitive sentence to be his lawful wife and he her lawful husband. When questioned about the contract, Joan confessed that they contracted in this form and no other: John asked her in this form: "Dost thou want to have me as husband (*vis tu habere me in virum*)?" and she replied, "Yes," and that it pleased her.[69] Joan also confessed that afterwards they took care to have the banns published in the face of the church. Whence the following day in the above place was set down and assigned to the same John and Joan to show reasonable cause, if they have one, why they should not be judged married according to their confessions. On which day and place before us, Thomas Gloucestre, commissary of the lord official of Ely, the parties appeared personally. Joan proposed that at the time she contracted, before and after, John was and still is a serf, neif, and of servile condition (*servus et nativus et servilis condicionis*). Ignorant of his condition, she contracted with him as aforesaid; otherwise she would not have contracted. She also alleged that from the time the servile condition became apparent to her, she immediately repented, said the opposite, and dissented, and that she repents at the present time, says the opposite, and dissents. Further, John confessed that he is a serf and of servile condition, but said by way of replication that Joan knew him to be a serf long before the contract and after. The parties on each side swore against calumny, to tell the truth, and against malice. A

[67] *Everard c Beneyt* (n. 48), T&C no. 419. All the substantive proceedings were oral, so Foxton could not rely on any written documents, which would now be lost.

[68] Foxton was rather careless with his tenses. I have converted some unusual present tenses to past tenses.

[69] Lit. T&C no. 419, n. 2.

day was given in the next consistory [13.xi.76] in St Michael's church, Cambridge, to prove on each side their propositions.

[13.xi.76, in St Michael's, Cambridge] . . . the parties appeared by proctors. No witnesses were produced by John and Joan or by either of them. A day was given in the next [consistory, 4.xii.76] for the second production.

. . . [The parties appeared personally before the official in Holy Trinity, Ely, on 17.xii.76.] No witnesses were produced by the parties or either of them, but some positions were made by us [Scrope] to the same parties for the information of our conscience, viz., to John whether he then was and now is a serf, neif, and of servile condition, and to Joan whether at the time of the contract confessed between them she knew this John to be of servile condition. John and Joan were sworn to tell the truth in this matter and questioned about the positions. John confessed that he then was and now is a serf and of servile condition. Joan confessed that at the time of the contract, before and after, she knew that he was of servile condition and that notwithstanding the condition they contracted with each other as previously described and had marriage banns between them publicly published in the face of the church. We declared a conclusion in the case because the parties proposed nothing effectual whereby marriage between them ought not be adjudged, and we set and assigned the hour of third bell after dinner on this Wednesday in the same place to hear the definitive sentence in the case. At which time and place the parties appeared personally before us, the official, and asked again whether they knew anything to propose ?aloud[70] why judgment should not be rendered in favor of the marriage according to their confessions poured out before us in court, they say that they do not know anything to propose except that they have changed their minds because they believe they do not love each other as a result of the resistance Joan has made. . . . [*Sentence*:] Since we find that John has founded and proved well and sufficiently his intention brought [before us] and that no canonical impediment stands in the way, we adjudge in this writing by sentence and definitively that John is Joan's lawful husband and Joan John's lawful wife, decreeing that the marriage be solemnized between them in the face of the church at an appropriate time and place.

Whether the words that Joan admits to having exchanged with John amount to words of the present tense is not completely clear, but nothing is made of this. It is significant that Joan does not present her defense until after a recess, and we might imagine that she consulted with someone who knew more about the law than she did.[71] When she returns, she has it right: In order for the impediment of servile condition to be operative, the non-servile party must be unaware of the status at the time of the contract. She is unable to produce witnesses, however. The fact that the parties do not appear at the only regular session of the case, the one at St Michael's Cambridge, even though they did appear by proctors, suggests that the journey may have been beyond their means. So the official comes to them (as he had when he first heard the case).[72] He holds them to an *ex officio* oath, and under the pressure of the oath, Joan admits that she knew of John's status when she contracted with him. She now has no

[70] See T&C no. 419, n. 4.
[71] Disc. T&C no. 420.
[72] Disc. T&C no. 421.

case, though she may not have realized this when she swore.[73] The couple quite frankly admit that they no longer love each other, but the official pushes them into the marriage.

To call the action of the official oppressive would certainly be to exaggerate; 'paternalistic' might be a better word.[74] Joan's residence with Robert Beneyt suggests that she was not an independent woman; John was, by his own admission, a villein, though his residence in Ely suggests that he was not living and acting as a peasant. Joan knew or found out something about how to defend her case, but she did not find out enough. Or, perhaps, her fear of the oath and the ambiguity of her feelings toward John ultimately led her to give up. One may suspect that a rather unhappy couple left Holy Trinity, Ely, in the dark of the late afternoon of 17 December 1376. They may have made up, but of their future lives we know nothing. What the records give us reason to suspect is that the official would not, and could not, have behaved in a similar fashion with people of higher status, those with greater knowledge or more assistance.

Our examination of the two-party cases suggests that our notion that male plaintiffs were more persistent in instance litigation at Ely may be a chimera. There are some cases that suggest this, but there are many other factors that may be producing this seeming result. The persistence might be that of the court rather than that of either of the parties; the distinction between instance and office/instance litigation was sufficiently permeable that it is unclear that statements should be made about straight-instance litigation; noncooperation of one or both of the parties is likely to produce distorted persistence statistics.

As was the case at York, so too at Ely, three-party cases are more complex. Ten of them involve male plaintiffs, five instance and five office, though one, as suggested earlier, could well be classified as instance. Five result in sentences for at least one of the male plaintiffs, two in sentences for the defendant(s); two have continuations beyond the chronological range of the book, and one disappears from view. Classification problems abound with three-party cases. As noted, the records classify some as marriage-and-divorce cases and some as competitor cases. The reality is more ambiguous. Rare is the marriage-and-divorce case in which the couple are equally assiduous in defending their marriage, so much so that one of them, almost always the woman, frequently emerges as a 'competitor'. Rare, too, is the competitor case where the defendant is defending each suit equally vigorously. In many cases, he or she will concede one suit and defend the other. In the tables, we have drawn the distinction between the two types of cases on the basis of whether or not a divorce sentence would have to accompany the sentence for the successful plaintiff (even if such a sentence was not given). Even this distinction runs into difficulties because there are cases in which a competitor and a defendant marry (wrongfully) *pendente lite*, and, hence, a judgment adverse to the couple will order marriage and divorce, even though that judgment could not have been predicted at the beginning of the

[73] Disc. and lit. T&C no. 422.

[74] Disc. T&C no. 423.

case. The following account seeks to tell the story of each suit, proceeding from the least to the most complicated without drawing any distinction between the two types of cases. It will take some time; three-party cases at Ely tell us more than do two-party cases.

The simplest three-party case brought by a male plaintiff takes just three days to resolve. John Rolf of Grantchester reclaimed against the banns of Alice Northern of Grantchester and Robert Myntemor of Trumpington. All three were cited by the official for a day out of session.[75] Robert and Alice confessed to a contract by words of the present tense followed by intercourse; John claimed that he had precontracted with Alice, an allegation which she denied. (She also denied that she had had intercourse with John, though he had not alleged that.) John produced two witnesses and Robert six. Three days later the testimony is published and the court rules that Robert has proven his claim and that John has not proven his. Robert and Alice are adjudged to be husband and wife.

No proctors are mentioned any place in the record. While the parties may have consulted with one, one can imagine that the preparation for the case was done with the assistance of the parish priest(s) at either Trumpington or Grantchester or both. When John made his reclamation, he was told that he would be cited to appear before the official in Cambridge (both towns are in the environs of Cambridge) and that he would need witnesses. Robert and Alice were told the same. Hence, the parties came prepared with their witnesses, and the whole affair was over remarkably quickly, much to the delight of Robert and Alice, but perhaps also with the grudging acquiescence of John. Whatever his relations with Alice, it was certainly important for him, too, to know that he had no case, as the record certainly suggests.

If *Rolf and Myntemor c Northern* shows how expeditious the court could be when the parties were cooperative, *Kirkeby c Poket* shows how frustrated it was when they were not.[76] William Kirkeby of Barnwell (just northeast of Cambridge) and Margaret Poket of the same place were cited before the official concerning a contract of marriage. At the beginning of February, 1380, they appeared in Chesterton church (near Barnwell) before the official where they admitted that they had contracted marriage with words of the present tense followed by intercourse. The court had also learned that Margaret had precontracted with one Thomas Swon. She admitted to a contract six years previously, although there was some ambiguity in the wording.[77] Intercourse, however, had followed, and so under the law, the parties would have been deemed to have waived any condition in their contract. William is ordered to prove his contract with Margaret, Margaret that with Thomas. At the next session the parties are contumacious; they are suspended from entry into the church. The suspension is executed at the next session. The parties reappear in April, and nothing is said about the suspension. They are once more contumacious and are cited to

75 *Rolf and Myntemor c Northern* (10.v.80 to 13.v.80), fol. 137v.
76 *Kirkeby c Poket* (3.ii.80 to 25.x.80), fol. 129r–144v.
77 T&C no. 424, with disc.

proceed according to the past acts. This entry is repeated at each session until October, when the case disappears from view.

There is more that the court could have done in this case. As we learn from other cases, contumacy could be punished by suspension, excommunication, aggravated excommunication, and, ultimately, caption by the secular arm. There were also more vigorous forms of citation that could be used before these steps were taken. While it is possible that William and Margaret had fled, there is nothing in the record to suggest that they were not still living in Barnwell, and Barnwell is within easy walking distance of where the court was sitting. Perhaps we should revisit our record to see if it contains any hints as to why the court was so passive in this particular case (though, as we will see, it was not in others).

William and Margaret had contracted marriage and had had intercourse. There is no particular reason to doubt their word, despite the fact that they showed no eagerness to solemnize the marriage. One suspects that the reason they showed no eagerness to solemnize it is that they knew very well about Thomas. Margaret obviously did, and if William did too (or suspected something along these lines), that would account for his not moving toward solemnization. Banns would bring out the facts (or suspicions) about Thomas. Someone, in fact, did know about Thomas and told the official about him. Margaret is honest. She is quite willing to admit what happened between Thomas and her, but Thomas is no place to be found, and she may well have no proof of what happened six years ago. Even if she does have proof, what incentive does she have to present it? What use to her is a judgment that she is married to a man who has disappeared and that she cannot solemnize her marriage to a man who is very much present and seems to want to marry her?

A more cynical couple might have presented incontrovertible proof of their current marriage and then deliberately failed in their proof of the prior one. That, of course, would run the risk of someone else being able to prove the contract with Thomas (or of Thomas himself returning, like Martin Guerre), but neither possibility seems very likely. Margaret, however, was not that kind of a woman. She confessed the marriage to Thomas when she was under no compulsion, other than the beady eye of the official, to do so. Besides, now that the facts have been confessed in open court, William's attitude may have changed, for it is now clear that he is not just engaged in an informal marriage; he is committing adultery. In short, William and Margaret are in a real dilemma, a dilemma that their straightforward acknowledgment of the facts to the official have gotten them into.[78]

Now if this reconstruction of the facts is plausible, then we may have an explanation of why John Newton, the official of Ely at this point, did not pursue this particular couple with any vigor. Proof of the contract between William and Margaret, without proof of the contract between Thomas and Margaret, would lead to judgment that they should marry, a ruling that would clearly be

[78] Disc. T&C no. 425.

against Margaret's conscience, and which ought to be against William's and John Newton's own. Proof of the contract between Thomas and Margaret, with or without proof of the contract between William and Margaret, would mean that William and Margaret could not solemnize their marriage, but that is not going to happen anyway. Margaret has said enough (and it is in Foxton's record) that her marriage to William will not proceed without proof either that she was mistaken when she said that she contracted with Thomas or that Thomas is dead. If William and Margaret live together openly and scandalously, the archdeacon will take care of them. Perhaps the rest should be left to their consciences.

The next three-party case is relatively simple when it reaches the Ely consistory, but it had a prehistory of unknown length before the official of the archdeacon. Matilda Tyd, widow of John Tyd, appealed from a judgment in favor of Walter Quernepekkere of Cambridge late in July of 1379. Walter, we learn from the final sentence in the case, had claimed that he had precontracted with Matilda before she contracted with one John Alderford.[79] (John does not appear in the proceedings, though he may have been supporting Matilda behind the scenes.) Walter confesses that the appeal was properly taken, and the *processus* is ordered from the archdeacon's court. Remarkably, it arrives in four days. Matilda produces four witnesses over the course of the summer and fall. On January 12, the consistory court renders judgment:

> [Because] we have found that the definitive sentence [of the archdeacon's official] was given rashly and wickedly by an incompetent judge, [a sentence] not having legal power and without lawful proofs, contrary to the law, in prejudice of the marriage of another, [a marriage] entered into and confessed and proved between Matilda and John Alderford – [a sentence] in unwritten form and otherwise contrary to due process of law – . . . and because we have found that Walter has insufficiently founded and proved the marriage contracted between him and Matilda, the marriage between John and Matilda entered into and clearly proved standing in the way, we dismiss and absolve this Matilda from Walter's petition and instance by this our definitive sentence, leaving [the rest] to their consciences.[80]

Some of this must be understood in the light of the dispute between the consistory court and the court of the archdeacon. When the dispute was finally resolved by Archbishop Arundel in 1400, the archdeacon's court was declared incompetent to give judgments in marriage cases. Echoes of that claim of incompetence are found in this case, although there are other cases in the book where judgments of the archdeacon's court in marriage cases are upheld. There is, however, language in this sentence that suggests that John Newton thought that the judgment of the archdeacon's official was incompetent in a more colloquial sense. The diplomatic of sentences of reversal tends to be strong. "Rashly and wickedly" (*temere et inique*) and "against due process" (*contra debitum iuris processum*, normally *contra iuris ordinem*) are quite standard phrases, but

[79] *Quernepekkere c Tyd* (21.vii.79 to 12.i.80), fol. 119r–126r.
[80] Fol. 126r, T&C no. 426.

"without lawful proofs," "in prejudice of the confessed and proved marriage entered into between Matilda and John Alderford," and "in unwritten form" are not standard phrases. Clearly, Newton thought that the archdeacon's official had botched the job.[81] But John Newton may also have had his doubts. Other sentences of absolution specifically leave the matter to the parties' consciences, but the phrase does not appear often. While we cannot exclude the possibility that Foxton left out what was a standard piece of diplomatic, Foxton's careful record keeping does not make that possibility likely. That in turn suggests that sometimes the official put the phrase in his sentences, but often he did not. It is hence possible that where he did so, he did it because for some reason his conscience was troubled by what he had seen.

That, in turn, brings us to Walter. He had pursued the case before the archdeacon's official, but before the consistory court he is remarkably passive. He consents to the appeal, and when the *processus* is received, he offers, so far as we can tell, no testimony and no arguments in its defense. The burden of presentation was on Matilda. She was the one who had to invalidate the sentence. Nonetheless, Walter's pursuit of the case does not look very vigorous. He does not even hire a proctor, and there is nothing in the record to suggest that he could not afford one. It is possible that once he saw how determined Matilda was to marry John Alderford, he decided that he was well enough rid of her, but if he had precontracted with her, his moral situation and that of Matilda and John were precarious indeed.

Our fourth case is more complicated: On 16 April 1381, John Webstere of Ely brought instance proceedings out of session in the hospital of St John at Ely asking that Isabel daughter of John Herberd of Walden, resident in Ely, be adjudged his wife.[82] No citation was necessary because Isabel was already present in court to answer an *ex officio* citation about a marriage between her and Robert de Sampford former servant of Richard Rugman now residing with Roger Bolleman cordwainer of St Ives. John alleges that he and Isabel contracted *de presenti* on the previous Michaelmas and that intercourse followed. Isabel admits this allegation. Isabel also admits that she had contracted with Robert two years previously and that intercourse had followed, but she alleges that this marriage cannot stand because Robert had previously contracted with Beatrix de Sampford. Two witnesses to Isabel's precontract are admitted "for the information of the court's conscience (*pro informacione consciencie nostre*)." (This last phrase may mean that they were produced *ex officio*, though we may suspect that Isabel was instrumental in getting them there. It clearly expresses the principle that the court will not rule on the confession of the parties alone when the rights of third parties are at stake.)

The case is set down for a day out of session in Cambridge (to which Robert is to be cited "if he can be found") but does not, in fact, reappear until the regular session of the court at the beginning of May. John appears personally

[81] Further examples T&C no. 427.

[82] *Webstere and Sampford c Herberd* (16.iv.81 to 16.i.82), fol. 149r–159v; lit. T&C no. 428.

and Isabel by a proctor, but no further witnesses are produced. Two more sessions produce no further witnesses. Finally, at a regular session at the end of October, Isabel excepts that before she and Robert contracted, Robert and Alice Whiston of Hildersham had contracted marriage, a contract that impedes hers with Robert. Two witnesses are produced; their examination is committed to the archdeacon's official; the testimony is returned and published, and in the middle of January 1382, the court rules that Isabel and John are husband and wife, Isabel's previous marriage to Robert being specifically invalidated because of his precontract with Alice.

Geography lends plausibility to Isabel's account of Robert's activities. Hailing from Sampford (in Essex, but fairly close to the southern border of Cambridgeshire), he abandons a woman from his hometown and another from a Cambridgeshire town about 10 miles from Sampford in order to enter into a term of service in Ely in the northern part of the diocese. Having contracted a third relationship with Isabel (whose father [and perhaps she] comes from Walden in Essex, which is quite close to Sampford), he abandons her after his term of service in order to take up residence, perhaps an apprenticeship, with a cordwainer in St Ives in the western part of the diocese, near Huntingdon. None of these places is that far from one another, but they are far enough that they would afford some refuge for a young man who needed to 'get out of town'.

Isabel was apparently unable to prove the relationship between Robert and Beatrix of Sampford, but the court accepted her two witnesses (a married couple from Ely) about his relationship with Alice of Hildersham. Robert never appears in the case (the remark in the record that he is to be cited "if he can be found" suggests that the court was well aware that he would have reasons not to be found). His appearance might have clarified the matter considerably, but it could also have added an element of complexity, for he might have had a different story from that of Isabel, and that story, in turn, would need to be verified with the other women whom he was alleged to have wronged. The court's failure to pursue Robert may have been motivated, if only subconsciously, by a desire to let Isabel tell her story of a woman wronged and get on with her life.

What this case does tell us is that it is possible sometimes to develop story-patterns from records that we find in the act book. And it also tells us that simply looking at who is suing whom and what they are claiming is not enough. In particular, John, the nominal plaintiff in the case, is almost a cipher (he does appear personally at most of the sessions). It is Isabel who hires a proctor; Isabel who sees to it that the case proceeds, and she tells a typically female story.

The male plaintiffs in *John Pottere of Carlton and Thomas atte Pool of Wilbraham c Alice Briggeman of Carlton* (two towns to the east of Cambridge about five miles apart) are more active, but not much more.[83] John is cited *ex officio* at a regular session of the court in May of 1381 to show cause why he is impeding the marriage of Thomas and Alice. Thomas appears out of session

[83] *Pottere and Pool c Briggeman* (2.v.81 to 27.ii.82), fol. 150r–161v.

six days later and brings an instance matrimonial action against Alice. All three appear at the next session of the court at the end of May. Both men allege a 'formula' marriage with Alice. Alice concedes that in both cases she contracted marriage with them, with John in Easter week of 1380 and with Thomas on 2 February 1381. She denies intercourse with either of them, explicitly in the case of Thomas and implicitly in the case of John. Fearing that they will flee, the court cites them to all acts and enjoins them not to proceed further with the contracts *pendente lite*.

The court's fears were well founded. It takes an excommunication to get them to reappear in court, which they do six months later. At this point John calls a priest as a witness, who, with John's consent, is allowed to reveal the contents of John's confession to him.[84] Thomas, on his side, calls John as a witness. At the next session, a man of Wilbraham is produced (the record does not say by whom) and another is to be compelled to come to testify. That man is then contumacious, and an entry in the last session recorded in the book (March 1382) indicates that he is still being sought.

This record tells us less than does that in *Webstere and Sampford c Herberd*, but it tells us something. The fact that the parties are uniformly contumacious for six months (none of them appears at any session for which they were called) and then uniformly appear at all sessions suggest that they had gotten together and decided that the case had to be settled by the consistory court. (Of course, their excommunication probably played some role in their decision.) The fact that Thomas calls John as a witness (a highly unusual move; I cannot recall ever having seen it elsewhere) also suggests that they knew each other and were cooperating (I am not suggesting colluding) in getting the matter resolved. The fact that John needs to call his confessor suggests that his problem (and perhaps Alice's, of whose role and desires we can be less sure) is that he has no witnesses. Finally, the fact that it is men of Wilbraham who are being called as witnesses at the end suggests that the question now is whether Thomas can prove his marriage. If Thomas cannot prove his marriage, then Alice and John are free to marry, her confession of the marriage to Thomas notwithstanding, because her confession makes clear that her marriage to Thomas was subsequent to that with John.

If this is the assumption under which the case is proceeding (and we cannot be sure because the case does not reach the sentence), then we have a rather interesting application of the principle of hierarchy of proof as it applies to marriage cases. If Thomas and Alice had publicly married in the face of the church, then John would have to have two witnesses to prove his prior marriage to Alice. The occult does not prejudice the manifest (*occulta manifestis non preiudicant*). But John got in in time and 'impeded' the marriage of Thomas and Alice, and so the question is what standard of proof the court will insist upon when we are dealing with two informal marriages. If one can be proven by two witnesses and the other cannot, then that one will prevail. This much seems

[84] Disc. T&C no 429.

clear by the way that the court is proceeding. The way that it is proceeding also suggests that Alice's confession in court, plus John's confession to his priest, may prevail over the later marriage to Thomas, if Thomas cannot prove that marriage by two witnesses.

The next case has entries running over more than a year and was still technically active when the act book ends. It begins with *ex officio* citations of Nicholas Mansonn of Barnwell (adjoining Cambridge to the east) and Agnes Coo of Arrington (about 10 miles to the west of Cambridge) to respond concerning a contract of marriage.[85] A similar citation was issued to Robert Bakere of Cambridge and the same Agnes. The men both appear at a regular session of the court at the end of January, 1381. Nicholas alleges that he contracted marriage *de presenti* with Agnes the previous Pentecost, Robert that they contracted *de presenti*, had intercourse, and that their banns were published sometime in the previous autumn.

Agnes, who was not present at the first session, appears at the second. She denies ever having contracted with Nicholas or having had intercourse with him (something he had not alleged). She admits having contracted with Robert, but alleges that the contract was conditional on her father's consent, which was not forthcoming. Then she had intercourse with Robert. This last admission, though she may not have known it, vitiated her argument of conditional consent because the law presumed that if the parties had intercourse after they had contracted conditionally, they waived the condition. The case does not proceed on this point, however, because Agnes's father, who is present in court, says under oath that he consented to the marriage and was pleased by it. Agnes then excepts that Robert had and still has a legal wife in London, and that he had also contracted with another woman, Matilda servant of John Clerk of Cambridge, who is still living. Robert denies the contract with Matilda (he says nothing about the wife in London). The case is set down for proof. Agnes names as a "necessary witness" (*testem sibi neccesarium*, apparently the prelude to an order compelling him to appear) a man who is a servant in Steeple Morden (a village about five miles southwest of Arrington). Robert is to exhibit a letter from London, where he used to live, stating that he is free to marry. Because the court fears that Agnes will flee, she is ordered to appear at all sessions.

The court's fears were justified; Agnes never appears again. Robert appears at one, perhaps two, more sessions, where nothing happens. Then he fails to appear and the case closes with a long series of entries, including one in the last session in the book, that Robert's suspension and Agnes's is to be executed. While it is possible that the court got the case going again, that does not seem likely. It is not clear that Nicholas appears at all of these sessions, but he may have appeared by the proctor whom he appointed early on.

One thing is reasonably clear from this messy record: Agnes did not want to marry either Nicholas or Robert. Her father was quite happy with the stranger from London and betrayed his daughter to say so, but Agnes was adamant.

[85] *Masonn and Bakere c Coo* (31.i.81 to 27.ii.82), fol. 147r–161v.

She may have contracted with and have had intercourse with Robert, but now she alleges that he is a double bigamist. Her allegations give us a glimpse into a world of rumors, where men from London have a checkered past (and living wives in the big city) and servant girls in Cambridge contract marriage with them. Another servant now working on the western border of the diocese (but still less that 15 miles from Cambridge) is a necessary witness to all this.

We may suspect that the court did not take Agnes at her word, but it had to give her an opportunity to prove these allegations. Agnes took advantage of the opportunity to disappear. The border of Lincoln diocese is close by Arrington, and she may have slipped across it. Writing entries in a court book that her suspension from entering the church is to be 'executed', however, is not very strong medicine (even if the order was communicated to the parish priest of Arrington). If we look to the male plaintiffs, perhaps we can find a reason why the court did not take stronger measures. Nicholas had an opportunity to prove his contract with Agnes, but he does not come forward with any witnesses. Something may have happened between Agnes and him, but when she denies it, he needs witnesses, or he has no case. Something pretty clearly did happen between Robert and Agnes, but serious doubts have been raised about Robert's past. He could have obtained a letter of freedom to marry from the official of London, but he did not when he was ordered to do so. Once it was apparent that Agnes had disappeared, Robert, too, disappeared. The authority of the court is maintained by repeated entries in the court book that Robert and Agnes cannot enter the church, and Nicholas is left to pay his proctor's bill.

John Wedone jr c Geoffrey Cobbe of Wimpole and Eleanor Franceys de facto wife of Geoffrey Cobbe was begun, as we noted earlier, with a delegation of the case from the bishop's audience to the official of the consistory court, Richard Scrope, and two men who had been serving as commissaries of the court, Thomas Gloucestre and John Newton.[86] The last-named presides at a number of the sessions and is ultimately authorized by the bishop to give sentence. Eleanor's appearance in the case is never recorded (Newton holds her contumacious a number of times, but ultimately does not force the issue). The case proceeds strictly in accordance with the *ordo*, without the elements of summary process that are usual in many Ely marriage cases. Over the course of more than a year, John produces a chaplain as a witness. He obtains the compulsion of one John Morden of Boxworth (Wimpole and Boxworth are both within 10 miles of Cambridge on the west side of the town) and one Henry Milk, whose place of residence is not identified. He also obtains a *missio* to London to examine one Margaret, a former servant of Eleanor, and, perhaps, a *missio* to examine Eleanor herself.[87] It is unclear whether any of these witnesses was examined. No publication of testimony is mentioned, and one entry, quite close to the end, specifically says that John has not procured the examination

86 See at n. 35; lit. T&C no. 430.
87 Disc. T&C no. 431.

of the witnesses. Ultimately, Newton holds that John has not proven his claim and condemns him to pay Geoffrey and Eleanor their costs "because of his rash importunity and unjust vexation."[88]

Much in this case would suggest that the parties were of a higher social station than those with whom we have dealt previously. The fact that the case is begun in the bishop's audience (and that he reserves the right to render sentence until the very end of the case); the delicate treatment of Eleanor's contumacy; the equally delicate treatment of her former servant, resident in London; the fact that Eleanor herself may be resident in London; the use of long-form procedure throughout the case, and the fact that the parties, when they appear, always do so by proctors all point to this conclusion. Whether there was anything to John's claim we will never know. What we do know is that he was given ample opportunity to build a case (the court questions whether he should be granted a *missio* in his third term to produce witnesses but ultimately allows it), and that he failed quite decisively to do so. He failed so decisively that the court characterized his behavior as "vexatious" and awarded costs, something that is not a usual feature in sentences for defendants in marriage cases.

In July of 1380, Stephen Gobat of Sawston was cited before the consistory court (the entry does not say that the citation was *ex officio*; it may have been, but the case is treated as an instance case) for failing to obey the bishop's order that he marry Julia Bygot of Sawston.[89] He alleges that he cannot do so because Julia had previously had intercourse with William atte Moore of Sawston, who is related to Gobat within the prohibited degrees. Witnesses are produced and examined over the summer recess. An entry in October records the publication of their testimony and the case is set down for definitive sentence. Contrary to Foxton's usual practice, nothing about the case is recorded in the entries for the next session.

Indeed, nothing is recorded until March of 1381 when Stephen Pertesen of Pampisford (the village is adjacent to Sawston, both lying about five miles south of Cambridge) files an instance suit claiming Julia as his wife. He introduces witnesses who are examined on the spot and their testimony published. At the next session, nothing is said against the witnesses and their testimony, but Gobat and Julia appear and claim that they precontracted and that the consistory had adjudged their marriage valid despite the alleged affinity by illicit intercourse, because William was not in fact related to Gobat within the prohibited degrees. They introduce witnesses but then fail to appear at the next session of court, for which contumacy they are suspended. They appear personally at the next session, and Julia introduces further witnesses about her exception. Gobat and Julia are absolved of their suspension but ordered to be whipped three times around the church for their contumacy. They also admit (the record does not say how the court knew to ask the question) that they had solemnized their marriage two weeks previously in the church of Westley Waterless (about 10 miles

[88] T&C no. 432.

[89] *Gobat and Pertesen c Bygot* (23.vii.80 to 6.ii.82), fol. 143v–160v; lit. T&C no. 433.

northeast of Sawston), subjecting themselves to a major excommunication for illegal solemnization.

Gobat and Julia are once again contumacious. Over the course of the next sessions (with the intervening summer recess), the testimony of the witnesses is published and the case set down for sentencing, which occurs in November: The testimony has revealed that Gobat and William atte Moore are related to each other within the fourth degree. Gobat's marriage to Julia is dissolved and Pertesen's declared valid. At the end of November, Pertesen (who had also been absent from the sentencing) appears and accedes to the judgment. Gobat and Julia are excommunicated. Execution of the sentence is ordered at the next two sessions, and in the next to last session recorded in the book, the case is inhibited by the court of Canterbury.

Indications of the social standing of the parties to this case are ambiguous. The facts that Gobat and Julia are first ordered to get married by the bishop and that they ultimately appeal to the court of Canterbury suggest a level of sophistication higher than that of, to take the polar opposite, John Everard and Joan residing with Robert Beneyt. Gobat and Julia are never, however, represented by proctors. This is odd because there is nothing that suggests that they could not have afforded a proctor (Pertesen is, at one point, represented by a proctor). We do not know how closely Gobat and atte Moore were related, but the fact that their relationship was in doubt suggests that they were second or third cousins. Third- and fourth-degree affinity were eminently dispensable impediments, at least for those who had the money and the persistence to apply for a dispensation, but there is no suggestion that Gobat and Julia even tried to obtain one.

The record suggests that there were ambiguities in the relationship between Gobat and Julia. The bishop orders them to marry, an order that Gobat at first attempts to resist by raising the issue of affinity by illicit intercourse. It may well be that it was during this period, when Julia could not be sure of Gobat's commitment to her, that she formed her relationship with Pertesen, one which she later denies but for which there seems to be firm evidence. Gobat then changes his mind, but by this time Pertesen is in court seeking to enforce his contract with Julia. Gobat and Julia then find a priest who is willing to solemnize their marriage, but this, of course, simply gets them into deeper trouble. They disappear; so does Pertesen, but the three of them have left enough evidence in the court's possession that it can, in their absence, render a judgment invalidating the marriage of Gobat and Julia and affirming that of Pertesen and Julia. That is all very well with Pertesen, but Gobat and Julia appeal to the court of Canterbury, and we do not know what happened there.

What of the role of the court in all this? Clearly, the court thought that Gobat and Julia were defying its authority. The penance for their initial contumacy in Pertesen's case is unusual. Normally, when someone fails to appear at the beginning of a proceeding and is suspended but then appears in the next session, the court simply absolves them. Here, it orders them whipped around the church three times. Of course, by this time the court knew that they had solemnized their marriage and thus were subject to much more serious sanctions than those for contumacy. They continued to defy the court's authority, and their ultimate excommunication is not surprising. This excommunication seems to have brought them to the realization that something had to be done about their situation, and hence the appeal to the court of Canterbury.

One more piece of evidence about what the court did is more ambiguous but worth suggesting: When Gobat and Julia appeared to defend Pertesen's case, they argued that the consistory court had held that their marriage was lawful and that William atte Moore was not related to Gobat within the prohibited degrees. The record that we now have has no indication that the court had so ruled (the case is simply set down for sentence and no sentence is recorded). But the record that we have is odd. The case is set down for sentencing, but not only does no sentence appear at the next session (or at any session between that time and the time that Pertesen brings suit five months later), but Foxton also did not enter, as was his normal practice, any indication of a continuation of the case. It is possible that the court told them to get married (the bishop had, after all, ordered them to do so), but was reluctant to record a judgment about the charge of affinity by illicit intercourse, either because the testimony on the topic was unclear or, perhaps, because it was clear that William was something like Gobat's third cousin. In short, the court may have been giving them a dispensation 'under the table'.

If something along these lines did happen, then Julia got herself into deep trouble by forming (or having formed, we do not know when it happened) the relationship with Pertesen. Once Pertesen has sued, the court cannot quietly let the matter of the affinity drop. The relationship between atte Moore and Gobat must be proven, and Gobat and Julia's marriage is an 'illegal solemnization'. Hence, the whipping order is not just a penalty for contumacy but an expression of the court's pique that they did not take advantage of its previous indulgence.[90]

A final word on Gobat and Julia: They seem remarkably alone in the world. Not only did they never hire a proctor, but over the course of a rather long record, we also get only one indication that either of them has any family. That indication comes in the mention of who was present at the illegal solemnization: John Gobat of Sawston, William Webbe of Sawston, and Dulcia his wife. John may be Stephen Gobat's father or brother. William and Dulcia (elsewhere called 'Lucia') are almost certainly the couple whom Gobat and Julia first produce as witnesses in defending the suit by Pertesen. Dulcia may have been related to Julia (a sister or a mother who has remarried). The impression remains, however, that Gobat and Julia do not have much help. Trying to handle their affairs on their own, they do a rather bad job of it.

None of the cases that we have considered so far has entries in the record for as much as two years. We now consider two, one of which has entries for four years and four months and is still proceeding (though not very actively) when the book ends, and the other of which takes a week short of six years to resolve.

[90] Lit. T&C no. 434.

Both are instance cases; both involve widows, and both involve proceedings for illegal solemnization in addition to the basic instance case.

The simpler of the two cases is *John Fisschere of Wilburton c John son of John Frost of Wilburton and Amy widow of Robert Brid.*[91] Indeed, so far as we can tell, the fundamental issue is classically simple: Did Fisschere marry Amy before she married Frost? The basic case takes slightly over a year to resolve (December 1377 to March 1379) and involves two moves: Fisschere's presentation of his witnesses and Frost's and Amy's exceptions to those witnesses on the grounds that they perjured themselves. As with all the cases that go down on basic factual disputes, the act book tells us little about the underlying claims. It does tell us, however, that sentence was ultimately rendered by the bishop himself, and that Frost's marriage to Amy was dissolved and she and Fisschere were ordered to solemnize.

Four separate cases of illegal solemnization (all brought in December or January of 1377) are joined to this suit, two against chaplains, one against Frost and Amy, and one against Frost's father. They tell us more. The article against Robert Mustell chaplain of Wilburton charges him with having persuaded Fisschere and Amy, though he knew that they had contracted marriage, to remit that contract and to bind each other under penalty not to pursue that marriage in the future. Furthermore, although Fisschere had reclaimed the banns of Frost and Amy and had claimed precontract with Amy in a suit pending in the consistory court, Robert had the marriage of Frost and Amy solemnized in the face of Wilburton church, despite his knowledge of the precontract, the reclamation, and the suit. As the article concludes, by authority of John Stratford's constitution *Humana concupiscentia* (of which more later),[92] Robert should be suspended from office for three years and excommunicated for his contempt and because of the scandal.

These are serious charges indeed. It takes until July to resolve them, when the bishop enjoins penance on the chaplain, but does not impose the full sanction because he finds that the chaplain acted out of ignorance. A second chaplain, who was also present at the solemnization, is allowed to purge himself. Frost, senior and junior, and Amy are enjoined to do penance by the official.

All of this seems straightforward enough. That the bishop should get involved in the punishment of the chaplain who seems to have played the key role in an illegal solemnization is not at all surprising. We might wonder why the bishop got involved in the basic case. At a minimum, that would suggest that these are people of some stature, a suspicion confirmed by the fact that the long-form procedure is used and proctors are employed.[93]

Whatever the merits of the judgment in the original case, it did not sit well with Fisschere and Amy. They were back in court in May 1380, petitioning to have the bishop's sentence nullified. Four witnesses were produced; their

[91] *Fisschere c Frost and Brid* (3.xii.77 to 27.ii.82), fol. 82v–151v; lit. T&C no. 435.

[92] At n. 189.

[93] Fol. 82v–83r; lit. T&C no. 436.

testimony was published, and in December the case was set down for definitive sentence in the absence of Fisschere. This entry is then repeated in every session until the end of the book.

There is not much to go on here, but perhaps there is enough for some speculation. Frost and Amy made a big mistake when they had their marriage solemnized despite Fisschere's reclamation of their banns. (I suspect he said a great deal more at the reclamation than what Frost's father alleges he said: "They will have no joy together.")[94] That move got them decidedly off on the wrong footing when Fisschere got them into court. They made another tactical error when they chose to defend the first suit on the ground that Fisschere's witnesses were lying. They may have been lying, but the proceedings in the second case suggest that they had a better defense. Those proceedings were based on the proposition that Frost and Amy married informally before any contract was made with Fisschere. They have four witnesses to this effect, one of whom is, admittedly, Frost's father, but the others of whom look as if they are independent. When Fisschere sees the publication of the testimony, he disappears. That puts the court in a bind. It is always reluctant to render judgment in the absence of one of the parties (though sometimes it will), and to do so in this case would involve reversing a judgment that had been rendered by the bishop. One thing is clear from the long string of continuances to hear the definitive sentence: The court is not going to enforce the bishop's original judgment of its own motion. At a minimum, that means that Amy will not be forced to solemnize her marriage with Fisschere, and it may mean that Frost and Amy can resume cohabitation, quietly.

We first see *William son of Henry Anegold of Chesterton and William Schanbery of Chesterton c Margaret widow of Geoffrey Grantesden* in March of 1374, when Margaret is appealing from a judgment of the archdeacon's official, which, as we later learn, ordered her to solemnize her marriage with Anegold.[95] On the same day, an *ex officio* action is brought against Margaret, Schanbery, and one Geoffrey Smith of Chesterton. This is not said to be an action for illegal solemnization (the record simply says "in a matter of correction," *in negotio correctionis*), and the case ends in the following month without any substance being revealed. In July, however, the same three parties are back in court to answer *ex officio* charges that Schanbery and Margaret, with Smith's connivance and aid, left the diocese and had their marriage solemnized while Anegold's case was pending before the archdeacon's official. They appear by proctor, propose some dilatory exceptions, and fail to return; the court does not pursue the matter further.

In the meantime, the basic case proceeds at a glacial pace. When the *processus* is received from the archdeacon's court (the fuller version, because the first version turned out to be incomplete), Schanbery and Margaret put in their

[94] Text and disc. T&C no. 437.

[95] *Anegold and Schanbery c Grantesden* (24.iii.74 to 16.iii.80), fol. 5v–133r; disc. with lit. T&C no. 438.

claim of precontract; witnesses are introduced and examined. In November, the official admits Anegold's exceptions to the witnesses and commissions Mr John Potton to hear the case. Before Potton, Anegold introduces some witnesses; there is a byplay about their expenses and a series of delays caused apparently by Potton's illness. Ultimately, the case is set down for sentence on 3 April 1376; a space is left blank for the sentence in the record, but no sentence is entered.

On 24 April, Schanbery and Margaret were back in court appealing to the official from Potton's sentence. Since there was no record of the sentence nor of the appeal, both had to be proven, which they were. Then some testimony was introduced. In September we learn that Schanbery has died. In December of 1376, the official warns both Anegold and Margaret not to marry other people, as he hears that they are planning to do. In May of 1377, the proctors of Anegold and Margaret want to withdraw from the case, claiming that their proxies have been revoked. The official tells them that they cannot do this since issue has been joined. The official sets the case down for sentence, and this entry is made in every session from June of 1377 until March of 1380. On 16 March 1380, the official summarizes the case. The reason that Potton had ruled against Schanbery and Margaret, he tells us, is that the witnesses to their precontract were excommunicates. With the parties' consent, the official absolves the witnesses of their excommunication, reexamines them, and finds that Schanbery and Margaret did, indeed, precontract. Margaret is absolved from Anegold's suit.

Some of the delay in this case can be explained by the fact that Thomas Gloucestre, the commissary of the court, served as its only judge from the last appearance of Richard Scrope as official on 8 April 1378 until the appointment of John Newton as official (first sitting, 22 September 1379). But Thomas, as we learn in one of the entries in the case, was the official of the archdeacon who rendered the original judgment; he was thus incompetent to hear the appeal. Indeed, the fact that Thomas was incompetent to hear the case probably accounts for Scrope's commissioning John Potton to hear it. Potton's illness (for that probably accounts for the absence of his sentence from the record and the fact that both the sentence and the appeal had to be proven) was another cause of delay.[96]

That still does not account for all the delay in this case, however. The fact is that with the death of Schanbery (first reported in September of 1376), Margaret and Anegold lose interest in the case. Hardly anything happens, though the proctors keep coming back (and are told by Scrope in May of 1377 that they cannot withdraw). We may suspect that both Margaret and Anegold married others, as they were apparently threatening to do in December of 1377. For a period of more than a year, the court was in the hands of a man who was disabled from acting on the case. When John Newton becomes official, he finally

[96] Potton's illness was not fatal; he is again commissioned in *Pope and Dreu c Dreu and Newton* (n. 122).

gets around to cleaning up the record. Since no citation is mentioned, it seems that the parties came to court voluntarily. If they have married others, they, too, would have an interest in not having an outstanding judgment that they marry each other.[97]

There can be little doubt that the parties to this case were substantial people in Chesterton. The long-form procedure, the extensive use of proctors, and the court's reluctance to punish them all point to this conclusion. There is also another reason why the court would not want to enforce the judgment of both the archdeacon's official and the court's own commissary: Everyone knew that it was wrong, though not in a technical sense. As Newton's final judgment points out, if the marriage to Anegold was proven by witnesses "beyond any exception" (*omni excepcione maiores*) (and there is no reason to doubt that it was), and if the precontract between Schanbery and Margaret was proven by excommunicates (who may have been excommunicates because they had participated in the illegal solemnization), then the rules of proof dictated that the latter witnesses should not be believed. But the rules of proof lead to unconscionable results if one is convinced that what the excommunicates are saying is true, for then the rules of proof will require that Anegold and Margaret be compelled to live in an adulterous union. John Newton saw that, and he also saw that the system had a way to avoid that result, the one he ultimately used: absolution of the excommunicate for the purpose of allowing him to testify. The odd thing is that Richard Scrope did not see the same thing sometime between learning of Schanbery's death in September of 1376 and leaving office in April of 1378.[98]

Three of the cases brought by male plaintiffs are instance divorce cases. On 24 April 1381, William Kele of the village of Balsham (about eight miles southwest of Cambridge) sued his wife for divorce out of session.[99] He alleges that he had precontracted marriage followed by intercourse with Alice Burgoyne of Hockham (six miles west of Attleborough, Norf). Alice later married Robert Disse, a cottar of Bury (St Edmunds, Suff, about 15 miles from Balsham). Ellen admits only that she and William were solemnly married. The case is set down for proof in a month (also out of session), and nothing further is recorded. This is the first case we have seen in which we get any indication that the parties were peasants. Of course, the fact (if we can believe it) that Alice married a cottar does not necessarily mean that her family were cottars, much less that William and Ellen were, but it is likely that they all were of roughly the same social status. That William precontracted with a woman who came from a town 40 miles from where he now lives is not impossible, but it is a different marriage pattern from the ones that we have seen in the other cases, where the parties, particularly those of lower station, tend to contract with people who live quite close by.

97 Disc. T&C no. 439.

98 Disc. T&C no. 440.

99 *Kele c Kele* (24.iv.81), fol. 149v.

Two factors probably help to explain the court's disposition (it might be called non-disposition) of the case, skepticism and the fact that divorce cases in the Ely court were 'pure' instance cases. If the parties did not pursue them, the court would not. We might imagine a conversation between the judge and William along these lines: "I must confess, William, that I'm skeptical of your story. Granted that Ellen will not support you in the story, you are going to have to get two unimpeachable witnesses who will swear that you married Alice before you married Ellen and before she married Robert." Perhaps he neglected to mention that the court could commission the taking of testimony in another diocese, even though it could not summon people from another diocese to come before the court. Faced with the formidable task of developing a case on his own, the peasant from Balsham does not come back on the appointed day, and Foxton allows the case to drop from view.[100]

If Kele's case shows how ordinary people could fail to get what they wanted in the court, *Robert Marion of Melbourn c Agnes Umphrey of Melbourn de facto wife of Robert Marion*, shows how they could succeed.[101] In October of 1377, Robert Marion appeared before the court petitioning for a divorce between himself and his wife, Agnes Umphrey. He claims that prior to his marriage with Agnes, he had had intercourse with Katherine Brid of Whittlesford, who is Agnes's second cousin. Agnes contests the suit affirmatively. Katherine appears and confesses the intercourse and the relationship. Robert produces five witnesses: Robert vicar of Meldreth, William Aleyn of Kelsale (Suff), Peter William of the same, John Grene of Melbourn, and John Rumbold of the same. At the next session of the court, the testimony is published, the parties renounce further terms, and John Newton, acting as commissary, pronounces them divorced.

There is no reason to believe that these people were of much higher station than the Keles, but they put together a much better case. When they arrive in court, Agnes has agreed to the divorce; the woman with whom the illicit intercourse is alleged to have occurred appears with them, prepared to confess that it all happened, and there are five witnesses, including a local priest. What the function of the two witnesses from Kelsale (almost 50 miles from Cambridge near the Suffolk coast) is we cannot tell, but their presence need not provoke suspicion, when two local men and a local priest are also among the witnesses.[102] Lacking the depositions, we cannot tell how much evidence the court required. Almost certainly the witnesses were asked to confirm that Katherine and Agnes were second cousins. Whether they also were required to testify to the intercourse we can be less sure. If they were not, the case proceeded on the agreement of three people, perhaps not enough to provoke strong suspicions of collusion but enough to raise the question.

[100] Lit. T&C no. 441.

[101] *Marion c Umphrey* (2.x.77 to 22.x.77), fol. 80r–80v. See Sheehan, "Formation," 71.

[102] Whittlesford, Meldreth and Melbourn all lie about 10 miles south of Cambridge and are quite close to one another.

Robert Puf of Little Shelford and his wife, Ivette, were cited for not treating each other with marital affection in a marriage of 30 years standing. Robert claims that the marriage cannot stand because he precontracted with Marjorie Benet of Comberton, who is still alive and living in London.[103] Ivette contests negatively, and Marjorie appears and contests affirmatively. A commission is sent to the official of London to examine witnesses. When the commission is returned, the court orders the witnesses reexamined, stating that it is suspicious of the testimony from London because the witnesses do not, in fact, reside in London but locally. In the meantime, Ivette has not appeared for some time. The case may continue beyond the period of the register, but Robert may have dropped it when the fraud was discovered.[104]

Let us return to the question that we initially posed: Does a more careful examination of the underlying records confirm that men were more persistent at Ely than they were at York, as suggested by the fact that more cases involving male plaintiffs resulted in judgments at Ely than they did at York? The answer must be a qualified 'no'. There are cases, particularly those involving the pursuit of widows or higher-status women, where the male plaintiffs were persistent, but such cases also exist at York.[105] But some of the cases involving male plaintiffs that were ultimately brought to judgment turn out, on more careful examination, to have been so brought by the *rea*, who, having been sued, pursued her defense to judgment either at first instance or on appeal. In some of the cases, it is the court that forces the issue, even if it is, as it was in Anegold's case, by keeping the case on the books long enough that the parties can finally come back for a final judgment.

Our examination of these cases also confirms what our statistical analysis showed: that marriage litigation at Ely and at York was similar in the types of situations that are revealed by the litigation. We cannot always tell as much from the Ely record as we can from that at York, but everything that the record does show – and in some cases it shows quite a bit – confirms the basic similarity in the factual patterns that were presented.

CASES INVOLVING FEMALE PLAINTIFFS

We could examine systematically the cases brought by female plaintiffs, but it would not produce enough enlightenment to justify the amount of space it would take. Where the record allows us to penetrate behind legal formulae that are its principal means of communication, we see a world very similar to that at York, with perhaps somewhat less legal sophistication. A few words are, however, in order about the cases generally and about those that present unusual features.

103 *Puf c Puf and Benet* (10.x.81 to 27.ii.82), fol. 153v–162r.

104 Disc. T&C no. 442.

105 We will consider one more office/instance case that might be regarded as having a male plaintiff: *Office c Poynaunt, Swan, Goby and Pybbel* (at nn. 248–54).

A striking feature of the instance cases brought by female plaintiffs is the large number (7 of 35, 20%) in which one or the other or both parties are described as servants. In the case of the male plaintiffs, we noted that servants were not involved in the instance cases, though they were involved in the cases begun by office citations. If servants or those who claimed to have married servants sometimes needed the extra push of an office citation, that is not evident in this group. Nor are we dealing with a gender difference peculiar to plaintiffs, since there are as many cases brought by servants as there are those brought against them.

Joan Braunche of Kings Lynn, Norwich diocese, residing in Elm c John son of Thomas Dellay of Elm[106] is hardly a case at all. Joan appears and alleges a *de presenti* marriage followed by intercourse. John admits the intercourse and denies the marriage. Joan produces three witnesses on the spot, including the chaplain and vicar of Elm, and obtains a *missio* to three local clergy who are to examine other chaplains (unnamed). What is unusual about the case is that two priests who appear in court are to be examined about matters revealed to them in confession, and so are the chaplains who are to be examined on commission. In the first case, this is said expressly to be by the consent of the parties, and in the second, the parties are said to consent to the *missio*, which presumably contained instructions to reveal the matters confessed.[107] Either John was remarkably ill-informed about the consequences of his consent to this procedure (I know of only two other cases in the Ely records in which it is done)[108] or he was already having qualms of conscience about his denial. Whatever the case, at the next hearing he agrees to solemnize his marriage with Joan, and the testimony is never published.

One instance case brought to enforce a marriage formed by abjuration *sub pena nubendi* followed by intercourse contains an unusual defense. Adam servant of John Smyth of Barnwell concedes both the abjuration and the intercourse, but alleges that he told the plaintiff, Rose Rouse of Barnwell, before they had intercourse that he did not want to make her his wife.[109] The case proceeds for more than a year (15 March 1380 to 12 November 1381). At first the case is committed to the commissary, Thomas Gloucestre, who renders sentence in Adam's absence one day after the case starts. Adam then appeals to the official. Most of the time in the case is taken up with the absence of one or the other party, but the fact that it takes so long may be an indication that, as at York, some of the personnel of the court, perhaps even John Newton, had doubts about the legitimacy of abjuration *sub pena nubendi*.[110] Adam is represented by a proctor in part of the proceedings. Adam eventually loses. His exception could have been naïve, but it also could have been quite sophisticated.

106 *Braunche c Dellay* (23.ii.80 to 15.iii.80), fol. 132r–135v. See Sheehan, "Formation," 61.
107 T&C no. 443.
108 See at n. 84.
109 *Rouse c Smyth* (15.iii.80 to 12.xi.81), fol. 135v–155r; text and lit. T&C no. 444.
110 Another example T&C no. 445.

Marjorie Bradenham of Swavesey c John son of Thomas Bette of Swavesey contains the clearest indications that we have seen at Ely of property negotiations attendant upon a marriage.[111] Marjorie alleges a *de presenti* contract (there is no allegation of intercourse). John admits that they contracted but under the condition that Hugh Bradenham, Marjorie's brother, give to them a dowry of half a piece of land that he had at Swavesey, or 100s. The condition was never fulfilled, nor removed, and so John claims they should not be judged married.[112] Marjorie produces three witnesses: Joan Bradenham, William Fayrchild, and John Royner of Swavesey. John produces three witnesses concerning the exception: Thomas Bette, Marjorie Porter, and Hugh Bradenham of Swavesey. Sentence follows in six weeks. John has proved the condition and is absolved from the suit. The witness lists on both sides suggest some discord between the male and female members of the Bradenham family.

On 22 June 1375 Anna daughter of John Sergeaunt of Ely was cited before the official at the instance of Robert Clerk *alias* Cartere, clerk and steward of the bishop in the city of Ely, in an appeal from the definitive sentence given in Anna's favor by the sacristan of Ely in a marriage case.[113] Officers of the bishop were apparently privileged to have their cases heard before the sacristan.[114] The parties are represented by proctors throughout the proceedings; the *processus* is received from the sacristan; no objections are made to it, and on 3 April 1376, a sentence is rendered confirming the sacristan's sentence, which, as we learn from the final entry, adjudged Anna and Robert to be husband and wife. If Clerk expected favorable treatment because of his position with the bishop, he did not get it.

Bringing the appeal may be nothing more than a delaying tactic by Clerk. Little in the record suggests that he pursued the case very vigorously. There is, however, one clue that suggests a substantive issue. The official's sentence specifically states that the sacristan of Ely was competent to render the judgment.[115] Unrecorded arguments in the case may have turned on that question. If this is correct, then the entry that says that no objections were made to the *processus* in the court below is to be taken in a rather narrow sense:[116] The *processus* itself was unobjectionable, but the person who rendered the judgment was arguably incompetent to do so.

If we wonder whether the competence to render sentences in marriage cases of a court lower than the consistory was questioned in Clerk's case, there is more evidence that it was questioned in *Isabel Spynnere of Bourn c Nicholas Deye of Bourn*.[117] The record in that case tells us that Nicholas appealed from

[111] *Bradenham c Bette* (4.x.80 to 19.xi.80), fol. 144r–145r. Swavensy is a village about six miles northwest of Cambridge off the road to Huntingdon.

[112] T&C no. 446.

[113] *Sergeaunt c Clerk* (22.vi.75 to 3.iv.76), fol. 26v–44v.

[114] Lit. T&C no. 447.

[115] T&C no. 448.

[116] Fol. 36r: *nullo dicto seu proposito contra processum.*

[117] *Spynnere c Deye* (17.vii.74 to 4.v.75), fol. 10r–22v.

the court of the archdeacon and claimed that the entire *processus* in the court below was void. It seems, however, that the issue is not whether the archdeacon or even his official was competent to render such judgments but whether the archdeacon's official's commissary, Thomas Gloucestre, had been specifically authorized to do so. Isabel, by her proctor, says that he was so authorized, although that authorization was not specifically stated in his commission, and she offers to prove it. The case goes on for almost a year, but in May of 1375, Nicholas Roos, the official, renders a judgment upholding the sentence below, after Nicholas's proctor refuses to swear that his claim of the nullity of the *processus* below was not raised maliciously.[118]

On 24 July 1377, Alice Geffrey of Trumpington had John Myntemoor of Trumpington, priest and Austin canon of Anglesey Priory, cited in a marriage case. She petitioned that John be degraded from holy orders, absolved of his oath of obedience to the priory's rule, and deprived of the habit and tonsure of a priest and canon because prior to his profession and ordination, he and she had contracted marriage (she employs a variation of the 'formula' libel).[119] John contested the case affirmatively. Alice produced one witness, William Killerwyk of Trumpington, who may be the same William Killerwyk who was one of the regular proctors of the court. The case was set to propose and for a second term to produce, and then it drops out of sight.

The record in this case tells us so little that any attempt to reconstruct the facts is dangerous. At a minimum, we can say that John did not object to being called from the priory because he contested the case affirmatively. Whether he connived with Alice to bring the case we cannot say.[120] When she failed to return for the next session, the court did nothing to pursue the matter. Perhaps like us, it had doubts about the validity of the claim.[121]

John Pope of Newton and Katherine daughter of John Dreu of Newton c Katherine daughter of John Dreu of Newton and Elias son of John Newton is one of only two examples that I have found in the Ely cases of what we might call an 'interlocking' competitor case, where the defendant in one action is the plaintiff in the other.[122] In this case, John sued Katherine, and Katherine sued Elias. Katherine plays the leading role in both cases. There seems to be little reason to doubt that she did contract with John; she excepts on the grounds of force and consanguinity. There may be some doubt whether she contracted with Elias. Elias spends most of the sessions being contumacious, but at one point he does except against Katherine's witnesses for unstated grounds. About 18 months after the case has begun, John Newton commissions John Potton to render sentence in the case, and Katherine wins all around. Her marriage to Pope cannot stand because of the force, because of the consanguinity, and

118 Texts and disc. T&C no. 449.
119 *Geffrey c Myntemoor* (24.vii.77), fol. 78r; text and lit. T&C no. 450.
120 Lit. T&C no. 451.
121 See at n. 146 for another case where the court seems to have preferred to just let matters lie.
122 *Pope and Dreu c Dreu and Newton* (8.vii.78 to 3.xi.79), fol. 95r–123v; disc. T&C no. 452.

because of the marriage to Elias. The marriage to Elias has been proven.[123] Ominously, Elias is not present at the sentence. Katherine's legal victory may not have led to a real victory.

Alice Bakewhyt of Malmesbury [Wilts] c Hugh Mayhen of Trumpington and Isabel Loot of Trumpington wife of Hugh Mayhen is an unusual marriage-and-divorce case in that Hugh's more recent wife is suing him and his former wife to establish their marriage and annul hers.[124] On 25 May 1380, Alice proposes orally that although she and Hugh contracted and solemnized marriage before the church, their marriage cannot stand because prior to her contract with Hugh, Hugh and Isabel had contracted and solemnized marriage in Trumpington church, consummated the marriage, and lived as husband and wife. Alice asks that her marriage to Hugh be annulled. Hugh contests the suit affirmatively. Isabel admits that she and Hugh married 30 years earlier in Trumpington church. Alice produces five witnesses, William Bernard of Trumpington, Katherine wife of John Thresschere, Marjorie wife of Thomas Serle of Trumpington, Richard Benethewode of Malmesbury, and Alice wife of John atte Halle of Malmesbury. They are examined and their testimony published. On 26 May, Thomas Gloucestre renders sentence for Alice. The marriage and solemnization of Hugh and Isabel are declared valid; their marriage is reintegrated and they are to live as spouses, treating each other with marital affection.

Obviously, there was little dispute between the parties at this point. They prepared well. The toponyms of the witnesses suggest that in addition to the confession of the parties, we have three witnesses to the marriage in Trumpington and two to that in Malmesbury. The result is such a foregone conclusion that Alice does not even bother to stay the extra day in Cambridge to hear the sentence. She appoints a priest as her proctor to do so.[125]

The fact that this is such an easy case leads one to question whether what we have here is a case like *Ingoly c Midelton, Esyngwald and Wright*, where the whole affair was probably a sham.[126] It may be, but we may doubt it, because a plausible story lies behind the facts recited in this case, as there does not in *Ingoly*. Sometime over the course of 30 years, Hugh left Trumpington and traveled to the west country. We know that men and women were on the move in the late fourteenth century, and Hugh may have been one of them.[127] He settled in Malmesbury where he met Alice. They married in Malmesbury church; banns were proclaimed, but, of course, no one from Trumpington was there to ask what had happened to Isabel. Sometime later, Hugh abandoned Alice and returned to Trumpington, where he may have resumed cohabitation with Isabel. (This would account for the fact that she is called his wife at the beginning of the case and would make the final judgment of 'reintegration' a

[123] T&C no. 453, with disc.
[124] *Bakewhyt c Mayhen and Loot* (25.v.80 to 26.v.80), fol. 138v.
[125] Disc. T&C no. 454.
[126] Lit. T&C no. 455.
[127] Lit. T&C no. 456.

formality.) Alice could not have been pleased with these events, but if she was going to get on with her life, she needed a judgment to bring back to Malmesbury that her public marriage to Hugh was invalid. Although she conducted the case herself, she had obviously received good advice as to what she needed to get such a judgment. Hugh cooperates; of course, Isabel cooperates. The only indication that the whole settlement was not totally amicable – and, of course, legally quite correct – is the fact that Alice commissions a proctor to come to the sentence. It is possible that she did not want to be in Hugh's presence any more than was absolutely necessary.

On 1 April 1377, Alice daughter of Robert Borewell brought a suit against John Russel of Ely and Katherine Selvald his wife, alleging that she had precontracted with John, and hence he should be divorced from Katherine and made to marry her.[128] John admitted that he contracted with Alice by saying "I wish to have you (*volo te habere*) as my wife," and intercourse followed.[129] Katherine requested permission to prove her contract and solemnization with John, so that he and Alice could not collude against her; she was admitted. She introduced two witnesses, whose testimony was published. Alice admitted that she had no witnesses. The court rendered sentence for Katherine, all, so far as we can tell, in one session.

Alice was badly advised (or she was not advised at all). As we have seen, the court frequently required proof even when the parties conceded a point; where one of the parties did not concede the point, it always required proof.[130] While this may be a case in which John and Alice were colluding in a fabrication so that John could rid himself of Katherine, it may be just what it seems to be. John and Alice married informally. John later married Katherine formally. He now has qualms of conscience about what he has done, but it is too late. The confession of the parties, absent independent evidence, cannot prejudice the right of third parties (Katherine, in this case).

If the record in the first *Borewell* case could lead to the conclusion that everyone was telling the truth, the record in the second *Borewell* case does not. In October of 1378, Alice was back in court, once more suing John and Katherine. John once more conceded Alice's suit, but Katherine contested it (both parties employed proctors in this case). Over the course of three terms, Alice produced six witnesses to support her claim. The case was concluded in April of 1379, but sentence was not rendered until March of 1380.[131] In John's absence, the court ruled that Alice had not proven her case.

The court obviously was not impressed with Alice's witnesses. Lacking the depositions, we cannot be sure why, but there is reason right on the face of the record why we should be skeptical about them. If Alice admitted she had no

[128] *Borewell c Russel and Selvald* (1.iv.77 to 15.iii.80), fol. 67v–134r.

[129] T&C no. 457.

[130] Lit. T&C no. 458.

[131] This gap includes the long period between the departure of Richard Scrope and the appointment of John Newton as official.

witnesses in April of 1377, how did she manage to find witnesses in the intervening year and a half?[132] It may well be that the six men (five of whom were from Ely) whom she produced believed her. We need not necessarily assume bribery. But canonical witnesses in a marriage case were not oath-helpers. They were required to testify to what they had seen and heard, and Alice had already confessed that there were no witnesses to her marriage to John.

Assuming that Alice and John were telling the truth, their moral situation was precarious indeed. Some writers in the internal forum advised people who were in such a situation to flee.[133] It may be that John took their advice.

Matilda Cattesos of Lincoln diocese c John Brigham of Cambridge and Alice Pyttok his wife takes almost two years to resolve, but the underlying facts are not complicated.[134] Matilda, who is said to be from Lincoln diocese but never precisely from where in the diocese, claimed that John had married her before he married Alice, and that this marriage had been confirmed by the judgment of a competent judge. John contested the suit affirmatively, Alice negatively. At the next session Matilda does not appear, and since she is out of the diocese she cannot be cited. Ultimately, however, she appoints a proctor who requests that testimony be taken before the archdeacon of East Riding at York. This testimony is ultimately transmitted to the court, and exceptions are raised to it.[135] The nature of the exceptions is not stated, but witnesses are introduced about them. Shortly before the conclusion of the case, John produces a letter patent from the archdeacon of East Riding, which apparently certified that he had judged Matilda and John's marriage valid. At the final session of the case (28 May 1379), the court introduces an *ex officio* witness to get on the record some proof of the second marriage.[136] Then, in the presence of Matilda and of John and Alice's proctors, it proceeds to render a judgment divorcing John and Alice and declaring Matilda and John husband and wife.

The case illustrates the fact that while there were difficulties with multijurisdictional marriages and litigation about them, the system could handle such difficulties if given sufficient time. Perhaps more interesting is the ambiguity of John's position in the litigation. He is, it would seem, a bigamist, one of those medieval men who took advantage of the mobility of the age to marry a woman in one ecclesiastical province and then marry another woman in another province.[137] When Matilda brings suit, he contests it affirmatively. But when the testimony is returned from York, he and Alice are said to except to it. This may be simply a statement of form; since John is one of the defendants, any exception would be formally made on his behalf, as well as on that of Alice. Certainly the fact that John is the one who presents the letter patent of

132 Lit. T&C no. 459.
133 E.g., Peter the Chanter, *Summa* § 351, ed. cit. at 3:464.
134 *Cattesos c Brigham and Pyttok* (30.vii.77 to 12.xi.81), fol. 79r–154v.
135 Disc. T&C no. 460.
136 Disc. T&C no. 461.
137 Disc. T&C no. 462.

the archdeacon to the court, a letter which seems (though the record does not quite say this)[138] to confirm Matilda's story that the archdeacon had judged her marriage to John valid, would suggest that at this point he is supporting Matilda. When sentence is rendered in the next session, however, it is specifically stated that John's proctor appeals. Perhaps the ambivalence of the record reflects a real ambivalence on John's part as to what he should do about an awkward situation.

On 9 January 1381, Matilda, now described as being of Chesterton, is back in court, along with Geoffrey Bernesdale, William vicar of Chesterton, and John Grantham, chaplain. Geoffrey and Matilda are charged *ex officio* with having contracted and solemnized marriage without publication of banns, after Matilda had been judged by the court to be the wife of John Brigham and while an appeal of the case was pending in the court of Canterbury. William is charged with having solemnized the marriage, with knowledge of the judgment, and John with having been present. William alleges that he was not present at the solemnization and knows nothing about it. His explanation is apparently accepted, because nothing more is said of him. John Grantham, too, having been cited one more time, drops from view.[139] On 24 May 1381, Geoffrey and Matilda appear and admit the charges. On 10 October, they appear by proctor, are declared subject to major excommunication, request absolution, and are ordered to carry a candle in the church in the manner of public penitents.[140] On 31 October, the court is certified that the penance was performed. Nothing is said about enforcing the judgment or about divorcing Geoffrey and Matilda, and it is possible that in the rather long intervening period, the court of Canterbury had reversed the sentence of the consistory court.

Just as there is some doubt as to the position that John Brigham took when faced with two women both of whom claimed that he had married them, so, too, there is some doubt about the position taken by John Draper, tailor of Cambridge. Sued on 6 June 1376 by Agnes Duraunt of Orwell and Alice Cakebred of Barley (Orwell is about six miles south of Royston; Barley is in Hertfordshire, and, hence, in London diocese, but it is quite close to Orwell), John negatively contests Agnes's suit and affirmatively contests Alice's.[141] Agnes asks for summary procedure "according to the new constitutions," and she gets it.[142] She produces two witnesses, one from Orwell and one from Cambridge, and sentence is rendered in her favor by a special commissary of the official on 24 July, from which John appeals. In the meantime, Alice has produced three witnesses on her behalf, but she fails to appear at the sentencing (also on 24 July), and the case goes against her.

138 Text T&C no. 463.

139 It is possible that the bishop handled this, though the record does not say so.

140 Fol. 153r: *iniugimus sibi quod deferant unam candelam publice in ecclesia in more publice penitentium*.

141 *Duraunt and Cakebred c Draper* (6.vi.76 to 25.x.80), fol. 48r–144v; lit. T&C no. 464.

142 T&C no. 465, with disc.

The reason why she does not appear becomes apparent in separate proceedings that are brought against John and Alice on 3 July for having illegally solemnized their marriage in Barley. After some delay they are pronounced excommunicate on 21 July.

John's appeal is not recorded until April of 1377, when he is described as a resident of Barley. Although three sessions of the case are recorded, no libel is ever given, and the record ends with a note that John and Alice are excommunicated as before.

Nothing more is heard of the case until 5 April 1380, when John and Agnes are cited before the official *ex officio* to explain why they had not married in compliance with the sentence. At the only session at which she appears personally (in a previous session she is said to be hiding),[143] Agnes proposes that she and one Henry Walter of Orwell had agreed to marry before the sentence was rendered and that they in fact had married after the sentence had been rendered. If the language of the entry is to be believed,[144] Agnes is confessing to a *de futuro* contract prior to the sentence and a *de presenti* one after the sentence. Such a marriage cannot impede the sentence, and it is not surprising that the court orders the sentence executed. It does so four more times at sessions at which it is not clear that the parties are present,[145] and the case disappears from view in October of 1380.

The record obviously leaves many questions unresolved, not the least of which is what happened to Alice. She may have died in the intervening years, or her marriage to John may have broken up. John returns to Cambridgeshire, perhaps for economic reasons, and offers no objection to the proposed execution of the sentence. He may even have prompted the *ex officio* citation. But Agnes has married another man. I am inclined to believe her story of the marriage to Henry because it is not a valid defense to the charge. Agnes 'hedged her bets' while she was suing John by getting Henry to agree to marry her. We might call this her 'contingency plan'. When John disappears over the border into Barley after the sentence, Agnes marries Henry. Now John is back and, quite understandably, Agnes wants none of him.

Again, we must ask why the court was so passive. Five entries of orders of execution is not particularly strong medicine, when excommunication followed by caption by the secular arm was an option open to it. There is at least one marriage case where the court does this, and it seems to produce the desired result.[146] We may be dealing here with a difference in judicial personalities. I cannot recall that John Newton, the official who heard the enforcement case, ever ordered caption by the secular arm in a civil dispute. But the reason may

143 Fol. 137r: *Predicto Johanne personaliter comparente, Agnete Duraunt nullo modo nec citata, ideo citetur viis et modis ad proximum quia latitat.*

144 T&C no. 466.

145 The entry says simply (e.g., fol. 140v): *fiat execucio sententie diffinitive.*

146 *Attepool c Frebern of Fulbourn* (21.ii.77 to 26.ii.77), fol. 64v–65v; lit. with another example T&C no. 467.

lie elsewhere. Agnes's initial case was heard by summary procedure, the judge who rendered the sentence was a special commissary, and John did not pursue his appeal. Newton may have looked at the record of the case and had doubts (as he certainly did in *Anegold and Schanbery c Grantesden*) that the right thing had been done. Certainly, John is not an appealing character. Having fled the diocese to marry Alice, he now seems to want Agnes back. Agnes has married another. She should not have done this, but perhaps this is a matter better left to her and her confessor.

The cases in which a female plaintiff emerges from an office citation need to be examined systematically. This type of case has an extraordinarily high rate of sentence (100%), and this type of case does not exist at York. If any group of cases is going to show us differences from the York litigation patterns, this group should be the one.

The cases are, in fact, somewhat different from those at York, though the difference is a relatively subtle one. As we might expect, cases that are begun with an *ex officio* citation are pursued somewhat more aggressively by the court than are the exclusively instance cases at York or, indeed, the instance cases at Ely. There is also evidence in at least some of the cases that the parties were causing a public scandal.

The element of scandal is quite clear in a case that begins "Thomas Barbour of St Benet's parish, Cambridge, and Joan Seustere his longtime concubine, were cited, on the basis of *publica fama* [for 10 March 1376]... for having entered into a contract of marriage and for subsequent intercourse."[147] Joan proposes a 'formula' marriage; Thomas confesses to something that looks very much like *de futuro* consent followed by intercourse. (Joan was about to leave him; he became depressed and suicidal; he promised to marry her; then they had intercourse, but he never intended to marry her, only to retain her as his concubine.)[148] The court orders them to abjure each other *sub pena nubendi*, but was apparently unwilling to rule in Joan's favor on the basis of Thomas's confession alone.[149] It takes a while for Joan to get her witnesses.[150] (Many of them have to be compelled, and some look like men of relatively high station.)[151] In May of 1377, Thomas proposes that the marriage cannot stand because Joan had precontracted with one Ralph Bressingham. There is further delay for Thomas to produce witnesses, but in April of 1378, slightly more than two years after the case was begun, sentence is rendered for Joan.

In December of 1377, the official (Scrope) cites Thomas in a straight-office case for adultery with Joan, who is described as a married woman. Thomas takes an appeal to the provincial court, which is called frivolous. Finally, in February, he renounces his appeal, agrees to do penance, and reimburses the

147 *Seustere c Barbour* (10.iii.76 to 29.iv.78), fol. 39v–91v; T&C no. 468.
148 T&C no. 469, with lit.
149 Disc. T&C no. 470.
150 Formula of abjuration quoted in Sheehan, "Formation," 67, n. 105.
151 Disc. T&C no. 471.

official for his costs of the appeal. When Thomas pays the official 13s 4d, the official declares that Thomas did not appeal maliciously but from bad counsel and commutes the public penance into private penance and returns 6s 8d to Thomas.

It is difficult to reconcile these proceedings with the ultimate judgment in what became a civil case. There may be an element of hoisting Thomas on his own petard: "OK, Thomas, you claim that you can't marry Joan because she's married to Ralph. Then, when Joan was your concubine, you were committing adultery." Clearly, Thomas cannot defend the adultery case without destroying his position in the matrimonial litigation. That Thomas comes up with a relatively large sum of money quickly, and that the official commutes the public penance into a private one, may be indications that Thomas is of relatively high station.

There are also indications in *Alice Borewell of Barnwell c Thomas Bileye of Cambridge* that the parties, or at least the man, is of relatively high station.[152] The case arises on reclamation of banns, where it "was found" (again in the passive voice) that Alice had had intercourse with one Thomas Clerk of Barnwell, who was related to Bileye within the fourth degree of consanguinity.[153] The parties, including Clerk, basically admit this, and the witnesses to the consanguinity, in addition to Bileye's mother, include a Carmelite friar (who appears with permission of his prior) and a scholar. While the case is pending, Bileye also raises the objection that Alice precontracted with one Richard Webster. Alice admits this, but alleges that at the time Webster was married, and also that she had been the godmother to his child (thus impeding the marriage on the ground of spiritual affinity). The truth of these claims is never decided. The court rules against the marriage of Alice and Bileye on the ground of affinity by illicit intercourse, saying specifically that this ruling is against Alice's wishes.[154]

While the record does not tell us nearly enough as we would like to know, it certainly suggests that Bileye, at this point, is trying to get out of the marriage. He contracted with Alice and had intercourse with her; they both admit that. But Alice is a woman with a decidedly checkered past, and she may not be the sort of woman whom a man with a cousin in the Carmelites and another a Cambridge scholar should be marrying.[155] The interesting question is why Bileye also raises the problem of the precontract with Webster, since he seems to have an airtight case (granted that he does not want to ask for a dispensation) on the basis of affinity by illicit intercourse. We saw at least one case in which the court (quietly) seems to have ignored affinity by illicit intercourse in the remote degrees. Bileye (or his advisers)[156] may have had doubts that the court would accept their proof of the relationship. Raising the issue of Webster produces an

[152] *Borewell c Bileye* (5.iv.80 to 23.vii.80), fol. 136v–143r.
[153] Fol. 136v; T&C no. 472.
[154] Text and lit. T&C no. 473.
[155] Disc. T&C no. 474.
[156] Proctors are never mentioned, but it seems likely that Bileye was getting advice.

interesting dénouement. Alice, who seems willing to admit all about her past, admits the contract with Richard but then raises issues that would have taken quite a bit of time to prove. Faced with the possibility that the case will drag on endlessly, the court cuts the Gordian knot and rules against the marriage on the basis of the affinity.

We may have some sympathy for Alice. Not only does she lose the man whom she clearly wants, but her revelations about her past with Webster have also put her in a position where she cannot marry him either. That she became Richard's spiritual relative after she had contracted with him is irrelevant to the validity of her marriage to him in the past. (Subsequent spiritual affinity does not bar a present consent marriage.) It is, however, relevant to whether she can marry him now that she has lost Bileye. Unless she can show that the prior marriage to Richard was valid, she cannot contract marriage with him now because of the copaternity. She would have been well advised not to mention the spiritual affinity (it could do her no good in the current case and might do her a harm later). The fact that she did so suggests that she was operating on her own without advice.

The title of *Agnes Knotte widow of Ralph Clerk c William de Potton son of Nicholas de Potton subdeacon and brother of Hospital of St John Cambridge* tells all.[157] The couple were cited *ex officio* for clandestine contract of marriage plus intercourse. It immediately turns into an instance case brought by Agnes, aided by a proctor, against William. William concedes the contract and the intercourse, and the case concludes summarily[158] with a sentence that absolves William of his religious vows and declares that he and Agnes are husband and wife.[159] The whole case is very straightforward, perhaps a bit too straightforward.

The remaining seven office/instance cases in which a woman emerges as the plaintiff divide rather neatly into four in which the woman pursues the matter and the man offers a weak defense and three in which the woman does not pursue the matter at all vigorously and the man has a good defense. Not surprisingly, the first four result in sentences for the plaintiff and the last three in sentences for the defendant. All but one are decided within a month of their being brought, and some contain indications that the parties are not of particularly high status. In two cases, one of the parties is a servant. In one, the defendant is a ploughwright. In another, the plaintiff is a tavern keeper for a woman (probably of Cambridge; the plaintiff herself coming from Wisbech) and the man is a wright of Cambridge. Only one, brought unsuccessfully against a clerk, contains any indications of higher status. Six of the cases are summarized in the margin.[160] We treat here the one that lasts longer than a month.

157 *Knotte c Potton* (17.v.80 to 8.vi.80), fol. 139r; lit. T&C no. 475.

158 The Clementines *Dispendiosam*, Clem. 5.11.2, and *Saepe*, Clem. 2.1.2, are specifically mentioned. The witnesses are a summoner, a tailor, and a wright.

159 No order to solemnize, but she is a widow; William is not present at the sentence.

160 See T&C no. 476.

Marion Pulter of Swavesey c John Castre servant of the vicar of Swavesey takes slightly less than a year to resolve.[161] The couple are cited for clandestine contract of marriage followed by intercourse, and when Marion first appears, she puts in a libel "in certain form" (which may mean what we have called the 'formula' libel).[162] John denies the contract and raises an exception of force. He says that one night when he was sleeping with Marion, some people from Hugh de Souche's household (*familia*) broke down the door, entered their room, and forced him to betroth her by threatening him with mutilation and by beating him.[163] Over the course of the next year John produces four witnesses, Marion only one. Nonetheless, Thomas Gloucestre, the commissary general, renders sentence for Marion. No mention is made of John's exception.

Without knowing what the witnesses said, it is difficult to know what motivated the court. At a minimum we can say that this case shows, as have others, that force was not an easy defense to prove. What John alleges should have been enough to make out the defense as a matter of law, but proving it is another matter. We may suspect, though we cannot prove, that the court was inclined to favor Marion. She has only one witness, and John denies the contract entirely (though his defense of force contains an implied admission that there was a contract). Marion probably should have been put to proof of the contract, and unless John's witnesses supported her, her claim should have failed for want of proof. But John admitted that he had been having intercourse with Marion for more than a year. He ought to marry her. The behavior of the members of Hugh de Souche's *familia* may have been crude, but absent clear evidence of credible threats or physical force or, better yet, both, John's contract will stand. Embarrassment is not enough to invalidate a contract of marriage.[164]

As with the cases involving male plaintiffs, some of the cases with female plaintiffs that also involve three parties are more complicated. Four of them seem quite straightforward and are discussed in the margin. They do, however, seem to illustrate the proposition that a competitor has to have some proof of her claim before she can demand that a couple who confess that they married prove theirs.[165]

John son of Thomas Lystere of Cambridge and Margaret stepdaughter of Robert Ballard of Cambridge were cited to appear on 16 May 1376 concerning a clandestine contract of marriage.[166] They appear personally and admit under oath that they contracted *de presenti* "but not clandestinely but publicly, with witnesses at hand and the requisite publication of banns," which revealed no impediment. The record then proceeds to record a sentence in their favor: "the

[161] *Pulter c Castre* (30.iv.78 to 21.iv.79), fol. 93r–113v.
[162] Fol. 93v: *libellatoque per dictam Marionam oretenus sub certa forma.*
[163] Text and ref. T&C no. 477.
[164] Lit. and disc. T&C no. 478.
[165] Ref. and disc. T&C no. 479.
[166] *Sadelere c Lystere and Ballard* (16.v.76 to 30.v.76), fol. 47r–47v. See Sheehan, "Formation," 47 and n. 32.

reclamation of Alice Sadelere notwithstanding."[167] What that is all about is explained in the next entry: Alice Sadelere, residing with Walter Smyth of St Andrew's, Cambridge, was cited before Thomas Gloucestre, commissary of the official, on 30 May 1376 (out of session) to explain why she reclaimed against the banns of John and Margaret. She appears and enters a 'formula' libel. John contests the suit negatively, and Alice produces two witnesses, Thomas Lystere of Cambridge and Marion his wife. The witnesses are examined; the testimony is published, and the case is concluded with the parties' consent. The court proceeds to the definitive sentence: Because Alice has not proved her case, John is dismissed from her suit and absolved, the matter being left to their consciences.

Thomas and Marion were almost certainly John's parents. They may have originally favored the marriage with Alice. They may still favor it, but not enough to support her claim. That is not the only possible conclusion from this record, but it seems to be the most likely. What needs explaining about this record is why John and Margaret were not put to the proof of their contract. They alleged that they had witnesses, but they are never asked to produce them. (They also alleged that no impediment was revealed by the banns, but the court found out that Alice reclaimed against the banns.) Some words probably were exchanged between John and Alice in the presence of his parents. When the parents were called to testify about it, however, we must assume that what they testified to did not amount to a *de presenti* contract, and may not have amounted to a contract at all. On that record, then, there was nothing to put John and Margaret to the proof of their contract because clearly they wanted to contract now. The parents' role is key, and if they wanted to support their son, it would have been tempting to testify to less than what was actually said. This possibility, however, still does not tell us what role the parents played in the marriage of their son. They may have decided that John was better off marrying Margaret than Alice, or he may have decided that he was better off marrying Margaret than Alice. Alice almost certainly felt betrayed not only by John but also by his parents. That they were present at whatever words were exchanged between John and her certainly suggests that they were not opposed to the marriage at the time. What we cannot tell, however, is whether they testified to less than was actually said or whether they did not testify to more, as she hoped they would. There is, of course, a third possibility: Their memory and understanding of what was said were not the same as Alice's.

Agnes Pateshull, residing with Stephen Morice of Cambridge, was called by the official, for 13 November 1376, to explain why she reclaimed the banns of Hugh Candelesby, registrar of the archdeacon, and Alice widow of Jacob le Eyr fisher (Fysshere) of Cambridge.[168] She appears and proposes a 'formula' libel. She also asks for an interdict and inhibition against Hugh and Alice because, she says, she fears that they will solemnize their marriage, notwithstanding her

[167] Text at T&C no. 480.

[168] *Pateshull c Candelesby and Eyr* (13.xi.76 to 24.i.77), fol. 57v–62r; lit. T&C no. 481.

reclamation. On 3 December, Agnes and Hugh appear before Thomas Gloucestre and John Newton, commissaries of the official. Hugh contests the suit negatively. Agnes claims she is not able to prove the contract. Sworn about malice and collusion, they repeat their statements. Sentence is rendered for Hugh.

Agnes had no case. We suspect that Hugh, who, in addition to being the archdeacon's registrar was also an experienced proctor in the Ely consistory, knew that, too.[169] As a result, he got cocky. In between the time of Agnes's reclaimation and his favorable sentence, he solemnized his marriage with Alice. This was a mistake, particularly considering the strained relations between the consistory court and the archdeacon's court.[170]

On 4 December William [. . .] chaplain of the chantry in St Clement's, Cambridge, appeared personally before the official, Richard Scrope. He explains that by tacit consent, he was responsible for the contract and solemnization of marriage between Hugh and Alice, despite the interdict and pending suit. Although he neither advised the marriage nor was present at it, he had been troubled by his conscience for his consent. He requests absolution from any censure he might have incurred and swears to uphold church mandates. Ultimately finding him not delinquent, Scrope absolves him and orders a salutary penance.

Hugh himself also appeared on 4 December at Scrope's residence in Cambridge. He admits that he contracted and solemnized marriage with Alice despite his knowledge of the interdict, inhibition, and pending case. He submits himself to Scrope's grace, requests absolution, and swears to uphold church mandates and complete any penance given to him. Scrope absolves Hugh and reserves his order of penance at his pleasure. The registrar of the archdeacon's official is now in Scrope's power.

The man whom, we may suspect, Scrope most wanted to get did not appear before him until 24 January 1377. John de Grebby, priest and commissary general of the archdeacon's official, was called to court *ex officio* to respond to the following charges: Although they were not his parishioners, he solemnized marriage between Hugh and Alice. He did this without any publication of banns or license of those who had cure of Hugh's and Alice's souls, at an inappropriate time and contrary to church interdict and Scrope's inhibition. John swears obedience and submits himself to Scrope's grace, promising to perform penance. He is ordered to go to St Etheldreda's shrine by the middle of Lent, walking through the village of Wichford as far as the shrine, and to offer there four pence. He is to go to the bishop for absolution from the excommunication that he had incurred under the provincial constitution.[171]

John Lovechild of Littleport and Tilla Taillor of Littleport were cited before the official (Newton) on 26 April 1380 concerning a contract of marriage.[172]

[169] Disc. T&C no. 482.
[170] Lit. T&C no. 483.
[171] T&C no. 484. See at nn. 201–4.
[172] *Taillor and Smerles c Lovechild and Taillor* (26.iv.80 to 7.xi.80), fol. 137v–144v.

They appear personally and are sworn. Tilla admits that they contracted on 17 October 1379 by saying, in turn, "I take you as my wife" and "I take you as my husband." John claims that he said "I will have you (*volo te habere*) as my wife," and Tilla consented. He admits that he had had the banns published, but he denies "the other things" (*alia*).[173] The case is set down for proof. At the next session, John is absent and Tilla, by proctor, produces a chaplain as a witness. The remaining sessions before the summer recess are devoted to trying to obtain John's presence. He is suspended, and the suspension ordered executed. On 25 October, Robert Smerles of Little Downham appears and asserts that he and Tilla contracted marriage, followed by intercourse. She contests the suit affirmatively.[174] The court sets the case down for 29 October in the chapel of Downham manor to propose and the second term to produce. John is to be called to be present if he wishes.

On 29 October, John, Robert, and Tilla appear personally. Robert produces four witnesses: John Taillor of Littleport, Katherine his wife, John Estcroft, and Agnes his wife. With the parties' consent, the case is concluded and set for 7 November, again, in the manor chapel. On 7 November, the official renders sentence. John and Tilla's contract has been proved to be prior to that of Robert and Tilla. John and Tilla are adjudged to be husband and wife; their marriage is ordered solemnized at an appropriate time and place. Robert appeals.

There is much about this case that is puzzling. The words to which John confesses at the first session are normally taken as words of the present tense. If that is the case, then one wonders why the case was set down for proof.[175] It is possible that Newton took the formula as one of future consent, or close enough to future consent that the matter needed clarifying. It is also possible that he knew something about Robert. Newton's adjourning the case to Downham chapel was an important element in bringing the case to resolution. Littleport is in the fen country, north of Ely, and Downham is even further north. Newton may well have suspected that John's nonappearance was not contumacy in the normal sense of the word but was prompted by his inability to get to Cambridge for the regular sessions of the court. Tilla, though she had a proctor, was able to produce only one witness in Cambridge. As soon as Robert appeared, Newton knew that he had a case best resolved locally. Whether his resolution was the correct one we cannot tell from the face of the record. What we can tell is that he allowed the confession of the parties and one witness to overcome the testimony of the four witnesses whom Robert produced (though those four witnesses may have said something that proved the prior marriage to John).

Tilla's role in the whole affair is interesting. She may have forced the issue by contracting with Robert, for there seems to be little doubt that such a contract did occur. (If she cannot get John, she is going to get a husband, come what may.) By forcing the issue, she provoked Newton into spending some chilly late

[173] Text and lit. T&C no. 485.

[174] Disc. T&C no. 486.

[175] The record says that it was done "out of abundance of caution" (*ex habundanti*).

fall evenings in the bishop's manor at Downham to find out what was really going on, and the result was what we may suspect that she wanted all along, a judgment that John should marry her. If that is what was happening, then Robert was duped. He appeals, though we doubt whether the appeal was ever pursued.

Margaret Blofeld of Chatteris and Katherine daughter of Ed[mund] Reder of Chatteris c John de Lile of Chatteris took more than two years to resolve (25 February 1378 to 15 March 1380).[176] As in *Taillor c Lovechild*, part of the problem seems to have been geography. (Chatteris is also in the fen country, about 10 miles west of Ely.) Part of the problem was also the long and awkward hiatus between the departure of Richard Scrope and the appointment of John Newton as official. So far as we can tell from the record, the case was a straightforward matter of proof. Margaret was cited before the official to explain why she reclaimed against the banns of Katherine and John. She alleges a 'formula' marriage, which John denies. Two sessions later, Katherine appears and alleges a marriage, which John affirmatively contests. The rector of Doddington (about five miles north of Chatteris) and a *magister* are commissioned to take testimony. It takes until November of 1378 to return it. The case then goes into a long period of hiatus, although the parties seem to be maintaining continuity through proctors. At the next to last session, Katherine asks to produce two more witnesses, which she seems to have at hand. The final session in this stage of the case takes place in the presence of the proctors. Katherine is declared to have proved her claim, and Margaret not to have proved hers. Her proctor appeals. The appeal must have failed because when we next see the case, John is resisting a court order to marry Katherine on the ground that the marriage is impeded by affinity by illicit intercourse (his own with one Alice, whose relationship to Katherine is not specified).[177] The proceedings are still continuing when the register ends.

The most complicated case in this material involves three women all seeking to marry a single man. On 14 March 1376, Adam Savage serjeant (Sargeaunt) and Christine Wafrer were cited before the official about intercourse known to the court through *publica fama*.[178] They admit to having contracted marriage the previous Christmas, followed by intercourse. On the same day,[179] Matilda de Wereslee spinner *alias* Warde de Hokyton of Cambridge and Agnes Dallynge of Cambridge were also cited, along with Adam, to answer about the contract of marriage followed by intercourse. Both women propose 'formula' marriages, and Adam contests both negatively. The cases proceed summarily out of session, and all three women produce witnesses. The first case to be resolved is Agnes's. Although she has produced two witnesses, the court declares on 19 March 1376 that she has failed to prove her case. The other two cases proceed in tandem,

[176] *Blofeld and Reder c Lile* (25.ii.78 to 28.ii.82), fol. 90r–162r.
[177] Lit. T&C no. 487.
[178] *Wafrer, Wereslee and Dallynge c Savage* (14.iii.76 to 15.v.77), fol. 43v–70v.
[179] The record does not say this but the entries follow right after the preceding one.

including meetings out of session during the summer recess. On 23 August, Mr John Potton rules that Matilda has proved her claim and Christine has failed to prove hers. Matilda and Adam are adjudged to be husband and wife and are ordered to solemnize their marriage.

On 21 November 1376, Agnes is back in court, once more seeking Adam as a husband. Adam concedes the contract but argues that it was not valid because he had a wife (one Alice) living at the time. Agnes replies that Adam's marriage to Alice was invalid because Alice had a husband living at the time. Matilda is brought into the suit, and she seems to carry much of the burden of defending it. It is finally resolved on 15 May 1377, with a judgment that Matilda's marriage to Adam was prior to the one with Agnes, and nothing is said about either the exception or the replication.

A ruling in the final session about a repeated witness allows us to see that Matilda and Adam were alleging a marriage that had taken place three years previously. This would explain why the marriage to Christine cannot stand. Since the marriage to Agnes is specifically said to have come after that, the ruling is clearly based on priority. We will never know about the mysterious Alice, who may or may not have been Adam's wife in the interim. Whatever the truth of the allegations, they were clearly not proven.

Adam certainly does not emerge as a very attractive character. We have reasonably firm evidence that over the course of three years, he contracted marriage with at least three different women, and he may have contracted with four. When he cannot have Christine, he seems to have concocted Alice in order to escape from Agnes, and perhaps also from Matilda. That, in turn, raises the question of why these women found him attractive. Since we do not possess his portrait (nor a record of his sweet talk), we are obviously hampered in trying to determine this. But there is one piece of evidence that is given in the record. Adam is described as a 'serjeant', as are several of the witnesses. Unfortunately, that word can mean many things, but if we take it to mean 'a person of military status roughly equivalent to a squire' (as opposed to 'a common solider'),[180] we have some indication of why he might have been thought to be a desirable match. Matilda, who is one of the few women in the Ely record who is given an occupation name, would be moving up in the world if she changed from being a spinner to being the wife of a man the social equivalent of a squire.[181]

There is one divorce case brought by a woman, and it is of some interest. On 18 March 1378, Joan daughter of Robert Pyncote of Kingston (about seven miles west of Cambridge) was cited for nonresidence with her husband John Maddyngle of Kingston.[182] Both appear and Joan immediately alleges that John is impotent and asks that the marriage be annulled. Over the course of the next several sessions, she produces four female witnesses; she asks that midwives be selected to examine her and that John be examined. The midwives are selected,

180 Disc. T&C no. 488.

181 Disc. T&C no. 489.

182 *Pyncote c Maddyngle* (18.iii.78 to 30.x.81), fol. 91r–154r; lit. T&C no. 490.

and John hides. He is excommunicated, but he apparently never appears to be examined.[183] The court seems unwilling to proceed to sentence without this examination, and so on 14 June 1380, Joan proposes that she and John are related within the fourth degree of consanguinity and produces four witnesses to that effect. It still takes a while to get a sentence, but on 30 October 1381, Newton renders sentence in favor of Joan annulling the marriage and ordering John to pay Joan's costs of litigation.

We can have little doubt that John was impotent. That the court was unwilling to render a default judgment against him attests both to the court's general reluctance to award default judgments and to its reluctance to dissolve ongoing marriages, particularly solemnized ones. That the consanguinity was an afterthought is also clear. Whether the court allowed something less than full canonical proof of the consanguinity we do not know. We do know that John's proctor objected to the witnesses, and the court overruled those objections. Morally certain that John was impotent, the court may well have allowed a divorce for consanguinity to go through in circumstances that it would not otherwise have allowed. This may also be a case in which the witnesses stretched the truth about the consanguinity because of their moral certainty about Joan's situation.

THE OFFICE CASES

The Ely act book allows us to see an example of an English ecclesiastical court exercising its office jurisdiction. We have already examined those cases that were begun with office citations but then turned into instance cases. We should now look briefly at those cases that never became instance cases. Before we do that, let us focus on the grounds given for office citations. I have counted 87 office citations in marriage matters in the Ely act book, as shown in Table 6.7.

Care should be taken not to assume that the nature of the office citation is always a good predictor of what the case is ultimately going to be about. There are, for example, seven cases in the register that we have classified as straight-office cases of divorce, but they are begun with widely varying forms of *ex officio* citation: two for illegal solemnization, one as a result of the bishop's inquiry into an instance sentence of divorce granted by the archdeacon, one for bigamy (the one that would most obviously lead to a judgment of divorce), one for refusal to solemnize, one for clandestine contract of marriage followed by intercourse, and one that has no citation because it begins before the register begins.[184]

Table 6.7 shows that almost half of the office citations (38/87, 44%) are for some form of "contract of marriage" with or without the additional elements

[183] He continues to appear by a proctor. One entry in the record suggests that he fled to Huntingdon. T&C no. 491.

[184] Ref. T&C no. 493.

TABLE 6.7. Ex officio *Citations in Marriage Matters at Ely (1374–1381)*

Ex officio Citation for	Straight Instance	Office/ Instance	Straight Office	Total
Contract of marriage	0	16	3	19
Clandestine contract of marriage	0	2	0	2
Contract of marriage plus intercourse	0	4	5	9
Clandestine contract of marriage plus intercourse	0	4	4	8
Reclamation of banns[a]	1	4	2	7
Nonresidence with spouse	0	2	0	2
Violation of court order to solemnize	2	1	1	4
Illegal solemnization	9	3	3	15
Appeal *ex officio*[b]	0	0	5	5
Adultery	0	1	6	7
Bigamy[c]	0	0	2	2
False appeal	0	0	1	1
Fornication	1	1	3	5
Wife beating	0	0	1	1
TOTAL	13	38	36	87

Note: These citations do not, of course, correspond to 87 separate cases because of the way in which we have combined proceedings to arrive at an overall case. The table lists initial citations in separate proceedings. These proceedings may, in turn, be part of a larger case. This is particularly true in citations for illegal solemnization. The header rows ('Straight Instance', etc.) indicate the nature of the overall case and not necessarily of the proceedings for which the *ex officio* citation was made.

For notes *a–c*, see T&C no. 492.

Source: CUL, DMA, D2/1; Stentz, *Calendar.*

of "clandestine" or "plus intercourse." Nine of these cases also add that the matter is "known to the court by *publica fama*," and one citation in an ordinary instance case adds that the matter was known to the court by report of the community.[185] What is the implication of such a citation, and is there any difference in the types of citations? In the case of illegal solemnization, adultery, and fornication, we are clearly dealing with ecclesiastical crimes. If a person cited for such things is found guilty, he or she will have to undergo penance. As we have seen, failure to marry solemnly (at a minimum, after publication of banns or after the banns had been dispensed) was also an ecclesiastical crime, both under the provisions of the canon *Cum inihibitio* of the Fourth Lateran Council and under English conciliar canons. Admittedly, this legislation does not specify, except in the case of participating clergy, the penalty for the offense, but then again, the canons do not specify the penalty for adultery either. That was a matter for the judge, taking into account the circumstances of the individual case.

[185] Ref. and disc. T&C no. 494.

The striking thing about the cases involving these *ex officio* citations for informal marriages is that in none of them does the Ely court impose a penance on the couple for having so contracted.[186] Occasionally, the couple will confess to intercourse but deny the contract, in which case, of course, they have committed fornication, for which the court will impose a penance. But in the vast majority of cases, the issue is whether there was a contract. If that is conceded, the couple will be ordered to solemnize. If it is not conceded, the matter will be put to proof, and if the party asserting the contract is successful, the couple will normally be ordered to solemnize. (Where they are not so ordered, it may be that Foxton simply neglected to record it, but of this we cannot be sure.) Where the contract is not shown, the couple is dismissed.

The Ely record, then, suggests that the court viewed its role as providing a forum in which the facts of an informal marriage could come to light and, if they did, getting the couple to solemnize that marriage. The court did not think that its job was to punish people for having contracted informally. To this statement we might add one caveat. Foxton did not record the fees that the court imposed. It is hard to imagine that it did not charge fees (all medieval courts charged fees, except, apparently, those in Sweden), but we do not know what they were.[187] Even if the fees charged to a couple who appeared in court and confessed an informal contract, which they then agreed to solemnize, were relatively small, it might have been perceived as a burden by those of modest means. There is also some evidence that one of the reasons why some English men and women delayed solemnizing marriages is that they did not want to pay the 'offering' to the priest that such solemnization entailed.[188] Hence, it is possible that some couples who were the subjects of such proceedings perceived that they were being punished for having gotten married informally because they had to pay the court fees and the oblation for solemnization. Nonetheless, even if this were regarded as a sanction (which legally it was not), it could not have been regarded as a particularly severe one.

Having determined that the consequences of a citation for "contract of marriage" was the opening of an investigation into whether an informal marriage had taken place, with a subsequent order to solemnize if it was determined that it had, I can say with some confidence that it made no practical difference whether this citation was simply for "contract of marriage" or contained the full rhetorical panoply that Foxton had at his command: "clandestine contract of marriage followed by intercourse known to the court by *publica fama*." The additional rhetoric may reflect additional language in the citation itself, which, in turn, may reflect that level of anxiety of the person who reported the matter to the court, but it made no difference in the results, and, so far as I have been able to tell, it does not correspond to any difference in the patterns of facts that ultimately emerged.

[186] Lit. T&C no. 495.
[187] Disc. and lit. T&C no. 496.
[188] Lit. T&C no. 497.

The next largest group of *ex officio* citations (15/87, 17%) is for what we have called 'illegal solemnization', proceedings under John Stratford's constitution *Humana concupiscentia* (1342). We have already seen that many of them can be connected with instance cases or office/instance cases that were proceeding before the court, although the proceedings themselves were in straight-office form. We focus here on the interpretation that the Ely court gave to this constitution by gathering together the proceedings under this constitution without regard to whether they proceeded independently or were part of a larger case. The operative words of Stratford's constitution are:

from henceforth those who contract marriages and have them solemnized between themselves, knowing that any impediments exist in the matter or having a likely presumption (*praesumptio verisimilis*) of them, and also priests who hereafter are knowingly present at the solemnizations of this sort of marriages or also of licit marriages between other than their parishioners, not having obtained special license of their bishops or those who have care of their souls, also those who hereafter have clandestine marriages solemnized . . . or are present at them, anyone who knowingly does any of these things incurs *ipso facto* a sentence of major excommunication.[189]

The 15 citations for illegal solemnization in our records are found in eight different cases.[190] As we have already mentioned, *Fisschere c Frost and Brid* has four of them, and *Pateshull c Candelesby and Eyr* has three. There are two each in *Bonde c Yutte* and in the related cases of *Office c Slory and Feltewell* and *Office c Anegold and Andren.*

As in a number of the entries involving *Humana concupiscentia*, those in *Office c John Slory of Chesterton and Joan widow of John de Feltewell of Chesterton*[191] begin with an explanation of the constitution:

The general council has accordingly established that when marriages are to be contracted, they shall be announced by the priest in the churches, with an adequate term fixed beforehand within which whoever wishes and is able to may adduce a lawful impediment in opposition to the marriage. The priests themselves shall also investigate whether any impediment stands in the way [of the proposed marriage]. When there appears a credible reason against the proposed union, the contract shall be expressly forbidden until there has been established by clear documents what should be done about it. Any and every person who contracts marriage with another, has it solemnized, or is present at the solemnization of such a marriage who knows of a lawful impediment or has a reasonable (*verisimilem*) suspicion thereof shall, and does, incur a sentence of major excommunication in accordance with the provincial constitution.[192]

The problem with this explanation is that the first three sentences quote the canon *Cum inihibitio* of the Fourth Lateran Council, while the last describes, more loosely, Stratford's constitution. The two constitutions are clearly related.

189 Ref. and full text T&C nos. 498–9.
190 Disc. and lit. T&C no. 500.
191 *Office c Slory and Feltewell* (31.i.79 to 20.iii.82), fol. 108r–162r. See Sheehan, "Formation," 46, 51–2.
192 T&C no. 501.

What is not clear is that Stratford and his council intended that sanction of automatic excommunication to apply to those who married during the pendency of the investigation or even in violation of the inhibition described in *Cum inihibitio*.

In the *Slory* case, the extension that the Ely court made of Stratford's constitution probably made little difference. In the second of two sets of proceedings, John Anegold of Chesterton and John Andren of Chesterton were cited before the commissary for 31 Jan 1379 to show why they should not be subject to major excommunication.[193] Knowing there was an impediment, interdiction, and no license, they arranged the solemnization of John Slory's and Joan Feltewell's marriage outside the diocese (where the constitution is also in effect) and were present at it.[194] They admitted that they were present at the solemnization in Muston church (Leics) while knowing of the impediment. They were pronounced excommunicate, and their excommunication was to be announced at an appropriate time and place. At the next session, at the request of one William Dengayne, intervening for them, the denunciation was omitted. They were enjoined to circle Chesterton church before the procession, wearing only their shirts and carrying candles, a priest carrying a staff to follow them.[195] Afterwards, the court modified the penance out of respect for Hugh la Souche (Zouche),[196] whose servants they claimed to be. They were to circle the church on one Sunday with bare heads, carrying a candle. The reason for their penance was to be published so that there would be no doubt about the cause. The vicar of Chesterton certified that the penance was humbly completed on 27 February 1379.

The first set of proceedings was more substantial. John and Joan were cited before Thomas Gloucestre, commissary of the bishop, for 31 January 1379, to show why they should not be subject to major excommunication according to *Humana concupiscentia*. Their banns had been proclaimed in Chesterton church and no one had reclaimed, but the vicar had refused to solemnize the marriage because he had learned that Joan had had intercourse with one John Lee, who was a relative of John Slory. Joan admitted the intercourse, but the couple denied the consanguinity. The court introduced *ex officio* witnesses (ultimately nine, probably provided by the vicar). It is only after the testimony was taken and published (3 November) that the excommunication was ordered and the divorce pronounced on the basis of affinity by illicit intercourse in the third degree (23 February 1380). In May of 1381, the couple were back before the court for continuing to live together after the divorce. They claimed to have a dispensation from the papal legate in England, but when given an opportunity to produce it, they failed to appear. The execution of the sentence of excommunication is being ordered when the act book ends.

193 *Office c Anegold and Andren* (31.i.79 to 27.ii.79), fol. 108v–110r; disc. and lit. T&C no. 502.
194 Text, T&C no. 503.
195 Text, T&C no. 504.
196 For Hugh de Souche (la Zouche), see n. 163.

Whatever we may think of a legal system that would prohibit a marriage because one of the couple had committed fornication with the second cousin of the other, John and Joan were clearly defying the authority of the court. As we saw in *Fisschere c Frost and Brid*, *Pateshull c Candelesby and Eyr*, *Anegold and Schanbery c Grantesden*, *Duraunt and Cakebred c Draper*, and *Cattesos c Brigham and Pyttok*, going off and getting married while a case was pending was behavior that provoked stern responses.[197] There are two differences between those cases and this one. In the previous cases, the court had stretched the law probably beyond where it ought to have gone. Stratford's constitution visits automatic excommunication on those who, knowing of an impediment (or having a reasonable suspicion of one), have their marriages solemnized anyway. Hugh Candelesby, to take the most extreme of the previous cases, knew of no impediment, and events quickly proved that there was none, at least not one that could be proved. Stratford's constitution does not say that those who have their marriages solemnized during the pendency of proceedings to determine whether there is an impediment should be automatically excommunicated, although it seems that that was how the court interpreted the constitution in all five of the previous cases. Newton behaved differently in *Office c Slory and Feltewell* and *Office c Anegold and Andren*.[198] He waited until the impediment was proven before he ruled against the couple. *Slory* also differs from the previous cases in that in all of them, there was a suggestion that ultimately the court allowed the parties to go their own way. Here, the court is insisting that they divorce despite the fact that they claimed to have a dispensation. At least when the book ends, the court is still insisting on execution of the sentence.

There is an aura of local politics about this case, the precise import of which we cannot quite recover. Hugh la Souche's men arranged a quick trip to Leicestershire for a couple whom the vicar determined cannot validly marry. Nine witnesses appear remarkably quickly to challenge the marriage; the dispensation claimed to have been granted by the cardinal of Ravenna is never produced. Perhaps most important, John Newton here shows no willingness to 'dissimulate', to use Alexander III's word, to let matters be, as he does in other cases. The suspicion, then, is that John and Joan are caught up in a local power struggle between Souche and the vicar, and which may go as high as being a struggle between the bishop (the brother of the earl of Arundel) and Souche's (unknown) patrons.

If we suspected in the *Candelesby* case that the real issue was the dispute between the consistory court and that of the archdeacon, there can be little doubt that that dispute underlies the illegal solemnization citation in *Agnes Bonde of Wimpole c John Yutte of Wendy*.[199] Agnes appealed from the official of the archdeacon, who had ruled against her in a marriage case. The next entry in the case suggests that the ruling was correct. Agnes admits that she has

[197] E.g., at nn. 91, 95, 141, 168.
[198] Nn. 191, 193.
[199] *Bonde c Yutte* (19.x.74 to 14.xi.74), fol. 11r–18r.

no proof, and her case is dismissed.[200] While the appeal is pending, however, the vicar of Wendy solemnizes a marriage between John and Joan daughter of William Molt of Wendy. He is cited for violation of *Humana concupiscentia* and also for refusal to cite John in the appeal case. He justifies the latter action on the ground that after he received the inhibition from the consistory, he received a mandate from the archdeacon's official to proceed despite Agnes's reclamation. This excuse is deemed insufficient, and the vicar submitts himself to punishment for contempt. The case is set down for determining his punishment, both for the admitted violation of *Humana concupiscentia* and for the contempt. When the vicar returns, he displays a dispensation from the violation of *Humana concupiscentia* that he obtained from the papal nuncio. The court defers to this, but imposes penance on him for his contempt.[201]

Penalties for the clergy for violating either *Cum inihibitio* or *Humana concupiscentia* were serious. In addition to the automatic excommunication (which, until lifted, would prevent the clergyman from functioning in his office) under the latter, there was, under the former, an automatic three-year suspension from office. We must be careful, however, to distinguish the different offenses. The suspension of *Cum inihibitio* is for priests who fail to prohibit "such unions" or clergy who "presume to be present at them."[202] The nearest referent for "such unions" is "clandestine marriages" (defined as those for which banns had not been proclaimed) and "forbidden marriages within a prohibited degree." There is no question that the vicar of Wendy was "present" at John and Joan's marriage. He had solemnized it and said the nuptial mass after the solemnization. But it was not at all clear that the union was clandestine (indeed, the mention of "reclamation" suggests that banns were proclaimed),[203] and there is no suggestion that it was within the prohibited degrees (the problem, if there was one, was precontract). Stratford's constitution, with reference back to that of Simon Meopham, contains a one-year suspension from office for clergy who solemnize without license a marriage outside a parish church or chapel with parochial rights. Again, there is no suggestion that the vicar had done this. Indeed, it would seem that the solemnization had taken place in Wendy church. Hence, it is not surprising that the official (Roos) accepts the dispensation and focuses on the contempt, for which he enjoins a penance but no suspension.

In *Gobat and Pertesen c Bygot*, Julia Bygot and Stephen Gobat solemnized their marriage during the pendency of the litigation.[204] This fact is noted in the record, as is the fact that they are subject to major excommunication under *Humana concupiscentia*, but nothing is done about it.[205] In *Saffrey c Molt*, as we have seen, the couple who solemnized their marriage during the pendency of

[200] We must, of course, consider the possibility that despite her oath that she was not colluding with John, she had in fact settled with him.

[201] Lit. T&C no. 505.

[202] Ch 1, n. 77.

[203] Fol. 11r: *non obstante reclamatione dicte* [*AB*].

[204] N. 89.

[205] There is no *ex officio* citation in this case.

the litigation claim that the archdeacon has cognizance of the matter.[206] So far as we can tell, the court accepts this argument. What both cases show is that the court did not always pursue violations of *Humana concupiscentia* vigorously.

The only case under *Humana concupiscentia* that does not have an accompanying marriage litigation is *Office promoted by Robert vicar of Bassingbourn c John Gilberd chaplain of Bassingbourn.*[207] John was cited for 18 June 1377 before the commissary (Gloucestre) because he had aided, advised, and been present at the solemnization of marriage in Bassingbourn church on 31 January 1377 between Warren White and Agnes widow of Simon Foulere both of Bassingbourn. The solemnization took place without the license of those who had the cure of Warren's and Agnes's souls or the appropriate publication of banns, and contrary to a reclamation made by John de la Gore at the publication of the banns between Warren and Agnes, at which Gore claimed precontract and about which a case was pending undecided in court. Endangering his soul further, the same John had been a common dealer in malt and other merchandise, frequenting markets, buying and displaying goods for resale, and being involved in various worldly deals, contrary to his clerical status and bringing disrespect on the clerical order.[208] On 9 July, it is announced that peace has been restored between the vicar and chaplain (this is the first that we learn that the vicar was promoting the case). John is called to respond *ex officio*. Later he appears, denies the article, and purges himself.

If any case was pending between Gore and the couple, as alleged, it was not pending in the consistory court because we certainly would have had a record of it. Perhaps it was pending in the archdeacon's court, though we may have reason to doubt even this. The fact that the court allows a simple purgation once the vicar has dropped the case suggests that the court suspected that what was involved here was probably a dispute between the vicar and the chaplain about who was authorized to solemnize marriages and, perhaps, who was entitled to the oblation. So far as the charge of conducting business is concerned, we will see that that charge was also present in *Office c Netherstrete* (2), where it seems to have been a make-weight.[209] Once the vicar and the chaplain have settled their dispute, a simple purgation suffices to clear the record.

The rest of the straight-office cases divide rather nicely into two groups, cases that could have become instance cases but did not either because (1a) the parties basically conceded the case when they came to court or (1b) the parties were jointly resisting the charge and the court or the community had to pursue it, and (2) cases that never could have become instance cases because the charge was one that was purely criminal.

Office c John Bokesworth of Sutton and Christine Messager of Sutton is typical of type 1a cases.[210] The parties were cited *ex officio* for 2 October

[206] N. 55.

[207] *Office and Bassingbourn (vicar) c Gilberd* (18.vi.77 to 9.vii.77), fol. 75v–77r.

[208] T&C no. 506.

[209] N. 238.

[210] *Office c Bokesworth and Messager* (2.x.76 to 2.x.76), fol. 55Ar.

1376 about a contract of marriage. They appeared in court and confessed to a *de futuro* contract. On the spot, they agreed to a *de presenti* contract, and the commissary (Gloucestre) pronounced them husband and wife.[211] An order to solemnize is not mentioned, probably because it was quite clear that this couple did not need to be encouraged to solemnize. What lies behind this case is, of course, impossible to tell from such a skimpy record. It could be that someone, either one or both families or one of the parties, was hesitating about the contract or even resisting. It could be that the marriage was a foregone conclusion, but members of the community thought that it was proceeding too slowly (and that John and Christine's relationship was becoming scandalous). Whatever prompted the *ex officio* citation, it is clear that all that was required was the brief appearance before the commissary to turn this relationship into a public marriage.

Three cases with a similar pattern are set forth in the margin.[212] One deserves treatment in the text: Alexander Wrighte and Isabel daughter of John de Wysbech of Cambridge and stepdaughter of William Walden of Cambridge were cited *ex officio* before the official (Roos) for 29 May 1375 concerning a contract of marriage. They admitted that Alexander asked Isabel "Do you wish (*vis*) to be my wife?" and she accepted. They joined hands and he pledged to take her as his wife, giving her a kerchief and a purse as gifts.[213] The case was set for 13 July to hear pronouncement on the confessions. On 13 July with the parties' consent, 4 October was assigned to hear the pronouncement. There follow 72 entries in which we are informed that the case is set to hear the pronouncement, until it finally disappears from view after 25 October 1380.

The ceremony that Alexander and Isabel describe is one familiar to us from the York records and from other sources. It is a rather charming version of a 'handfasting'. We have seen that at York, this ceremony was normally taken to be *de presenti* marriage, whatever may have been the social understanding of it. Roos may have had his doubts, and it is probably significant that no intercourse is mentioned or confessed. (It is also possible that however willing Alexander and Isabel were to get married, there were those, such as their families, who opposed the marriage.) There is no suggestion that the couple were contumacious. We cannot imagine that they appeared at all 72 sessions, but there is no mention of their being cited again. Perhaps they went ahead and got married and did not inform the court. Only Foxton's compulsiveness allows us to see that so far as the court was concerned, the case was unresolved.[214]

Office c Adam Barbour of Thorney and Agnes Whitheved of Chatteris, residing in Whittlesey is typical of the type 1b cases.[215] Adam and Agnes were cited *ex officio* for 9 September 1381, concerning a contract of marriage followed

[211] Transcript in Sheehan, "Formation," 66 n. 101.
[212] See T&C no. 507.
[213] *Office c Wrighte and Wysbech* (29.v.75 to 25.x.80), fol. 25v–144v; disc. T&C no. 508.
[214] Lit. T&C no. 509.
[215] *Office c Barbour and Whitheved* (14.vi.81 to 10.ix.81), fol. 152r.

by intercourse. They confess to a *de presenti* contract followed by intercourse. They had proceeded to the promulgation of banns and no one had objected, but the dean of Ely inhibited the solemnization on the ground that Adam had had intercourse with Alice Cok of Chatteris, who was alleged to be a consanguine of Agnes. Adam admitted the intercourse, but the couple alleged that they knew of no relationship between Alice and Agnes. The case was adjourned for the next day in Chatteris church.[216] Alice appeared (but not Adam and Agnes); Alice admitted the intercourse and the consanguinity and produced two witnesses to this effect. The court, however, called the vicar of Chatteris, the parish clerk, and four elderly men and women from Agnes's *parentela*. The witnesses were examined and their testimony published on the spot. The court then ruled that the relationship had not been proven; the solemnization of Agnes and Adam's marriage was ordered, and Alice was ordered beaten three times around Chatteris church for the intercourse. The fact that only Alice is ordered to do penance and not Adam suggests that Newton regarded her claim of consanguinity as bordering on the specious (though we cannot exclude the possibility of an application of a double standard).[217]

On 2 May 1381, Robert Andren and Alice Edyng of Swavesey were cited to show cause why they reclaimed against the banns of Nicholas Andren of Swavesey and Marjorie Solsa of Swavesey.[218] They appear (as did Nicholas but not Marjorie) and propose that while Nicholas's wife was still living, he committed adultery with Marjorie and they plotted his wife's death. They also claim that Walter Grym, related to Nicholas within the fourth degree, had intercourse with Marjorie and contracted marriage with her. They produce two witnesses, both men of Swavesy. At the next session (where Marjorie does appear), Robert and Alice produce three additional men of Swavesy as witnesses. After the summer recess, Robert and Alice fail to appear, the testimony is published, and the case is set, first to speak against the witnesses and then to hear definitive sentence. It is still being continued, in the absence of Robert and Alice, on 27 March 1382, when the act book ends.

It seems likely, though we cannot be sure, that had the published testimony clearly demonstrated either the impediment of crime or that of affinity by illicit intercourse or public honesty (the relationship with Grym),[219] the court would have proceeded *ex officio* to require Nicholas and Marjorie to answer these charges. As it is, we cannot be sure that any of the parties was present after the publication of the testimony, and the court makes no effort to cite them. Whether the court would have proceeded against Nicholas and Marjorie under *Humana concupiscentia* if they had solemnized their marriage during the pendency of the proceedings we do not know, but its behavior in other cases suggests

[216] Disc. T&C no. 510.

[217] Disc. and lit. T&C no. 511.

[218] *Office and Andren and Edyng c Andren and Solsa* (2.v.81 to 27.ii.82), fol. 154v–161v; lit. T&C no. 512.

[219] Lit. T&C no. 513.

that there was some risk that it would. We may also suspect that if Nicholas and Marjorie had appeared and asked for a sentence, they would have been able to obtain one, even in the absence of Robert and Alice. That happens sometimes in instance cases, and this case was probably regarded as *ex officio promoto*. That, in turn, allows us to speculate about the nature of the testimony. There probably was something to it (as to which impediment, of course, we cannot tell). Nicholas and Marjorie did not want to take the litigation risk of forcing the case to the judgment. Whether they took the risk of getting their marriage solemnized or whether they simply dropped the project we cannot tell.

Thomas Wolron, servant of Richard Leycestre, parishioner of Holy Trinity, Ely, and Margaret, servant of the same Richard, were cited before one of the commissaries (Gloucestre) for 2 October 1376, concerning a contract of marriage followed by intercourse.[220] They admitted that they had had a sexual relationship for two years without correction. With their consent, they contracted marriage in the common form. In another case, John Heneye of Cambridge and Marjorie Baldok were cited before the commissary (Gloucestre) for 15 May 1377, concerning a contract of marriage followed by intercourse.[221] They admitted the intercourse but denied the contract. The record says that they willingly abjured each other *sub pena nubendi*. In both of these cases, Gloucestre obviously has no evidence of the contract. If the parties would not admit it, the best that he can do is ensure that if they continue their relationship, they will be married. No correction is ordered other than the abjuration, although the second record says that their intercourse made them subject to correction.

The one attempt to enforce *ex officio* a marriage formed by abjuration and subsequent intercourse does not seem to succeed. Upon inspection of the register of corrections from the vacancy following John Barnet's death, the official (Roos) found that John Robynesson senior of Swaffham Prior and Joan daughter of Geoffrey Moryce of Swaffham Prior had been cited *ex officio* for the crime of fornication, notoriously committed and continued, uncorrected, for five years.[222] They had appeared 14 March 1374 before the keeper of spiritualities of the city and diocese of Ely and confessed to having committed the crime for three continuous years, to having been corrected and inhibited often by the archdeacon's official, and to having offended since their last correction. They then abjured each other *sub pena nubendi*. Roos cited them to appear on 5 Oct 1374. They appeared and admitted that they contracted in court and that afterwards they slept together alone and naked on two nights, but they denied that they had intercourse. The case was set down for 14 October to hear pronouncement on their confessions, but the couple did not appear. The case was set again for pronouncement and then disappears from the record.

220 *Office c Wolron and Leycestre* (2.x.76), fol. 55Ar. See n. 212 for a case almost certainly involving another of Richard's servants.

221 *Office c Heneye and Baldok* (15.v.77), fol. 72.

222 *Office c Robynesson and Moryce* (5.x.74 to 14.x.74), fol. 12v. See Sheehan, "Formation," 68 n. 109.

The proceedings in *Office c Richard Galion woolman of St Neots [Hunts] and Matilda Phelip his de facto wife* are complicated, but the basic story is relatively simple.[223] Richard and Matilda were cited before the official (and apparently also before the official of the archdeacon) for bigamy, Richard having married one Matilda Sped of Heacham (Norf) 27 years previously. Richard admits that he solemnized the marriage with Sped, but the couple defends the charge on the ground that their contract was the prior one. We see the case first in July of 1378 as an appeal from the official of the archdeacon, where Richard is described as a resident of St Neots (Hunts). In October the case is said to be discontinued because of the nonappearance of the official.[224] Leaving aside a defamation action against Hugh Candelesby, the registrar of the archdeacon, which may not involve the same man and which ends after an aborted appeal to the provincial court,[225] the next time we see the case is in June of 1379 when Richard, now described as being of Cambridge, and Phelip are cited before the official, once more for bigamy. The case is set down for proof of the precontract and disappears from view. It is back in September of 1379 in an appeal from the official of the archdeacon. This appeal is aborted when the official, who is said to have left office and the diocese, fails to appear. Richard and Phelip are cited before the official once again for the same reasons in May of 1380. This time, Richard is asked to produce witnesses about the contract with Sped. He asks for a long term to do so because the witnesses live far away, and the case disappears from view in October without any witnesses being produced. The case is once more back in court in October of 1381 as an appeal from the official of the archdeacon and is still active when the act book ends in the spring of 1382.[226] Concomitant with this appeal are *ex officio* proceedings against the archdeacon's official for failure to obey the consistory's inhibition and against the dean of Cambridge for failure to serve Richard's libel on the archdeacon's official.

Richard was a man of some stature. He is described as a "woolman" (sometimes that is given as his surname), which probably means that he is a wool merchant. We know little about Phelip, except that she solemnized her marriage to Richard in Cambridge. Neither of them was young. Richard solemnized a marriage in a small town on the Norfolk coast 27 years previously, and Phelip must have been approximately his age in order for the claim of precontract to be plausible. It is probably significant that neither Richard nor Phelip claims that the solemnization of their marriage took place before the solemnization of the marriage with Sped, and from this fact we may reconstruct a plausible, if not inevitable, series of events. Richard, the wool merchant from Huntingdonshire,

[223] *Office c Galion and Phelip* (29.vii.78 to 27.ii.82), fol. 96v–162r; see n. 127.

[224] This is what the entry says, and it is odd. 'Discontinuance' normally implies the failure of the plaintiff (here the appellant) to pursue the case.

[225] *Galion c Candelesby* (29.vii.78 to 21.x.78), fol. 97r–99v.

[226] It is possible that the basic case between Richard and Phelip was renewed at this time. See n. 104.

contracted marriage informally with a Cambridge woman (though we do not know that she was a Cambridge woman at the time) and solemnized one with a Norfolkshire woman. He then came to live in Cambridge where he solemnized the marriage with the local woman. Someone found out about the woman in Norfolkshire, and this rumor (which we should probably take to be a fact, granted Richard's confession of it) subjected the couple to continual harassment both by the archdeacon's official and by the official of the consistory. Proof was, however, difficult to come by. The events happened long ago; the contract with Sped took place far away, and we have no idea where the informal contract with Phelip took place. The question then becomes who has the burden of proof, and the record suggests that there was some doubt about this question. Whatever the archdeacon's court may have been willing to do, we suspect that the consistory would have been reluctant to divorce a couple who had been living in a long-term solemnized marriage without clear proof of the bigamy. Richard and Phelip, however, could not protect themselves against continual harassment unless they had clear proof of their precontract, which they pretty clearly did not have. One can, of course, say that they have only themselves to blame. Their failure to solemnize their marriage when they entered into it was the root cause of the problem, coupled by Richard's inexcusable behavior with regard to Sped, inexcusable even if we accept his version of the facts.[227]

Two cases involve what seem to be relatively straightforward issues of consanguinity. In the first case, John vicar of Bourn is cited for 8 July 1378 for refusing to solemnize the marriage of Thomas son of John Stanhard and Agnes daughter of John Molt, both of Bourn.[228] The vicar appears and alleges that five male parishioners had reclaimed the banns on the ground of the consanguinity of the couple. Four of the five appear and testify, and when Thomas and Agnes appear at the end of the month with no counterproof, their marriage, if any, is declared void for consanguinity (the degrees not being stated).

John son of William Symond of Leverington and Alice daughter of William Page of Leverington were called before the official (Roos) for 26 July 1375 in Wisbech, concerning a clandestine contract of marriage followed by intercourse.[229] They confess to a *de presenti* marriage followed by intercourse.[230] John's father appears and alleges that the marriage cannot take place because the couple are second cousins once removed. The case then proceeds as if it were an instance case between the father and the couple (technically, office promoted, but this is not said). The father produces eight witnesses to this effect; the couple apparently have no answer. The official orders a divorce.

The most spectacular case in this group is *Office c William Chilterne de Leverington of Ely, Amy Neve of Ely and Joan Spynnere of Whittlesey alias*

227 Lit. and disc. T&C no. 514.

228 *Office c Bourn (vicar)* (8.vii.78 to 29.vii.79), fol. 95v–119v; lit. T&C no. 515.

229 *Office c Symond and Page* (26.vii.75 to 28.vii.75), fol. 28v.

230 Transcription of the confession in Sheehan, "Formation," 55 n. 58.

Squyer of Kirkby.[231] The defendants were cited before the bishop for 14 September 1378 for having collusively obtained a divorce before Mr William de Rookhawe, former official of the archdeacon. William and Amy had been married for many years and had had children. The divorce was obtained on the ground of precontract with Joan. The bishop commissions John Newton to hear the case. It takes some time to establish what happened before the archdeacon's official, because there is no record of it. Eventually, the archdeacon's registrar (Candelesby) and another establish that Rookhawe had proceeded orally and had taken no testimony other than the confessions of the parties. William now confesses that he colluded with Joan out of spite for Amy. Joan, though cited, never appears. On 4 December, Newton quashes Rookhawe's sentence in stern language and reinstates William and Amy's marriage.[232] William's confession is obviously key in this case. He may well have had qualms of conscience.[233] Whether Amy had proof of the collusion we do not know, nor do we know Joan's version of the story. We do know, however, that Rookhawe's procedure had been shockingly sloppy. This was probably enough for Newton to rule against the sentence. That would shift the burden of proof to those who wanted to defend the divorce, and no such person appeared before the court.

In addition to the illegal solemnization cases discussed here, the Ely court in this period heard seven *ex officio* adultery cases; there were three citations for fornication (two of which, as we shall see, could be regarded as one), and one case for spousal abuse. The adultery cases have elements that suggest that routine adultery cases were within the purview of the archdeacon's court and that only those that had some aggravating factor were normally heard by the consistory court. Two of these cases involve priests and were begun in the bishop's audience. In the first case (27 June 1377), the bishop ordered Robert vicar of Bassingbourn to purge himself with six honorable clerics before the commissary (Gloucestre), of the charge that he had abducted Alice wife of William Adekyn of Bassingbourn against William's will and committed adultery with her.[234] The previous month, Robert had brought a defamation action against William for having accused him of committing adultery with his wife.[235] William appears at the purgation and offers to prove the charge (thus blocking the purgation). Both cases continue over the summer; William does produce witnesses, but on the date scheduled for publication of the testimony, he does not appear, and the case is held to be in abeyance pending prosecution by either party. At the same session, the defamation case also goes into abeyance. It seems unlikely that the witnesses provided solid proof of the truth of the charges and likely that William and Robert reached some kind of compromise.

231 *Office c Chilterne, Neve and Spynnere* (14.ix.78 to 4.xii.78), fol. 103r–104r; disc. at length in Aston, *Arundel*, 104–6; Sheehan, "Formation," 63–4.
232 T&C no. 516.
233 Compare *Palmere c Brunne and Suthburn* (Ch 4, n. 191).
234 *Office and Adekyn c Bassingbourn* (*vicar*) (27.vi.77 to 22.x.77), fol. 75v–77r.
235 *Bassingbourn* (*vicar*) *c Adekyn* (29.v.77 to 1.x.77), fol. 74v–79v.

In the second case, Alice wife of Thomas Gritford of Doddington was cited before the bishop for 10 June 1380, concerning the crime of adultery with a priest.[236] She purged herself with 12 women compurgators. On the same day the bishop imposed a penance on John Hervy of Doddington, who was cited for the same day in a defamation action brought against him by Alice: The next Sunday in Doddington church John should seek from Alice forgiveness, saying before the congregation that he did not say the words (which must have been the accusation of adultery) because they were true but because he had been provoked while angry.[237]

A third case of adultery involving a priest may be part of a much larger dispute that William Netherstrete, chaplain of Fulbourn, among others, was promoting as an office case against the vicar of Hinton.[238] William was cited *ex officio* for correction before the official (Scrope) for 14 Dec 1377. The charges against him are substantial: (1) adultery with Alice wife of Richard Fuller, now a resident of Balsham; (2) practice of divination (having employed incantations to entice Katherine wife of Henry Molle of Fulbourn to come to his room at night so he could violently force her into adultery); (3) assault against John Petyt senior of Fulbourn (priest), Roger in le Netherstrete (clerk), and John Baldewyn of Fulbourn (clerk) in St Vigor of Fulbourn (a sacred place); (4) solicitation of Isabel wife of Richard atte Wich in order to seduce her; (5) intercourse with Eleanor Attepool; (6) keeping a concubine (Agnes, widow of Robert Godsped of Wilburton, whose female member he cut off because he suspected her of committing adultery with John Alston of Wilburton); (7) frequenting common taverns by day and night with ribald and suspicious people, contrary to the honor of his order; and (8) being a common dealer in corn.[239] William (1) admitted that he and Alice committed adultery, but claimed that he was corrected 13 years earlier for that crime and denied the crime since then; (2) denied the divination; (3) denied the assault on Petyt and Baldewyne, and admitted violence against Netherstrete, but claimed that he acted in self-defense; (4) denied soliciting Isabel; (5) admitted that he had intercourse with Elenore two years earlier, but alleged that he was corrected by the archdeacon's official and that he had not committed the crime since then; (6) admitted he had been corrected 15 years earlier for the offense with Agnes, but denied the crime since then; (7) denied going to taverns; but (8) admitted to dealing in corn.

On the day assigned (7 January) to William to purge himself with 12 honorable people for the crimes denied by him; to prove his alleged corrections and, if proved, to purge himself for the crimes committed since his corrections; to prove the self-defense, and to receive punishment for his negotiations in corn, William is absent. The record says that he does not dare to appear because

236 *Office c Gritford*; *Gritford c Hervy* (10.vi.80), fol. 140r. See Aston, *Arundel*, 40–1.
237 Text and disc. T&C no. 517.
238 *Office c Netherstrete* (2) (14.xii.77), fol. 84v–88r. For Netherstrete, see T&C no. 518.
239 T&C no. 519.

he is pursued by his enemies (by royal writ); someone, probably his proctor, takes an oath about this. On 14 January, he appears, produces compurgators, and offers to purge himself. John Baldewyn of Fulbourn (one of the men he is alleged to have assaulted) appears and is prepared to prove the matter. At the next session, however, John and William are alleged to have compromised. The case is set down for proof of the compromise or of the crimes, but then disappears from view.

Were it not for the fact that William was also involved in other litigation, litigation that may have prompted these charges against him, we would wonder why the bishop did not take up the matter personally. Perhaps he did. As it is, however, the court may have suspected that his enemies, and he clearly had many, had dug up a whole of group of charges, some true but going a long way back and some the product of the local rumor mill. So long as William could produce compurgators (as he did), the court was willing to let the charges drop when the man who said he could prove them failed to do so.

The act book also contains two related cases of clerical fornication. In one, a woman accused of fornication with two different priests (the vicar of Littleport and his chaplain) purges herself.[240] In another, the vicar of Littleport is cited for both fornication and incest with the same woman.[241] (The grounds for the latter charge are not reported, but the fact that the vicar and the woman have the same surname, Lakyngheth, suggests that they were consanguine). After contumacy and a frivolous appeal, the vicar submits, does penance for contumacy, purges himself, and promises to remove the woman from his house.[242]

In two adultery cases involving lay people, it seems likely that the reason the consistory court took original jurisdiction of the case was that not only was adultery involved but also incest. Stephen Bernewelle of Cambridge, poulterer and married man, and Isabel Tavern of Cambridge, who accepted Stephen's two children from the baptismal font, were cited *ex officio* for 21 July 1374, charged with adultery and incest.[243] They spend the better part of 18 months resisting the charges. There is a frivolous appeal in the middle of the case, they are excommunicated for contumacy, and, ultimately (perhaps at the advice of Henry Bowet, their advocate), they put themselves on the mercy of the court, are absolved, purge themselves, and get off with a threat of severe punishment if they sin again.

John son of Adam Joseph senior of Castle Camps (deep in the country near Haverill and the Suffolk border) and Alice wife of John Coupere of Castle Camps (John Joseph's uncle) were called before Thomas Gloucestre on 16 April 1378 because they had committed the crime of adultery and incest for many years.[244] They had three children, and Alice was pregnant with a fourth. (Her

[240] *Office c Lakyngheth* (1) (9.i.76), fol. 35r.
[241] *Office c Lakyngheth* (2) (19.i.76), fol. 34v.
[242] Disc. T&C no. 520.
[243] *Office c Bernewelle and Tavern* (21.vii.74 to 11.i.76), fol. 8v–33v.
[244] *Office c Joseph and Coupere* (16.iv.78 to 15.viii.78), fol. 97r–97v.

appearance is apparently excused because of her condition, and she never appears.) For the crime already committed, John was ordered beaten three days round Camps church, one day round Cambridge market, and one round Linton (a more substantial place between Camps and Cambridge) market, in the manner of a public penitent. He refused to perform the penance, was excommunicated, and remained obdurate for 40 days. The bishop requested his caption by the secular arm, and after four days in the jail of Cambridge castle, John submitted and performed his penance. In parallel proceedings in July, John was ordered to pay the expenses of Edward chaplain of Camps and Rose wife of Robert Bygge of Camps, whom he had had cited before the provincial court of Canterbury for falsely accusing him of the offense, a citation (connected with an appeal) which the provincial court had remitted when John failed to pursue the appeal.

Joan Fyskerton of Cambridge, alias Cornwaille, had been cited before the official for the crime of adultery committed with John Erneys, servant of John Barker of Cambridge, and with John Chapman, servant of Richard March of Cambridge.[245] The crime had been brought to the court's attention by *publica fama*. When we first see the case, Joan has appealed to the court of Canterbury (apparently in March of 1376); she has failed to prove her appeal, and the appellate court, by letters dated 7 October 1376, has remitted the case to the consistory. Ultimately, Joan appears before the court on 6 December and pays five shillings to the official for his expenses. She is assigned 10 January to receive her penance, but no further entry has been found.

If it seems reasonably clear that the aggravating factor in the two previous cases was incest (coupled, in *Office c Joseph and Coupere*, by the blatant nature of the relationship), it is less easy to see what it was in this case. If we focus on the fact that the two men with whom Joan was accused of committing adultery were both servants, we may suspect that she was thought to be seducing men younger than she.

In all three cases, the defendants resist and take appeals to the court of Canterbury. This suggests that they had at least enough money to pursue the appeal, although they may not have had enough money to pursue it very vigorously because in all three cases, the provincial court remits the case, and the defendants are condemned to pay expenses for a frivolous appeal. It should also be noted that only in Joseph's case do we have evidence that a defendant ever did the penance. Bernewell and Tavern pay the expenses of a frivolous appeal and are let go without a penance (the man had purged himself) under a threat of a much more serious sanction if they offend again. Fyskerton may or may not have been assigned a penance (it is possible, though not likely, that Foxton neglected to record it). It is also possible that any penance assigned to her was a private one (and deliberately not recorded). This would also suggest that she was a woman of some standing.

The final adultery case tells us something about appellate practice in *ex officio* cases. Bartholomew Chaundeler of Cambridge and Katherine Hostiler

245 *Office c Fyskerton* (7.x.76 to 10.i.77), fol. 55Br.

appealed from Mr John de Pynkeston, the archdeacon's official.[246] They had been accused of adultery, and they allege that Mr John had assigned to them an excessive number of compurgators. Mr John fails to appear; it is reported that he has left office and the diocese, and the case is dropped.

Richard Fysshere of Chatteris was cited before the bishop in the conventual church of Chatteris because he mistreated his wife, breaking her leg and causing her other injuries, in a case not permitted by law.[247] He appeared on 9 June 1380 and admitted the article. He swore to treat his wife with marital affection in the future and to obtain medical treatment to cure her, as much as this was possible. As penance, he was ordered to circle the parish church of Chatteris on three Sundays before the procession, carrying a candle in the manner of a penitent, and to pay 20 shillings to the church fabric within a year. He was also ordered to circle the church of Ely, deposed of his clothing, in the same manner on 23 June (the patronal feast of St Etheldreda).

It is hard to imagine that this was the only case of spousal abuse to occur in Ely diocese over an eight-year period. The archdeacon may have heard others; indeed, the bishop may have heard others, for we do not know why Foxton recorded this particular case. The penance imposed here is quite severe (we do not know if it was performed), but the abuse also seems to have been extreme. The promise to amend, as we saw in the cases at York, was standard. When we look at the Paris register, we will see many more cases of this type.

We have saved for last the third citation for fornication, the only one involving a layman, because fornication was the least of the problems of John Poynaunt of Thriplow.[248] When John was cited on 21 October 1378 for fornication with Isabel Pybbel, the court was already aware that John had been divorced by the archdeacon's official from Joan Swan on the ground of John's impotence. Following the divorce, Robert Goby married Joan. John and Isabel admit that they had intercourse; indeed, she says that she is pregnant by him and has known no other man. They also allege that they contracted marriage. When asked why the divorce should not be revoked, John says that he cannot return to Joan because she and Isabel are related within the forbidden degrees.[249] The argument is a sophisticated one. Since, under the assumptions of the case, the marriage with Joan was never consummated, John is arguing that it should be dissolved on the ground of supervenient affinity. This is not the classical law of the church as defined by Innocent III, but prior to Innocent's time, such arguments had been heard, and there were those who argued, even in this period, that unconsummated marriages were not absolutely indissoluble.[250]

After the introduction of one witness (a chaplain, whom John authorizes to reveal the contents of his confession),[251] the case goes into abeyance until

[246] *Office c Chaundeler and Hostiler* (22.ix.79 to 13.x.79), fol. 120v–121v.
[247] *Office c Fysshere* (9.vi.80), fol. 140r; text, disc. and lit. T&C no. 521.
[248] *Office c Poynaunt, Swan, Goby and Pybbel* (21.x.78 to 23.vii.80), fol. 100r–142r; disc. T&C no. 522.
[249] T&C no. 523.
[250] See Ch 1, at nn. 5–6.
[251] See at n. 84.

23 February 1380, when John and Isabel, by their proctors, once more admit the intercourse (they now have children). Joan's proctor produces documentary proof of the divorce and once more asserts that she and Robert have married. John is given a day to prove the intercourse and the consanguinity of Isabel and Joan. Out of term, with just John and Robert present, four more witnesses are introduced, including another chaplain who is authorized to testify to what was said in confession. The case once more goes into abeyance, although on 14 June, a brief entry says that John has undergone palpation and has been proven potent.[252] On 23 July, with only John present, Newton renders a judgment that the church was deceived in granting the divorce (there is no suggestion that John and Joan did the deceiving); the marriage of Robert and Joan is dissolved, and Joan and John are ordered to treat each other with marital affection. Nothing is said about Isabel in the entry other than that she and John had intercourse often.

Although two careful scholars have dealt with this case as simply a correction of an erroneous judgment of the archdeacon's official, it is hard to imagine that it is not more complicated than that.[253] From November of 1378 to February of 1380, nothing happens in the case. At a minimum, that suggests that if the parties do not pursue the case, Newton will not make them pursue it. When Newton sets the case down for proof on 23 February, he seems to be prepared to hold that if John's intercourse with Isabel and her relationship with Joan can be proven, then John has a case. That would be a daring move granted the state of the law, but the situation of the parties demands that, if possible, something be found to avoid the harsh judgment that eventually follows, particularly, as seems possible, if John and Joan's marriage never was consummated. That John is willing to reveal the contents of his confessions suggests that at least he is trying to do the right thing.[254] At the simplest level what may have happened is that his case collapsed when he could not prove the relationship between Isabel and Joan. But there may be more. Isabel has not appeared in court since November of 1378. She may have gone missing; she may even be dead. Newton has medical evidence that John is not impotent. John may or may not have had intercourse with Isabel 'often', but that is beside the point. The divorce for impotence is an erroneous judgment and must be quashed on the record. As for Joan and Robert, perhaps they left the diocese. That there are no further entries in the case may be evidence that neither Newton nor John saw fit to pursue the matter any further.

CONCLUSION

A number of our conclusions have already been anticipated. The evidence of the Ely register supports that of the York cause papers. Although we know less about the stories that the parties told at Ely than we do about those told at York,

[252] Fol. 140v: *commissa palpitacione viri, certificatum est nobis de eius sufficienti potencia.*
[253] Aston, *Arundel*, 102 n. 2; Sheehan, "Formation," 74.
[254] This is a rare procedure at Ely, but this is not the only example. See at n. 108.

the similarity in types of cases and what we can see when the veil of formulaic language is lifted suggest that the stories were probably quite similar to those told at York. The presence of the office citations and office cases shows us a court that was a bit more proactive than the York consistory seems to have been (we should recall, however, that we know relatively little of the archdeacons' activities in York diocese). The Ely court is somewhat more an enforcer of the law than an arbiter between arguing parties, but only somewhat more.

Whether the attitude of the parties toward marriage merits the phrase 'astonishingly individualistic' that Michael Sheehan used to describe it is a matter about which we may have more doubt.[255] What astonishes depends on what one is expecting, and when Sheehan wrote, it was generally accepted that marriage choice in the Middle Ages was not within the control of the parties to the marriage. True, we do see the intervention of parents and occasionally of other social superiors in the Ely cases, but such intervention is quite rare. Indeed, there is less evidence of third-party involvement and arranged marriages in the Ely register than there is in the York cause papers because far fewer Ely cases are defended on the ground of force and none are defended on the ground of nonage. Even if we increase the number of cases involving third parties by an order of magnitude to make up for the situations where parents or lords are working behind the scenes, we still end up with a large number of couples who seem to be operating entirely on their own.[256]

The evidence of the Ely register allows us to add one more aspect to the picture that we painted for York. The court itself played some role, if not in marriage choice, at least once that choice had been made. There is somewhat more enforcement of the rules about consanguinity and affinity at Ely than there is at York, though not much more. There is evidence at Ely, as there is not at York, that the court was putting some pressure on couples to solemnize their marriages. The pressure was, however, quite gentle. Absent an illegal solemnization (which, as we have seen, the court interpreted as being a solemnization during the pendency of a case), the pressure was by way of court order to solemnize an informal marriage once it was proven, not by way of penalizing couples to an informal marriage.

The number of cases in which no resolution is reached is relatively high at Ely, as it was at York. Since the York court that we see in the cause papers does not seem to have been engaged in law enforcement at all, the fact that some cases were not resolved did not surprise us. When the conduct of a case is entirely within the control of the parties, we would suspect, and indeed we find in virtually every legal system that has such cases, that the parties will drop the case either because they have reached a satisfactory compromise or because they have run out of money, patience, or energy. We have seen that the Ely court will pursue a case when the parties seem to have lost interest, but it is rare for it to use the full panoply of mechanisms at its disposal, notably caption by the

255 Sheehan, "Formation," 76.
256 Disc. T&C no. 524.

secular arm. Those who were determined to evade the court could and did flee, and in a small diocese, flight beyond the boundaries of the diocese might take such parties but a few miles from home. So far as we can tell, the court never pursued a party into another diocese, though mechanisms for doing so were available.[257]

The end result, then, is that, so far as we can tell from the court record, management of marital matters in the Ely diocese of the late fourteenth century was pretty much a matter for the parties to work out, aided, of course, by a dispute-resolution mechanism that the court provided and occasionally more active enforcement. That, in turn, raises the question, as it did at York, of who these people were who were in many instances – so far as we can tell – arranging their own marriages.

Since we can be reasonably confident that everyone who came before the consistory[258] in the eight years in question was recorded by Foxton, and since Foxton almost always tells us where the parties came from, we probably have better data for Ely than we do for York about the geographical dispersion of the parties. We have 117 cases that we have classified as 'marriage cases'. These 117 cases yield the names of 258 parties, all but 14 of which have a toponym associated with them.[259] Table 6.8 lists the places from which more than one party came, from the most frequent to the least.

As might be expected, Cambridge and Ely account for more than a quarter of the parties in the cases. Almost all of the regular sittings of the court took place in Cambridge, and Cambridge and Ely were the only areas in the diocese that could be called urban in the fourteenth century. They were also the ecclesiastical centers of the diocese. There is reason to believe that the numbers given in the table understate the dominance of Cambridge in marriage litigation in this period. Six of the 14 parties who are not identified in a case probably came from Cambridge (because the other parties to the cases came from Cambridge), and towns in the immediate environs of Cambridge also account for substantial number of parties: Barnwell (9), Trumpington (7), Chesterton (6), Grantchester (3), Madingley (3), and Newnham (2). If we add these parties to those that we know came from Cambridge itself, we get a total of 86, or 35 percent of the parties that have toponyms.[260] But if 35 percent of the parties came from areas that might generously be described as urban, 65 percent did not. Also, unlike York, the entire diocese of Ely (which is admittedly quite small) is represented in these cases.

As at York, the 'middling sort' of people seem to be the parties in these cases. Although we suspected that some were of higher station than the record

[257] Disc. T&C no. 525.

[258] 'Came before' is important. Foxton does not seem to have recorded initial citations where none of the parties appeared.

[259] Disc. T&C no. 526.

[260] If we leave out Trumpington, Grantchester, and Madingley on the ground that they are too far away to count as part of Cambridge, we get 73 or 30%.

TABLE 6.8. *Parties' Place of Residence in Marriage Cases at Ely (1374–1381)*

Place	No.	%	Place	No.	%
Cambridge	50	19	Hardwick	3	1
Ely	24	9	Madingley	3	1
Chatteris	10	4	March	3	1
Swavesey	10	4	Newton	3	1
Barnwell	9	3	Sutton	3	1
Bourn	7	3	Wendy	3	1
Trumpington	7	3	Wilbraham	3	1
Bassingbourn	6	2	Arrington	2	1
Chesterton	6	2	Balsham	2	1
Fulbourn	6	2	Carlton	2	1
Wimpole	6	2	Castle Camps	2	1
Littleport	5	2	Clopton	2	1
Thriplow	5	2	Doddington	2	1
Wisbech	5	2	Elm	2	1
Emneth	4	2	Kingston	2	1
Lolworth	4	2	Leverington	2	1
Melbourn	4	2	Newnham	2	1
Sawston	4	2	Swaffham	2	1
Shelford, Little	4	2	Swaffham Prior	2	1
Stretham	4	2	Westley Waterless	2	1
Downham, Little	3	1	Whittlesford Bridge	2	1
Grantchester	3	1	Wilburton	2	1

Note: Single instances listed T&C no. 527.
Source: CUL, DMA, D2/1; Stentz, *Calendar*.

showed, the highest lay social ranking that we find mentioned in the records is the ambiguous 'serjeant'. Below or perhaps equal to that is the 'woolman', who may have been a wool merchant. On approximately the same social plane, perhaps slightly higher, are the steward of the bishop of Ely and the registrar of the archdeacon's official. There is, as we have seen, one case where one of the parties is alleged to have married a cottar, and one where one of the parties is clearly a villein (but resident in Ely). The other indications that we get of occupation fall in between. There are 7 male and 10 female servants (to these we might add the one man and three women who are described as 'residing with' someone who does not look like a relative). There are three tailors, two cordwainers, one wright, one ploughwright, one poulterer, one leach, one dyer (lystere), two female taverners, and one female spinner. On the clerical side, there are two Austin canons (a subdeacon and a priest) and one undifferentiated clerk.

That adds up to approximately 40 (of 258, 16%) parties about whom we have some idea of their occupations. We can expand this if we are willing to look at the surnames. Here, we are not talking about occupation (for there is little doubt that most of the surnames we have here are genuine surnames)[261] but about likely social status. In all probability, someone in the person's patriline in the not-too-distant past was engaged in the occupation that gave the family its surname. Our group of parties includes (with various spellings) seven Tailors, three Fishers (one of which may be a genuine occupation), three Lysters, two Pages, two Barbers, two Spinners, and one each of the following: Potter, Mason, Baker, Chapman, Webster, Smith, Reader, Sargent, Wafer, Draper, Garthmaker, Painter, Saddler, Poulter, Butcher, Taverner, Messenger, Chandler, Ostler, Squire, Lockyer, Cooper, and Wright. That adds another 42 indications of class or status to our list, and these indications are quite consistent with the actual occupations that are given for some of the parties. Another indication, at least of a lack of high status, is that there are very few surnames that reflect Norman placenames, or, more broadly, that seem to be Anglo-Norman names.[262]

All the evidence, then, points in the direction of what we described as the 'middling sort' of people. The problem is that we do not have this type of evidence for approximately two-thirds of our group. Michael Sheehan faced the same problem (he was, perhaps, unaware of how many of the parties could be given a social standing) and surmised that the unidentified parties were peasants.[263] That depends on how one defines 'peasants'. In the first place, we have a substantial number of people from Cambridge and Ely, people who are unlikely to have been engaged in full-time farming. Second, the information that we do have suggests a status slightly above that of the ordinary peasant. Third, although we have not systematically examined the information given about witnesses, most of them, where we can tell, seem to be of roughly the same range of statuses as the parties, and that, in turn, would suggest that where we have these indications for the witnesses and not for the parties, the status of the parties was similar. Fourth, the Ely litigants are quite sophisticated. Even where they conduct their cases themselves, they have a pretty good idea of what to say; many of them can afford proctors, at least for part of the case; and a substantial number are able to afford the expenses of an appeal.

All of this would suggest, though it does not quite prove, that the litigants before the consistory of Ely were, on the average, of somewhat higher status and income than that of ordinary Cambridgeshire peasants. Those that came from rural areas and are not identified by occupation were probably 'peasants', if one wants to use that term for anyone who worked at farming by himself or herself, but they were probably of the upper strata of peasants, the sort of people who will be called 'yeomen' in the fifteenth century.

We suggested in the case of York that the evidence of the cause papers tended to confirm the recent suggestion that some women were on the move in the late fourteenth and early fifteenth centuries, and that being a servant gave these

261 Disc. T&C no. 528.

262 Disc. T&C no. 529.

263 Sheehan, "Formation," 44 ("Scores seem to be peasants attached to manors in the countryside").

women more choice of marriage partner than they might otherwise have had. We doubted, however, that there was as much of a distinction between rural and urban as has recently been suggested. While there were cases from rural areas that suggested arranged marriages and substantial parental involvement in marriage choice, such cases were also to be found in urban areas. Conversely, there were also rural cases in which the couple seems to have been doing the arranging by themselves. Whether this is because the high mortality rate of the second half of the fourteenth century left many young people of marriageable age without immediate family, or because at least some Yorkshire parents left their children to choose a marriage partner pretty much on their own, or both, we cannot say.

If the York evidence leads us to doubt how great the difference was between urban and rural marriage practices, the Ely evidence (where, admittedly we have fewer circumstantial accounts of what happened) tends to confirm those doubts. If *Everard c Beneyt* looks like a typical story of deracinated young people in an urban setting contracting marriage pretty much on their own, *Gobat and Pertesen c Bygot* suggests a quite similar story from a largely rural setting.[264] We should have no doubt that life-cycle servanthood contributed to the independence of marriage choice in England (and also to young people getting in trouble). The York and Ely evidence is quite convincing in this regard. What we may doubt is whether it was the only factor. This is an issue to which we will have to return after we look at some arguments about marriage on the other side of the English Channel.

[264] See text following n. 67; text following n. 89.

7

Paris

THE BUSINESS OF THE COURT OF PARIS

In the late fourteenth century Paris was the largest city in Europe north of the Alps. It may have been the largest city in Europe. Its population was more than an order of magnitude greater than that of York or Cambridge. It was the center of the French royal government, the seat of the largest university in northern Europe, and a bustling commercial center. It was, however, the see of only a bishop.[1] The metropolitical see was at Sens. Because of the large population of Paris (and of the large number of clergy that were resident in the town), the ecclesiastical courts of Paris probably had more business than any of the other ecclesiastical courts in France. There were three archidiaconal courts in addition to the court of the bishop's official.[2] Two exempt jurisdictions within the city have also left a few surviving records.[3]

Time has not been kind to the medieval records of the Paris officiality. There does, however, survive one remarkable register containing entries dating from November of 1384 to September of 1387, 319 folios in the original and 538 columns in the modern edition, approximately 3,250 entries all told.[4] Despite the fact that the register has been in print since 1919, relatively little use has been made of it by modern scholars.[5] The reasons are not hard to find. Like the Ely act book, the Paris register contains no depositions, making it difficult at times to get at the reality that lies behind its formulaic language. Unlike the Ely act book, the Paris register contains relatively few sentences. It seems clear that at least in cases that proceeded by long-form procedure, a separate register of

[1] From 1384 to 1406, the period of our records, the bishop was Pierre d'Orgemont, son of Charles V's chancellor, but he does not figure in our records.

[2] Pommeray, *Officialité archidiaconale*, 3.

[3] See Donahue, ed., *Records 1*, 105–9.

[4] *Registre de Paris*, ed. Joseph Petit. The figure is extrapolated from a sample of all the cases in 1385.

[5] The only systematic study of it that I know of is Lévy, "Officialité de Paris."

sentences was being kept. A few of these have survived (bound, apparently by mistake, in the back of the main register), but for the most part, the main register allows us only to follow the procedural steps in a contested case, and when the court sets the case down for sentencing, it disappears from view. The surviving sentences reveal another distressing fact. There are 15 sentences, all dating from the period of the main register, but only two of them are for cases mentioned in the register. Clearly, the notary of the register, who appears to have been, at least for most of the register, one Jean de Villemaden, was not recording everything.[6] This impression is confirmed by the fact that cases appear that have clearly had some unrecorded past. Sometimes cases disappear and then reappear some months later, having reached a different stage. Villemaden does not seem to have had the devotion to his task that characterized Robert Foxton of Ely.

We should have some sympathy for Villemaden. He had a much bigger job. In a small diocese with a relatively small case load, Foxton was able, it would seem, to record all the business that came before the consistory court (and, as we have seen, some of the business that came before the bishop's audience as well). The Paris court had, in addition to the official himself, at least one auditor of causes (by the sixteenth century there will be two such auditors) who functioned like the commissaries at Ely. Villemaden made no attempt to record business that came before the auditor(s).[7] As there was at Ely, so too at Paris there was a separate register of fines (which has not survived). Indeed, there may have been more than one such register. A number of entries suggest that each of the promotors kept his own register of fines. These registers may also have contained records of the more routine criminal matters, for although some criminal matters are recorded in the main register, there do not seem to be very many of them.

The final reason why no one has given the Paris register the attention that it deserves is that it contains too much data to control (Villemaden made entries for more cases in the Paris court in one year than Foxton made for eight years in the Ely act book) without the use of a computer. We have not coded everything that might be coded in this book. More work needs to be done with the names of the parties and with the cases that do not concern marriage. We have, however, made a start, and that start suggests that the Paris consistory was a very different type of court from that either at Ely (the record for which is almost exactly contemporary) or at York.

To get some idea of how different the Paris court was, let us look at the types of cases it was hearing over the course of one year, 1385, the year that left the largest number of entries (despite the fact that there is about a week missing

[6] Disc. T&C no. 530.

[7] To put it positively, this is a register of matters that came before the official himself: Guillaume de Boudreville, for a brief period at the beginning of the register; N. Domicelli, a *locum tenens* during an equally brief period of Boudreville's illness and following his death; and from 9 January 1385, Robert de Dours.

TABLE 7.1. *The Business of the Court of Paris in 1385*

Type of Case	No.	MaxEn	AvgEn	% Cases	% Entries
Unknown	93	7	1.39	13	9
Appeal	9	9	3.22	1	2
Ex officio	60	3	1.13	8	5
Debt	84	9	2.18	11	13
Ecclesiastical	81	13	1.67	11	10
Injury	49	15	3.00	7	10
Miscellaneous	8	2	1.14	1	1
Matrimonial	181	31	2.55	24	32
Proxy	12	3	1.25	2	1
Security	122	4	1.11	16	10
Testamentary	44	27	2.50	6	8
TOTAL	743			100	100

Notes: Where 'No.' = the number of cases; 'MaxEn' = the maximum number of entries for cases of this type; 'AvgEn' = the average number of entries for cases of this type; '% Cases' = the percentage of cases represented by this type; '% Entries' = the percentage of entries represented by cases of this type.
Source: Registre de Paris.

at the end of the year). The recorded business of the court during this year is summarized in Table 7.1.

The basic unit here is the 'case', though unlike Ely, there are very few cases that involve more than one type of proceeding. Ninety-three cases give us no indication of the substance involved, although the vast majority of them seem to be instance cases. In about half of these entries, one of the parties fails to appear, and nothing more is recorded about the case. In the other half, a procedural step is recorded, but nothing is recorded about the case either before or after the entry. Nine cases involve appeals, normally from one of the archdeacons, but the substance of the case cannot be discerned. (Where the substance can be discerned, the case is classified under the substantive category.) Sixty cases are *ex officio*, usually brought by one of the promotors of the court. Most of these give no indication of the substance of the crime; a few tell us that they involve violence, sometimes violence against a clerk. (If the case involves a sexual offense, it is classified with matrimonial.) There are 84 cases of debt, including 15 cases of absolution (i.e., from excommunication for nonpayment of the debt), a number of which result in a *cessio bonorum* made by the debtor (other cases of absolution are classified with the substantive area for which the excommunication was given), and 7 noncontentious recognizances of debt. Eighty-one cases deal with a wide range of ecclesiastical matters, including the noncontentious approval of the election of church wardens and approvals of transfers of property belonging to churches. There are also 12 contested benefice cases, but no cases involving tithes. Forty-nine cases involve *iniuria*, normally physical violence, but occasionally, it would seem, verbal assaults. There are 122 cases in which a clerk posts security, an institution that was dependent upon the custom of the court (the entries specifically say so). Many of these cases suggest that the clerk posted security before the official of Paris so that he would not be compelled to do so before the Châtelet. Clerical posting of security is an institution that merits more attention than it has received. It is sometimes found connected with cases of injury (in which case it is classified under that category), but it is in itself a noncontentious procedure: The clerk never argues that he need not post security. Forty-four cases involve testamentary matters, including litigation about testaments and the routine appointment of tutors and curators for orphans. That leaves the largest single category, matrimonial cases, which, as in the case of York and Ely, were classified broadly to include matrimonial litigation in the narrow sense, cases of divorce and separation, and criminal prosecution for sexual offenses. This category will be subdivided further in the next section.

This analysis suggests that the characterization that the original editor, Joseph Petit, gave to this register as 'civil' is misleading. That word does not appear in the brief description of the register that appears on the front cover, nor, so far as I am aware, is the word used in the register.[8] Not only is there no evidence that the civil–criminal distinction was in Villemaden's mind, but the contents of the register also belie the notion that he was deliberately excluding matters that we would call criminal. As suggested, I suspect that Villemaden was trying to record all matters that came before the official (as opposed to various other officers of the court), at least in formal session. That he did not succeed is painfully obvious, but there appears to be no substantive pattern in his omissions. It is possible that there is a pattern to his omissions, though it may not be completely recoverable. The fees that Villemaden records in the margin (though he is not consistent about this either) suggest that there may have been a fee for recording the results of a session in the register. If the party did not pay, the session was not recorded.[9]

The table also shows that another characterization of the book, for which I must confess responsibility, is also misleading.[10] Matters concerning marriage do not predominate in the book, at least if one takes 'predominate' to mean more than half of the cases or entries. Marriage matters account for 24 percent of the cases and 32 percent of the entries. They are the single largest substantive category, but they account for fewer cases and fewer entries than do cases involving the law of obligations (debt, injury, and security combined, 255 cases, 34% of cases, 33% of entries).

It is this focus on obligations, what in England would be called 'personal actions', that distinguishes the Paris court both from that at Ely and from that at York. York and Ely both have cases of what we would call contractual obligation (breach of faith in both courts, court officers' fees at Ely), but they represent a far smaller proportion of the cases than they do at Paris. Similarly,

[8] Text and disc. T&C no. 531.
[9] Disc. T&C no. 532.
[10] See Donahue, ed., *Records 1*, 106.

TABLE 7.2. *York Cause Papers (Fourteenth Century), Ely Act Book (1374–1381), and Paris Register (1384–1387) – Comparison of Proportions of Types of Cases*

	York	Ely Total	Ely Instance	Paris
Type of Case	% Total	% Total	% Total	% Total
Unknown	2	8	0	22
Obligation	15	24	44	34
Court	0	7	5	2
Ecclesiastical	40	25	16	11
Miscellaneous	0	1	1	1
Matrimonial	34	24	23	24
Testamentary	9	11	11	6
TOTAL	100	100	100	100

Source: Tables e3.App.1, 6.1; *Registre de Paris.*

York and Ely both have cases of delictual obligation, but it is almost exclusively confined to verbal, as opposed to physical, assault (defamation, but see the cases of 'violence' at Ely).

While this difference probably cannot be fully accounted for by the way in which jurisdiction was divided between the ecclesiastical and secular courts in the two areas, that division was probably influential in producing the result that we see. In particular, the virtual absence of cases of physical violence from the York and Ely courts probably reflects the substantial amount, one might say the virtual monopoly, of cases of this sort in both the English central royal courts (trespass) and, by the late fourteenth century, the courts of the justices of the peace. The Châtelet in Paris heard such cases as well, but it does not seem to have monopolized them in the way that English secular courts did. Not all the defendants in such cases in the Paris court are clerks, but a number of them are, and all the security cases involve clerks. Hence, the Paris ecclesiastical court seems to have been more successful than the English courts were in maintaining a jurisdiction *ratione personae*, the *persona* in this case being a clerk.

Despite these important differences, we should not lose sight of the similarities. Table 7.2 shows that the broad substantive categories within which the three courts were operating are similar. Our comparison is hampered by the fact that we do not know the substantive category for more than a fifth of Paris cases, but where we do know the substantive category,[11] it is comparable, at least at a relatively high level of generality. There were substantial differences in the types of cases that the three courts were hearing when we get below the broad category. (One wonders, for example, where tithes litigation was being heard in the Paris diocese, because it pretty clearly was not being heard in the court of the bishop's official.) The fact that we cannot tell in most security

[11] Disc. T&C no. 533.

cases in the Paris court whether the underlying matter is one of contractual or delictual obligation requires that we go up to the next higher level of generality, obscuring in the process the different types of cases of obligation that were heard in the three courts, but the basic jurisdictional categories hold up reasonably well.

Particularly notable is the fact that marriage litigation, broadly conceived, occupies approximately the same proportion of cases at Paris as it does at Ely (about a quarter). The greater proportion of cases of obligation heard in the Paris court does not produce a corresponding reduction in marriage litigation. Rather it affects the other categories, notably ecclesiastical and testamentary.

Before turning more specifically to the marriage cases, we should pause to ask whether we can be confident that the sample of one year's worth of litigation before the court is likely to be representative of the whole. Extrapolating from that year to the rest of the book (controlling for the fact that each of the other years occupies less space than does 1385), we predict that 1384 will have 17 marriage cases, 1386 will have 140, and 1387 will have 91. The actual count is 12, 140, and 99, respectively. In short, the prediction turns out to be remarkably accurate.[12]

THE MARRIAGE CASES

If the overall categories with which the Paris court was dealing are recognizable from what we learned from the cases at York and Ely, neither the categories in which matrimonial litigation falls nor their proportions are anything like what we would expect on the basis of York and Ely, as can be seen in Table 7.3.

This is so different from what we find at York and Ely that we must emphasize a few points of similarity. As at York and Ely, a large majority of the cases at Paris are cases to establish a marriage (what we have called, using the later English term, 'spousals' litigation). These represent 254 (out of 410, 62%) of the cases. As at York and Ely, divorce cases are rare (10/410, 2%). In marked contrast to York and Ely, separation cases represent 25 percent of the total (102/410), and the great majority of these (72/102, 71%) are in a category that we have not seen before: 'separation of goods'. Even more surprising are the claims being made in the spousals litigation. Seventy-five percent of them (190/254) are for the enforcement of *sponsalia de futuro* unaccompanied by sexual intercourse, *re integra*, as the records call it.[13] A further 15 percent (37/254) are for the enforcement of a marriage formed by *de futuro* consent plus intercourse. The remainder are divided between cases in which a *de presenti* marriage may be involved, cases in which we cannot tell what type of *sponsalia* are sought to be enforced, and cases of jactitation of marriage, a category that we do not find at York or Ely, but which can be found in English spousals litigation in the early

[12] Disc. T&C no. 534.

[13] A few records make clear that this is a shorthand for the expression *re integra quoad carnalem copulam*.

TABLE 7.3. *Types of Marriage Cases in the Court of Paris (1384–1387)*

Type of Case	No.	% Total Cases
Unknown	16	4
Ex officio	24	6
Spousals		
De futuro		
Confessed	6	1
Contested	31	8
Deferred	91	22
Dissolution	15	4
Remitted	47	11
SUBTOTAL	190	46
De futuro plus *copula*		
Confessed	6	1
Contested	15	4
Deferred	16	4
SUBTOTAL	37	9
De presenti	7	2
Jactitation	9	2
Undifferentiated	11	3
SUBTOTAL (Spousals)	254	62
Divorce	10	2
Separation		
Bed	15	4
Goods	72	18
Uncertain	15	4
SUBTOTAL	102	25
Miscellaneous instance	4	1
TOTAL	410	100

Source: Registre de Paris.

modern period. As the name implies, this is an action brought against someone who is publicly claiming to have married or to have contracted marriage with the plaintiff, and the plaintiff seeks to put the claim to rest, frequently when he or she wants to marry someone else.[14]

The *ex officio* cases involving marital matters at Paris fall into more familiar categories: There are eight cases of wife beating, five of adultery, four of paternity, three of concubinage, one of bigamy, one of criminal contempt for violating an order not to marry *pendente lite*, one case of clerical fornication that resulted in the pregnancy of the woman, and one to compel a couple to cohabit. As at Ely there are a number of cases that mix office and instance procedure. Hence, all the office cases are best treated with their corresponding

[14] Lit. T&C no. 535.

substantive categories. The miscellaneous instance cases include two cases of opposition to banns (which could well be classified with the spousals litigation), one *causa alimentaria* (which seems to be a case of child support), and one case of *repetitio uxoris* (which seems to be a case of restoration of conjugal rights).

As will become apparent when we examine the contents of the register in more detail, counting the sentences in the Paris register is difficult, and dividing them between male and female plaintiffs is even more difficult. The record frequently gives us a result without telling us who asked for it. Sometimes this is because the case contains *ex officio* elements; sometimes it is because there was not much dispute (this is particularly true in separation cases, and in spousals cases that were confessed or remitted); sometimes, we suspect, it is because Villemaden simply failed to record who was the moving party. Sometimes we know, or strongly suspect, that the court rendered a sentence, but we do not know what it was because it was recorded in the separate register of sentences. Table 7.4, therefore, is incomplete, and it probably contains some mistakes. We have, on occasion, surmised who was the moving party or what was the result on the basis of the entire record, including who paid the fees. The results, however, are so different from York and Ely that they are unlikely to be wrong as a statistical matter.

Comparing this table to Table 6.5, the differences are so great that, once more, we must begin by emphasizing the similarities. Despite the number of Paris cases in which there may have been a sentence but we could not guess what it was, Paris litigation shows an overall ratio of judgments to cases (including those cases in which we know there was a judgment even though we cannot not tell the gender of the person who obtained it) that is comparable to York's in the fourteenth century (74% vs 73%), higher than York's in the fifteenth century (58%), though lower than that of Ely (82%). The suspicion that the lower rate for York in the fifteenth century was the product of poor record keeping, rather than of fewer judgments, is confirmed by the Ely/Paris comparison (Foxton kept better records than Villemaden). The relatively high Paris rate of judgments also tends to confirm the notion that medieval marriage cases produced more judgments than other types of cases.

The ratio of female plaintiffs to male is significantly lower than it is at Ely or at York in either century (52% vs 64%, 73%, 61%, respectively).[15] Here we are hampered by the fact that in 88 cases (21%) we do not know the gender of the moving party. It is unlikely, however, that the gender ratio differed significantly in those cases in which Villemaden chose to tell us who the moving party was from those in which he did not.[16] What is dramatically different from the situation at either York or Ely is the types of cases in which women dominate the litigation and those in which men do. In spousals cases in which *copula* is not alleged, women represent only one-third of the plaintiffs (33%, 63/190). In

[15] Statistical disc. T&C no. 536.
[16] Disc. T&C no. 537.

TABLE 7.4. *Gender Ratios and Judgments in the Court of Paris (1384–1387)*

Type of Case	FP	MP	% F	SFP	SMP	Total Cases	SFD	SMD	Total Cases	S	noS	GTOT
Unknown	8	8	50	0	0	0	0	0	0	0	16	16
Ex officio	0	0	0	0	0	0	0	0	0	23	1	24
Spousals												
De futuro												
Confessed	2	3	40	2	3	5	0	0	0	1	0	6
Contested	6	25	19	1	3	4	7	1	8	0	19	31
Deferred	23	68	25	0	0	0	68	23	91	0	0	91
Dissolution	7	6	54	6	8	14	0	0	0	0	1	15
Remitted	10	13	43	0	0	0	14	10	24	23	0	47
SUBTOTAL	48	115	29	9	14	23	89	34	123	24	20	190
De futuro plus *copula*												
Confessed	3	0	100	3	0	3	0	0	0	3	0	6
Contested	12	3	80	1	1	2	1	3	4	0	9	15
Deferred	16	0	100	1	0	1	0	15	15	0	0	16
SUBTOTAL	31	3	91	5	1	6	1	18	19	3	9	37
De presenti	3	4	43	0	2	2	1	3	4	0	1	7
Jactitation	5	4	56	5	4	9	0	0	0	0	0	9
Undifferentiated	7	4	64	0	0	0	0	0	0	0	11	11
SUBTOTAL (Spousals)	94	130	42	19	21	40	91	55	146	27	41	254
Divorce	3	1	75	2	1	3	0	0	0	6	1	10
Separation												
Bed	4	9	31	3	5	8	0	0	0	0	7	15
Goods	48	4	92	31	2	33	0	0	0	16	23	72
Uncertain	10	2	83	0	0	0	0	0	0	0	15	15
SUBTOTAL	62	15	81	34	7	41	0	0	0	16	45	102
Miscellaneous instance	1	2	33	0	0	0	1	0	1	0	3	4
TOTAL	168	156	52	55	29	84	92	55	147	72	107	410

Notes: Layout as in Table 6.5. S = a definitive sentence in a case where the plaintiff cannot be identified; noS = a case in which no definitive sentence is reported. Other abbreviations as in Table 3.5.

Ratio of judgments to cases: 74% (303/410).
Ratio of FPs to total Ps: 52% (168/324).
Ratio of successful FPs to total successful Ps: 65% (55/84).
Female plaintiff success rate: 50% (55 won, 55 lost).
Male plaintiff success rate: 25% (29 won, 92 lost).
Overall plaintiff success rate: 36% (84 won, 147 lost).

Source: Registre de Paris.

divorce and separation cases, however, women are four-fifths of the plaintiffs (80%, 65/81). This is the opposite of the pattern that we saw at York and Ely, where women sued more often to get into a marriage and men to get out of one. The only pattern that corresponds to that at York and Ely is the dominance of women in cases to establish a marriage in which intercourse is alleged. Women bring 91 percent of such cases at Paris (31/34).

The courts of York in both centuries and of Ely were decidedly friendly to plaintiffs without regard to the gender of the plaintiff (plaintiffs' success rates: 60%, 80%, and 78%, respectively). The same was not true of late fourteenth-century Paris, where plaintiffs had an overall success rate of only 36 percent (84/231). Once more when we break this litigation down by types of cases, even more dramatic differences appear. Plaintiffs' overall success rate in spousals litigation was a dismal 15 percent (31/213).[17] Plaintiffs fared considerably better in divorce and separation litigation, obtaining a divorce or separation in 59% of the cases (66/112).[18] Granted the dominance of men as plaintiffs in spousals litigation and the dominance of women in litigation for divorce or separation, it is not at all surprising that the overall female plaintiffs' success rate was twice that of the men (50% vs 25%).

SPONSALIA DE FUTURO RE INTEGRA

Turning to the largest category within the spousals litigation, that of *sponsalia de futuro re integra*, we see that in a few cases (5) the defendant confessed the action. Such couples were ordered to solemnize their marriages. In 15 cases, the action was brought or defended on the ground that the *sponsalia* ought to be dissolved on such grounds as the absence of the fiancé, prior *sponsalia* with another, nonage, and so on. In 31 cases, the action was contested and set down for proof. In 45 cases, the couple appeared before the court and admitted that they had contracted but mutually discharged each other of the obligation. In 91 cases, the defendant contested the case negatively; the plaintiff admitted that he or she had no proof and deferred the decisory oath to the defendant. The defendant took the oath and was discharged, normally in one session. A similar pattern of resolution can be seen in the cases of *sponsalia* plus *copula*, except that here, remission was not possible.

Deferred

Any hope that we have of understanding what is going on in the Paris court and why it is so different from what we see in the English courts rests on our being able to determine what is at stake in these cases of *sponsalia de futuro*, virtually half of all the marriage cases, and in the cases involving the decisory

[17] Disc. T&C no. 538.
[18] Disc. T&C no. 539.

oath, virtually a quarter of all the marriage cases. The formula for the entry in the latter form of case is not particularly helpful:

There appearing Jean Orillat, plaintiff in a matrimonial cause, and Marion *fille de* Simon Malice, defendant on the other [side], the plaintiff proposed *sponsalia de futuro re integra*; the defendant denied everything, and the plaintiff, saying that he had no witnesses, deferred the oath to the defendant, which defendant swore that she never contracted any *sponsalia* or pledged faith with the plaintiff; and this being the situation we absolved the defendant, etc., giving [*dantes*] license to each of them, etc.; 8 *deniers*; defendant 2 *sous*.[19]

Variations of the formula include a statement that "the defendant contested negatively" (*lite ex parte rei negative contestata*), rather than that he or she denied all. (This is probably more common than simply "denied," and lets us know that the case is proceeding according to the *ordo*.) Sometimes (perhaps more often) the plaintiff "asserts" (*asserens*) that he has no witnesses; occasionally he or she swears to the fact, but there are also cases where he or she simply defers "immediately" (*statim*) or simply defers without more. The plaintiff sometimes defers to the oath of the defendant "in place of all proof" (*pro omni probatione*). The content of the oath sometimes differs, the most common variant being "never contracted *sponsalia* or had marital promises with the plaintiff" (*se nunquam contraxisse aliqua sponsalia nec promissiones matrimoniales habuisse cum dicto actore*). The first "etc." is sometimes filled in with "from the plaintiff's claim" (*ab impetione actoris*). The second "etc." is never spelled out, but it is almost certainly something like "to contract elsewhere" (*alibi contrahendi*).[20]

If any of these variations has significance, it is probably lost. It is possible, for example, that the court insisted on an oath from the plaintiff that he or she had no proof where it suspected that there was proof. If there were proof, then the defendant could be committing perjury in taking the decisory oath. Similarly, the substitution of *promissiones matrimoniales* for *fideidationes* may have been the result of a more informal recital by the plaintiff of what he or she thought had actually happened. We cannot, however, be sure that what we are seeing is not simply artistic variation by the notary. The formula was not firmly fixed, and the notary relieved his boredom by varying it.[21]

We can be somewhat more confident that another variation does have some significance. A few, but only a few, of the cases add at the end of the formula "leaving the rest to their consciences" (*cetera eorum conscienciis relinquentes*).[22] While it is possible that this is supposed to be present in all cases, buried in the final "etc.,"[23] its presence in just a few cases suggests that these

[19] *Orillat c Malice* (26.viii.85), col. 180/1, T&C no. 540 with disc. of citation form.

[20] Disc. T&C no. 541.

[21] Disc. T&C no. 542.

[22] Examples T&C no. 543.

[23] It also sometimes appears before the *dantes* clause. Unfortunately, we frequently find an "etc." here too.

were cases where the court thought that the conscience of the oath-taker (for it is hard to see how the plaintiff had done anything that might trouble his or her conscience) ought to be troubled.[24] In one case this formula appears after the plaintiff had produced some witnesses.[25] Although these witnesses did not prove the plaintiff's case (hence her deferral), they may have said enough to provoke suspicion in the official that there was a real but unprovable contract here. In another case, this formula appears after the defendant concedes that her father had arranged a marriage with the plaintiff, but she says that she never ratified it.[26]

Similarly, it is surely significant that in one case, the court refuses to give the couple license (to marry elsewhere). This is said to be done *ex causa*, but the *causa* is not stated.[27]

Some of the cases in which the decisory oath is taken tell us more: *Pierre de Coesmes domicilié à la maison de maître Jean Paquete, rue de Quincampoix, paroisse de Saint-Nicolas-des-Champs c Colette fille de Colin Poulain* took two sessions to resolve. The plaintiff proposed *sponsalia de futuro* and pledges of faith (*fideidationes*) and said that he had given the defendant a *virga* of silver as a token of marriage.[28] The defendant confessed that the plaintiff had asked him to be his wife and that she well wanted to do so if it pleased her father and her relatives (*amici*), and that she took the *virga* under that condition. The father appeared and said that it did not please him, and the case was set down for making positions. At the second session, the plaintiff deferred to the defendant the oath whether the promise was unconditional or whether it was conditional on her father's approval. She swore to the latter; the father once more expressed his displeasure. The defendant was absolved and the plaintiff was condemned to pay her expenses.[29] The condemnation to pay expenses (as opposed to fees) is not standard and may indicate that the court thought the plaintiff's claim frivolous.[30]

Similar claims by a *rea* that the promise was conditional on the approval of her father, mother, and/or her relatives are made in 10 other cases:

1. *Jean Gorget c Marion fille de Guillaume le Fauconier* (27.vi.85),[31]
2. *Vionnet Parvi domicilié à la maison de maître P. Cramete c Jeanette fille du défunt Jean Charronis* (21–29.vii.1385),[32]
3. *Guillaume le Cesne c Margot fille de Simon Trilloye* (13.x.85),[33]

[24] Disc. T&C no. 544.
[25] *Keroursil c Gerbe* (5.v.85), col. 112/8.
[26] *Preudhomme c Tueil* (20.vi.86), col. 320/3. See at nn. 46–7.
[27] *Croso c Havini* (25.v.86), col. 310/3, T&C no. 545.
[28] Classically this would be a rod or a pin; it may be a ring. See DuCange, s.v.
[29] (10–17.v.85), col. 115/1, 119/4, T&C no. 546.
[30] It may also be because she, or her father, hired an advocate. In the *Parvi* case, which is similar, no advocate will be mentioned.
[31] Col. 144/5.
[32] Col. 161/5, 165/4.
[33] Col. 202/1.

4. *Robin de Champront c Gilette de Valle* (30.iv.86),[34]
5. *Huguelin Burgondi c Perette fille de Jean Fusée* (27.vi.1386),[35]
6. *Henri de Trois Maisons c Margot fille de Henri de Beaumarchais* (15.iv.87),[36]
7. *Baudet d'Autreau c Margot fille de Jean Doublet* (16.iv.87),[37]
8. *Colin Hardi c Huguette fille de Jean le Chapellier* (16.iv.87),[38]
9. *Jean Garderel c Simonette fille de Pierre Pavot* (13.vi.87),[39] and
10. *Robin Caudin c Gilette fille de Jean Housel* (22.vi.87).[40]

It will be noted that in all of these cases a male plaintiff is suing a woman, who in all but one case is named as the daughter of some man (even if the man is dead). It will also be noted that five of these cases come from the spring of 1387, a fact which raises the possibility that the pattern noted in the next paragraph existed in other cases that are more cryptically noted.[41]

These cases have a distinct pattern that is best illustrated by a series of formulae that appear in *Garderel c Pavot*:

> The *actor* proposed *sponsalia de futuro re integra*. The *rea* confessed that the *actor* had required of her and had spoken to her about contracting marriage. She then replied that she would do what pleased her father and relatives, denying the rest. The *actor* deferred the oath to the *rea*, who swore that she never contracted with the *actor*, and, further, her father said that it did not nor does it please him, etc. And therefore we absolved the *rea* from the claim of the *actor*, giving both of them license, etc.[42]

Sometimes the claim appears as part of the *litis contestatio* and is then confirmed by the decisory oath; sometimes it appears in the decisory oath after a negative contest. In almost all the cases someone, usually the father, appears and denies having consented or refuses to consent now. The form in which the statement of the condition and the relatives' denial is given varies, suggesting that we are dealing with variations that may conform to the facts, at least as they were stated in court. In *Gorget c le Fauconier*, the woman claims that she said that she would do nothing against the wishes of her father and relatives (*quod nihil faceret absque voluntate patris et amicorum suorum*), and her father and some (*quidam*) of the relatives appear and say that they had consented to nothing (*nihil non consenserunt* [sic]). In *Parvi c Charronis*, the woman, lacking a father, claims that when the man spoke to her many times (*pluries*) about contracting *sponsalia*, she always replied that she would do nothing that did not please her mother and her relatives. This case takes two sessions to resolve,

[34] Col. 297/2.
[35] Col. 324/3.
[36] Col. 453/3.
[37] Col. 455/5.
[38] Col. 456/1.
[39] Col. 481/7.
[40] Col. 486/1.
[41] For the possible significance of this, see at n. 70.
[42] Col. 481/7, T&C no. 547.

with the decisory oath taken at the second session, the only session at which the dissent of the relatives is mentioned (*quia amicis non placet*).[43] In *Cesne c Trilloye*, the woman claims that she told the man that she would do the will of her father and mother (*quod faceret voluntatem patris sui et matris*). Her father appears and refuses his consent and then says that this is the first time he has heard about any marriage between Guillaume and his daughter. She had never spoken to him about it.[44] In *Champront c Valle*, the *rea* is particularly firm that a marriage to the *actor* is not to her liking. Having confessed that the *actor* asked her to marry him and having said that she would do what pleased her relatives (she is the one *rea* who is not described as the daughter of someone), she swears "that her relatives never said to her that it pleased them, nor did it please her."[45] No mention is made of the appearance of the relatives. *Burgondi c Fusée* involves the same claim by the woman, about which she takes the decisory oath. Here, the man then confesses that the relatives did not consent. In *Maisons c Beaumarchais*, the woman swears that she never contracted or had marital promises with the man, but only once, while he was speaking to her about contracting marriage, she said that she would do what pleased her father and mother. Her father appears in court and recites the formula of dissent. In *Hardi c Chapellier*, the girl claims that she said that she would do what pleased her relatives, and her mother and relatives appear and withhold their consent. Perhaps the notary failed to enter that her father was dead, or perhaps he was ill. In *Caudin c Housel*, the woman is a bit more forthcoming, confessing that she told the man that the marriage was pleasing to her so long as it was pleasing to her father, mother, and relatives. The father appears and denies his consent, and the decisory oath is taken specifically on the question of whether she promised simply (*simpliciter*) or as she had previously confessed.

If we wondered in *Champront c Valle* whether the woman's choice was not perhaps the decisive factor in the plaintiff's failure to obtain a judgment, there can be little doubt that that was the case in *Jean Preudhomme c Amelotte du Tueil*.[46] Jean proposed that Amelotte's father promised to give her to him as wife and that she had ratified the arrangement. She, in turn, took the decisory oath that "although the *actor* had spoken to the same father of the girl about a contract of marriage with this girl, she never ratified it nor consented to it, nor did she have any *sponsalia* or marital promises with the *actor*."[47]

Guillaume de Leonibus c Agnesotte veuve du défunt Simon de Maubeuge[48] also involves a woman who clearly had a mind of her own. To the *actor*'s standard-form proposal, Agnesotte confessed that her brother, a master in theology, had spoken to her about whether she would take Guillaume as spouse.

43 Disc. T&C no. 548.
44 Col. 201/1, T&C no. 549.
45 Col. 297/2, T&C no. 550.
46 (20.vi.86), col. 320/3. This is a case where the matter is explicitly left "to the conscience." See at nn. 22–6, and n. 47.
47 *Id.*, T&C no. 551, with disc. of another example.
48 (19.vii.87), col. 499/4.

She always replied that it was not pleasing to her, nor did it ever please her. Once, however, her brother put her hand into Guillaume's hand, she unwilling. She denied everything else that was alleged. She then swore that she never contracted espousals with Guillaume nor was it her intention to contract with him.[49]

Matrimonial negotiations involving relatives are also mentioned in *Richardette fille de Gervais de Servaise* [*sic*] *c Jean Huberti alias Normanni*:[50] "The defendant confessed that the relatives of these parties had talked together about a marriage contract between these parties, but nothing was agreed. He denies *sponsalia*." The plaintiff's statement that she has no witnesses would seem to be particularly inappropriate here, but the usual formulaic decisory oath follows.

If there is a suggestion of force in *Leonibus c Maubeuge*, there is more than a suggestion of it in *Foursia de Louyse c Pierre Doujan*.[51] Foursia claims not only that Pierre contracted *sponsalia de futuro* with her but also that he attempted to rape her (*quod postmodum idem vir temptavit eam cognoscere, ipsa invita*). On the contract claim, she defers to Pierre's oath, and he is absolved of this claim. On the rape claim (*super residuo*), the court assigns a day for both the parties and the promotor to present their case. On that day Pierre appears, accompanied by an advocate, but Foursia does not (the promotor is not mentioned), and the case disappears from view.[52]

Jeanne *fille de* Jean de Sartouville has the most dramatic allegation of force. She confessed that while she and the plaintiff were going to look for straw for someone at the house of one master F. in the town of Argenteuil, a gang of men came up to her with swords unsheathed threatening to kill her unless she pledged faith to the plaintiff. Out of terror of the gang, she promised them that she would take the plaintiff as husband, and then immediately reclaimed. The plaintiff deferred to her oath, and she swore as previously and was absolved.[53]

The formula used in *Perette la Clergesse c Hans Pruce*[54] is different from what we find in other cases, although this may be because a different court officer recorded the entry. What appears at the end of the entry, however, clearly tells us more than we normally learn:[55]

> The *actrix* proposed *sponsalia* and matrimonial pledges of faith (*fideidationes matrimoniales*); the *reus* contested negatively saying that although the parties had spoken together about contracting marriage with each other, he had never contracted with the *actrix* nor pledged faith to her, and because, the oath having been deferred to him by the *actrix*, he swore to this, the same *reus* was absolved, etc. Each of them 2 *sous*. The same man is condemned to pay to Perette 27 gold *francs* and two pairs of linen cloths, on the basis of the confession of the man. Note this; Forestarii.[56]

[49] Col. 499/4, T&C no. 552.
[50] (9.iv.86), col. 289/4, T&C no. 553.
[51] (22.xi.85), col. 224/1.
[52] (29.xi.85), col. 228/4.
[53] *Kaerauroez c Sartouville* (8.ii.85), col. 50/1, T&C no. 554.
[54] (4–7.v.85), col. 300/2, 302/5.
[55] Col. 302/5, T&C no. 555.
[56] For Forestarii, see T&C no. 556.

Perette and Hans may or may not have contracted marriage, but their relationship had gone beyond simple talk, for what he owes her looks like the repayment of a substantial dowry.[57]

The longest case in this group is *Agnesotte la Demandresse c Simon Touart*,[58] which takes more than a month to resolve and has six entries. The case begins with a standard-form proposal of *sponsalia de futuro re integra*. There is a negative contest, the *reus* appearing with an advocate, the *actrix*, so far as we can tell, by herself. At the next session the *actrix* produces a husband and wife as witnesses, and their examination is committed to Alain Forestarii. The testimony of the witnesses is published, and at the next session, the *actrix* defers the decisory oath to the *reus*. Pretty clearly, her witnesses had not proved what she hoped they would prove.

Pierre Reaudeau clerc domicilié à la maison de Gervais Gonterii, paroisse de Saint-Germain-l'Auxerrois c Maline fille de Jean Sampsonis gives us some procedural details that we do not get in other cases.[59] On 2 October 1386, Pierre was examined *ex officio*, but apparently not under oath, by the official at the request of Jean, and apparently not in the presence of Maline. Pierre said that he had pledged faith with Maline (*se affidasse dictam filiam*) and had contracted *sponsalia de futuro* with her. He swore to prosecute the case and pay expenses if he lost the case (*si subcombat*), and he chose a domicile.[60] The case was set to proceed. The parties were ordered not to contract elsewhere under a penalty of 100 *livres*,[61] and the record tells us that the girl was inhibited personally the next day. On the next day, the couple appeared with advocates (Jean is not mentioned). Pierre proposed as before, and Maline excepted that he could not bring the suit because he was excommunicated by the authority of the official at the instance of the receiver of fines of the court of Paris.[62] The case was set down for the next day to prove the exception. The next day nothing was said about the exception, and the case turned into a standard case of deferral, with the only slight variation of the formula being that Pierre said that "he cannot fully prove," rather than the usual that he has no witnesses or no proof.

The case was heard during the vintage vacation,[63] and one of the reasons why we have as much as we do for this case may be that Villemaden did not have much else to record. Some of the procedural elements present in this case, we may suspect, were quite standard. An initial appearance accompanied by an order not to contract elsewhere *pendente lite* is found in one other case in this group, and it may have occurred in other cases, though not recorded.[64]

[57] Disc. T&C no. 557.
[58] (22.v.87 to 28.vi.87), refs. in TCas.
[59] (2–4.x.86), col. 371/3, 371/4, 372/2.
[60] Disc. T&C no. 558.
[61] This is much higher than the usual 40 *livres*, suggesting that these parties are of some wealth.
[62] Col. 371/4, T&C no. 559.
[63] The Paris court took a vacation for harvest and, somewhat later, for vintage.
[64] Other examples T&C no. 560.

What is probably not usual in this case is that Pierre, though he is described as plaintiff from the beginning, does not seem to be pursuing the case very aggressively. It is Maline's father who seems to have been the moving party at the first appearance. A reason that Pierre may have been reluctant to appear before the court is suggested by Maline's exception. Although she ultimately does not pursue it, it may have had some basis in truth. Another reason why Pierre might not have wanted to pursue the case is that he is a clerk. If he marries, he will not be eligible for promotion to higher orders.

The rest must remain speculative, but it is at least possible that the parties got exactly what they all wanted in this case. There may well have been some kind of dealings between Pierre and Maline, perhaps involving her father. Ultimately, they decided to call it off, but enough had been said that they needed a public record that there was no espousal. It is also possible that Jean was pursuing the contract with Pierre and that Maline opposed and ultimately thwarted his wishes. Jean's behavior is consistent with either possibility. Whether he wants to clear the record or to push the couple into a contract, the correct first move is to get Pierre to acknowledge before the court that a contract was, in Pierre's view, made. Maline may not have wanted the matter to be brought to a head so quickly, hence her exception. The next day, however, she is firm. The exception is forgotten, and she takes the decisory oath.[65]

Guiot Morelli c Laurencette de Aitrio[66] begins with a quite routine deferral, puzzling only in the fact that only the defendant is given license to contract elsewhere. A note appended to the case tells us why: "Note that the promotor wants to prosecute double *sponsalia*. Pilays."[67]

Jean Radulphi c Jeanette fille de Robert de la Saussaye[68] combines elements of a deferral case with elements of a remittance case. When the *actor* defers the oath, the *rea* quite frankly says that "she does not remember that she had any marital promises with the *actor* and it was never her intention to contract with him." "Thereupon," the entry continues, "the parties remitted each to the other on both sides any marital promises or words, if there were any between them, that savored of the force of *sponsalia*." The official "tolerates the acquittance in patience," gives each of them license to contract elsewhere, and leaves the rest to their consciences.[69]

All told, we have found additional information beyond the bare formulae of deferral in 22 cases, approximately one-quarter of the total (91). This additional information gives us something that may allow us to make some generalizations, and may allow us to generalize about this group of cases as a whole. Of our 22 cases, 16 show the involvement of parents and relatives in the

65 Disc. T&C no. 561.
66 *Morelli c Aitrio* (23.i.87), col. 418/7.
67 Col. 481/7, T&C no. 562.
68 *Radulphi c Saussaye* (30.v.87), col. 475/4.
69 Col. 475/4, T&C no. 563. The formula here is standard in remittance cases; see at n. 77 and the following section.

marriage choices of the women involved (all of the parental condition cases [11], *Preudhomme*, *Bourges*, *Leonibus*, *Servaise*, and *Reaudeau*). In all but three of these cases (*Champront*, *Preudhomme*, and *Leonibus*), the woman's name is given in terms of her father's name (*fille d'un tel*). In the three cases where the name is not so attached, the woman is emphatic about her own choice, and in *Preudhomme* and *Leonibus*, the woman rejects the choice of her relatives. In this regard, the pattern of naming in *Preudhomme* is particularly significant, because Amelotte du Tueil did have a living father (who had promised to give her to Jean Preudhomme); she rejected her father's choice. Gillette de Valle (in *Champront*) may not have had living parents (none is mentioned; she speaks only of the choice of her relatives). Agnesotte Maubeuge (in *Leonibus*) was a widow, and the male relative whose choice she rejected was her brother, a master of theology.

This is not much to go on, but it is enough at least to suggest that the women named as *fille d'un tel* are young, living with their parents, and subject, in a substantial measure, to their control, at least so far as marriage choice is concerned.[70] Those not so described are more independent, perhaps older, perhaps not living with their parents. They have more to say about their marriage choice. This is certainly the case with Agnesotte Maubeuge, probably the case with Gillette de Valle. Of Amelotte du Tueil we can be less sure. She may have been a woman who knew her own mind despite the fact that she was young and living with her father.[71]

Some confirmation of this hypothesis is found in the six cases that show no evidence in the record of parental involvement. Foursia de Louyse, who accused her putative fiancé of attempted rape, Agnesotte la Demandresse, who tried to prove her espousals but then had defer to the defendant's oath, and Perette la Clergesse, who got back the advance on her dowry from her putative fiancé, are not identified by their father's names and are behaving more like the female plaintiffs at York and Ely. Laurencette de Aitrio not only got out of an engagement that she seems not to have wanted but may also have been the source of the information that led the promotor to want to prosecute the man for double espousals. We can tell less about the two women defendants who are identified by their father's names – Jeanne *fille de* Jean de Satrouville, the country woman who alleged that she was forced into contracting *sponsalia* by a local gang, and Jeanette *fille de* Robert de la Saussaye, whose decisory oath turned into a remittance – but their stories are not inconsistent with their being quite young. In Jeanne's case, the problem may well have been that there was no parental involvement in the arrangement, and in Jeanette's case, the parties, perhaps including their parents, seem to have been quite happy to break off whatever kind of arrangement had been made.

Another pattern emerges from these cases: Only one of them has a specifically rural setting, *Kaerauroez c Satrouville*, the case of the allegedly forced

[70] Disc. T&C no. 564.
[71] Another example T&C no. 565.

espousals. In two cases, the plaintiff elects a domicile specifically said to be in Paris. In another, the plaintiff elects a domicile in the house of one "*maître* P. Cramete," which was almost certainly in Paris. We probably can go further (an impression based on more than this group of cases). It seems likely that the overwhelming majority of the parties to the cases were Parisians. This impression is based on the fact that people who do not come from Paris are always so identified at the beginning of the case. (There are never any surprises.) And people who are not identified as to a place turn out to be Parisians if an identification of place occurs later in the case.

One more probable conclusion can be drawn from these cases. The number of cases that involved a condition of parental consent was probably larger than the 11 (12%) for which we have records. One could probably honestly take the decisory oath in the simple form, "never contracted *sponsalia* or had marital promises," if the facts were that one had contracted conditionally and the condition was not fulfilled. If the condition is regarded as a precedent one (the obligation does not arise until the parental consent is had), then one could quite honestly say that there were no *sponsalia* or promises of marriage because the precedent condition had not been fulfilled. Of course, we have no way of knowing whether anyone took advantage of this argument, but it is hard to imagine that some of the defendants were not so advised by their advocates. Further, as noted earlier, almost half of the conditional promise cases come from a three month period in 1387. Such a distribution is unlikely to be the result of random variation in the timing of the cases.[72] When we couple this fact with the fact that there was not so much business to record in 1387 as there was in 1385 and 1386, we come to the possibility that some of the formulaic cases of deferral in those earlier years were, in fact, more complicated, conditional cases, but that Villemaden only recorded the formula because that was all that he needed to have for his records. The decisory oath was taken; the court absolved the defendant from the suit and gave the parties license to marry others. That was what needed to be known. How that result was reached did not have to be recorded.

With these conclusions in mind we can look to the cases of deferral as a whole. The first thing to notice is that a large percentage of them are brought by men (68/91, 75%). This is, of course, a quite different gender ratio from what we find at York and Ely.

There are 26 of the 'straight' deferral cases in which a man sues a woman named as someone's daughter (including four whose fathers are deceased) for *sponsalia de futuro re integra*.[73] Both of the parties in all of these cases seem to be Parisians, although in most of the cases we have to rely on the fact that no place outside of Paris is given. If we add these cases to the 13 discussed previously, we have a substantial fraction of the deferral cases (39/91, 43%) that seem to involve the *fiançailles* of young Parisian women living with their parents. While this guess is probably wrong as to some of these cases, we also

72 Statistical disc. T&C no. 566.
73 Listed in T&C no. 567.

know, from the cases where more of the circumstances are given, that women whose fathers were arranging their marriages are not always described as *fille d'un tel*. Hence, the percentage may be close to correct even if we have not counted all the right cases to make it up.[74]

Not all of the cases involve young women living with their parents, however. As we saw, one of the circumstantial cases involves a widow whose brother is attempting to arrange her marriage. Five of the 'straight' deferral cases are also brought against widows, including two cases brought by different men against the same widow, one day apart.[75] And it is at least worth suggesting that the surname of the defendant in *Jean le Museur c Jeanne la Riche Femme* is a nickname that tells us something about her status.[76]

We have thus been able to derive some social information from the bare Paris record, but we are still left with the legal puzzle: Why are these parties bringing these suits? What was the legal result that the plaintiff sought to achieve? In order to begin to answer this question we must look at the other possible results of a case brought to enforce *sponsalia de futuro re integra*.

Remitted

The 45 cases in which the parties acknowledge the obligation but remit it are most like the 'straight' cases in which the oath is deferred. The result is a foregone conclusion; the parties will be given license to contract elsewhere. The formula entered varies somewhat, but the following includes all the elements that are sometimes omitted in the others, with or without an "etc.":[77]

There appearing *maître* Guillaume Lot *alias* de Luca, plaintiff, against *demoiselle* Jeanette *fille du défunt maître* Jean Corderii, defendant, in a case of marriage or espousals, they remitted each to the other the promises and pledges of faith of matrimony that they had had and had contracted with each other, *re integra* as to carnal intercourse, and they acquitted each other of the costs and legal proceedings that thereafter followed, which remission and acquittance, for certain reasons prompting us to this, we admit and tolerate in patience, giving to both of them license to contract elsewhere, etc., leaving the rest to their consciences.

An alternative form reads:[78]

Today *maître* Pierre Gaupin and Jeanne la Chapelue remitted each to the other the *sponsalia* contracted between them *per verba de futuro*, *re integra* as to carnal intercourse, and acquitted each other, asking us that we would deign to admit this acquittance and remission and tolerate [it] in patience. We therefore admit and tolerate the same, and

[74] Other examples T&C no. 568.
[75] Listed T&C no. 569.
[76] (26.i.87), col. 420/5. Indeed, both names may be out of Molière, *Idler vs Rich Woman*. I have similar suspicions about 'Agnesotte la Demandresse'.
[77] *Lot c Corderii* (23.viii.86), col. 354/2, T&C no. 570.
[78] *Chapelue c Gaupin* (22.iv.85), col. 102/2, T&C no. 571.

for cause (*et ex causa*), giving them license to contract elsewhere or,[79] etc. The woman, 2 *sous*.

The first form has an element in it that is specific to the case. There is evidence that there had been litigation between this couple about these espousals before they finally agreed to remit them.[80] Whether the explicit reference to conscience is also specific to the case we cannot be sure. It appears about as often in remittance cases as it does in the deferral cases and may have been a standard part of the formula otherwise incorporated in the almost ubiquitous final "etc."[81] In one of the cases that includes the clause (in addition to *Lot c Corderii*), there are strong indications that the judge knew more about the case than he normally did because there had been previous proceedings in it.[82] In another, there may have been previous proceedings, or the couple was not offering very powerful reasons why they should not proceed with the contract.[83] In the other two cases, we simply cannot tell why the phrase is included here and not elsewhere.[84] Hence, as in the case of deferrals, there is some, but not overpowering, evidence that the official knew something about the case that led him to put the phrase in.

The formula in *Lot c Corderii* tells us who the initial plaintiff was, but that in *Chapelue c Gaupin* does not. We have styled the latter case *Chapelue c Gaupin* because at the end, the woman is charged a fee and no fee for the man is mentioned. As will be discussed, there is much about the fees of the Paris court that we do not know, but in one of the cases in which we know from its style that the man is the moving party, only the man is charged the fee, and there are none in which the only party to be charged a fee is otherwise known to be the defendant.[85] On the basis of the assumption that where only one party is charged a fee he or she was the original plaintiff, and adding to that the cases in which the style of the entries allows us to tell who was the moving party, we arrive at a gender ratio of 60 percent (13 male plaintiffs and 9 female), lower than the gender ratio for the deferral cases (75%), but still quite different from that at York and Ely.[86]

The formulae for entries in remittance cases suggest dispensation, particularly in the phrase "tolerate in patience" (which appears in 18 of them) and "for a cause" (which appears in 11). (These phrases may be assumed to have been absorbed in the "etc." in other cases, for some are quite radically abbreviated.) The use of these phrases should give us pause, for the learned law did not speak in terms of dispensation in such cases. *Sponsalia de futuro* were like a contractual promise. If the promisee wanted to release the promisor, he or

79 Disc. T&C no. 572.
80 *Lot c Corderii* (20.viii.86), col. 352/8.
81 Disc. T&C no. 573.
82 *Bonete et Dol* (12.vii.87), col. 496/2; citation form disc. T&C no. 574.
83 *Torneur et Caraiere* (21.i.85), col. 35/4.
84 *Aumosne et Boisleaue* (2.vi.85), col. 126/4; *Pajot et Montibus* (13.ix.85), col. 189/2.
85 *Firmini c Buve* (17.ii.86 to 3.iii.86), refs. in TCas, disc. T&C no. 575.
86 Disc. T&C no. 576.

she could. That this should be done in the presence of a judge was frequently stated, but the reason for this recommendation was publicity. No dispensation was required, except perhaps in the case where the promise had been accompanied by a vow. Four of our cases do mention *fideidationes*; perhaps that is to be assumed in other cases and these pledges of faith may have been treated as vows. Whatever lies behind the practice of the Paris court, it is clear that it took *sponsalia de futuro* seriously.

Some of our cases give an indication of the sort of *causa* for breaking an engagement that the court thought to be appropriate ones. The age of the parties, either at the time of the contract or now, is mentioned five times: "Considering the youth of the man and the age of the woman,"[87] or "considering the age of the parties," we admit, and so on.[88] The parties said that "three years ago, they being of a childish age, they had some words between them about contracting marriage, although they did not intend to contract. These words, to the extent that they savored of the force of *sponsalia* or marriage, they remitted each to the other," and so on.[89] This last case is harder than it looks. If the couple were over the age of puberty and they exchanged words that "savored of the force of marriage," they were married. The learned law on the topic of exchanges of present consent that are not meant to create a marriage tended to prefer the visible to the inner intention. It may have been perfectly obvious, however, that this couple three years previously had not reached the age of puberty, in which case, even if they had exchanged words of present consent, they would be treated as words of future consent that could be revoked upon reaching puberty.

In some cases the *causa* is one that could have given rise to action for dissolution of the *sponsalia*, or even to dissolution of a marriage subsequently contracted: "On account of adultery committed on both sides, they remitted each to the other, for which act they paid a fine."[90] "They said that it was not beneficial (*utile*) for them to proceed further to the solemnization of the marriage, considering that the [woman] had sinned against the law of espousals with Jean Ludovici and others.... The woman... paid a fine for the act."[91] The use of the word "adultery" to describe the behavior of the first couple is startling and telling. For an espoused woman to have sexual intercourse with a man other than her fiancé was adultery in the law of the Hebrew Bible. It may have been considered adultery in the canon law of the early Middle Ages for either an engaged man or an engaged woman to have sexual intercourse with someone else, but in the classical canon law, an engaged couple were not married, and the behavior described here was, at worst, aggravated fornication. The phrase "sinned against the law of *sponsalia*" in the second case is a much more accurate description of the state of the law.

87 *Jovine c Robache* (28.i.85), col. 41/1, T&C no. 577.
88 *Bouchere c Houx* (5.vi.86), col. 315/4, T&C no. 578.
89 *Prepositi et Chamoncel* (5.vii.86), col. 329/3, T&C no. 579.
90 *Aumuciere c Lorrain* (20.v.85), col. 121/4, T&C no. 580.
91 *Portier et Malevaude* (4.xii.85), col. 231/3, T&C no. 581.

The situation in *Pierre Gaillart et Margot fille de Jean Ragne* is more straightforward: "Considering that the same man by means of an oath asserted that he had had carnal knowledge of Jeanne de Biaufort, aunt of the girl, and that Jeanne, having been summoned about this so that the truth of the matter could be known, did not appear," we remitted, and so on.[92] Affinity by illicit intercourse in the first and second degrees, as we have seen, was a diriment impediment to marriage and probably, as a practical matter, indispensable. To dissolve a marriage on this basis would probably have required more proof than the man's oath, but this was not marriage; the couple wanted to remit their vows, and the aunt's nonappearance suggests that she had something to hide.

For the rest, it is quite vague. Jean le Torneur and Jeannette la Caraiere are allowed to remit their *sponsalia* "because they do not wish to proceed further, nor does it seem beneficial to them." The matter is left to their consciences.[93] Michel Lavandier and Jeanne la Royne alias la Magdelene are allowed to remit "for certain reasons prompting them."[94] And the vast majority of cases give no reason at all. It is, of course, possible that the rest of the couples were subjected to hard questioning that is not recorded, or that Villemaden only entered the admission of the remission when it was granted, not when it was denied. The record we have before us, however, suggests that despite the rhetoric of cause and dispensation, any couple who wanted to break their engagement could do so as long as the matter was *res integra*.

This last requirement is, of course, important. If the couple had had intercourse after the promise, they were not engaged; they were married. Almost all of the records mention that the matter is *res integra*, and eight mention that the couple had taken an oath to that effect.[95] In one of them the couple came quite close to being married, but the court accepted their oath that they had had intercourse only before they contracted and not after.[96] As is the case with other elements that appear in some entries but not in others, we cannot tell whether it can be assumed to have been taken in all cases, although the number of cases in which it is mentioned is sufficiently small that we may doubt that it was. What the official might have required the oath in some cases but not in others can only be guessed. It may be significant that the oath is not mentioned in any of the cases that refer to the youth of the parties, suggesting that they may have been below the age of puberty even when they appeared, and that the oath is not mentioned in the couple of cases where the parties can be shown to be of a relatively high station.[97]

As was true in some of the deferral cases, a few entries in the remittance cases tell us more because, it would seem, they did not quite fit the basic pattern.

92 (19.viii.87), col. 509/3, T&C no. 582.
93 Col. 35/4, T&C no. 583.
94 *Lavandier et Royne* (16.ii.86), col. 264/3, T&C no. 584.
95 Listed T&C no. 585.
96 *Bonete c Dol* (12.vii.87), col. 496/2, T&C no. 586.
97 See, e.g., *Stainville, Houx, Monete et* [...], at n. 102; cases cited in nn. 77, 87–9, and 114.

Jeanne la Esveillée c Reginald Bontrelli domicilié à la maison d'Étienne Britonis à la signe du Dé, rue Saint-Germain-l'Auxerrois begins like a normal remittance case in which there had been previous litigation about the espousals. The couple had decided to remit whatever espousals they had contracted, and the official is more than usually full in admitting the remission: "considering that the *res* is *integra* insofar as carnal intercourse is concerned and that forced nuptials have difficult results and lest worse occur from this, etc., we have admitted," and so on.[98] The additional language may be the result of the fact that the defendant was represented by a proctor at the session at which the remission took place. Be that as it may, the additional phrases come straight out of the decretals, where they appear in the context of cases in which the pope is expressing considerable doubt as to whether it is wise specifically to enforce *sponsalia de futuro*.[99] As we shall see, the Paris court does seem to have enforced such *sponsalia* in a few instances, but it was aware of a contrary tradition, and that tradition came into play in situations where neither of the parties wanted them enforced.

Roger l'Oiselet c Guillaume le Ganter père de Perette le Ganter[100] is an odd case because so far as we can tell, it is never even alleged that Perette consented, and she does not appear. Rather, Roger "says in court that although [Guillaume] had previously promised the same [Roger] that he would give him the girl as spouse, the girl being absent, he does not intend to prosecute the girl about this promise nor can he prove it, as he says." The father, in turn, denies the promise before the judge and swears that he never promised. Someone, the record does not say who, is to pay a fee of two *sous*.

Jean Boujou c Jeanettte fille de Simon le Varlet proceeds like a defaulted lawsuit rather than a formally accepted remission, but the effect is the same: "[Jean] proposed that [Simon] had promised the same plaintiff the girl as spouse and wife and that the girl has ratified this. The girl said and asserted that she never made the promise; rather, she replied to her said father that she would not have him. And because the same plaintiff did not want to prove further, the defendant was absolved from the claim of the plaintiff."[101]

The following entry is bizarre: "There appearing Isabelle de Stainville, Jean du Houx, Guillaume Monete and [name illegible] who previously had contracted *sponsalia*, they acquitted themselves on each side. We admitted this [acquittance], considering [their] youth, etc. Jean 8 *deniers*."[102] If the gender of the illegible name is male, then Isabelle somehow got involved with three different men. If it is female, then either we are involved in some complicated arrangement of interlocking double *sponsalia*, or two couples found a way to save themselves fees by having their remissions recorded as one entry. (Why

98 (12.iv.87), col. 453/2, T&C no. 587.

99 X 4.1.2 (Alexander III, *Super eo. Praeterea hi*, WH 101) (*ne forte deterius inde contingat*); X 4.1.17 (Lucius III, *Requisivit*) (see Ch 9, n. 152).

100 (24.x.86), col. 382/5, T&C no. 588.

101 (30.x.86), col. 385/3, T&C no. 589.

102 (12.xii.86), col. 403/5, T&C no. 590.

Jean ends up paying the fee I do not know. Perhaps he brought the action that uncovered the mess.) In any case, they are all young; they want to seek other partners, and they probably do not have much money. A sketchy entry, made perhaps with an indulgent smile, will suffice for them (and no one is concerned about the puzzlement of future historians).

As we have seen in previous cases, couples sometimes wanted to assert that they really had not contracted *sponsalia* and to remit them if they had: "Bertrand de Aqua and Perette la Champione of Saint-Maur-des-Fossés (Val-de-Marne) appear and assert that they had some words between themselves that savored the force of *sponsalia de futuro*, although it was not then nor is it [now] their intention to contract with each other."[103] The case then proceeds as a regular remission case, which the official tolerates in patience "considering both the youth of the parties and that they have sworn that the *res* is *integra* insofar as carnal intercourse is concerned."[104]

Colin de Puteo and Catherine la Taverée are even more firm that they did not contract: "They assert on both sides that many are whispering that these parties have had marital promises with each other. These parties have not had them, as they say, and if they had any between themselves or their relatives [had any], they remit them each to the other."[105]

This last entry is telling because it provides a clue as to the motivation of the parties for going through the procedure of remittance. If one is seeking a marriage partner, even if one just wants to be free to do so, it does not help to have rumors around that one has contracted with someone else. We have already seen that double espousals was an offense for which one could be prosecuted. In at least one case, a priest refuses to solemnize a marriage where a third party alleges that one of the couple had *sponsalia de futuro* with him.[106] We may suspect, however, that there was more to the fear of having rumors of a contract around than simply the legal consequences. As the misuse of the word "adultery" in *Aumuciere c Lorrain* shows,[107] late fourteenth-century Parisians, or at least some of them, did not regard *sponsalia de futuro* as simply a contract. It was more serious than that, more like an 'initiate marriage', a phrase that had pretty much dropped out of the canonical literature after Gratian's solution to the problem of the *sponsa duorum* had been rejected in the late twelfth century.

As was the situation with the deferred cases, the remission cases give us some hints as to the age, status, and residence of the parties. In the five cases in which the age of the parties is mentioned as a motivating factor for admitting the remission, the parties are probably all quite young, except for the woman who is specifically stated to be older than the boy.[108] To these we may add the seven cases in which the woman is named as the daughter of some man, and

[103] (13.x.86), col. 377/5, T&C no. 591.
[104] *Id.*, T&C no. 592.
[105] (27.xi.85), col. 225/2, T&C no. 593, with disc. of another example.
[106] *Voisin c Furno* (27.x.85), col. 205/4. Another example T&C no. 594.
[107] See at n. 90.
[108] See at nn. 87–9.

the case in which the woman is not even a party.[109] That still gives us a lower percentage of young women whose fathers or relatives are, or are expected to be, arranging their marriages than we found in the deferral cases (12/45, 27% vs 39/91, 43%). On the other side, there are four widows, a slightly higher percentage than we found in the deferral cases (4/45, 9% vs 6/91, 7%).[110] There is enough here to suggest that the parties in remission cases may have been a bit older and bit more independent than those in deferral cases.

One *reus* in this group has chosen a domicile that is obviously in Paris, and a woman is given a street address in Paris when she is fined.[111] One *actrix* is described as being of the diocese of Séez and another woman as being of the village Saint-Maur-des-Fossés (Val-de-Marne).[112] For the rest we must presume, as we did with the deferral cases, that most, if not all, of the parties unidentified as to place come from Paris.

The remission cases give us one of the rare indications of a man's trade, Matthieu Rochet, pewterer.[113] *Maître* Guillaume Lot, *alias* de Luca, and *demoiselle* Jeanette *fille du défunt maître* Jean Corderii may have operated in professional circles.[114] At one point in the case, Jeanette appoints seven proctors. The defendant in another case is styled as *magister*.[115] A mysterious note at the end of the remission of Rémi Ogeri and Colette la Maigniere suggests that one "*maître* Ja[?cques]" owes the fee.[116] The couple may have worked for him.

Confessed

There are only five actions for *sponsalia de futuro re integra* that are confessed. In all but one of them, they result in an order to solemnize the marriage, within quite a short time. The actions are thus like the remission actions, in that the parties come to an agreement, but different in that they have the opposite result.

The standard form in confessed actions is well illustrated by *Perette la Truiere c Laurence Johannis*:[117]

> Concerning [PT], plaintiff in a marriage case against [LJ], defendant, the plaintiff proposed *sponsalia de futuro* and matrimonial pledges of faith. The defendant confessed, etc. He was condemned to solemnize the marriage in the face of the church [within six weeks], etc., which the same man promised to do. Plaintiff, 12 *deniers*.

Two other cases have shorter entries but are to the same effect.[118]

[109] Listed T&C no. 595.
[110] Listed T&C no. 596.
[111] Ref. T&C no. 597.
[112] Colette la Soupparde (n. 95); Perette la Champione (n. 103).
[113] *Rochet c Chouine* (13.iii.86), col. 276/5.
[114] See at n. 77. The plaintiff may have been of Italian origin. While both *maître* and *demoiselle* indicate a higher social status, they are quite vague as to what status.
[115] *Maître* Pierre Gaupin (n. 78).
[116] (16.xii.84), col. 12/5, T&C no. 598.
[117] (7.vi.85), col. 130/3, T&C no. 599.
[118] Listed T&C no. 600.

We might think that *Truiere c Johannis* was a case in which a woman, on her own, was using the court to provide the necessary shove to get her fiancé to solemnize the marriage, and perhaps it was. But in another case, we know that there was parental involvement. The entry in *Catherine fille de Jean Miole et Jean Tissay clerc* is simple: "Today, having heard the confession of [CM], [CM] was adjudged the *sponsa* of [JT] and they were affianced to each other by their common consent. And it was enjoined upon them that they solemnize the marriage within a month, etc."[119] Because Tissay was a clerk, we know what we would not have known had he been a layman. In the previous entry, Jean Miole took security from him according to the custom of the court of Paris. Tissay was enjoined not to do wrong to Jean Miole under penalty of excommunication and 40 Paris *livres*. Six months later Jean Miole released the security, and we may well imagine that the solemnization happened.[120]

Jean de l'Aumosne le jeune c Robinette la Charretiere is a quite different kind of case.[121] Robinette confesses the *sponsalia* but immediately alleges that Jean had previously espoused another woman. The case is set down for two days later for Jean to take an oath that the previous *sponsalia* were remitted.[122] When the day comes for him to do so he does not appear, and the case disappears from view. Both parties are represented by advocates; perhaps Jean's told him that he did not have a case.

Dissolved

Many of the 15 cases of dissolution of *sponsalia* have a criminal element in them, particularly the 8 that involve attempted bigamy. They thus do not normally have a 'plaintiff', although we may suspect that in at least some of the cases, the innocent party was responsible for bringing the case to light.

Office c Margot l'Uillere de Lagny (Seine-et-Marne) et Denis Toussans (13.iii.85) is typical:[123] "Today the *sponsalia de futuro re integra* between [MU] and [DT] were declared null, considering that the same man had previously contracted *sponsalia* with Perette [la Migrenote], carnal intercourse thereupon following. The same man made amends as is contained in the register of those imprisoned."

Some light is shed on this case by an entry in the session for 27 February 1385, in which Denis Toussains (who must be the same man) and Perette la Migrenote are petitioning the court: "[T]hey say that they had pledged faith to each other, and afterwards had had carnal matter. Then they were declared married by the official of Meaux, but after that adjudication they had not

[119] *Miole et Tissay* (7.x.85), col. 198/1, T&C no. 601.
[120] *Id.* col. 197/10, disc. T&C no. 602.
[121] *Aumosne c Charretiere* (13–15.xii.85), col. 235/1, 236/3.
[122] Col. 235/1, T&C no. 603.
[123] Col. 76/2, T&C no. 604.

had intercourse, but Perette had several times had intercourse with Hanequin Hurtaut, a resident of Meaux. Therefore they did not wish to proceed further." This last remark is strange. It is almost as if they thought that somehow the official could dissolve their marriage. The official is about to make a decree, perhaps of separation from bed and board, but the entry breaks off.[124]

Sometime between 27 February and 13 March, the court found out about Margot, and Denis ended up in the bishop's prison. The declaration of nullity of his attempted *sponsalia* with Margot is now a foregone conclusion. That is the least of his problems.

The entry in *Sibel fille de Bertin le Valyte* [*de Gretz* (*Seine-et-Marne*)] *et Jean Sapientis du diocèse de Besançon* is much less criminal, though it may be an office case:[125] "Today, considering the confession of [JS] who confessed that he had contracted marriage in the face of the church with [name garbled] and afterwards that he had contracted *sponsalia de futuro* with [SV] in Gretz on [25.ix.85], we declared that the espousals are null, etc., giving the same girl license to contract elsewhere."

One can imagine a story that would account for the fact that Jean Sapientis is let off, so far as we can tell, without even paying a fine, whereas Denis Toussains ends up in the bishop's prison. Perhaps Jean thought that his wife in far-off Besançon was dead, and when he discovered that she was alive, he came into court of his own accord and begged to be forgiven.[126] He certainly had not, as may have happened in Denis's case, attempted to get the judgment of another bishop's official reversed and, when he failed to do so, gone out and brazenly attempted to marry another woman. There are, however, many other possibilities. The entry in this case contains an obvious error (the garble of the other woman's name), a fact that suggests that Villemaden was not paying much attention to his task. He could just have forgotten to enter the punishment, which, as we know from other entries, would have been recorded elsewhere as well.

We cannot tell whether *Loret le Lonc et Edelotte fille de Jean le Gaignier de Vaudherland* (*Val-d'Oise*)[127] is an instance case brought by Loret that turns into an office case or an office case promoted by Loret. That he was actively involved in the prosecution of the case, however, is indicated by the fact that Edelotte is, among other things, condemned to pay his costs for the day in court. Edelotte confesses on oath that she contracted *sponsalia de futuro* and pledged faith to Jean Hardy of Gonesse (Val-d'Oise) on 2 October 1385. Jean swore to the same thing. On 18 November, the court declares that the espousals (not specifically said to be *de futuro*) that Edelotte had contracted with Loret on 10 November are null, and Loret is given license to contract

124 Col. 65/4, T&C no. 605.
125 (7.x.85), col. 198/8, T&C no. 606.
126 Reconstruction suggested by *Falampin et Falaise* at n. 134.
127 (18.xi.85), col. 221/2.

elsewhere. Edelotte and Jean are to make amends for "clandestine *sponsalia*"; Edelotte is to make amends for double *sponsalia* "as is secured in the register of Nicolas Charronis," one of the promotors of the court. She is charged a fee of two *sous* and Loret a fee of twelve *deniers*. A marginal note suggests that the amends were paid.[128]

Other cases of double *sponsalia* by a woman give us less detail. In one it would seem that on the confession of the woman alone, the current *sponsalia* were dissolved, and the man given license to contract elsewhere. The man is to pay the court fee, and the woman is to make amends for the double *sponsalia*.[129] In another case, the first of two men whom Marguerite *fille d'*Honorati Marescalli espoused appears and proposes that he had affianced her (*affidavit*) three months previously, and that the second man had affianced her in the face of the church the previous Sunday. Marguerite confesses all this, and court declares the first *sponsalia* valid, the second null, and gives license to the second man to contract elsewhere. Marguerite is to make amends for double *sponsalia*, and someone, the record does not say who, is to pay a fee of two *sous*.[130] One wonders what Honorati thought of all of this. We may speculate that he preferred the man whom his daughter had publicly espoused, and he may not even have known about the other one.

If *Lonc et Gaignier* raises questions of whether subsequent *sponsalia de presenti* could overcome prior *sponsalia de futuro*, *Jean Pelliparii et Jeanette fille d'Étienne Perrisel* leaves no doubt that subsequent marriage (however defined) would.[131] The court finds (*quia nobis constat*) that after contracting *sponsalia de futuro re integra* with Jean, Jeanette has "consummated marriage" (*matrimonium consumasse*) with one Pierre Heude. Jean is given license to contract elsewhere. Someone (probably Jeanette) is to pay a fee of two *sous*, and Jeanette is to make amends "as is secured in the paper [register] of Alain Audren," a proctor of the court and one of the numerous keepers of registers.[132]

We do not know what sorts of fines the women involved in double espousals paid, but there is no indication that any of them was imprisoned. The court was harsher with men (though it might be more cautious to say that it was harsher with two of the three men it caught). Étienne Jouvin of Chevreuse (Yvelines) confessed to having contracted *sponsalia* (of uncertain verb tense) with Agnesotte la Bouchere about a year before he contracted them with Perette *fille de* Jean la Cheuvre. The second *sponsalia* were declared null, and Étienne was imprisoned. Two weeks later he made amends by promising to pay six *francs* within two months. A fellow townsman went surety for him, and a marginal note indicates that the money was paid.[133]

128 *Id.*, T&C no. 607.
129 *Ancien et Templiere* (23.ii.87), col. 432/7, T&C no. 608.
130 *Huguelin, Olearii et Marescalli* (13.iii.86), col. 276/1, T&C no. 609.
131 (27.xi.85), col. 226/4.
132 E.g., col. 6, 243; col. 226/4, T&C no. 610.
133 *Cheuvre c Jouvin* (24.i.86), col. 250/4, T&C no. 611.

We cannot be sure, however, that all who contracted double *sponsalia*, even if they were potential bigamists, were punished. The entire entry on 19 October 1386 in *Cassin Falampin et Perette la Falaise* reads: "[PF], who contracted new *sponsalia de futuro* with [CF] was enjoined to provide assurance (*faciet fidem*) about the death of her first husband before Christmas; otherwise [CF] will have license to contract elsewhere, etc.; 12 *deniers*."[134]

As in the case of Jean Sapientis, it is possible that the penalty for Perette was recorded elsewhere and not here. We can imagine, however, that if Perette had been forthcoming about the existence of the prior husband and her belief in his death, the court might not have penalized her but simply required that she come up with some convincing evidence of his death.

There is one example of *sponsalia* dissolved on the basis of the incest rules. Those of Jean de Rivers and Marion la Contesse de Pentino were dissolved on the ground that Jean's former wife, Sancelotte, was the second cousin once removed of Marion.[135] Both were given license to contract elsewhere, and Jean paid a fee of two *sous*, a fact that suggests that he was the moving party.

Four women petition for dissolution of their *sponsalia* and license to marry another because of the absence of their fiancés. In all four cases the petition is granted, at least in part, but in some cases it takes some doing to get it. The greatest amount of detail is given in *Jeanette fille d'Étienne Carnificis de Vémars (Val-d'Oise) c Guillaume Regis de la région d'Anjou*:[136]

> Today [JC] appeared and asserted that five years ago a certain young man named [GR] from the region of Anjou, who was then staying in the town of Vémars, asked the mother of the girl to grant her to him as *sponsa*. The mother promised to give the same girl to the man as wife, there being no other promises or pledges of faith between this girl and the man, although she ratified the promise of her said mother. Shortly afterwards the man absented himself from the village and the surrounding area and went to foreign parts. Therefore, she had him called in the village, in the place where she [? it could be "he"] was then living and from the pulpit of the church, at four intervals, at which he did not appear. Therefore, the girl, considering the foregoing, asks for license to contract [elsewhere], and she swore that she had never had sexual intercourse with the man. Considering this oath and the other matters foregoing, we admitted the summonses and the oath, and we admitted her conscience. We neither give nor do we deny her license. 2 *sous*.

We have no idea why Jeanette's mother rather than her father made the promise. It could be that Villemaden neglected to note that the father was dead, but perhaps the point is that the mother made the promise, not the father. Jeanette, in turn, ratified her mother's promise, but there was no *affidatio*. Guillaume departed for parts unknown. Jeanette had him summoned, and swore that she never had intercourse with him. The official's response strikes me as niggardly. Perhaps he did not believe Jeanette when she said that she had not had intercourse with Guillaume. As it is, she will probably have to come back

[134] (19.x.86), col. 379/8, T&C no. 612.
[135] (27.x.85), col. 209/2, T&C no. 613, with disc.
[136] (2.vi.86), col. 314/2, T&C no. 614.

to court when her banns are proclaimed, something that she would not have to do if the official had given her license (unless, of course, Guillaume appeared and claimed that they did have intercourse).

In three other cases, the license is given. In one, the girl claims that the man has not been found after a year and that she wants to become a mother. She swears that the *sponsalia de futuro* were *re integra*, that the four summonses were made, and that the *sponsalia* were made conditional on the approval of her relatives. The girl is charged the quite high fee of four *sous*.[137] In another, the man has been banished from the kingdom for his crimes. This seems to be an easy case, and no fee is mentioned, although even here four summonses were made.[138] The last case is even easier. Isabelle *fille de* Jean Charronis is granted license to contract "where she will," notwithstanding her *sponsalia de futuro re integra* with Robin Anglici a year earlier, because the man had absented himself and did not appear when called at three intervals.[139]

One dissolution case casts doubt on whether there was anything to dissolve. Pierre Fabri and Jeanette *fille de* Jean de Moriaut are granted license to contract elsewhere, "because they had not had any *sponsalia*, although their fathers had had some words between them about giving one to the other."[140]

The final dissolution case is contested. It raises a number of interesting issues but disappears from view before we can get any sense of what the court will make of them. Henri Rouet, residing at the house of Brice Podeur (almost certainly in Paris), brings an action alleging that the deceased father and the mother of Agnesotte *fille du défunt* Simon de Longuerue had promised their daughter to him, had granted her to him (*concesserunt*), and had affianced her to him (*affidaverunt*), on the basis of a contract that they had between them. Agnesotte denies the pledges of faith, and says that if her father and mother promised anything to Henri, she was not pleased and was not of age at the time. Now she reclaims: "as quickly as she could find him so quickly would she reclaim" (a garbled phrase but that is probably what it means). Both parties are represented by advocates, and the mother and tutors of the girl are inhibited from binding her to anyone else *pendente lite*.[141] In the next session, Henri produces five witnesses; an examiner is commissioned. Agnesotte reclaims, and someone (probably Henri) produces "letters or a brevet from the Châtelet" purporting to be a contract between Agnesotte's father and Henri. Although the case is set for the following Monday, no further entries are to be found.

It is striking how many of these cases of dissolution of *sponsalia* come from outside of the city of Paris. Four of the double espousals cases do so, as do

137 *Rouge c Carnoto* (18.iv.87), col. 457/2, T&C no. 615. The man's name suggests that he came from Chartres.

138 *Cularse c Pelliparsi* (3.vii.87), col. 492/1, T&C no. 616.

139 (4.v.86), col. 300/6. Three intervals (*tres dilationes*) is probably the same as four summonses (*quatuor evocationes*).

140 (2.iii.87), col. 436/4, T&C no. 617.

141 *Rouet c Longuerue* (25–27.x.85), col. 208/4 (T&C no. 618), 209/4.

three of the non-bigamy cases (if we accept the identification of "de Pentino" in *Rivers et Contesse*).[142] These cases remind us more of the English cases in the issues that they raise: double espousals, nonage, whether the words exchanged constitute *sponsalia*. Perhaps French men and women who lived in rural areas engaged in the kind of behavior that got them into marital difficulties like those found in England more often than did those who lived in the big city of Paris.[143] Of course, when they got to court the *sponsalia* that they alleged were *de futuro* rather than *de presenti*. We will have occasion to explore these similarities and differences in more depth in a later section.

Contested

Thirty-one of the cases seeking to enforce *sponsalia de futuro re integra* are contested and not deferred, at least initially, to the decisory oath. A few do not get very far, a couple give us a result, and we can be reasonably confident that a result was reached in a number of them but that the sentence was recorded elsewhere. These cases took up a lot of the court's time. There are 196 entries for our 31 cases, an average of 6.3 entries per case. This did not mean that such cases extended over a long period of time. The Paris court was in session virtually continuously, and while some cases were postponed over the harvest and vintage vacations, most marriage cases were not. At Ely a postponement from session to session would mean that a case would meet at three-week intervals. At Paris it was much more common for a marriage case to meet every week.

The tendency of male plaintiffs to dominate marriage litigation, which we noted in other types of cases, is particularly notable in the contested cases. Eighty-one percent of the plaintiffs (25/31) in contested cases of *sponsalia de futuro re integra* are male.

Contested cases in the Paris register are disappointing in the amount of substantive information that they reveal. We follow the parties through numerous procedural steps. Sometimes the defendant is contumacious, witnesses are introduced and their depositions published, and various procedural arguments take place. Information about the substance of the claims, much less about what the argument was really all about, is hard to come by.

Twelve of the cases give us no substantive information other than that the plaintiff was claiming *sponsalia de futuro*, which the defendant denied. Most of these cases disappear after one, two, or three sessions, usually following the nonappearance of the plaintiff and before any witnesses are introduced.[144] One is resolved by the deferral of the decisory oath to the defendant after

[142] See n. 135, disc. T&C no. 619.

[143] That Parisians could also, on occasion, engage in such behavior is suggested by *Huguelin, Olearii et Marescalli* (n. 130).

[144] Listed T&C no. 620.

witnesses are introduced,[145] and one is remitted after witnesses are introduced.[146] To this we may add the one case in which the plaintiff fails to appear after having produced witnesses.[147] In all of these latter cases we may suspect that the witnesses did not prove what the plaintiff hoped they would prove.

Some of these cases give us some social information, even though they do not tell us what the dispute was about. *Maître* Jean Fernicle took security from Guillaume le Paige, clerk.[148] On the same day, Burgotte, Jean's daughter, sued Guillaume, alleging *sponsalia de futuro*. The case was set for a session to determine the mode of procedure (probably whether it would be long form or summary), but no further entries are recorded.[149] It was probably settled.

Dame Jeanne de Senay dame de Vienne (Val-d'Oise) c Bartholome de la Pierre involves parties at the highest social level that we have seen.[150] After indecisive proceedings in the spring of 1385, in which it is unclear whether Jeanne is suing Bartholome or he suing her, the case begins in earnest on 10 June, with the jurisdiction of the court founded on the basis of letters of citation from the king himself. The entry describes the case as one that "has been initiated for a long time or is hoped to be initiated."[151] In July, Jeanne's proctor proposes *sponsalia de futuro*, which Barthomole's proctor denies, and the case then disappears from view.

In *Denis le Bryais c Julianne fille du défunt Jean Chapon*, a case that disappears after the plaintiff's non-appearance at the third session, the defendant denies *sponsalia de futuro*, but then says that "she does not know whether the plaintiff took her by the hand or not."[152] Whether he took her by the hand or not is probably legally irrelevant, but the mention of it suggests, as do a number of other cases in the register, that handfasting was not a custom confined to England.[153]

The most frustrating case in this group is *Colin Eliart c demoiselle Guillemette fille de Raoul Gosse*.[154] Twenty-nine sessions over the course of almost 15 months tell us virtually nothing about what the case was about. It is finally set down for an interlocutory sentence, the subject of which is not given, but it may have resolved the case. Guillemette constitutes six proctors at the beginning of the case, and she also has more than one advocate over the course of the proceedings. It seems fairly clear that she was attempting to delay the

145 *Chemin c Chapelle* (16.viii.86 to 14.v.87), refs. in TCas, disc. T&C no. 621.

146 *Ruella c Provins* (1.vi.87 to 26.viii.87), refs. in TCas.

147 *Hugot c Furno* (10.iv.85 to 2.v.85), col. 92/5, 97/6, 103/3, 109/7.

148 *Fernicle c Paige* (1) (21.iv.85), col. 101/4.

149 *Fernicle c Paige* (2) (21.iv.85), col. 102/1.

150 (17.iii.85 to 3.vii.85), refs. in TCas.

151 Col. 132/1: *in quadam causa matrimoniali mota diu est seu moveri sperata*. For this formula, see Donahue and Gordus, "Case from Stratford's Act Book," 52.

152 (16.iv.87), col. 455/4 (T&C no. 622), 461/3, 463/5.

153 For another example, see *Odin et Thiefre c Blagi* (n. 180).

154 (9.i.86 to 29.iii.87), refs. in TCas.

proceedings. Colin, who is also represented, may have just allowed the proceedings to carry on for as long as they did, or the case may illustrate how slow long-form Romano-canonical procedure could be if committed to skilled lawyers. At one point, Colin's advocate argues that Guillemette's exceptions to his witnesses are "frivolous and inept," and a later entry tells us that she accused them of being criminals.[155] The potential of this exception for delay had become so notorious by the early modern period that efforts were made to restrict its use.[156] In the autumn of 1386, there is a new *litis contestatio* on facts proposed by Guillemette. This suggests that Colin had proved his basic case and may suggest, as do other cases, that it had become a case about whether the conditions of the contract had been fulfilled.

Marion la Ligniere fille de Jean Chateaufort c Jean Colasse (*Ser*[*ur*]*arii*) *?apprenti* (*famulus*) *de Guillaume le Serreurier*[157] is similarly frustrating in the amount of substantive information that it gives. The result in the case, if there was one, lies beyond the chronological limits of the book. What is interesting about the case is that the parties seem to be more like those whom we saw at York and Ely. Here, a young woman is suing to establish a marriage with the apprentice (if I am reading *famulus* right) of a man who may well be a locksmith.[158] The fact that later in the case Jean is called Jean "le Serrurier" suggests that he may have left his apprenticeship and become a locksmith himself. Marion has three witnesses, all women, one married, and her father is not in evidence. Both parties have hired advocates. Jean, at one point, is represented by a proctor. These people are not of the social level of Colin Eliart and *demoiselle* Guillemette *fille de* Raoul Gosse, but the court is open to them, and they know how to handle themselves in it.

Of the 19 contested cases about which we know more about the issues than just that they involve *sponsalia de futuro re integra*, 17 concern either parental consent or the financial arrangements for the marriage. Let us look first at the parental consent cases.

Thomas Domont c Perrette la Cousine[159] has a pattern of pleading similar to that which we saw in some of the deferral cases. Thomas claims *sponsalia de futuro re integra*. Perette confesses that he spoke to her about marriage, and she replied that she would do nothing unless it pleased her father. The father appears and says that he was not, and is not, pleased. An entry is missing, but we see that Thomas produced witnesses, perhaps on the question of whether the father had consented, but more likely on the question of whether Perette's consent was conditional in the first place. The testimony is ultimately published, a conclusion is declared in the case, and it is set "to hear the law." It then disappears

155 Col. 336/3 (read *actor dixit* for *rea dixit*), 369/3.
156 E.g., Maranta, *Speculum aureum*, pars 6, tit. *De repulsa testium*, pp. 384–6; Ordonnance du roi pour la procédure civile (1667), tit. 23, in *Recueil des grandes ordonnances*, 464.
157 (30.iv.87 to 19.viii.87), refs. in TCas.
158 Disc. T&C no. 623.
159 (2.i.85 to 20.ii.85), refs. in TCas.

from view. It could have been compromised,[160] but considering the presence of a separate register of sentences, it is equally likely that the result was recorded elsewhere.

A number of other cases produce variations on this basic theme. In *Colin Oliverii c Jeanette la Bouchere*,[161] Colin claims that "*sponsalia per verba de futuro* were contracted between him and the relatives of the defendant, which this defendant before and afterwards ratified, and that he contracted with her." She "confessed that the plaintiff had spoken with her and that she said that she would do nothing except at the will of her relatives."[162] Colin produces 10 witnesses (all men) who are examined and whose testimony is published. He is asked to produce them again, but after the vacations for harvest and vintage, the parties remit their contract. The fact that Jeanette and not Colin is charged a fee (admittedly a modest one) for the remittance suggests that Colin had a case. It is probably significant that the relatives never appear, as they do in most such cases, to deny that they ever consented.

Pierre Vauvere c Jeanette Maindieu[163] is more cryptic. Pierre claims *sponsalia de futuro* and matrimonial pledges of faith. Jeanette claims that they were conditioned on the approval of her relatives. Two of the relatives appear and say that they did not and do not approve.[164] At the next substantive session, the couple are enjoined from contracting elsewhere *pendente lite*, and Jeanette's father appears and adds his disapproval to the list.[165] Pierre produces six witnesses whose testimony is published, and the case is set down for conclusion. A sentence may have been rendered, or the case may have been compromised; there is less indication in this case than there is in some of the others that the court was ready to render sentence.[166]

Other cases take fewer sessions to resolve, although they seem to raise the same basic issue. Françoise *fille de* Guillaume Grivel says that she replied to Odinet Tassin's request that she be his wife that she would do what pleased her father and mother. The father swears to his displeasure in the standard form, and she is absolved from Odinet's suit.[167] Apparently Odinet had no proof to the contrary, though this is not mentioned. A pair of incomplete entries in another case suggest that the same result followed when the claim was that the relatives had to be pleased.[168] In a third case, the plaintiff alleges that the consent was obtained: "The plaintiff proposed that he contracted *sponsalia de futuro re integra* with this defendant, and the mother of the defendant agreed

[160] Text and disc. T&C no. 624.
[161] (26.v. to 21.x.85), refs. in TCas.
[162] Col. 123/8, T&C no. 625.
[163] (22.vi.85 to 19.viii.85), col. refs. in TCas.
[164] Col. 141/1, T&C no. 626.
[165] Col. 146/4, disc. T&C no. 627.
[166] This is because the case is not set down *ad audiendum ius*, and no *collatio* is ordered. See n. 160.
[167] (28.viii.86), col. 358/3, T&C no. 628.
[168] *Paillart c Grolée* (3.ii.86), col. 256/3, 257/4, disc. T&C no. 629.

that she [the defendant] be wife to the plaintiff, and afterwards the defendant, ratifying this, affianced the plaintiff." The defendant denies all; the case is set down for proof and disappears after the second entry.[169] In a fourth case that disappears without a resolution, the defendant answers the plaintiff's claim that she had pledges of faith and *sponsalia de futuro re integra* with him by saying that "she confessed that he had proposed to her and had spoken with her about contracting and that she had replied that she would do what pleased her mother and relatives and what belonged to them."[170] The last phrase is not standard and hence quite telling.

Gilda *fille* [*du défunt*] Jean Bigot replies to the claim of Jean de Sancto Mederico not only that her consent was conditional on that of her relatives but also that she was "seduced" into consenting by Jean's father, that she was 11 years old at the time, and that she reclaimed. Her tutors appear and say that they did not and do not consent.[171] Jean introduces witnesses, but in the fourth session of the case the court renders sentence:[172]

Considering that the same plaintiff previously proposed *sponsalia de futuro re integra*, etc., and the defendant confessed that by the seduction of the father of the plaintiff she had made a marital promise with the same plaintiff, and that this was out of fear and not otherwise, which *sponsalia* she protested that she would reclaim when she became of marriageable age,[173] which defendant also swore today before us that she had not otherwise contracted or made marital promises with the plaintiff, considering also the oath of [four men, including a priest], witnesses who were examined today and testified to the same thing, we absolve the defendant from the claim of the plaintiff, giving license to both, etc.

If we can doubt whether Gilda Bigot was even "of marriageable age," there is no doubt that Agnesotte *veuve du défunt* Guillaume du Pré *alias* Charron was a mature woman whose ambiguous marriage negotiations with Monet Foueti (Fouest) are at least hinted at in the pleadings and positions of the case that he brought against her:[174]

The plaintiff proposed that previously (*alias*) they had made many marital promises and finally in the garden of the woman this woman said that she would "lead" (*duceret*) the plaintiff as husband even without the consent of her relatives if they do not want to consent to this, etc., and the plaintiff also promised to take her (*ducere*) as wife. The defendant confessed that they had previously had words about contracting marriage and that she said to the plaintiff that if it pleased the relatives of this defendant she would contract marriage with this plaintiff and not otherwise.

169 *Andree c Pigne* (16–23.i.86), col. 246/2 (T&C no. 630), 249/3.
170 *Gallon c Godée* (16–23.vii.87), col. 498/2 (T&C no. 631), 501/5.
171 (23.ix.85), col. 192/4, 194/7, 198/3, 203/4.
172 Col. 203/4, T&C no. 632.
173 This suggests that she is not yet 12, though we cannot always be confident that the notaries got their tenses right.
174 (27.vii.87 to 5.ix.87), refs. in TCas.

The parties are inhibited from contracting elsewhere *pendente lite* under penalty of 40 *livres*, and the woman introduces her relatives to the court (four men, one of whom is a Raoul du Pré). The record does not say that they dissented, but they probably did.[175]

The entry in which the defendant clarifies the "doubted" positions previously entered into by her proctor[176] tells us a bit more:

To the position that begins [i.e., the position originally said]: "And again, that the plaintiff came again to the defendant on the Monday next following and asked of her whether she wished to take [*accipere*] the plaintiff as husband or not. She doubts." – she [now] replies, "She believes [so]." [To the position that begins:] "And again, that at that time the plaintiff said to the same defendant that the same plaintiff would not have his relatives come until he knew exactly what the defendant wanted, and that he did not wish to labor further in vain at the word "she doubts," – she [now] replies "She does not believe [it is so] as it is stated." [To the position that begins:] "And again, thirdly, that the plaintiff also promised the same defendant likewise that he would take her and 'lead' her (*ipsam caperet et duceret*) as wife and that nonetheless he would, out of abundance [of caution], take steps to seek her through her relatives, as this defendant wished. She doubts." – she [now] replies, "She believes that [it was so] in the situation in which it pleased her relatives and not otherwise."[177]

While we must fill in what is missing with details from the pleadings, a consistent picture emerges. Monet is arguing that on a particular occasion, Agnesotte had agreed to a marriage without requiring the consent of her relatives. This happened, he says, on a Monday in her garden. Dispensing with the relatives' consent was not his idea, but he did not want to call his relatives, unless he was sure that she was willing to go through with the contract. He even suggested that she call her relatives "out of abundance of caution" (*ex habundanti*).[178]

Monet produces two witnesses, both men, and seeks the compulsion of two others, both married women. These witnesses are still being examined when the register ends, and so we have no idea how the case was resolved. What we do have, however, tells us more than do most of the Paris cases. Agnesotte is an independent woman (*mulier*, not *filia*), though she need not have been very old. She has her own garden, and she may have been of somewhat higher station than Monet. The phrase in the pleadings "that she said that she would lead the plaintiff as husband" (*quod ipsa dictum actorem duceret in maritum*) is a striking piece of Latin, for in both classical and medieval Latin, the husband "leads" the wife (i.e., to his house), not vice versa, except, so far as I am aware, in one passage in the *Codex* where a free woman led a slave as husband, not knowing that he was a slave.[179] It also seems clear that Monet and Agnesotte had discussed the possibility of agreeing to marriage without the consent of

175 Col. 502/3, T&C no. 633.
176 Disc. T&C no. 634.
177 Col. 508/1, T&C no. 635.
178 The meaning here is least certain because the Latin does not quite parse. See text at T&C no. 636.
179 C.5.18.3.

their relatives, except, perhaps, having them come in at the end to witness what had already taken place. It seems reasonably clear that this latter is what Monet had in mind. He may even have genuinely thought that that was what was agreed to. Of Agnesotte we can be less sure. She may have agreed to Monet's proposal and then thought better of it, perhaps under the influence of her relatives, or it may have been a genuine misunderstanding. What is clear is that it was a plausible argument for a respectable widow to make that she would not negotiate her own remarriage without requiring the consent of her relatives.

Two cases contain strong indications that the woman is resisting the marital choice of her relatives. *Jean Odin et Alison veuve du défunt Robin Thiefre c Laurence de Blagi*[180] is the simpler of the two cases:

[JO] and [AT] asserted that they contracted espousals of the future tense on Sunday [2.ix.86] and that on [18.ix.86] a certain godfather (*compater*) of the woman took the hands of this woman and [LB] and put one in the other saying that he was affiancing them, and for this purpose he was [acting as] priest, etc. Considering the confession of the parties, we decreed that the first espousals were valid and the second were not, giving license to [LB], etc. The woman four *sous*.

It cost Alison twice the usual fee to clear the record caused by the arrogant behavior of her godfather, but there is no evidence that she could not afford it. It will be noted that no proof, other than the confession of the parties, is required of the prior *sponsalia*, as there probably would have been if we had been dealing with *sponsalia de presenti*. Indeed, there is little indication that the *sponsalia* with Laurence were anyone's idea other than the godfather's. Laurence puts up no resistance and may even have actively cooperated in obtaining the judgment. (This depends on who is being referred to by "the confession of the parties.") Finally, it will be noted that other than the high fee, there is no indication that Alison has to make amends for double *sponsalia*. To put it another way, she was not expected to resist her godfather's bullying, which may have been a sort of crude joke. She does not, however, confess that she said anything that indicated her consent.

The record in *Jean Blondel c Jacquelotte fille ainée de maître Michel Tybert*[181] is more complicated and more ambiguous than that in *Marguonet c Belot*, but it seems clear that here, too, the woman is resisting the choice of her relatives. Jean proposes

that the father of this defendant and the same plaintiff had contracted *sponsalia per verba de futuro* between the same plaintiff and defendant with the common consent of the relatives of both parties, although the defendant was at that time absent, the father, however, saying that he was doing this with the consent of his said daughter, etc., and that afterwards the same daughter ratified and accepted this and affianced the same plaintiff by hand (*manualiter*), and the defendant promised this to certain persons appointed by the plaintiff.

180 (6.x.86), col. 372/6, T&C no. 637.
181 (17.i.87 to 5.vii.87), refs. in TCas.

Jacquelotte "confessed that her father and others had talked to her about these matters, and although she had told her father that she would do his will, she never had the will to contract *sponsalia* with the plaintiff nor with anyone else, but he always displeased her and he displeases her [now], etc., and she denies everything else."[182]

The parties are of some status. They engage advocates and are represented by proctors throughout most of the proceedings, which follow the long form. The court sets the penalty for disobeying the injunction not to contract elsewhere *pendente lite* at 100 *livres*, rather than the usual 40. All of this is what we would expect for the eldest daughter of a man who calls himself *magister*.

The greater detail given in the pleadings also gives us some idea of how marriage negotiations were expected to proceed at this level of society. An agreement is reached with the father of the prospective bride and the prospective groom, aided by their *amici*. The prospective bride is then asked what she thinks of all of this, and she is expected to say that she will do the will of her father. The parties are then affianced by a version of the ceremony of handfasting. Whether the discussion with the representatives of the prospective groom and the prospective bride was also standard we can be less sure. If it was, we may suspect that it came before the ceremony of affiancing.

Somehow in this case it did not work. We do not know why. It may have been that Michel thought better of the arrangement and instructed his daughter to say that she never consented, but that is not the impression that the record gives, which is that Jacquelotte, having made the standard statement that she would do the will of her father, took a dislike to Jean. There is even a hint in her insistence that she never had the will to contract with Jean, or with any other man, that she had decided against marriage, perhaps in favor of the religious life.

The pleadings themselves raise an interesting legal issue. Could Jacquelotte have authorized her father to contract on her behalf without knowing with whom he would contract? It was clear, after some discussion, that in the case of *sponsalia de presenti*, a third party could be deputized to enter into the *sponsalia*, but the canonists insisted that the person with whom the contract was to be made by the proctor be a single identifiable person.[183] The issue was less often discussed in the context of *sponsalia de futuro*, but it would seem that the same rule applied.[184]

Whether the long series of proceedings that followed raised these issues we do not know. The one entry that tells us something more than the procedural steps is a long entry in which Jacquelotte makes some changes in detail to the positions to which, apparently, her proctor had sworn at an otherwise unrecorded session.[185] Otherwise, we learn that Jean produced four witnesses,

[182] Col. 416/2, T&C no. 638.
[183] See Sánchez, *Disputationes de matrimonio*, 2.11 nu. 4, pp. 1:124b–125a, with references.
[184] *Id.*, 1.7 nu. 4, p. 1:19a; disc. T&C no. 639.
[185] Col. 423/2.

two of whom look like his relatives. They are examined and their testimony is published. Jacquelotte proposes an exception.[186] Approximately six months after the case is begun, Jacquelotte is contumacious, and the case disappears from view.[187] Unfortunately, this record does not give us enough information even to guess what may have been the result of the case.

The litigation pattern in *Jean Vaquier c Jeannette la Hesseline fille de Jean Hesselin*[188] is different, but the substantive issue is the same. The pleadings in the case lie before the beginning of the book, but they probably alleged *sponsalia de futuro re integra*, which were simply denied. Jean produces four witnesses, whose testimony is ultimately published. Jeanette then introduces her substantive defense: "if the parties ever contracted any *sponsalia* or marital promises with each other, Jean Hesselin and Marie his wife, parents of the defendant, disavowed this defendant and do so now, and that these [*sponsalia* and promises] did not please them nor do they please them, nor did they nor do they ratify them."[189] A commissary is to take the parents' oaths, and he reports back that Jean and Marie swore that "if the parties had had any *sponsalia* or marital promises, they never pleased the same parents nor do they please them, rather they displeased and displease."[190] The case is then concluded and set for sentencing.

The wording of Jeanette's exception is startling, because nowhere does it mention that the *sponsalia* were conditional on her parents' consent. The way the exception is worded makes it look as if it were in the power of parents to "disavow" their daughter and hence her promises, whether she had made them conditional or not. That was emphatically not the law, and most of the rest of the cases of parental consent are phrased in conditional terms. We should recall, moreover, that we do not have the pleadings in the case, nor do we know what the testimony revealed. As it is, the exception is, at least, a telling slip that tells us about social expectations, and it may tell us something about the law that the court was in fact applying, as opposed to what it ought to have been applying.

Yet another litigation pattern is revealed in *Colin le Voisin c Jeanette fille de Reinald de Furno*.[191] Colin and Jeanette appear in October of 1385, having been sent by the *curé* of Le Tremblay (Maine-et-Loire) because Colin had reclaimed against the banns of Jeanette and Odin Bricii on the ground that he had a previously contracted *sponsalia de futuro re integra* with her. Jeanette said that when Colin asked her to marry him, she had replied that it pleased her so long as it pleased her father and her relatives.[192] The case proceeds through

186 Col. 463/3. The record calls this a *factum contrarium*, a term that is normally associated with summary procedure, which this emphatically was not.
187 Disc. T&C no. 640.
188 (22.xii.84 to 22.iii.85), refs. in TCas.
189 Col. 78/4, T&C no. 641.
190 Col. 79/8, T&C no. 642.
191 (20.x.85 to 10.ii.86), refs. in TCas.
192 Col. 205/4, T&C no. 643.

the regular admission, examination, and publication of witnesses, the plaintiff always appearing in person, the defendant normally by proctors. Odin joins the suit as plaintiff in January. In February, quite suddenly, we find the following sentence: "Today having heard the confession of [JF] who confessed that she contracted *sponsalia* with [CV] in the middle of Lent a year ago [19.ii.85], we adjudge her spouse of the same [CV], decreeing that the *sponsalia* afterwards contracted between her and [OB] are null. And she made amends for the second *sponsalia* as is secured in the register of Alain Audren and Alain Forestarii."[193]

The absence of the father throughout the proceedings in this case is unusual. It is possible that he never knew about Colin until he got a rude shock at the proclamation of the banns, but then one wonders why he did not appear and support his daughter's claim by refusing to consent. Jeanette may have been persuaded to make up the story about parental consent, a story that others (proctors) then pursued until she was finally able to appear and tell the truth. On balance, however, I am inclined to think that both father and daughter were negotiating with two different men. Odin first forced the matter by getting the banns proclaimed; then Colin raised the stakes by reclaiming. By January, the du Four family was inclined to Colin, perhaps because he had made a better financial offer. Now it was Odin's turn to try to raise the stakes, but he failed when Jeanette confessed to an unconditional precontract with Colin. Not knowing what the fine was for *bina sponsalia* (it is striking that it is never stated for a woman), we do not know how much this cost. We do know that Colin was charged a relatively high fee for his first appearance (3 *sous*). That certainly suggests that he was not poor, and it may suggest that the court sensed that there was a considerable amount of maneuvering going on in the case.

Perette veuve du défunt Étienenne le Marguonet c Guillaume Belot[194] is the only case in which the parental consent of the man is at stake. Perette may have been older than Guillaume:

> The plaintiff proposed that the same defendant last Christmas affianced her in the house of Isabelle de Rieu and promised the same plaintiff that he would take her as wife and that he would never have another woman except for her, and this plaintiff promised the same to the same defendant on her side. The defendant confessed that he would take her as wife so long as it pleased his father, and he denies everything else.[195]

The case gets into a minor procedural snarl in the next session. In the third, the plaintiff produces five witnesses (including Isabelle) in the absence of the defendant, and the case disappears from view.

As in *Voisin c Furno*, the father never appears. Unlike *Voisin c Furno*, we have no reason to suspect in this case that he was operating in the background. The record, unfortunately, gives us nothing to let us guess which of the numerous possibilities accounts for the disappearance of a case in which the plaintiff

[193] Col. 261/7, T&C no. 644.
[194] (15.v.86 to 2.vi.86), col. 306/7, 309/8, 314/3.
[195] Col. 306/7, T&C no. 645.

seemed to be doing quite well. The pleadings, however, have a kind of specificity that is lacking in other cases.[196]

The three brief entries in *Jean de Parisius c Isabelle la Giffarde et [...] son père*[197] are important for what they tell us not only about this case but also about what may have been going on in other cases where the record is less forthcoming. The beginning of the case is not recorded. Jean probably alleged *sponsalia de futuro re integra.* When we first see the case, the court orders the father to appear because he had promised Jean his daughter, together with "certain goods to be handed over" within a term now passed, which he has not done.[198] Jean is asking either for license to contract elsewhere or that Isabelle's father fulfill his promise. A week later, the court gives the father another week to fulfill his promise (which is taken as having been made; there seems to be no issue about that); otherwise, license is given "from this time forward" (*ex nunc*).[199] A week later, the "conditional espousals contracted between [JP] and [IG] and the father of the girl were declared null" and license given to Jean to contract elsewhere, if the condition were not fulfilled by the end of the day. Jean pays a fee of two *sous*.[200]

Were it not for the fact that Jean was willing to go through with the arrangement if the father fulfilled his side of the bargain, this could have been a remission case. Were it not for the fact that (apparently) the Giffardes admitted what the arrangement was, this could have been a deferral case. The question that cannot be answered is how many remission and deferral cases are really cases of marriage arrangements that broke down over the financial arrangements, but we may suspect that it was considerably more than appear to be so on the face of the record.

Other cases give us details about the financial aspects of *sponsalia*. In April of 1385, Marguerite de Carnoto proposed that Manuel Torin had contracted *sponsalia de futuro* with her with the consent of their relatives and in the hands of a priest (*per manus presbiteri*) during the previous Christmas season. Manuel replied that the arrangement was conditional on her giving him 100 *francs* and on her being free of all debts by 15 January.[201] The case has no further entries.

The greatest amount of detail about the financial arrangements is found in *Denisette Critin c Jean Helias*:[202]

The defendant confessed that he and the relatives of the plaintiff had words about [his] contracting marriage with the defendant, and he promised to take her as wife, the relatives saying that they would give him the girl with all her goods free and unbound from all servitudes and debts, and along with this they would give him 100 *francs* which the brother of the girl promised, etc., and a half of a house, and this [happened] about two years ago, and afterwards they did not perform the promise.

196 Disc. T&C no. 646.
197 (29.iv.– 29.v.85), col. 107/3, 113/5, 125/1.
198 Col. 107/3, T&C no. 647.
199 Col. 113/5, T&C no. 648.
200 Col. 125/1, T&C no. 649.
201 (9.iv.85), col. 92/2.
202 (8–12.iii.86), col. 272/4, 275/8.

The plaintiff "confessed the promises, except for the half of a house, and she offered herself as ready to perform the promises, except for the half of a house. She also proposed that afterwards the defendant promised simply, without any condition being imposed, to take her as wife. The defendant denied this."[203] At the next session, the parties remit the contract, which remission, of course, the court accepts.

Even at the distance of more than six hundred years, this looks like a deal that might have happened. As it was, under the pressure of a lawsuit, the parties could not come to some kind of compromise about the house and decided to call the whole thing off. It will be noted that Jean's description of the deal puts Denisette in a passive role. It is what the relatives will do, not what she will do, that is important. In Denisette's version, it is she who will perform the promises. We may be looking at differences in perceptions based on gender, but it is also possible that, two years later, Denisette is more mature and more in control of her own affairs.

There are only two contested cases in which we have some sense of the issue and in which the issue turns out not to be parental consent or the property aspects of the transaction. *Pierre Midi domicilié à la maison de la Contesse à la signe de la Boulaie, paroisse de Saint-Eustache c Jeanette la Drouete*[204] looks like a straightforward factual dispute about who said what: "The plaintiff proposed that he promised the defendant to take her as spouse, and the defendant promised the same on her side, and that the defendant said afterwards that if the plaintiff wanted to contract with another woman, she could impede him. The defendant confessed that the same plaintiff asked her if she wished to be his spouse. She replied to him that she did not."[205] The plaintiff's second claim is significant, for it shows us that whatever the law might have been, the parties who appeared before the court of Paris thought that prior *sponsalia de futuro* impeded a subsequent marriage. In the event, the plaintiff produces six witnesses, who are examined and whose testimony is published. In the later sessions, Jeanette's father, Jean, acts as her proctor. Less than three months after the case has begun, a conclusion is called for and the case is set *ad audiendum ius*. The plaintiff may well have had a case, for no defense is apparent.[206]

Agnesotte la Tristelle c Perrin le Mouscheur clerc[207] is more like the kind of case that we would find at York or Ely. Most of the substantive information about it is found in the initial pleadings:

The plaintiff proposed *sponsalia per verba de futuro*, viz., the same defendant, four years or thereabouts ago, promised the same plaintiff that he would take her to wife and that he would never have another woman as long [as he lived], etc., and that afterwards the same defendant, confessing these things, took many delays in solemnizing this marriage,

[203] Col. 275/8, T&C no. 650.
[204] (20.iii.86 to 1.vi.86), refs. in TCas.
[205] Col. 279/5, T&C no. 651.
[206] Disc. T&C no. 652.
[207] (26.iv.85 to 23.v.86), refs. in TCas.

and he confessed before many that he had affianced this plaintiff, etc. The defendant, joining issue, confessed that [he said] that if he ever took a wife he would never take any woman other than this plaintiff, [and he] denies the rest. [208]

Both parties have both advocates and proctors. Agnesotte produces four witnesses relatively quickly, and their testimony is published. Perrin then goes into 'delay mode'. The second time that he fails to appear, Agnesotte takes security from him, showing clearly that he is a clerk.[209] The case is finally concluded 13 months after it began, and it looks as if Agnesotte has a winning case.[210]

SPONSALIA DE FUTURO CARNALI COPULA SECUTA

As Table 7.3 shows, there are 37 cases in which allegations are made of a marriage formed by *sponsalia de futuro* followed by sexual intercourse. The overwhelming proportion of these cases are brought by women. In the 33 cases that have an identifiable plaintiff, 30 are women (91%), and we will see that even this number probably understates the proportion of female plaintiffs. The table also shows that in 6 of these cases the action is confessed; 16 are deferred to the decisory oath, 15 to the defendant, and 1, quite dramatically, to the plaintiff; 15 of them are contested. Let us consider them in that order.

Four of the six cases that were confessed give no indication of having a plaintiff and were probably brought as office cases, although in all but one, we may suspect that the woman was instrumental in getting the prosecution brought. *Office c Ives Henrici et Martine la Buissonne*[211] is typical:

Considering the confessions of [IH] and [MB] who confessed on either side that they contracted *sponsalia de futuro* around three years ago, sexual intercourse having followed and offspring begotten, they were adjudged one to the other, viz., the woman as wife to the man and the same man as husband to the woman, and they were enjoined under penalty of excommunication and 40 Paris *livres* to have the marriage solemnized in the face of the church within a fortnight, etc.[212]

Office c Martin Couet et Jeanette la Boursiere[213] is similar although it mentions the confession only of the man, does not specify when the *sponsalia* were made, and contains no order to solemnize (which may be buried in the "etc."). *Office c Jean Jaqueti et Adette veuve du défunt Pierre Biaux Hoste*[214] is similar to *Henrici et Buissonne* without the mention of offspring or that the *sponsalia* were *de futuro*, but here the woman is specifically described as "plaintiff," and she pays a fee of 16 *deniers*.

208 Col. 104/2, T&C no. 653.
209 Col. 181/7.
210 Disc. T&C no. 654.
211 (15.vi.85), col. 136/7.
212 Col. 136/7, T&C no. 655.
213 (3.vii.85), col. 148/1, T&C no. 656.
214 (21.v.87), col. 474/2, T&C no. 657.

Jean Couron et Jacquette la Saquete[215] may have begun as an instance case brought by Jacquette, but what we see could equally well have been an office prosecution in which Jean counterclaims for separation, or simply an action by Jean for separation following an otherwise unrecorded judgment of marriage:

There appearing [JC], on one side, and [JS], on the other, who previously had *sponsalia per verba de futuro* between them, sexual intercourse having followed thereupon, [thus] consummating marriage between them, because the woman confessed that afterwards she had committed adultery with Guillaume Boudet, thus sinning against the law of marriage, they were separated by us from goods and bed, etc., [we] decreeing that they ought to live apart. The woman made amends as is contained in the register of Nicolas Charronis. The woman 8 *deniers*; the man 12 *deniers*.

The other two cases that are confessed are clearly instance cases. On 17 February 1386, Colette de Trepye proposed *sponsalia de futuro carnali copula secuta*. Guillaume de Ruppe

confessed that he and the plaintiff had marital promises and dealings (*tractatus*). In these marital dealings, the mother of the said [?plaintiff] promised the defendant twenty *francs*, a furnished bed, and half of the household goods of the mother. In consideration of this promise, he promised to take her [Colette] as wife and not otherwise. Afterwards he knew her carnally once, viz., on [8.vii.85]. He says he is ready to solemnize marriage, satisfaction being made to him about the promise. The plaintiff said that the condition was purified by the sexual intercourse, etc. Hearing this we adjudge this plaintiff to the same [defendant] as spouse and wife, and we adjudge the defendant to the same plaintiff as husband, etc. Each of them, 12 *deniers*.[216]

Colette had the law right, and Guillaume had it rather badly wrong. If Colette knew the law at the time she had intercourse with Guillaume, we might describe her behavior as, at best, underhanded. She may, however, have been told what the law was later. Whichever was the case, Guillaume was quite clearly trapped by his own admission – could we say "his boast of his conquest?" – in court. These parties do not seem to be of very high station or great sophistication. Colette's dowry is modest. (Her father may be dead, though this is not said.) The fees are modest, and the notary took little care with the entry. Nonetheless, the law was applied correctly.

The entry in *Gilette Angot c Giles Vignereux* is similar to that in *Henrici et Buissonne*, with the following exceptions:[217] This is clearly an instance case. Gilette proposes *sponsalia de futuro*, sexual intercourse, and offspring. Giles "confessed that he promised the same plaintiff to take her as wife, so long as this plaintiff did his will, and afterwards he carnally knew her." The couple are pronounced husband and wife, and the defendant is enjoined to solemnize marriage with the plaintiff within a fortnight under penalty of excommunication:

215 (24.iv.85), col. 103/7, T&C no. 658.
216 *Trepye c Ruppe* (17.ii.86), col. 264/6, T&C no. 659.
217 (26.vi.86), col. 323/2, T&C no. 660.

"They make amends for the sexual intercourse as is secured in the register of Ives Caponis."

This is the only case in this group in which it is recorded that the couple are to make amends for the intercourse. While we have seen that amends may not be consistently recorded, it is possible that the court did not regard the formation of a marriage by *sponsalia de futuro* followed by intercourse as necessarily meriting the making of amends. In this regard we might note that the events described by Giles look more like a seduction than an attempt to form a marriage in an informal way. The fact that both are to make amends probably means that the court did not think that Gilette should have allowed herself to be seduced, but the key to the court's attitude, how much each must pay in amends, is missing.

One case not in our group because we classified it as *ex officio* also involves a confession and a fine, but it is a confession by both parties that they did not contract *sponsalia*.[218] It is an odd case from a procedural point of view because it begins with a recognizance. Marguerite d'Auvers quitclaims Jean de Veteriponte of any claim for salary during the period that she stayed with him or otherwise, and Jean quitclaims Marguerite of any claim whatsoever. Marguerite was probably some sort of servant of Jean's. Then Marguerite and Jean assert (no oath is mentioned) that they never made marital promises or pledges of faith, nor did they contract *sponsalia*. They do, however, make amends for concubinage, with a fine being taxed at one *franc* each. Each of them then chooses a domicile, the man at the sign of the Key, in the rue de la Harpe, parish of Saint-Séverin, and the woman before the butcher shop (or the meat market, *Carnificeria*) in the parish of Saint-Christophe, in the City. These places are within walking distance of each other, but the court has at least ensured that they were not claiming to live in the same place and that their claimed residences were separated by a branch of the Seine.[219]

Like the cases of *sponsalia de futuro re integra* where the decisory oath is deferred to the defendant, most of the cases of claims of *sponsalia de futuro carnali copula subsecuta* where the decisory oath is deferred tell us relatively little. The similarity of the formula is apparent from *Jeanne veuve du défunt maître Michel Charronis c Jacques Dourdin*:[220]

In a marriage case the plaintiff proposed *sponsalia per verba de futuro* and marital pledges of faith followed by sexual intercourse. The defendant confessed the carnal matter, denying the rest. Issue having been joined, the plaintiff, asserting by way of an oath that she had no witnesses, deferred the oath to the defendant who swore that he had never contracted *sponsalia* with the plaintiff nor had marital promises [with her], etc. Considering this oath, we absolved the defendant from the claim of the plaintiff, giving [license], etc.

218 (10.i.85), col. 27/4, T&C no. 661.
219 Disc. T&C no. 662.
220 (13.v.85), col. 117/4, T&C no. 663.

As was the situation with deferral cases where the claim was *sponsalia de futuro re integra*, there are minor differences in wording in the formula that probably do not reflect any underlying substantive difference. Sometimes, for example, instead of swearing that she has no witnesses, the plaintiff simply "asserts" (*asserens*) it or "says" (*dicens*) it or just simply defers, or the deferral is grounded in the fact that she has no witnesses ("because she has no witnesses, she deferred").[221]

Two entries radically truncate the form and in the process fail to mention whether the defendant confessed to the intercourse.[222] We suspect that he did not. In one other case with a fuller entry, the defendant denies both the *sponsalia* and the intercourse.[223] These entries also do not mention that license was given.

In two other cases in which license is not mentioned, there are suggestions that the court had doubts about the defendant's oath. In one, the court leaves the matter to the parties' consciences; in the other, it "leaves the other things to him [the defendant]."[224] In one case, heard before the former official, the court says that it neither grants nor denies license.[225]

In fact, the cases that mention the license are a distinct minority. In the three cases in which we know to whom license was given, it is only to the defendant, and in one of these, the grant is quite reluctant: "giving to the man license to contract elsewhere, unless etc. [?he is otherwise impeded], leaving the other things to his conscience."[226] It is not hard to see why license would not be given to the woman in this situation. She has claimed that she is married to the man. She has no witnesses, but presumably in her conscience she believes herself to be married. The decisory oath decides the case, but it does not prove that there was no marriage. This situation is quite different from the case of *sponsalia de futuro re integra*, where the decisory oath may be taken as dissolving any *sponsalia* that there might have been. Whether the fact that the woman does not get license to marry means that she was practically impeded from contracting elsewhere is a difficult question to answer. On a social level, we might wonder whether a woman who had confessed to having intercourse with one man might have difficulty finding another to marry her. On a legal level, we might wonder whether her banns could be reclaimed. This latter possibility does not seem very likely. The most likely reclaimant would be the now-defendant, and in order to reclaim he would have to confess to perjury. While it is possible that witnesses to the prior *sponsalia* and intercourse might appear, the now-plaintiff has been unable to find such witnesses, and so the possibility of their eventual appearance seems remote. Other than the social barriers, then, the largest barrier to the

221 Examples T&C no. 664.

222 *Quintino c Blondelet* (6.viii.87), col. 505/2; *Escrivaigne c Trect* (25.v.85), col. 311/4; both T&C no. 665.

223 *Perigote c Magistri* (n. 221).

224 *Hardie c Cruce* (n. 221) (*cetera sibi relinquendo*); *Doucete c Cambier* (n. 221) (*cetera eorum conscientie* [sic] *relinquentes*).

225 *Fevrier c Drouardi* (17.xi.84), col. 1/1.

226 *Guillarde c Limoges* (27.viii.86), col. 355/3, T&C no. 666, with other examples.

now-plaintiff's contracting elsewhere is likely to have been her conscience and whatever advice she received from her confessor.

As was the case at York with female allegations of *sponsalia de futuro* and intercourse, the man normally admits the intercourse. Sometimes, as in *Charronis c Dourdin*, nothing more is said about this. In eight cases, however, it is specifically said that the parties are to make amends as is secured in one of the registers of amends, and in three we have notes suggesting that the amends were, in fact, made.[227] In one of these cases it is specifically said that the amends are to be made for sexual intercourse (*copula carnalis*), in two it is said to be for concubinage (one under unusual circumstances to be discussed), and in one it is said simply to be for the deed (*factum*) and only the man makes amends.

A few entries tell us more and suggest some variation in fact-patterns. Thomasette *fille de* Jean de Nicochet brought a standard allegation of *sponsalia de futuro carnali copula secuta* against Jean Parvi. He confessed both sexual intercourse and deflowering,[228] denying the *sponsalia*. She deferred the oath to him about the espousals, and, dramatically, he confessed that they had taken place. The parties then voluntarily (*sponte*) affiance each other in court. Then one Jean Blondelli and Thomasette say that Blondelli had spoken to her father about a marriage contract and that the father had promised her to him, on the condition that the relatives of parties on both sides consent. The mother of Blondelli appears and says that the contract does not please her. "Considering the bond, and the sexual intercourse had with [JP]," the entry continues, "him [presumably JB] . . . ," and then the entry breaks off.[229] The only possible result is that Blondelli is absolved from any contractual obligation and that Thomasette and Parvi are ordered to solemnize. Perhaps the official could not make up his mind whether to penalize Thomasette or Blondelli or both.

On its face, it looks as if Parvi, faced with the prospect of perjuring himself, did the right thing. It is just possible, however, that the whole dramatic scene was prearranged. We know that had Thomasette and Parvi simply contracted *re integra*, the court would have dissolved any subsequent contract with Blondelli, even if the contract were not conditional and the conditions not fulfilled. But Thomasette and Parvi may not have known that, and the contract with Parvi may have postdated that with Blondelli. They also may have had no way of knowing what Blondelli's mother was going to say. Indeed, she may not have made up her mind until she heard what Thomasette and Parvi had to say. Once we begin thinking of the possibility that Thomasette and Parvi may have been conspiring, we must also think of the possibility that everything to which they confess is a charade. Did they contract? Did they have intercourse? Perhaps, perhaps not. But if they wanted to thwart what were clearly Jean de Nicochet's plans for Thomasette, the best way to do it, granted the way the Paris court

227 Listed T&C no. 667.

228 For actions where this is an issue, see at nn. 235–50.

229 (4.vi.87), col. 478/6, T&C no. 668.

operated, was to confess to *sponsalia de futuro copula carnali secuta* and to confess in such a way that it looked as if Parvi were reluctant to admit it.

Our estimate of how sophisticated the parties were about the law will also determine our understanding of *Jacquette de Perona résident à la maison de maître Jean de Vesines c Jean Hessepillart résident dans la rue des Rosiers.*[230] The entry is simple: Jacquette proposed *sponsalia de futuro carnali copula secuta* both during the lifetime of her first husband and after his death. Jean confessed the sexual intercourse and denied the rest. Taking the decisory oath, he swore that he never contracted with her. He is absolved from her claim, and the couple make amends for concubinage.

Jacquette might not have known that under her claim as she stated it, she could not have Jean as husband. The marriage is impeded by the diriment impediment of crime (adultery plus promise of marriage during the lifetime of her husband). We can, however, explain her behavior even if she knew about the impediment of crime. Adultery during the lifetime of her husband does not alone impede her subsequent marriage to Jean. It is possible that this was, in modern terminology, a "strike suit." Planning on marrying and knowing that someone will raise the impediment of crime, Jean and Jacquette get a judgment that there was no contract and hence their marriage is not impeded. They have to pay the fine for adultery (called "concubinage"), which they do, but now they have at least an argument that they may marry.

In *Olivette la Rousse c Thomas Voisin alias le Baleur*,[231] the defendant deferred the decisory oath to the plaintiff, who, as one might expect, "swore that they contracted *sponsalia* together, followed by sexual intercourse." "Considering the oath and the confession of the defendant," the entry continues, "who confessed the sexual intercourse, we adjudge ... " And then the entry breaks off. There can be only one result on this record, an adjudication that Olivette and Thomas are husband and wife. If it is not the result of scribal carelessness, the absence of the complete entry may, as in *Nicochet c Parvi*, reflect an indecision on the part of the court as to whether to punish the couple.

Thomas's behavior suggests something that may have been operative in other deferral cases. Thomas took his oath seriously. He was quite willing to admit that he had intercourse with Olivette; he was not willing to admit that he contracted with her. (There may have been some ambiguity about the contract.) He was not, however, willing to imperil his soul by swearing that he did not contract with her. Indeed, if she is willing to put her soul at risk, he will marry her.

Demoiselle Jeanette de Marcheis attempts to prove her case against Martin Sapientis.[232] She introduces five witnesses, but ultimately the court rules that they do not prove the case, and she has to defer to Martin's oath.[233] In addition

230 (21.vi.87), col. 485/3, T&C no. 669.
231 (19.i.87), col. 417/5, T&C no. 670.
232 (30.x.85 to 29.i.86), refs. in TCas.
233 Col. 253/1, T&C no. 671.

to Jeanette's title, there are other indications in this case that the parties are of relatively high status. They both are represented by advocates. The defendant constitutes three proctors and is represented by them for much of the case. He also pays the unusually high fee of four *sous* to take the decisory oath and get his judgment. A hint as to what is involved in this case may be found in the second entry, where the couple, having both admitted that they had intercourse, make amends for "concubinage."[234] While we cannot be sure of the precise import of the term, it normally implies a long-term relationship. Jeanette was Martin's mistress, she wanted to become his wife, and she did not succeed.

Of the 15 contested cases that allege *sponsalia de futuro carnali copula secuta*, 7 involve claims for deflowering or paternity or both. While some of these cases also involve a deferral to a decisory oath, we have grouped them together because of the similarity of the issues that they raise.

Florie la Closiere c Oger le Cordier[235] gives us the most detail about how cases of deflowering were handled in the court of Paris:

> [FC] proposed *sponsalia per verba de futuro carnali copula secuta* and deflowering. The defendant confessed the sexual intercourse and denied the rest. The plaintiff, asserting that she did not have witnesses, deferred the oath to the defendant asking that this defendant be compelled to endow her, etc. The defendant then saying that he could not prove that she was defamed by another deferred the oath to the plaintiff about the deflowering. The oath having been taken on both sides by the parties, etc., we absolved the defendant from the claim of the plaintiff so far as *sponsalia* were concerned but condemned him to endow the girl according to her status.[236]

A day is then set to hear the official's ordinance about the dowry (*super dotem*). The couple make amends for the sexual intercourse as is secured in the register of Alain Audren. Significantly, Audren also serves as Florie's proctor. Florie pays a fee of two *sous*. A week later, the case, described as "a case of dowry" (*causa dotis*), is set down for the following day at prime, with both parties represented by advocates.[237] The following day, Oger is condemned to pay Florie ten *francs* gold for the endowment (*dotalitio*), and to pay half the expenses of maintaining (*nutritura*) their child.[238]

One gets the impression that this couple are of a relatively high status. Florie can afford the standard fee and both an advocate and a proctor (though the latter may have served as her proctor in connection with his duties as a promotor of the court). Perhaps more significant, ten *francs* is a substantial sum of money. It is even possible that the ordinance was made early in the morning to save the couple some embarrassment.

234 Col. 212/1, T&C no. 672.
235 (22–30.x.86), col. 381/4, 384/3, 384/7.
236 Col. 381/4, T&C no. 673.
237 Col. 384/3, T&C no. 674.
238 Col. 384/7, T&C no. 675.

Further light on the nature of this *causa dotis* is cast by *Jaquette Turbete c Robin Jolis clerc*:[239]

The plaintiff proposed that the same defendant had deflowered her, promising to take her as spouse. The defendant denied the *sponsalia* and swore that he never had marital promises with her, and he confessed the carnal matter, not confessing, however, the deflowering. And because the same defendant said the he could not prove that the plaintiff was deflowered by another he was condemned to endow her according to the means and status of each party or to take her as wife. Defendant 2 *deniers*; plaintiff 16 *deniers*.[240]

Robin then gives Jaquette security in the standard form. At the next session Robin is contumacious, but a day later Jaquette appears and acquits Robin generally, saying that she has received six *francs* from him for the deflowering.

This action is not well attested in the canonists and seems to have operated largely on the basis of the practice of individual courts. "Deflowering" (*defloratio*) presumably means having sexual intercourse with a female virgin. Florie also became pregnant as a result of this event, but so far as we can tell, Jacquette did not, and it probably would have been mentioned, and an allocation of costs made for caring for the child, if she had. The question is whether there were any other requirements that the woman had to meet in order to make the claim, such as being under a certain age or in paternal power. No additional requirements are mentioned in the six deflowering cases that we have, though others may have been assumed.[241] Another way of posing this question is to note that 37 women are involved in claims of *sponsalia de futuro carnali copula secuta*. Virtually all the men in these cases confess to the sexual intercourse; did only six of these women have plausible claims to having been virgins at the time?

What the two cases described here do show is that where the woman claims to have been deflowered and the man admits the intercourse, the man has the burden of coming forward with evidence that she was not a virgin at the time. In the first case, the man defers the decisory oath on this issue to the plaintiff; in the second case, the entry simply says that because he had no proof that she was not a virgin, he is condemned to pay the dowry.[242]

That the court did not always put the burden of producing evidence about virginity on the man is indicated by *Cassotte la Joye c Jean Ayore*,[243] where Cassotte claimed *sponsalia de futuro cum carnali copula*, deflowering, and subsequent offspring. The man confessed the intercourse and the offspring, took the decisory oath on the *sponsalia*, and was absolved with a highly unusual note "and the woman was inhibited from getting in the man's way (*ne impediat*) any further."[244] The only reason I can think of for the difference in the way that

239 (9–22.iii.85), col. 73/2, 84/2, 85/6.
240 Col. 73/2, T&C no. 676.
241 The five cases discussed here and *Nicochet c Parvi* (n. 229).
242 Disc. T&C no. 677.
243 *Joye c Ayore* (20.xii.86), col. 405/3.
244 Col. 405/3, T&C no. 678.

this case was handled vis-à-vis the two previous cases was that the court knew that Cassotte was not a virgin at the time (a possibility that may be suggested by her surname) or, more broadly, that she was not the sort of woman who could claim to have been deflowered.

The other two cases of claimed deflowering do not add much to our knowledge of how the action regularly proceeded. Jeanette la Gabonne claimed against Jean Haudria *sponsalia de futuro carnali copula secuta* and deflowering. Jean confessed the intercourse and denied the *sponsalia* and the deflowering, but the entry does not go beyond the pleading stage to tell us who had to prove what and how.[245]

Similarly, on 7 December 1386, Margot la Goudine claimed *sponsalia de futuro carnali copula secuta* against Guillaume Lamberti, clerk.[246] Guillaume confessed that he had carnal knowledge of Margot in August three years previously and denied the rest. (The reason for the specificity about this will become apparent shortly.) After the case was set for making positions, Margot "protested" (a word that normally means reserving the right to raise an issue at a later time) concerning dowry for deflowering. The entry also tells us that Margot was represented by an advocate. After one entry in which Margot excused herself for reasons unstated, the case was postponed until February, *ex officio*, by reason of the fact that Margot was engaged in childbirth.[247] We can be confident that this child was not the result of the intercourse to which Guillaume confessed. In February, Guillaume fails to appear and the case does not get going again until March, at which point Margot drops her claim of *sponsalia* and claims forty *livres* for dowry and deflowering.[248] The same entry tells that Guillaume gave security to one Jean du Fossé, who is otherwise unidentified. A couple of sessions are devoted to Guillaume's claim that he should be reimbursed for his expenses in defending the part of the suit that was dropped. In June, Margot fails to appear, and the case disappears from view.

We cannot tell why it is that Margot, with the advice of counsel, did not present her claim for deflowering as part of the initial lawsuit, nor can we be sure that Jean du Fossé was involved in Margot's action. (Jean could simply have taken advantage of Guillaume's appearance in court to take security about an unrelated matter.) If, however, Jean was the father of Margot's current child, there is a plausible explanation for how this litigation proceeded. Jean is willing, perhaps reluctantly, to do right by Margot, perhaps even to marry her. But he knows that Margot has a past, and he insists that she get what she can from Guillaume. If she can get him to marry her, then Jean is off the hook. But by March it is apparent that Guillaume is not willing to marry her, and Margot has no proof of her claim. Hence, the next best thing is to put pressure on Guillaume by an exaggerated claim for a dowry (a claim quite out of proportion with the

245 (7.xii.85), col. 233/2.
246 (7.xii.86 to 7.vi.87), col. 400/1 (T&C no. 679); further refs. in TCas.
247 Col. 406/1, T&C no. 680.
248 Col. 440/9, T&C no. 681.

awards that we know the court usually gave). We do not know how the case came out, but we may suspect that it was compromised.

A case that I have classified as *ex officio* (and hence is not included in group of cases of *sponsalia carnali copula secuta*) shows how the elements of deflowering, paternity, and *sponsalia* could be combined:

> Today, considering the confession of Étienne Anselli of Quiers [Seine-et-Marne]... who confessed that he had known the girl [Jeanette *fille de* Milet Malyverne] carnally and that he had not heard or knew that she was defamed by anyone else, as he says, denying *sponsalia*, he was condemned to endow the girl, to guide (*gubernandam*) her in childbirth, to pay half the expenses of maintaining the daughter procreated by him, and he made amends for the deed.... Afterwards, because he promised that he would take the girl to wife, the fine was remitted."[249]

The fact that the court knows that the child is a girl suggests that the "guidance" that Étienne is to give Jeanette in childbirth is financial.

Another *ex officio* case brought against Jean Treachedenier involves elements of adultery (and, hence, not of *sponsalia*), deflowering, and paternity:[250]

> Today, [JT] made amends for adultery with [Jeanette la Piquete] and the deflowering of this [JP], as is secured in the register of [Gautier de Lingonis], and [JP] appeared and said that she did not intend to stand in the way of (*impedire*) or prosecute this [JT] by reason of her said deflowering and this was by the will and consent of this [JP], etc. [JT] moreover promised to pay the same [JP] ten *livres* at the will of this [JP] for the deflowering, and sustain her in childbirth and to have her churched out of his money.

The care with which Jeanette's will is consulted, at least in the rhetoric of the entry, will be noted, as will the fact that Jean did not agree to pay for the maintenance of the child. Instead, he agreed to a substantial capital sum plus the expenses of childbirth and churching. (The latter could not have been an expensive proposition, and the fact that it is mentioned suggests that the settlement was carefully negotiated.)

Two other contested cases of *sponsalia de futuro carnali copula secuta* involve claims of paternity, without a claim of deflowering. *Eloïse de Villaribus domicilié à sa maison à la signe de l'Horloge dans la rue des Arcis, paroisse de Saint-Merry c Jean Tartas*[251] is the less interesting of the two. On 26 August 1385, Eloïse entered a standard claim to which Jean replied with the standard response, denying the *sponsalia* but confessing the intercourse. Both parties are represented by advocates. After the case is set for making positions, the entry notes that "[t]he plaintiff asserted that she is pregnant by the man, and the same man confessed that he had known her carnally; the offspring was adjudged, etc. (*fuit adiudicatus partus*)."[252] This would suggest that where a woman claimed paternity and the man admitted that he had intercourse with

[249] (10.x.85), col. 200/3, T&C no. 682.
[250] (19.iv.85), col. 100/2, T&C no. 683.
[251] (19.viii.85 to 27.i.86), refs. in TCas.
[252] Col. 176/3, T&C no. 684.

her, no further inquiry was made as to whether the offspring was the man's child. It was so adjudged, and as a consequence, other cases suggest, the man paid for the expenses of the woman's lying-in and half the cost of maintaining the child.[253]

The rest of the case is long and uninformative. The plaintiff produced two witnesses quite quickly, and their testimony was published. In the middle of September, the plaintiff constituted a proctor, another indication along with her residence and her appointment of an advocate that she was not poor. On 14 October, the case was set as it had been before "in hope of peace."[254] But peace did not result. Rather, the defendant introduced new facts (which are not stated), and witnesses were introduced, examined, and, apparently, published about them. At the end of January, the case was set for sentencing and, as is usual, we do not know what the sentence was.

Isabelle veuve du défunt Colin Chambellant c Colin Monachi[255] tells us more in less space. Isabelle proposed that during the lifetime of her husband she and the defendant made marital promises to each other, followed by sexual intercourse and the begetting of offspring. Colin admitted the intercourse, both before and after the death of the husband, and that he told Isabelle before the death of her husband that if he knew her husband was dead, he would contract with her. But then the husband appeared and resumed cohabitation with her.[256] A subsequent entry tells us that Isabelle deferred the decisory oath to Colin, but we do not know the contents of the oath. Rather, the final entry gives us the result:[257]

> Today we declared the *sponsalia* and marriage [contracted] *de facto* between [IC] and [CM] with sexual intercourse, etc., to be null, considering that during the lifetime of the first husband of the *actrix* the parties had marital promises with each other, followed then by sexual intercourse; in costs having been compensated, etc.[258] The same man is condemned to pay half the costs of maintaining a certain daughter procreated between them, whom the woman swore was engendered by the man, etc., with the parties supported on both sides by advocates.

Both parties were represented by advocates, it would seem, from the beginning of the case. Hence, it is hard to believe that Isabelle did not know that what she alleged could not result in a marriage between them because, as was finally adjudicated, of the impediment of crime. Perhaps she did know this but was too honest not to say what had really happened. Perhaps, too, her motivation for bringing the suit was to get what she finally achieved, a judgment of paternity and child support. It is even possible that she wanted a judgment that

253 There are three paternity cases in the register in which marriage is not implicated. See T&C no. 685.
254 Col. 202/5, T&C no. 686.
255 (12.i.86 to 6.ii.86), col. 245/1, 248/5, 256/4, 259/7.
256 Col. 245/1, T&C no. 687.
257 Col. 259/7, T&C no. 688.
258 Disc. T&C no. 689.

she did not have to marry Colin. Colin's initial response is more likely to have been what his advocate told him to say. By alleging the ambiguous promise, he is setting himself up to move in a number of different directions: First, the marriage is not impeded by the impediment of crime because either (a) they did not actually promise or (b) he did not know that she had a living husband. Second, since he has an argument that he never promised, he could be arguing that he has no obligation to marry Isabelle now. It then turns out that Isabelle offers no proof, and all will depend on Colin's oath. At this point, however, it would seem, considering the result in the case, that Colin has to admit that what Isabelle says is true. They did promise during the lifetime of her husband, and so marriage between them is not possible. Judgment on the question of paternity then turns on Isabelle's oath. There is no suggestion that because she had a living husband, he is presumed to be the father.

A number of the contested cases of *sponsalia de futuro carnali copula secuta* that do not allege deflowering or paternity raise interesting complexities. To Jeanette de Curte's standard-form complaint that they had contracted and had intercourse a year previously in Lent,[259] Étienne Ruffit replied that he had promised to take her as wife so long as her husband was dead at that time, and intercourse followed.[260] "And to the end that he might be absolved, etc.," the entry continues, "he proposed that her husband was then alive and still lived, the plaintiff asserting to the contrary." The entry later notes that she said that her husband had died five years previously. The couple made amends for the deed (*factum*), and the case was set down for a month later, both for the court to inform itself about the death of the husband and for the plaintiff to prove it. But at the next session, where Jeanette is described as the daughter of the deceased Étienne l'Escot, and the wife of "the deceased, as is said on her side," Guillaume de Curte, Jeanette does not appear, and the case disappears from view.[261]

Both parties were represented by advocates and, as in *Chambellant c Monachi*, the pleading, particularly on the man's side, is interesting. In order to avoid the impediment of crime, we might imagine, Étienne alleges that his promise was conditional. If the condition has not been fulfilled, he, of course, is not married to Jeanette, but he still may marry her. He is, in short, keeping his options open. If this is the nature of the argument, it is certainly a dangerous argument because the subsequent intercourse would normally have purged the condition, making the couple now open to the charge that marriage between them now would be impeded by the impediment of crime. Also interesting is the statement that Étienne pleaded that Guillaume was alive, "to the end that he be absolved," presumably of his contract. This suggests that he was not asserting the truth of his statement, perhaps in order to avoid confessing adultery. That,

[259] Disc. T&C no. 690.
[260] (18.vi.–23.vii.86), col. 319/1 (T&C no. 691), 342/1.
[261] Col. 342/1, T&C no. 692.

in turn, raises the question of just what "the deed" (*factum*) was for which they made amends. The phrase seems to have a wide semantic range;[262] here, it may refer to attempting to marry without knowing whether the woman's former husband is dead.

Was Guillaume de Curte dead? We cannot know. On this record, however, it is probably safe to say that Jeanette could not prove that he was dead. The other possibility, that Étienne persuaded her not to come back to court so that he would not have to marry her, seems far-fetched on this record.

Jean Milot c Thomasette fille du défunt Théobald le Champenoys[263] is unusual in this group of cases because it was brought by a man. To a standard-form complaint Thomasette replies that Jean raped her (*eam carnaliter cognoverat ipsa invita*) and that there were no *sponsalia*. Jean, alone, makes amends for the sexual intercourse. (Nothing is said about the rape, but that may have been taken into account in setting the fine, which he apparently paid.) He is also inhibited under penalty of excommunication and 10 *livres* not to defame or assault (*ne diffamet aut iniuriet*) Thomasette in any way. He fails to appear at the next session, and the case disappears from view.

We have the impression that Jean, despite the fact that he can afford an advocate, does not have much money. The penal sum that the court sets is lower than most (40 *livres* is standard, and one does find 100 *livres*). We also have the impression that the court did not take the charge of rape very seriously. Jean does not, for example, have to buy his way out of the bishop's prison, as do some bigamists. This lack of seriousness may have been produced by one or some combination of the following facts: that the court did not believe Thomasette (although it believed her enough not to require her to make amends for the sexual intercourse), that she did not allege physical force, that responsibility for punishing rape lay with the secular courts, or that the law on the topic was unclear.[264]

To Jeannette la Bretelle's allegations of *sponsalia de futuro*, pledges of faith in the face of the church, and subsequent sexual intercourse, Pierre Cochon confesses all.[265] The court orders him to solemnize the marriage but apparently suspends its order to allow him to propose facts to impede the marriage. We never find out what these facts were (the entry where they should have been proposed is not recorded), but they were clearly enough, on their face, to constitute a diriment impediment because he is allowed, over the course of the next month, to introduce nine witnesses to them. The case is set to publish the testimony when it disappears from view. Of numerous possible outcomes, it seems most likely that Pierre realized that his witnesses had not proven what he hoped they would prove. Whether this means that he settled with Jeanette

[262] Examples T&C no. 693.
[263] (6–13.vii.86), col. 331/5 (T&C no. 694), 335/6.
[264] Disc. T&C no. 695.
[265] (2.i.–10.ii.85), col. 21/5 (T&C no. 696), 40/4, 46/1, 51/3.

financially or actually married her we cannot tell. It may have been the latter, because the procedural posture of the case was that he was under an order to solemnize unless he could prove facts to impede the marriage.

Another case brought by a man is an appeal, though the record does not say from whom. Pierre d'Abbeville claimed that he had had intercourse with Guillemette la Clemente after *sponsalia* and petitioned that he be allowed to visit her.[266] One Odin Ravenel, who claims to be Guillemette's proctor (he is not one of the regular proctors of the court), argues that the petition should not be granted. Odin is enjoined not to marry Guillemette to someone else *pendente lite*. (This order suggests that he is her guardian.) The court sets the case to join issue on a petition handed over in the interim "by the means of an act" (*per modum acti*). This phrase is unclear, but it may mean that the libel or petition in the lower court is to be reduced to the form of a judicial act, on which the joinder of issue will take place. Guillemette is ordered to appear "if conveniently, etc." (*si comode* [sic], *etc*). Whether this means that she is ill, pregnant, very young, or of such high status that it would be embarrassing for her to appear is unclear. Guillemette does not appear at the next session, but she does appear at the third, the only one at which Pierre does not appear. In the meantime, the litigation goes badly for Pierre. At the second session, he is condemned to pay Guillemette's proctor expenses because he has failed to produce the *actum*. At the third session, he fails to appear. At the fourth, he renounces the litigation and the appeal.

We will never know what happened between Guillemette and Pierre. What does seem clear is that those around her are making some effort to prevent her from seeing Pierre. They seem to have succeeded, and Pierre gives up.

Two other cases give us some detail in the pleadings. Marion la Hutine *domiciliée à la rue du Plâtre-au-Marais* claimed against Jaquin Gast that four years previously they had contracted marriage by *sponsalia* followed by sexual intercourse and that on the preceding Wednesday they had kissed and called each other married. Jaquin confessed to having had intercourse with Marion once and denied the *sponsalia*.[267] The case does not get beyond the positions, and Marion apparently abandons it after four sessions. The interest in it lies in the detail that Marion provides about what happened the previous Wednesday. It is legally irrelevant, except perhaps as an element of proof. It may not, however, be socially irrelevant. Marion seems to have been willing to forget the events that happened four years previously until her hopes were raised by Jaquin's behavior toward her the Wednesday before she appeared in court.

Argentine Martine alleged that *maître* Thomas Guist had affianced her 16 years previously in Bruges.[268] Sexual intercourse followed, the date of which is vague. The fact, however, that the couple are said to have "otherwise made amends for the sexual intercourse, as is secured in the register of *maître* Jacques

[266] (31.iii.–23.v.86), col. 285/4 (T&C no. 697), 292/1, 297/4, 310/1.
[267] (3–23.ii.86), col. 256/5 (T&C no. 698), 261/6, 264/2, 268/2.
[268] (27.ii.– 30.iv.86), col. 268/8 (T&C no. 699), 271/5, 276/4, 297/5.

de Tornaco"[269] suggests that it took place in Paris and probably relatively recently. Thomas concedes the intercourse and denies the *sponsalia*. Argentine produces four witnesses, and the parties agree on an examiner for the witnesses outside the diocese.[270] Argentine then apparently abandons the case.

As we noted in the case of Ely, proving events that took place out of the jurisdiction of the court was difficult but not impossible. When we combine this fact with the difficulty of proving something that had happened 16 years previously, we can see why Argentine may have abandoned her case. It would have been particularly difficult for someone who was poor to do so, but there is no evidence that this was Argentine's situation. Indeed, one of her witnesses calls himself *magister* and another describes herself as *domina de la Selle*.[271]

Guiot aux Feves c Guillemette la Guimpliere[272] is the strangest case in this group, and the legal maneuverings that it involves are not completely recoverable from the record. On 11 November 1385, Guiot brought "a case of absolution" against Guillemette, and he began by confessing that he had sexual intercourse with her after *sponsalia* had been contracted. The case is set to declare Guiot's petition. Over the next couple of entries it appears that his claim is that Guillemette committed adultery. Issue is joined on this question, and Guiot is absolved on the condition that he prove the adultery within a month. (After this the record calls the case a "marriage case.")[273] Guiot produces 15 witnesses whose testimony is, apparently, published. At this point Guillemette goes into 'delay mode', and she ultimately fails to appear in two sessions at the end of January and the beginning of February 1386. The case is not recorded again until 30 October, where we read: "Today we decreed that [GG], who had been excommunicated, aggravated and reaggravated by our authority for debt (*pro re*) at the instance of [GF], be absolved, on the ground of the wretched *cessio bonorum* that she made today, saving nonetheless the principal and expenses, and [GG] consented that the expenses be taxed in her absence, etc., which are taxed at five *sous* and in letters *nisi*, twelve *livres*."[274]

In the practice of the court of Paris, a case of absolution was a case brought by someone who had been excommunicated, frequently for debt. He sought to be absolved from the excommunication, and he often got this absolution by making a cession of goods (only in this case is it called "wretched" [*miserabilis*]), a kind of bankruptcy, which served to lift the excommunication but left the remaining obligation if the plaintiff in the absolution case came into better fortune.[275] This case begins as one of absolution, and it ends with a cession of goods, but its pattern is far from that of regular absolution cases. Guiot

269 One of the promotors of the court, e.g., col. 141, 144.
270 Jean Colombier, col. 271/5, disc. T&C no. 700.
271 Col. 271/5, T&C no. 701.
272 (11.xi.85), refs. in TCas.
273 Col. 230/5.
274 Col. 384/6, T&C no. 702.
275 Even this is not completely clear, but it seems to be the main thrust of the entries in these cases. Listed T&C no. 703.

confesses at the beginning of the case that he is married to Guillemette. He may not have confessed this before, and any previous litigation between them probably lies before the beginning of the book. He is seeking absolution, presumably from excommunication, but it is an absolution that he seeks to obtain by showing that Guillemette committed adultery. So far as I know, the only obligations that could be dissolved by adultery were the obligations to solemnize a marriage or to cohabit after a marriage, and we may strongly suspect that the excommunication from which Guiot sought absolution was an excommunication for failure to do one or the other. That this was the excommunication in question is certainly suggested by the court's order that Guiot be absolved so long as he proves the adultery within a month "otherwise he is to be forced back into the present sentence," that is, that he is excommunicated until he obeys the order that gave rise to the excommunication.[276]

Apparently, the 15 witnesses proved the adultery, though no ruling to that effect is recorded, because Guillemette immediately goes on the defensive and ultimately disappears. The final entry, separated from the previous one by more than eight months, suggests that in the intervening period Guillemette had been excommunicated. (The sentences were probably recorded in the register of sentences.) She could have been excommunicated for her contumacy, but it is hard to see how that would have led to a cession of goods, and the entry specifically says that she was excommunicated *pro re*, a phrase that in other entries seems to mean "for debt." She does not have the wherewithal to pay; she is absolved of her excommunication by making a cession of goods, but she remains liable for five *sous* in costs and for twelve *livres* that are secured by penal letters *nisi*.[277] What is the source of this debt, the principal sum of which seems to be twelve *livres*? The record does not say, but it could have been payments that Guiot made to Guillemette in connection with the marriage or her dowry (which she would have forfeited to Guiot for adultery), which she somehow had lost before it was transferred to Guiot. The former seems to be slightly more likely.

Guillemette's adultery cost her dearly. The record suggests that she was too ashamed to appear at the final session of the case.

Alison la Maillarde c Robin Anglici[278] is the longest case in this group (31 entries over 10 months), but the record tells us relatively little. The pleadings are standard: Alison proposes *sponsalia de futuro carnali copula secuta*; Robin admits the intercourse and denies the *sponsalia*. Robin corrects an answer that he made to a position, a correction that allows us to see that among other things, the positions required the parties to assess the characters of the adversaries.[279] Alison produces four or five witnesses (the record is a bit unclear) whose testimony is ultimately published. Robin requests that the witnesses be

[276] Col. 220/1, T&C no. 704.
[277] Disc. T&C no. 705.
[278] (4.i.85 to 7.x.85), refs. in TCas.
[279] Col. 26/9, T&C no. 706.

reexamined, a request the ruling on which is never given. Ultimately, he produces seven witnesses on his side, and the case ends with the publication of his witnesses.

Toward the end of the case, there is one indication that the court was getting annoyed with the delay: "and the defendant shall take care to have his witnesses [before the examiner]; otherwise they [the witnesses previously examined] will be published," an event that would preclude his producing more.[280] The threat, however, is mild and produces the desired effect. The line between a careful defense and delay is a thin one, and Robin and his proctor did not go far over the line.

Alison is well represented throughout the case. At one point she constitutes four proctors.[281] Robin has proctorial representation, and at one point he confesses that N. Domicelli is not his advocate, suggesting that he may have consulted him. Domicelli served as *locumtenens* for the official and, as such, must have been one of the senior advocates of the court.[282] All of this suggests that the parties knew what they were doing, so that when the case disappeared from view after the witnesses on both sides had been published, they had a pretty good idea what the result was going to be. The problem with such a record, of course, is that we do not.

Sexual intercourse, unaccompanied by any suggestion of marital promises, was, of course, fornication, an ecclesiastical crime. The Paris court seems not to have concerned itself with routine fornication prosecutions. These, we might imagine, were dealt with by the archdeacons, as they clearly were in a later period,[283] and they may also have been dealt with by the promotors of the court in their registers and not entered in the register of the official. There are three cases of prosecution for concubinage in the register. One has been treated already because it involved possible *sponsalia*.[284] In another we are informed that Marguerite Guilloti, the servant of *dominus* Guillaume, the farmer of the church of Saint-Josse, made amends for concubinage with the deceased Vital de Brucelles 10 years previously.[285] She is, "in place of fine and as a measure of the fault to place a candle of one pound of wax before the church of Sainte-Marie of [. . .]," and here the entry breaks off. We may suspect that this case came before the court because a priest could not have such a woman as a servant if the offense had gone unamended.

The third case gives us interesting details about the couple but no indication why the couple came before the court. Jean le Gaigneur, a weaver of cloth, who chose his domicile in the house at (the sign of) the shield of Flanders in the rue de la Grande-Truanderie, and Gilette la Badoise, residing near the sign of

280 Col. 193/1, T&C no. 707.
281 Col. 92/1.
282 Col. 4, 45, 128.
283 See Pommeray, *Officialité archidiaconale*, 372–400; disc. T&C no. 708.
284 *Office c Veteriponte et Auvers* (at nn. 218–19).
285 (31.vii.87), col. 504/5, T&C no. 709.

the Bear and the Lion, in the parish of Saint-Pierre-aux-Boeufs (la Cité) made amends for concubinage together.[286] They apparently paid the fine, but that is all that is said.

SPONSALIA DE PRESENTI AND AMBIGUOUS *SPONSALIA*; MISCELLANEOUS TYPES OF SPOUSALS LITIGATION

We group together here cases in which *sponsalia de presenti* are alleged or may have been alleged and miscellaneous types of spousals litigation, notably cases of jactitation. We have already noted that cases involving *sponsalia de presenti* are rare, certainly when compared to English cases in which such allegations are found. The fullest such case also contains indications as to why the allegation is so rarely found.

On 6 February 1385, Huet Ringart, *clerc domicilié à la maison à la signe du Gros tournois dans la rue des Prêcheurs, paroisse de Saint-Eustache*, brought suit against Étiennette *fille de* Gérard Bersaut with a complaint that looks like a quite standard one of *sponsalia de futuro*.[287] Étiennette's response is also quite standard: "She confessed that he asked her to be his spouse, and that she replied to him that she would do nothing without the consent of her father and mother, and that she would do what pleased them."[288] As was quite common in such cases, the father and mother appear and swear that the marriage does not please them. Somewhat less common, but certainly not unprecedented, is Étiennette's final "protestation" that if she said any words savoring of the force of espousals she reserved the right to revoke and renounce them because she is [or was] under age.[289]

Two entries 11 days later cast a quite different light on Huet's claim:

> Because the plaintiff had proposed in his act [this could refer to the positions that were then being answered, or it could refer to the complaint that Villemaden had "sanitized" before he entered it] that he had contracted clandestine marriage with the defendant, viz., by *verba de presenti*, the defendant by voice of her counsel asked that the plaintiff be declared excommunicate, since by the synodal statutes, those who contract clandestine marriage are excommunicated, etc., and be precluded from bringing the case (*repelli ab agendo*), this sentence of excommunication standing in the way.... We, however, informed about the synodal statutes, declared that the plaintiff, excommunicated by the authority of the synodal statutes, be absolved, there intervening a fine that he has pledged, as is secured in the register of Alain Audren.[290]

From a procedural point of view, the exception is well taken. A person who was excommunicated could not plead in an ecclesiastical court (indeed, he or

286 (21.iii.85), col. 83/1.

287 (6.ii.85 to 6.x.85), refs. in TCas. That Huet is a clerk is indicated by the standard-form security that he gives to Gérard Bersaut, col. 130/2.

288 Col. 47/4, T&C no. 710.

289 Col. 47/4, T&C no. 711.

290 The entries are in reverse order but are clearly to be read together. See T&C no. 712.

she was not supposed to be able to plead in any court). We have already seen the statutes (or their ancestors) to which Éienette's counsel was referring.[291] The procedure, however, was flexible. A court could absolve someone from an excommunication temporarily in order to allow him to bring a case, or, as here, it could absolve him permanently upon his making amends. We will have occasion to discuss later how serious a barrier these statutes posed to the bringing of spousals litigation in the Paris court. Suffice it to say here that it was a barrier, a barrier that might have encouraged litigants to frame their complaints in terms of *sponsalia de futuro*, where it would not have made a difference in the result.[292]

The rest of the case seems to focus more on Étienette's age than on the nature of the *sponsalia*, although the entries are sufficiently cryptic that it is hard to tell. Étienette reclaims the contract on no less than four separate occasions, something which she, of course, could do if she were underage at the time she made it.[293] Huet produces seven witnesses, one of whom claims to be the servant-woman of the herald of France at the gate of Paris (*pedisecca scuti Francie in porta Parisius*), and Étienette, with her father's permission, constitutes four proctors.[294] Ultimately, Huet also constitutes a proctor. Further entries mention three more witnesses of Huet, including two women, one a former servant of Gérard, who are said to be "in remote parts."[295] The deposition of at least one of these is ultimately published, as are, apparently, the depositions of all the other witnesses. In June, Huet gives security to Gérard. The last entry, on 6 October 1385, sets the case down for an interlocutory sentence, which, apparently, effectively decided the case, because no more is heard of it thereafter.

It looks as if Huet had a plausible case. He may well have contracted with Étienette *per verba de presenti*. She, in turn, cannot have been much older than 12 in order to make her claim that she is (or was) underage plausible. Her father, at least initially, is adamantly opposed to the marriage. The fact that he takes security from Huet toward the end of the case, however, suggests that some financial negotiations were taking place between them. Étienette, so far as the record shows, never presented witnesses. She may not have had any, but that seems unlikely considering that she is defending the case on the grounds of nonage. It may well be that the case was compromised, though whether that compromise resulted in a marriage we cannot tell.

The other two cases that contain specific mention of *sponsalia de presenti* are less informative. Annette la Bordiere, *domiciliée à la maison l'Alemant à Choisy-le-Roi* (Val-de-Marne), proposed *sponsalia per verba de presenti*, which Jean le Normant denied, but at the second session she had to defer the decisory oath to Jean, and both parties were given license, as in a standard

291 Ch 1, at nn. 85–6.
292 See the discussion in the conclusion to this chapter.
293 Col. 64/8, 81/4, 98/4, 115/2.
294 Col. 64/8.
295 T&C no. 713, with disc.

de futuro deferral case.[296] Jean Bernardi's claim against Marion *fille de* Jean le Coeffier *alias* le Champenoys was more successful. He proposed *sponsalia de futuro* and *de presenti*, which she confessed. The couple was ordered to solemnize within a month.[297] Neither case mentions a penalty for clandestinely contracting marriage.

Annette was a country woman, who may have been misinformed about what to say. She also may have been poor. She was never charged a fee, whereas Jean was charged eight *deniers* for the first session and two *sous* for the second. The court treated the case exactly as it would have treated a deferred case of *sponsalia de futuro*. We can be less sure that Jean Bernardi was ill-informed. He may have deliberately raised the stakes in the face of unrecorded parental resistance. Again, however, the court behaved exactly as it would have in a case of confessed *sponsalia de futuro*.[298]

There are four cases in which the *sponsalia* are not described as *de presenti*, but the way in which they were described suggests that they might have been. *Jeanne fille de Guillaume de Coloigne c Jacquet de Bouloigne* is the clearest of these cases.[299] On 31 January 1386, Jeanne proposed "that the parties and their relatives in their names made marital promises with each other, and then the defendant took the hand of the plaintiff saying to her that from that time (*ex tunc*) he would hold her and take her as wife." This formula is one that many canonists would have regarded as a present one, though it is not mentioned that Jeanne said the same thing. Jacquet has a somewhat different version of the story:

> The defendant confessed that the relatives of the plaintiff and defendant made promises of marriage to be contracted between the parties, if this condition were fulfilled, viz., that the father of the girl promised to hand over to him [the defendant] 50 *livres* of Paris before the contract and promised to pay 50 more after the contract, viz., before the feast of St John the Baptist next to come, and the same father had to oblige himself to this along with another guarantor, etc. He denied the rest.

Jacquet's pleading is not completely clear. He could be claiming that the conditions were to be fulfilled by the previous feast of St John (24 June 1385) and, hence, that he is no longer obliged, or he could be claiming that they had to be filled by the coming feast of St John (24 June 1386), in which case he is claiming that he is not yet obliged. Whether the words spoken were one of the present or future tenses would make no difference as to the obligation, but if they were of the present tense and if the conditions were future ones, he would be more than obliged if they were fulfilled; he would be married. After positions were exchanged, the parties came to a clarification of the issue: Jacquet now may be speaking only of 50 *livres*, and he says that he is prepared to marry

[296] (13–23.vi.85), col. 135/3 (*actor proposuit sponsalia per verba de presenti; lite ex parte rei negative contestata . . .*), 142/1.

[297] (10.x.85), col. 200/1, T&C no. 714.

[298] Disc. T&C no. 715.

[299] *Coloigne c Bouloigne* (31.i.–17.xi.86), col. 255/1 (T&C no. 716); further refs. in TCas.

Jeanne if they are paid. Jeanne insists that "he promised to take her to wife, simply and without condition."[300] This clarification of the issue has all the hallmarks of a compromise. Jacquet gives up his claim to the 50 *livres*, and Jeanne hers to the *de presenti* contract.

The case does not get very far with the proof stage. Jacquet fails to appear on 30 April, and the case does not appear again until 17 November, when Jeanne and Jacquet enter a standard-form remission of their "promises by words of the future tense," which the court admits.[301]

Did Jeanne and Jacquet exchange words of the present tense? They may have, but the financial arrangements were important to Jacquet, and they were probably important to Jeanne, too. If the financial arrangements could not be worked out, as clearly they were not, then they are better off having conditional *sponsalia de futuro*, because we know that the Paris court routinely allowed a couple to remit such *sponsalia*. It probably would have dissolved conditional *sponsalia de presenti* if the condition were not fulfilled, but it might have insisted on clear proof of the conditions and their nonfulfillment. Casting the case in terms of conditional *sponsalia de futuro* probably gave the couple (and their relatives) more flexibility. It was a flexibility of which they took advantage.

If the handfasting described in *Coloigne c Bouloigne* is similar to that which we find in some of the English cases, and perhaps quite traditional, the next two cases give us details about handfastings that suggest customary arrangements that could not be generalized. Jean Tiphania and Amelotte la Fevresse, whom we later learn was the widow of one Chrétien (Pierre) Fabri, appeared before the official on 30 June 1386 and told the following strange story:[302]

> While they were staying together in the house of Étienne de Meneville at Domont (Val-d'Oise) last Lent, and their master (?Étienne) bought them some shoes, the woman said to the same Jean that her[303] shoes were too small and that the shoes of Jean were good for her. The same man said that if she wished they would exchange their shoes in the name of marriage. [But] they did not exchange shoes. [Rather,] they then exchanged hands in the name of matrimony. They asked that license be given them to contract elsewhere if that were possible and to acquit each other of this. They wished nonetheless, etc. [?to do what was right].

The final "etc." in this entry is annoying, but if we have filled it in correctly, we can imagine that the official told them either that they had contracted *de presenti* or that the obligations of handfasting were serious ones that they ought not remit. Whichever it was, when we next see the case, Jean is described as plaintiff and Amelotte is to obtain a certificate of the death of her former husband. This is obtained, and in the next entry, Amelotte and Jean are adjudged to be *sponsi* on the basis of testimonial letters from the *curé* of Roman (Eure) approved by letters of the official of Évreux. The naïve couple from the country,

300 Col. 263/1, T&C no. 717.
301 Col. 392/4, T&C no. 718.
302 (30.v to 16.vii.86), col. 326/4 (T&C no. 719), 327/2, 336/7.
303 Disc. T&C no. 720.

who seem to have thought that exchanging shoes might have something to do with getting married, prove themselves to be quite competent when it comes to bringing in proof of the death of the woman's first husband.[304]

Étienne Derot *domicilié à sa maison à la signe de l'image de saint Jean dans la rue Saint-Denis*, *paroisse de Saint-Sauveur* claimed *sponsalia de futuro* against Laurence Chippon.[305] She, in turn, confessed that she had gone to the house of her godmother (*matrina*), who had given a loaf of bread to the plaintiff. The plaintiff had, in turn, handed over to her a piece of the bread which she took and for which she thanked him. Afterwards the plaintiff said that he had done it in the name of matrimony, but it was never her intention to have the plaintiff as husband. At the next session, Étienne defers the oath to Laurence, which she takes and is absolved.

Like the proposed exchange of shoes in *Tiphania c Fevresse*, the exchange of bread described in this case suggests some sort of customary ceremony that accompanied handfasting. The law did not forbid such ceremonies, though it encouraged couples to become engaged in the face of the church, and many canonists suggested that the customary understanding of particular words could be used to determine whether the *sponsalia* were of the present or of the future tenses. In *Derot c Chippon*, however, at least if we believe Laurence, there are no words to interpret. There was some debate among the canonists whether a couple could contract using signs rather than words, if they were capable of speech. The mainstream opinion suggested that they could not, even if that was their intention.[306] Laurence's statement in this case that it was not her intention to have Étienne as husband, then, is part of an *ipso fortiori* argument: "*Sponsalia* cannot be contracted by signs alone where the couple are capable of speech, and even if they could be, they must intend to contract, which I did not in this case." There is even a suggestion that Étienne was trying to trick her by saying, in effect: "If I did that in the name of marriage, we're married."

Of course, we do not know that there were no words. All that we know is that Laurence said that there were no words and no handfasting. The fact, however, that Étienne defers the oath to Laurence when we know that there was at least one witness, the godmother, who could have testified to what happened, suggests that Laurence's version of the story is likely to be closer to the truth.

The last case that may have involved *sponsalia de presenti* is illustrative of a larger group. We have already seen that some cases claim *sponsalia* without specifying the tense, and we will see that in a number of cases we know that spousals litigation was taking place but have no record of the claims and defenses.[307] Since the overwhelming majority of cases that do specify the tense

[304] One is reminded of the sandals that sealed the contract in the book of Ruth (Ru 4:7–8), but that arrangement was between two men.

[305] (27.viii.86 to 3.ix.86), col. 355/2 (T&C no. 721), 359/3.

[306] Disc. T&C no. 722.

[307] Disc. T&C no. 723.

of the verbs are *de futuro*, the probabilities are that they also involve *sponsalia de futuro*. We have also just seen, however, that it could be dangerous to specify that the *sponsalia* were *de presenti*. One might find oneself declared excommunicate and subject, at a minimum, to paying a fine. Hence, cases in which the tense of the verbs of the *sponsalia* are not specified or in which we do not have the pleadings may be cases of *sponsalia de presenti*. Indeed, as we saw in *Coloigne c Bouloigne*, some of the cases in which the claim is of *sponsalia de futuro* may in fact involve *sponsalia de presenti*.

How many cases are like this we cannot tell, but there is a case that gives us a hint that it may be one of them. The pleadings in *Marion Ladriome c Roger Errau* lie before the beginning of the register. When we first see the case, arrangements are being made to examine two witnesses in Paris and an unspecified number of them before the official of Chartres.[308] In the next entry, Marion gives up, swears that she cannot prove her case, and defers the decisory oath to Roger. The official absolves Roger, considering both his oath and "that the plaintiff swore that no collusion was present nor that she had anything from the same [defendant] for this."[309] As we have seen, parties were routinely allowed to remit *sponsalia de futuro*. If the *sponsalia* were *de presenti*, on the other hand, they should not have been allowed to remit. A marriage once formed cannot be dissolved by mutual consent. The official may have insisted on the extra oath in this case (the only case in which such an oath is recorded) because he knew or suspected that the *sponsalia* were *de presenti*.[310]

The nine jactitation cases are of some interest because they illustrate the different ways in which couples could get the same issues before the court, and because they cast some light both on their underlying motivations and on the role that the court played. No two of them are quite alike. The earliest, *Emangone fille de Thomas Guerin de Noisy-le-Grand (Seine-Saint-Denis) et Alain Quideau ?apprenti [famulus] de Pierre Genart*,[311] states the motivation for the action quite clearly:[312]

> Today [AQ] and [EG] appeared, and the girl said that she was planning to contract marriage with [PB], that many in the town were whispering and saying that the same [AQ] had boasted that he had contracted *sponsalia* with this [EG], wherefore she asked whether he wished to propose anything, etc., and [asked] that he speak the truth. [AQ] on his side, questioned under oath and interrogated, said and deposed that he never made nor contracted *sponsalia* with the girl nor did he boast, etc., and if he had had any [promises], he remitted them to her. The man, 16 *deniers*.

The case nowhere says that this was an instance action brought by Emangone against Alain, but there is nothing that suggests that there was an *ex officio* citation. Hence, this case is very much like a standard remission case. The

308 (18.xi.84 to 10.xii.84), col. 3/2, 9/3.
309 Col. 9/3, T&C no. 724.
310 Disc. T&C no. 725.
311 (30.v.85), col. 125/3. On *famulus*, see at n. 158.
312 Col. 125/3, T&C no. 726.

difference presumably lies in the fact that in most remission cases, there is at least a suggestion that the couple have indeed contracted. Here, they are at pains to establish that they did not. Whether this is a situation in which the local rumor mill simply got it wrong, or whether there really was something between Emangone and Alain that they now want to suppress, we cannot tell. The court seems willing to let the matter be, upon receipt of a relatively modest fee from the man.

There is more of a suggestion of proceedings *ex officio* in *Jeanette la Sigoignée et Bertaud de Ranville*:[313] "Today [BR] cited because he falsely boasted that he had affianced [JS], nonetheless deposed by means of an oath that he had not affianced said girl nor made marital promises with her. Considering this oath, license was given to the girl to contract elsewhere, etc." One can certainly imagine that falsely boasting that one had affianced someone would be an offense for which a penalty was owed. Apparently, however, if one were willing to clear the record when cited for the offense, nothing more would be done.

Arnoleta fille de Roland du Perier et Roger Barberii is more like *Guerin et Quideau* than like *Sigoignée et Ranville* in that the parties appear, so far as we can tell, without citation, and there is no suggestion of a possible penalty for false boasting.[314] In this case, after the man's negative oath the court decrees "that there is no impediment on this ground that would prevent [AP] from contracting elsewhere." The use of the word "impediment" is telling. Of course, it was a fundamental legal principle that prior *sponsalia de presenti* were a diriment impediment to subsequent *sponsalia* of any type. But it was also a fundamental principle that prior *sponsalia de futuro* unaccompanied by intercourse were not a diriment impediment to subsequent *sponsalia de presenti*, though they might have been regarded as an impedient impediment. The picture that is emerging from our survey of the Paris cases suggests not that the Paris court was violating either of these fundamental principles but that it was developing a third one: Prior *sponsalia de futuro* are a diriment impediment to subsequent *sponsalia de futuro* and, at least, an impedient impediment to subsequent *sponsalia de presenti*, and that both impediments will be enforced judicially. This is an issue to which we will have to return.

Other cases are more like *Sigoignée et Ranville*. *Sedile fille d'Henri du Martray et Phelisot Frapillon*[315] is exactly like it, except that Phelisot also swears that he never boasted of having contracted *sponsalia* with Sedile. In *Colin Thomassin et Jeanette la Guione*, Jeanette swears that "although she had otherwise boasted that [CT] had affianced her, he never affianced her, nor did they make marital promises with each other."[316] Colin "swore similarly," a phrase that does not allow us to tell whether he also had been boasting of the

[313] (13.vi.85), col. 135/4, T&C no. 727.
[314] (23.vi.85), col. 142/4, T&C no. 728.
[315] (29.xi.85), col. 228/1.
[316] (14.vi.86), col. 317/2, T&C no. 729.

relationship. Both are given license to contract elsewhere, and the man pays a fee of two *sous*. In *Engerran Gonterii et Jeanette de Varenges*, the entry specifically tells us that Jeanette's boast is "impeding a good marriage" of Engerran. She swears that there was no contract and that she had not boasted that there was, and Engerran gets his license for 12 *deniers*.[317]

In *Pierre le Hideux et Jeanne la Bouvyere*,[318] one of the two entries is similar to what we have seen. Jeanne is cited because she boasted that Pierre had contracted with her and to show cause why he cannot contract elsewhere. She appears and says that she does not wish to propose anything or to impede Pierre from contracting elsewhere. This entry does not result in a court order, but a week later we learn that the court had ordered an investigation: "Today, considering the information made by *maître* Jean Caretti, a promotor of the court, about the fact that it was asserted that [PH] had contracted espousals with [JB], sexual intercourse following, nothing is found against him, and because the woman does not wish to prosecute this [matter], we gave license to [PH] to contract elsewhere unless something else stands in the way, etc., [leaving] the rest [to their consciences]."[319]

The matter here is more serious. If, as local rumor had it (*asserebatur*), Jeanette and Pierre had had intercourse following *sponsalia*, they are married, and Pierre cannot be given license to contract elsewhere. But Jean Caretti can find no evidence of it, at least not without the cooperation of Jeanette. The matter is left to their consciences.

Perette l'Esveillée was given license to contract *sponsalia per verba de futuro* with Jean Maillefer, notwithstanding the fact that Jean Rappe had otherwise boasted of having so contracted with her.[320] Rappe is absent, though he had been formally cited. The license is also given "notwithstanding the young age of the girl, 12 years." The law did not require a license for a girl of that age to contract *sponsalia*, even *sponsalia de presenti*. The fact that such a license is thought appropriate indicates that it was not normal for girls of such an age to so contract.

The last jactitation case is the strangest. "Today, Margotte, wife of Richard de Camera, who boasted, as was said, [to have contracted with] Jean de Bruire, etc., and the same Jean appeared before us and swore that they had never contracted *sponsalia* nor made marital promises with each other, and therefore the marital promises, if they had any between them, we leave to their consciences and burden their consciences [with them]. Each one 12 *deniers*."[321]

In the other jactitation cases, it is clear that at least one and perhaps both of the parties wish to be free of the contract of which one is said to have spoken ("boasted," though that is what *se iactare* means, seems almost too strong

[317] (22.v.87), col. 474/4, T&C no. 730.
[318] (16–23.iii.87), col. 445/4, 449/2.
[319] Col. 449/2, T&C no. 731.
[320] (1.vi.87), col. 477/4, T&C no. 732.
[321] (8.vii.87), col. 493/8, T&C no. 733.

in some of these contexts). In most of the cases, it seems clear that the party who wants to be free is contemplating marriage with someone else. Indeed, that person's name is given in a number of the cases. Here, however, Margotte is married. How could her boast impede Jean from marrying another? One possibility is that the marriage contract of which they are speaking antedated the contract with Richard and that it was *de presenti*. This would, of course, mean that Margotte is not married to Richard; she is married to Jean, and he cannot marry someone else.

There is another possibility suggested by the fact that the record in no place says that a contract between Margotte and Jean casts doubt on her marriage to Richard. Margotte and Jean have formed a relationship either in Richard's absence or during his sickness. They hope to receive news of his death. But they cannot marry after his death if they have contracted during his lifetime and have committed adultery. This may be a 'strike suit' to establish their freedom from a contract, pending Richard's death.

Whichever possibility it is, the court is clearly troubled. The language by which it burdens Margotte's and Jean's consciences is the strongest that we find in the register. That language would slightly tip the balance toward the first possibility, for if Margotte and Jean contracted *de presenti* prior to her marriage with Richard, she is living in sin with Richard, and Jean will be living in sin if he contracts elsewhere.

The two cases that suggest an action derived from opposition to banns tell us little. In *Pierre Porcherii c Jeanette fille du défunt Richard le Bouc et Jean Seigneur*, "license was given to [JB] to contract with [JS], etc., notwithstanding the impediment put up by [PP], because it is null."[322] This would suggest that Pierre was ill-informed about what constituted an impediment. *Office c Étienne Malpetit prêtre chapelain de Groslay (Val-d'Oise)* tells us even less: "[EM] made amends because through inadvertence he assigned to [Simon Belot] [26.x.85] in a case of opposition [instead of] putting the date in the opposition [31.x.85]."[323] Without much confidence, we may suggest that the chaplain cited Belot for the wrong day. The case itself is not recorded.

There is one more *ex officio* case that refers to prior spousals litigation. On 22 April 1385, Simon Contesse, a resident of Maisons-Alfort (Val-de-Marne), made amends for his wife Jeanne, who had married him in the face of the church in violation of an inhibition that she not marry during the pendency of a matrimonial case brought against her by one Jean Guerini.[324] The litigation itself probably lies before the beginning of the register, so that we cannot tell whether Simon and Jeanne's marriage was valid because Jean's claim failed or whether it was valid because Jean claimed *sponsalia de futuro* and their marriage was, of course, by *sponsalia de presenti*.[325] The presence of this case

[322] (8.xi.85), col. 214/4, T&C no. 734.
[323] (26.x.85), col. 208/6, T&C no. 735.
[324] (22.iv.85), col. 102/3.
[325] Disc. T&C no. 736.

shows that the court took these inhibitions seriously. It also shows, however, that it could be manipulated. The entry closes with a note: "Her fine was remitted out of consideration for the *seigneur* of Essars."[326]

DIVORCE FROM THE BOND

There are 10 cases of *divortium a vinculo* in the Paris register, two of which are on the ground of male impotence. Both of them take only one entry, and both suggest that the practice of the court of Paris is such cases was fixed and effective: On 23 March 1385, the court decreed that the marriage contracted between Jeanne la Houdourone de Lagny-sur-Marne (Seine-et-Marne) and Jean Carre 13 months previously was null on the basis of Jean's "frigidity, inability, and impotence."[327] The decision offers three motivations: (1) a report of two masters of medicine and of Michel de Pisis, "our sworn surgeon," who had visited the man and reported that he was unable to have intercourse with a woman; (2) the oath of Jeanne, who swore that he was unable and impotent, and that she had exposed herself to him and tried to have him know her, and (3) the oaths of six men living in Lagny, who swore on the Gospels that they believed Jeanne's oath, and that they had never heard of Jean's having carnal knowledge of a woman. Jeanne was given license to marry elsewhere, and paid the quite high fee of six *sous*.

In comparison with the procedure that we have seen in England, with its embarrassing tests and equally embarrassing testimony, this procedure seems quite civilized, and the reason for the difference is not hard to find. Fourteenth-century Paris was well supplied with medical specialists, and the court had confidence in them. The necessity of paying the experts may be the reason for the high fee. The confidence in the experts may also account for the fact that the court waives the requirement found in some of the canonic sources that the couple attempt to have intercourse for three years before a marriage could be dissolved on these grounds. Of course, we do not know what would have happened if the man had not cooperated, or if the medical practice of the day could not tell whether he was impotent.

Philippe Natalis was even more cooperative than Jean Carre. He joined his putative wife, Raosia *fille d'*Adanet Petitbon, in swearing that they had been unable to have intercourse after six years of marriage.[328] In this case, the report of a single master of medicine and one in surgery, together with the oaths of five men who both support the couple's oath and report on the *publica vox et fama*, suffice to ground the sentence of nullity. Raosia is given license to marry elsewhere, a matter that may have been of some urgency because she has confessed to having been deflowered by one Pierre Parvi. Her fine for this is remitted in the event that Pierre marries her.

[326] Col. 102/3, T&C no. 737.

[327] (23.iii.85), col. 86/1, T&C no. 738.

[328] (2.xii.85), col. 229/2, T&C no. 739.

Another case tells us nothing except that it is a case of divorce. It disappears before the libel is delivered.[329]

In the remaining seven cases, the ground claimed for the divorce is *ligamen*, prior bond. In many of these cases, the penal element is strong; in some it is not. The records give us only hints as to why that might be so.

On 28 March 1387, the court declared the marriage contracted *de facto* and not *de iure* between Pierre Regis and Marion Grante Enpaille on 15 January 1387 to be null "considering that the first husband of the woman, called Janson le Natier, is still living."[330] Pierre was given license to contract elsewhere, and Marion was "kept as a prisoner." This is the most severe penalty that we find in this group of cases, and it is the only marriage case that we have found in which a woman is put in the bishop's prison. Otherwise, however, the case is typical. Obviously, there was an investigation and probably proceedings that came before this entry. Someone had authorized Marion's arrest, for the entry indicates that she was already in prison. These proceedings may have been the result of the activities of one of the promotors of the court, who developed the facts and then a record on which the sentence was based. That this entry is found in the official's register suggests that only he had the power to issue an order dissolving a marriage.

The result in *Office c Jeanne Bataille et dominus Guillaume Maloy* is quite different, but the case begins with the same formula as the previous one: "Today, we declared the second marriage between [JB] and [GM] contracted *de facto* 15 years ago was and is null considering that Gobin de Sivri, the first husband of [JB] with whom she contracted 21 years ago still lives, etc., giving the same [GM] license to contract elsewhere, etc."[331] Rather than proceeding to say how Jeanne would be punished, however, the entry tells us that "*Dominus* [GM] acquitted the woman of all the common goods that they had together, on this condition that the woman will be bound to maintain the three children that they had together, and he demised the goods to her, etc. Each of them 2 *sous*."

How can we account for the difference in the way in which Jeanne Bataille and Marion Grante Enpaille were treated? A cynic might suggest that the *de facto* wife of someone who calls himself *dominus*, even if she committed bigamy, will not be put in the bishop's prison. Exactly what *dominus* means in this context is unclear, but we probably should be thinking along the lines of *chevalier* or *seigneur*. It may well be that the wife, even the *de facto* wife, of such a man would not normally be put in the bishop's prison, but as we shall see in other cases, making amends short of imprisonment was a decided possibility in this type of case. That suggests that we should look elsewhere for an explanation of why no punishment for Jeanne is indicated. The fact that she was able to marry Guillaume and stay with him for 15 years and have three children by

329 *Metis c Metis* (13.ii.87), col. 428/5; disc. T&C no. 740.
330 (28.iii.87), col. 451/2, T&C no. 741.
331 (1.vii.87), col. 491/3, T&C no. 742.

him suggests that no one knew that Gobin was alive. Indeed, she may have thought him dead. But someone found out that he was alive, and unlike Enoch Arden, this person felt it necessary to reveal the fact. Marion Grante Enpaille, by contrast, may well have married knowing that Janson was alive.

If Jeanne's situation was tragic rather than criminal, that could also account for Guillaume's generous settlement. He gives her all the community property (he probably had ancestral lands that he could not share with her) and the three children.

Other bigamists were punished, though none of them, so far as we can tell, as severely as Marion Grante Enpaille. Jean Bayart tailor (*custurarius*) of Cambrai diocese and Margot la Hemarde appeared before the court and confessed that Jean had married Denise *fille de* Noël le Cousturier 11 years earlier and that Jean and Margot had contracted marriage *de facto* 8 years previously while Denise was alive. The official declares the second marriage void. Even if Denise is no longer alive, the marriage cannot be sustained because of the impediment of crime, assuming that Margot knew about Denise when she married Jean. Neither party is expressly given license to contract elsewhere, and the record tells us that the man had elsewhere (*alias*) made amends for the deed.[332]

That the tailor from Cambrai diocese deceived a woman of Paris about the fact that he had married a woman who looks like another tailor's daughter in Cambrai is certainly possible on this record. That would account for the fact that Jean made amends, and no amends for Margot are mentioned. If, however, Margot was deceived, then her marriage to Jean can be sustained, if Denise is no longer alive. Perhaps the reason that this record says so little is that whether Denise was still alive was a matter under investigation.

Meeting on the feast of the Exaltation of the Holy Cross (14 September 1385), the court nullified the marriage contracted between Perette la Gaignerresse and Berthelin de Tomailles 6 years previously because 24 years previously, Berthelin had contracted with Jeanette la Miresse solemnly (*rite*) in the face of the church.[333] The case was brought by an unnamed *actor* (probably one of the promotors of the court), and both women and the man were present. Perette was given license to contract elsewhere. Berthelin avoided the penalty of being exposed on the ladder of justice (and being whipped thereafter)[334] by paying ten *francs* to the almonry of the bishop. Berthelin seems to have been a man of some substance, and it was probably he who paid the (again, quite high) fee of four *sous*.

One case suggests that there were problems of proof.[335] On 15 April 1385, the court separates in goods Antoine Johannis and Jeanne la Serreuriere, his putative wife, because Jeanne has confessed that Colin le Serreurier is alive.

[332] *Bayart et Hemarde* (7.ii.85), col. 49/3, T&C no. 743.
[333] (14.ix.85), col. 189/3, T&C no. 744.
[334] Disc. T&C no. 745.
[335] (15.iv.85), col. 97/3, T&C no. 746.

Colin's relation to Jeanne is not stated in this entry, but their common surnames suggest that they are married. Colin, however, cannot be found, and the court offers this as a motivation for its sentence of separation. Jeanne makes amends, not for bigamy but for double espousals, and the couple swear to separate their common goods.

We will see in Chapter 10 that the Paris court regularly granted separation of goods to couples who did not qualify for separation from bed, but who found life with each other intolerable. These separations never seem to be granted unless the couple ask for it. That would, in turn, suggest that this couple was seeking to dissolve their marriage. They do not succeed. The court would seem to require more proof than simply Jeanne's confession that Colin was still alive for it to dissolve the marriage. The court will, however, allow the couple to live apart, a kind of compromise. The penalty for double espousals is, I would suggest, also a kind of compromise. Jeanne has confessed to bigamy. She is not punished for bigamy, however, but for contracting *sponsalia* with two different men.

Some light is shed on this case by an entry that appears in the register a month earlier (9 March 1385).[336] Jeanne la Charrone appeared in court without being cited (*sponte*) and made amends because she had espoused Colin le Serreurier in the face of the church of Sainte-Croix-sur-Buchy (Seine-Inférieure, Rouen diocese) 19 years previously. Her husband (*maritus*) left her within 3 years and no news was heard of him for 16 years. Although Colin was still living, she contracted marriage *de facto* with Antoine Johannis in the parish of Gouvernes (Seine-et-Marne, Paris diocese) the previous May. The court imposed a fine of six *francs* on her, to be paid in two installments by 9 April, and a priest named Pierre de Aulo, the governor of the *maison de Dieu* in Lagny-sur-Marne (Seine-et-Marne), went surety for her. Jeanne was said to be living at the *maison*, and she choose her domicile there. A final cryptic note says: "She has made amends; she lacks." (*Emendavit; caret.*)

There can be little doubt that Jeanne la Charrone is the same person as Jeanne la Serreuriere in the entry of 15 April. What the entry of 9 March tells us in many ways confirms our speculations about the entry of 15 April. Jeanne confessed that Colin was still alive and that she had committed bigamy. But Colin has not been heard of for 16 years. How does she know that he is alive? She should not have married Antoine without some evidence that Colin was dead, and she certainly should not have married him if she was convinced in her conscience that he was alive. But that is a matter best left to her and her confessor, who may well be Pierre de Aulo. In the external forum, the court will not dissolve a public marriage on the basis of the confession, however conscientiously made, of the existence of a person who has not been heard of for 16 years.

The previous entry also opens further possibilities that we would not have expected from the entry of 15 April. Jeanne is not living with Antoine; she

[336] (9.iii.85), col. 72/2, T&C no. 747.

is living in the *maison de Dieu* in Lagny. She may be ill, and she is almost certainly poor.[337] Her residence in the *maison de Dieu* suggests that, and the final cryptic note in the entry for 9 March probably means that she was forgiven some or all of the payment of the fine because she has no money. But she does have a potential source of some money, the community property that she accumulated with Antoine during their year of marriage. It may not be much but it is something, and if she is going to live at the *maison de Dieu*, Pierre de Aulo may be entitled to whatever it is that she has. But these possibilities also raise the possibility that Jeanne's conviction that Colin is still alive may have been prompted by her perceived need to dissolve her marriage with Antoine in order to get the property that she has with him.

We cannot tell precisely what motivated Jeanne's confession of 9 March, and we suspect that the court could not be sure of her motivation either. What the court does, then, is to solve the problem of getting Jeanne her share of the community property without having to dissolve the marriage with Antoine. It does this by ordering a separation of goods.

That ruling, of course, leaves Antoine still married to Jeanne. Of him the record tells us nothing, though the court may have known about him. He may not have been a good husband.[338] Jeanne's residence at the *maison de Dieu* suggests as much, and that would have been an additional reason why a separation would be appropriate. It may also be that if Jeanne is in poor health, Antoine will not have to wait for long before he can marry someone else. All that the record tells us, however, is that the court will not dissolve his marriage to Jeanne on the evidence before it.

Two cases, in addition to *Bataille et Malloy*, do not mention any penalty. The marriage of Jeanne de Sancto Martino and Jean Naquet goldsmith was declared null on the basis of Jean's previous marriage to one Marota, but the entry is cut off, and so we do not know whether he was penalized.[339]

In the other case, the entry is complete, and it tells a strange story.[340] Gérard de Brulleto of the diocese of Limoges confessed before the court that seven years previously, he had promised Marion la Gregoire, also of the diocese of Limoges, that "if it pleased him, Gérard, he would take her as wife." Marion also confessed the same thing. Afterwards, Gérard had had intercourse with Marion, had lived with her for a long time, and had offspring by her. On the basis of these confessions, the court declared null the *de facto* marriage that Gérard had contracted the same day as the sentence (*hodie*), followed by sexual intercourse, with Guillemette la Heraude. The court also declared that the marriage with Marion was valid and binding, and Guillemette was given license to contract elsewhere.

337 It is also possible that she was a prostitute in the intervening years between Colin's abandoning her and her marrying Antoine.

338 More sinister possibilities are suggested in the previous note.

339 (14.vii.85), col. 156/6, T&C no. 748.

340 (12.xii.85), col. 234/1, T&C no. 749.

One may imagine that a dramatic scene occurred when Marion arrived from Limoges on Gérard's wedding day after he and Guillemette had retired to the bridal chamber. We do not know who persuaded the three of them to go see the official; it may have been the priest who officiated at Gérard and Guillemette's marriage. Guillemette, however, may have been the person who insisted that they go see the priest. Gérard's behavior was inexcusable; yet the record does not mention that he was punished. A clue as to why may lie in the fact that alone among these cases, the court in this one specifically declares that the marriage with Marion is valid. Gérard's carefully worded promise to Marion is, of course, no promise: "I promise to marry you, if I choose to do so." Probably correctly, the court deemed that the condition was purged by the subsequent intercourse, but Gérard may not have known this piece of legal doctrine. Indeed, none of the parties may have known it. Hence, they went to the official and asked him what they should do. If three rather naïve people appeared before the official, confessed all, and asked him what was the proper thing to do in their situation, we may imagine why the official, having made his ruling, decided not to penalize anyone. They had already had quite a day.

CONCLUSION

We are not quite finished with the Paris marriage cases. The rather large number of separation cases, together with the related *ex officio* actions (e.g., adultery and spousal abuse) are more conveniently treated in Chapter 10. The time has come, however, to face directly an issue that we have noted with some puzzlement as we proceeded. What accounts for the overwhelming proportion of cases of *sponsalia de futuro* and the virtual absence of cases of *sponsalia de presenti* in the Paris register?

We have already seen one possible reason. In Paris, in marked contrast to Ely and York, a person who alleged informal *sponsalia de presenti* could be declared automatically excommunicate by synodal statute.[341] We say 'could' because we have seen cases in which *sponsalia de presenti* were alleged and nothing is said about excommunication. Nonetheless, the fact that it could happen might well have shaped the way in which cases were brought, particularly if the party wishing to bring the case consulted with a lawyer before appearing in court. Since a great many of the parties to the cases in the Paris register are represented by proctors or advocates or both, it seems highly likely that many of them did consult with lawyers before formulating their complaints.

Let us imagine a man or a woman who wanted to bring spousals litigation in the Paris court consulting a lawyer. The lawyer will first ask precisely what was said. If the party then describes a handfasting in which words of the present tense were employed, the lawyer will say, "Are you sure that that is what was said? Because if it was, you are excommunicate under the statutes of Eudes de Sully. If you say that in court, the other side may ask that you be declared

[341] *Ringart c Bersaut* (at nn. 287–94), lit. T&C no. 750.

excommunicate. The court will declare you excommunicate, although it will probably absolve you *ad cautelam*, perhaps completely. But you will have to make amends, and the case will be delayed. If, however, you say that the two of you said, 'I promise to marry you', and you can prove it, then the court will order you to solemnize your marriage and will declare any subsequent promise that your partner made void."

Thus, the litigation risk of alleging *sponsalia de presenti*, coupled with the willingness of the court specifically to enforce *sponsalia de futuro*, may have led plaintiffs who had exchanged words of the present tense to say that the words were future ones only. If the court would enforce a simple contract to marry by means of a court order backed ultimately by excommunication and serious secular sanctions, a prosecution for failure to fulfill a marriage contract would, in most circumstances, be just as good as a prosecution for a *de presenti* marriage.

It would not be as good in two types of situations: (1) where the defendant had contracted *de futuro* with someone else prior to contracting *de presenti* with the plaintiff, and (2) where the defendant, subsequent to the *de presenti* contract with the plaintiff, had gone out and married someone else either *de presenti* or by words of the future tense followed by intercourse. As we have seen, there are cases that allege a prior *de futuro* contract and those that allege a subsequent marriage. In all of these cases, the fact that the plaintiff alleged only a *de futuro* contract may have hampered his or her ability fully to present the case, but such cases are rare.

The reason why they are rare is that in both types of cases, the defense creates a considerable litigation risk for the defendant. By alleging prior *sponsalia de futuro*, the defendant would be exposing him- or herself to the charge of double espousals, a charge that could result in quite severe penalties. An allegation of a subsequent marriage also presents risks. In the first place, it would seem that this too would subject one to the penalties for double espousals. Further, that marriage would be either formal or informal. If it were formal, the prior spouse would have an opportunity to object to the banns, and we have seen that a number of them did. If it were informal, the same difficulties would exist with admitting that marriage as there would be with admitting the initial *de presenti* marriage.

Because of these difficulties, three-party marriage cases are quite rare on the Paris records. They exist, but they are far less common than they are in England in the same period. We might imagine that someone who had contracted a *de presenti* marriage but alleged that it was *de futuro*, could, when faced with a defense either of prior *de futuro* espousals or subsequent marriage, raise the stakes by changing the plea to one of *de presenti* marriage (or introducing proof that the marriage was, in fact, *de presenti*), but so far as we can tell, no one in 410 Paris marriage cases did this, and, again so far as we can tell, no one had to do this.[342] As a practical matter, an allegation of *sponsalia de futuro* is as good as an allegation of *sponsalia de presenti*.

342 Disc. T&C no. 751.

So far the argument has proceeded on the assumption that the social practice was the same in both England and in Paris. The litigation patterns were different, I have argued, because of differences in the ways in which the law was enforced in the two places. We will see in the following chapters that two key features of the Paris practice, automatic excommunication for clandestine *de presenti* contracts and a dominance of litigation about *de futuro* ones, can be generalized to the whole of what we will call the 'Franco-Belgian region'. Hence, the social question can be broadened to the two regions. But the assumption just made that the underlying social practice about marriage was the same in the two regions involves the further assumption that there were massive amounts of perjury before the church courts in the later Middle Ages. If we assume that the social practice was the same in the two regions, then the English must have lied almost always when they said there had been a *de presenti* marriage, or the Franco-Belgians must have lied almost always when they said there had been a *de futuro* one, or the Franco-Belgian and English witnesses must have lied an exactly corresponding percentage of the time. Exact correspondence of lies defies the laws of statistics. That most of the Franco-Belgian witnesses (but not the English witnesses) or most of the English witnesses (but not the Franco-Belgian witnesses) were lying is possible statistically, but also seems unlikely. While there can be no doubt that there was a considerable amount of perjury before both sets of courts (someone, for example, must have been lying in *Dolling c Smith*), it seems unlikely that it could have been on the scale necessary to produce the striking differences we see in the records.[343] More cases would probably have crept through in which the witnesses told the truth.

We cannot avoid the social question, moreover, even if we assume – as I have suggested that we cannot – that the underlying social practices were the same but that different legal institutions make the records generated by the courts dealing with those practices look very different. The institutional explanation simply puts the social question at one further remove: Why did Franco-Belgian society in the later Middle Ages create legal institutions so different from those in England?

This last question is one to which we will return in Chapter 12. For the time being, we can probably proceed on the assumption that there are more *de presenti* marriages than appear on the face of the Paris register. There may have been more even by an order of magnitude, but if that extrapolation gives us 30 or 40 cases of *de presenti* contracts, it leaves 215 or 225 cases of *de futuro* contracts. We might even be willing to expand this number. As we have seen, there are 37 cases in which the plaintiff alleges not only *sponsalia de futuro* but also subsequent intercourse. In this situation it makes no difference whether the *sponsalia* were *de presenti* or *de futuro*. These events make a marriage, not a contract to marry, and they can be overcome only by a prior marriage. Even if we are willing to say, however, that all the cases of *sponsalia* plus intercourse

343 For evidence from the secular law that *de presenti* informal marriages did indeed exist in France, see Turlan, "Recherches," 503–16.

were really cases of *de presenti* consent (as they were in law), that still leaves us with almost 200 cases of *sponsalia de futuro*, approximately 70 percent of the total (255) cases of spousals litigation. What does this very large number of *de futuro* contracts tell us?

We noted that the cases of *sponsalia de futuro* plus intercourse look much more like the English spousals cases than do the cases of *sponsalia de futuro re integra*. The former type of case is largely brought by women, and when we can see what the issues were, they look like those in England. Unlike the English cases, they all allege that the *sponsalia* were *de futuro*, but that fact makes no legal difference, and we have already seen that there are institutional reasons why the pleading always takes that form. What is different about the Paris spousals cases is the very large number of *sponsalia de futuro re integra*. What can we tell about these cases, particularly in the light of the social information that we can derive from them?

The first thing we might note about these cases is that the plaintiffs (who, as we have seen, are mostly men) have a dismal rate of success. Of 172 such cases (excluding the dissolution cases), five were confessed and the plaintiff got a favorable judgment in one of the contested cases and may have gotten such a judgment in a half dozen more. That is a success rate, at best, of 7 percent.[344] In over half the cases (53%), the defendant took the decisory oath, normally, as we have seen, in the same session where the claim was presented, and in slightly more than a quarter of the cases (26%), the parties remitted any promises that they may have made. While it is possible that some of the men who brought these cases hoped that the woman would confess or were unaware that they needed proof, it seems likely that most of the plaintiffs who appeared in deferral and remission cases knew what was going to happen.

That realization, in turn, leads us to ask whether these plaintiffs can be said to have 'lost'. This is particularly true of the remission cases, the record of which frequently does not tell us who brought the case and, indeed, suggests that in many cases the couple appeared voluntarily, both asking that their remission be 'admitted' by the court. But the statement that the plaintiff did not 'lose' may also be true of the deferral cases. If the plaintiff was aware, as we may suspect most of them were, that the result was going to be a judgment for the defendant on the basis of the decisory oath, can they be said to have 'lost' when they got what they knew was going to happen?

That question leads us to inquire into the motivations of the plaintiffs in the deferral cases. We have seen that a few of them thought they had proof, though it turned out that they did not have convincing proof, and so they had to defer, but this is a very small percentage of the total number of cases. We have also seen that there was another possibility if the result (no *sponsalia*) was totally agreed upon: Both the potential plaintiff and the potential defendant could have come into court and remitted. Why did so many plaintiffs bring an action that they knew was going to result in a judgment for the defendant?

[344] Disc. T&C no. 752.

The records, of course, do not say. What the record in some cases does say, and in many more suggests, is that they were brought by men who had been negotiating with the fathers of young women and, at least in some cases, with the young women themselves. Perhaps these negotiations had resulted in an unprovable contract; perhaps the existence of a contract was a matter that could be disputed between the parties; perhaps the father had committed to the contract and the young woman had not, or vice versa. The precise details will always escape us and probably varied from case to case. The point, however, is that negotiations had been taking place, and this fact was known to a fairly wide circle of people, not only the parties but also at least some of their *amici*, probably neighbors and friends, and so on. Granted the penalties for double *sponsalia* and the fact that prior *sponsalia* could impede a marriage to someone else, it was in everyone's interest that if Jean were not going to marry Jeanne, there be a public record that there were no *sponsalia* between them.

Now this situation is one in which a remission would provide an effective record freeing the parties from any obligations of *sponsalia*, but remission involved a kind of commitment. The couple had to agree to it, and most of the remission cases imply that there had been a contract (a few are carefully worded conditionally), whereas all the defendants in the deferral cases were willing to put their souls on the line that there had not been. Bringing a suit that was certain to result in a deferral was the only option open to the plaintiff in a number of different situations: (1) where negotiations had broken down so badly that the parties could not even agree to a mutual release; (2) where the young woman was being kept away from talking to the man (this could, of course, be a variant of situation 1); (3) where the father or the young woman or both were delaying in answering the man's proposal and he wanted to force an answer, positive or negative, and (4) where the man was convinced that there was a contract and the young woman or her family was equally convinced that there was not. This, of course, does not exhaust the possibilities but these seem to be among the more likely.

Perhaps we can go a step further, although these suggestions do not depend, as do the previous ones, on classically 'rational' behavior but more on guesses as to what may have been at stake in fourteenth-century Paris. The fee for taking the decisory oath was almost always two *sous*. Sometimes the plaintiff also paid a fee, but that was usually quite small. The fee in remission cases varied and frequently was not mentioned at all; usually it was small, and it was, I believe, almost always shared by the couple. Two *sous* is not a large amount, particularly if our guesses as to the social status of most of these parties are correct, but it is not a derisory sum either. There may have been a slight element in the fee structure, if the plaintiff knew about it, of making the defendant pay to get out of the contract.

There was more than a slight element of making the defendant pay in what she had to do. As we have said, she had to put her soul on the line. In at least some of these cases, the plaintiff may, in effect, have been saying to the defendant, "After all that you said to me, I am going to make you jeopardize your salvation, if you want to get out of it."

So far as the other option, remission, is concerned, there may have been social factors that made the defendants reluctant to choose it. As we have said, remission normally involved an admission that there had been a contract. The existence of the impediment of public honesty suggests that there were some who regarded affiancing as more like marriage than did the developed canon law. There may have been a vague sense among some fourteenth-century Parisians that a young woman who was physically a virgin was not really a virgin if she had been affianced to another man. There might even have been suspicions that if she had been affianced to another man she might not be physically a virgin. Having made this suggestion, I would want to be very cautious about it. Despite the presence of the deflowering cases, there is not the evidence for fourteenth-century Paris that there is for, say, some places in the Mediterranean world of heightened concern about female virginity.

Prescinding for now from these speculations, let us return to more solid ground. If we are willing to read the evidence of those cases where we have some sense of what the issues were, and/or of what the social situation of the parties was, into the rather large number of cases where we have no such evidence, the Paris cases of *sponsalia de futuro re integra* suggest that we are looking at a type of dispute seen only rarely in the English cases, disputes about arranged marriages. Just as we asked regarding the English cases whether we may be seeing in the litigation a disproportionate number of marriages that were not arranged, so too we must ask whether we may be seeing a disproportionate number of arranged marriages in the Paris cases. That may be the case, although we have reason to doubt it because the modal Paris case of an arranged marriage is one where the arrangement has, for some reason, gone awry. This, then, necessitates establishing a record either that there was no contract or that any contract was remitted. It is likely that the proportion of cases in which the arrangement went awry is small compared to the number in which the social steps toward marriage outlined in the cases that give us the details resulted in marriages that did not have to be litigated.

Not all Parisians followed these steps. There are cases of women who arranged their own marriages, particularly, but not exclusively, widows, and of country people who seemed to be behaving more like the English couples. We cannot say that the cases of *sponsalia de futuro re integra* show us *the* marriage pattern in the diocese of Paris or even that in Paris itself. What we can say is that one of the Paris marriage patterns – one that seems to be evidenced among people of somewhat higher social status – was for a young woman to be espoused by her father and relatives to a man somewhat older than she. She had to consent, and sometimes she did not, but the initial choice was not hers. Another pattern in the same group (and the two patterns could blend) was for the man to approach the young woman first, obtain her consent, and then negotiate with her father or relatives. The distinction is a subtle one, and in both cases we probably should speak of arranged marriages. Much depends on something that the records never tell us: whether the man first obtained permission from the family to talk to the young woman. The second variation, however, does give the woman a somewhat greater range of choice.

If the pattern of marriage suggested in the previous paragraph reminds one more of Italy than it does of the 'northwest European marriage pattern', as it has come to be known in the literature, it should.[345] That urban Parisians were behaving more like urban Italians in the later Middle Ages, at least when it came to marriage, than like the largely rural populations that surrounded them would not be surprising. We cannot, however, be sure how much of a 'marriage pattern' this was on the basis of the evidence before us. The Paris register never gives us the age of the parties. In only two cases is nonage claimed.[346] We do not know the age of the men who were plaintiffs, though we suspect that most of them were over 20 and many may have been older than 25. So the suggestion that here we are looking at a marriage pattern quite different from that which we have come to expect for northwest Europe in this period must remain just that, a suggestion.[347]

345 See Richard M. Smith, "Geographical Diversity," with references.

346 *Rouet c Longuerue* (n. 141); *Ringart c Bersaut* (n. 287).

347 Lit. T&C no. 753.

8

Cambrai and Brussels

The Courts and the Numbers

INTRODUCTION

In the late Middle Ages, the diocese of Cambrai was large. It extended from the county of Cambrai in the southwest, across a large swath in the central part of modern Belgium, to Antwerp in the northeast. It thus included, in addition to Cambrai itself, the towns of Valenciennes (Nord), Mons, the part of Tournai on the right bank of the Scheldt, and Brussels. A survey in the fifteenth century counted 1,029 parishes, divided into 18 deaneries and 6 archdeaconries. The official, who held court at Cambrai, was assisted by a delegate at Brussels. In 1448, the official at Brussels became an official principal, equal in rank to that at Cambrai. The jurisdiction of the official at Brussels covered the three northern archdeaconries, that of Antwerp, Brussels, and Brabant, roughly corresponding to the Flemish-speaking areas, while the official in Cambrai retained jurisdiction over the three southern archdeaconries, Cambrai, Valenciennes, and Hainault, roughly corresponding to the French-speaking areas.[1]

These officialities have left a collection of registers of sentences, dating from the middle of the fifteenth century. Those from the city of Cambrai bear dates from 1438 to 1453, though there are gaps, while that from Brussels bears dates from 1448 to 1459 and seems to be complete. The sentences thus allow us to see the activity of the officials of Cambrai both before and after the division of the diocese and that of the officials of Brussels just after the division of the diocese.

During the period covered by our sentences, the see of Cambrai was occupied by two bishops, Jean (V) de Lens and Jean (VI) de Bourgogne. The former died on 30 March 1439. The latter, the bastard son of John the Fearless of Burgundy, was elected in April, confirmed by the pope, and consecrated in May; he entered Cambrai in July and, after some administrative acts in August, departed the city

[1] Lit. T&C no. 754.

rarely to return. He governed the diocese through what today would be called auxiliary bishops. After a long and disgraceful life, he died in 1479.

The official of Jean de Lens during the period covered by our registers was *maître* Oudard Divitis (Le Riche). He continued as official *sede vacante*, but Jean de Bourgogne replaced him with Grégoire Nicolaï, who served as official of Cambrai until 1466. The officials of Brussels during the period of our sentences were Jan Rodolphi *alias* Flamingi, from November of 1448 through September of 1452, and Jan de Platea *alias* de Lira (Lier), for the remaining seven years of the register.

The Cambrai sentence books, indeed all sentence books, are, in many ways, curious documents. One can see, of course, why a court might want to keep a register of its judgments, particularly its final judgments, for purposes of determining the application of the doctrine of *res iudicata*, the notion that once a case is decided finally it cannot be relitigated between the same parties. We have already seen that this doctrine was only imperfectly applied in marriage cases, but it was clearly relevant even in such cases. To relitigate a marriage case, one had to demonstrate 'that the church was deceived' in the previous case, and a record of what was done in the previous case was useful.

What is curious, then, about the Cambrai sentence books is not that records of judgments were being kept but the way in which they were being kept. A much shorter entry would have sufficed to convey all the information about the judgment that is contained in sentences like the following:[2]

In a case initiated and pending before us the official of Cambrai between Jeanne Rattine, party plaintiff on the one side, and Colin l'Oyseleur, party defendant on the other, having seen the petition of the plaintiff shown before us in court, the oaths, assertions, and replies of the parties, and other things moving us and our soul, supported by the seasoned advice of those who are expert in the law, the name of Christ having been invoked, because it was and is apparent to us that the defendant entered into and made clandestine marital promises by words of the future tense suitable for and capable of such things and had deflowered and carnally known the plaintiff and had brought forth a child from her, on account of these things we condemn the defendant to proceed further to the solemnization of the marriage with the plaintiff – as is customary and is normally done – in the hand of a priest and in the face of the church, issuing a definitive sentence in this writing.

The information contained in this mass of verbiage can be reduced to "Jeanne Rattine c Colin l'Oyseleur, clan[destine] [*sponsalia*] *d*[*e*] *f* [*uturo*] + deflowering, one child, confessed, ordered to solemnize." (That the action was confessed can be inferred from the fact that no proofs other than those supplied by the parties themselves are mentioned.) For purposes of coding, this information can be placed in fields labeled "Plaintiff," "Defendant," "Claim," "Defense" (none in this case), "Process," and "Sentence." This stripped-down entry tells us everything that seems to be legally relevant in the sentence.[3] It does not,

[2] *Rattine c Oyseleur* (26.vii.38), no. 20, T&C no. 755.
[3] Disc. T&C no. 756.

however, tell us everything that is legally relevant about what happened. For this we need a marginal note, which, in this case, the register supplies: "The parties are held to the laws (*tenentur ad leges*) for making clandestine [*sponsalia*] and not renewing them, and because they did not proceed [to solemnization] within the time defined by law, sexual intercourse following, in such a way that the defendant deflowered the plaintiff. At Lahamaide [Ellezelles, prov. Hainaut, Belgium]."[4]

This cryptic note tells us more than does the whole sentence. In addition to being ordered to solemnize, the parties were also penalized (though exactly how is by no means clear from the phrase "are held to the laws") for what looks like four potentially separate offenses: (1) clandestine *sponsalia* not renewed (presumably publicly), (2) failure to solemnize within a legally defined period (presumably after the *sponsalia*), (3) consummating their marriage before it was solemnized, and (4) deflowering. It also tells us where the parties come from (presumably for the purposes of collecting the fines).

The kind of information that is contained in the note and the style in which it is recorded is typical of what we find in registers of the period, particularly registers that are mostly or entirely devoted to office cases.[5] What is surprising, then, is not that we find such notes in the Cambrai register (and it is not clear that this type of information was always recorded)[6] but that we do not find the sentences similarly reduced to their bare legal minimum.

The man who was responsible for redacting this sentence was named Jean Carlerii. Jean went on a trip to Italy during the period covered by the registers, and when he returned he crossed out one of the sentences of his substitute, Raoul Hennoque, and wrote a caustic remark about it in the margin.[7] We can still read the crossed-out sentence, and it looks very much like the ones that Carlerii registered, but it clearly was not up to Carlerii's standards. This tells us that there was a bureaucratic tradition at Cambrai concerning the maintenance of these sentence registers in a particular way, but it does not tell us how the tradition started and what its purpose was.

Although nothing quite like the sentence registers of the Cambrai diocese has yet been found elsewhere, we know that the tradition of writing sentences in highly formal and rhetorical language was characteristic of Romano-canonical procedure as it was practiced in the ecclesiastical courts in the later Middle Ages. The quire of sentences found in the Paris register are in the same style, as are the individual sentences found in the cause papers of the higher ecclesiastical courts in England. They give an impression of seriousness and solemnity, an impression that was clearly their purpose to produce. We are probably correct in imagining that they were read out in court, and if we read them aloud we find that they

[4] *Rattine c Oyseleur* (n. 2), T&C no. 757.

[5] E.g., Hereford Record Office, "Acts of Office," Donahue, ed., *Records 2*, 170–1; CCA, *Ex officio* Act Books, *id.*, 105–8; A.D. Marne, G 922 to G 934, Donahue, ed., *Records 1*, 97.

[6] See App. e9.1, "*Non sunt leges* or None Mentioned" (T&C no. 1054).

[7] *Douvel et Becforte* (4.viii.39), no. 253, T&C no. 758.

make an aural impression, even on those who do not know Latin. For those who did know Latin (the officers and personnel of the court certainly, attendant clergy, and perhaps some educated lay people), they probably seemed a bit pompous, but they may have had a kind of reassuring quality, like good liturgy. It is important to emphasize, however, that the reassurance is not produced by a demonstration of the compelling reasons that led the court to act as it did. Motivations, though occasionally present, are relatively rare in these and similar sentences. Rather, the reassurance lies in the recitation of the steps of the *ordo* that have been followed, the findings of the court, and the inevitable conclusion that follows from those findings. The reassurance, then, is a reassurance of the fundamental notion of the rule of law.

The reading of the sentence in court was, of course, a fleeting moment, but the act of reading the sentence was the most solemn act that the court did. The registers of sentences, then, are records of these solemn acts, preserved, we might suggest, not so much as precedents (although any notary who wanted to learn how to write sentences would find good examples in these registers) but more for the purpose of preserving and passing on to future generations the tradition of the court as an authoritative embodiment of the rule of law.

The rhetoric of the sentences themselves is mostly formulaic. Like the formulae of a Homeric poem, a repertoire of stock phrases and half-phrases can be stitched together to fit the circumstances of the case. The existence of this repertoire of stock phrases suggests the possibility that the sentences themselves were composed orally by the official as he rendered them. It also means that the notary, by deft use of abbreviations, for example, "X" for *Christi nomine invocato*, could take down the sentence word for word as it was being given. Whether this is in fact the case with the sentences in the Cambrai register I am not sure.[8] There are changes in the style of the sentences over the course of the registers that seem to reflect more a change in notarial practice than anything that might be attributed to a particular official. For example, the early sentences in the register in office cases begin: "In an office case, initiated and pending before us, the official of Cambrai, between the promotor of cases of our office, acting in the name of and for the sake of his office, plaintiff, on the one side, and on the other side, the defendants, [JH] and [JH]."[9] Six months later this formula has been reduced and changed to "Having seen the articles of the promotor of our office brought against the defendants, [JR] and [JC]."[10] Three years later (there is a substantial intervening gap), this formula has been expanded to "Having seen the articles of the promotor of our office brought against the defendants, [JW] and [CP], who are subject to our jurisdiction."[11] This last remains the formula for the next 10 years. It is also the basic formula in the Brussels register, though there are variations. Certain changes in the rhetoric seem to be specific to particular cases, however, and probably reflected

[8] Disc. T&C no. 759.
[9] *Office c Hayette et Hongroise* (13.xii.38), no. 90, T&C no. 760.
[10] *Office c Roussiau et Comte* (30.vi.39), no. 250, T&C no. 761.
[11] *Office c Wyet et Paiebien* (13.vii.42), no. 280, T&C no. 762.

what the official wanted to say about that case. We will see, for example, that it is characteristic of cases that seem to involve very serious offenses, such as bigamy, for a heightened rhetoric to be employed, and we will see in Chapter 10 that changes in the rhetoric of separation sentences almost certainly reflects the unease of the officials with what they were doing with an increasing number of basically consensual separations *a thoro*.[12]

These changes in rhetoric mean that we cannot simply give the standard form of sentence for each type of case and then count the number of cases of each type. This is unfortunate because with close to three thousand sentences, analyzing every one of them is out of the question. What I did, therefore, was to sample, beginning with 10 percent (146) of the sentences in the registers from the city of Cambrai and using this sample to test the variations in case types. I then drew samples just of the marriage cases, as will be explained later. I also drew samples of the Brussels cases for purposes of comparison, though the focus was somewhat more on Cambrai than on Brussels.[13]

Much of the marriage litigation at Cambrai, particularly the office cases, involves violations of local legislation. A brief rehearsal of that legislation is necessary in order to understand what follows. The distinctive approach of the area to the regulation of *sponsalia* is already to be seen in the synodal statutes of Guiard de Laon, bishop of Cambrai, 1238–48, which can be dated with some confidence between 1238 and 1240:[14]

[89] Priests shall prohibit their subjects (*subditis*) from giving faith of contracting marriage mutually except before the priest of either of them who wish [so] to contract and in public before the people, and if they give faith between themselves it shall not be valid.

[90] We command that no priest should, without the license of the bishop, dare to celebrate banns or edicts or solemnize marriage between them [i.e., those who violate c. 89] even if they should wish to affiance themselves again. If, moreover, a priest presumes to celebrate marriage between anyone against this precept, let him know that by that very act he is suspended.

[91] Let them be excommunicated and denounced as excommunicate those who contract clandestine marriages, and let the priest who celebrates this sort of marriage also be denounced as excommunicate. Whoever, clerk, layman or woman, presume to join any persons in this manner, let them also be denounced as excommunicate.

[92] Let them be excommunicate and denounced as excommunicate those who after clandestine affiancing know each other carnally. Whoever are present at clandestine marriages celebrated before a priest or another, we excommunicate them unless they reveal [this] to the bishop or his official within 15 days.

[93] We excommunicate [those] who give faith, or take it, or give a gift or take it for concealing impediments to marriage. Let this excommunication be often announced by every priest in [their] parishes.

12 The highest level of rhetoric is found in *Office c Roders* (2.vii.46), no. 951, a prosecution for, among other things, sorcery.

13 Disc. T&C no. 763.

14 *Statuts synodaux français IV*, 45–7; text and disc. T&C no. 764.

After a paraphrase of the canon *Cum inihibitio* of the Fourth Lateran Council,[15] the statutes continue:

[96] If anyone gives faith to another to contract marriage by words of the future tense, and before sexual intercourse they mutually wish to remit the faith, such quittance should not be done except by the bishop or his official.

We have already seen that the Paris statutes on the topic of clandestine marriage were strict.[16] Such marriages subjected the parties to automatic excommunication. What is different about the Cambrai statutes is that they also insist that the *sponsalia de futuro* be public. In the thirteenth century, they do not excommunicate those who contract *sponsalia de futuro* privately, but they do excommunicate those who, having contracted them, then form a marriage by subsequent intercourse. The control over *sponsalia de futuro* is exercised in a different way (c. 89–90). First, private *sponsalia de futuro* are prohibited; indeed they are said to be invalid. Second, the parish priest may not proclaim the banns or solemnize the marriage of those who have so contracted without license from the bishop. This may not be a direct violation of Alexander III's decretal *Quod nobis ex tua parte*, but it is certainly in a different spirit.[17]

Further emendation to these canons followed in the compilation of synodal statutes made in 1287–8 and again in the early years of the fourteenth century. In particular, what we labeled canons 89–90 in the quotation was amended to read as follows:[18]

[65] [80] Parish priests shall prohibit their subjects (*subditis*) from contracting *sponsalia* or giving faith of contracting marriage to each other (*fidem de matrimonio inter eos pariter contrahendo*), except, at a minimum, before the priest of one of those who wishes to contract (*nisi coram presbytero alterius saltem contrahere volentium*), and this should be in a public place, a church, for example, or a cemetery or a chapel and before many other trustworthy people. And if they otherwise contract *sponsalia*, unless they repeat them within eight days before any of the above priests, the priest should not proceed to the proclamation of the banns or the solemnization of them without our special license [i.e., of the bishop] or that of our official. And anyone who presumes to do this [knowingly] shall know himself suspended by this very fact.

This is, in many ways, an improvement from the point of view of legislative drafting. The sanction for not so contracting is changed from invalidity of the *sponsalia* (something that was probably not within the power of the synod to do) to the requirement that a special license be obtained from the bishop or his official (on which occasion, presumably, a penance could be imposed) in order to proceed with the proclamation of the banns and the solemnization. Perhaps most important and by way of concession to the fact that medieval people, like

[15] Ch 1, at n. 77.
[16] Ch 1, at nn. 85–7.
[17] X 4.3.2 (Ch 1, at n. 74).
[18] *Statuts synodaux français IV*, 118, 160; text and disc. T&C no. 765.

modern, normally first found out whether someone was willing to marry them in a private setting, clandestine *sponsalia de futuro* were not forbidden. Rather, the couple were enjoined to publicize them within a week after they were made. This period of a week remained a feature of the Cambrai legislation throughout the Middle Ages and was being enforced in the mid-fifteenth-century sentences that we see in our registers.

As we saw and will also see in the cases that follow, the Cambrai court regularly fined couples for failure to solemnize their marriages after *sponsalia* had been entered into, and the fines mention a period "fixed by law." That the failure to solemnize *sponsalia* (unless they were remitted before the bishop or his official) would be an offense is clearly implied in the legislation, but no fixed period for solemnization is laid down. We have been unable to find such legislation, though we have no doubt that it existed. Because we have been unable to find the legislation, we do not know what the period was as it is never given in the sentences.[19] It could have been as short as a month from the time of solemnization of the *sponsalia* because that would have given ample time for the three successive proclamations of the banns on Sundays or feast days called for in *Cum inihibitio*. Clearly, this legislation was designed to turn marriage promises into solemnized marriages quickly.

Not every diocese in the region seems to have adopted these provisions. For example, if we can rely on an older printed edition, the diocese of Soissons in the year 1403 adopted a reasonably systematic collection of synodal statutes that were divided into *consilia* and *praecepta*. Classified as a *consilium* and not a *praeceptum* was the following provision that seems to have been adapted from Cambrai: "Let priests frequently prohibit lay people, under excommunication, from giving faith to themselves of contracting [marriage] unless a priest is present, and many others, and if they do so in his absence, let him [the priest] not make edicts or banns."[20] This probably refers to *sponsalia de futuro*; the reference to excommunication is vague. It might have been necessary to impose the sentence rather than the parties' incurring it automatically (technically an *excommuncatio ferendae sententiae* rather than *latae sententiae*). The fact that the whole thing is called a *consilium* suggests that it is considerably less binding than the Cambrai statutes.[21] Around 1454, the bishop of Amiens adopted a collection of synodal statutes that said nothing about the celebration of *sponsalia de futuro*, excommunicated those who contracted *per verba de presenti* clandestinely, but then repeated the injunction of *Quod nobis ex tua parte*[22] that those who wish to publicize such marriages be received by the church and blessed.[23]

[19] Disc. T&C no. 766.

[20] Soissons (1403), c. 50, in *Actes de Reims*, 2:631; T&C no. 767.

[21] By contrast, clandestine marriages seem to be punished with automatic excommunication. *Id.*, c. 55, in *id.*, 2:632; cf. *id.*, c. 48, in *id.*, 2:631.

[22] X 4.3.2 (Ch 1, at n. 74).

[23] Statutes of Jean Avantage (c. 1454), c. 5.10, in *Actes de Reims*, 2:712.

There is one further statute of possible relevance to our cases, appearing first in this form in the Cambrai collection of 1287–8 and carried over into that of the early fourteenth century:[24]

[71] [83] Item, we excommunicate all those who propose false impediments against marriages, or who knowingly [*scienter*] conceal the truth, out of affection, [superior] order or favor, or for any other reason, and will that priests frequently denounce them as excommunicate for this reason. Even if no one offers opposition at the proclamation of the banns, but the priest has a probable or true suspicion (*versimilem aut veram coniecturam*) against the marriage, he should not proceed to solemnize the marriage without consulting with us or our official of Cambrai about this. If he does to the contrary, he will be held to the penalty for [performing a] clandestine marriage.

The general thrust of this statute is clearly designed to encourage the raising of objections, but it could be used to penalize those who raise objections that turn out not to be provable, particularly since the *scienter* requirement does not have to be taken as applying to "those who propose false impediments." This statute may be the authority for a penalty that we find quite often in the cases, imposed for "frivolous opposition" to a marriage.

Two relevant additions to the basic statutes of Cambrai are recorded in the fourteenth century. In one, the canon complains that because of the "simplicity of priests," couples who wish to contract *de futuro* are being given the form to contract *de presenti*. It recommends the form "I promise that I will take Bertha as wife, if a canonical impediment does not stand in the way."[25] In 1315, a synod imposed *ipso facto* excommunication on those who separated themselves without judgment of the church.[26] This canon was being applied in our fifteenth-century cases.

THE BUSINESS OF THE ECCLESIASTICAL COURTS OF CAMBRAI AND BRUSSELS

Our initial sample of 146 cases from the registers of the court of Cambrai at Cambrai yielded the types of cases shown in Table 8.1. The numbers are dramatically different from those of the other courts that we have examined. Marriage cases (including prosecutions for sexual offenses, such as adultery) account for 70 percent of the total, as opposed to 38 percent at York, 23 percent at Ely, and 23 percent at Paris. The disparity is even more dramatic (79%) if we include, as we did with the other courts, the cases of clerical discipline that involve sexual offenses. But if 79 percent of the Cambrai sentences involved matrimonial or sexual matters, 21 percent did not, and 21 percent of 1,455 sentences is 306 sentences. Clearly, the court of Cambrai was not dealing only with matrimonial and sexual matters. The fact that only records of sentences have survived probably means that the number of such cases is understated

24 *Statuts synodaux français IV*, 119; text and disc. T&C no. 768.

25 (c. 1310), in *id.*, 2:492–3.

26 *Id.*, 2:502.

TABLE 8.1. *The Business of the Court of Cambrai at Cambrai (1438–1453)*

Type of Case[a]	No.	% Total
Ecclesiastical		
Clerical discipline	4	3
Clerical discipline (sexual)	13	9
Other[b]	6	4
SUBTOTAL	23	16
Matrimonial[b]	102	70
Obligation		
Arbitration	1	1
Cession	2	1
Debt	4	3
Debt appeal	1	1
SUBTOTAL	8	5
Testamentary		
Renunciation	6	4
Other[b]	3	2
SUBTOTAL	8	6
Miscellaneous		
Unknown	1	1
Injury	1	1
Spoliation	1	1
Witchcraft	1	1
SUBTOTAL	4	3
TOTAL	145	100

Notes: 'Clerical discipline' = an office proceeding against a member of the clergy for conduct unfitting to his order. Where 'sexual' is added, the case involves, at least in part, a sexual offense.

For notes and literature, see T&C no. 769.

Source: Registres de Cambrai.

because, as we have noted, matrimonial cases tend to have a higher rate of sentences than do other types of cases.[27]

We can be less sure of the proportions of the other types of cases that the Cambrai court was hearing. Many of the sentences in our sample have only one or two examples, a fact that makes extrapolation from the sample to the total population problematical. For this reason, we have gathered the other types of cases into groups. Six percent of the Cambrai cases involve the law of obligations broadly conceived, of which the overwhelming proportion involve contractual obligations (8/9, 89%). This is less than the 16 percent at York, 24 percent at Ely, and 34 percent at Paris, but the Cambrai court clearly had jurisdiction over such cases. The relative absence of cases involving delictual

[27] Disc. T&C no. 770.

obligations may tell us something about the activity of the secular courts in the diocese and the way in which jurisdiction was divided between the two sets of courts. Six percent of the Cambrai cases involve testamentary matters broadly conceived. This is, in fact, not much different from York (9%), Ely (11%), and Paris (6%).[28] A substantial portion of these cases (6/9, 67%) are cases of "renunciation." It is not completely clear what these routine entries mean, but the fact that it is always a widow who does the renouncing suggests that what is being renounced is the widow's rights in the community property. Perhaps she is renouncing them because she does not want to share in the obligations.

The proportion of "ecclesiastical cases" at Cambrai is substantially lower than that at York, Ely, and Paris, particularly if we exclude cases of clerical discipline that involve sexual matters (7% vs 40%, 25%, and 11%, respectively). The Cambrai court did not record in its sentence book much in the way of routine matters of ecclesiastical administration (such as the appointments of administrators for sick priests at Ely or the approvals of the election of church wardens at Paris). Such matters may have been recorded in another book. (It seems unlikely that they were handled by another officer of the bishop, since officials in French-speaking areas tended to have at least as wide, if not wider, jurisdiction over such matters than did those in England.) The Cambrai court clearly did not entertain as much litigation about benefices as did the court of York, but as we have seen, it is the York court that is unusual here. There is not nearly so much business of this type at Ely and Paris. Our sample of Cambrai cases does include two tithe cases and one case in which a clerk whose letters of tonsure have been lost in a fire obtains another copy. It is also possible that the interlocutory sentence in a spoliation case included in the "Miscellaneous" category is a benefice matter because the defendant is styled *maître*, but there is no indication that the plaintiff is a clerk.

Another striking difference between the sentences recorded at Cambrai and the matters recorded in the York cause papers and the Ely and Paris act books is the dominance of office cases. There are, for all practical purposes, no office cases in the York cause papers, and the Paris office cases are, as we have seen, imperfectly reported. Ely does have office cases but not nearly so many. At Cambrai almost two-thirds (65%) of the cases are office or office promoted; at Ely they represent slightly more than a quarter (26%).[29] Conversely, at Ely over half (54%) of the cases are brought as instance cases, while at Cambrai the proportion is less than 30 percent (29%). The difference is less dramatic but still noticeable in the marriage cases. At Cambrai almost three-quarters of them are office or office promoted (83/115, 72%), while at Ely fewer than one-half are office cases (66/135, 49%).[30]

[28] Disc. T&C no. 771.
[29] Details and disc. T&C no. 772.
[30] The Ely numbers predate the consolidation of cases that combined office and instance cases that involved the same matter.

TABLE 8.2. *The Business of the Court of Cambrai at Brussels (1448–1459)*

Type of Case[a]	No	% Total
Ecclesiastical		
Clerical discipline	2	3
Other	4	5
SUBTOTAL	6	8
Obligation:	3	4
Debt		
Debt appeal	2	3
SUBTOTAL	5	6
Matrimonial	57	74
Testamentary	8	10
Miscellaneous		
injury/debt	1	1
TOTAL	77	100

Notes: For the layout, see Table 8.1.
For note and literature, see T&C no. 773.
Source: Liber van Brussel.

In order to provide a cross-check on our results for Cambrai, we drew a sample of 77 sentences from the court of Cambrai at Brussels, as can be seen in Table 8.2. Clearly, the types of cases heard by the Brussels court and their proportions were quite similar to those heard in the court at Cambrai. There is the same dominance of matrimonial matters broadly conceived (74% and 70%, respectively). Litigation about obligations is not dominant, but it is there (7%, of which 1% contains noncontractual elements, vs 6%, of which 1% is noncontractual). "Ecclesiastical" cases broadly defined are less well represented at Brussels than at Cambrai (8% vs 16%), but this discrepancy is more than accounted for by the total absence from our Brussels sample of cases involving sexual offenses of the clergy. This discrepancy is made up for by the larger proportion of testamentary cases (10% vs 6%) and the larger proportion of matrimonial cases already noted.

Most notable among the differences is the aforementioned total absence from the sample of cases involving sexual offenses of the clergy. The index to the Brussels register reports four such cases, but they are very much the exceptions that prove the rule.[31] The unusual nature of most of these cases and their scarcity contrasts sharply with the numerous routine cases of clerical concubinage, fornication, and adultery that we find at Cambrai. It is possible, though it seems highly unlikely, that clerks in the Flemish-speaking parts of Cambrai diocese in the mid-fifteenth century were more chaste than their counterparts in the French-speaking parts. Slightly more likely, but still quite improbable, is that the ecclesiastical officers in the area of the Brussels officiality had decided

[31] Listed with disc. T&C no. 774.

not to pursue routine cases of clerical sexual misconduct. It seems most likely, however, that in this part of the diocese routine discipline of the clergy about sexual offenses was handled by lower-level officers, probably the deans.[32] When we get to the marriage cases, we will see that routine fornication and adultery cases were also not a regular part of the Brussels court's jurisdiction, and such cases, which almost certainly existed, must have been handled in lower-level courts, perhaps in secular courts.[33]

The other differences between the recorded business of the court at Cambrai and that at Brussels are more subtle, but they probably tell us something about record keeping. There are few, if any, cases in the Brussels sample that were not, or at least could not have been, contentious matters. Particularly notable in this regard is the absence of any cases of widows' renunciations, cases that formed a large part of the Cambrai testamentary jurisdiction. This means that the proportion of genuinely contested testamentary matters is quite a bit higher at Brussels than it was at Cambrai (10% vs 2%). That, in turn, suggests that secular jurisdiction may have been less involved in testamentary matters in this area, though we know that it was involved.[34] There are no cases of cession of obligations in our Brussels sample. There is one case where a marriage contract is registered in the sentence book totally, it would seem, without controversy, but a similar case shows that controversy could arise on such occasions.[35] We noted that our sample of "ecclesiastical" cases from Cambrai included one totally noncontentious case in which a clerk obtains another copy of his letters of tonsure, the original having been lost in a fire. There are no such cases in the Brussels sample. All of this would tend to suggest that it is even more likely at Brussels than it was at Cambrai that a separate book of noncontentious matters was being kept.[36]

Two features predominate when we come to compare the types of procedure employed at Brussels with that at Cambrai. One we have already anticipated. There are very few, if any, "administrative" cases in our sample of Brussels cases, whereas 6 percent of the Cambrai cases are of this type.[37] There is a substantially greater proportion of sentences in instance cases (51% vs 29%). This proportion, however, is largely accounted for by the greater proportion of types of instance cases other than matrimonial.[38] While there is a greater proportion of instance marriage cases at Brussels than at Cambrai (27% of total cases vs 22%) and a considerably smaller proportion of office marriage sentences (55% vs 43%), the former gap is not large and the latter gap can be accounted for by the Cambrai cases of clerical incontinence, a category that, as we have seen, is missing from our Brussels sample and largely missing from the

32 Disc. T&C no. 775.

33 Disc. T&C no. 776.

34 See the references to city officials in a number of the testamentary cases.

35 Ref. and disc. T&C no. 777.

36 For an example of a book largely devoted to such matters, see A.D. Aube, G 4170, ed. as *Registre de Troyes*.

37 Disc. T&C no. 778.

38 Disc. T&C no. 779.

book.[39] When we come to analyze the marriage sentences themselves, we will see both at Cambrai and at Brussels that office cases and instance cases tend to blur and that the promotor was quite active in marriage litigation in both places. Indeed, we will eventually argue that he was more active in matrimonial matters, particularly those with regard to the formation of marriage, at Brussels than he was at Cambrai.

MARRIAGE LITIGATION AT CAMBRAI AND BRUSSELS – A LOOK AT THE NUMBERS

We will have occasion in Chapter 12 to explore the possible significance of the greater proportion of office cases in the mid-fifteenth-century diocese of Cambrai. Let us turn here to the marriage cases themselves, beginning with the instance cases, because the patterns of litigation here will be somewhat familiar from those at Paris.

Because the total number of instance marriage cases in our first Cambrai sample was relatively small, I drew a second sample, entirely of marriage cases (excluding cases of clerical discipline involving sexual matters). The results of this draw were encouraging. The first sample had 102 marriage cases (excluding cases of clerical discipline). Of these, 33 (32%) were straight-instance cases. The second sample drew 145 marriage cases of which 49 (34%) were straight-instance cases. Clearly, both samples were drawn from the same world. As I got down into the smaller cells, however, there were substantial differences between the two samples. This was particularly true of the instance cases, which was already the smaller group. For this reason I drew a third sample consisting of 49 straight-instance cases concerning marriage.[40] The combined results of the instance cases in the three samples may be further subdivided, as shown in Table 8.3, making use of categories that we employed in dealing with the Paris cases.

As at York, Ely, and Paris, so too at Cambrai the vast bulk of instance marriage litigation concerns the formation of marriage ("Spousals"). The proportion of such litigation at Cambrai is closer to that at Paris than it is to that at York and Ely (69% vs 69%, 81%, and 86%, respectively). Instance cases of divorce from the bond are rare at York, Ely, and Paris; they are very rare at Cambrai.[41] Most of the rest of the instance litigation at Cambrai is taken up with separation cases (26%). In this respect, Cambrai is more like Paris (27%) than it is like York and Ely (3% and 0%, respectively).

If we look to the spousals cases, those at Cambrai are more like those at Paris than they are like those at York and Ely. Our Cambrai sample contains only one case in which a *de presenti* marriage is alleged.[42] This is, of course, a marked contrast with York and Ely and much more like Paris. As at Paris,

[39] Data T&C no. 780.
[40] Disc. of samples T&C no. 782.
[41] Disc. T&C no. 783.
[42] *Heylen et André c Wituenne* (24.vii.44), no. 505, disc. T&C no. 784.

TABLE 8.3. *Instance Marriage Cases at Cambrai – Subject Matter (1438–1453)*

Type of Case	No.	% Cambrai	% Paris[a]
Spousals			
De futuro (two-party)[b]			
Contested	17	13	13
Deferred	1	1	25
Dissolution	7	5	4
Remitted[c]	25	19	13
De futuro (three-party)[d]	22	17	?
SUBTOTAL	72	55	54
De futuro plus *copula* (two-party)	7	5	
De futuro plus *copula* (three-party)	7	5	
SUBTOTAL	14	11	10
De presenti plus *copula* (three-party)[e]	1	1	2
Jactitation	3	2	2
SUBTOTAL (Spousals)	90	69	69
Divorce	1	1	3
Separation			
of bed?	34	26	4
of goods	0	0	23
SUBTOTAL (Separation & divorce)	35	27	30
Miscellaneous instance	5	4	1
GRAND TOTAL	130	100	100

Notes: '% Cambrai' = proportion of sample of Cambrai instance cases; '% Paris' = proportion of Paris instance cases (excludes *ex officio* and 'uncertain', n = 370). The Paris spousals cases of uncertain type have been arbitrarily assigned to '*de futuro*: contested' and the separation cases of uncertain type to 'separation: of goods'. Because of rounding, the percentages do not always add up precisely to the subtotal or total.

For Notes *a–e*, see T&C no. 781.

Source: Registres de Cambrai; Table 7.3.

some cases at Cambrai concerning *de futuro* spousals result in a deferral of the decisory oath to the defendant, some ask for dissolution of the espousals for cause, some seek the admission of a mutual agreement to abandon the espousals, and some contest the existence of the espousals. As at Paris, there is at Cambrai an occasional case of jactitation. But the proportion of some of these types of litigation is quite different at Cambrai from what it is at Paris. Only one case in the Cambrai sample is deferred (1%), as opposed to fully one-quarter of all the Paris marriage litigation. The proportion of dissolution and remission cases is roughly similar (5% vs 4% and 19% vs 13%, respectively), but the proportion of contested cases is much higher (30% [combining the 2–party and 3–party cases] vs 13% [combining the "contested" Paris cases with those that were confessed, as, in essence, some of the Cambrai cases were]). What causes this much higher proportion of contested cases at Cambrai is the large number of three-party cases (17% of the marriage cases in the sample, not counting those involving *copula*, which adds another 5%). (We did not count three-party cases separately at Paris; there are very few of them, and they are all in the "contested" category.)

The larger proportion of contested cases at Cambrai is not the only important difference between the litigation patterns in the two places. The Paris cases differentiate between cases of separation of goods and cases of separation from bed, whereas those at Cambrai do not. At Cambrai, all separation cases seem to be separations from bed and board. We will deal with this difference in Chapter 10.

The differences between Paris and Cambrai instance litigation patterns are not exhausted by what can be seen in Table 8.3. The greater proportion of contested cases at Cambrai and the fact that all of the Cambrai cases are evidenced by a sentence (almost always a definitive sentence) means that virtually all the Cambrai cases have winners and losers. We must be careful in making a comparison here because we do not know how many Cambrai cases were abandoned before reaching the sentence stage, although the proportion may be lower than that at Paris.

The reason for believing that the Cambrai court allowed fewer cases to be abandoned is due to a second major difference between the Paris and Cambrai instance litigation patterns that is not reflected in the table. Virtually all of the Cambrai spousals cases result not only in a judgment as to the existence or nonexistence of the spousals but also in a fine for one or both of the parties. Such fines are also found at Paris (and at Ely), but they are relatively rare. At Cambrai they are so common that we will need to discuss what is happening in the relatively few cases where they are not mentioned.[43] If the court is going to be able to collect a fine as a result of instance spousals litigation, it has a reason not to allow it to be abandoned. Like the Ely court, the Cambrai court was probably more proactive in instance spousals litigation than were the Paris and York courts. This inference is made even more likely by the nature of the fines that could be collected and the presence at Cambrai of an active prosecutorial staff. Both of these features of Cambrai litigation will be discussed more fully.

To return to our comparison of Cambrai and Paris in terms of winners and losers, we noted that at Paris male plaintiffs tended to dominate in most of the categories of spousals litigation and that they had a dismal success rate. It was so dismal that we suggested that frequently these plaintiffs were litigating in order to get the result that they got: a judgment that they had not contracted *sponsalia* with the *rea*. At Cambrai the proportion of female plaintiffs is higher and their success rate is higher.

Table 8.4 shows that overall, the 130 cases in the sample produced 101 plaintiffs identifiable to a single gender. Their male/female gender ratio (48%) is slightly unbalanced toward the female side. Overall, too, these 102 cases give us 99 definitive sentences, with a plaintiffs' success rate of 59 percent (58/99). These overall statistics obscure a much more diverse underlying reality. Women dominate separation and divorce litigation (25/34, 74%), and plaintiffs' success

[43] See App. e9.1.

TABLE 8.4. *Instance Marriage Cases at Cambrai – Gender Ratios and Judgments (1438–1453)*

Type of Case[a]	FP	MP	%F	SFP	SMP	Total Cases	SFD	SMD	Total Cases	S	noS	GTOT
Spousals												
De futuro (two-party)												
Contested[b,c]	3	14	18	0	5	5	9	2	11	0	1	17
Deferred	1	0	100	0	0	0	0	1	1	0	0	1
Dissolution[d]	3	3	50	3	3	6	0	0	0	1	0	7
Remitted[d]	1	1	50	0	0	0	1	1	2	23	0	25
De futuro (three-party)[e]	3	19	14	1	4	5	15	2	17	0	0	22
SUBTOTAL	11	37	23	4	12	16	25	6	31	24	1	72
De futuro plus *copula* (two-party)[f]	7	0	100	2	0	2	0	5	5	0	0	7
De futuro plus *copula* (three-party)	7	0	100	2	0	2	0	5	5	0	0	7
SUBTOTAL	14	0	100	4	0	4	0	10	10	0	0	14
De presenti plus *copula* (three-party)[f]	1	0	100	1	0	1	0	0	0	0	0	1
Jactitation	1	2	33	1	2	3	0	0	0	0	0	3
SUBTOTAL (Spousals)	27	39	41	10	14	24	25	16	41	24	1	90
Divorce[g]	1	0	100	1	0	1	0	0	0	0	0	1
Separation of bed[b,d]	24	9	73	23	9	32	0	0	0	1	1	34
Miscellaneous instance[b,d]	1	0	100	1	0	1	0	0	0	3	1	5
GRAND TOTAL	53	48	52	35	23	58	25	16	41	28	3	130

Notes: For the layout, see Table 7.4.
Ratio of FPs to total Ps: 52% (53/101).
Ratio of successful FPs to total successful Ps: 60% (35/58).
Female plaintiff success rate: 69% (35 won, 16 lost).
Male plaintiff success rate: 48% (23 won, 25 lost).
Overall plaintiff success rate: 59% (58 won, 41 lost).
For notes *a–g*, see T&C no. 785.

Source: Registres de Cambrai.

rate in such litigation is virtually 100 percent (as already noted, one case has only an interlocutory sentence, and the divorce case fails, but the *actrix* obtains a separation). Women also dominate litigation in which intercourse is alleged, bringing all 15 of these cases. Their success rate in such litigation, however, is fairly low; they prevail in five of the cases (5/15, 33%). (It should be noted, however, that in some of the cases in which the woman fails to establish a marriage, she does receive a dowry for having been deflowered.)

Litigation about spousals in which intercourse is not alleged has a very different gender ratio. In such litigation men dominate (39/51, 76%). Plaintiffs' success rate in such litigation, as we might expect from the Paris cases, is considerably lower than their overall success rate in the entire sample (38% vs 59%). Here, the female plaintiffs seem to have done somewhat better than male (45% success rate vs 36%), but the numbers in the cells are sufficiently small that we should be cautious about drawing any firm conclusions.

Dissolution and jactitation cases are, of course, cases in which the plaintiff is not trying to establish or enforce *sponsalia* but to dissolve them or to deny their existence. If we exclude cases of these types from our calculation and focus only on those in which the plaintiff is seeking to establish *sponsalia*, we get, again as we might expect from the Paris cases, an even lower plaintiffs' success rate (5/17, 29%, for cases not involving intercourse; 10/32, 31%, if we include the cases involving intercourse). The numbers in the cells have become sufficiently small that we should not attempt to calculate any difference between male and female litigants.

At least two patterns emerge from these statistics. First, it was much easier to get the Cambrai court to separate a marriage, dissolve *sponsalia*, or declare that they did not exist than it was to establish *sponsalia*. Plaintiffs in separation, dissolution of *sponsalia*, and jactitation cases had virtually a 100 percent success rate. (Indeed, they may have had a 100% success rate if we treat the unsuccessful divorce case as a successful separation case, which it was, and assume that the separation case that has an interlocutory but no definitive sentence ended in a judgment of separation as did the 32 other separation cases for which we have definitive sentences.) Second, although men and women tended to be represented equally as plaintiffs if we look to marriage litigation overall, gender ratios were decidedly unbalanced when we look to different types of marriage litigation. Women occupied the field to the exclusion of men in the case of spousals litigation where intercourse was alleged, and constituted three-fourths of the plaintiffs in separation litigation. Men, however, constituted more than three-fourths of the plaintiffs in other kinds of spousals litigation. These two factors combine to produce a higher overall success rate of female plaintiffs (35/51, 69%) than of male plaintiffs (23/48, 48%).

We must postpone asking what all this might mean until after we have examined the sentences in more detail, but in Table 8.5 we can compare the gender ratios and success rates for the Cambrai instance cases to those that we calculated for Paris, Ely, and York.

TABLE 8.5. *Instance Marriage Cases at Cambrai (1438–1453), Paris (1384–1387), Ely (1374–1381), and York (1300–1499) – Gender Ratios and Judgments*

	Cambrai Instance										
Type of Case[a]	FP	%FP	SFP	%SFP	SMP	%SMP	TSP	%SP	S	noS	GTOT
Spousals											
Two-party – no *copula*	8	16	3	43	8	44	11	44	24	1	50
Two-party – plus *copula*	7	100	2	29	0	0	2	29	0	0	7
SUBTOTAL (two-party)	15	26	5	36	8	44	13	41	24	1	57
Three-party – no *copula*	3	14	1	33	4	21	5	23	0	0	22
Three-party – plus *copula*	8	100	3	38	0	0	3	100	0	0	8
SUBTOTAL (three-party)	11	37	4	36	4	21	8	27	0	0	30
SUBTOTAL (*copula*)	15	100	5	33	0	0	5	20	0	0	15
Jactitation	1	33	1	100	2	100	3	100	0	0	3
SUBTOTAL (spousals)	27	30	10	38	14	36	24	37	24	1	90
Divorce	1	100	1	100	0	0	1	100	0	0	1
Separation (bed)	24	71	23	100	9	100	32	100	1	1	34
SUBTOTAL (Div. & sep.)	25	71	24	100	9	100	33	100	1	1	35
GRAND TOTAL	52	42	34	68	23	48	57	58	25	2	125

	Paris										
Type of Case	FP	%FP	SFP	%SFP	SMP	%SMP	TSP	%SP	S	noS	GTOT
Spousals											
Two-party – no *copula*	58	32	9	20	16	15	25	16	24	32	208
Two-party – plus *copula*	31	91	5	22	1	50	6	24	3	9	37
SUBTOTAL (two-party)	89	41	14	20	17	16	31	18	27	41	245
Three-party – no *copula*											
Three-party – plus *copula*											
SUBTOTAL (three-party)											
SUBTOTAL (*copula*)					(same as two-party – plus *copula*)						
Jactitation	5	56	5	100	4	100	9	100	0	0	9
SUBTOTAL (Spousals)	94	42	19	26	21	19	40	22	27	41	254
Divorce	3	75	2	100	1	100	3	100	6	1	10
Separation (both)	62	81	34	100	7	100	41	100	16	45	102
SUBTOTAL (Div. & sep.)	65	80	36	100	8	100	44	100	22	46	112
GRAND TOTAL	159	52	55	50	29	24	84	37	49	87	366

Type of Case	Ely Combined									
	FP	%FP	SFP	%SFP	SMP	%SMP	TS	%SP	noS	GTOT
Spousals										
Two-party – no *copula*	14	47	5	45	6	50	23	48	7	30
Two-party – plus *copula*	15	94	8	53	0	0	15	53	1	16
SUBTOTAL (two-party)	29	63	13	50	6	46	39	49	7	46
Three-party – no *copula*	24	75	15	68	4	80	27	70	5	32
Three-party – plus *copula*	1	33	1	100	1	50	3	67	0	3
SUBTOTAL (three-party)	25	71	16	70	5	71	30	70	5	35
SUBTOTAL (*copula*)	16	89	9	56	1	50	18	56	0	18
Jactitation	0	0	0	0	0	0	0	0	0	0
SUBTOTAL (spousals)	54	67	29	59	11	55	69	58	12	81
Divorce	2	33	1	0	1	0	2	0	4	6
Separation (both)	0		0		0		0		0	0
SUBTOTAL (Div. & sep.)	2	33	1	67	1	0	2	0	4	6
GRAND TOTAL	56	64	30	60	12	57	42	59	45	87

Type of Case	York 14th c									
	FP	%FP	SFP	%SFP	SMP	%SMP	TS	%SP	noS	GTOT
Spousals										
Two-party – no *copula*	13	68	11	100	2	67	14	93	5	19
Two-party – plus *copula*	24	92	15	75	1	100	21	76	5	26
SUBTOTAL (two-party)	37	82	26	84	3	75	35	83	10	45
Three-party – no *copula*	4	40	3	100	5	100	8	100	2	10
Three-party – plus *copula*	9	90	6	67	1	100	10	70	0	10
SUBTOTAL (three-party)	13	65	9	75	6	100	18	83	2	20
SUBTOTAL (*copula*)	33	92	21	72	2	100	31	74	5	36
Jactitation	0	0	0	0	0	0	0	0	0	0
SUBTOTAL (Spousals)	50	77	35	81	9	90	53	83	12	65
Divorce	7	44	3	75	8	100	11	100	5	16
Separation (both)	3	100	0	0	0	0	1	0	0	0
SUBTOTAL (Div. & sep.)	10	53	3	60	8	100	12	92	7	19
GRAND TOTAL	60	71	38	79	17	94	65	85	20	85

(continued)

TABLE 8.5 *(continued)*

	York 15th c									
Type of Case	FP	%FP	SFP	%SFP	SMP	%SMP	TS	%SP	noS	GTOT
Spousals										
Two-party – no *copula*	26	59	6	75	5	56	17	65	27	44
Two-party – plus *copula*	12	60	5	50	3	100	13	62	7	20
SUBTOTAL (two-party)	38	59	11	61	8	67	30	63	34	64
Three-party – no *copula*	16	53	11	85	9	100	22	91	8	30
Three-party – plus *copula*	7	88	5	83	1	100	7	86	1	8
SUBTOTAL (three-party)	23	61	16	84	10	100	29	90	9	38
SUBTOTAL (*copula*)	19	68	10	63	4	100	20	70	8	28
Jactitation	0	0	0	0	0	0	0	0	0	0
SUBTOTAL (spousals)	61	60	27	73	18	82	59	76	43	102
Divorce	10	67	6	100	4	80	11	91	4	15
Separation (both)	4	100	1	0	0	50	2	50	0	0
SUBTOTAL (Div. & sep.)	14	78	7	88	4	80	13	85	5	18
GRAND TOTAL	75	63	34	76	22	81	72	78	48	120

Notes: For the basic layout, see Table 8.4. TS = total sentences; TSP = total sentences for plaintiffs; GTOT = grand total of cases.
Notes: See T&C no. 786.
Source: Tables 3.5, 3.6, 6.5, 7.4, 8.4.

What the table shows is that while Cambrai has some features in common with the English records that make it different from Paris, the litigation pattern in instance cases at Cambrai is more like Paris than it is like that at York or Ely. The features that it has in common with the English records is the presence, already noted, of a relatively large number of three-party cases. What Paris and Cambrai have in common, however, seems far more important. Notable is the lower proportion of female plaintiffs (52% and 42% vs 64%, 71%, and 63%). This difference becomes particularly dramatic if we focus on spousals litigation (42% and 30% vs 77%, 60%, 67%), and even more dramatic if we exclude litigation in which *copula* is alleged (20% and 16% vs 60%, 59%, and 57%), which in all places had a high proportion of female plaintiffs (91% and 100% vs 89%, 92%, and 68%). The other characteristic that Paris and Cambrai have in common is that both courts were less friendly to plaintiffs than were the courts at Ely and York (plaintiffs' success rate: 37% and 58% vs 59%, 85%, and 78%). Once more this difference becomes dramatic if we exclude separation and divorce litigation (particularly the former) and focus instead on spousals litigation (22% and 37% vs 58%, 83%, and 76%). We will return to these differences after we consider the Brussels cases and again in Chapter 12.

There is one more data set that needs to be explored here, that of the court at Brussels. Our relatively small sample of Brussels cases suggested that there was approximately the same proportion of instance marriage cases at Brussels as there was at Cambrai. If anything, the proportion was slightly higher (27% of total cases vs 22%).[44] The subject matter of these cases, however, differs quite a bit from that at Cambrai. The sample includes 18 instance marriage cases, 2 of which do not reveal anything further about their subject matter. Of the remaining 16, almost half deal with property (7/16, 44%), 2 cases in which the plaintiff seeks a dowry for deflowering, and 5 in which the parties, sometimes multiple parties, are litigating about marriage settlements. Such cases exist at Cambrai, but there are so few of them that we classified them with the "Miscellaneous." Five of the cases (31%) deal with issues of separation, approximately the same proportion as at Cambrai (27%), and three (18%) are remissions or consensual dissolutions of *sponsalia*, again approximately the same percentage as at Cambrai (18%). That leaves only one case (6%) in which there is a genuine contest about the existence *vel non* of *sponsalia* or a marriage.

There is reason to believe that this number greatly understates the amount of such litigation at Brussels. We have noted that it was the practice at Cambrai to record in the margins of the sentence books the fines that were imposed on the parties in cases in which the sentence was worded as if it were a straight-instance case. We have found one such entry in the Brussels sentence book, toward the beginning.[45] Later on in the book, however, virtually all matrimonial litigation is brought in the name of the promotor (and hence is classified as an office case),

[44] See at n. 39.
[45] *Molenbeke c Hochstrate* (18.i.49), no. 20.

and the fines are made a part of the sentence itself. In three cases in our sample, what is begun as an instance case is transformed into an office case for the final sentence.[46] In one marriage case in our sample, one of the defendants is formally joined with the professional promotor as a promoting party.[47] In an additional 10 cases, there is unmistakable evidence that one of the nominal defendants was, in fact, taking the lead in the prosecution.[48] (These are frequently cases in which one of the defendants is described as the "opponent" of the proposed marriage of two other defendants.) If we add these cases to our sample, we begin to see subjects that remind us of instance litigation at Cambrai. There is one case in which the promotor and a private party seek the enforcement of *sponsalia* (probably *de futuro*), a two-party case in which subsequent *copula* is not alleged, and four similar cases in which *copula* is alleged. There are two three-party cases involving the priority of *sponsalia de futuro* and six three-party cases alleging the priority of *sponsalia de futuro* plus *copula*, and there is one spectacular four-party case involving three sets of alleged *sponsalia*, one of which was accompanied by abduction and *copula* and another of which was *de presenti* and accompanied by *copula*.[49]

What this means, of course, is that if we want to compare comparable types of cases at Brussels and Cambrai, we should expand the Brussels sample to include the *ex officio* cases. We should also expand the Cambrai sample to include the *ex officio* cases, just to make sure that the spousals litigation found there gets its fair share. With this in mind, I reconstituted the samples to include all three procedural types, instance, office, and mixed. The following discussion is based on a sample of 259 marriage cases from Cambrai and 157 such cases from Brussels.[50]

As can be seen from Table 8.6, the instance mode of proceeding dominated non-spousals matrimonial litigation at Brussels. Of the 41 such cases in the sample, only 3 (7%) were office cases. Separation litigation (and its converse, suits for restoration of conjugal rights) and litigation about marital property make up the vast bulk of non-spousal matrimonial litigation in this court, and all of these cases are straight-instance cases. There is one element in the table that is misleading. The number of cases involving dowry for deflowering is greatly understated because only those cases in which the plaintiff's sole object is such a dowry are listed. When we come to analyze the spousals cases more carefully, we will see that a large number of them involve a claimed spousal that fails, but the unsuccessful claimant (always a woman) is then awarded a dowry for deflowering.[51]

Spousals litigation is quite different. Of the 116 spousals cases in the sample, 107 (92%) have sentences in the office form.[52] Relatively few of these, however,

[46] Listed T&C no. 787.
[47] *Officie en Tieselinc c Tieselinc en Outerstrate* (9.v.52), no. 370.
[48] Listed T&C no. 788.
[49] Listed T&C no. 789.
[50] Disc. of sample T&C no. 790.
[51] E.g., text following Ch 9, n. 222.
[52] Derived from Table 8.6.

TABLE 8.6. *Marriage Cases at Brussels – Types of Cases (1448–1459)*

Type of Case	Procedure[a]	No.	%
De futuro, two-party, contest	Instance	1	
	Office/instance	3	
	Office	1	
SUBTOTAL		5	3
De futuro, two-party, dissolutionl[b]	Office/instance	4	
	Office	7	
SUBTOTAL		11	7
De futuro, two-party, remission	Instance	4	
SUBTOTAL		4	3
De futuro, three-party[c]	Instance	2	
	Office/instance	10	
	Office	1	
SUBTOTAL		13	8
SUBTOTAL (*de futuro*, no *cop*)		33	21
De futuro cop, two-party[d]	Office/instance	20	
	Office	13	
SUBTOTAL		33	21
De futuro cop, three-party[e]	Instance	2	
	Office/instance	44	
	Office	2	
SUBTOTAL		48	31
SUBTOTAL (*de futuro*, plus *cop*)		81	52
Miscellaneous spousals, *de presenti*[f]	Office	2	1
SUBTOTAL (Spousals)		116	74
Divorce[g]	Instance	1	
	Office	1	
Restoration of conjugal rights	Instance	5	
Separation	Instance	13	
SUBTOTAL		20	13
Dowry			
Deflowering[h]	Instance	6	
Dos seu donatio[i]	Instance	13	
SUBTOTAL		19	12
Miscellaneous nonspousals[j]	Office	2	1
SUBTOTAL (Nonspousals)		41	26
GRAND TOTAL		157	100

Notes: For the basic layout, see Table 8.4.
For notes *a–j* and literature, see T&C no. 791.
Source: Liber van Brussel.

are pure office cases. In 81 cases (70% of the total), we know that one of the defendants was, in fact, assisting the promotor. There is reason to believe that this number understates the proportion of such cases. Normally, we learn of the fact that one of the defendants was assisting the promotor because he or she (it is usually "she") fails and is, for example, fined for "frivolous opposition." If the spousals litigation is successful in its aim, the record will not mention that one of the defendants was responsible for the success. In 8 of the 11 straight-office two-party cases alleging future consent plus *copula*, the official finds that a presumptive marriage has taken place and orders the couple to solemnize it. It is hard to imagine that in at least some, if not most, of these cases one of the parties, probably the woman, joined with the promotor in bringing the reluctant man to court. In short, these cases may be much like the instance cases alleging a future promise plus *copula* that we find in England, at Paris, and at Cambrai.

Once we pierce the veil of the procedural form, what we see at Brussels is not too far different from what we saw in the Cambrai instance cases. Spousals litigation makes up a bit less than three-quarters of the total (69% at Cambrai, 74% at Brussels), with separation litigation and litigation about marital property taking up most of the rest. There are some differences, however. As we have already noted, there was considerably more litigation about marital property at Brussels than there was at Cambrai. There was also considerably more litigation about marriages allegedly formed by an exchange of future consent plus *copula* (11% at Cambrai, 52% at Brussels). In order to see if this difference is a real one and not one that is peculiar to Cambrai instance cases, we need to add the Cambrai office cases to the sample.[53]

Table 8.7 confirms a number of features of matrimonial litigation at Cambrai that we had suspected from our smaller sample of all types of Cambrai cases and from our larger sample solely of instance cases. First, prosecution of sexual offenses was an important part of matrimonial litigation, broadly defined, at Cambrai. Such cases represent 20 percent of our sample. The notes to that portion of the table suggest that the Cambrai court confined itself to the more serious of such offenses. Many of the adultery cases have aggravating factors; all but two of the fornication cases do. Probably the more routine fornication cases, and perhaps the more routine adultery cases, were handled in lower-level courts.[54] Since our sample of Brussels cases contains no prosecutions for sexual offenses (and, as we have seen, there are virtually no such prosecutions recorded in the register), we need to exclude these prosecutions from the Cambrai cases in order to compare what is jurisdictionally similar between the two courts.

The last two columns of percentages in Table 8.7 make this comparison. The similarity that we had suspected when we looked at only the instance Cambrai cases is confirmed by the comparison. The proportion of spousals cases to the total number of marriage cases is virtually the same (Cambrai 75% vs Brussels 74%). Within the spousals cases, however, the proportion of cases involving *copula* is much lower at Cambrai than it is at Brussels (27% vs 52%), while the proportion of cases not involving *copula* is correspondingly higher (48% vs 21%).[55] We can also identify where this difference lies. Two-party

[53] See at n. 50 for how this sample was drawn.

[54] Disc. T&C no. 793.

[55] The totals here do not always add up to the sum of their parts because of the 'miscellaneous' spousals cases at Brussels.

TABLE 8.7. *Marriage Cases at Cambrai – Types of Cases (1438–1453)*

Type of Case[a]	Procedure	No.	% Total	%TOT-S	%T/B
Sexual offenses					
Adultery[b]	Office	29			
Bigamy	Office	2			
Clerical[c]	Office	13			
Fornication[d]	Office	8			
SUBTOTAL		52	20		
De futuro, two-party, contest	Instance[e]	13			
	Office/instance[f]	14			
	Office[g]	10			
SUBTOTAL		37	14	18	3
De futuro, two-party, dissolution	Instance	4			
	Office/instance	5			
	Office	8			
SUBTOTAL		17	7	8	7
De futuro, two-party, remission	Instance	11			
	Office/instance	5			
SUBTOTAL		16	6	8	3
De futuro, three-party	Instance[h]	17			
	Office/instance[i]	7			
	Office	5			
SUBTOTAL		29	11	14	8
SUBTOTAL (*De futuro*, no *cop*)		99	38	48	21
De futuro cop, two-party	Instance[j]	5			
	Office/instance	13			
	Office[k]	20			
SUBTOTAL		38	15	18	21
De futuro cop, three-party	Instance	7			
	Office/instance	6			
	Office	5			
SUBTOTAL		18	7	9	31
SUBTOTAL (*De futuro*, plus *cop*)		56	22	27	52
SUBTOTAL (Spousals)		155		75	74
Divorce	Office[l]	12	5	6	1
Separation	Instance[m]	19			
	Office/instance[n]	12			
	Office	1			
SUBTOTAL		32	12	15	11
SUBTOTAL (Div. & sep.)		44	17	21	13
Miscellaneous	Instance[o]	4		2	12
	Office[p]	4		2	1
SUBTOTAL		8	3	4	13
SUBTOTAL (Nonspousals)[q]		52		25	26
GRAND TOTAL		259	100	100	100

Notes: For the basic layout, see Table 8.4. % Total = percentage of total cases; %TOT-S = percentage of total cases less prosecutions for sexual offenses only; %T/B = comparable percentage of Brussels cases.

For notes *a–g* and literature, see T&C no. 792.

Source: Registres de Cambrai; Table 8.6.

cases alleging *copula* are in approximately the same proportions at Cambrai and Brussels (18% vs 21%); the difference lies in the three-party cases (9% vs 31%). The proportion of two-party cases seeking the dissolution of *sponsalia* is approximately the same at Cambrai as at Brussels (8% vs 9%). What gives Cambrai its greater proportion of non-*copula* cases is the large difference in the proportion of two-party contested cases (18% vs 3%) and the smaller, but still significant, differences in the proportion of two-party remission cases (8% vs 3%) and three-party cases (14% vs 8%).[56]

There are also substantial differences in the proportions of non-spousals matrimonial cases. As noted, litigation about marital property is found in the Cambrai court, but it makes up only a tiny fraction of the matrimonial cases,[57] whereas it represents 12 percent of the Brussels cases. The proportion of Cambrai divorce cases (6% vs 1%, the former all office) and separation cases (15% vs 11%) is correspondingly higher, and the remaining difference is accounted for by a miscellaneous collection of actions (e.g., jactitation, impeding a marriage) that do not appear in our Brussels sample.

We have already noted the differences in the procedural forms in matrimonial cases in Cambrai and Brussels. Table 8.7 confirms those differences. Virtually all of the non-spousals matrimonial litigation at Brussels was in straight-instance form. At Cambrai only 44 percent of it was straight instance (23/52), while 33 percent was straight office (17/52) and 23 percent was mixed (12/52). Part of this difference is accounted for by the fact that the Cambrai court entertained prosecutions for adultery, and a number of these ended up as separation cases.[58] But this fact accounts for only part of the difference. All 12 of the actions for divorce *a vinculo* in our Cambrai sample were also straight-office actions (12/52, 23%).

At Brussels spousals litigation was dominantly in the mixed form. As we have seen, we know that in 70 percent of the cases, one of the defendants in an office case was assisting the prosecutor, and we suspected that the percentage was higher than this.[59] At Cambrai the corresponding percentage is 32 (49/155); 37 percent of the spousals cases were straight instance (57/155, vs 8% at Brussels) and 32 percent straight office (49/155, vs 22% at Brussels).[60] Thus, if we confine ourselves to comparable types of cases, the overall percentage of straight-instance matrimonial cases was higher at Cambrai than it was at Brussels (39% vs 30%), and these cases were divided among types in very different ways.[61]

It is unlikely that any single factor accounts for all of these differences. I have already suggested that differences in the way that business was divided between

56 Statistical disc. T&C no. 794.
57 Disc. T&C no. 795.
58 See n. 54.
59 See at n. 52.
60 Derived from Tables 8.6 and 8.7.
61 Disc. T&C no. 796.

the secular and ecclesiastical courts may account for the larger proportion of cases about marital property that we find at Brussels, and that the way that business was divided between higher- and lower-level ecclesiastical courts may account for the larger proportion of cases involving sexual offenses that we find at Cambrai. This latter difference could also account for the somewhat greater proportion of separation cases that we see at Cambrai.[62]

There remain, however, differences that are unlikely to be accounted for, at least in any simple way, by jurisdictional divisions. The differences are both procedural (far greater involvement of the promotor in spousals litigation at Brussels, and substantially greater involvement of the promotor in separation and divorce litigation at Cambrai) and substantive (more three-party cases at Brussels, more cases involving *copula* at Brussels, more two-party contested cases at Cambrai, more remission cases at Cambrai). There are *a priori* reasons for thinking that these phenomena might be related. A potential marriage is at stake in all cases involving *copula*; one could see why the official and his promotors might not want to leave such matters just to the parties. The potential problem was even more serious in three-party cases involving *copula*. In three-party cases not involving *copula*, one might be concerned that two of the parties could conspire to defeat the rights of a third; the intervention of the promotor in such cases might serve to redress the balance.

If thoughts like these were motivating the officials and their promotors, we would expect to find more intervention of the promotor in these sensitive areas. Such is not the case, however. At Brussels the promotor is involved in virtually all of the spousals litigation. Except for the remission cases, there is no category of spousals cases that has any appreciable percentage of straight-instance actions. At Cambrai, too, the remission cases are dominated by instance actions, but the pattern of prosecutorial intervention in other types of cases is not what we would expect on the basis of the motivations suggested here. True, the promotor dominates the two-party actions involving *copula* (33/38, 87%, office and office/instance), but he is evident in only about three-fifths of the three-party actions involving *copula* (11/18, 61%, office and office/instance). About three-fifths of the three-party cases not involving *copula* are straight-instance actions (17/29, 59%), but the promotor is involved in about two-thirds of the two-party non-*copula* contested cases (24/37, 65%, office and office/instance).

We thus lack any evidence that the promotors became involved in spousals litigation because they were particularly concerned about cases involving *copula* or cases involving three parties, or both. The fact remains, however, that there were more such cases at Brussels than there were at Cambrai. It is possible that there were more because there were more such cases, that is, that the problems and disputes evidenced in these cases were more common in the Flemish-speaking areas of the diocese than they were in the French-speaking areas. It is also possible that there were more such cases because the promotors pursued them more vigorously. Having become involved in spousals litigation on

[62] Ch 10 will suggest other reasons, principally the views of the different judges.

a much broader scale than they were in Cambrai, they particularly sought out such cases or particularly reacted to them when they came to their attention. This argument is different from the one suggested earlier because it does not posit that the reason why the promotors became involved had anything to do with their concern about cases of this particular type. (They could have become more involved simply because they did not have to spend the time on sexual offenses, as did their brothers at Cambrai.) A closer look at the sentences themselves may give us some evidence as to which is more likely to be the case.

Before we do that, however, we should ask what adding the category of office/instance to the Cambrai cases does to the tentative conclusions that we drew about gender ratios and plaintiffs' success rates on the basis of just the straight-instance cases. We can also compare those results to similar data from Brussels. (Calculating this data for Brussels on the basis of the straight-instance cases alone would be pointless because there are so few such cases in the spousals area.) Gender ratios for office/instance cases are relatively easy to calculate because normally, only one of the two or three defendants joins with the promotor in pursuing the case. Calculating success rates is more difficult. In one sense, the plaintiff won virtually all of them because the promotor almost always was awarded his costs, and in all but a few cases he found something for which to fine the parties. That cannot always be counted as a win for the defendant who joined with the promotor, however. That defendant was almost always seeking to establish *sponsalia* or a marriage with the defendant or one of the defendants. Sometimes the defendant/plaintiff (always a woman) failed to establish the *sponsalia* or the marriage but was awarded a dowry for having been deflowered. We will have occasion to look at such cases later on, but here we confine ourselves to asking whether the defendant/plaintiff succeeded in establishing what he or she was trying to establish, *sponsalia* or a marriage. We will see that that was rarely the case.

The results given in Table 8.8 are somewhat different from those given in Table 8.4. The overall proportion of female plaintiffs has gone up from 52 percent to 58 percent, and the overall plaintiffs' success rate has gone down from 59 percent to 52 percent (47% if we exclude the uncontested cases).[63] That the addition of the office/instance cases is what is causing these differences is clear enough when we compare the straight-instance cases to the office/instance cases in this sample.[64] This sample has approximately the same proportion of female plaintiffs in straight-instance cases as does that in Table 8.4 (51% vs 52%), but female plaintiffs dominate the office/instance sample (66%). Similarly, the plaintiffs' success rate in the straight-instance cases is approximately the same in this sample as it was in Table 8.4 (59% vs 60%), but their success rate in office/instance cases is significantly lower (42%).[65]

[63] They are already excluded in Table 8.4, in all cases but one. If we exclude that one, the rate in Table 8.4 goes down to 58%.

[64] These figures are all derived from Table 8.8.

[65] $z = 2.02$, significant at .96.

TABLE 8.8. *Marriage Cases at Cambrai – Gender Ratios and Judgments (1438–1453)*

Type of Case	Procedure	FP	%F	SFP	%SFP	SMP	%SMP	SP	%TSP	SPro	%SPro	noS	GTOT
Sexual offenses:													
Adultery[a]	Office	1	100	1	100	0			100	25	89	0	29
Bigamy	Office	0		0		0				1	100	1	2
Clerical[b]	Office	0	0	0		0	0			12	92	0	13
Fornication	Office	0		0		0				7	88	0	8
SUBTOTAL		1	50	1	100	0			100	45	90	1	52
De futuro, two-party, contest[c]	Instance	3	23	0	0	3	30		25	0		1	13
	Office/instance	6	43	0	0	1	13		7	0		0	14
	Office	0		0		0				4	40	0	10
SUBTOTAL		9	33	0	0	4	22		15	4	40	1	37
De futuro, two-party, dissolution	Instance	1	33	1	100	2	100		100	0		1	4
	Office/instance	3	60	3	100	1	50		80	0		0	5
	Office[d]	0		0		0				5	63	0	8
SUBTOTAL		4	50	4	100	3	75		88	5	63	1	17
De futuro, two-party, remission	Instance	1	50	1	100	1	100	9	100	0		0	11
	Office/instance	1	33	1	100	2	100	2	100	0		0	5
SUBTOTAL		2	40	2	100	3	100	11	100	0		0	16
De futuro, three-party	Instance[e]	3	18	1	33	2	14		18	0		0	17
	Office/instance[f]	2	33	0	0	1	20		14	0		0	7
	Office	0		0		0				3	60	0	5
SUBTOTAL		5	22	1	20	3	16		17	3	60	0	29
SUBTOTAL (*de futuro*, no *cop*)		20	32	7	37	13	30	11	42	12	52	2	99
De futuro cop, two-party	Instance	5	100	2	40	0			40	0		0	5
	Office/instance	13	100	2	15	0			15	0		0	13
	Office	0		0		0				11	55	0	20
SUBTOTAL		18	100	4	22	0			22	11	55	0	38

(*continued*)

TABLE 8.8 *(continued)*

Type of Case	Procedure	FP	%F	SFP	%SFP	SMP	%SMP	SP	%TSP	SPro	%SPro	noS	GTOT
De futuro cop, three-party	Instance	7	100	2	29	0			29	0		0	7
	Office/instance[g]	6	100	1	17	0			17	0		0	6
	Office	0		0		0				3	75	1	5
SUBTOTAL		13	100	3	23	0			23	3	75	1	18
SUBTOTAL (*de futuro*, plus *cop*)		31	100	7	23	0			23	14	58	1	56
SUBTOTAL (Spousals)		51	54	14	28	13	30	11	62	26	55	3	155
Divorce	Office	0		0		0				2	17	0	12
Separation	Instance	13	72	12	100	5	100	1	100	0		1	19
	Office/instance	8	67	8	100	4	100		100	0		0	12
	Office	0		0		0				1	100	0	1
SUBTOTAL		21	70	20	100	9	100	1	100	1	50	1	32
SUBTOTAL (Div. & sep.)		21	70	20	100	9	100	1	100	3	21	1	44
Miscellaneous	Instance	2	67	1	100	1	100	1	100	0		1	4
	Office[h]	1	100	1	100	0			100	3	100	0	4
SUBTOTAL		3	75	2	100	1	100	1	100	3	75	1	8
SUBTOTAL (Nonspousals)		24	71	22	100	10	100	2	100	6	33	2	52
GRAND TOTAL		76	58	37	51	23	43	13	52	77	61	6	259

Notes: For the basic layout, see Table 8.4. The layout of this table differs somewhat from previous tables on this topic in order to accommodate the role of the promotor. As before, 'FP' gives the number of female plaintiffs in the category, '%FP' the female/male gender ratio, excluding those cases that have multiple plaintiffs. (This is a significant factor only in the remission cases, where 11 of them result from joint petitions of the espoused.) As before, SFP and SMP give the sentences for male and female plaintiffs, respectively, while '%SFP' and '%SMP' give the success ratios for each (SFP/[SFP + SMD], SMP/[SMP + SFD]). 'SP' gives the sentences for those plaintiffs in cases where there are multiple plaintiffs, but '%TSP' gives the total success ratio for all plaintiffs in the category – (SFP + SMP + SP)/(SFP + SMP + SP + SMD + SFD) (there being no sentences for defendants in cases with multiple plaintiffs). 'SPro' gives the sentences for the promotor in those cases where a nonprofessional plaintiff cannot be identified (more on the coding of this in the text at nn. 74–7), and '%SPro' gives the promotor's success ratio in such cases. 'noS' gives the few cases that have no definitive sentence, with the total number of cases in the last column. '0%' is genuine (if the fraction has no denominator, the cell is left blank). The notes give the denominators where they are not obvious from the percentages.

For notes *a–h*, see T&C no. 797.

Source: Registres de Cambrai.

As was the case in Table 8.4, these aggregates conceal a much more diverse reality. As in Table 8.4, women dominate in separation litigation (72% in Table 8.8 vs 73% in Table 8.4); the addition of the office/instance cases actually brings their participation down just a bit (72% vs 67%, office/instance). Plaintiffs' success rate in such cases is 100 percent. Women also totally dominate in litigation in which *copula* is alleged, bringing it on their own or aiding the promotor in 100 percent of the cases. Here, however, there is a significant difference in their success rate, depending on which form of procedure is used. As in Table 8.4, they prevail in 33 percent of the straight-instance cases, but are able to establish a marriage in only 11 percent of the office/instance cases.[66]

As in Table 8.4, men dominate in straight-instance cases about spousals where *copula* is not alleged (77% in both cases). Plaintiffs' success rate in such litigation is higher than it was in Table 8.4 (47% vs 34%), and as in Table 8.4, women's success rate is no worse than men's.[67] Women make up somewhat less than half of the plaintiffs in the office/instance cases where *copula* is not alleged (43%). The overall plaintiffs' success rate in such cases is somewhat lower than in the straight-instance cases (35%), but the women, once more, do no worse than the men.[68]

Extreme caution is again in order when dealing with these numbers because the sample sizes in each cell are small. With all due caution, however, we can say that most of the conclusions that we drew from Table 8.4 remain intact. It was much easier at Cambrai to get the court to separate a marriage, dissolve *sponsalia*, or declare that they did not exist than it was to establish *sponsalia*. The intervention of the promotor did not alter this tendency; if anything, it exaggerated it. The numbers are here so small as to become almost anecdotal, but they all point in the same direction. On their own, women prevailed in two of five two-party cases involving *copula* (40%) and two of seven such three-party cases (29%). Joined with the promotor they lost 11 of 13 such two-party cases (15% success rate) and 5 of 6 such three-party cases (17% success rate). Ten men and three women brought straight-instance two-party actions to establish *sponsalia*. Three of the men and none of the women prevailed; defendants got judgments in nine cases, and one had no final judgment (25% success rate). Joined with the promotor, six women and eight men brought similar actions. One of the men prevailed, and the defendants got 13 judgments (7% success rate).

These facts raise questions that the numbers alone cannot answer. Two sets of motivations are at stake, those of the promotor and those of the parties. An analysis of the straight-office cases will give us some clues as to what they might have been, as will the sentences themselves. But before we look at them, we need to look at a table comparable to Table 8.8 but drawn from the Brussels register, Table 8.9.

[66] Disc. T&C no. 798.
[67] Disc. T&C no. 799.
[68] Disc. T&C no. 800.

TABLE 8.9. *Marriage Cases at Brussels – Gender Ratios and Judgments (1448–1459)*

Type of Case[a]	Procedure	FP	%F	SFP	%SFP	SMP	%SMP	SP	%TSP	SPro	%SPro	noS	GTOT
De futuro, two-party, contest[b]	Instance	1	100	0	0	0		0	0	0		0	1
	Office/instance	1	33	0	0	1	50	0	33	0		0	3
	Office	0		0		0		0		0	0	0	1
SUBTOTAL		2	50	0	0	1	50	0	25	0	0	0	5
De futuro, two-party, dissolution[c]	Office/instance	2	50	1	50	0	0	0	25	0		0	4
	Office	0		0		0		0		1	14	0	7
SUBTOTAL		2	50	1	50	0	0	0	25	1	14	0	11
De futuro, two-party, remission[d]	Instance	0	0	0		1	100	3	100	0		0	4
SUBTOTAL		0	0	0		1	100	3	100	0		0	4
De futuro, three-party[e]	Instance	1	50	0	0	0	0	0	0	0		0	2
	Office/instance	3	33	0	0	0	0	0	0	0		0	10
	Office	0		0		0		0		1	100	0	1
SUBTOTAL		4	36	0	0	0	0	0	0	1	100	0	13
SUBTOTAL (*de futuro*, no *cop*)		8	40	1	13	2	15	3	25	2	22	0	33
De futuro cop, two-party[f]	Office/instance	18	90	3	17	0	0	0	15	0		0	20
	Office	0		0		0		0		7	54	0	13
SUBTOTAL		18	90	3	17	0	0	0	15	7	54	0	33
De futuro cop, three-party[g]	Instance	2	100	0	0	0		0	0	0		0	2
	Office/instance	32	74	5	15	3	27	0	18	0		0	44
	Office	0		0		0		0		2	100	0	2
SUBTOTAL		34	76	5	14	3	27	0	17	2	100	0	48
SUBTOTAL (*de futuro*, plus *cop*)		52	80	8	15	3	23	0	17	9	60	0	81

Miscellaneous spousals	Office	0		0		0		0		1	50	0	2
SUBTOTAL (Spousals)		70	82	11	15	3	20	0	16	17	57	0	116
Divorce[b]	Instance	0	0	0		0	0	0	0	0		0	1
	Office	0		0		0		0		1	100	0	1
Restoration	Instance	2	40	1	50	2	67	0	60	0		0	5
Separation	Instance	9	75	8	100	3	100	1	100	0		1	13
SUBTOTAL (Div., rest., & sep.)		11	61	9	90	5	71	1	83	1	100	1	20
Dowry													
Deflowering	Instance	6	100	4	80	0		0	80	0		1	6
Dos seu donatio	Instance	1	20	1	100	3	100	6	100	0		3	13
SUBTOTAL		7	64	5	83	3	100	6	93	0		4	19
Miscellaneous	Office	0		0		0		0		2	100	0	2
SUBTOTAL (Nonspousals)		18	62	14	88	8	80	7	88	3	100	5	41
GRAND TOTAL		88	77	25	29	11	44	7	36	20	61	5	157

Notes: For the basic layout, see Tables 8.4 and 8.8.
For note *a–h*, see T&C no. 801.
Source: Liber van Brussel.

There are only 11 instance cases about spousals in Table 8.9's sample, far too few to do any statistical analysis, but it is clear enough what is not there. Unlike the court at Cambrai, the court at Brussels did very little instance spousals business. What this means is that a substantial portion of litigation in which men played a dominant role at Cambrai is absent. What is left are office/instance cases in which women play a dominant role (82% of all spousals litigation). In such cases plaintiffs have a low success rate (15%). As they were at Cambrai, women were also dominant in other types of matrimonial litigation. They brought three-quarters of the separation suits and all of the suits for dowry for deflowering. Men were dominant in the relatively few dowry suits not for deflowering that have only one plaintiff (most are brought by the couple) and in the relatively few suits for restoration of conjugal rights (which can be viewed as inverse separation actions). The end result is a lower female/male gender ratio in non-spousals litigation than in spousals (62% vs 82%). Plaintiffs' success rate in non-spousals matrimonial litigation (all of which is brought in straight-instance form) is high (88%). This has the effect of pulling up plaintiffs' overall success rate, but it is still significantly lower than it is at Cambrai (36% vs 52%).[69]

We need one more number to complete the numerical picture. We have said that the promotor almost always found something for which to fine the defendants in any kind of office action. We have also said that in office/instance spousals actions, he was singularly unsuccessful in establishing *sponsalia* for the defendant who joined him in the action. The question remains whether he was any more successful in those cases where a defendant did not join him in the action. The question is easier to ask than it is to answer because it is not always clear that the promotor is trying to establish *sponsalia*. Indeed, in many cases he seems to be trying to dissolve them for some alleged impediment. Further, in three-party cases, some *sponsalia* are almost always confirmed; the question is which, and again it is not always clear what side the promotor is taking. Hence, the coding in what follows calls for some judgment.

Leaving aside the three-party cases, the numbers, though small, do point in certain directions. In the Brussels sample, there are 21 straight-office two-party spousals cases. In only one of them is the promotor trying to establish *sponsalia* where *copula* is not also alleged. He fails.[70] In seven he is trying to dissolve unconsummated *sponsalia* that the parties admit have taken place. He fails in all but one of these cases.[71] He is also trying to dissolve five sets of conceded *sponsalia* that have been consummated. He succeeds in two of these cases and fails in three.[72] In another eight cases, it looks as if he is attempting to establish a presumptive marriage between the couple. He succeeds in five

[69] $z = 2.30$, significant at .98.

[70] *Officie c Rampenberch en Bossche* (29.vii.57), no. 1190.

[71] Listed T&C no. 802.

[72] Listed T&C no. 803.

cases and fails in three.[73] It will be noted that this last is the only type of case in which the promotor by himself has a higher success rate than he does when he joins with one of the parties. Since one of the reasons we know that a party has joined with the promotor is when that party is fined for a frivolous allegation of *sponsalia*, it is possible that in some or all of the cases the promotor won, he was being aided by one of the parties but that fact was not recorded.

The Cambrai numbers point in the same direction. There are 11 two-party cases in the sample where the promotor seems to be trying to establish *sponsalia* where *copula* is not also alleged. He succeeds in four cases and fails in seven.[74] In seven cases he is trying to dissolve unconsummated *sponsalia* that the parties admit have taken place. He succeeds in five cases and fails in two.[75] He is also trying to dissolve three sets of conceded *sponsalia* that have been consummated and is probably trying to do so in another such case. He succeeds in one of these cases and fails in three.[76] In another 16 cases, it looks as if he is attempting to establish a presumptive marriage between the couple. He succeeds in nine cases and fails in seven.[77] While in a number of types of cases the promotor by himself has a higher success rate in the Cambrai sample than he does when he joins with one of the parties, his rate is certainly not high (50%, 19/38 vs 90%, 45/50 in straight cases of sexual offenses), and once again it is possible that in some or all of the cases the promotor won, he was being aided by one of the parties.

To return, just briefly, to the comparison that we made between Cambrai instance matrimonial litigation and that at Paris, Ely and York (Table 8.4), what the addition of the *ex officio* cases at Cambrai and Brussels does to that comparison is to eliminate the difference in the gender ratio of spousals litigation at Cambrai (and Brussels) and that at Ely and York. It does not, however, eliminate the difference in the success ratios. If anything, it makes it wider. Once more, the significance of these findings will be postponed to Chapter 12.

RURAL VERSUS URBAN

The Cambrai sentences quite frequently do not give us the place of residence of the parties; the Brussels sentences are even more deficient in this regard. Place of residence is almost always reported when the imposition of *leges* is noted in the margin, and we can infer what it was when a couple are said to have solemnized their espousals in a particular church (if there is no indication that they deliberately went someplace else to do so in order to avoid local objections to their marriage). Because there are more indications of place of

[73] Listed T&C no. 804.
[74] Listed T&C no. 805.
[75] Listed T&C no. 806.
[76] Listed T&C no. 807.
[77] Listed T&C no. 808.

residence in the Cambrai registers and because, until 1448, the Cambrai court was hearing cases from the whole diocese, we coded the placenames from the index of *Registres de Cambrai*. Approximately a third (496/1,455, 34%) of the cases yielded some information about the residence of one or both of the parties. The proportion of marriage cases (including cases of adultery but excluding clerical sexual offenses) was lower, approximately a quarter (264/1,019 [est.], 26%). There are a number of reasons for this discrepancy, but one of the most important is that almost all of the cases that involve members of the clergy give the name of the parish or religious house to which the cleric belonged.

As is discussed more fully in Appendix e9.1, the entry or nonentry of the marginal *leges* in the Cambrai sentence books is somewhat puzzling, and practice may have changed over the course of the period of the surviving registers. We assume here that the presence or absence of such an entry or other indication of the residence of the parties is not biased with regard to whether the residence was urban or rural. It is possible that no entry of residence was recorded if the person being fined paid the fine on the spot, in which case there might be some bias in favor of (i.e., omitting) the well informed and the wealthy, which category might correlate with urban residence, but an entry of residence would also not be made if the court did not know what it was because the person had disappeared, and that category might correlate with rural residence. We offer in Table 8.10, then, the data that we have on the ground that it gives us some evidence of the balance between urban and rural residence of the parties.

The findings here are similar to those for Ely. Cambrai, Valenciennes, Mons, and Tournai certainly qualify as urban (U), but they account for only 21 percent of the places of residence. We may add to them places that are sufficiently close that today they are brought within their governmental units (U1), and that raises the urban residents to 31 percent. We can repeat the process for the seats of the deaneries (U2) and the places that today are within their governmental units (U3), and that will add another 11 percent. One might argue that certain towns (e.g., Ath) that were not seats of deans should be included within the group, but one could also argue that some of the seats of the deans (e.g., Avesnes-sur-Helpe) should not be. A number of towns along the Scheldt were engaged in manufacture of, and trading in, cloth in the mid-fifteenth century, only to suffer before the end of the century in the wars of Louis XI. The possibility that we have missed one or more of such towns is balanced by the fact that some of the towns that are now within the governmental areas of the larger ones were probably quite rural in the mid-fifteenth century. All told, it is unlikely that the proportion of urban residents, narrowly defined, exceeds 30 percent by much and, more generously defined, by 40 percent. This would make the litigants before the court at Cambrai somewhat more urban than those before the court of Ely (roughly 30%), but not so urban as those before the court of York (roughly 50%) and certainly not so urban as those before the court of Paris (probably in excess of 90%).

TABLE 8.10. *Parties' Place of Residence in Marriage Cases in Southern Cambrai Diocese (1438–1453)*

Place	Country	P/D	Unit1	Unit2	U/R	No.
Cambrai	F	Nord	Cambrai		U	20
Valenciennes	F	Nord	Valenciennes		U	15
Mons	B	Hainaut	Mons		U	12
Tournai	B	Hainaut	Tournai		U	3
SUBTOTAL					21%	50
Ghlin	B	Hainaut	(Mons)		U1	3
Curgies	F	Nord	Valenciennes	Valenciennes est	U1	2
Escanaffles	B	Hainaut	Tournai	Tournai 1	U1	2
Quarouble	F	Nord	Valenciennes	Valenciennes est	U1	2
Abancourt	F	Nord	Cambrai	Cambrai ouest	U1	1
Amougies	B	Hainaut	Tournai	Tournai 1	U1	1
Anseroeul	B	Hainaut	Tournai	Tournai 1	U1	1
Ciply	B	Hainaut	Mons	Mons 2	U1	1
Harmignies	B	Hainaut	Mons	Mons 2	U1	1
Hyon	B	Hainaut	(Mons)		U1	1
Kain	B	Hainaut	Tournai	Tournai 1	U1	1
Pottes	B	Hainaut	Tournai	Tournai 1	U1	1
Thieusies	B	Hainaut	Soignies	Mons 1	U1	1
Trith-Saint-Léger	F	Nord	Valenciennes	Valenciennes sud	U1	1
Verchain	F	Nord	Valenciennes	Valenciennes sud	U1	1
Warchin	B	Hainaut	Tournai	Tournai 1	U1	1
Wattripont	B	Hainaut	Ath	Tournai 1	U1	1
SUBTOTAL					31%	72
Maubeuge	F	Nord	Avesnes-sur-Helpe	Maubeuge	U2	6
Avesnes-sur-Helpe	F	Nord	Avesnes-sur-Helpe		U2	3

(continued)

TABLE 8.10 *(continued)*

Place	Country	P/D	Unit1	Unit2	U/R	No.
Binche	B	Hainaut	Thuin	Binche	U2	3
Chièvres	B	Hainaut	Ath	Lens	U2	1
SUBTOTAL					36%	85
Hon	F	Nord	Avesnes-sur-Helpe	Bavay	U3	2
Houdain-lez-Bavay	F	Nord	Avesnes-sur-Helpe	Bavay	U3	2
Câtillon-sur-Sambre	F	Nord	Cambrai	Le Cateau-Cambrésis	U3	1
Estinnes-au-Mont	B	Hainaut	Thuin	Binche	U3	1
Étrœungt	F	Nord	Avesnes-sur-Helpe	Avesnes-sur-Helpe Sud	U3	1
Le Cateau-Cambrésis	F	Nord	Cambrai	Le Cateau-Cambrésis	U3	1
Ors	F	Nord	Cambrai	Le Cateau-Cambrésis	U3	1
Saint-Souplet	F	Nord	Cambrai	Le Cateau-Cambrésis	U3	1
Semousies	F	Nord	Avesnes-sur-Helpe	Avesnes-sur-Helpe Nord	U3	1
Taisnières-en-Thiérache	F	Nord	Avesnes-sur-Helpe	Avesnes-sur-Helpe Nord	U3	1
Vellereille-les-Brayeux	B	Hainaut	Thuin	Binche	U3	1
SUBTOTAL					42%	98
Oisy	F	Pas-de-Calais	Arras	Marquion	R	6
Le Quesnoy	F	Nord	Avesnes-sur-Helpe	Le Quesnoy	R	5
Lessines	B	Hainaut	Soignies	Lessines	R	5
Ath	B	Hainaut	Ath		R	4
Ellezelles	B	Hainaut	Ath	Lessines	R	4
Lahamaide	B	Hainaut	Ath	Ath	R	4
Crespin	F	Nord	Valenciennes	Condé-sur-l'Escaut	R	3
Frasnes-lez-Buissenal	B	Hainaut	Ath	Leuze	R	3
Leuze	B	Hainaut	Tournai	Leuze	R	3

Wodecq	B	Hainaut	Ath	Lessines	R	3
Acren	B	Hainaut	Soignies	Lessines	R	2
Aubigny-en-Artois	F	Pas-de-Calais	Arras	Aubigny-en-Artois	R	2
Avesnes-lès-Aubert	F	Nord	Cambrai	Carnières	R	2
Avesnes-le-Sec	F	Nord	Valenciennes	Bouchain	R	2
Bancourt	F	Pas-de-Calais	Arras	Bapaume	R	2
Condé-sur-l'Escaut	F	Nord	Valenciennes	Condé-sur-l'Escaut	R	2
Crèvecœur-sur-l'Escaut	F	Nord	Cambrai	Marcoing	R	2
Ellgnies-Saint-Anne	B	Hainaut	Ath	Quevaucamps	R	2
Ghislenghien	B	Hainaut	Ath	Ath	R	2
Hacquegnies	B	Hainaut	Ath	Leuze	R	2
Honnecourt-sur-l'Escaut	F	Nord	Cambrai	Marcoing	R	2
Horrues	B	Hainaut	Soignies	Soignies	R	2
Isières	B	Hainaut	Ath	Ath	R	2
Marcq	F	Nord	Cambrai	Marcoing	R	2
Meslin-l'Évêque	B	Hainaut	Ath	Ath	R	2
Rebecq	B	Brabant wallon	Nivelles	Tubize	R	2
Roucourt	B	Hainaut	Tournai	Péruwelz	R	2
Soignies	B	Hainaut	Soignies		R	2
The 62 rural places that appear only once are given in the margin.[a]					R	62
TOTAL					100%	235

Notes: The subtotals are cumulative, and the proportions are of the total. No. = the number of parties who are identified to this place; P/D = modern province in the case of Belgium, *département* in the case of France; unit1 and unit2 = the modern units of government below the provincial/departmental level. Not all the names have survived to today, but all the places exist under one name or another, except for two in Mons that are indicated by 'Mons' in parentheses.

For note *a*, see T&C no. 809.

Source: Registres de Cambrai.

TABLE 8.11. *Parties' Place of Residence in Marriage Cases in Northern Cambrai Diocese (1438–1453)*

Place	Country	P/D	Unit1	Unit2	U/R	No.
Antwerpen	B	Antwerpen			U	3
Mechelen	B	Antwerpen	Mechelen		U	2
Brussel	B	Brussel Hoofdstad			U	1
SUBTOTAL					11%	6
Baaigem	B	Oost-Vlaanderen	Gent	Gent 6	U1	1
Dikkelvenne	B	Oost-Vlaanderen	Gent	Gent 6	U1	1
Vorst	B	Brussel Hoofdstad	Brussel Hoofdstad	Ukkel	U1	1
Lemberge	B	Oost-Vlaanderen	Gent	Gent 6	U1	1
Schelderode	B	Oost-Vlaanderen	Gent	Gent 6	U1	1
Scheldewindeke	B	Oost-Vlaanderen	Gent	Gent 6	U1	1
SUBTOTAL					21%	12
Geraardsbergen	B	Oost-Vlaanderen	Aalst	Geraardsbergen	U2	4
Aalst	B	Oost-Vlaanderen	Aalst		U2	2
Pamel	B	Oost-Vlaanderen	Oudenarde		U2	2
SUBTOTAL					35%	20
Moorsel	B	Oost-Vlaanderen	Aalst	Aalst 2	U3	1
Ophasselt	B	Oost-Vlaanderen	Aalst	Geraardsbergen	U3	1
Welle	B	Oost-Vlaanderen	Aalst	Aalst 2	U3	1
SUBTOTAL					40%	23
Herne	B	Vlaams-Brabant	Halle-Vilvorde	Herne	R	4
Kwaremont	B	Oost-Vlaanderen	Oudenarde	Ronse	R	3
Bever	B	Vlaams-Brabant	Halle-Vilvorde	Herne	R	2
Dendermonde	B	Oost-Vlaanderen	Dendermonde		R	2
The 23 rural places that appear only once are given in the margin.[a]					R	23
TOTAL					100%	57

Notes: The layout of this table is the same as Table 8.10.
For note, see T&C no. 810.
Source: Registres de Cambrai.

The list for the northern part of the diocese, as shown in Table 8.11, is even more problematical. The division between the two halves of the diocese was made acccording to the modern provinces. This does not quite correspond to the medieval ecclesiastical division, but it is close enough for statistical purposes.[78] The division between the two parts of the diocese was not rigid. Couples, one of whom gives a place of residence in the southern and the other in the northern half, appear in our tables (each in his/her own half).[79] After the establishment of the independent officiality in Brussels in 1448, cases from the northern half of the diocese tended not to appear in the court at Cambrai, but some did.[80] Prior to the establishment of the independent officiality in Brussels, there was a subordinate officiality there. This fact probably accounts for the fact that only one party known to be from Brussels appears in the Cambrai registers, and it may account for the relative absence of cases from the north generally. Overall, the two tables illustrate a phenomenon that we noted at York. The farther away geographically the place of residence of the parties, the less likely it is that they will appear in the court. The whole modern province of Antwerp, which contained two towns that certainly qualify as urban, Antwerp and Mechelen, accounts for only seven cases, while the town of Maubeuge, barely urban by any standard but much closer to Cambrai, accounts for six.

As is the case with the southern half of the diocese, one can doubt some of the classifications of urban and rural. Herne, though it was not the seat of a dean, might be raised to urban status. Then again, the places in the canton of Ghent known as 'Gent 6' are quite far from the medieval center of the town, and probably did not have an urban culture in the fifteenth century. Overall, discounting for the virtual absence of Brussels, we probably should raise the proportion of clearly urban litigants who appeared before some officiality, be it that at Cambrai or that at Brussels, to 30 percent, perhaps more. Stretching the definition of 'urban', we might get to 50 percent, but all we have evidence for is 40 percent, roughly the same proportion as in the southern half of the diocese.

[78] The northern parts of the modern provinces of Hainaut and Brabant wallon were in the archdeaconry of Brabant and, hence, under the jurisdiction of the officiality of Brussels.

[79] Listed at T&C no. 811.

[80] Listed at T&C no. 812.

9

Cambrai and Brussels

The Content of the Sentences

The numbers that we explored in the preceding chapter left us with several questions. There were differences between Cambrai and Brussels that were hard to account for on the basis of our speculations about differing roles of the secular and the lower ecclesiastical courts. Prominent among these was the greater involvement of the promotor in spousals cases at Brussels and the greater involvement of the promotor in separation and divorce cases at Cambrai. Underlying this difference was a difference between the courts of Cambrai diocese and that of other ecclesiastical courts that we have examined: the far greater role of the promotor generally. We sought, without success on *a priori* grounds, to sort out the motivations of the promotors and the parties, some of whom joined with the promotor and some of whom did not. Because of the formulaic nature of the only record we have, the sentences, we may not be able to penetrate as deeply into what is happening in matrimonial litigation in Cambrai diocese as we were in York, Ely, and Paris, but the sentences themselves do tell us something, and it is to these that we now turn.

TWO-PARTY SPOUSALS CASES NOT ALLEGING *COPULA*

Contested – Cambrai

As Tables 8.7 and 8.8 show, there are in our sample of Cambrai cases 70 two-party spousals cases where *copula* was not alleged. The cases are about evenly divided between those in which the existence of the espousals is at stake (37/70, 53%), on the one hand, and those in which conceded espousals are sought to be dissolved or remitted (dissolution: 17/70, 24%; remission: 16/70, 23%), on the other.

As we have seen, male plaintiffs dominate the straight-instance actions in which the existence of the espousals is at stake (10/13, 77%); the cases in which the promotor joined with one of the defendants show less male dominance, but it is still greater than one-half (8/14, 57%). There are also 10 such cases brought by the promotor, without, so far as we can tell, the participation of either of the defendants. The three types of procedure thus make up roughly equal proportions of this type of litigation (35%, 38%, 27%). Plaintiffs' success rate in this type of litigation is low. It is highest in the straight-office actions (40%, success being here measured by whether the promotor succeeded in establishing the *sponsalia*, not whether he got the parties fined or obtained his costs [the latter being something that happened in virtually all the cases he brought]), next highest in the straight-instance actions (30%), and lowest in the combined actions (8%).

Oudard Divitis, the official who rendered the sentences recorded in 1438–9, rendered sentence in five straight-instance actions in which the issue was the existence of the espousals, two straight-office cases, and one mixed. Since Divitis accounts for 19 percent of the sentences in the surviving registers, his proportion of this type of case (21%) is about what we would expect. His proportions of types of procedure, however, is not what we would expect, though the numbers in the cells are small. He seems to have heard a greater proportion of instance actions of this type and correspondingly lower proportion of actions involving the promotor.[1] This means, of course, that his successor, Grégoire Nicolaï, heard more than his share of such cases in a criminal or quasi-criminal mode.

Divitis's sentences tend to be quite cryptic. His first sentence in a straight-instance two-party case in which the plaintiff sought to establish *sponsalia* is typical:[2]

> In a case initiated and pending before us the official of Cambrai between the parties, [JL], plaintiff on the one side, and [JH] defendant, on the other, having seen the petition of the plaintiff, the oaths, assertions, confessions, and replies of the parties and other things moving us and our soul, supported by the seasoned advice of those who are expert in the law, the name of Christ having been invoked, we absolve the defendant from the promises of marriage proposed and alleged by the same plaintiff, condemning the plaintiff [to pay] the costs of the defendant, and reserving to our judgment the taxation [of these costs], and granting, moreover, to the defendant the capacity (*facultatem*) to marry another, if she should wish to marry in the Lord, issuing a definitive sentence in this writing.

This sentence will be seen to have a number of elements in common with the sentence quoted at the beginning of the last chapter.[3] There is a formal recital of the name of the case, a rehearsal of the elements of the *ordo* that were followed, an assertion that there were, in addition to the *acta*, other things (*alia*) that moved the judge and his conscience, an assertion that the *iurisperiti* had been consulted, and an invocation of the divine name. Some fairly formal

[1] Instance: 5/13, 38%; office and office/instance: 3/25, 12%.

[2] *Laugoinge c Hennin* (8.xi.38), no. 53, T&C no. 813.

[3] Ch 8, at n. 2.

indication of the parties' names, the rehearsal of the elements of the *ordo*, an invocation of the divine name, and the final phrase are found in virtually every Cambrai definitive sentence, whether the case is instance, office, or mixed. Certain changes, such as putting the "having seen" clause first, omitting the formal "In a case initiated" clause, and inserting the name of the parties in the description of the process are, so far as we can tell, matters of style. We can be less sure about the omission of the "and other things" clause or the clause about consultation with the *iurisperiti*. These clauses are not found in most of Nicolaï's sentences, and where they are found, their presence may indicate that the case was particularly serious, difficult, or important. We can be quite sure that changes in the recital of the elements of the *ordo* do tell us something. There are a sufficient number of sentences that mention witnesses and counter-witnesses, documents, and/or *ex offico* oaths that we can be reasonably confident that where these are not mentioned, they were not present. Hence, we can also be reasonably confident that there was relatively little process in this case. The plaintiff made a petition (probably oral); the parties swore to their positions (*sacramentis*); there were various charges, admissions, and countercharges (*assertionibus, confessionibus, et responsionibus*).[4] These last could have been in writing, like the positions and articles in the court of York, but they may well have been oral. Hence, it is possible that the whole proceeding took no more than one session of court.

What follows is the heart of the sentence: The defendant was "absolved from the proposed promises." This wording is a little odd. Absolution suggests to us criminal charges, which these were clearly not, but the word is often found in instance sentences.[5] What we have been used to from England, however, is that the defendant is absolved from the 'petition' or 'instance' of the plaintiff and that this absolution is normally preceded by a motivation clause: "because we find that the plaintiff has insufficiently founded and proven the matrimonial contract," and so on.[6] That this is to be assumed here is clear enough from the marginal note telling us that the plaintiff was "held to the laws" for "clandestine [espousals] frivolously alleged."[7]

There is much about the practice of "holding to the laws" that is unclear from the registers. Both the instance and the office cases use the words *leges* and *emende* to describe what seem to be fines for various kinds of misconduct.[8] The sentences normally speak of *emende*, occasionally offering them as an alternative to corporal penance.[9] The marginalia usually speak of *leges*. This suggests that the fines were statutorily fixed, although I have found no evidence

4 Sometimes *allegationibus* is substituted for *assertionibus*. So far as I can tell, these terms were synonymous, and they will be treated as such.

5 E.g., Ch 6, n. 80.

6 *Ibid.*

7 *Tenetur actor ad leges pro clandestinis cum rea frivole allegatis.*

8 See text before n. 5.

9 E.g., *Officie c Drivere*, at nn. 408–9 (*ad penitentiam iuxta nostrum arbitrium moderandam aut alias ad leges et emendas*). Disc. and refs. T&C no. 814.

of it in the synodal statutes that I have examined.[10] There does not seem to be any difference between the two words. Offenses for which a person is held to amend in a sentence will appear in the marginalia as those for which a party is "held to the laws." The words were probably interchangeable, and any difference in nuance between the two cannot be recovered from the records as we now have them.

Even more serious is the fact that we have no direct evidence of how much the fines were.[11] They probably varied depending on the perceived seriousness of the offense. They probably were not particularly high for some of the lesser offenses, such as here, for espousals frivolously alleged. We will see later that they probably were not very high for failure to publicize clandestine espousals or failure to solemnize within the fixed period, for we find many people willing to run the risk of having to pay such fines (indeed, we find people bringing cases when there was a virtual certainty that they would have to pay such fines). Aside from a few very serious cases where corporal penance is ordered (and the option to pay a fine is apparently not given),[12] there is only one element in the fines that is ever specified. In some cases, the guilty party is ordered, in addition to paying the fine, to contribute wax, usually a pound or two of it, to the chapel of the officiality. There are relatively few such cases in our sample, but there are a number of them outside the sample. I have gone through a group and can report that there seems to be little pattern to when it is ordered and when it is not, except that it tends to occur in the more serious cases. But there are equally or more serious cases where a contribution of wax is not ordered. What may be involved here is a perception by the court that the guilty party could well afford to come up with a pound of wax in addition to the fine, or it may simply be that the sacristan told the official when he was going to court in the morning that the stock of candles was running low.

Despite the uncertainties as to precisely what was involved, these marginal indications of the *leges* are valuable. In the first place, they tell us that relatively few instance matrimonial cases at Cambrai were really totally instance. Many sentences that look on their surface as if they were simply instance judgments have marginal *leges*. Hence, the movement across time toward a greater criminalization of the process of matrimonial litigation is a direction in which the court was heading when it was still hearing a number of cases in which the promotor was not a formal party. Further, the *leges* frequently give us important details that are not found in the sentences themselves. Here, for example, we learn that what the plaintiff had alleged was a clandestine exchange of *sponsalia* and that the court considered him so far from proving it that it was willing to

[10] See Niermeyer, s.v. *lex*, meaning 23, for numerous examples of the word being used to mean a fixed penalty.

[11] App. e9.2, "What Can We Learn from the Tournai Account Books?" (see T&C no. 1055), suggests that we can get some idea of their range from the roughly contemporary account books of Tournai diocese. Lit. and disc. T&C no. 815.

[12] E.g., *Office c Wyet et Paiebien* (Ch X, at n. 195) (attempted bigamy); *Office c Lienard* (14.v.46), no. 920 (contempt).

call the allegation 'frivolous'. (We will have occasion to return to this charge and the amends for it a number of times in this chapter.)[13]

In the sample of cases in which the existence of *sponsalia* is contested, no two of Divitis's sentences have quite the same fact-pattern or quite the same result. In the second straight-instance action of this type, a couple, having previously been sentenced to solemnize their marriage in what was probably a straight-instance action, appear before the court and remit their contract.[14] The wording of this sentence is best treated with the other remission cases,[15] but the entry tells us something about the preceding case (which probably appeared in a register that is now lost). The marginalia indicate that there were no *leges* for the *actor* because he had previously satisfied for them "as is apparent by the first sealed sentence." The *rea*, however, is fined for not having proceeded, that is, to solemnize the *sponsalia*. Hence, we conclude that in the first case, the man was the plaintiff (the record of the remission sentence has no indication of who was plaintiff and who defendant; both parties, it would seem, requested the remission). Further, the reference to the "first sealed sentence" suggests that the court did collect the fines and that the successful party did not get the sentence sealed until he or she had paid them or otherwise compounded for them. Perhaps more important, concern with maximizing revenues is indicated by the *leges* imposed on the *rea*. Apparently the court had forgotten to fine her the first time around and took the opportunity of her return to court to extract a fine for not having proceeded to solemnize the *sponsalia* that both parties now wanted to remit.[16]

In the third straight-instance action, the court finds for the *rea* and tells us more than it usually does as to why: "We absolve the *rea* from the promises of marriage proposed and alleged by [the plaintiff] against her, because she was deceived by the plaintiff so far as his wealth (*facultates*) is concerned and she does not want to contract with him."[17] Costs are divided between the parties, and no *leges* are mentioned.[18] Process in this case is minimal; no proof other than the "oaths, confessions, and replies" of the parties is mentioned. The court obviously believed that the *rea* had been deceived by the *actor*, but the deception may not have been deliberate. Had the *actor* clearly been lying, it is hard to imagine that there would not have been some sort of fine or that he would, at least, have been required to pay the *rea*'s costs. Indeed, the fact that the court absolves the *rea* rather than dissolves the *sponsalia* suggests that it viewed the case as one in which no *sponsalia* had been formed because of the *rea*'s mistake. This kind of error was not sufficient to upset a *de presenti* marriage,[19] and the Cambrai court's practice of treating virtually all *sponsalia*

13 E.g., see text following n. 153.
14 *Jolin et Gillette* (28.xi.38), no. 82.
15 At nn. 120–30.
16 Disc. T&C no. 816.
17 *Flaminc c Pinkers* (18.vii.39), no. 263, T&C no. 817.
18 *expensas hincinde factas compensantes*. This may mean that the party who incurred the costs bore them, but that is not the natural meaning of *compensare*.
19 See Ch 1, at n. 30.

as *de futuro* makes this judgment legally possible. The fact that the court holds that there were no *sponsalia* may explain why there were no fines of the kind that we normally associate with clandestine *sponsalia*, but we will see that in many cases, such fines are found even where the *sponsalia* are not proven. This suggests either that these *sponsalia* were not clandestine or that the parties got into court within eight days of making them. A final inference: The fact that this is the only case in the sample that is grounded on a legal deficiency in the contract (the doctrine of *error*) suggests that in most, perhaps all, of the other cases where *sponsalia* are not found, the reason for the finding is that there was insufficient proof of the contract.

In the fourth straight-instance action, the parties are ordered to solemnize their *sponsalia*: "[W]e pronounce and decree that the *rea* proceed further to solemnizing the marriage with the plaintiff in the hand of the priest and the face of the church – as is customary and is normally done...."[20] Both parties are fined for not having renewed their clandestine contract publicly and for not having proceeded to solemnization. Judicial enforcement of *sponsalia de futuro* at Cambrai is fairly rare, but it could happen. Since the process here consisted only of the "oaths, assertions, confessions, and replies" of the parties, we must imagine that the *rea* either confessed or said something that made it clear that she had contracted. It is even possible that she got the result she wanted, that is, that the reason why the *actor* had to sue her was that the *rea*'s family, not the *rea*, was opposed to the marriage.

The fifth straight-instance case in this series has only an interlocutory sentence.[21] (The definitive sentence, if there was one, probably came in the gap that exists between the sentences in 1439 and those in 1442.) It does, however, tell us something. The *actrix* is admitted to the proof of her case. Serious contests about the existence *vel non* of *sponsalia* could occur at Cambrai.

The only mixed office/instance case for the enforcement of *sponsalia* in our sample of Divitis's sentences is quite similar to the first straight-instance case just discussed.[22] The *reus* is absolved; the *rea* is fined for frivolously alleging clandestine *sponsalia*. There are also differences: The sentence begins with the style normally used by Divitis in this period for office cases. The *reus* is absolved from the "promises of marriage proposed and alleged by the promotor and the *correa*." The latter is specifically condemned to make "fitting amends." Only the *reus* is given license to marry another Both *rei* are charged with the costs of the promotor. The marginal *leges* state specifically that the *reus* was not charged with any. The final and perhaps most important difference is that the promoting *correa* was a woman, as was the *actrix* in the fifth straight-instance case.[23]

In the first of the two straight-office cases of this type, the official has issued a 'commission', probably to a promotor, to prosecute the case.[24] The *rea* is

[20] *Gousset c Cauvinne* (18.iv.39), no. 201, T&C no. 818.
[21] *Cordière c Pasquart* (30.iv.39), no. 212.
[22] *Office c Creteur et Formanoire* (10.i.39), no. 110.
[23] *Ibid.*, T&C no. 819.
[24] *Office c Speckenen et Vettekens* (14.iii.39), no. 170; disc. of commissions T&C no. 820.

contumacious, and the promotor introduces witnesses. The official finds that the *rei* "had entered into and had maintained [*habuisse*] *sponsalia* by words suitable and fitting for this, had not renewed them within the required time, nor had they proceeded to solemnizing the marriage within the fixed times." He therefore orders them, in language quite similar to the instance case with the same result, to solemnize the marriage, and condemns them to pay him amends and the promotor's costs.[25] In the other case, the promotor is less successful. On the basis of the "oaths, confessions and replies" of the *rei*, the official absolves the *rei* of the promises of marriage proposed by the promotor against them, but he does condemn them to pay the promotor's costs. The couple are not specifically licensed to marry others.[26]

These three cases have many characteristics of the office cases found in the rest of the Cambrai registers. The wording of the sentences is sufficiently constant that we should note where it differs. In the office/instance case, the woman clearly wanted the marriage to proceed and the man did not. She sought the aid of the promotor and got it, but she had no proof, at least when the man would not confess. So she lost and had to pay a fine for 'frivolous' allegations, and both of them had to pay the promotor's costs. Assuming that the costs were really compensatory (and that there was a reasonable chance that they would be paid), the promotor took no risk in joining in the woman's allegation. She, in turn, though she did take a financial risk, got some expert legal advice. If she won, she would not have had to pay for it. If she lost (as she did), the man would normally have had to share in paying for it. No mention was made of the man's costs in this case, and though they may have been minimal, he probably had to bear them. In the instance case with the same result, the unsuccessful *actrix* not only had to pay her own costs but she also had to pay those of the *reus*.[27] Hence, in the instance case, the unsuccessful plaintiff had to pay more. If this were the normal practice, one has to wonder why anyone, except those who were ill-advised, brought an instance case.

We will see that this was the normal practice, but there was considerable variation about the awarding of costs, particularly those between the parties. We have already seen one straight-instance case in which they were probably divided ('compensated') between the parties, even though the *actrix* was successful.[28] The judge seems to have had considerable discretion about awarding the parties' costs, and he always reserves the taxation of both the parties' and promotor's costs to himself, a process that, unfortunately, our records do not report. Almost always in straight-office and office/instance cases, however, all defendants were charged with the promotor's costs. Hence, there was an incentive to use this method of proceeding, rather than the straight-instance method. This incentive might have operated particularly strongly in

[25] *Ibid.*, T&C no. 821. Cf. *Gousset c Cauvinne* (n. 20).

[26] *Office c Cambre et Crocq* (14.vii.39), no. 260, T&C no. 822.

[27] *Laugoinge c Hennin* (at n. 2).

[28] *Flaminc c Pinkers* (at nn. 17–18).

the case of women, who, as a general matter, may have had less access to ready cash.

The successful office case has a number of unusual features, including the commission and the fact that the *rea* was contumacious. It is almost certainly because of this last fact that the promotor had to introduce witnesses, who, apparently, confirmed that the couple had, indeed, contracted. More ambiguous is the role of the *reus*. There is nothing in the sentence to suggest that he was 'friendly' to the promotor's charges, except for the fact that he did not present any counterproof. Someone, however, must have come all the way from Mechelen to get the official to issue the commission, and the most likely candidate is the *reus*. (Recall that the reason we normally know that one of the *rei* has sided with the promotor is that this person is fined for 'frivolous' allegations. The allegation that this couple had contracted was clearly not frivolous.)

If this speculation is correct, then our last case is quite different. The couple resisted the promotor's allegations successfully. That fact, in turn, raises the question of how the promotor knew about them. Unfortunately, our record gives us no indication, other than the fact that the couple have to pay the promotor's costs and that they are not given license to marry others. The license is present in some cases and absent from others. It could have simply been omitted (the sentence is otherwise quite cryptic), but it is possible that the official thought that there might be unprovable *sponsalia* between this couple. Divitis does not say why he charged the promotor's costs to the couple, but Nicolaï did, on occasion, say that it was "on account of the *fama*."[29] We will see that on other occasions, people were fined for allowing *publica fama* of an offense to arise, even though they had not committed one.

We have already seen that Grégoire Nicolaï renders a disproportionate number of sentences in office cases where the issue was the existence or nonexistence of *sponsalia*. He also, however, rendered sentences in eight such instance cases in the sample. Three seem quite routine and have no process beyond the usual petition, oaths, assertions, confessions, and responses. One of these results in an order to solemnize.[30] The wording of the sentence is a bit different from that of the similar sentence of Divitis in that the couple are specifically ordered to solemnize within 40 days and the *rea* is ordered to treat the *actor* thereafter with marital affection.[31] In the other two cases, the *rea* is absolved and given license. In one, in which the *actor* was contumacious, the *rea* is specifically awarded costs; in the other, costs are not mentioned.[32] In all three cases, the *actor* is fined for not renewing clandestine *sponsalia* publicly and for failure to proceed to solemnization; in the last case, he is also fined for frivolous allegation of *sponsalia*.

29 See cases discussed in n. 72 and at nn. 168–70.
30 *Beccut c Miquielle* (12.ix.44), no. 530.
31 Disc. T&C no. 823.
32 Listed T&C no. 824.

That someone should be fined for not renewing clandestine *sponsalia* publicly and for failure to proceed to solemnization and also for frivolous allegation of *sponsalia* might strike us as an irony worthy of *Catch-22*. That someone should be fined for the first two offenses and also be faced with a judgment in which the *rea* is absolved of any obligation to marry him is only slightly less ironic. One can certainly imagine the unsuccessful *actor* asking "What more could I have done?" The answer is not easy, but there are hints of it in some of the sentences. In one of the office/instance cases, Nicolaï condemns the promoting *reus* to amend "because he took no care to renew the words that he asserted and to proceed within the required time to contract marriage with the *correa* or at least have her brought to court because of this."[33] Similar language is found in two other cases in the sample.[34] It would seem, then, that the court was interpreting the synodal statutes very strictly. Private *sponsalia* had to be publicly renewed within eight days; if one of the couple refused to do this, the other had to bring suit, perhaps within eight days. If the rejected party did not do so and ultimately brought suit, he or she would have to pay a fine even if the suit was successful.

Looking at the situation from a moral point of view, perhaps we can find some justification for the practice. The court will assume that the party alleging *sponsalia* is doing so in good faith. Even if it ultimately concludes that the allegation is 'frivolous', that could simply mean that the party making the allegation had no proof. The espousals may well have taken place, or at least the alleging party may have thought that they did. If the alleging party thought so, then he or she should have done something about them before the suit was instituted. This may be the reason why the party who alleges *sponsalia* is not, so far as I am aware, ever given license to marry another. Perhaps the notion is that he or she is still bound in conscience, even if the other party is not.

Despite these possible justifications for the practice, it is hard to escape the conclusion that the underlying motivation for it was simply to collect money from the parties before the court. It may even have troubled some of the judges. In none of the cases in the sample does Divitis fine a party who unsuccessfully alleges *sponsalia* either for not renewing or for not proceeding (though he does do so for frivolous allegation). Jan Rodolphi, the first of the two Brussels officials, does not do it in any of the cases in our samples; Jan Platea, the second of the two, does it once, early in his term of office, but then seems to have abandoned the practice in his later sentences.[35]

The other five straight-instance cases before Nicolaï give indications of a more elaborate process. In the first, the *actor* produced witnesses whose depositions were taken; the parties produced written documents impugning, on the one side, and saving, on the other, the testimony in the depositions (we are

[33] *Office c Comte et Corelle* (26.i.46), no. 870, T&C no. 825.

[34] *Office c Gobert et Cange* (22.xi.49), no. 1230; *Office c Mote et Gavielle* (10.ii.53), no. 1410.

[35] The exceptional case is *Officie c Meyman, Eechoute en Haucx* (at n. 313). Fines for frivolous opposition without fines for nonrenewal are quite common in the sentences of all four judges.

reminded here of the *exceptiones contra testes* and the answering replication of English practice), and the *actor* also produced documentary evidence, the nature of which is not stated. In somewhat heightened rhetoric, the court ordered the couple to solemnize their marriage, adding that this had to be done within 40 days, and enjoining the woman thereafter to treat the man with marital affection.[36] The *rea* was condemned to pay the *actor*'s costs, and nothing was said about *leges* or *emende*. There are indications in this that the parties are of somewhat higher status; the woman is called *domicella*, though it is unclear precisely what that means. The higher status almost certainly explains how the parties were able to afford the more elaborate process; that process probably accounts for the somewhat heightened rhetoric of the sentence. Whether the status of the parties also accounts for the fact that *leges* were not imposed, and whether it indicates that the unspecified documentary evidence was, in fact, the draft of a written marriage contract, are less clear.

In the other four cases, the plaintiff is unsuccessful. In the first, the *actor* is given a term to prove the asserted contract; he is contumacious, and the *rea* is absolved, awarded costs, and given license.[37] Once more *leges* are not mentioned, and once more the woman is described as *domicella*. The fact that the *actor* is given a term to prove the contract suggests that what was said in the initial court appearance indicated that he might have had a case. In the second, the *actor* produced witnesses whose depositions were taken, the *rea* excepted to the witnesses (called here a *factum*, reminiscent of the *factum contrarium seu exclusorium* of summary procedure), and witnesses were heard on the *factum*. In the end the official defers the oath to the *rea*; she takes it, and the official absolves her and gives her license. Costs are, however, divided between the parties, and no mention is made of *leges*.[38] Virtually the same procedure is followed in the third case (the only difference is that the exceptions to witnesses and the replication are called *impugnationes* and *salvationes*, rather than *factum in testes* and *responsio*). The *rea* is once more absolved and given license, but this time she is granted her costs, and the *actor* is fined for frivolous allegation.[39] In the last case, the only one in this group with a female plaintiff, we know less about the process because the sentence simply says that the judge has examined the *processus*. He finds for the *reus* and gives him license; no *leges* are mentioned, and the official adds the unusual note "keeping silent about the costs incurred on this occasion in this *processus* and for cause."[40]

These cases raise a number of issues, not the least of which is why we find fines recorded in some of them and not in others. In all five of the instance cases discussed in the preceding paragraphs, they could have been imposed on the

[36] *Heghes c Cache* (26.vi.45), no. 722, T&C no. 826.
[37] *Baillon c Doncke* (4.ii.47), no. 1090, T&C no. 827.
[38] *Gillebert c Try* (23.vi.47), no. 1170, T&C no. 828.
[39] *Louroit c Espoulette* (24.xi.49), no. 1231, T&C no. 829.
[40] *Estricourt c Roy* (15.vii.52), no. 1332, T&C no. 830.

party alleging the *sponsalia* for failure to publicize and failure to proceed.[41] We cannot exclude the possibility that in some cases, they were imposed and the scribe forgot to record them, but there are enough cases in the sample in which they are not mentioned that it seems unlikely that scribal negligence accounts for all of them.[42] A tentative explanation for this phenomenon has already been suggested. If one were cautious about costs, it would make sense to go to the promotor and join with him in bringing the case. The parties who brought the five cases discussed here were not cautious about costs, as is witnessed both by the fact that they did not go to the promotor and by the extensive process in which they engaged. In two cases we have at least some indications that they were of some wealth. They may have been in others. The criminalization of the process of matrimonial litigation at Cambrai may not have affected all social classes equally. The wealthier may still have chosen to sue at instance, at least in some cases. When dealing with such people, the official and the promotors may not have been quite so insistent on imposing every possible fine.[43]

These cases confirm our earlier impression that the official had considerable discretion as to what to do about the parties' costs.[44] He could award them to the winning party; he could divide them between the winning party and the losing party (*compensare*), or he could, as in the last case, let them fall on the party who had incurred them. This last option, though not often used, does occur in other cases both within and outside of the sample.[45]

The record does not tell us why the official chose among the various options that he had about costs (and in a number of cases costs are not mentioned). In some cases it may have depended on what the official thought the parties could afford, and in most cases we have little or no information about the relative wealth of the parties. In some cases, however, the record gives us some hints as to the motivation. It is probably not by chance that in one case just rehearsed, after an elaborate process, the official imposed no *leges* and ordered the costs compensated, while in another, after a similarly elaborate process, he ordered the unsuccessful plaintiff to pay the defendant's costs and fined him for a frivolous allegation.[46] We can probably tentatively conclude, in the absence of other evidence, that in most of the cases in which the costs are compensated or allowed to lie where they are, the official thought that the losing party had a plausible case.

41 Assuming, as seems safe to assume, that most, if not all, of these plaintiffs did not come to court within eight days of the alleged *sponsalia*.

42 See App. e9.1, "*Non Sunt Leges* or None Mentioned" (T&C no. 1054), where we expand the sample and draw some general conclusions about cases where *leges* are not mentioned.

43 This observation should be contrasted with our examination of the pattern of fining at Tournai (App. e9.2), where there seems to be a tendency to charge wealthy parties more.

44 At n. 28; disc. T&C no. 831.

45 *Registres de Cambrai*, s.v., *subticere* (9 instances of the word, all in sentences of Nicolaï), T&C no. 832.

46 Compare *Gillebert c Try* (n. 38) with *Louroit c Espoulette* (n. 39).

The two cases mentioned in the preceding paragraph raise another issue. In both of them the official defers the oath to the *rea*. This practice, which we have seen was quite common at Paris, does not seem to have been nearly so common at Cambrai. The two cases also suggest that the oath was used in a somewhat different context at Cambrai. At Paris, the oath was used where the plaintiff admits that he has no proof; in our two Cambrai cases it is used only after both the plaintiff and the defendant have produced proof. In Paris the oath is truly decisory; at Cambrai the wording of the sentences suggests that it is but one of a number of factors that the official took into account in rendering his sentence.[47] The first of the two Cambrai cases suggests that the oath was used in particularly difficult cases, where it was unclear where the balance of proof lay. The second of the two cases undercuts this inference because ultimately, the official fined the plaintiff for frivolous allegation.

An examination of the cases where the oath is used, both in and out of the sample (including a major dowry case and a number of debt cases), suggests that neither of the previous suggestions quite captures the practice.[48] The oath is never used in a case where there was no other proof; indeed, in most of the cases there was a considerable amount of proof, and in all of them there was at least one set of witnesses. The oath is always listed along with other things that "moved" the official. The full rhetoric describing its granting is quite elaborate and fairly consistently used.[49] That it is done by the office of the judge (and not by the request of the parties) is always stated; frequently the official adds that he had reasonable grounds to do so.

On the basis of the few cases that tell us a bit more[50] and of the general pattern of these cases, we can draw some tentative conclusions about the practice of deferring the *ex officio* oath. We have had occasion previously in this book to discuss the canonical conception of proof.[51] At first, it seems quite mechanical. Two unexceptionable eyewitnesses to each necessary element in a claim or defense were preferred, but in various circumstances presumptions, circumstantial evidence, and *fama* could make up a "half-proof." Documents could also make a up a half-proof and, in some instances, a full proof. The reality – and this was a reality of which the more sophisticated proceduralists were aware – was more complicated. It was relatively easy to defeat a case; the judge simply had to say, in effect, that he did not believe the plaintiff's witnesses. It was harder to sustain a judgment for the plaintiff where the legal standard of proof had not been met, but grounds for discretion were there, too. We have seen how judges seem quite frequently to take proven exceptions to witnesses as going to their credibility and not to their admissibility. Half-proofs were not

47 Disc. with examples T&C no. 833.

48 See *Registres de Cambrai*, s.v. *iuramentum veritatis* (22 instances); disc. T&C no. 834.

49 That given in *Gillebert c Try* (n. 38) is typical; sometimes the *certis de causis* clause is omitted as in *Louroit c Espoulette* (n. 39).

50 Disc. with examples T&C no. 835.

51 E.g., Ch 5, at n. 48.

that hard to find. One such half-proof was the formal oath of one of the parties, the *ex officio* oath practiced here. It differed from the formal decisory oath in that it was within the discretion of the judge as to which party should take it. Obviously, this discretion could be abused, but there is no evidence that Nicolaï (the only Cambrai official who uses it) was abusing it. He uses it in very few cases; in most of these cases proof has been introduced by, or on behalf of, the party who is given the opportunity to take the oath.[52] What I think we are to imagine is that in these cases something was missing; it could have been as little as a second witness or an unexceptionable witness on a relatively minor, but necessary, element in the case. It could even have been, as it may have been in the dowry case mentioned earlier, an element that was necessary to prove a negative ("I never agreed to take less") or a negative element in the debt cases ("I never received payment").

If this is what is involved in these cases, then we can begin to see how it is that in two instances, Nicolaï could both have deferred the oath to the defendant in a marriage case and have fined the plaintiff for frivolous allegation of espousals. In the case discussed earlier,[53] the plaintiff had introduced witnesses; the defendant had excepted to them and had introduced witnesses on the exceptions. If the official did not believe the plaintiff's witnesses but the exception witnesses did not quite prove that these witnesses could not, as a matter of law, be admitted, we can well imagine how he could both have deferred the oath to the *rea* and have thought that the plaintiff's case was frivolous (indeed, corrupt, but the *leges* never say that). In the other case,[54] the reason for the deferral is even easier to see. The *actrix* had introduced witnesses; the *reus* had not. The official, however, had made an *ex officio* inquiry from which, we may imagine, he came to the conclusion that there was nothing to the plaintiff's story that she and the *reus* had contracted marriage, although they had, as they may have confessed, had intercourse. The evidence of the inquiry was hearsay, not enough to overcome the plaintiff's witnesses as a technical matter; so the official deferred the oath to the defendant. He then fined the plaintiff for frivolous opposition, fined both of them for fornication, and, perhaps out of sympathy for the woman's position, ordered the costs compensated.

Nicolaï rendered sentence in 13 mixed office/instance cases in the sample in which two parties were contesting the existence of *sponsalia* and not alleging intercourse. All but one resulted in a judgment absolving the party from the *sponsalia* alleged against him or her. (The one exception ended in a remission.)[55] In all of the absolution cases but one, the absolved party was given license to marry another, and in all of the absolution cases but one, the party asserting the marriage contract was fined for not having publicized it and for not proceeding to solemnization. In none of the absolution cases was the party asserting the

[52] Disc. T&C no. 836.

[53] *Louroit c Espoulette* (n. 39).

[54] *Motoise c Dent et Braconnière* (17.x.42), no. 355 (a case of opposition to banns of a type discussed in the section on three-party cases).

[55] *Office et Donne c Flanniele* (at nn. 61–8).

marriage contract fined for frivolous allegations. In most, there was no process beyond the articles of the promotor and the mutual assertions and confessions of the parties.[56]

The case in which the absolved party was not specifically given license and that in which the party asserting the contract was fined only for non-publication and not for failure to solemnize are the same case.[57] The fact that the parties in this case are called *fils de* and *fille de*, respectively, suggests that they were quite young. The *rea* is expressly stated to have confessed a clandestine agreement and that she had not renewed it publicly within the required time. For this she is condemned to pay amends and the costs both of the promotor and the *correus*. She is also, somewhat unusually, "absolved from the necessity of proceeding further with the same *reus*."[58]

The latter formula is found in two other cases in the same year.[59] In the first of the two cases, it is the *reus* who is absolved of the necessity of proceeding; both parties are ordered to pay the costs of the promotor, and, unique among the cases of this type in the sample, both parties are given license to marry others. In the other case, the *reus* is said to have boasted (*iactavit*) of having made a clandestine agreement with the *correa* (who is described as *fille d'un tel*). Both parties are to pay the costs of the promotor. The *reus* is to pay the *correa*'s costs, she alone is given license, and the *reus* is, once more, absolved of the necessity of proceeding.[60]

There are at least hints here of what may have underlain these judgments. In all three cases, there was nothing that warranted a legal proceeding about the existence of the *sponsalia*. In all three cases, therefore, the alleging party must pay the other party's costs. In the first case, we may suspect that it is not just a question of proof; the official thought that what the *rea* thought was a contract really was not, and so she must pay the costs of the promotor. She is, however, not malicious, simply naïve. She will not be fined to the fullest extent possible, and she will be told that she needs not pursue the matter further. In the other two cases, the official suspected that there was something there, but it could not be proven. The couple must together pay the costs of the promotor, but because it cannot be proven, the alleging party must pay the absolved party's costs. In both cases the alleging party will be told that he need not pursue the matter, but the man who boasted of the contract will not be expressly given license to marry another; he may marry another, but the official is not going to give him the satisfaction of hearing that in court.

One of the office/instance cases is quite different.[61] It is one of the few cases in which the party asserting the *sponsalia* is expressly described as a formal party along with the promotor.[62] This suggests that the promotor was less involved

[56] In five cases depositions were taken, listed T&C no. 837.
[57] *Office c Cauchiot et Fèvre* (10.i.50), no. 1241.
[58] *Id.*, T&C no. 838.
[59] *Office c Copin et Morielle* (7.xi.49), no. 1221; *Office c Coulon et Fontaine* (25.iii.50), no. 1272.
[60] Disc. of similar cases at T&C no. 839.
[61] *Office et Donne c Flanniele* (13.xi.45 to 14.vi.47), nos. 821, 1164.
[62] *Id.*, no. 821, T&C no. 840.

in the case than he was in the normal mixed case, a suggestion that is confirmed by the fact that the case is styled in the second sentence as if it were straight instance.[63] The case also contains the highest indications of social status that we find in the sample. The man is called "the noble Jean de le Donne," and is styled as "the bastard of Rabecque"; the woman is called *honesta iuvencula* Joye Flannielle, a title that may or may not indicate higher status than the *domicella* that we find fairly frequently. She comes from the city of Cambrai. The interlocutory sentence indicates an elaborate process. According to the decrees of the holy fathers, the official tells, "he who is judging ought to examine everything to the bottom and weigh the *ordo* of things with full inquisition."[64] As a result, the court orders that the four of nine witnesses for Jean and two exception witnesses, all of whom have remained unexamined, should be examined. Joye's two witnesses are named: Béatrice, a servant in the house of the woman's parents, and Belote, recently a servant at the inn (*cabareti*) called "Roma," giving us at least a hint of the kind of issues that were being litigated.

The final sentence comes more than a year and a half later. In the meantime, Joye appealed from the *advocatio* of the case by the bishop of Cambrai to the provincial court at Rheims.[65] There, both parties proceeded concerning "the proffering of a sentence."[66] Now, however, appearing before the official, they [*sic*] renounce the appeal. Jurisdiction has therefore devolved on the official, and they ask that their espousals be remitted. In a formal letter patent, the official accepts the remission in the standard language that he uses in such cases, and the parties are held to *leges* for clandestine promises not publicized and for not proceeding to solemnization.

If I am reading the reference to the *advocatio* of the bishop correctly, what happened here is that after the interlocutory sentence, the bishop removed the case to his audience court.[67] He was probably about to hold for Jean, because Joye appealed to Rheims. There, the couple dickered about the form a sentence should take (*citra cuiusvis sententie prolationem*, the indefinite adjective indicating that no sentence yet existed). Ultimately, however, they agreed to remit their espousals. On the basis of this record, it seems relatively clear that Jean had a case.[68] For some reason, Joye, having clandestinely agreed to a marriage, decided that she did not want "the bastard of Rabecque" as a husband, or, perhaps more likely, her parents did not want him as a son-in-law. About what was at stake in these negotiations we can only speculate, but the evidence is consistent with the possibility that this was a case of an impoverished and illegitimate nobleman attempting to marry a rich *bourgeoise*.

[63] *Id.*, no. 1164.
[64] *Id.*, no. 821, T&C no. 841.
[65] *Id.*, no. 1164, T&C no. 842.
[66] *Ibid.*, T&C no. 843.
[67] Lit. T&C no. 844.
[68] For this reason, I have coded it as an office/instance case in which the party asserting the espousals succeeds.

Nicolaï rendered sentence in eight office cases in the sample in which the existence of *sponsalia* unaccompanied by *copula* was at stake. In two of them the alleged *sponsalia* are found: The couple are fined for failing to publicize clandestine promises and for failing to proceed to solemnize; they are to pay the costs of the promotor and to proceed to solemnization within 40 days and treat each other with marital affection thereafter.[69] In both cases depositions are taken; in one, in addition to the articles of the promotor and the usual oaths, replies, and confessions of the parties, the official grounds his decision on the mutual allegations, petitions, and conclusions of the parties.[70] This indicates that at least one of the parties, and perhaps both, were supporting the *sponsalia*. The other case does not contain that recitation, but we know from the remission cases that even if the parties had contracted, they could have remitted the *sponsalia* if neither of them wanted the marriage.

One case contains no *leges* but does contain an order that the couple solemnize their marriage. The wording of the sentence indicates fairly clearly what had happened. On the basis of the couple's oaths, confessions, and responses, they were absolved from the promotor's charge of *neglegentia* (probably to publicize their espousals); they did, however, have to pay the promotor's costs *propter aliqualem famam*, which they had confessed. The official then found, again on the basis of their confessions, that they had exchanged clandestine consent the previous day.[71] He found the consent valid and ordered the marriage to proceed. This couple pretty clearly had decided to get married, though it may have required the citation of the promotor to galvanize them into doing it. We will recall that they had eight days under the statutes to publicize their *sponsalia*, and clearly they were in court within the requisite time. That suggests that the *fama* of which the court speaks was that they had contracted at an earlier time. There may have been something to that *fama*, but once the couple had decided that they were going to get married anyway (and granted that there were no witnesses), they seem to have been able to avoid the imposition of the *leges* by denying the earlier contract but admitting one that would not subject them to *leges*.

In the other five cases, the couple are absolved from the articles of the promotor; no *leges* are mentioned, but the couple does have to pay the promotor's costs. The sentences in these cases tell us something about the role of *fama*.[72] In the cases in which there were depositions, we may assume that the witnesses at least confirmed the existence of the *fama*. In the cases where there were no witnesses, we must wonder how the official knew that there was *fama*. Perhaps the couple confessed to it, as in the case described in the previous paragraph;[73] perhaps the official took the promotor's word for it. The wording

[69] Listed T&C no. 845.
[70] *Office c Staelkins et Velde* (n. 69).
[71] *Office c Enfant et Mairesse* (23.xi.52), no. 1381.
[72] Details at T&C no. 846.
[73] See at n. 71.

of the sentences shows that Nicolaï felt some need to justify the imposition of costs when the couple were absolved. The sentences themselves, however, show that one way or another, the promotor would normally get his costs.

Contested – Brussels

As Table 8.6 shows, there are only five cases (4%) in our sample of Brussels cases in which the existence of espousals is contested and *copula* is not alleged. Three of these cases took place while Rodolphi was official and only two while Platea was official. While the small number of cases should make us hesitant to draw any statistical conclusions from this fact, the proportion of such cases in which Rodolphi rendered sentence (60%) is quite different from the proportion of all sentences he rendered (402/1590, 25%).

Two of the cases are begun as straight-instance actions. One ends there. Although she produced witnesses, the *actrix* fails to establish the *sponsalia*, and in a skimpy sentence, Rodolphi absolves the *reus* but orders the costs compensated.[74] The next case tells us more. After "propositions, allegations, and assertions" of the *actor*, "responses" of the *rea*, and "solemn oaths" taken by the parties, the *actor* produced witnesses. On the basis of this record, Rodolphi adjudged the couple *sponsi* and ordered them to solemnize within 40 days. Costs are not mentioned, but *leges* were imposed on both of them for failure to publicize their clandestine espousals.[75] Ten months later the couple are back in court being prosecuted by the promotor, together with a male third party. In the meantime, the original *rea* had appealed to the Apostolic See but had failed to perfect her appeal within the time fixed; she had also contracted *sponsalia* with the third party and banns had been proclaimed on them, but there had been no sexual intercourse between them. Rodolphi orders the original couple, once more, to solemnize their *sponsalia*, annuls the second *sponsalia*, gives the third party license to contract elsewhere, and orders the woman to make amends for failure to solemnize and for double espousals and to pay costs of the case and the third party's damages. Considering the nature of the offense, the level of rhetoric is fairly low.[76]

The two cases in which the promotor joins with one of the parties in seeking to establish the *sponsalia* fail. In the first, the promoting male party is to make amends for failure to publicize and failure to solemnize and to pay the costs of both the promotor and the *rea*.[77] In the second, Platea imposes silence on both the promotor and the female promoting party, and the latter is ordered to do penance or to make amends for "rash allegations" and to pay the costs of the promotor, but costs between the parties are compensated "for a reason moving [the official's] soul."[78]

[74] *Gragem c Ghisteren* (8.xi.48), no. 2, T&C no. 847.
[75] *Craynem c Raegmans* (7.ii.49), no. 30, T&C no. 848.
[76] *Officie c Crayehem, Raechmans en Visch* (21.xi.49), no. 116, T&C no. 849.
[77] *Officie c Fiermans en Pijcmans* (26.ix.49), no. 100, T&C no. 850.
[78] *Officie c Sibille en Fossiaul* (30.ix.58), no. 1360, T&C no. 851.

In the last sentence, so far as we can tell, the promotor is proceeding without the assistance of either of the parties. On the basis of the oaths and allegations of the parties, Platea absolves them of the charge of having contracted clandestine promises of marriage and imposes silence on the promotor. He, nonetheless, "enjoins the *rei* to proceed within the appropriate time to their affiancing in accordance with the matrimonial negotiations (*tractatus*) had and held between them and their friends." Nothing is said of costs, and it would seem that this is one of very few cases in which the promotor did not get his costs.[79] While it is possible that something more complicated lies behind this cryptic sentence (such as that one of the parties joined with the promotor initially but then changed his or her mind), it seems best to take it as it appears on the surface: There was an agreement to have an engagement (hence, the parties are "enjoined," not simply given liberty, to proceed), but there was no engagement. The fact that the court was willing to make this distinction, and that it was unwilling to allow the promotor his costs when he failed, may go some way to explaining why there are so few cases of this type at Brussels.

Instance cases at Brussels are uncommon, but they do exist. The second of our two instance cases shows that they could be won, and that the promotor would intervene to help enforce the judgment. The two mixed cases show that the promotors would, occasionally, intervene to assist a party alleging *sponsalia*, even where there was no proof of intercourse nor any third party involved. It is, of course, possible that there were further aggravating factors even in these cases. That seems virtually certain in the first of them, because the *rea* is absolved of "the other things alleged by the promotor and the *reus*." It will also be noted that in the unsuccessful straight-instance case and in the second of the two promoted cases, costs are compensated between the parties, a fact that suggests that the official thought that there was something to the promoting party's allegations. Finally, Platea's sentencing style is a bit different from that of Rodolphi, who, in turn, seems to follow the forms that we have found at Cambrai. For example, unlike Rodolphi, Platea makes clear that penance and amends are alternatives;[80] Platea also imposes silence on the losing party.

Dissolution – Cambrai

We have classified 17 cases in our Cambrai sample as two-party actions for the dissolution of *sponsalia* where *copula* was not alleged: 4 straight instance, 5 mixed, and 8 straight office. As we will see, there are problems with the classification of some of them, but there are no such problems with the four instance cases. They begin with one sentence of Divitis in his usual cryptic style:[81]

Considering the oaths and responses of [Jacques Maire] and [Catherine Faveresse] who entered into *sponsalia* with each other in the hand of the priest and the face of the church,

[79] *Officie c Rampenberch en Bossche* (29.vii.57), no. 1190, T&C no. 852.
[80] See at n. 9.
[81] *Maire et Faveresse* (13.xi.38), no. 61, T&C no. 853.

because it was and is apparent to us that [JM] and [CF] entered into such *sponsalia* before [JM] was properly certified of the death of Marguerite, his first wife, for these [reasons] we dissolve and annul the *sponsalia* at the instance of the [parties], granting license to [CF] to marry another in the Lord, if she wishes to marry, condemning moreover this [JM] to an appropriate penalty, issuing a definitive sentence in this writing.

The wording of the sentence is a bit odd. Of course, Jacques should not have entered into *sponsalia* if his first wife was still alive, and he should have made sure that she was not. If the wife was still alive, his entering into such *sponsalia* would be treated like attempted bigamy.[82] The fact that the sentence said that he entered into the *sponsalia* before he was certified that she was dead suggests that, in fact, she is dead, and the *sponsalia* are being dissolved on the quite technical ground that they should not have been entered into before the certification had been received. Since both parties now want to dissolve the *sponsalia*, one wonders why they simply did not come before the official and remit. The answer to that question may be that Catherine was sufficiently angry at what Jacques did that she wanted to see him punished, or that she had to bring him to court on some ground in order to get him to agree to dissolve the *sponsalia*. It is also possible, however, that the official was unwilling to take a remission in this case either because granting a remission implied that the *sponsalia* had been valid or that granting it might have suggested that both were free to marry. That would not be the case if it were still unclear whether the former wife of Jacques was still alive.

Nicolaï's three instance sentences in which it is clear the plaintiff sought dissolution of the *sponsalia* from the beginning are more complicated in their wording and less complicated in their facts. All of them begin with a formal recital of the fact that this is *causa dissolutionis sponsalium*. In two there are a libel or petition of the plaintiff, a response of the *reus*, and oaths, assertions, confessions, and conclusions of the parties – much verbiage that still may not have added up to more than one session of court. In both cases the official dissolves the *sponsalia* on the basis of the fornication of the woman with another man: "on account of the sin of the *rea* committed against the law of this sort of *sponsalia*"; both of the couple are given license, the *rea* is charged with the costs of the *actor*, and, strikingly, no *leges* are mentioned. One sentence specifically mentions that the contract was one *per verba de futuro* and that the *rea* confessed her sin and that both asked for the dissolution; the other mentions none of these things.[83] In the third the *reus* is contumacious. The official dissolves *sponsalia* on which three banns had been proclaimed; he specifically mentions that there had been no intercourse between the couple and that the *actrix* is free from the obligation of the *sponsalia* and free to marry another. The *reus* is charged with costs, but the *marginalia* note that "the *reus* is a vagabond."[84]

[82] See *Office c Gruarde et Sivery* (n. 107).

[83] *Douriau c Malette* (30.iv.45), no. 690; *Fortin c Boursière* (11.ix.45), no. 782; both T&C no. 854.

[84] *Ymberde c Dent* (24.ix.46), no. 1020, T&C no. 855.

Both infidelity and long absence were grounds recognized by the formal law for dissolution of *sponsalia de futuro*. Other than the absence of mention of *leges*, a feature that is best treated generally when we can look at more cases in which they are not mentioned,[85] the result in the two cases of infidelity is totally unsurprising. Since we know that in at least one of the cases the *rea* was willing to accept the dissolution, we once more must ask why the couple just did not remit. Here it seems even more likely that the man was sufficiently angry at what the woman had done that he wanted to make a public spectacle of her. If that is the case, then the absence of *leges* may indicate that the official did not want to make things any harder for her. The case of the contumacious *reus* is a bit more difficult. The law spoke in terms of long absence, and there is no indication here that the *reus* had been gone for a long time. Here the marginal note helps, and perhaps we can imagine a man who appeared out of nowhere, stayed long enough at Honnecourt to contract a marriage with three banns, and then disappeared again. The official was trying to help the woman out, and he added an element that is normally found only in remission cases: that the *sponsalia* had not been consummated.

The five office/instance dissolution cases are more complicated because it is unclear in some of them who was trying to achieve what. The first sentence of Divitis in this type of case is illustrative. A commission was issued; the *rei* entered their usual oaths, confessions, and responses, and witnesses were examined. Divitis then absolved the woman from the matrimonial agreements alleged by both the *reus* and the promotor and gave her license to marry another. Turning to the *reus*, he found, in strong language, that he had enticed the wife of one Willebrod, had taken her away from the consortium of her husband, and had known her carnally many times. He was condemned to make amends; the *rei* were condemned to pay the costs of the promotor, and the *reus* was condemned to pay the *rea*'s costs.[86]

There is nothing about the facts of this case that would have prevented it from being a prosecution for adultery (of the *reus* with the wife of Willebrod) promoted by the *rea* in order to obtain a judgment of dissolution of her *sponsalia*. That is not, however, how the sentence is worded, and I am inclined to think that the official is unlikely to have worded the sentence this way had that been the case. What he says is that the *reus* had supported the promotor in his charge that the couple had exchanged words of matrimonial consent, and his language in absolving the *rea* of the charge is the standard language used in cases where the existence of *sponsalia* are contested and the judge finds that they have not been proven. There is nothing in the sentence that speaks of dissolution; rather, what it seems to say is that there were no *sponsalia* to dissolve. Someone must have approached the official to obtain the commission. It could have been Willebrod, but if that were the case, it is a bit difficult to see why the *rea* was cited at all. While it is conceivable that some concerned member or members of

[85] See at n. 92; App. e9.1.

[86] *Office c Bueken et* [...] (5.vii.38), no. 2, T&C no. 856.

the community brought both the possibility of the *sponsalia* and the adultery to the court's attention, I think it more likely that it was the *reus* himself (who, of course, did not mention the adultery).[87] If so, he failed spectacularly. The *rea* not only succeeded in convincing the court that there had been no *sponsalia*, but she may also have been instrumental in getting the *reus* convicted of adultery. Cited by the court in a case of clandestine *sponsalia*, we might imagine, she came prepared to defend on two grounds: the *sponsalia* did not exist and if they did, they ought to be dissolved because of the man's infidelity.

The other of Divitis's sentences in an office/instance dissolution case and one of Nicolaï's both involve fact situations similar to that in Nicolaï's third instance sentence.[88] In both cases *sponsalia* have concededly occurred, clandestinely in one case, publicly with three banns proclaimed in the other. In both cases the *reus* is contumacious, and the official dissolves the *sponsalia*, gives the *rea* license to marry another, and condemns her to pay the costs of the promotor.[89] We may suspect that in both of these cases and in the corresponding instance case, the woman's fiancé has disappeared. We may speculate why the women used different forms of procedure,[90] but however they got there, all three women were helped by the court once there. As we have seen, it was by no means clear that these women were entitled to a dissolution of their *sponsalia* as a matter of law. When we combine these three cases, it seems relatively clear that the court took the position that a contumacious defendant in a *de futuro* spousals case where no intercourse was present would be regarded as absent 'for a long time' if the party who was present wanted those espousals dissolved.

Another sentence of Nicolaï in an office/instance case involves much clearer grounds for dissolution. In one the couple was fined for clandestine promises not renewed and for not proceeding to solemnization; the *sponsalia* were dissolved *propter peccatum viri*, which he confessed. Both were given license, both were to pay the promotor's costs, and the court was expressly silent about the costs between them.[91] The procedure in this case was interesting. There are said to have been two commissions, one issued at the instance of the promotor, one at the instance of the *rea*. It seems relatively clear in this case that when the *rea* found out that she was going to be prosecuted for clandestine promises, she sought to combine her action for dissolution of those promises with the prosecution, a move that was almost certainly designed to save costs. The official may have been somewhat disapproving of this move, and by letting the costs between the parties fall where they lay, he seems to have made the *rea* pay more than she would have had to pay had she been successful in an instance action.

[87] Disc. T&C no. 857.
[88] *Ymberde c Dent* (n. 84).
[89] Refs. and details T&C no. 858.
[90] Disc. at T&C no. 859.
[91] *Office c Cuppere et Moens* (n. 45).

At this point, we should face squarely the fact that no *leges* are mentioned in this case as having been imposed on the man for his fornication and couple that with the fact that in two of the instance cases for dissolution of *sponsalia*, no mention is made of *leges* being imposed on the *rea* for a similar offense. While we treat the issue of missing *leges* in general terms in Appendix e9.1, there is reason to believe that something quite specific to this type of case is at stake here. We have already noted that the Cambrai court did not prosecute routine fornication cases. All of the fornication cases in our sample involved some aggravating factor: incest, clerical involvement, deflowering, or long-term cohabitation and concubinage.[92] The impression of the sample is confirmed by checking the 10 places in which the words *fornicari* or *fornicatio* appear in the sentences in the book.[93] There are, however, 17 cases in which one (or both) of an engaged couple are said to have violated the *lex sponsalium*.[94] In addition to the three cases already mentioned, there is only one other in which the *fiancé(e)* who had committed fornication was not fined for it. In that case, it was not proven that the *rea* had committed fornication; she was contumacious, and it was simply presumed that she had.[95]

We thus have one case in which we can be reasonably confident that *leges* were not imposed and that we know the reason why: The *rea* was presumed to have fornicated; it was not proven that she had. We have another case in which we can suspect at least a part of the reason: The official disapproved of the way in which the *rea* was proceeding.[96] When we combine these cases with the 13 in which *leges* were imposed, a pattern begins to emerge: All but 3 of the 13 cases involve an aggravated form of fornication. The first two cases are typical. In the first, the man promoted a prosecution of the *rea* for clandestine *sponsalia*.[97] As in the case of the man who had committed adultery with another man's wife,[98] the strategy backfired. The woman was able to convince the court that the man had "carnally known a certain Marguerite tsHazen often and very often and also many other women."[99] In an office dissolution case four months later, Divitis finds that after three banns had been proclaimed in the face of the church concerning her espousals with the plaintiff, the woman had "sinned by allowing herself to be abducted, deflowered and carnally known by one Thomas Rauet."[100] Still later, Nicolaï followed the wording that Divitis had used in the same situation: "[T]he *rea* allowed herself to be abducted, deflowered, dishonored and many times carnally known, thus sinning against

92 Ch 8, at n. 54.
93 *Registres de Cambrai*, s.vv.
94 *Id.*, s.v.
95 *Lièvre c Fagotee* (18.vii.39), no. 267, T&C no. 860.
96 *Office c Cuppere et Moens* (at n. 91).
97 *Office et Onckerzele c Hanen* (5.vii.38), no. 4.
98 *Office c Bueken et* [...] (n. 86).
99 *Office et Onckerzele c Hanen* (n. 97), T&C no. 861, with details.
100 *Espaigne c Formanoir* (8.xi.38), no. 55, T&C no. 862 (not in current sample, but in instance sample).

the law of the espousals."[101] This is the first time that we have encountered the word *abducere* in a Cambrai sentence. We have already seen that fifteenth-century York is notable for a number of cases in which abduction was alleged.[102] The same is true of Cambrai, but the allegation does not appear very often. Other than these two sentences, the word occurs in only five others.[103] What is at stake in these two cases is clearly not something that happened against the will of the woman; she "allowed herself to be abducted."

Of the three cases in which there is no indication that the fornication was aggravated, two are standard instance remissions where the sentence says nothing about the fornication and the *leges* "for sin against the law of espousals" are noted cryptically in the margin.[104] The third is an instance dissolution case where the *leges* pick up an equally cryptic remark in the sentence.[105] There could have been aggravating factors in these cases; we just do not know. The evidence is thus consistent with the proposition that the judges, in accordance with their pattern of sentencing in criminal fornication cases, did not think it necessary to impose a fine in every case in which *sponsalia* were dissolved for "sin against the law of espousals," absent aggravating factors. This possibility should be balanced against the evidence that we find elsewhere that the Cambrai judges fined for every possible offense, even where doing this involved the imposition of inconsistent fines.[106]

Nicolaï's last sentence in an office/instance dissolution case has some aspects of a straight-office case, but the *reus*, at least ultimately, is said to have presented a conclusion and a petition to the court and the *rea*, again ultimately, is ordered to pay his costs.[107] The substantive part of the sentence begins with a finding that the *rea* "grievously sinning against the law of her marriage allowed herself to be polluted in adulterous coitus by a certain man named in the articles."[108] This is not the usual language in cases of dissolution of *sponsalia*, and the reason for it becomes immediately apparent. The *rei*, "there still living and in a place not far distant from their residence – at least easily findable – the husband of the same *rea*, presumed to enter into promises of marriage *de facto*, even in the hand of a priest and the face of the church, three banns, to the extent that they could, being proclaimed thereupon."[109] Not only that but "they would have proceeded further to contract this pretended marriage – insofar as they could – had publication of the [news] of the life of this man not prevented it, and by

[101] *Office c Romain et Iongen* (26.i.43), no. 410, T&C no. 863.
[102] See Ch 5, text following n. 70.
[103] Listed T&C no. 864.
[104] Ref. T&C no. 865.
[105] *Hennon c Cauvenene* (24.iv.45), no. 685, T&C no. 866.
[106] At nn. 32–5.
[107] *Office c Gruarde et Sivery* (14.iv.53), no. 1422. The *correus*'s testimony may have been crucial because no witnesses are mentioned.
[108] *Id.*, T&C no. 867.
[109] *Id.*, T&C no. 868.

this they showed themselves zealous seekers after damned nuptials, thereby most grievously failing and breaking the law."[110] The *sponsalia* are dissolved; indeed, the official is at pains to say that he is simply declaring that they are null, and the *reus* is given license to marry another.

The level of the rhetoric is as high in this sentence as in any that we find in matrimonial cases in the Cambrai court. It is higher than that found in the straight-office dissolution cases for attempted incest with which we will deal in Chapter 11. It reflects, perhaps, a genuine horror of bigamy, a horror that we also noted, at least in some cases, in the records of the Paris court.[111]

Of the eight straight-office two-party dissolution cases in the sample, one is quite similar to the instance and office/instance dissolution cases that we have been examining, except that there is no indication that the *reus* either asked for or obtained dissolution of the *sponsalia*. The *rea* is fined for not having proceeded to solemnize her *sponsalia* and for, in language already quoted, having run off and having had intercourse with one Gilles Withamers.[112] The *reus* is absolved from the promotor's articles (we are not told what they were); he and the *rea* are to share paying the promotor's costs, but the *rea* is to pay the *reus*'s costs. There is almost certainly more to this story than is told here. The most likely of a number of possibilities is that the promotor was attempting to prove that the couple had had intercourse, and thus had a presumptive marriage that could not be dissolved by the *rea*'s infidelity. If that is what the promotor was trying to prove, he failed.

The remaining seven straight-office two-party dissolution cases involve the complicated law of incest. In five of the seven, the promotor succeeds in dissolving the *sponsalia* of a couple who, so far as we can tell, are seeking to maintain them. In two cases the couple succeeds in maintaining them. We defer more detailed discussion of these cases to Chapter 11.

Dissolution – Brussels

As Table 8.6 shows, the Brussels sample contains 11 cases of dissolution of *sponsalia* where no *copula* is alleged, 4 mixed office/instance, and 7 straight office. Platea accounts for three of the sentences in the mixed cases but only three of the sentences in the office cases, whereas he accounts for fully three-quarters of the sentences in the register.[113]

The mixed cases offer a variety of grounds. In the first, Rodolphi dissolves the *sponsalia* and condemns the *reus* both to make amends and to pay the costs of the promotor and the *rea* and the *rea*'s damages because "with a strong hand he presumed to take the *rea* to various places, indeed, rather, to abduct her."

110 *Id.*, T&C no. 869.
111 See Ch 7, at nn. 330–40.
112 *Office c Romain et Iongen* (n. 101).
113 See text preceding n. 74.

The sentence begins by reminding us that "according to the canonical sanctions marriages ought to be free"; the ground for the dissolution is expressly said to be fear (*metus*), and the *rea* is given license.[114]

In the next two cases, Platea dissolves the *sponsalia* on the ground of the infidelity of the man in the first case and of the woman in the second. In the first case, the language of the sentence is reminiscent of remission cases: "[O]n account of the sin committed by the [*reus*] with [BL] against the law of these [promises], with the consent of these *rei* who wish to release themselves from and about the promises, considering also that there did not intervene between them fraud, deceit, any illicit agreement, or sexual intercourse and that unwilling marriages commonly have bad ends, we dissolve," and so on.[115] Both parties are given license. The man is to make amends for having had intercourse with the other woman "many times, even to the procreation of two children" and for failing to renew and to proceed to solemnization of his promises. He also is to pay the expenses of the promotor, and those of the *rea* are not mentioned.[116]

The language of the second sentence is more reminiscent of separation cases:

> [W]e absolve [JD] ... from the promises of marriage alleged against him by [MN] ... on account of the sin against the law of the espousals committed and confessed by [MN] with [GV] ... imposing perpetual silence on the promotor and [MN] about them, and also we admit and tolerate in patience the quittance of such promises that they made and passed on each side by their own rashness – burdening the consciences of the *correi* about it and ours completely unburdening – particularly because of the discord of their *mores*.[117]

Why their consciences might be burdened by this quittance is elaborated earlier in the sentence: "notwithstanding the sexual intercourse attempted with [MN] by [JD] while he was drunk, and oath about the truth of the sexual intercourse having been previously deferred to him and taken by him." Had they succeeded in having intercourse, of course, they would have been married, and the promises could not have been dissolved.[118] As it is, they are to make amends for clandestine espousals, for remitting them without judicial license, and for unchastely attempting carnal intercourse. The *rea* is to make amends for her intercourse with the other man, thereby furnishing the occasion for the dissolution of the *sponsalia*, and both are to pay the promotor's costs. They are free to marry others, though license is not expressly given.[119]

In a further case, Platea denies the dissolution and orders the couple to solemnize their marriage. The man's allegations against the espousals are not

[114] *Officie en Tieselinc c Tieselinc en Outerstrate* (9.v.52), no. 370, T&C no. 870. The Brussels abduction cases are listed in n. 414, with cross-references.

[115] Cf. at n. 131.

[116] *Officie c Lisen en Ghosens* (12.v.53), no. 491, T&C no. 871.

[117] Cf. Ch 10, text following n. 140.

[118] Prescinding from the complexities to which the drunkenness might have given rise. See Ch 5, at n. 105.

[119] *Officie c Diels en Nouts* (5.vii.54), no. 641, T&C no. 872; cf. Officie c Lauwers en Winnen (15.xi.54), no. 720, next paragraph and T&C no. 872.

specified but are said to be "frivolous and not lawful." He is to make amends for not proceeding to the solemnization and to pay the costs of the promotor.

The seven straight-office dissolution cases are of a quite different nature. Six are grounded on consanguinity or affinity, one in the impediment of vow. Dissolution is ordered in one of the consanguinity cases. In all of the others the promotor fails. Once more, we will defer more detailed discussion of them, including the case of vow, which is best treated in the context of the incest cases, to Chapter 11.

Remission – Cambrai

The Cambrai sample contains 11 cases in which a couple remit their *sponsalia* civilly and 5 in which they remit them after having been prosecuted and convicted of not publicizing clandestine *sponsalia* and also, in all but one, for not proceeding to solemnize these *sponsalia*.[120] Proceeding at instance did not necessarily allow the couple to avoid such fines. One or the other or both are imposed as *leges* in all but three of the instance cases. In two of the three cases, the *sponsalia* were public, and they may have been in the third; the sentence simply does not say.[121] In all three cases, it is possible that the couple came to court to remit their *sponsalia* within the (apparently) 40-day period within which they were supposed to solemnize them. The advantage, then, of proceeding at instance and not waiting to be prosecuted is that one did not have to pay the promotor's costs. That these would, in most cases, be higher than the costs of proceeding at instance in such a case is suggested by the fact that in the relatively few cases in which the process is given, it consists simply of a joint petition for release and the "oaths, assertions and replies" of the parties.[122] That fact then raises the question of why anyone waited to be prosecuted. A number of motivations can be imagined, but there are three that, singly or in combination, appear the most likely: ignorance (the couple simply did not know of the less costly alternative), thinking that they could get away with it (having contracted clandestinely and having decided to remit privately, they thought that the promotor would not find out about it), and hesitancy (one or both had not decided to remit until they were forced to make up their minds by the court appearance).

The operative language of sentences of remission is standard and almost inevitable. The official "admits" the "quittance," "considering that there did not intervene in it fraud, deceit or illicit agreement, or sexual intercourse," and the couple are given license to marry others.[123] That the couple had to be found not to have had intercourse is obvious enough; if they had, they would be married, and they could not remit. Why the absence of "fraud, deceit, or illicit

[120] Ref. T&C no. 873.
[121] Listed T&C no. 874.
[122] Examples T&C no. 875.
[123] E.g., *Horiau et Martine* (n. 121), T&C no. 876.

agreement" is also mentioned is less clear. These were all, of course, grounds that could vitiate an agreement, but they are not the only such grounds. Force and error (at least in some circumstances) could also vitiate an agreement, as could lack of capacity (insanity or nonage), but these are never mentioned. One sentence adds simony to the list.[124] This is puzzling, for it is hard to see how such an agreement, even if money were paid for it, could be regarded as simoniacal. Another case adds *parentas* to the list.[125] This word is not found in any of the standard dictionaries of either classical or medieval Latin, but is probably a back-formation from French *parenté*, 'relationship'. This is even more puzzling, because one would have thought that *parenté* between the couple would have been a reason for dissolving the *sponsalia*, not for denying the parties remission of it.

I have no explanation for the one mention of simony. It could be that the judge or the scribe was momentarily confused, or it could be that the judge was considering the possibility of denying to couples the right to buy their way out of an obligation to marry. There was a moment in the twelfth century when concern about simony was at its height, when some canonists and theologians thought that the sacrament of marriage did not impart grace, perhaps because of the financial transactions that normally accompanied it.[126]

There is, I think, a possible explanation for the much more common "fraud, deceit or illicit agreement." If we recall that an indissoluble marriage could be formed by present consent unaccompanied by intercourse,[127] then the phrase becomes more understandable. The couple swore that they had contracted by words of the future tense. When the court finds no fraud, deceit, or illicit agreement, it is finding that it believed them. The judge finds that they were not committing a fraud on the court or deceiving the court when they said this; they did not make an illicit agreement to dissolve a *de presenti* marriage. It is even possible that in the case that says *quevis alia parentas*, the scribe misheard the official and what he in fact said was *quevis verba de presenti*.[128] The fact that the court uses this circumlocution, rather than the more straightforward direct expression of the requirement, may indicate its reluctance regularly and publicly to admit that indissoluble marriages could be formed *verba de presenti* unaccompanied by intercourse.

The five remission cases that begin as office prosecutions for clandestine *sponsalia* not renewed employ the same wording so far as the remission is concerned. In one, only the man is fined for nonrenewal and failure to proceed to solemnization, and only he is condemned to pay the promotor's expenses.

[124] *Roussiel et Fèvre* (3.xii.42), no. 391.

[125] *Doyse et Fenee* (16.v.43), no. 470, T&C no. 877.

[126] This was, for example, the view of Peter Abelard, *Epitome*, c. 31.

[127] Disc. T&C no. 878.

[128] If this is the case, then it is evidence that the sentences were written down as they were being spoken. See Ch 8, at n. 8.

No witnesses are mentioned, and it looks as if the man was unable to prove his charges; so his agreement to the remission avoided an adverse judgment. He is made to swear solemnly that there was no "fraud, deceit or sexual intercourse" in his agreement and is then given license, along with the woman, to marry another. Costs are compensated, a fact that suggests that the official thought there was something to the man's charges.[129] The entire process is consistent with, though it certainly does not prove, the argument we just made that the real concern here was that there had been no words of the present tense.

Another case tells us nothing more about this but does show that in some circumstances the remission was an afterthought. After witnesses are introduced, the parties are fined for nonrenewal and failure to proceed. They then "at the end of the process" ask to remit. The remission is granted in the usual form, but the woman is ordered to pay the man's costs up to the time of remission. This strongly suggests that she was resisting his charges but that he had proven them. Having gotten the record straight, he then relented and, rather than forcing her into an unwanted marriage, remitted.[130]

Remission – Brussels

There are in the Brussels sample four civil two-party remission cases in which *copula* is not mentioned and no office cases of this type. The official in all four cases is Platea. Like the Cambrai remission cases, they all give the parties license to contract with others, and one of them, like the Cambrai cases, contains a full recital of findings: "especially since fraud, deceit, collusion or any illicit pact, or sexual intercourse after such affiancing did not intervene in the premises."[131] The other cases do not contain such findings, although one specifies that the espousals were "without sexual intercourse."[132] We can assume that that was found in the other cases as well. What is striking about these sentences is how closely they echo the language of Platea's separation sentences that we will examine in Chapter 10. Sometimes the emphasis is on the will of the parties: "[W]e declare that the *correi* can freely recede from the contract of matrimony otherwise had and held between them with the consent of all their relatives, and absolve each other from the same, and neither is obliged to marry the other, but rather we grant license to them, even if the other is unwilling, to marry in the Lord wherever one or both of them wish."[133] All three of the later cases, however, though they mention the consent of the parties are also grounded in the "discord of *mores* and mutual dislike" (*morum discrepantia et mutua displicentia*) of the couple, and two of them darkly warn of the ill that

[129] *Office c Parmentiere et Donnucle* (7.xii.46), no. 1057.
[130] *Office c Mathieu et Fourment* (21.vii.49), no. 1190.
[131] *Godezele en Willeghen* (28.i.55), no. 752, T&C no. 879.
[132] *Olmen c Aeede* (30.vi.58), no. 1330, T&C no. 880.
[133] *Boxhorens en Spaens* (27.ix.54), no. 690, T&C no. 881.

could result from requiring their marriage: "lest it might happen that a man or woman should marry someone whom he or she pursues with a quite genuine hate."[134]

We will see in Chapter 10 that the courts of Cambrai diocese developed an extensive jurisprudence by which they separated married couples on the ground of *morum discrepantia*. This jurisprudence is obviously playing back into Platea's remission sentences. If married couples could be separated on this ground, even more so could couples who were only espoused. The fact is, however, that only Platea regularly uses separation language in remission cases. We have seen that both judges at Cambrai employed a different formula: They admitted the couples' "quittance," normally with a finding that there was no fraud, deceit, or illicit pact and, of course, no intercourse subsequent to the pact. They also made such couples make amends for failure to proceed with their espousals and sometimes for having remitted their espousals without getting a court order.

Remission cases that use language like that at Cambrai are rare in our Brussels sample, but there are 19 cases in the register that do employ such language, and they give us a better sense of remission practice at Brussels.[135] Twelve of these sentences are by Rodolphi and only seven by Platea, who, as we will recall, accounts for three-quarters of the sentences in the register.[136] The last of these sentences in chronological order is dated 5 July 1454,[137] although more than half of the sentences in the register are found from that date until the end of the register in December of 1459.

What happened, of course, was not that Platea ceased to allow couples to remit their espousals. He ceased using the language of quittance and remission that both the Cambrai officials and Rodolphi had employed and began, instead, to deal with such cases with the language of separation. We can even date when this happened with some precision. The last of the sentences that employs language of quittance and remission is, to repeat, dated 5 July 1454; the first of the sentences in the sample employing language of separation is dated 27 September 1454.[138]

The question is whether this change in sentencing style made any substantive difference to the couples involved. We saw that at Cambrai, remissions were often granted after the promotor had successfully prosecuted the couple for failure to follow through with their espousals. Even where the matter was pursued at instance by the couple, amends were quite frequently imposed for the same offense. While there are a number of factual variations in Rodolphi's remission sentences, four of them were rendered after the couple had been prosecuted, made amends, and were ordered to solemnize, and one of them could have been

[134] *Grimberghen c Gheraets* (20.vii.59), no. 1510, T&C no. 882.
[135] Disc. T&C no. 883.
[136] Listed T&C no. 884.
[137] *Officie c Diels en Nouts* (n. 119).
[138] *Boxhorens en Spaens* (n. 133).

rendered in such circumstances.[139] An additional three were granted when the couple remitted on the spot without having to be ordered to solemnize, but after they have been ordered to make amends for failure to solemnize.[140] Not all the prosecutions that resulted in remissions also resulted in amends, however. In two cases, Rodolphi neither imposed amends nor awarded the promotor his costs; in another he did the latter but not the former.[141] This could have been because the promotor had a particularly weak case, but there must have been at least a suspicion of espousals to warrant the remission. Rodolphi may have been coming to doubt the wisdom of vigorously pursuing couples who emphatically did not want to marry.

While they continue to employ the language of quittance and remission, Platea's early remission sentences also borrow from separation sentences language that suggests doubts about the wisdom of forcing unwilling couples to live together: "We dissolve the promises of marriage, such as they are, alleged and presumed between the *rei*, which seem to have the force of espousals, they being unwilling mutually to accept each other on account of the discord of their *mores*,[142] having been previously warned and carefully induced by us to contract, lest it should happen that someone should marry a woman whom he hates, since unwilling marriages often have harsh ends." This was certainly a strange case. The couple are to make amends for "having abducted themselves mutually and rashly without the license and knowledge of their relatives, for having had suspicious and suspect dealings in various places, and otherwise having failed grievously with respect to a sacrament of the church." Further, while the man is given license, the woman is neither given it nor denied it but is told to inform her conscience with a discrete priest.[143] Platea may be applying a social double standard here, although it is possible that what she told him led him to believe that she thought she exchanged words of the present tense with the man.

In four more sentences Platea employs similar language about separation. None of these have the feature of the runaway marriage or the difference in the moral advice given to the man and woman. In two cases the couple are to make amends for not having publicized their clandestine espousals, and in one for having had intercourse before the espousals. In the other two cases the couple are to make amends for having privately remitted their promises.[144]

In none of the sample remission sentences in which Platea employed the language of separation were the parties required to make amends.[145] Examination of cases outside of the sample shows that he continued to do so where he

[139] Listed T&C no. 885.
[140] Listed T&C no. 886.
[141] Listed T&C no. 887.
[142] For possible meanings of these phrases, see Ch 10, at nn. 139–40, 161–2, 180–2.
[143] *Officie c Stenereren en Bollents* (n. 136), T&C no. 888.
[144] Listed T&C no. 889.
[145] See at nn. 133–4.

thought it appropriate.[146] There are, however, a number of cases outside of the sample where amends are not imposed.[147] While most of these are instance cases (suggesting that a couple who wished to dissolve their espousals were well advised to come to court before the promotor found them), there are office cases in which no amends are imposed,[148] and there is at least one instance case in which they are.[149]

All of this suggests that Platea's move to treat remission cases like separation cases did not have a radical effect on the usual practice of the court. It may, however, have had a somewhat subtler effect, leading to more situations in which a couple could remit without penalty.

THREE-PARTY SPOUSALS CASES NOT ALLEGING *COPULA*

Cambrai

We have noted that in marked contrast to Paris but more like York and Ely, the courts of Cambrai diocese entertained a rather large number of spousals cases involving three parties. In our sample of Cambrai cases, there are 29 such cases not involving allegations of intercourse, 17 straight instance, 5 straight office, and 7 mixed. The form of the instance actions reminds us of the York marriage-and-divorce cases where a single plaintiff is suing a couple. Here, however, the suit is to dissolve their *sponsalia*, not to dissolve their marriage.

Most, if not all, of the instance cases come up in the form of opposition to banns (styled in one case as *causa oppositionis matrimonialis*).[150] The following sentence by Nicolaï is typical:[151]

> Having seen the opposition of [PR] who opposed the *sponsalia* entered into and maintained between [AP] and [JG], the parties desirous of contracting, in the hand of the priest and the face of the church of Quaermont in the diocese of Cambrai, [having seen] the replies of [AP], one of those desirous of contracting, and [having seen] the oaths, confessions and replies of these parties . . . having invoked the name of Christ, we say and declare that the contract and solemnization of marriage by and between those desirous of contracting should proceed, the opposition of the opponent – which we consider frivolous – notwithstanding, condemning on account of this the same opponent [to pay] the *rea* [AP's] costs, damages, and interest sustained and suffered on this occasion.

The marginal *leges* indicate that the *actor* was fined for "frivolous opposition."

The fact that only the replies of the *rea* are mentioned (and, indeed, she seems to be the only formal party defendant) strongly suggests that the opposition was based on a precontract with the *actor* (and that the subsequent contract of the

[146] Examples T&C no. 890.
[147] Examples T&C no. 891.
[148] Examples T&C no. 892.
[149] *Lionis en Wijsbeke* (12.v.58), no. 1313, disc. T&C no. 893.
[150] *Moru c Mellée et Boussieres* (2.ix.44), no. 523.
[151] *Rocque c Piers* (17.v.43), no. 471, T&C no. 894.

rea was uncontroversial). This is characteristic of most of the cases in this group. It is also characteristic of these cases that plaintiffs have a very low success rate. Of the 17 straight-instance sentences, 14 are for the defendant(s). The style of the parties in these cases suggests one of the reasons why; the plaintiff is called "the opponent" (*opponens*), the defendants "those desirous of contracting" (*contrahere volentes*). The decretals tell us that "compelled [marriages] frequently have bad ends"; Roman law opines that "marriages ought to be free," and on the basis of the unwillingness of Roman law specifically to enforce *sponsalia*, some canonists argued that the church should do likewise.[152] That was not the practice in Cambrai diocese, but the plaintiff who was seeking to upset public *sponsalia* between a couple who wanted to marry each other and force one of them to marry him had a high barrier to overcome, one that few overcame.

The pattern of fining in these sentences varies. The most common fine is *pro frivola oppositione*, which we find in 9 of the 14 sentences in favor of the defendant(s).[153] This means, of course, that in five cases that result in favorable sentences for the defendant, no such fine is mentioned; yet in the sentence of all five, the official finds the opposition "frivolous." In one of them we can be quite sure that no fine was imposed because there is a marginal annotation *non sunt leges*.[154] In another, it seems likely that the scribe forgot to note it because there is a marginal annotation that *leges* were not imposed on the parties "desirous of contracting."[155] In the other three no mention is made of *leges*. It is possible that here, too, there was a scribal error, but we know from the first case that a finding in the sentence of frivolous opposition did not always lead to imposition of *leges*, and it is possible that none were imposed in these cases as well.[156] All of this would tend to suggest that a finding of frivolous opposition in the sentence was another way of saying that the claim failed of proof, and the imposition of *leges* for frivolous opposition suggests, at a minimum, that the opponent had no proof at all and perhaps even that the official thought that the claim was made in bad faith.

In three cases in which there was a judgment for the defendant(s), the plaintiff is fined not only for frivolous opposition but also for failing to publicize clandestine *sponsalia*, and in two of these for failing to proceed to solemnization.[157] This "Catch-22" type of penalty has already been discussed in the context of two-party cases.[158] We should resist the temptation that it is being used here to impose additional penalties on a plaintiff who had a particularly weak case (or just to raise money), because in one of the cases there is evidence that the plaintiff had quite a strong case.[159] Normally, this type of case is decided on the basis

[152] Texts and ref. T&C no. 895.
[153] Listed T&C no. 896.
[154] *Bastard c Potine* (12.ix.44), no. 531, disc. T&C no. 897.
[155] *Estrut c Flamencq et Fournière* (30.vii.46), no. 982; further examples T&C no. 898.
[156] Listed T&C no. 899.
[157] *Evrart c Orfèvre* (n. 153); *Weez c Gauyelle* (n. 153); *Estréez c Moquielle* (n. 153).
[158] At n. 33. All of these "Catch-22" sentences are sentences of Nicolaï.
[159] *Evrart c Orfèvre* (n. 153).

of the "oaths, confessions, and replies" of the parties. In this one the plaintiff produced witnesses. Not only that but the costs were compensated between the parties rather than being charged, as was normal, to the unsuccessful plaintiff, and *leges* were imposed on the couple who succeeded in the litigation. We are not told what these *leges* were for because they had paid them by the time the scribe made the entry, but they were not for clandestine *sponsalia*; the sentence tells us that the *sponsalia* had been published in the church of Beaurevoir. The most obvious alternative is that the couple were fined for having contracted knowing of the *fama* of the precontract. Hence, we might speculate that this was a case in which the official was reasonably sure that the precontract had happened. He could not enforce it because there was insufficient proof, but this was a particularly appropriate case for fining the plaintiff; his failure to publicize the contract and proceed with solemnization was the reason why the couple were able to engage in bigamous *sponsalia*.

In three cases the plaintiff obtained a favorable judgment. The circumstances were a bit different in each case. In the first, process consisted of "oaths, assertions, confessions, and responses" of the parties and, notably, the consent of the *reus*. On the basis of this, the prior clandestine *de futuro sponsalia* of the *actor* and *rea* were held to prevail over the subsequent public *sponsalia* of the *correi*. The *actor* and *rea* were ordered to solemnize; the *rea* was ordered to pay the *reus*'s costs, and he was given license to marry another. *Leges* were imposed on the *actor* and *rea* for nonrenewal of their clandestine *sponsalia*, on the *rea* for double *sponsalia*, and expressly not on the *reus*.[160]

It seems relatively clear that what happened was that when the *rea* was summoned before the court, she admitted that she had contracted with the *actor*. The confession of the parties, however, could not prejudice the rights of third parties unless there was independent proof, and there probably was not. Hence, the consent of the *reus* was critical. He could waive the rights that he had acquired by *sponsalia de futuro* (as he could not, had the *sponsalia* been *de presenti*). He did waive (though he may have hesitated; there is mention of contrary "propositions" that he made), and the final result was a foregone conclusion. It also seems reasonably clear that the *reus* had known nothing about the previous contract; hence, only the *rea* was fined for double espousals.

The second case is quite similar to the first except that the consent of the *reus* is not mentioned. Rather, in addition to the usual "oaths, assertions, propositions, responses, and confessions" of the parties, the official had the answers to interrogatories that he had put to the *reus*. On the basis of this, the official found that the apparently clandestine *de futuro sponsalia* of the *actor* and *rea* antedated those of the *rei*. He ordered the former to solemnize, gave the *reus* license, and ordered the *rea* to pay his costs and damages. No *leges* are mentioned, though they certainly could have been imposed.[161]

160 *Engles c Jacotte et Bourgois* (20.xi.38), no. 70.
161 *Moru c Mellée et Boussieres* (2.ix.44), no. 523, disc. T&C no. 900.

At first glance, this seems inconsistent with the first case. There is no indication that there was any proof of the first contract other than the confession of the parties, but the consent of the second man is not, so far as we can tell, obtained. Since the first sentence is one of Divitis and the second one of Nicolaï, it is possible that the two judges had different views about the quantum of proof necessary in such cases. We can, however, reconcile the two cases on their facts. In the first case, the second *sponsalia* were public. Ample proof of them existed. In this case, both sets of *sponsalia* seem to have been clandestine. The *actor* confessed to one set, the *reus* to another, and the *rea* to both.[162] The proofs were thus evenly balanced. (It is possible that there were witnesses to both, which the official did not insist on hearing because it was obvious what they were going to say.) The purpose of the interrogatories that the official put to the *reus* was probably to determine the date of his alleged *sponsalia*. Once he had admitted that they were later, the official was not going to allow his clandestine *sponsalia* to prevail over another set of clandestine *sponsalia*, which the couple had admitted.[163]

The third case is quite different.[164] The definitive sentence gives us no indication that a third party was involved. We only know of her from an interlocutory sentence in which she was ordered to appear and answer interrogatories under oath because she was alleged to have entered into promises of marriage with the *reus*.[165] Depositions were produced on behalf of the *actrix*, the *reus* excepted to the witnesses, and the *actrix* replied to the exceptions. The third party was probably interrogated, though this is not mentioned in the final sentence. Ultimately, the official defers the oath to the *actrix*,[166] adjudges her the *sponsa* of the *reus*, orders the couple to solemnize within 40 days, and orders the *reus* to treat her thereafter with conjugal affection. No *leges* are mentioned.

The fact that the woman with whom the *reus* is alleged to have contracted has to be summoned to answer interrogatories suggests that we are not dealing here, as we were in the other cases, with a couple who are 'desirous of contracting' and a third person who wants to break it up. Rather, this looks much more like a case in which the man, in order to escape from his obligations to the *actrix*, defended on the ground of a precontract, one which neither he nor the woman with whom he is alleged to have precontracted had any intention of performing. We do not know whether she appeared or what she said if she did. It seems likely, however, that if she appeared, she either denied the contract or confessed to a contract that postdated the one at stake here. That would then bring us back to the question of whether the *actrix* had sufficiently proven her contract. The fact that the *reus* does not offer witnesses to his exceptions to her

162 Disc. T&C no. 901.

163 See the office cases at n. 176 where clandestine espousals do prevail over public, with further discussion of such cases in n. 179.

164 *Varlut c Hauwe* (18.ii.47 to 1.iv.47), nos. 1100, 1121.

165 Disc. T&C no. 902.

166 For this practice, see at nn. 47–56.

witnesses suggests that his objections to them were obvious: They were related to her, or they did not testify to the same event, or only one of them testified to the event and the others to *fama*. The *ex officio* oath that the official allowed her supplies the necessary quantum of proof, and she wins.

Six of the seven cases in the sample in which the promotor brings the action, along with the opponent of the *sponsalia* of another couple, have similar results to those of the straight-instance actions. In all six of the actions, the couple are ordered or given license to solemnize their marriage, and the opponent's case fails. In all six cases the opponent must make amends. In two cases it is not said for what; in one case it is for not publicizing clandestine espousals and not proceeding to solemnization and for frivolous opposition; in two cases it is for not publicizing and not proceeding but not for frivolous opposition, and in one case for frivolous opposition only.[167] The two cases that do not specify what the amends are for say either that the contracting parties or just the one who is alleged to have precontracted is also to make amends and to share with the opponent in paying the promotor's costs, and the costs of the parties are not mentioned. In the others, the couple is not ordered to make amends, but in three of the four the party who is alleged to have precontracted shares with the opponent in paying the promotor's costs (in one it is said to be *propter famam*), and in all four the opponent pays that party's costs (in one it is said to be *propter frivolam oppositionem*, though the opponent does not have to make amends for that). In three of the cases, including the two with nonspecific amends, the *sponsalia* of the contracting parties are specifically said to have been in the face of the church; in the other three that quality is not mentioned.

When we put these details together, some patterns emerge that allow us to make probabilistic judgments about what may have been involved. The two cases with nonspecific amends (a practice that seems to be confined to Divitis) and the case in which the *rea* has to share in the promotor's costs *propter famam* are the three cases in which the sentence specifically mentions that the *sponsalia* of the *rei* were solemn.[168] In all three cases we imagine that the offense of the contracting parties, or at least of the one with whom the precontract was said to have been made, was publishing their espousals knowing of the *fama* of the precontract. The case where the opponent makes amends *propter frivolam oppositionem* alone is also the case in which the other party does not have to share in paying the promotor's costs.[169] This is probably a case in which the official thought that there was just nothing to support the opponent's case, perhaps even that the charge was malicious. In the other three cases where the winning party's costs are paid by the opponent, the winning party has to share in the promotor's costs. That suggests there was something to the charge. In one case we know that that something was *fama*, and it may have been the case in

[167] Listed T&C no. 903.
[168] Listed T&C no. 904.
[169] *Office c Petit et Brunielle* (n. 167).

the other two as well.[170] In all three of these cases, the opponent made amends for non-publication and non-proceeding. That suggests the official thought that there may have been something more than *fama*. But the proof ultimately failed, and as a general matter, when this happens the winning party was entitled to costs. In one case, we might imagine, it failed quite spectacularly, and in this case the opponent was also fined for frivolous opposition.

One of the mixed office/instance cases in the sample is quite different and is one of the most dramatic. Two of the three sentences rendered on the same day are in instance spousals actions, one brought by Aymeric *dit* Patin against Agnès Burye and the other by Agnès against Hacquinet du Prijer.[171] The form of the action is thus what we called in Chapter 6 a case of 'interlocking competitors'. Since the second case is called a *causa oppositionis*, we are probably to imagine that Hacquinet is trying to marry someone else. Hence, this is, at least potentially, a four-party case. In the first case, the *actor* produced witnesses whose depositions were taken, and some of whom the official recalled and reexamined. The *rea* produced written objections to the witnesses and depositions were taken on these objections. On the basis of this, the official finds that Aymeric and Agnès are *sponsi*; she is ordered to solemnize her marriage with Aymeric within 40 days, to treat him with marital affection thereafter, and to pay his litigation costs. In the second case, the official mentions only the petition of the *actrix* and the response of the *reus*. On the basis of the *processus* in the previous case, the official finds that *sponsalia* found to have occurred in that case antedated the ones alleged in this case. He absolves Hacquinet from the pretended promises asserted by Agnès and from her petition, orders her to pay the costs that he incurred because of her frivolous opposition, and gives him license to marry another.

Agnès was not a woman to be trifled with. In the third sentence, the promotor alleges, and the official finds, that when Agnès learned of the depositions in the first case, she had some of the witnesses who had testified on behalf of Aymeric jailed in a secular jail, ill-treated in jail, and ultimately branded in the face for having committed perjury.[172] She also threatened potential witnesses in the second case with the same treatment. By these acts she

> not little harmed, damaged, and very much contemned the spiritual jurisdiction of the most reverend our lord of Cambrai and the authority of this his court, and detracted from its honor, glorying in the alleged things with a malice by her otherwise newly devised, likewise perpetrating a crime of most pernicious example – by which, to wit, hereafter, witnesses to be produced before us might be struck by such fear that they could not enjoy the full liberty of exonerating their consciences, and otherwise in many ways most grievously breaking both the civil and the moral law.[173]

170 Listed T&C no. 905.

171 *Patin c Burye*; *Burye c Prijer*; *Office c Burye* (10.ix.46), nos. 1000–1002.

172 *Office c Burye* (n. 171), no. 1002, T&C no. 906.

173 *Ibid.*, T&C no. 907.

For this she was condemned to make amends, pay two pounds of wax to the chapel, and pay the promotor's costs.

The level of the rhetoric of this sentence is the most overblown that we have seen. It is higher in the description of what Agnès threatened to do to the potential witnesses (witnesses who, as we have seen, were ultimately not necessary) than it is in its description of what she did to the actual witnesses.[174] This suggests that the court was genuinely concerned, as it says in its sentence, about the potential intimidation of witnesses. The concern was not misplaced, granted how dependent the court was on witness testimony. But we have also seen that perjury was not uncommon in the ecclesiastical courts. Agnès was, no doubt, well connected. The question is whether she was so well connected that she could have had the witnesses branded for perjury if there were no indication that they had committed it. We will recall that the official in the first case ordered Aymeric's witnesses reexamined. This frequently happens when we have reason to suspect that the judge suspected perjury.[175] Ultimately, he decided that they were telling the truth, and for Agnès to have brought them before the secular authorities, in essence appealing the official's decision to them, was contempt.

What happened afterwards the record does not say. We may doubt, however, that she thereafter treated Aymeric 'with marital affection'.

There are five cases in the sample in which the promotor proceeds in potential cases of double *sponsalia* without, so far as the sentence says, any participation by one of the parties or any allegation of *copula*. In two of them prior clandestine *sponsalia* prevail over subsequent public ones. The couple are fined for not publicizing the clandestine *sponsalia* and for not proceeding to solemnization and are condemned to pay the promotor's costs; the *rea* is also fined for double *sponsalia* and condemned to pay both the costs and damages of her second partner (who was not made a formal party and was, in both cases, said to be have been deceived by the *rea*).[176] In two other cases, the promotor alleges that one of the parties to a clandestine contract had previously contracted (probably also clandestinely) with someone else. In both cases, the court absolves the third party from the charges of the promotor and orders the clandestinely contracting couple to solemnize within 40 days.[177] In the fifth case, no *sponsalia* are found; all three parties are absolved of all the promotor's charges.[178] There are other differences among these cases that allow us to speculate about what actually happened and about the kinds of proof that were required, but these details are best left to the margin.[179]

174 Compare T&C no. 906 with T&C no. 908.
175 *Dolling c Smith* is a good example.
176 *Office c Mont et Aredenoise* (28.ix.42), no. 341; *Office c Barat et Brule* (24.xii.46), no. 1070.
177 Listed T&C no. 909.
178 *Office c Lentout, Coesins et Haremans* (6.ii.45), no. 641.
179 Disc. T&C no. 910.

Brussels

There are 13 three-party spousals cases in our sample of Brussels cases in which *copula* is not alleged: 2 straight instance, 10 office/instance, and 1 straight office. All but one of these cases can be characterized as oppositions to public espousals, and in none of them does the opponent (10 men and 3 women) succeed. The difficulty that opponents had at Cambrai when they could not allege a presumptive marriage was repeated at Brussels. As at Cambrai, so too at Brussels, the pattern of fining and imposition of costs allows us to speculate about how plausible the opponent's case was. Some of the Brussels opposition cases also provide us better glimpses into what may have been going on socially than do those at Cambrai.

Both of the instance cases came before Rodolphi. In one of them, he defers the oath to the *reus*, and on the basis of this deferral he orders the public espousals of the *reus* with another woman to be solemnized. While he finds the plaintiff's case "insufficient," he does not order her to make amends for her opposition.[180] In the other case, he finds the male plaintiff's opposition to the public espousals of a widow described as *domicella* "frivolous" and orders him to make amends for it.[181]

Eight years later, the widow is back in court suing the man to whom she was engaged in the earlier case. In an interlocutory sentence, Platea orders the woman or her proctor to exhibit the originals and the execution of the "inhibitory letters" that he previously issued at her instance. If they are not exhibited, they will be revoked from the time of the sentence. Whether the reference to the "inhibitory letters" is to the judgment in the previous case (in which case the court cannot find, or will not rely on, the registered sentence), or whether it is to some order against the erstwhile fiancé that was not recorded (more likely), we cannot tell. In either case, however, the sentence suggests that her relations with him were not totally happy.[182]

An angry mother almost certainly lies behind the one straight-office case in our group, heard fairly early in Platea's career. On the basis of the oaths, replies, and confessions of the parties, Platea finds that the public espousals of the *rea* with the second *reus*, three banns having followed, are to be solemnized, notwithstanding the "dealings between the first *reus* and the *rea* at one time held and maintained with their common relatives, but not carried forward or having achieved their end." The first *reus* is absolved from the complaint of the promotor, but the *rea* is to make amends "for having gone off with [the second *reus*] without her mother's knowledge and allowing herself to be affianced" and is to pay the costs of the promotor. There can be little doubt that the mother got the promotor to bring the case, and there is no indication that the first *reus* wanted to pursue the matter. In these circumstances, a public espousal will not

180 *Vrients c Smeekaert* (26.i.50), no. 130, T&C no. 911.
181 *Roevere c Bolenbeke* (9.i.49), no. 15.
182 *Bolenbeke c Jan* (4.xi.57), no. 1240, T&C no. 912.

be upset, though the mother will be given the satisfaction of seeing her errant daughter (but not her future son-in-law) fined.[183]

The sentences in the more routine opposition cases brought in the office/instance mode show Platea's increasing concern about frivolous opposition. In the first sentence in such a case, he orders the opposing *rea* to make amends and pay the costs of the promotor and the *reus*.[184] His next two such sentences raise the stakes by declaring that the opponent had incurred excommunication by "to no avail and *de facto*" opposing the marriage or simply by "less than lawfully" opposing it.[185] Another sentence contains a reference to synodal statutes against frivolous opposition.[186] These statutes are probably the source of the idea in the previous sentence that someone who did this was excommunicate. In his final two sentences of this type, Platea adds another feature. The opposing *reus* is not only to make amends for frivolous opposition and pay the promotor's costs and those of the couple, but he is also pay damages to the *rea* to repair her honor, these damages to be taxed by arbitrators.[187] It is possible that in these two cases, the opposing *reus* had alleged not only that he had contracted with the *rea* but also that he had had sexual relations with her, but the pattern is definitely one of increasing concern about false allegations in opposition to marriage.

Not all unsuccessful opponents were punished, however. In one case it is the successful couple who have to make amends for having publicly espoused each other during the pendency of a case brought by the first *reus* against the *rea*. They are the ones who have to pay the costs of the promotor, and costs between the parties are compensated. There was something to the first *reus*'s case, although Platea ultimately finds on the basis of their replies, oaths, and allegations, that it was "some words about espousals" rather than espousals themselves.[188]

A few of the cases fall outside of the usual pattern. In one, neither alleged espousal was public. Hence, neither espousal was entitled to the presumption that normally attached to public espousals. The man and his fiancée, however, confessed to one espousal, and he denied the other. That put the *rea* to her proof, and in an interlocutory sentence, she is admitted to her proof. She obviously had none, and four days later the sentence goes against her. The successful couple does, however, have to make amends for the clandestine espousals. They all share in the costs of the promotor, and no mention is made of the costs of the parties.[189]

In three cases, it seems reasonably clear, as we suspected in one of the Cambrai cases,[190] that the opponent is one of the parties to the public espousals, who

[183] *Officie c Codde, Henricrus en Heckleghem* (19.i.54), no. 570, T&C no. 913.
[184] *Officie c Nichils en Roelants* (12.vi.53), no. 500.
[185] Listed T&C no. 914.
[186] *Officie c Bodevaerts en Heyns* (28.i.58), no. 1270, T&C no. 915, with disc.
[187] *Officie c Favele, Oys en Scroten* (27.x.58), no. 1380, T&C no. 916.
[188] *Officie c Wante, Verre en Molen* (30.vii.56), no. 1000, T&C no. 917.
[189] *Officie c Mota, Nijs en Hermani* (n. 185).
[190] *Varlut c Hauwe* (n. 164).

is now trying to get out of them by alleging a clandestine precontract with the other *rea*. In no case does the ploy work. In the first case the man is condemned to make amends for "certain words sounding with the force of promises of marriage alleged by him and not proven and because, without having brought the [*rea*] before a competent judge he affianced [CO] in the hand of the priest and in the face of the church." The *rea* is absolved of the promises proposed against her, and the man is to pay the promotor's costs.[191]

In the second case the man went further. Not only did he get the promotor to prosecute him and the woman with whom he had allegedly precontracted but that woman was also his fiancée's sister. If the contract had been proven, not only would it have been prior in time but it would also have given rise to the impediment of public honesty, which would have prevented his marrying the sister.[192] The fiancée's sister also apparently agreed to support his story. How Platea found out that it was all a lie we do not know. The sentence recites no more proof than the oaths, responses, and confessions of the parties. Perhaps the sister broke down when faced with hard questioning by the judge. In the event, Platea orders the public espousals solemnized (something that he had not done in the previous case, and something that he may not have been authorized to do, because the fiancée was not a party to the case). The man is to make amends for "falsely and rashly asserting that there were such promises between him and [JG], his fiancée's sister," and the sister is to make amends for "consenting that the same be asserted of her." What kind of family relations these people had with one another after all of this was over the record, of course, does not say.[193]

The final case has a ring of truth about it. The *rea* is at least as active as the *reus* in promoting the case; witnesses are heard, and a love letter (*littera amoris*) that the *reus* wrote the *rea* is introduced into evidence and acknowledged by him. Ultimately, however, Platea orders the public espousals solemnized (an order that, once more, may not technically be within his power because the *reus*'s fiancée is not a party to the case). Platea's language suggests that he thought it was a hard case. The *sponsalia* alleged by the *rea* are not only not frivolous, but "in order to avoid perils and scandals" and assuring us that he had found out all about them (*de quibus nos sufficienter fuimus informati*), he specifically quashes and annuls them (implying that there was something there to quash and annul). The *rea* is specifically given license to contract elsewhere. The *reus* must make amends because having promised to God and the saints that he would contract with the *rea*, he went off and contracted with his fiancée, thus committing double espousals (to the extent that he was capable) and violating his oath to God and the saints. The couple are also to make amends for not having publicized their espousals "such as they were." But Platea seems to be convinced that the couple did not contract because "he offered his faith to her clandestinely, but she did not properly accept it." Those familiar with the

191 *Officie c Hoemakere en Luis* (10.xii.51), no. 330, T&C no. 918.
192 See Ch 1, at nn. 71–2; Ch 6, at n. 219.
193 *Officie c Rosijn en Goffaert* (11.i.55), no. 741, T&C no. 919.

Anglo-American contract doctrine of offer and acceptance will recognize the deficiency here, as will those who remember that *sponsalia* are derived from a form of the Roman contract of stipulation. In a final concession to the situation of the *rea*, Platea orders the *reus* to pay both the promotor's costs and her costs.[194]

It is rare that we have so much information about what happened between the couples who appear in these registers. The *rea* in this case was fortunate to have considerable evidence that was admissible in court, and we must imagine that the *reus*, perhaps because of qualms of conscience, perhaps because he was having second thoughts about his impending marriage to the other woman, was forthcoming. But the *rea*, to her credit, was also honest. Neither she nor the *reus* was able to testify that she said "yes" at the crucial moment. We probably should imagine that many of the cases that have less full records involved ambiguous relationships like the one quite vividly described here.

One of the cases of frivolous opposition, so frivolous that the opponent has to pay damages to the *rea*, has a rather unusual end. Less than two months after the engaged couple are ordered to solemnize, they appear in court and remit their espousals, a remission that Platea grants with his usual separation language. It is hard to know what happened here. Perhaps the man did not think that the opponent's opposition was as frivolous as Platea thought it was; that is to say, the very damage to the woman's honor that Platea feared would happen, happened. It is also possible, however, that the woman was being pursued by the opponent. To escape him she got engaged to another man. Once the opponent had lost his suit, there was no need for her to go through with the marriage to the other man. Our assessment of the case depends greatly on how sophisticated we imagine the parties might have been. All that the record tells us is that they came from Brussels. Hence, they could have known that if one wanted to resist an unwanted lawsuit for espousals, it was a good idea to have a public espousal to raise in opposition to it.[195]

TWO-PARTY SPOUSALS CASES ALLEGING *COPULA*

Cambrai

Somewhat more than a third of the spousals cases in the Cambrai sample allege *copula* (36% 56/155).[196] Table 8.8 shows that those in which only two parties are involved are heavily dominated by the promotor (20 straight office, 13 office/instance, and only 5 straight instance), that in the instance and office/instance cases the woman is always the moving party, that their success rate in such cases was low (2 instance and 2 office/instance cases won, for an overall success rate of 22%). We also saw that when we added the straight-office

[194] *Officie c Timmerman en Rutsemeels* (15.xi.55), no. 882, T&C no. 920.
[195] *Heyden en Waghesteit* (23.xi.59), no. 1574; cf. at n. 187.
[196] Table 8.7

cases in which the promotor was attempting to establish a presumptive marriage, his success rate was considerably higher (9/16, 56%).[197]

The wording of the sentences tends to confirm my speculation that in many, perhaps all, of the straight-office cases in which a presumptive marriage is found, the woman brought the matter to the attention of the promotor and aided him in the prosecution. Here is a typical sentence of Nicolaï in an office/instance case where a presumptive marriage is not found:[198]

Having seen the articles of the promotor . . . and the oaths, responses and confessions of the same *rei*, the allegations, petitions, and conclusions mutually given by and between the same *rei*, the depositions of the witnesses produced at the instance of the promotor and [MM], the *correa*, who was adhering to the same promotor, the writings impugning such depositions given on behalf of [JC], the response of the promotor and [MM] to them, and the depositions of the witnesses thereupon . . . we absolve [JC] the *reus* from the promises of marriage and the other things alleged and requested by the promotor and [MM], and grant on account of this to the same [JC] free capacity to marry in the Lord wherever and whenever he wants, condemning him, nonetheless, for certain reasonable grounds moving us and our conscience, [to pay] the costs of the promotor. . . . We condemn [MM] to make appropriate amends because after the promises of marriage that she asserted, she did not take care to proceed by force of them to the contract and solemnization of them with [MM] within due time, indeed she confessed that she, in this situation, allowed herself to be carnally known by the same *reus* and wanted to transform the asserted promises, insofar as she could, into the force of a presumptive marriage, and [we condemn] her [to pay] the costs of the promotor and also those of the *reus*, who has been absolved of the claim of this *correa* as justice requires . . . and we absolve the same woman from the necessity of proceeding further with the *reus* and from the other things asked by the promotor.

There are a number of special features of this sentence to which we will have to return,[199] but the important thing to note here is that when a presumptive marriage is not found, it is almost impossible to write the sentence without mentioning the party who favored it. Even if the procedure was less elaborate than it was in this case (so that there would be no mention at whose instance the witnesses were produced), and even if the moving party was not fined for her role in the case, the rhetoric still calls for naming who, in addition to the promotor, was alleging the presumptive marriage so that the moved-against party could be freed from her charge.

The following is a typical sentence of Nicolaï in a straight-office case in which a presumptive marriage was found:[200]

Having seen the articles of the promotor . . . and the oaths, responses, and confessions of the same *rei*, the allegations, petitions, and conclusions mutually given by and between the same *rei*, the depositions of the witnesses who were produced . . . because they did

[197] Disc. T&C no. 921.
[198] *Office c Cherchy et Mairesse* (18.iv.50), no. 1280, T&C no. 922.
[199] At nn. 240–2.
[200] *Office c Besghe et Fayt* (6.vi.50), no. 1310, T&C no. 923.

not take any care to renew [publicly] the promises of marriage that they began by and between themselves nor to proceed by force of them to the contract and solemnization of the marriage within due time, or at least to ask for and obtain a judicial declaration about them, indeed, in this situation, they many times had sexual relations between them thereby transforming the promises into the force of a presumptive marriage – such as we also declare it – we condemn the *rei* to make amends fitting for such violations, and [we condemn] them to proceed to the publication and solemnization in the face of the church – as is customary – of their presumptive marriage such as we have declared it within 40 days from now and to treat each other in the future with conjugal affection [and to pay] the costs of this litigation.

This case had more process than some, and the name of the producing party could have been included with recital of the witnesses, but it was not. Otherwise, there is no place for it. The fines, the order to solemnize, and the allocation of costs are all charged against both *rei*. While it is possible that in some of these cases both *rei* were resisting the promotor's charges, it seems unlikely that that was so in many of them.[201] To the extent that these cases were contested (and it seems that this one was), we are probably to imagine that only one of the parties was contesting it. Granted the gender ratios in the instance and office/instance cases, it seems likely that in most if not all of them, the moving party was the woman.

On this assumption, the overall success rate of the women who were seeking to enforce a presumptive marriage is considerably higher than it was if we look at just the instance and office/instance cases (13/35, 37% vs 4/19, 21%). The question is what accounts for the success of these women in slightly more than one-third of the cases and the failure of the moving parties in the other two-thirds.

In some cases the man seems to have confessed or, at least, admitted the woman's case after some wrangling. *Rattine c l'Oyseleur*, quoted at the beginning of Chapter 8, is a good example.[202] Other cases were fully litigated. In *Office c Henri de Fenain et Marie le Nain*, in addition to the usual "oaths and replies" we find "mutual allegations, petitions, conclusions, responses, and confessions of the *rei* given between and against each other," "depositions of witnesses against the [*reus*] on behalf of the promotor and the [*rea*]," "certain writings given on both sides by the parties to impugn and save such witnesses and depositions," "an allegation of fact proposed by the [*reus*]," "the response of the *correa* to it," "depositions of the witnesses thereupon produced on behalf of the [*reus*]," and "an oath of truth deferred to the [rea] by our office for certain rational causes moving us and our conscience and by her accepted and taken."[203] In addition to the usual fines for not renewing publicly clandestine promises, not proceeding to solemnization, and having sexual intercourse following clandestine promises, the man was fined for deflowering, persistent

[201] Disc. T&C no. 924.
[202] Ch 8, at n. 2.
[203] (4.vii.44), no. 490, T&C no. 925. Was Marie a dwarf?

fornication, and impregnating the woman, and the woman for allowing it to happen. That probably provides a clue as to why she was pursuing the matter so vigorously. The order to solemnize contains a telling and unusual phrase: The man is to solemnize with the woman, "which she is prepared to fulfill."[204] She also has a copy of the sentence engrossed for her use, and the man is ordered to pay her costs. If he did not marry her, it was not for her lack of trying.

Both cases discussed in the previous paragraph involve deflowering, as do many of the other cases in this group. The deferral of the oath to the woman in the second case may have to do with this issue. It was the practice of the court of Cambrai to defer the oath to the woman on the question of whether she was a virgin prior to the intercourse. If it had not done so, she would normally have been in the position of having to prove a negative.

Cases like *Rattine c l'Oyseleur*, where there was no real dispute about the facts, are as common as, perhaps a bit more common than, cases like *Office c Fenain et Nain*. In addition to *Rattine*, six, probably seven, cases go down on the "oaths, confessions, and responses" of the parties, one adding "mutual petitions and conclusions."[205] One specifically mentions that the parties willingly accepted the order to solemnize.[206] In addition to *Fenain et Nain*, six cases required depositions, though none is as elaborate procedurally as *Fenain et Nain*.[207]

In three of the confessed cases (including the one that had mutual petitions and conclusions) and two of the cases where depositions of witnesses were necessary, the sentence, and probably the facts found, proceed in a somewhat different order from that of the aforementioned sentences.[208] Rather than finding first that the *rei* had entered into clandestine promises of marriage, which they did not publicize or proceed to solemnize, and then had intercourse, thus converting the promises into a presumptive marriage, the court finds that they had first committed fornication and then entered into the agreement, which was subsequently consummated. In three of the confessed cases (one of which is in reverse order) and, as we have seen, in one bitterly contested case, the woman is found to have been deflowered.[209] The pattern of fining generally follows that of Nicolaï's sentence quoted earlier[210] without regard to whether the case was confessed or contested: failure to publicize, failure to proceed to solemnization, and consummation of the *sponsalia*. The deflowering cases and the cases in which fornication preceded the *sponsalia* have additional penalties for these crimes. Two couples are not fined for failure to publicize but only for failure to proceed. In one of these cases the *sponsalia* were public, but in

204 *Ibid.*, T&C no. 926.
205 Listed T&C no. 927.
206 *Office c Ravin et Bridarde* (n. 205).
207 Listed T&C no. 928.
208 Listed T&C no. 929.
209 Listed T&C no. 930.
210 At n. 200.

the other they were not.[211] The couple whose willingness to solemnize was expressly stated were not fined for either; their *sponsalia* had been public, and they may have consummated them within the 40-day period.[212] There is also one case where the *sponsalia* were clandestine and neither of the penalties for clandestine *sponsalia* was imposed.[213]

Three cases, two confessed and one requiring witnesses, feature additional penalties for one or both of the parties for sexual relations with others than each other. In two of the cases, the court clearly regards this as adultery following a presumptive marriage.[214] In the third case, the relationship may have occurred before the presumptive marriage, and the focus of the sentence is on incest: The woman was also alleged to be a consanguine of the man, and although it was not proven that she was, because there was *fama* that she was, the man was fined for committing incest "at least mentally."[215]

The rhetoric of these sentences is not particularly strong. *Office c Fenain et Nain* finds that the couple has "most grievously violated the moral and criminal law" (*gravissime delinquendo et excedendo*)[216] and orders them to make amends "appropriate for such great offenses" (*tantis excessibus correspondentibus*). More often the superlative is not used; the couple is found simply to have "grievously violated the moral and criminal law" or simply to have violated it without the adverb, and to make amends "corresponding to such offenses" (*in emendis excessibus huiusmodi correspondentibus*) or simply to make amends.[217] Entering into a presumptive marriage was an offense that incurred automatic excommunication under the synodal statutes, but that fact is not mentioned in any of these sentences.[218] When this fact is coupled with the rather high number of confessed cases and cases that do not require much process, and with the occasional lightening of the sentences, we might be able to draw the conclusion that the court was not greatly concerned with presumptive marriage if it proceeded to a more regular marriage.[219] Many of these couples got the normal order of the marital process mixed up, at least from the point of view of the church's rules, but most them seem to be headed in the direction of marriage in their own way. They have to pay various fines along the way, but the way is clearly in the direction of a relationship of which the church could approve. There are, of course, exceptions. One does wonder where the

[211] *Office c Roy et Barbiresse* (n. 207) (clandestine; Divitis); *Office c Bonvarlet et Bridainne* (n. 205) (public).

[212] *Office c Ravin et Bridarde* (n. 205).

[213] *Office c Belleken et Capellen* (n. 205), disc. T&C no. 931.

[214] *Office c Moyart et Boulette* (n. 205) (confessed, T&C no. 932); *Office c Lambert et Journette*, (n. 205) (confessed, T&C no. 932).

[215] *Office c Brisemoustier et Buisson* (n. 207) (contested, T&C no. 933, with disc.).

[216] Disc. T&C no. 934.

[217] E.g., *Office c Besghe et Fayt* (n. 200), T&C no. 935; *Office c Ravin et Bridarde* (n. 205), T&C no. 935.

[218] It is mentioned in a dissolution case that has a considerably higher level of rhetoric, *Officie c Drivere* (n. 408).

[219] The pattern of fining at Tournai may point in a different direction. See App. e9.2.

couple in *Office c Fenain et Nain*, the most bitterly litigated case, are heading, and perhaps a similar concern by the court accounts for the somewhat more elevated rhetoric of the sentence. One also wonders about the future of the couples who are found to have been having sexual relations with others. These cases, however, are the exception, not the norm.

In one case the attitudes of the couple, the promotor, and the court are considerably more ambiguous, but it probably should be classed with cases in which the couple are moving in the direction of a relationship of which the church could approve, though perhaps not one of which society approved. Divitis's sentence is cryptic and dramatic: "[DE], *correus*, enticed the [BC], *correa*, with sweet talk, abducted and at length deflowered her and deprived her of the flower of her virginity, entered into and made promises of marriage with her, and also did not renew the promises nor proceed to the solemnization of marriage within the fixed time." He orders the couple to solemnize, to make amends, and to pay the costs of the promotor.[220] The promotor had to introduce witnesses in this case, and so someone was resisting something. It could be, as we saw in the abduction cases at York, that the issue was whether the woman had freely consented, in which case either she or her relatives (as is suggested by the use of the word *abducere*) were resisting the marriage. We cannot tell whether the promotor's position was for or against the marriage. It will be noted that the findings are directed entirely against the man, though the couple are together ordered to make amends and pay the promotor's costs. It will also be noted that it is not clear whether there was a presumptive marriage here. The way the sentence is worded suggests that the intercourse came before the promises of marriage.[221] The couple here came from Burst, today a borough of Erpe-Mere in Oost-Vlaanderen, a place that in the fifteenth century would have been deep in the countryside.

If the couples in many or most of the cases in which a presumptive marriage is found are heading in the direction of a relationship of which the church could approve, then something quite different seems to be happening in the cases where it is not found. There are 20 cases in the sample in which the woman or the promotor or both fail in their attempt to establish a presumptive marriage. In 10 of these cases, the woman is found to have been deflowered. Nicolaï's sentence in *Office c Alardin Granwiau et Colette Courbos*, a mixed office/instance case, is typical:[222]

> [B]ecause the *reus* presumed by an act of fornication outside of the good and honor of marriage to commit *stuprum* and deflower [CC] who was then an incorrupt virgin and afterwards to know her ["many times" may be missing here]...and because the *correa* took no care – at least as is apparent – to have the clandestine promises of marriage that she alleges renewed or to proceed by force of them to contracting and solemnizing marriage, but rather, in this situation, she allowed herself to be deflowered

[220] *Office c Eddeghem et Couwenberghe* (31.i.39), no. 131, T&C no. 936.
[221] Disc. T&C no. 937.
[222] (27.v.47), no. 1150, T&C no. 938.

by the same *reus* and afterwards to be known carnally many times, transforming the asserted promises, insofar as she could, into the force of a presumptive marriage, . . . we condemn the same *rei* to make amends corresponding to these excesses to us and [to pay] the costs of the promotor. . . . [B]etween the parties, moreover, [we condemn] the *reus*, on account of the deflowering to endow the *correa* according to the dignity of her birth and the amount of goods of this *reus* and [to pay her] costs, absolving the *reus* of the alleged promises.

Each of the elements in this sentence is typical, but the elements are not universal. One instance case has no *leges* mentioned, but simply absolves the *reus* from the promises of marriage and condemns the *reus* to endow the *rea* and pay the costs of her lying-in, maintenance for their son, "as the laws wish," and the costs of the litigation.[223] In two mixed office/instance cases, the man is so condemned (except that there is no child), and the *rei* seem to be required to make amends only for the sexual offense.[224] In these cases, the man is expressly given license to marry elsewhere. In another instance case, the man is condemned as in the previous cases and is fined for deflowering the *rea*; she is fined for having converted, insofar as possible, the clandestine promises into a presumptive marriage and for allowing herself to be deflowered and known many times, but she is not fined for non-publication and not proceeding.[225] One case follows exactly the same pattern as *Office c Granwiau et Courbos*, except that the expenses of lying-in and child maintenance are also added to the man's charge, and he is expressly given license to marry elsewhere.[226] In two straight-office cases, the couple are to make amends for the sexual offense only, both are absolved of the allegations of promises of marriage made by the promotor, and nothing is said about dowry.[227]

Some of these variations are probably random, scribal, or attributable to the style of two different judges.[228] Some of them, however, probably point to differences at least in the parties' litigation style, if not to the underlying reality. As we might expect, there is little proof presented in these cases. In only one are witnesses mentioned, and that was one of the cases in which only the promotor seems to have been alleging the presumptive marriage.[229] This means that it is likely in all of these cases that the man confessed the intercourse; he may even have confessed the deflowering. The only disputed issue was whether there were clandestine *sponsalia* that preceded the intercourse. It is probably not by chance that the two cases in which the woman is not alleging the *sponsalia* are also the two in which nothing is said about a dowry. At least in law, the dowry for

223 *Raymbarde c Buigimont* (18.xi.52), no. 1380: (*uti iura volunt*). Elsewhere we are told that maintenance 'as the laws wish' is half the cost of maintaining the child.

224 *Office c Cambron et Sadone* (21.iii.39), no. 181, disc. with another example T&C no. 939.

225 *Enghien c Goubaut* (8.v.50), no. 1293, disc. with another example T&C no. 940.

226 *Office c Pinchelart et Callekin* (6.vi.50), no. 1312.

227 *Office c Herdit et Compaings* (6.iii.45), no. 661; *Office c Machon et Poullande* (22.i.50), no. 1251.

228 Disc. T&C no. 941.

229 *Office c Herdit et Compaings* (n. 227).

deflowering had nothing to do with a presumptive marriage; the deflowered woman was entitled to it without regard to whether there had been a promise of marriage. It seems likely in these cases that nothing was said about a dowry because the woman did not ask for one, and the reason why she did not do so may have been that she had already received one.[230] Part of the consideration for the man's giving her the dowry without her having to litigate for it may have been that she not make any allegation of marital promises. That left the promotor high and dry; he could not, at least not normally, win such a case without the woman's cooperation.

The woman who had been deflowered was in a strong position. Not only was she entitled to a dowry but she could also make allegations of marital promises without being concerned about paying the costs if the allegations failed. In all the cases of deflowering where the woman makes the allegations, even if she fails, she is awarded her costs by the official. This may explain why it is that Nicolaï (Divitis does not do this) adopted the practice of multiplying the *leges* against the woman who made allegations of marital promises and then failed to prove them. That he did not always do it may indicate that in some cases he thought there was something to the charges.

In four cases, the man is expressly given license to marry elsewhere. This may be something that one had to ask for, perhaps even pay for. That the man should want it may indicate his station in life was such that he might have to prove his freedom to marry by a written instrument. The woman is never given license. In all but two cases, she has confessed to a presumptive marriage. That marriage cannot be proven, but in the face of the confession the court is not free to give her license.[231]

Three of the cases have aggravating factors. In *Office c Granwiau et Courbos*, the man was also charged with having ignored the official's sentence of excommunication for a year.[232] The sentence may have been related to the matter principally before the court, although there is nothing in the wording of the sentence that suggests that it was. The woman in the same case had also committed fornication "with a certain canon."[233] In another case, the man had been living in adulterous relationship with another married woman.[234] All three offenses occasion a heightened level of rhetoric. Of the third case we can be less sure, but the judge's description of the man's offense goes beyond what we normally find in these cases.[235]

We have saved for last a case that has a quite different pattern from the others. The couple are found to have committed fornication many times, on the first occasion of which the woman was deflowered. They then contracted

230 Disc. T&C no. 942.
231 This is confirmed by the case discussed at n. 236.
232 N. 222, T&C no. 943.
233 *Ibid.*, T&C no. 944.
234 *Office c Pinchelart et Callekin* (n. 226), T&C no. 945.
235 *Office c Apelheren et Claus* (n. 224), T&C no. 946.

marriage and one bann was proclaimed on it, but they failed to proceed to solemnization within 40 days. According to the *rea*, they then once more had intercourse, converting their espousals into a presumptive marriage. She also confessed to having sexual intercourse with another married man, and the *reus* confessed to have "many times sinned against the law of such espousals." For these offenses they are condemned to make amends and pay the costs of the promotor. The promises of marriage between the couple are dissolved, and the *reus* is given license to marry another. The *rea* is not given license, nor is she denied it; rather, she is left to her conscience "on account of the sexual intercourse which she alleges intervened after the promises."[236] Nothing is said either of dowry for deflowering or of the costs that the parties incurred.

Since there were no witnesses in this case, it is relatively easy to reconstruct what happened. In marked contrast to the other cases in this group, the promises of marriage were public, and so there was no issue that they had taken place. Since both parties confessed to "having sinned against the law of espousals," we would expect that the promises would be dissolved, certainly at the request of both of the parties, perhaps at the request of either of them.[237] Here, however, the woman alleged that they had had intercourse after the promises. Though he confessed to the initial fornication and deflowering, the man denied this intercourse, and the woman could not prove it. Hence, the promises were dissolved and the man given license, but the woman was left to her conscience.

There are 10 cases in the sample in which the promotor fails to establish a presumptive marriage and deflowering is not found. In 6 of these cases the promotor is joined in the allegation of the presumptive marriage by the *rea*; in 4 he is not. In all but one the couple are fined for fornication.[238] Most of the cases are decided on the basis of the "oaths, allegations, and responses" of the parties without any testimony being taken, meaning that both parties confessed to the intercourse. The only issue is whether there were marital promises.

We have discussed before why in our other courts men who are trying to get out of a presumptive marriage rarely deny that intercourse has taken place.[239] Since sexual intercourse is frequently difficult to prove, one would have thought that more men would deny that it had taken place. We have no better explanation of why this is so at Cambrai than of why it is so at York, Ely, and Paris. We speculated that most defendants could not reconcile an outright denial of intercourse with their consciences. To this we might add a possible element of machismo (men boasting of their 'conquests') coupled perhaps with conventions about gender relations. Convention dictates that the woman should be more ashamed to admit sexual relations; if she admits it, the manly thing to do is not to deny it.

236 *Office c Saint Pol et Grande* (26.vii.49), no. 1191, T&C no. 947.
237 Disc. T&C no. 948.
238 The exception is *Cherchy et Mairesse*, discussed at n. 240, where only the woman is fined for fornication.
239 See Ch 4, at n. 125.

Since men rarely deny that intercourse has taken place, we should pause at the one case in this group of our sample where the man did. *Office c Jean de Cherchy et Marie Mairesse* was bitterly contested. After the usual oaths, responses, and confessions to the articles of the promotor and the relatively common mutual allegations, petitions, and conclusions of the parties, the promotor and Marie introduced witnesses whose depositions were taken. Jean filed written objections to the depositions, to which the promotor and Marie replied, and Jean had depositions taken of witnesses in support of his objections. The result is virtually a total victory for Jean. He is absolved of both the promises of marriage and everything else alleged by the promotor and Marie and given license to marry another, though he is "for certain reasonable causes moving our conscience" required to share with Marie in paying the promotor's costs. Marie, on the other hand, is to make amends for the full range of offenses to which she confessed: nonrenewal of clandestine promises, failure to solemnize within the statutory period, and allowing herself to be carnally known by Jean and thus transforming – to the extent that she could – the promises of marriage into a presumptive marriage. She is also – and this is quite unusual in this type of case – condemned to pay Jean's costs.[240]

Our first reaction to this record is that the official thought this a classic case of the woman wronging. Marie was out to get Jean, and she failed miserably. The official may even have thought that her witnesses were lying. Only two things stand in the way of this interpretation: the fact that Jean is required to share in the promotor's costs and the fact that the official absolves Marie of the necessity of proceeding further with the man. The former, as we have seen, probably does not stand in the way. On almost all occasions, the promotor is going to be allowed to get his costs from both *rei*.[241] If the official cannot find that there was *fama*, he will say that he awards the promotor's costs *certis rationalibus de causis animum nostrum ad id moventibus*. The latter, however, must give us pause. As we have seen, this phrase is included in such sentences relatively infrequently, and it may indicate that the official thought that Marie was pursuing the matter, however mistakenly, in good faith.[242]

In all of the cases in this group in which the woman joins with the promotor, she is condemned to make amends, in addition to those for the fornication, once for frivolous allegations (a Divitis sentence) and in all others for the full range of offenses to which she had confessed: nonrenewal of clandestine promises, failure to solemnize within the statutory period, and allowing herself to be carnally known by the man and thus transforming – to the extent that she could – the promises of marriage into a presumptive marriage. In three of these cases, the fornication resulted in the procreation of a child. In one such case, the *reus* is ordered to pay the *rea*'s litigation costs and her costs of lying-in; in

240 Quoted at n. 198.
241 Disc. T&C no. 949.
242 See at nn. 58–60.

another, the parties' litigation costs are to be compensated and the *reus* is to pay both the *rea*'s costs of lying-in and maintenance for the child.[243] In addition to *Office c Cherchy et Mairesse*, just discussed, there are two cases that do not mention the procreation of children. In one of them, the litigation costs are to be borne by the man; in the other they are to be compensated.[244]

The most obvious conclusion to draw from these variations is that *Cherchy et Mairesse* is, indeed, an unusual case. In all of the other cases where the woman joins with the promotor, she gets something, even if it is only a share of her litigation costs. This is almost certainly the result of the fact that in all the other cases, there was something there, fornication if not promises of marriage. Explaining the differences among these cases is more difficult. That the man in one case is ordered to pay only the costs of lying-in and not child maintenance and in another he is to pay both may be a result of scribal neglect; it may also be because the child in the first case did not survive birth. The two cases where costs are compensated are the only two in the group in which witnesses were introduced. An order to share the costs strikes a nice balance between discouraging a party from introducing witnesses unnecessarily and at the same time communicating that the official did not think the woman's claim frivolous in the normal sense of the term.

The fact is, however, that in all of these cases, the woman is fined to the full extent of the law. This may have posed a barrier to raising the issue of presumptive marriage. How high a barrier we cannot tell, because, as mentioned before, we do not know how high the fines were and how much effort was made to collect them. It is possible that in the four cases where the promotor but not the woman raised the issue of presumptive marriage, the woman was deterred from raising it by the knowledge that she would be fined (even if she were successful). It is possible, too, that the man paid her not to raise the issue. There is, however, indication in the cases themselves that something different is going on. All of these cases are, or could be, cases of concubinage.

This is easiest to conclude in the first such case because the *rei* are expressly ordered to make amends for concubinage in addition to making amends for fornication.[245] In two other cases the word is not used but the description of the relationship is the same: "for [a period of years] they stood together in the same house, bed, and board."[246] We can be less sure of the fourth case because the couple is to amend only for multiple fornications, but it could involve a similar relationship.[247]

In none of these cases is there an indication of any process beyond the oaths, replies, and confessions of the parties. One case does mention that there was *fama* of the promises of marriage, though the official does not say how he knew

243 Listed T&C no. 950.
244 Listed T&C no. 951.
245 *Office c Payge et Baillette* (23.iv.45), no. 681, T&C no. 952.
246 Listed T&C no. 953.
247 *Office c Putte et Yeghem* (6.v.47), no. 1130, T&C no. 954.

that.[248] We might imagine that the promotor fairly regularly added a charge of presumptive marriage to any case in which he had knowledge of persistent fornication. In some cases, the woman joined with him in the charge. In others, such as these, the social situation was quite different. We might imagine a class, if not a legal, barrier to marriage and a relationship recognized perhaps by some in the society, though not by the canon law.[249] Unfortunately, the entries give us no other indication of the social situation of the parties.

In three cases the presumptive marriage seems to be conceded – indeed, it seems to be desired by the parties – and the issue is whether it must be dissolved because of some impediment. In one of the cases, it is clear that the promotor is trying to get the marriage dissolved despite the wishes of the parties. In the other two, the role of the promotor is more ambiguous. They all involve incest and so will be treated more fully in Chapter 11.

Brussels

As Table 8.6 shows, there are 33 two-party cases in our sample of Brussels cases that raise issues of espousals between couples who are also alleged to have had intercourse with each other, approximately the same proportion of such cases as at Cambrai (21% vs 18%).[250] There are no straight-instance cases of this type at Brussels, and whereas at Cambrai the division between instance and office/instance, on the one hand, and straight office, on the other, is approximately equal (5 and 13 vs 20), the division between office/instance and straight office at Brussels strongly favors the former (20 vs 13). As at Cambrai, this division probably understates the number of cases in which one of the parties was aiding the promotor because the form of the sentence in which the promotor succeeds in establishing a presumptive marriage need not mention the name of the party who was helping him. (In one case the only reason we know that she was is that witnesses are introduced who are said to have been produced by the *rea*.)[251] Of the 8 straight-office cases in which the promotor seems to be attempting to establish a presumptive marriage, 5 result in a judgment that such a marriage exists, whereas only 3 of the 16 office/instance cases of this type result in such a judgment.[252] The remaining 9 of the 33 cases (4 office/instance and 5 straight office) are those that raise issues both of the existence of a presumptive marriage and of its dissolution.[253] The role of the promotor is less clear in these cases; he was probably supporting the dissolution in most of them. Suffice it to say here that dissolution is ordered in 4 of the 9 cases. Looking at it from the point of view of whether a presumptive marriage

248 *Office c Petit et Voye* (n. 246).
249 See Brundage, *Law, Sex*, 514–17 (with ample references), who also notes increasing efforts to repress concubinage in this period.
250 Disc. T&C no. 955.
251 *Officie c Verdonct en Voirde* (12.xi.56), no. 1050.
252 Listed T&C no. 956.
253 Listed T&C no. 957.

was established, the results at Brussels are approximately the same as they were at Cambrai.[254]

There are considerably more cases involving the potential dissolution of a presumptive marriage at Brussels than there were at Cambrai (9/33, 27% vs 3/38, 8%), and it is best to treat these after we treat the more usual case in which only the existence *vel non* of a presumptive marriage is at stake.

Three sentences of Rodolphi in two-party presumptive marriage cases not involving dissolution, and in which the presumptive marriage is not found, are similar to one another: The couple are ordered to make amends for fornication, the woman is ordered to make amends for failure to publicize and failure to solemnize her alleged promises, and the man is absolved from the promises alleged by the promotor and the *rea*.[255] One such sentence differs markedly from the others. There was no doubt about the intercourse ("many times up to the deflowering of the *rea*"), nor does there seem to have been any doubt that the couple had contracted. There was apparently, however, no proof that they had had intercourse after the contract, although one suspects that the witnesses introduced by the woman and the promotor were trying to prove just that. Rodolphi orders the couple to make amends for the intercourse, the clandestine promises, the failure to renew them, and the failure to proceed to solemnization. He then orders them to solemnize. A little more than a month later, the couple are back before the court; they remit their espousals, and Rodolphi accepts the remittance.[256] One could tell a story here of a man who, under pressure from the promotor, decided to make an honest woman of his mistress, but then changed his mind and talked, or bribed, her out of it as well. There is probably, however, not enough evidence from which to draw that conclusion firmly.

Eight cases find that there was a presumptive marriage, which the couple are ordered to solemnize. As was the case at Cambrai, the amount of proof required and the amends that were imposed varied considerably. Three of them remind us of the Cambrai cases in which the couple were proceeding, at least eventually, in the direction of a relationship of which the church could approve, though not in an order of which the church could approve. The details are best left to the margin.[257]

A fourth case is somewhat different. There seems to be no doubt about the promises and the intercourse; both are found on the basis of oaths, replies, allegations, and confessions of the parties, and the promises are specifically said to be confessed. Unlike what seems to have been the desire of the couples in the first two cases, however, and ultimately of the couple in the third case, this couple did not want to get married, and they tried to remit their promises

[254] Disc. T&C no. 958.

[255] Listed with details T&C no. 964.

[256] *Officie c Platea en Aa* (4.ix.50 to 9.x.50), nos. 190, 202, T&C no. 965.

[257] Disc. T&C no. 959.

after they had had intercourse. This, of course, they could not do, as Platea quite firmly told them.[258]

The other four cases in which a presumptive marriage is found were all resisted by the man. Proof in these cases tends to be fairly elaborate and is best detailed in the margin,[259] but one is particularly interesting because there is so little proof. On the basis of the oaths, replies, and confessions of the parties, Platea finds for the presumptive marriage and orders it solemnized. As is standard in this group, the couple are to make amends for not having proceeded to solemnization and for consummating their espousals, whereby they incurred excommunication; the deflowering and procreation of a female child, mentioned in the findings, are not included in the order to amend. The man appeals. He is granted *apostoli*, and there is no record of his having abandoned the appeal.[260]

As we have seen, a finding of presumptive marriage normally requires either the confession of the parties or testimony of witnesses. It is possible that the man confessed in this case and then changed his mind, but if that had happened, we would expect to find a record that he had either abandoned his appeal or that the court of Rheims had sent the case back. The fact that neither is recorded does not prove that the appeal was successful, but it is consistent with that possibility. The case came down when Platea had been in office for slightly over a year. The sample contains one prior case where he had already found a presumptive marriage (on the basis, admittedly, of considerably more proof).[261] That case, too, had been appealed, though the appeal was abandoned. We will see that after this time, the overwhelming majority of Platea's sentences are against a finding of presumptive marriage. Possibly, in this case Platea went too far. He believed the woman but not the man when the woman had no independent evidence to support her story. His subsequent behavior suggests that he realized that he had made a mistake.

Shortly after the sentence in which a finding by Platea of a presumptive marriage was appealed, perhaps successfully, he rendered one that suggests a different approach to this type of case:[262]

> [W]e declare that [Jan Broelants] is to be absolved, and we absolve [him], from and about the promises of marriage proposed and alleged by the promotor and [Beatrice Snit] but not sufficiently proven, there having been deferred to him judicially an oath of truth about showing his innocence about them, his extrajudicial confession in the absence of [BS] notwithstanding, imposing on the promotor and on [BS] perpetual silence about the pretended promises. Further, we condemn [JB] to endow [BS] concerning and about the flower of her virginity of which he deprived her, according to the dignity of the birth

258 *Officie c Kerchoven en Visschers* (13.iv.56), no. 950, T&C no. 960.
259 Disc. T&C no. 961.
260 Ref. T&C no. 962.
261 *Officie c Gheerts en Heiden* (n. 257); further examples T&C no. 963.
262 *Officie c Broelants en Snit* (19.iii.54), no. 592, T&C no. 966.

of [BS] and the availability of goods of [JB], an oath about this having been previously deferred to [BS] and taken by her, and [we condemn] them who commingled carnally outside the good of marriage up to the deflowering of [BS], thereby damnably committing *stuprum*... to *leges* and amends... along with the costs of the promotor and [BS].[263]

We have seen the imposition of a dowry for deflowering before in the practice at Cambrai.[264] What we have not seen is such a full explanation of what moved the judge. There was apparently testimony that Jan had admitted the promises (perhaps to friends or relations of Beatrice); there was, however, no direct evidence that they were ever made, other than Beatrice's word. In these circumstances, Jan will be made to put his soul on the line that there were no promises. If he does, he will not be forced into marriage with Beatrice. He will, however, have to pay her a dowry for deflowering her and, if we are reading the somewhat confused grammar right, her costs and those of the promotor. Beatrice and Jan will both have to make amends for the intercourse, but she will not have to make amends for the promises that she alleged. There are, of course, elements of a compromise in all this, but it is one that strikes us as rather nicely balancing the principle that marriages ought to be free with a humane consideration of Beatrice's plight.

This basic pattern of sentence – denial of the presumptive marriage and dowry for deflowering – is followed in an additional eight cases in the sample. There are variations. One case awards the woman her costs of lying-in, in addition to dowry for deflowering, the only case in the sample to do so.[265] In a straight-office case, another woman is awarded child support but not dowry for deflowering.[266] That child support is ordered in the second case but not in the first might be a result of the fact that the child in the first case did not survive, but that can hardly be the explanation for why the costs of lying-in are awarded the first case but not in the second. Indeed, neither award is common, considering the number of cases in which it could have been awarded.[267] While it is possible that such awards were made only to those women who were particularly persistent or particularly well connected, it is equally, perhaps more, likely that the dowry is only mentioned in cases where there could be controversy about it and that the payment was simply assumed in the more routine cases. This possibility is suggested by the fact that the case that mentions the costs of lying-in is one in which the *reus* or his mother had made some contribution to those costs, and it was necessary to say that that payment be deducted from the charge.[268] One case outside of the sample seems to condemn the *reus*

[263] The Latin is ambiguous as to who is to pay the costs, but I am reasonably confident that it is Jan Broelants.

[264] At nn. 223–30.

[265] *Officie c Chehain en Poliet* (20.v.57), no. 1158 (18.xi.57), no. 1251, T&C no. 967.

[266] *Officie c Coereman en Vos* (16.x.56), no. 1040; text and disc. T&C no. 968.

[267] See n. 260.

[268] *Officie c Chehain en Poliet* (n. 265).

to pay what he and the *rea* have already agreed would be an appropriate sum for the dowry and lying-in.[269]

Normally, the decision about the amount of the dowry takes place off our record (like the decision about how much the costs will be). Specific judgments in three of the cases of dowry for deflowering were, however, entered in the register. We will discuss these when we consider the instance cases seeking such dowry.[270]

One of the cases in which dowry for deflowering is awarded is quite different from the others. In this case it is the man who is claiming the promises of marriage and the woman who is denying them. Why it is he and not she who is claiming the promises of marriage seems clear enough from the fact that she is also to make amends for "having presumed to go off with the man without the consent of her relatives."[271] She may have wanted to marry him, but once she got back in the clutches of relatives they were able to persuade her not to.

One of the cases in which dowry is awarded for deflowering also, it would seem, orders the woman to make amends for having alleged the clandestine promises.[272] The official may have thought that she had a particularly weak case. In another case, one that does not involve dowry for deflowering, the *rea* is also condemned for having attempted to enter into clandestine promises.[273] This case was quite bitterly contested. An interlocutory sentence orders the parties to make specific their allegations (a rather unusual sentence, which suggests that the first oral session resulted in a hopeless wrangle). A second interlocutory sentence admits the *reus* to proof. The sentence informs us that there were witnesses on behalf of the *rea*; an exception against those witnesses, with a "salvation" (replication), followed by a duplication, triplication, and quadruplication; and witnesses on behalf of the *reus* and exceptions against them, with the oath finally being deferred to the *reus*. Despite all this process, the time from the first interlocutory sentence to the final sentence is less than two months, even though the Christmas holiday intervened in the period. In the end, the *reus* is absolved from any contract; the parties are to make amends for fornication, and the *rea*, as previously noted, for having tried to enter into clandestine promises. The costs of the parties are not mentioned. Clearly, Platea was requiring quite strict proof of the promises.

In one straight-office case, the promotor's failure is quite dramatic. On the basis of the replies of the parties, Platea finds that there was neither sexual intercourse nor clandestine promises. No amends are imposed, license is given, and, quite unusually, the promotor's costs are compensated with those of the

269 *Officie c Sandrijn en Tabbaerts* (17.viii.59), no. 1517.

270 Following n. 370.

271 *Officie c Riddere en Beken* (24.iii.58), no. 1292: *preter consensum suorum parentum cum prefato reo abire presumpsit.*

272 *Officie c Asselaer en Waghemans* (13.iv.59), no. 1451, T&C no. 969.

273 *Officie c Rutgeerts en Cudseghem* (21.xi.55 to 9.i.56), nos. 886, 890, 908, T&C no. 970. (Not included in the eight cases mentioned at n. 265.)

parties.[274] This may be a case in which the man settled with the woman before they got to court. Clearly, the promotor had not come to court with any proof other than what he thought the parties were going to say. When they did not 'propose' anything, he had nothing to go on.

Except for this case, the promotor always gets his costs, it would seem, from both parties. The allocation of costs among the *rei* is considerably more varied. To the extent that we can tell from our records, the decision about the parties' costs seems to have depended on the official's assessment of how plausible a case the party had.[275]

Nine cases in the sample raise issues about the dissolution of alleged presumptive marriages, five straight office and four office/instance. Most of these cases involve the rules about incest and will be considered in Chapter 11. Only three need concern us here.

One case is, at least from a modern point of view, straightforward. The *rei* had entered into clandestine promises and had then consummated them, turning them into a presumptive marriage. The *reus*, however, had previously been married in Ghent and had no evidence that his former wife was dead. The presumptive marriage is dissolved; the couple are to make amends for having transformed their clandestine promises into a presumptive marriage without having been certified of the death of the *reus*'s former wife, and the *rea* is expressly given license.[276]

It is not completely clear who was alleging what in this case, but there are hints. Silence is imposed on the *reus* and the promotor, indicating that they were supporting the presumptive marriage. The witnesses are expressly said to have been produced *ex nostro officio*, suggesting that it was the judge, rather than the parties or the promotor, who produced them. The question, of course, is who told the judge about the former wife? While it is possible that someone not involved in the case whispered in the judge's ear, it seems at least as likely that it was the *rea* who told him about her. That would account for the fact that, somewhat unusually in this type of case, the *rea* was given license. She does not seem to have been totally innocent, however, since she is to make amends for having engaged in a presumptive marriage without being certified of the death of the *reus*'s former wife. It is possible that the *reus* told her that his former wife was dead. It was not proved that she was alive. The law may have allowed one in certain circumstances to presume death, but Platea's ruling may take this possibility into account in an awkward phrase: "the marriage that [AP] previously... contracted...with [AT] and that is found never to have been dissolved (either by the death of [AT] that was or is apparent to us, or by some other canonical means)."[277] Whatever may have been her previous views

[274] *Officie c Couruyts en Waelravens* (26.x.53), no. 530, T&C no. 971.
[275] Details at T&C no. 972.
[276] *Officie c Pratere en Uden* (10.i.58), no. 1260, T&C no. 973.
[277] Disc. T&C no. 974.

on the matter, it seems likely that the *rea* decided that she did not want to be involved in a potential bigamy.

There is another case in which espousals are dissolved and a presumptive marriage is potentially involved, but, on balance, it would seem that the court did not find that the couple had had intercourse after the clandestine contract. The espousals are dissolved on the ground of the unfaithfulness of the woman, but the man is condemned to endow her for having deflowered her and to pay the costs of her lying-in "according to the custom of the place or as they amicably agree among themselves."[278]

In the remaining case, public espousals, followed by one bann, are ordered to proceed despite the impediment of fear that the *rea* had alleged, because the fear is found to be such that "worthily ought not fall upon a constant woman." The amends tell us more. The man is to make amends for having deflowered the *rea*, but the woman is not charged with the intercourse. This apparently occurred before the espousals, because there is no mention of presumptive marriage. Both *rei* are to make amends for having "presumed to abduct themselves mutually without the consent of the mother and relatives of the *correa*." The wording is, of course, odd; it would seem to describe consensual abduction. Something along these lines is involved because among the proofs are mentioned "recognitions before two feudatories of the powerful count of St Pol."[279] It seems that we are dealing with a feudal secular court that took cognizance (apparently lawfully, because there is no complaint about interference with ecclesiastical jurisdiction) of the abduction.[280] Costs between the parties are compensated; that is frequently, as we have seen, an indication that the official thought that there was something to the *rea*'s charges. The witnesses are produced by the man. Much lies hidden behind the face of this record, but it certainly looks as if this couple succeeded in running off and getting engaged after they had had a sexual relationship. Whether the woman regretted what she had done, or whether she was put up to defending the case by her relatives, we cannot tell, but Platea clearly thought that she had gone too far in circumstances that did not amount, in his view, to force.

THREE-PARTY SPOUSALS CASES ALLEGING *COPULA*

Cambrai

As noted in Table 8.7, the Cambrai sample contains 18 cases involving three parties in which *copula* is alleged to have followed one or both of the espousals. The cases are almost equally divided among instance, office/instance, and office (7,

278 *Officie c Rode en Vlamincx* (9.viii.54), no. 660, T&C no. 975. Godding, *Droit privé* does not report any customs on this topic, though the text here suggests that such customs existed.
279 *Officie c Clinkart en Lescole* (27.viii.56), no. 1010, T&C no. 976.
280 Disc. T&C no. 977.

6, and 5, respectively). Knowing the basic fact-pattern of the case might lead one to think that these are simply cases like the two-party cases that allege *copula*, with the additional element that the man has now gone off and contracted with someone else. That is the pattern of many, but not all, of them. Perhaps more important, the combination of infidelity and sexual intercourse in at least one, and sometimes both, of the relationships seems to have raised the emotional stakes for all concerned.

The sentence in the first case in the group chronologically reads like that in a typical three-party instance case of opposition to banns. The couple who publicly contracted are authorized to proceed to solemnize their marriage notwithstanding the opposition of the *actrix*. It is only when we look to the *leges* that we see that more was involved. The *reus* is fined for having deflowered the *actrix* and she for having allowed herself to be deflowered. (Nothing is said about dowry for the deflowering.) The *actrix* is also fined for frivolous opposition and condemned to pay the *reus*'s costs. The woman with whom he had contracted is not mentioned as a party to the case and may not have appeared. She may have had a reason not to appear; the *reus* is also fined for having deflowered her before he contracted with her.[281]

Four of the other instance cases follow the same pattern, except that in none of them is there any indication that the *reus* had sexual relations with the second woman.[282] In one, an action for deflowering is reserved to the *actrix*, and allocation of costs is postponed as well. No sentence in the dowry case is recorded, but approximately six months after the first sentence, the *actrix* is fined at the instance of the promotor for having had the *reus* taken by the secular authorities on a rape charge and imprisoned in the castle of Ath, where he had to pay damages of six *florins* and costs. She did this, the sentence says, for the purpose of defaming the *reus*, and in prejudice of the jurisdiction of the ecclesiastical court.[283]

In two of the instance cases the *actrix* is successful. In the first, a sentence of Divitis, on the basis of the confessions, oaths, and responses of the parties on which Marguerite, the *rea*, "totally rested and rests" (*se retulit totaliter et refert*), the court declares that the promises of marriage between Jeanne, the *actrix*, and Pierre, the *reus*, preceded those between Pierre and Marguerite "by which [promises] marriage between Jeanne and Pierre is deemed (*censetur*) to be and is presumed." Jeanne and Pierre are ordered to solemnize; Pierre is ordered to pay costs and damages to Marguerite who is given license, and Jeanne and Pierre are ordered to make amends, but it is not specified for what.[284]

Much about this sentence is puzzling. I take it that *se retulit totaliter et refert* means that Marguerite chose not to contest what Jeanne and Pierre had confessed. The sentence does not say that the promises between Jeanne and Pierre

[281] *Scallette c Mol et Francque* (20.xi.38), no. 72.
[282] Listed with details T&C no. 978.
[283] *Steenberghe c Ruvere et Brunne* (n. 282); disc. T&C no. 979.
[284] *Burielle c Fouret et Oiseleur* (20.vii.39), no. 270.

were clandestine and those of Pierre and Marguerite public, but it is likely that they were. Had Marguerite chosen not to concede the case, the confession of Jeanne and Pierre probably could not have overcome her opposition. *Clandestina manifestis non preiudicant*. We say 'probably' because we are not dealing here with the situation to which the maxim was normally applied, a clandestine marriage followed by a subsequent public one, for we must assume that the *sponsalia* of Pierre and Marguerite to which the court refers were, as was overwhelmingly the case at Cambrai, *sponsalia de futuro*. Indeed, we would normally assume that the *conventiones matrimoniales* between Jeanne and Pierre were also not a marriage but simply *sponsalia de futuro* were it not for the court's mysterious reference to *matrimonium presumptum*, mysterious because it is not accompanied by the normal finding that the couple had had intercourse after the promises and because the court does not find a *matrimonium presumptum* but says that one *censetur fuisse et esse*. Specific *leges* would have helped to clarify the situation but none are found; the scribe did not even record the name of the town from which the parties came.

While it is possible that these peculiar features are attributable to the cryptic style of Divitis's sentences, coupled with a somewhat unusual scribal negligence, I am inclined to think that it is more likely that something may be going on here that the court is taking some pains to conceal. Clearly, this case was not contested. Marguerite gets damages and license to marry another, and that was probably her price for not contesting the case more fully. As we will see in the next case, a number of different penalties could have been imposed on Jeanne and Pierre, but other than the court's vague reference to making amends, there is no specification of the penalties and none, so far as we can tell, were collected. The case reminds us more of an English case than it does of what we have come to expect at Cambrai. But if we start thinking along those lines, there is no reason not to think that other features of English matrimonial litigation may not be present here as well. This could be a case of two *de presenti* clandestine contracts. It could be a case of Pierre's entering into a clandestine marriage with Jeanne in order to escape from an arranged marriage with Marguerite, which it turned out that Marguerite also did not want. Whatever the underlying facts, when the three parties came to the court with a quite acceptable solution to a problem that the promotor had not been able to discover, the court chose to let them settle the matter as they wanted to and to let them off lightly.

The other instance case with a judgment for the plaintiff is much more typical of the kind of result that we have come to expect at Cambrai. Nicolaï fines the *actrix* and the *reus* for not renewing their promises, for failing to solemnize within the fixed period, and for deflowering and the *reus* for having made second espousals publicly. Nicolaï declares a presumptive marriage between the couple, orders them to solemnize it, annuls the second *sponsalia*, and orders the *reus* to treat the *actrix* with marital affection. Nothing is said about the *rea* or about the costs. The fact that the *reus* is ordered to treat the *actrix* with marital affection may indicate that he resisted her claims to start off with, but ultimately he must have confessed because no proof other than the statements and oaths of the parties is mentioned. We must assume also either that the *rea* consented or that Nicolaï thought that the maxim *clandestina manifestis non preiudicant* did not apply to this situation. The fact that she does not get license or damages and costs may indicate that these parties are of a somewhat lower station than those in the previous case, although at least the *actrix* had the wherewithal to bring a case on her own without the help of the promotor.[285]

There are six examples in the sample of office/instance cases involving three parties and an allegation of *copula*; all have slightly different patterns. In the earliest such case, Divitis, on the basis of the statements of the parties alone, finds that the *rea* and the first *reus* contracted clandestinely, had intercourse, and did not proceed within the time set by law. They are ordered to solemnize, to make amends, and pay the costs of the promotor. The second *reus* is absolved from the promises of marriage alleged by the promotor and given license. If the *rea* was trying to rid herself of the first *reus* and establish her relationship with the second, she failed. This may be because, when faced with the necessity of swearing, she could not deny either the promises or the intercourse with the first *reus*.[286]

Each of Nicolaï's sentences in this group has a somewhat different fact-pattern from the others. In his first sentence in chronological order, he finds:[287]

> The defendants, Colard and Pétronille, three years, or thereabouts, ago, had by an act of fornication sexual relations with each other, once and afterwards many times, even up to and including the procreation of two children. They did not renew the promises of marriage that they afterwards had between them with the spirit and intent of legitimizing their children, nor did they care to proceed on the strength of the [promises] further to contracting and solemnizing matrimony. Further, Colard secondarily contracted – *de facto* since he could not *de iure* considering the above – *sponsalia* with Marguerite in the hand of the priest and the face of church, one bann being proclaimed thereon, in such a way as he wished and tried to deceive Marguerite who at the time was unaware of what had gone before.

Colard and Pétronille are ordered to make amends for fornication "up to the begetting (*suscitationem*) of two children," for clandestine promises not renewed, and for failure to solemnize within the fixed period and to pay the costs of the promotor. Colard is to make amends for public secondary promises and having attempted to deceive Marguerite. The secondary promises are quashed as void. Colard and Pétronille are ordered to solemnize within 40 days and to treat each other with marital affection thereafter. Colard is ordered to pay Marguerite's costs, and she is given license.

It will be noted that nothing is said about Colard's and Pétronille's having had intercourse after the agreement or about presumptive marriage. That is not legally necessary for the resolution of the case because Colard's relationship with Marguerite had not proceeded beyond the *de futuro* stage. In

285 *Los c Roy et Waterlint* (24.xii.42), no. 400.

286 *Office c Bertremart, Pret et Roussiau* (5.vi.39), no. 231, T&C no. 980 with disc.

287 *Office c Rosse et Thenakere* (23.x.42), no. 370, T&C no. 981, with disc.

Cambrai, a prior *de futuro* contract trumps a subsequent one; indeed, the subsequent contract is said here to be void. Had it been clear that Colard and Pétronille had had intercourse after the contract, Nicolaï probably would have mentioned it, because that would have been an additional reason to fine them and would, under the synodal statutes in effect, have been grounds to hold them excommunicate. Since the case proceeds by the confessions of the parties, however (no other proof is mentioned), it is possible that Colard, Pétronille, and Marguerite struck a deal. Nothing would be said about the presumptive marriage; Marguerite would get her costs and freedom from Colard, which she probably by this time firmly desired, and Pétronille would get a husband. It is also possible, however, that Nicolaï ignored the presumptive marriage because the *reus* was, finally, prepared to do the right thing.

Colard's behavior may not be quite so inexcusable as the findings suggest. Nothing is said about the children being alive, and granted the rates of infant mortality in the fifteenth century, they could both be dead. Colard had agreed to marry Pétronille in order to legitimize their children. When the children died, we might speculate, he felt free to go off and marry Marguerite. That was not the way that Pétronille saw it. Nor was it the way the promotor, the official, and, we can also have little doubt, Marguerite saw it.

There is no doubt in the next case that the first woman played an active role in promoting it. She is said to have offered "allegations and conclusions" against the *reus*, and she may have been responsible for the witnesses whose depositions are mentioned right after. Nicolaï finds that she had contracted publicly with the *reus*, three banns having been proclaimed. After this, he had gone out and contracted with the second *rea* and had proceeded to consummate the union. He and the second *rea* are declared married and are ordered to solemnize and to treat each other with marital affection. The *rei* are absolved from other articles of the promotor (indicating that there were others).[288]

The fact that the promotor thought that there was more to this case than ultimately was proven gives us a hint, if only a hint, as to what may have been involved. The most obvious possibility is that the promotor thought that the relationship between the first *rea* and the *reus* had been consummated as well. If that had happened before the consummation of the relationship between the *reus* and the second *rea*, it would be the first relationship that would have been presumptive marriage and the second relationship adulterous. As in the previous case, the first *rea*'s damages and license may have been her price for not saying anything about the consummation, but this time her silence was more serious if it led to the wrong marriage being held valid. There are, however, less sinister possibilities. The fact that *sponsalia* of the *reus* and the first *rea* were public and followed by banns suggests, at a minimum, that their relatives approved of them. The couple may not have. The *reus* may genuinely have wanted to marry the second *rea*, and the first *rea* may have been willing to have him do so. If the promotor suspected that this was what was going on, his charge would have

[288] *Office c Scueren, Carrenbroec et Bouchout* (12.ii.43), no. 431; disc. T&C no. 982.

been that all three conspired to dissolve the first *sponsalia* without obtaining a court order doing so.

In the next case, the fines are even heavier. On the basis of the allegations and confessions of the parties and the depositions of witnesses, the *reus* is found to have deflowered the first *rea* and to have conceived a male child by her. Then he and the second *rea*, knowing that there was *fama* that he had promises of marriage with the first *rea*, entered into secondary clandestine promises and consummated them. (This, too, was a deflowering.) All three *rei* are condemned to make amends, pay the promotor's costs, and provide half a pound of wax for the chapel of the officiality. The *reus* and second *rea* are ordered to solemnize their marriage within 40 days, and the *reus* is ordered to endow the first *rea*, pay the costs of her lying-in and half the cost of maintaining the child, and, it would seem, all their litigation expenses.[289]

There can be little doubt that Nicolaï thought that the first *rea* had been victimized by the *reus*. Although she is fined for having allowed herself to be deflowered, for not having proceeded with her alleged promises of marriage, and for converting them, to the extent that she could, into a clandestine marriage, she received a substantial monetary award. Her allegations are not described as "frivolous." There was *fama* that she and the *reus* had contracted; it is even possible that they had, but she either could not prove it in the face of the *reus*'s denial or, perhaps slightly more likely, she could not prove that they contracted and then had intercourse before the *reus* and second *rea* did the same.

The *reus* in the next case behaved equally badly, but here it is the second *rea* who was the victim. After considerable process, including witnesses introduced by the promotor and the second *rea* and then by the *reus*, the official finds that 14 years previously, the *reus* had deflowered the first *rea*, entered into clandestine promises with her, had intercourse with her (converting the promises into a presumptive marriage), and proceeded to cohabit with her without the benefit of solemnization. Indeed, they still do cohabit. In the meantime, the *reus* also entered into clandestine promises with the second *rea* (which he acknowledged before trustworthy persons), deflowered her, and had intercourse with her many times. All three are ordered to make amends and pay the costs of the promotor. The *reus* and the first *rea* are ordered to solemnize, and nothing further is said about the second *rea*, other than that her allegations of promises of marriage are deemed frivolous.[290]

In the light of the way that Nicolaï treated the first *rea* in the previous case, his treatment of the second *rea* here seems inconsistent. While the second *rea* here is not saddled with a child, nothing is said of a dowry for her deflowering, and to call her allegations of promises of marriage "frivolous" seems odd since the promises pretty clearly happened. It is just that the *reus* was in no position to make them because he was already married to the first *rea*, as the sentence

289 *Office c Tieuwendriesche, Cauelette et Roelf* (11.ix.45), no. 779.
290 *Office c Brambosche, Peelken et Quisthous* (21.i.47), no. 1081.

points out. It is possible that Nicolaï was less sympathetic with the second *rea* than he had been with the first *rea* in the previous case because the second *rea* here knew about the relationship with the first *rea*, but normally Nicolaï mentions that fact as an aggravating circumstance. It seems more likely, as we have suspected in previous cases, that the second *rea* here is not entitled to a dowry because she is not of a class that is entitled to dowries or that the *reus* clearly cannot afford it, or both. If so, the *reus*'s relationship with the first *rea* may provide us with an insight into how at least some lower-class couples in the diocese of Cambrai got married, to the extent that they did.

The last of the cases in this group has a similar fact-pattern to the previous one, with the following exceptions. There was only one set of depositions. The first presumptive marriage took place only three years previously, and there is no indication the couple continued to cohabit. The second attempted presumptive marriage was accompanied by promises that the couple attempted to solemnize. They had had two banns declared, and at least the man was prepared to proceed to solemnizing the marriage had the *curé* not put a stop to it. (This may well have been because the first *rea* objected.) The result is that all three are ordered to make amends and pay the promotor's costs; the *reus* and first *rea* are ordered to solemnize, and the second *rea* is given license. She is also awarded costs from the first *reus*, though here, too, there is no mention of a dowry for deflowering.[291]

The cases that only the promotor is pursuing, so far as we can tell, build on the basic fact-patterns that we have already seen, but add aggravating factors. In the first case, the woman had been ordered to solemnize her presumptive marriage with a third party who does not appear in the case. Despite this sentence, she went off and contracted marriage publicly and in the face of the church with the *reus* and had intercourse with him. The official declares this marriage null and orders the *rea* to solemnize with the third party. Both *rei* are condemned to make amends, and to pay the costs of the promotor and two pounds of wax to the chapel. That the *reus* is also condemned indicates, though the sentence does not say so, that the *reus* was aware at least of the relationship that the *rea* had with the other man, if not of the previous sentence.[292]

As we have already noted, Divitis's sentences are quite cryptic, and this one is more cryptic than most. One wonders why this blatant case of bigamy did not bring forth stronger language. One also wonders where the third party is and how it is that the *curé* allowed this marriage to go ahead. It is possible that the third party had disappeared and that the *curé* was willing to indulge in a broad presumption that he was dead. Other than the usual oaths and confessions of the parties, the only proof mentioned is letters introduced by the promotor. These letters may have demonstrated that the third party was, in fact, alive, though we may doubt whether he is going to obey the order to solemnize with the *rea*.

291 *Office c Bury, Roucourt et Caremy* (18.iv.50), no. 1281.
292 *Office c Beys et Kicht* (14.ii.39), no. 142.

The next case chronologically, one of Nicolaï, has the longest sentence in this group and considerably heightened rhetoric. It has some elements of an office/instance case because Marie, the *rea*, seems to be alleging a presumptive marriage with Florent, the first *reus*, but it is not clear that that is the marriage that she wants to have sustained. The sentence contains a long recital of things for which the *rei* are to make amends, but it does not close with a definitive sentence about the second of the two possible marriages. Rather, we learn from the next entry in the register that the promotor was asked to produce more proof, and Élisabeth, the now-wife of Florent, was ordered cited. No further entries are found in the surviving registers; the case may ultimately have been resolved in the following year for which no register survives. The difficulty of the case for Nicolaï is indicated by the fact that he mentions that he consulted with the *iurisperiti*, and adds the unusual parenthetical "as the difficulty of the matter demanded."[293]

The sentence begins with a series of findings that are typical of cases of alleged presumptive marriage in which the marriage is going to fail and parties will be fined. Florent is found to have committed *stuprum* with and to have deflowered Marie. She is found not to have proceeded to solemnize the promises of marriage that they are alleged to have had, but rather to have allowed herself to be deflowered and known many times in her parents' house (a telling detail not found in many other cases), thus converting the asserted promises of marriage, as much as she could, into a presumptive marriage. The sentence then moves into hitherto unexplored territory:[294]

Not content with this Marie entered into other promises of marriage with Jean, the other *reus*, in the hand of the priest and the face of the church of Humbeek, diocese of Cambrai,[295] and three banns were proclaimed on them,[296] and – what is far more serious! – because the *curé* of Humbeek refused to allow the couple to contract and solemnize marriage, though they wished to do so *de facto*, because there was definite opposition to a pretended future marriage of this sort on account of the consanguinity in the fourth degree subsisting between Florent and Jean, *correos*, and from the affinity in a similar degree created between Jean and Marie, which would impede [their marriage], that resulted from the fact that Marie had been deflowered by Florent and known often – as they both confessed – [which consanguinity] was at that time sufficiently obvious to the same Marie, *rea*, and is now made clear to us in the present process, this Marie, like one deliberately ignorant,[297] presumed to transfer herself with her *correus* Jean, to a foreign parish and diocese, to wit, the town of Hulst, Utrecht diocese,[298] where true notice of the premises could not be had, and there, without asking for or obtaining any letters

[293] *Office c Tiestaert, Hove et Beckere* (20.x.42), nos. 360–1, T&C no. 983.
[294] *Ibid.*, T&C no. 984.
[295] Prov. Vlaams-Brabant, about halfway between Brussels and Mechelen.
[296] The word order of the Latin may suggest that the banns were proclaimed before the promises were made, but this would be most unusual.
[297] Literally, 'like a seeker after ignorance'. See Ch 11, at n. 118.
[298] Prov. Zeeland, the most southeasterly town in the province and hence the closest town to the border of Cambrai diocese.

from her diocesan or *curé*, to have recourse, by whatever means possible, to contracting and solemnizing marriage in the face of the church of the place, and, at length for the pleasure of her will by rash daring to consummate such pretended marriage by dwelling together in the flesh and incestuous commingling [with Jean]. Jean de Backere, moreover, not unaware, as he confesses, that the promises [of marriage] between Marie, *rea*, with Florent followed by sexual intercourse came before, entered into other promises with the same Marie, and subsequently learning of the consanguinity and affinity – which stood in the way of his achieving his purpose in his own place – took this Marie to the town of Hulst, and there, by all the things as are said above about Marie, did not blush to contract, solemnize, and consummate the pretended marriage, thus showing himself equally with Marie to be a seeker after and perpetrator of incestuous and otherwise prohibited commingling and nuptials.

The interlocutory sentence that follows is much shorter:[299]

So that we might be able to proceed in the matter of the bond (*federis*), the dissolution of which is being dealt with by the promotor, correctly and with that deliberation (*maturitate*) that the matter demands, we order and declare in these writings that witnesses and other – if they exist – fuller documents are and ought to be produced about the sexual intercourse alleged and confessed between Florent and Marie, and also that Élisabeth Joes with whom Florent is said to have contracted, insofar as possible, *sponsalia* and marriage is and ought to be called to law, produced, and called forth before us as a party having an interest in this matter.

The bond that the promotor is seeking to dissolve seems, at first glance, to be that between Marie and Jean. The question is why Nicolaï wants more proof about the intercourse between Florent and Marie. After all, he had said in the previous sentence that it was "made clear to us in the present process" (*nobis in presenti processu clare patefactam*). But the Latin is not ambiguous. What was made clear was not the intercourse (there being no *copulam* for *patefactam* to modify) but the consanguinity between Florent and Jean (*consanguinitatem* being the only feminine accusative noun that *patefactam* could modify).[300] So if it is clear that Florent and Jean were related, what more needs to be proved about the relationship between Florent and Marie? It is possible that the only evidence that they had had intercourse was their confession. Nicolaï was reluctant to dissolve the marriage, however irregular, between Jean and Marie, particularly if Jean was resisting it, on the basis of Florent and Marie's confession alone. For this to be possible, the witnesses that are mentioned in the beginning of the first sentence would have to have been witnesses to something other than the intercourse between Marie and Florent, but there was much else about which they could have testified, for example, the relationship between Florent and Jean. The interlocutory sentence, however, tells us that there was other evidence of the intercourse; there was documentary proof (perhaps evidence of a conviction for fornication), as indicated by the fact that Nicolaï asks for "other – if they exist – fuller documents."

[299] *Office c Tiestaert, Hove et Beckere*, at no. 361, T&C no. 985.
[300] Disc. T&C no. 986.

All of this would tend to suggest that what Nicolaï was seeking was not evidence of whether Florent and Marie had intercourse but when. This could be relevant for two purposes. If Florent and Marie did not have intercourse until after Marie and Jean married, then their marriage could not be dissolved on the basis of it. Marie would have committed incest with Florent, but this would not constitute preexisting affinity, which alone could make the marriage invalid. That possibility does not seem very likely, however, because the first sentence seems quite clear that all the events with Jean took place after Marie had consummated her relationship with Florent. The other possibility, of course, is that Florent and Marie did exchange words of future consent and the question is whether they had intercourse after that. That this is what is involved is suggested by the fact that the first sentence is silent on the question of whether the promises that Marie alleged with Florent were proven (he apparently did not admit them, but if the official thought that they did not exist he normally says so), by the fact that Jean is said to have known of the promises of marriage between Florent and Marie (not simply their *fama*), and, perhaps most significantly, by the fact that Élisabeth is to be cited as an interested party. She is not interested, in a technical sense, in her husband's premarital fornications, but she is certainly interested in whether her husband entered into a presumptive marriage with Marie before he married her because, if he did, her marriage to him is void. If this analysis is correct, then the *foedus* referred to at the beginning of the interlocutory sentence is not that between Marie and Jean. That one cannot stand, and the only issue is whether it is to be dissolved on the grounds of both preexisting affinity and prior bond or just on the former ground.[301] The *foedus* that is at stake is that between Florent and Élisabeth.

It is less clear why Nicolaï proceeds to impose amends on all three parties before he has all the facts. I suspect that he knows that it is going to take some time to bring out all the facts, if they ever can be known. In the meantime, Marie and Jean's behavior cannot go unpunished. It is not only that they entered into an incestuous, and possibly bigamous, union but it is also – *quod longe gravius est!* – that knowing that they could not solemnize their marriage in their home parish, they went to another diocese and in defiance of church authority solemnized their marriage there. One is reminded of John Stratford's constitution *Humana concupiscentia*.[302]

The next case is one in which what might have been happening in one of the previous cases[303] definitely was happening. The woman in this case emphatically did not want the first marriage and saw to it that she did not have to enter into it by contracting and having intercourse with the second man. Nicolaï was not pleased: "[O]n another day immediately following this renewal [of the first contract in the face of the church] they [the second couple] together

[301] Disc. T&C no. 987.
[302] Ch 6, at n. 189.
[303] *Office c Scueren, Carrenbroec et Bouchout* (at n. 288).

withdrew [from the first promises] and were not ashamed to enter into other *de facto* promises of marriage, sexual intercourse both preceding and following, transforming the secondary promises – insofar as they could – into a true presumptive marriage... most grievously breaking on both sides both the moral and criminal law." But there was nothing that Nicolaï could do about it other than fine them and order them to pay both the costs and the damages of the first man.[304]

The next case in this group is quite different from the others, though it shares with one of the others a fine, this time on the woman only, for having, in this case, made *sponsalia* and also contracting and consummating marriage with another man (who never appears), knowing that there was *fama* that she had previously contracted with the *reus*. The *rea*'s current marriage is expressly declared to be ratified and firm so long as she and her husband both live. On the basis, moreover, of the parties' confessions, the *reus* is fined for having deflowered the *rea* and having known her many times up to the procreation of a child and the *rea* for having allowed him to do this. The couple is freed, however, from the charge of having contracted *sponsalia* (which the intercourse would have turned into a presumptive marriage that would have upset the *rea*'s current marriage).[305]

The last case in this group shows us the Cambrai court enforcing its judgments. In November of 1438, Divitis rendered judgment in a case that bears some relationship to the later case concerning the couple who were in no hurry to solemnize their presumptive marriage.[306] Jean and Catherine had clandestinely contracted and had had intercourse, thereby creating presumptive marriage. Notwithstanding this, Jean went off and contracted solemnly with Pasque (though no banns are mentioned), while continuing to live with Catherine. Divitis declares the contract between Jean and Pasque void and orders Jean and Catherine to solemnize. All three are to make amends and pay the costs of the promotor, and Jean is to pay Pasque's costs.[307]

Almost eight years later, Jean and Catherine are back in court, in a case that appears in our sample.[308] They still have not solemnized their marriage, but rather "without solemnization of the marriage, they have cohabited in the manner of reprobate concubinage, in the same house, board and bed, rashly in contempt of the sentence and authority of this court."[309] They are to solemnize within 40 days, make amends, and pay the expenses of the promotor.

One case is not much to go on, and we should be cautious about generalizing. The couple in question came from Herne, a small place then and now, about

304 *Office c Hauens, Mortgate et Leysen* (13.iv.43), no. 450, T&C no. 988.
305 *Office c Witte et Vos* (25.ix.45), no. 790.
306 *Office c Oerens, Camérière et Barbiers* (15.xi.38), no. 65; cf. *Office c Brambosche, Peelken et Quisthous* (at n. 290).
307 *Office c Oerens, Camérière et Barbiers* (n. 306); disc. T&C no. 989.
308 *Office c Coppins et Camérière* (28.v.46), no. 931, disc. T&C no. 990.
309 *Ibid.*, T&C no. 991.

10 miles southwest of Brussels, near Halle.[310] It could be that when Divitis left office in 1439, the personnel of the court forgot about them, and that it was unusual for a sentence to go unenforced for so long. Jean's behavior gives some suggestion that he was living "in the manner of reprobate concubinage" because that is what he thought it was. His attempt to marry another woman eight years previously may suggest that he did not regard his relationship with Catherine as marriage. She and the court thought differently, but perhaps she was willing to let matters be once the court had declared them married. To go further would be total speculation, and perhaps even this is too much.

Brussels

As Table 8.6 notes, there are 48 cases in the Brussels sample in which three parties are at least potentially involved in a case in which intercourse is also alleged. This is a dramatically larger proportion of such cases than at Cambrai (31% vs 9%). The sentences are divided between the two judges, as we would expect on the basis of their share of the total number of sentences (12/48, 75%), but Rodolphi hears the only two straight-instance cases and the only two straight-office cases (in one of these we strongly suspect that one of the parties was also pursuing the matter).[311] All the rest are mixed office/instance.

Twenty-four of the cases, including both instance cases, fall into a pattern that is quite familiar from the Cambrai cases of a similar type. A man has entered into public espousals. A woman appears and objects that the man had previously contracted with her and had had intercourse with her. The intercourse is proven but not the contract, the public espousals are ordered to be solemnized, and the couple are to make amends for their previous illicit relationship. The vast majority of cases have no more process than the articles of the promotor and sworn responses and allegations of the parties. In 11 cases deflowering is found; in 3 an action for deflowering is reserved. In 22 cases, the woman is to make amends for frivolous allegations of the promises; in the 2 in which she is not, she is to make amends for not renewing and not solemnizing them.[312]

Four cases are quite similar to the previous group. The only difference is that the opponent is not seeking to upset public espousals; she is seeking to upset a subsequent presumptive marriage. In two cases this presumptive marriage was formed after clandestine espousals, in two cases after public espousals. In three cases the unsuccessful opponent is found to have been deflowered, and in the same three the woman whose presumptive marriage is to be solemnized had been deflowered as well.[313]

310 There are, however, four other cases from Herne in the Cambrai registers. See *Registres de Cambrai*, s.v.

311 Listed T&C no. 992.

312 Listed with disc. T&C no. 993.

313 Listed with disc. T&C no. 994.

Two other cases involve oppositions to presumptive marriages, but the fact-pattern here is different. There are two *rei* and one *rea*. In the first case a couple who had consummated their marriage after public espousals, followed by two banns, are ordered to solemnize, "notwithstanding the made-up and fictitious promises that the [*rea*] vainly boasted that she had with [*reus*2]." The second *reus* is absolved from these promises, and the promotor is silenced concerning them. The couple who are ordered to solemnize are also ordered to make amends for having consummated their marriage before its solemnization (by which the *rea* was deflowered), and the *rea* is to make amends for "having allowed herself to be voluntarily abducted by [*reus*1], against the will of her parents and relatives," thus (both of them) incurring excommunication and committing *stuprum*. The *rea* is also to make amends for having "'fictitiously' [i.e., by making up another contract] and rashly gone against her faith, insofar as it was possible for her" to do so.[314]

The presumptive marriage would, of course, take precedence over any promises that the *rea* had had with the second *reus*. Even if these second promises had been consummated, it is clear that they would have been to no avail so long as the intercourse with (and deflowering by) the first *reus* preceded the consummation of the second arrangement. That raises the question of why the *rea* bothered to boast (*iactavit*) of these second promises, and how Platea could possibly have known that they were *excogitatis et fictis* when there was no evidence taken other than the statements of the parties. The mention of the will of the relatives suggests a possible answer. The *rea* was allowed to contract publicly with the first *reus*, but the relatives decided to break up the relationship in favor of the second. The *rea* was persuaded to claim that she had promises with him, but this is not what she wanted, and she ran off and consummated her relationship with the first *reus*. The promotor got wind of at least some this and brought proceedings. When they are before the official, the *rea* admits both that the promises with the second *reus* never happened (a fact that the second *reus* confirms) and that she had intercourse with the first *reus* (a fact that the first *reus* confirms). On this record, there is nothing that the official can do about the marriage; it is a fact. He can and does, however, order the *rea* to make amends for all of the offenses she has committed.

If there is a plausible, though speculative, explanation for what is happening in the preceding case, it is much harder to figure out what is happening in the second. On the basis of the statements of the parties and of witnesses introduced by the parties (unfortunately, the record does not say by which parties), the official orders Jacob, the second *reus*, and Katherina to solemnize their presumptive marriage, formed by clandestine promises followed by intercourse, notwithstanding the promises alleged by Joost, the first *reus*, which the official deems frivolous, unproven, and inapt. The *correi* are then ordered to make amends for clandestine promises; Jacob and Katherina are ordered to make

[314] *Officie c Baserode, Kempeneere en Woters* (31.x.55), no. 871, T&C no. 995.

amends for sexual intercourse and deflowering, and Katherina is ordered to pay Joost's costs.[315]

This is certainly odd. It is so odd, in fact, that the editors thought that the name of the man who was ordered to make amends for sexual intercourse was an error and emended it to 'Joost'. That would turn the case into a quite typical opposition case, except that it is the man who is making the claim, rather than the woman. Joost and Katherina had sexual intercourse by which she was deflowered. She then went off and formed a relationship with Jacob, which was also consummated. When Joost objected, he could not prove the promises, and so he loses, but he had a sufficiently plausible claim that Katherina must pay his costs. That is a possible scenario, but it is not what the record says, and there are reasons, in addition to the fact that what the record says is the *lectio difficilior*, for believing that it is not what was meant: The *correi*, all of them apparently, are to make amends for having entered into clandestine promises. That suggests that there was more than something to Joost's allegations of the promises. They may actually have happened. That, in turn, makes it more plausible that Katherina should be compelled to pay his costs, a quite unusual order in this type of case. Further, it is quite understandable that Jacob and Katherina should have to make amends for illicit intercourse, for that is the foundation of their presumptive marriage. Hence, I am inclined to believe the record. Katherina probably contracted with two men, but she had intercourse with only one of them, Jacob. That is the presumptive marriage that must be solemnized. Admittedly, it is a bit odd that the official finds that the promises alleged by Joost were frivolous, unproven, and inapt, but, of course, they were so when compared to a presumptive marriage.

There are, in fact, 15 more cases in the sample where two sets of promises are found, or seem highly likely to have occurred, but only 1 of them is consummated and, hence, is the presumptive marriage that is to be solemnized. In 9 of the cases, the unconsummated promises are subsequent to the consummated ones; in 7 they precede the consummated ones, as in the case just discussed. In 2 of the latter cases, the process is straight office (both Rodolphi). The rest are office/instance, including two sentences of Rodolphi's and one case begun under Rodolphi but concluded under Platea.

While there is considerable variation in these cases, certain typical fact-patterns emerge. One pattern is that of a woman successfully opposing the banns of the man with another on the ground that she and he had engaged in prior presumptive marriage. There are five such cases. In three of them the opponent had witnesses; in two the man apparently confessed when he was brought into court. In all cases, the couple whose marriage is to be solemnized are to make amends for their clandestine promises and for consummating them, and the man is to make amends for entering into public, double, or secondary promises. In one, the second couple also have to make amends for clandestine promises before the public ones. In three cases the couple who have to solemnize

[315] *Officie c Faucoys, Haghen en Assche* (12.x.56), no. 1033, T&C no. 996.

are to pay the costs of the promotor and of the other woman, and in two cases damages to her as well.[316]

Two of Platea's sentences in such cases contain variants that may help to explain the social situation. In one case, the man is to make amends for having "permitted an affiancing" with the second woman. If this is not a mistake for "presumed to affiance" (which it may be), it suggests that he was under some pressure to do so.[317] It is possible that his friends and relatives were trying to break up his relationship with the first woman. Something along these lines may also account for the cases in which the woman had no witnesses and which, we must assume, the man could have defeated simply by denying her charges.[318] In another case, the couple are to make amends not only for having consummated their clandestine espousals but also for having committed *stuprum*.[319] The striking thing is that this is the only case in which the woman succeeds in establishing the presumptive marriage where this is mentioned, compared to the rather large number of unsuccessful cases where it is mentioned. It is possible that the successful women were somewhat older or, at least, more experienced (not the sort of person with whom sexual relations would be regarded as *stuprum*); hence, they took precautions that allowed them to prove their relationship when they were betrayed.

The four cases in which a presumed marriage prevails over later espousals that do not fall into the pattern just described involve two men. The basic pattern of the sentences follows that of the sentences concerning two women, with the genders reversed. There are variations, however, and the variations point to possible (or certain) variations in the underlying fact-patterns that merit some discussion.[320]

The first case is furthest away from the general pattern. When we first see it, it is an instance case between Pieter de Nova Villa and *domicella* Johanna de Boussout. Three interlocutory sentences, in March and June of 1453 and September of 1454, take the case back from an appeal to the bishop, order the publication of witnesses heard by the bishop's commissary, and admit Johanna to proof of an article on her exception to Pieter's witnesses. We next see the case in October of 1456, when the promotor has joined the case, proceeding against both parties. On the basis of the promotor's witnesses (and, presumably, also on the basis of the witnesses previously produced), Platea orders the couple to solemnize their presumptive marriage, notwithstanding Johanna's claim that litigation is still pending about her marriage to one Jan de Boulenghe "in his sickbed," because, he finds, that such marriage is not apparent in the acts of the present case and that the presumptive marriage long preceded it. The couple are ordered to make amends for their clandestine promises (their intercourse is

316 Listed with disc. T&C no. 997.
317 *Officie c Scrivere, Abele en Sporct* (n. 316), T&C no. 998.
318 Disc. T&C no. 1000.
319 *Officie c Waghels, Campe en Scoemans* (n. 316), T&C no. 1001.
320 Listed with disc. T&C no. 1002.

not mentioned), and Johanna is ordered to make amends for bigamy. A related entry in April of 1458 declares that Jacquelina Boulenghe is a bastard and not entitled to inherit from Jan, now deceased, because Jan's marriage to Johanna "on his sickbed" on 18 December 1448 was null.[321]

Clearly, much happened behind these terse records, about some of which it would be dangerous to speculate. If, however, the deathbed marriage of Johanna and Jan took place in December of 1448, Pieter seems to have taken his time to come to court. It is hard to imagine that the case began more than a year or two before the first sentence in March of 1453. At a minimum, that would suggest that he was not concerned to regularize his prior relationship with Johanna until something happened. One thing that pretty clearly happened was that Jan had died. But if all that was involved was the fact that Jan was now dead and so Johanna was free to marry Pieter, one wonders why Pieter bothered to allege a presumptive marriage that had occurred before the deathbed marriage of Jan and Johanna. Jacquelina had been conceived and born before the deathbed marriage.[322] The deathbed marriage was pretty clearly designed to legitimize her and, perhaps, to give Johanna a share in the community property, and would have had that effect were it not for Pieter's claim. That, in turn, suggests that the other heirs of Jan may have put Pieter up to making the claim. If the real focus of the litigation was the legitimacy of Jacqueline, that might explain why, in addition to the leniency about amends that we sometimes find for defendants of higher class, Platea did not bother to order Pieter and Johanna to make amends for their intercourse and why he orders the costs compensated. Johanna had already lost a great deal and, perhaps, unjustly.

The sentence in the next case is closer to the pattern that we have come to expect. One thing unusual about it is that the second *reus* does not get an award of costs. The reason seems reasonably clear: He and the *rea* have to make amends for having consummated their public espousals and, indeed, for having procreated a female child, although the prior consummated espousals that Platea finds were "clearly proven" (*lucide probatas*), presumably by the witnesses that both the first *reus* and the promotor introduced, were the "stronger bond" (*fortius vinculum*). This is also a case in which the couple ordered to solemnize do not have to make amends for clandestine promises, even though they were *lucide probatas*. Rather, they make amends for having mutually abducted themselves and for having carnal intercourse outside the good of marriage and committing *stuprum*. The *rea* made a claim of force, but Platea found that that was not proven.[323]

If the *rea* in the preceding case was denying the validity of the first promises and resisting the first *reus*, the *rea* in the next case did so only up to a point. At first she denied the promises, and then "in a change of heart" (*ad cor reversam* [read *reversum*]), she confessed them. The list of amends suggests that her

321 *Villa c Boussout* (n. 320).
322 *Id.*, no. 1299 (reading *nata* for *nota*).
323 *Officie c Hermans, Brixis en Logaert* (n. 320).

change of heart was about more than the existence of the promises. The couple who are ordered to solemnize are to make amends for having "mutually gone away despite the fact that litigation was pending before us undecided about their promises and mingled in the flesh, thus incurring excommunication."[324] The *rea* must make amends for the second promises in violation of the first, but what she did about the second promises, though not the subject of amends, is condemned in even stronger language, "spurned and damnably taken for naught" (*spreta et dampnabiliter presumpta*).[325] Not surprisingly, the second *reus* gets both damages and costs and does not have to share in paying the costs of the promotor. It seems fairly clear that the *rea*, having been talked into, perhaps even forced into, the second set of promises found a way, once the first *reus* made clear his commitment to her, to ensure that she would not have to go through with them.

The last case is the only one that is decided totally on the basis of the statements of the parties. This means, at a minimum, that the *rea* conceded both the promises and the intercourse. The couple who are ordered to solemnize are to pay not only the promotor's costs and those of the second *reus* but also the latter's damages and an amount "in repair of his honor." They do not, however, have to make amends for their intercourse, only for their clandestine promises. The *rea* also has to make amends for secondary promises; indeed, the sentence says, she would have proceeded to solemnize them had not the first *reus* made his opposition known.[326]

The *rea* in this case was a widow. That makes it somewhat less likely, though not impossible, that she was talked into or forced into the second promises. Perhaps we should take the court at its word. She would have married the second *reus* had the first one not opposed the promises. But that could mean that her entering into the promises with the second *reus* was designed to provoke just the behavior that it provoked. When the first *reus* opposed the second promises, she was only too willing to admit the truth of his allegations. That means, of course, that the second *reus* was in some sense used, particularly if he knew nothing about the first *reus*, as seems likely. The second *reus* is entitled to a quite unusual compensation for his honor, but mature persons and perhaps those of slightly higher station (the second *reus* has an honor that requires compensation), are not to be punished severely for entering into an informal marriage, particularly when they are willing to admit it with a minimum of fuss. Hence, they do not have to make amends for the intercourse.

There are seven cases in which a presumptive marriage takes precedence over earlier espousals. The fact-patterns vary considerably, as do the sentences. What they have in common is that two men and one woman are involved. In all cases, too, the unsuccessful claimant gets something, one or some combination of costs, damages, and/or express license to marry another. Four cases are decided

324 *Officie c Swalmen, Wittebroots en Meyere* (n. 320), T&C no. 1003.
325 This is admittedly not the normal meaning of *presumere*, but it seems to be what it means here.
326 *Officie c Peerman, Hoevinghen en Cesaris* (n. 320).

on the basis of the statements and oaths of the parties. This means, assuming that there was no proof at hand that would have been pointless to resist, that the *rea* had considerable discretion as to which man she was going to choose.

In four of the cases, the consummated promises were, or could be, styled as clandestine, and in all but one of them, the promises raised in opposition were as well. Perhaps more important, it seems reasonably clear in all four cases that the presumptive marriage was against the wishes of the *rea*'s parents and relatives. In the first such case, a straight-office case decided by Rodolphi, the amends ordered tell the story. The first *reus* and the *rea* entered into clandestine promises, notwithstanding an impediment of consanguinity "of the fourth degree." They then did not proceed to solemnize those promises or otherwise to have their validity judicially determined. The second *reus* abducted the *rea* without the consent of her parents and friends and deflowered her, and the *rea* allowed herself to be so abducted and deflowered. After having espoused each other, they then presumed to have carnal intercourse once. There can be little doubt that the second *reus* and the *rea* knew exactly what they were doing. By having intercourse once, after they had affianced, not only did they create a *fortius vinculum* that was proof against the promises that her relatives had almost certainly arranged with the first *reus*, but they also ensured that they would be ordered to solemnize a relationship that her relatives could not break up.[327] (Of course, the finding of consanguinity about the first relationship ensured that that one, absent dispensation, could not be solemnized, but the *rea* could not have been certain of that finding, and just dissolving those promises would not have guaranteed that she could contract with the second *reus*.)

The second case, an office/instance case also decided by Rodolphi, is almost the same as the first. The opposition of the *rea*'s parents and relatives is not specifically mentioned, but the same language of abduction is used, making it likely that the opposition was there.[328] The sentence in the third case is the same in all relevant aspects as that in the second, except that the couple who are to solemnize introduced witnesses, a fact that suggests that the first *reus* resisted their allegations.[329] The fourth case, this time by Platea, also is based on witness testimony. This time the first espousals were public, and hence amends do not have have to made for them. The couple whose presumptive marriage is to be solemnized are to make amends: "In prejudice of the [first] engagement, not asking the relatives of the *rea*, indeed without their knowledge and consent, they went off and contracted clandestinely and mingled with each other in the flesh many and repeated times, including the deflowering of the *rea*, standing and living together in the same house, table, and bed, to the prejudice of [first] *reus*, the fiancé, and in derogation of his honor."[330] The language about "the same house, table, and bed" is normally found in sentences about concubinage,

[327] *Officie c Hellenputten, Vleeshuere en Kerkofs* (10.vii.51), no. 290, T&C no. 1004.
[328] *Officie c Deckers, Godofridi en Ghiseghem* (2.viii.49), no. 81, T&C no. 1005.
[329] *Officie c Hulst, Spaenoghe en Mertens* (19.vi.50), no. 170.
[330] *Officie c Putkuyps, Muyden en Custodis* (17.v.54), no. 620, T&C no. 1006.

but it is clear that when they were challenged, this couple decided to call it a runaway marriage.[331]

The fact-pattern in the other three cases is different. In these cases, the first espousals were clandestine; the second were public, but it is the second that the couple turned into a presumptive marriage. These second espousals need not have been against the wishes of the *rea*'s relatives; indeed, in two cases, the fact that they were public suggests that at a minimum the relatives did not object. They could even have encouraged her relationship with the second man in order to get her away from the first. But the fact that she consummated her relationship with the second man illicitly before its solemnization suggests that at this point, it was the relationship that she wanted as well. While it is possible that she was so passionate about the second man that she simply could not wait, at least one case suggests that strategic considerations played a role. The couple are to make amends "in derision of the [?first] espousals and to the prejudice of pending litigation they mingled in the flesh before the solemnization of the marriage and did not proceed in due time, damnably committing *stuprum* and incurring excommunication." The first *reus* in this case had witnesses. It certainly looks as if the couple took matters into their own hands when he appeared and made sure that he did not have a case.[332]

In the second case in this group, Platea firmly holds that the couple's presumptive marriage constituted the *fortius vinculum* that overcame the previous clandestine promises, which seem pretty clearly to have been proven. (The opponent had introduced witnesses.) This case, however, had the additional features that the couple's relationship was against the will of her parents and had been entered into during the pendency of the litigation brought by the opponent. That the couple were able to get engaged in the face of the church despite the opposition of her relatives shows that this was possible, at least in the town of Brussels, but in addition to the pending lawsuit, they may also have feared that her relatives would be able to break up their engagement if they did not consummate it.[333]

Did these couples have to go this far in order to be sure of their success? One case suggests that they did not, at least so far as the court was concerned. Platea, faced with a couple that had done the same thing as in the previous cases (though it is less clear that their consummation of their public espousals was in reaction to the appearance of the first *reus*), holds that their "clandestine marriage" (he does not use the phrase *matrimonium presumptum*, though it clearly was) is to be solemnized, notwithstanding the previous clandestine promises, "which is publicly 'derogated from' in the contentious forum by the promises made in the face of the church."[334] Platea is clearly relying on the proposition that

[331] See *Liber van Brussel*, s.v. *cohabitare* (11 cases, most of which seem to be prosecutions for concubinage).

[332] *Officie c Perkementers, Godofridi en Beyghem* (7.ii.54), no. 580, T&C no. 1007.

[333] *Office c Linden, Coyermans en Luyten* (1.x.56), no. 1020.

[334] *Officie c Fore, Perremans en Gruenenwatere* (3.vii.59), no. 1490, T&C no. 1008.

clandestina manifestis non preiudicant. There were, however, no witnesses in this case, though there seemed to be no doubt that the clandestine promises had taken place. The couples in the previous cases, even if they had been well advised, could not be sure that the court would react the same way when there were witnesses to the clandestine espousals; perhaps that would have made them not 'clandestine' within the meaning of the maxim.

The case that holds that public espousals 'derogate' from clandestine ones, seemingly without regard to whether they had been consummated, is the only such case in the sample, but it is not the only such case in the register.[335] About nine months before Platea rendered the sentence in the sample case, he rendered one not in the sample that involved prior clandestine espousals and subsequent public ones with no allegation that sexual intercourse had taken place. Despite the fact that the couple who engaged in the clandestine espousals confessed to them, Platea ordered the public ones to be solemnized, "notwithstanding the prior clandestine espousals, entered into, maintained and confessed between [the *reus*] and [first *rea*], which are 'derogated from' by the engagement made publicly, from which we also absolve the [*reus*] and [first *rea*], imposing on our promotor perpetual silence about them."[336] Sixteen months previously, he had dissolved the prior clandestine espousals in a similar situation "on account of the following public engagement as a clearer bond (*lucidius vinculum*) and one 'derogating from' the promises or espousals."[337]

These cases are the only three that I have been able to find in which it is suggested that public espousals take precedence over clandestine ones, even if the latter can be proved. The force of the case in the sample is blunted by the fact that a *matrimonium presumptum* was found in that case, and the only thing that is odd about it is that Platea seems to rely on the public nature of the espousals that preceded the intercourse, rather than on the *fortius vinculum* created by the *matrimonium presumptum.* The force of the cases not in the sample is blunted by the fact that neither of the parties to the prior clandestine espousals is pursuing them. In the first case, only the pursuit of the promotor is mentioned. In the second case, the couple are expressly said to have consented to the dissolution, and it is the only case I have found in which even the promotor does not seem to support the charges, which are said to proceed *ex denunciatione* of a woman whose relation, if any, to the parties is not stated. The couples, then, who consummated their unions were probably right not to take a chance that the court would hold for them simply because their espousals had been public.

One more case not in the sample, once again strange not for its result but for the way it is reached, may cast some light on what Platea was thinking. In a case decided about a month before the first of the two out-of-sample cases just described, Platea was faced with a situation in which two women were alleging

[335] Derived from *Liber van Brussel*, s.vv. *verloving, clandestiene, ontbinding van.*
[336] *Office c Langhevelde en Egghericx* (27.vi.58), no. 1378, T&C no. 1009.
[337] *Office en Lathouwers c Gavere en Moerbeke* (20.vi.57), no. 1166, T&C no. 1010.

clandestine espousals with the same man. During the pendency of the litigation, one of the women and the man consummated the espousals that were second in time. The result in the case is a foregone conclusion; they will be ordered to solemnize, though, as we have seen, the punishments for such behavior could be severe. What Platea says, however, is odd: "[B]etween [the *reus*] and [the second *rea*] on account of their promises of marriage, followed by sexual intercourse, entered into clandestinely and proven lawfully by witnesses, true marriage, although presumed, is to be considered [to exist] . . . notwithstanding the prior promises of marriage also entered into clandestinely between [the *reus*] and [first *rea*] and confessed, which are 'derogated from', perhaps not by the law of heaven but [that of] the forum, by the later promises, as ones that are stronger."[338]

The question, of course, is what is meant by "not perhaps by the law of heaven but that of the forum"? The most obvious meaning – that for Platea, the doctrine that espousals of the future tense plus intercourse created an indissoluble marriage that took precedence over prior espousals of the future tense not followed by intercourse was positive canon law but not natural or moral law – is possible, and there is support for that proposition.[339] It seems more likely, however, that Platea was referring to some better-known conflict between the internal and external *fora*. A sharp one could have arisen if the *reus* and the first *rea* had confessed to a *de presenti* espousal. The rights of the second *rea*, proven as they were by lawful witnesses, could not be prejudiced in the external forum by the confession of the other couple. The second *rea* might not have a public marriage, but what she had would have been just as good in the external forum granted the proof. In the internal forum, however, the first couple would be married.

If we put these cases together, all of which appear over a relatively short period, and seem to be the only ones of this sort in the register, we can essay some tentative conclusions. We know from the three-party cases not involving *copula* that Platea was concerned about frivolous allegations of clandestine espousals prior to public ones. In none of the cases in the sample is the person alleging such clandestine espousals successful, and Platea's rhetoric against, and punishment of, 'frivolous' allegations becomes stronger and stronger.[340] While there is one case in which Platea seems to have come close to upholding such allegations,[341] it is possible that by the middle of 1457 (the first of our cases), he had come to the conclusion that a change in the standard of proof was called for. Public espousals 'derogate' from clandestine ones. One cannot allege clandestine espousals in the face of public ones. Had he adopted this standard (and we cannot be sure that he did, because the register ends shortly after these

338 *Officie c Verbilen, Scollaert en Peters* (15.ix.58), no. 1354, T&C no. 1011.

339 Theologians had doubts about *matrimonium presumptum*, throughout the pre-Tridentine period. See Dauvillier, *Mariage*, 70–5.

340 See at nn. 184–7.

341 *Officie c Timmerman en Rutsemeels* (n. 194).

cases), it would have involved a substantial change in the practice of the court. He chose, therefore, to announce this change in the context of cases where it did not make any difference; the cases would have come out the same way under the old standards. This subtle way of making a change was probably not lost on the personnel of the court and the promotors. We may have more doubt whether it could have affected the behavior of the parties, who, we suspect, did not normally seek legal advice before they acted.

Had Platea made this change (or if he did after the register ends),[342] it could have had another effect that he might have been able to foresee. As we have noted, a number of couples seem to have responded to opposition to their marriages by going out and consummating their promises, thus creating an indissoluble presumptive marriage. This was behavior of which Platea could hardly have approved, and his rhetoric in such cases shows that he did not. We have one case, and admittedly only one case, in which he seems to be saying that such behavior is unnecessary where the promises are public: They 'derogate' from clandestine ones. He may have been trying to encourage couples to take that route.

Two of the cases alleging *copula* involve four parties rather than three. One of them seems almost routine in its economy of words. In an office/instance case brought by the promotor against a man and three women, one of whom is described as the man's fiancée, the public espousals of the engaged couple are declared to be valid and ordered to be solemnized, notwithstanding the opposition of the other two women, which is deemed frivolous. All four are then condemned to make amends for sexual intercourse in which all three women were deflowered, and the two unsuccessful claimants are to make amends for the frivolous opposition. They both, however, get a dowry, and costs among the parties are compensated.[343] One is left to wonder in what the *reus*'s attraction consisted, but our records are not going to tell us that.[344]

The other four-party case is one of the most spectacular in the sample. It begins as a straight-instance case before Rodolphi. The sentence starts routinely enough with a declaration that Walter de Cotthem, *actor*, and Barbara Trullaerts, *rea*, contracted espousals by words of the future tense in the hand of the pastor of Gaasbeek.[345] The first hint we get that something peculiar may be going on is that the sentence then notes that many people were present at these espousals, and particularly the parents of Walter and Barbara, who consented to the espousals. That is the last that we hear of the espousals, for rather than ordering them solemnized, Rodolphi then proceeds to order Walter to make amends because "he tore a resisting Barbara from the hands of her parents, and with many associates took her away (*abducere*) to out-of-the-way

342 Disc. T&C no. 1012.

343 *Officie c Boelkens, Claes, Schueren en Baten* (23.xi.58), no. 1391, disc. T&C no. 1013.

344 See *Wafrer, Wereslee and Dallynge c Savage* (Ch 6, at n. 178).

345 Gaasbeek (gemeente Lennik), Vlaams-Brabant, just west of Brussels, the site of a medieval castle.

places, and after a number of days presumed rashly to know her carnally, committing *stuprum* upon her, and for many days and weeks held her with him successively in various places, and carnally knew her on repeated occasions." We are reminded of the abduction cases from York, which are roughly contemporary.[346] While we should perhaps discount part of this story because of the heightened rhetoric, I think it likely that something along these lines did happen.[347] Of course, if it happened, it happened before the espousals; otherwise, we would be dealing with a potential presumptive marriage.

We next see Walter and Barbara six months later, in a sentence in a case brought *ex officio* against Barbara, one Arnold Pauwels, and one Clara Simoens. The sentence is typical of three-party cases in which *copula* is alleged. On the basis of the sworn statements of the parties and of witnesses produced by Arnold and Barbara, Clara and Arnold are to make amends for having illicit intercourse that led to the procreation of a child; Arnold and Barbara are to make amends for clandestine promises and illicit intercourse, leading to a presumptive marriage. Arnold is absolved from the promises with Clara alleged by the promotor, and Arnold and Barbara (but not Clara) are to pay the promotor's costs. What is different about the case is its references to Walter. Arnold and Barbara are to make amends because "after the espousals between the same Barbara and Walter declared by our sentence, in prejudice of such sentence and of Walter, they presumed to enter into clandestine promises of marriage by words of the present tense and knew each other carnally on repeated occasions thereafter, transforming such promises into the force of a presumptive marriage and deceiving Walter." The promises between Walter and Barbara are then dissolved, on the ground of the "supervenient stronger bond," and Arnold and Barbara are condemned to pay Walter's damages and costs. This is the only explicit reference to promises by words of the present tense in the entire sample, and it is telling that Rodolphi chooses to dissolve the promises with Walter on the ground of presumptive marriage rather, than on the ground that present promises trump future ones.[348]

Eighteen months later, Arnold and Barbara are once more before the court, Platea in the meantime having replaced Rodolphi. The former renders a sentence that is unique in the sample and difficult to interpret. For this reason the translation is painstakingly literal:[349]

> The costs incurred by the late Walter in a marriage case litigated before our predecessor between the same Walter, *actor*, on the one, and Barbara and Arnold, *rei*, on the other side, to the payment of which together with the damages of this late Walter, the *rei* were condemned by our predecessor, with due moderation taken into account, we tax, at the sum of 32 *florins* of gold, called 'riders' or of their value, there having been included a half of the *leges* paid by the late Walter for himself and the same Barbara to the use of the

[346] Ch 5, at nn. 70–99.

[347] *Cotthem c Trullaerts* (19.iii.51, 5.xi.51), nos. 250, 319; T&C no. 1014.

[348] *Officie c Pauwels, Simoens en Trullaerts* (5.v.52), no. 375, T&C no. 1015.

[349] *Cotthem c Trullaerts en Pauwels* (1.xii.53), no. 550, T&C no. 1016.

reverend in Christ our father and lord of Cambrai, commuting the pilgrimages sought (*viagia petita*) on behalf of the late Walter to other pious works, considering the death of the same late Walter, as follows: that for the salvation of his soul Barbara and Arnold, a married couple, put in our hands between now and the feast of the purification of the Blessed Virgin Mary [2 February],7 like *florins* to be distributed by us in the presence of two common friends of the parties to any and all priests who wish to celebrate [Walter's] anniversaries and that there also be a general distribution of three bushels (*modii*) of white bread in the town of Sint-Martens-Lennik to be distributed by the provisors of the table of the Holy Spirit of the place to the poor streaming into the place.

A few things seem relatively obvious. Walter, who we have no reason to suspect was elderly (his parents consented to his espousals), is now dead. A violent man may have met a violent end. The costs and damages that he was awarded in the previous sentence are now, 18 months later, being taxed at 32 Burgundian *florins*. These costs are said to be for a marriage case that Walter brought against Barbara and Arnold, suggesting that the sentence in the instance case was not the final sentence in that case but that it continued and was finally resolved when the promotor intervened against Arnold, Barbara, and Clara.[350] The costs and damages taxed are also substantial; one could hire a skilled carpenter in Antwerp for 307 days for this sum.[351]

More difficult to interpret is the reference to the *leges*, half of which are said to be included in the sum of costs and damages, and which, if we have gotten the grammar right, have already been paid by Walter to the use of the bishop. The only *leges* imposed on Walter in the previous sentences are those imposed on him in the first sentence, and we must puzzle over why Barbara and Arnold should be required to pay half of those. Even more puzzling is the reference to the pilgrimages (*viagia*) that are "sought (*petita*) on behalf of the late Walter." These are now commuted, in consideration of Walter's death (again if we have gotten the grammar right), "to other pious works." A payment for masses and a distribution of bread to the poor is substituted, both to be offered for the salvation of Walter's soul.

Prescinding from the possibility that there were other *leges* imposed on Barbara and Walter that were not recorded, we can make sense of the *leges* if we assume that, though the instance sentence does not say so, they were, in fact, imposed on both Barbara and Walter. What that must mean is that even if Barbara was "torn resisting from the hands of her parents," she was not an unwilling participant in their wild jaunt around the Brabantine countryside. She was probably quite young and may even, as sometimes happens, have come to identify with her captor. To a late medieval judge, however, that would have looked like voluntary abduction, not rape. When Walter and Barbara got back, his parents and, significantly, hers consented to their marriage. Barbara, however, came to have different ideas. She formed a relationship with Arnold, displacing his mistress, Clara, and saw to it that her promises with

350 Disc. T&C no. 1017.
351 See n. 374.

Walter, carefully described as *per verba de futuro*, were superseded by promises *de presenti* followed by intercourse.

When Walter first brought suit against Barbara, Arnold was not yet in the picture, or, at a minimum, Walter did not know about him, because he did not join him as a party. Walter clearly was having difficulty getting Barbara to go through with the marriage, however, because he had to sue her. Rodolphi's attitude toward him is ambiguous. On the one hand, he finds for the promises and seems to hold that they are valid; on the other hand, he is decidedly hostile to the way in which Walter began the relationship, and he does not order the espousals solemnized. He was certainly aware that Barbara was resisting, and he may even have told Barbara how to rid herself of him by carefully designating the promises as future ones (a designation that does not appear in many sentences).

Walter then paid the *leges* on behalf of both himself and Barbara and thus restored himself to respectability in the eyes of the court. Barbara, however, went off and took the law into her own hands. Walter was now seen as the victim of Barbara and Arnold's machinations. Their marriage had to be allowed to stand, but Walter was owed compensation. By the time that a new judge calculated that compensation, Walter was dead, but we must imagine that his heir was seeking the reimbursement in his name. The heir also wanted Barbara and Arnold to do penance (*viagia*) for the damage that they had done to Walter's reputation. But since Walter is dead, Platea decides that it would be better for Barbara and Arnold to do something for the benefit of Walter's soul, and he comes up with the classically late-medieval coupling of masses and distribution of bread for the poor.

Obviously, what we have just said is not the only way to read this case. It is possible that Barbara was raped in the modern sense, that her parents abandoned her to Walter as damaged goods, and that she escaped from his clutches to a sympathetic Arnold. The court failed to sympathize with her and, as a result, she and Arnold had to pay dearly for what they did. All of this is possible, but I would suggest, the previous reading better reconciles all the evidence we have before us.

DIVORCE FROM THE BOND

Cambrai

Table 8.7 indicates that there are 12 cases of divorce from the bond in our sample, strikingly all office cases.[352] Strikingly, too, the promotor succeeds in dissolving the marriages in only 2 cases (17% success rate). In almost all the cases, however, he demonstrates something for which the parties must make amends, in most because they got married before it was determined that the impediment did not exist. Because so few marriages were dissolved, we cannot be completely

[352] Disc. T&C no. 1018.

sure what all the alleged grounds for dissolution were. (There is no need to be precise about the nature of the impediment if it does not, in fact, exist.) In 8 cases, it is described as affinity, in 1, consanguinity. These cases are best dealt with in Chapter 11. That leaves 3 cases, 1 of vow, 1 that seems to involve precontract, and 1 in which the nature of the impediment is not specified at all.

The cases in which the promotor sought dissolution of a marriage on grounds other than incest tell us less than those that do, but they fit the overall pattern of the incest cases. Nicolaï was not going to dissolve a marriage without clear proof of its invalidity. The one case of the impediment of vow is decided on legal grounds. The woman in question had promised her former husband while he was still alive that she would not take a second husband. The sentence expressly equates this promise with a simple vow of chastity. That was an impedient but not a diriment impediment. The woman must make amends for having broken her promise, but the marriage is allowed to stand.[353] A case that is probably based on the impediment of *ligamen* (prior bond) fails miserably, though the man and the woman to whom he is not married have to pay the promotor's costs.[354] The final case does not even tell us the nature of the alleged impediment. The *reus* is to pay the promotor's costs and make amends for having married knowing of the *fama* of an impediment that could impede the marriage, making him 'deliberately ignorant'.[355] The marriage is allowed to stand, and nothing is said about the woman.[356]

Brussels

As Table 8.6 shows, there are only two cases in the Brussels sample that raise issues of divorce from the bond. Since both of them also raise issues about separation, they will be discussed in Chapter 10.[357] Since the grounds alleged for dissolution is incest, they will also be discussed in Chapter 11.

MISCELLANEOUS CASES

Cambrai

Table 8.7 indicates that there are eight "miscellaneous" marriage cases in our sample, four straight instance, three straight office, and one promoted case in which the victim is made a formal party. They are, indeed, miscellaneous, and because they are, the sentences tend to tell us more than do those in cases of types that were routinely handled by the court.

Many of these cases concern out-of-court statements made by the defendants designed either to promote or impede a marriage. Of the two straight-instance

353 *Office c Male* (8.v.45), no. 692, disc. T&C no. 1019.
354 *Office c Rouge, Franchoise et Frasne* (25.viii.42), no. 312.
355 See n. 297.
356 *Office c Motten et Nols* (18.xii.45), no. 851.
357 Listed T&C no. 1020.

jactitation cases, the first, a sentence by Divitis, tells us simply that he absolves the *actrix* of the jactitation of promises of marriage made by the *reus*, gives her license to marry another, and condemns the *reus* to pay her costs.[358] The other case tells us more. On the basis of corroboration by the *curé* of Avesnes-lès-Aubert and the confessions of the parties, Nicolaï absolves the *actor* from the clandestine promises of marriage that the *rea* had alleged before the *curé*, gives him license to marry another, and condemns her to pay his costs. The sentence also tells us that the *rea* was contumacious, though she must have appeared at least once for her confession to have been taken. The *leges* tell us that she was fined for frivolous allegations and both parties were fined for fornication.[359] In both cases, the defendants were probably seeking to create a *fama* that would have impeded marriage of the plaintiffs to others. In neither case did they succeed, but the other party had to bring an action to ensure that they did not. On the one hand, one wonders, granted the requirements of the law of proof, whether the claims that the defendants made were as baseless as the court found them to be. On the other hand, one wonders how often such claims did succeed in the social realm when the other party was not so well informed or so capable of bringing an action as the plaintiffs in these cases were.

The promotor could be persuaded to get involved in such cases, at least where a third party was involved. Anne Bigotte was constituted a formal party along with the promotor to make a "denunciation" that, as the court found, Jean Crispelet in the pub called "London" in the market of Cambrai said a few days after Anne's engagement to Jean Vast had been announced: "He won't get a big kick out it because it won't be the first time." By this, Crispelet confessed, he meant that Anne had previously been known by one of his buddies, whom he named. By this, he also confessed, he had damaged the honor and reputation of Anne, who had been to that moment and is "honest [a word that probably has class connotations] and upright, an uncorrupt virgin, a young woman of good name and *fama (honestam ac probam bonorumque nominis et fame iuvenculam virginem et incorruptam)*." He is ordered to make amends, to pay a pound of wax to the chapel, to pay the promotor's and Anne's costs, and to appear within the next week in her parish church where he is to say before eight persons selected by Anne that he rashly said what he said, that it is not true, that he regrets it, that he never saw or heard anything but good of Anne, and that he begs her forgiveness. He is also to make a pilgrimage within the next six weeks to the church of Notre-Dame in Halle.[360] Whether as a result of the lingering effects of the defamation or not we cannot tell, but three months later, Jean Vaast (Vat) and Anne appear in court and remit their espousals after three banns have been published.[361]

A similar case, brought by the promotor alone, tells us less, perhaps because the woman in question was not of the same class as Anne. Baudouin de Honte,

358 *Latteresse c Pont* (17.xii.38), no. 91.
359 *Heugot c Pouparde* (27.i.53), no. 1400, disc. T&C no. 1021.
360 *Office et Bigotte c Crispelet* (24.xii.44), no. 621, disc. T&C no. 1022.
361 *Vat et Bigotte* (10.iv.45), no. 676.

in the presence of trustworthy people, boasted that he had carnally known Jeanne vander Base. As a result of the *fama* generated by this remark, Arnauld de Coebere refused to solemnize their marriage. Baudouin denied on oath that he had had sexual relations with Jeanne, and he was ordered to make amends for defamation and for impeding her marriage and to pay the promotor's costs.[362]

That impeding a marriage was a separate offense for which one could be prosecuted is confirmed by *Office c Jean Cornut, Jean de Rodegnies et Michel fils de Jean de Rodegnies*.[363] Nicolaï found that Cornut had done his best to impede the espousals between his daughter Marie and Pierre Thurin. He brought an action in the secular court of Tournai against Marie Carlière, Marie's aunt (*matertera*), in order to establish that she had forced Marie to enter into the espousals, thus to prevent the ecclesiastical court from establishing the truth of the matter. When his widowed stepmother intervened and gently suggested to him that he would do better if he allowed Marie and Pierre to marry, he replied: "Madam, shut up about this. I have given my soul to the devil to prevent my daughter from marrying him."[364] He was, Nicolaï tells us, "speaking irreverently, most dishonestly and irreligiously, and otherwise than is appropriate for a reply of a true zealot of the orthodox faith."[365] For all of this he is to make amends. So far as the other (unspecified) articles are concerned, he and his *correi* are to purge themselves four-handed. There is, however, no record of the purgation.

We have seen outbursts by fifteenth-century fathers like this before.[366] In this case, we may suspect that a major family squabble lies behind it. Marie's mother is not mentioned, and she may be dead. Marie Carlière is described by a word that classically means 'maternal aunt', a relationship that is also suggested by the fact that she does not have Jean Cornut's surname. Michel de Rodegnies may well be the man whom Jean Cornut had in mind for Marie. The women in the family had different ideas.

Jean Cammelin, the *curé* of Amougies, got into serious trouble for his handling of a marriage case. Knowing that Nicolaï had rendered a definitive sentence ordering Jean du Quesne *le jeune* and Jeanne Aleisen to solemnize their presumptive marriage, and knowing the *fama* that Jean du Quesne had been excommunicated, Jean Cammelin proclaimed two banns between Jean du Quesne and Marguerite sBucs, relying on the *fama*, which he alone asserted and did not investigate, that Jeanne had died in Tournai. After the second bann it became apparent that Jeanne was alive, and the warden (?sacristan) of the church, a relative of Jean du Quesne, made up letters in Jean Cammelin's name (which Jean Cammelin knew about) asserting that there was no impediment

362 *Office c Hont* (28.viii.44), no. 520.
363 (30.i.43), no. 420.
364 *Ibid.*, text and disc. T&C no. 1023.
365 *Ibid.*, T&C 1024.
366 E.g., Ch 5, nn. 191–3.

to the marriage of Jean and Marguerite, and sent the couple with the letters to Deinze (in the diocese of Tournai) where the *curé* solemnized their marriage, not knowing anything about the impediment. This caused a great scandal. Jean Cammelin also committed fornication with many women. For all of this he was to make amends and pay the promotor's costs.[367]

Although there are many cases of clerical discipline in our sample, this is the only proceeding brought against a *curé* for mishandling a marriage case. It was a particularly egregious case, both because it involved a dramatic flouting of one of Nicolaï's sentences (not otherwise recorded) and because of the scandal that it caused. We may suspect that similar behavior went undetected in less high-profile cases.

The other two miscellaneous cases can be treated more summarily. On 22 September 1452, Renaude Coppine obtained letters declaring that her husband had died on a pilgrimage to Rome during the Jubilee the previous year. She was given license to remarry.[368] A major dowry case, the only such case in the sample, is referred to in a previous section and discussed there in the margin.[369]

Brussels

Table 8.6 tells us that our sample of Brussels cases contains 19 instance actions for dowry (6 for deflowering and 13 'regular' dowry) and 2 miscellaneous office cases involving marriage. A comparison with Table 8.7 shows that the Brussels court did considerably more business involving marital property than did that at Cambrai, where there is only one dowry case in the sample, and we have already speculated that this difference may be the result of the way in which the secular and ecclesiastical courts divided jurisdiction in the two areas. Be that as it may, we can learn a considerable amount more about practices concerning marital property from the Brussels register than we can from the Cambrai registers.

We have already discussed the institution of dowry for deflowering in the context of spousals cases involving *copula* because many of the unsuccessful claimants in those cases were awarded such a dowry.[370] We begin here with three cases (not included in the numbers just given) in which there was a separate entry of a judgment of dowry for deflowering following an unsuccessful attempt to establish a marriage.

It is not completely clear why separate, specific judgments were entered in these cases and not in the others where a dowry for deflowering is awarded as part of the sentence in the main case. The first, a two-party case, is one in which Platea had expressly deferred making the order to pay the dowry, perhaps because he knew that this case was going to be particularly complicated or that

[367] *Office c Cammelin* (20.xii.49), no. 1240, disc. T&C no. 1025.
[368] *Coppine* (22.ix.52), no. 1344.
[369] *Messien et Daniels c Daniels* (n. 50; disc. T&C no. 835).
[370] See at nn. 229–30, 263–73, following n. 290, at n. 343.

the parties were unlikely to reach an agreement on their own.[371] In the second, also a two-party case, the man had died in the interim, and judgment had to be rendered against his widow.[372] The third, a three-party case, does not contain such hints as to why a separate judgment was necessary.[373] Since the woman, now an instance *actrix*, was awarded her costs in all three cases, we can imagine that there was some pressure on the *reus* to agree to a sum without the necessity of having to litigate the matter, but we are probably to imagine in all three cases that the parties simply could not agree.

The form of all three sentences is similar and complicated. In the first, the *reus* is given a choice of paying the *actrix*, within approximately a month, 16 *clinkaerts* of the money of Brabant,[374] or of paying her 2 *clinkaerts* a year, beginning a bit more than a year from the date of the sentence. The *reus* is given three weeks to make the election, and he then has a month from the election to find a sufficient surety (*sufficiens contrapignus*). In the second sentence, in addition to the fact that it is the *reus*'s widow rather than the *reus* who is condemned, there are differences in detail. The capital sum is 14 rather than 16 *clinkaerts*; she has two rather than three weeks to make the election, and the first payment of the installments (if that is what she chooses) is in somewhat more than six months, rather than slightly more than a year.[375] This second case was the one in which the *reus* or his mother had made voluntary contributions to the woman's costs of lying-in, and that may suggest that these differences were based more on the *bonorum facultas* of the *reus* than on the *natalium dignitas* of the woman.[376]

In the third case, the *reus* is to pay the capital sum within approximately two and a half months; if he chooses to pay in installments, the first is due in approximately six months. He has 12 days to make his election, and three weeks thereafter to come up with the *contrapignus*.[377] There is some difficulty figuring out the coin in which the payment is to be made: "18 peters, counting [one of] which for 18 *stufers*" (*octodecim petros semel, quem pro octodecim stuferis computando*). The text may be corrupt; it certainly does not easily parse. There does not seem to have been a coin in this period that was regularly referred to as a 'peter' (or a 'rock', if we change the gender), but the Tournai account books regularly use the term, apparently as a unit of account.[378] *Stufer*, however, is almost certainly *stuiver*, a very common silver and alloy coin (*blanc*) in the Burgundian Netherlands, also known as a *patard*. Our text seems to be telling us that a 'peter' is worth 18 *stuiver*, and in this period a *stuiver* was worth two groats. Thus, the 18 'peters' that this woman will receive if she

371 *Office c Goerten en Emeren* (19.v.58), no. 1316, T&C no. 1026.
372 *Officie c Chehain en Poliet* (n. 265).
373 *Officie c Bot, Buysschere en Gheersone* (n. 312).
374 Disc. T&C no. 1027.
375 *Officie c Chehain en Poliet* (n. 265) (18.xi.57), no. 1251, T&C no. 1028.
376 See at n. 262.
377 *Officie c Bot, Buysschere en Gheersone* (n. 312), T&C no. 1029.
378 Disc. T&C no. 1030.

gets a capital dowry is 648 groats, somewhat less than the 768 or 672 groats that the women in previous sentences will receive, but within the same general area.[379] If this is right, the rather substantial variations that we find in these sentences as to the timing of the election, the finding of the *contrapignus*, and the first installment payment may be as important, if not more important, than the variations in the sums involved.

The six cases in the sample that were not begun as spousals cases add something, but not a great deal, to our knowledge. Two have judgments that specify the amount of the dowry. Both are decisions of Rodolphi, and one shows the same basic pattern as do Platea's judgments given earlier, but without quite the precision. The *reus* is given the option of paying a capital sum (20 *riders*) or an annual amount for the life of the woman (2 *riders*); a term of 12 days is fixed as to when he is to make his choice, but the precision as to within what period after that he needs to find the *contrapignus* and when the payments of the annual sum are to be made is lacking. Perhaps these features were added as a result of experience with Rodolphi's sentences. Fourteen months after he rendered this sentence, Rodolphi had to issue letters of execution at the request of the *actrix*.[380]

The other judgment brings us into a different world. The *reus* is ordered to provide the *actrix* two bushels (*modii*) of rye[381] every year that she lives, and no capital sum is mentioned.[382] The parties in this case came from Vlezenbeek, which is actually quite close to Brussels, but was obviously at the time very much rural.[383] The parties in the first case came from Mechelen and Brussels. The difference is almost certainly not only that between town and country but also social classes. The *facultas* of the *reus* in the second case makes it unthinkable that he could discharge his obligation by paying a capital sum.

Three cases under Platea result in judgments that the *reus* is to endow the *actrix*, without there being any further judgment about the amounts.[384] Not all actions of this sort resulted in judgments for the *actrix*, however. In one case, a woman seeking child support (but not dowry for deflowering) fails. The sentence ends with a mysterious note "saving always the right [or duty] for the putative father of the child."[385] This probably means that the woman did not prove that the *reus* was the father, but that someone who claimed to be the father could still appear and claim the child (but also have the obligation of support). It may mean, however, that it was still open to the *reus* in the case to do the right thing.

[379] Disc. T&C no. 1031.

[380] Ref. T&C no. 1032 with disc.

[381] Disc. T&C no. 1033.

[382] *Bersele c Verheylweghen* (20.vi.52), no. 380, T&C no. 1034; (22.xii.52), no. 432 (AV's appeal declared abandoned for non-prosecution).

[383] Now Sint-Pieters-Leeuw in Sint-Kwintens-Lennick, Vlaams-Brabant.

[384] Listed T&C no. 1035.

[385] [...] *c Stillemans* (26.iv.57), no. 1140, T&C no. 1036.

The 13 cases involving dowry or *donatio propter nuptias* (the two phrases almost always appear together) involve considerable complexity, not the least because a number of them produce more than one judgment. Before we try to analyze the patterns of litigation about dowries, it seemed best to outline the contents of the dotal agreements alleged or proven in these cases.

We do not know the contents of some of the agreements that were litigated, and where we are told the contents some of them seem incomplete. Nonetheless, we do know quite a bit, and what we are told reveals a wide range of things that could be subjects of such agreements. Some reflect the pattern that we saw in the condemnations for dowry for deflowering, except that annual payments and a capital sum are sometimes combined. One of the least complicated called for a one-time payment of 12 'peters' and an annual pension for the life of the man of three bushels of rye.[386] Another called simply for five bushels of rye annually for the life of the man, but there may have been more to this agreement than that.[387] A third called for 20 bushels of rye for the life of the wife and an additional five sacks to be assigned, apparently from the rent or *cens* owed by one of the tenants of the woman's family. This agreement also called for the one-time transfer of four beds with the hangings for one bed and, if we are reading it right, a dozen raincoats (*duodena pluvinarium*), and there was certainly more to the agreement than that.[388] A fourth agreement seems to have called for a one-time payment of 40 groats and an annual payment of the same amount.[389] A fifth involved a one-time payment of 24 gold crowns, which probably translates to about 1,900 groats.[390]

Dotal agreements that involved interests in immovables could give rise to considerable complexities. In one case, the court orders that a house called "de Loyve," located near the bridge called "Tsmuyntersbrugge" in Brussels, be transferred as part of a dotal agreement to a couple, and it dismisses the claim of the guardians of the *béguinage* of Brussels to half of the house.[391] In another case, the defendants are ordered to pay the couple the value of half a building site that was found to be part of the dotal agreement but which the defendants had later transferred to the Benedictine abbey of Affligem.[392] Other issues raised in the case and a counterclaim allow us to see other elements in the agreement: The plaintiff was to be reimbursed for half the costs of the wedding and for what was probably a furred garment that he had purchased for his wife, two couches, two bolts of linen cloth, and two household utensils, whereas the plaintiff was to restore, redeem from the Lombards, or compensate the *rei* for a bed, iron breast-armor, three pounds of wool, and "other things mentioned

386 *Bivoet c Bivoets* (23.v.50), no. 160. For 'peters', see at n. 378; for *modii siliginis*, see n. 381.

387 *Ossele c Venne* (19.i.51), no. 240; (3.vii.51), no. 286; (31.vii.52), no. 393, T&C no. 1037.

388 *Bock c Castro en Godesans* (18.iv.55 to 27.vi.55), nos. 781, 809, T&C no. 1038.

389 *Huffele c Brouwere* (9.ii.59), no. 1422 (13.vii.59), nos. 1500, T&C no. 1039.

390 *Moernay en Herdewijck c Herdewijck* (31.iii.52 to 17.x.52), no. 365, 392, 410, disc. T&C no. 1040.

391 *Roode en Voort c Brussel* (*begijnhof*) (13.viii.59), no. 1501.

392 Oost-Vlaanderen, about a mile east of Aalst.

in the reconventional libel [roughly equivalent of our counterclaim]." This was also an agreement in which we can be reasonably certain that other items were involved.[393]

The usefulness of the money, the immovables, and some of the specific items is obvious enough, but two call for some discussion. "Bushels of rye" may be a unit of account, not necessarily intended for consumption. If we were right in our estimate that a woman could be sustained, or could come close to being sustained, on 2 bushels a year, one really has to wonder whether a man needed 5 bushels, and 20 seems like more than enough for a couple. This last couple is also the one that gets four beds and a dozen raincoats. They do seem to be the couple that is at the top of the economic scale with which we are dealing, and perhaps they needed these things not for themselves but for their servants. It is also possible, however, that some of these things were commercial items, just as it is possible that the breast-armor was valuable not for use but as an item that could be pawned "to the Lombards."

The relatives who make the dotal payments are quite varied, and the persons to whom the payments are to be made also show some variation. One man is suing for payments owed by his aunt; the payments were to be made to him alone and were to last for his life.[394] In another case where the payments are to be made to the man alone, they were agreed to by the maternal uncle (assuming that the classical meaning of the word is intended, an assumption that is supported by his surname) of the man's stepson and by the stepson. This was clearly a second marriage for the woman.[395] In one case, the payments owed from the man's mother-in-law are to last for the life of her daughter; in another case, the payments owed from the woman's grandfather or uncle are to last so long as the couple both live.[396] One of the cases in which the details of the dotal agreement are not given involves the grandfather or uncle of the bride (probably the latter and probably her maternal uncle, considering the divergence between her surname and his); another involves her maternal uncle, and a third involves the man's family.[397] The remaining cases in which the payers of the dowry can be identified involve the parents or a parent of the bride.

The issues in the cases varied. As we have seen, complicated agreements could have given rise to quite genuine misunderstandings as to what items were involved or whether the endowing parties had full rights in them. It is striking, however, how many of the cases involve multiple endowing parties one of whom has died. Not all of these cases were really contested. In one, the widowed *jonkvrouw* Elisabeth vanden Bloke, mother of a daughter also named Elisabeth, who had married twice, appears before two notaries commissioned by the court and introduces a document in Flemish (unfortunately, only the first

[393] *Gheele c Gheele en Ans* (17.x.55), no. 860, T&C no. 1041.
[394] *Bivoet c Bivoets* (n. 386).
[395] *Ossele c Venne* (n. 387).
[396] *Bock c Castro en Godesans* (n. 388); *Huffele c Brouwere* (n. 389).
[397] Listed T&C no. 1042.

and last sentences are given) to which her late husband had agreed with her consent; witnesses are heard, and the widow makes confessions or attestations, which the court regards as particularly important (*presertim*). The court orders the entire record of the proceedings to be made a public record, "lest the copy of the proof and recognition, which could be of interest to [the daughter] and her heirs, should fail with the passage of time," and that full faith be granted to the dotal agreement that was produced in the acts. These people may have been genuinely unclear as to what their rights and obligations were once the father had died and the daughter had remarried.[398]

Records of this sort could be useful. In December of 1450, Rodolphi rendered a sentence declaring that the "molestations, perturbations and inquietudes" that the *reus*, the *actrix*'s brother, was making about "the dotal goods that the late mother of the parties had designated in the acts of the case" were "frivolous, unjust, and *de facto* presumed." He ordered the brother to keep silent about them. Five years later, the sister now being dead, her daughters obtained a judgment from Platea against their uncle that the previous sentence was *res judicata*, and he could not relitigate the issue.[399] The passage of dotal goods through three generations in this way suggests a customary understanding that dotal goods, or at least certain kinds, passed in the female line. This understanding may be related to the fact that all of the uncles we have seen so far in these cases are, or seem to have been, maternal uncles.

In two other cases, litigation that hardly seems contested resulted in the recording of evidence of dotal agreements pursuant to language similar to that found in the *Bloke* case. In neither of these cases is it as clear as in *Bloke* why there is a concern to have a public record, but in both we can suspect the reason. One case involves a man who seems to be the woman's maternal uncle, and he is said to have "promised and stipulated" the dowry or *donatio propter nuptias* "with his niece (possibly granddaughter)."[400] That suggests that her father and perhaps also her mother were dead. The former would certainly be the one to promise his daughter if he were alive, and the latter would probably be involved if he were not. In the other case, a woman asks the court for permission to sue her mother. She gets permission, and nine months later (the summer vacation intervening) a similar agreement is recorded. The case never says that the mother is a widow, but it never says who her husband is either. In other cases, the endowed woman's husband will sue in her name, but not here, though it is clear that she has a husband.[401] Once more we may be dealing with property that passes in the female line, and one of the purposes of recording the agreement may be to make that clear.

Another case that ends in the redaction of documents in public form may have begun in a noncontentious mode but then became more contentious. In January

398 *Bloke en Bloke* (16.vii.56), no. 990, T&C no. 1043.
399 *Luytens, Luytens en Luytens c Luytens* (n. 397), T&C no. 1044.
400 *Eect en Zijpe c Bonne* (n. 397), T&C no. 1045.
401 *Coudenberghe c Coudenberghe* (4.ii.57 to 10.xi.57), nos. 1110, 1245.

of 1459, the court ordered *jonkvrouw* Maria Cluetincx, widow of Wenceslas Tserclaes, knight, and her son, also named Wenceslas, to produce within eight days anything that they had to say against the claims of Everard Tserclaes, also described as a knight. In March, the court ordered that a document, discovered in the *étude* (*in scrinio ubi sua prothocolla sunt et fuerunt sub custodia posita*) of a deceased notary, be redacted to public form. In March, Maria and Wenceslas appealed to the pope from this order, and *apostoli* were denied. In April, they were ordered either to acknowledge or deny the document. In September, the *rei* being contumacious, the court ordered that a public record be made of the document, saving the rights of the parties. The last entry elaborates on the description of the document. It was made between Wenceslas, senior, and *jonkvrouw* Elisabeth Tsertoghen, in the name of her daughter *jonkvrouw* Clara, who was Everard's mother.[402]

Any hope of figuring out what is going on in this case is dependent on identifying Everard's father, who, unfortunately, is never named and who is probably dead. Granted Everard's surname, the most obvious candidate for Everard's father would be a younger brother of Wenceslas senior (younger because Wenceslas senior was making arrangements for his marriage). That would mean that the dispute is about provisions in a dotal agreement made by Everard's uncle with his mother and her mother, which now inure to Everard's benefit (perhaps because he is planning to marry) and which his uncle's widow and his first cousin are resisting. The only bit of evidence against this supposition is that Everard is called "knight," and Wenceslas junior is not, though he is clearly of the knightly class. That may be because he is still too young to be a knight, something that is also suggested by the fact that his mother is joined as a defendant. That would suggest that Wenceslas senior did not produce his heir until fairly late in life, but that is certainly possible. In any event, Everard is no relation of Maria, and he is the son of Wenceslas junior's uncle, a man whom Wenceslas junior may never have known.[403]

Be that as it may, the court is clearly proceeding cautiously in dealing with a class of people with which it did not normally deal. After nine months of maneuvering, the court proceeds in the absence of the *rei*, making no attempt to force them to come to court, and enters the agreement, saving their rights. One gets the feeling that if Everard is going to get satisfaction, he will have to proceed in some other court. There may have been more to the case in this court, however: The last sentence recorded is very close to the end of the register.

Evidence abounds in the contested cases that the problem with the dotal payments arose when a key player in making the arrangements died. In one, the *actor*'s aunt (his father's sister, if we can rely on her surname and ignore the fact that she is called *matertera*) is ordered to pay arrearages in an annual payment that had not been paid since her husband died. Now the husband was, of course, the *actor*'s uncle, in modern terminology, but no blood relative of his.

402 *Erclaes c Cluetincx en Erclaes* (9.i.59 to 28.ix.59), nos. 1410, 1428, 1436, 1456, 1537.
403 Disc. T&C no. 1046.

Nonetheless, he seems to have been the person who made the arrangements and saw to it that the annual payments were made until he died. Apparently, however, he had not paid the capital sum, because the aunt is held obligated to pay this as well.[404]

A widow's maternal uncle, a priest, and her son arranged for a dowry for her remarriage. If there was a capital sum involved, it was paid, but the stepfather had to sue the stepson for the annual payments, which were to last for the life of the stepfather, once the priest and the woman were both dead.[405]

Two cases brought against widows of the father of the endowed woman both suggest that the arrangement broke down with the death of the father. There may have been genuine issues as to whether the widow was obligated or as to how much she was obligated. In one case, the widow had paid to her daughter 9 bushels of rye of the 40 that the court found that she owed and had ordered her tenant not to pay an additional five sacks of rye, which, again, the court found that she owed.[406] The other case involves a dowry for an illegitimate daughter, amounting to half of the father's goods, the payment of which the father's widow, it would seem quite understandably, bitterly resisted.[407]

There are two miscellaneous office cases in our sample. One calls forth the strongest language that we find Platea using. He condemns Egied de Drivere, the *reus*, to make amends for the following offenses:[408]

> [I]t is clear that he entered the cloister or *béguinage* of the beguines of the town of Aalst, in the diocese of Cambrai, at night time, secretly and surreptitiously, with the purpose and intent of taking and abducting *jonkvrouw* Katherina vander Hulst, the widow of the late Laurens Kareelbacker, and he took away from the house, raped and abducted this Katherina, who was lying in her bed, resisting and objecting, thereby damnably breaking, disturbing, and rashly violating the cloister, which was established under the defense of the reverend father in Christ the lord bishop of Cambrai and as a liberty for the purpose of serving God on behalf of the beguines dwelling there and others coming there, and endowed and privileged by pontifical authority, and infringing on its liberty and franchise, and also the same *reus*, casting aside the fear of God, put the same woman who had been, as was said, taken away, raped and abducted, into a certain boat at nighttime and, according to his rash design, took her publicly to wife outside of the diocese of Cambrai in the town of Hever in the diocese of Liège, rejecting and omitting the solemnities required in contracting marriage, no banns, at least on his side, being proclaimed or dispensed, to say the least, rashly going against the laws, truly also against the synodal statutes that enjoin this sort of marriage, thereby incurring excommunication.

The sentence raises geographical problems that are best treated in the margin.[409] Suffice it to say here that a boat trip from Aalst to Hever would have

[404] *Bivoet c Bivoets* (n. 386).
[405] *Ossele c Venne* (n. 387).
[406] *Bock c Castro en Godesans* (n. 388). This case begins with the man suing his wife, but the judgment is against the mother-in-law alone.
[407] *Joebens c Motten* (9.ii.59 to 27.xi.59), nos. 1423, 1441, 1522, 1546, 1581.
[408] *Officie c Drivere* (16.v.55 to 10.vi.55), nos. 795 (T&C no. 1047), 801.
[409] Disc. T&C no. 1048.

probably taken more than one night to accomplish. That raises a more fundamental question that we have encountered in other cases of abduction. (Rape, in the modern sense, seems out of the question here; the sentence would certainly have mentioned sexual intercourse if that had happened.) There can be little doubt that Egied violated the cloister of the *béguinage* of Aalst. There can also be little doubt that his marriage to Katherina was irregular, though the phrase "no banns, at least on his side" suggests that banns may have been proclaimed on hers. It is striking, however, that the marriage is not dissolved, and that would suggest that however startled Katherina was when Egied appeared in her bedroom at the *béguinage*, she had voluntarily consented to marry him by the time she engaged in a public ceremony with him at Hever. That also makes it likely that Katherina was not a Beguine; she was just staying at the *béguinage*. Egied appeals this sentence to Rome, and he is granted *apostoli* and a three-month term within which to perfect his appeal. If he can obtain absolution for violating what may have been a papally sanctioned cloister (*pontificali auctoritate* being ambiguous), he may simply have to do penance or pay a fine (the option is specifically given) for a marriage no more irregular than many and considerably more regular than some.

The other miscellaneous *ex officio* sentence gives us a glimpse into a legal possibility that we not have otherwise seen. In June of 1453, Platea enters an order *ex officio* admitting Arnold Frederix, plaintiff in a case against Giselbert de Sprengher, "to verify the *fama* otherwise confessed before us on the side of [GS], the defendant." The motivation of the sentence is that "it pertains to the judge to examine carefully the merits of cases and to track down what is of truth and lest the truth of the process had before us be obscured and [in order] to prevent danger to souls." In December, the thrust of these platitudes becomes a bit clearer. At the instance of the promotor and by his own confession, Giselbert is condemned for double adultery with Quenegonde, Arnold's wife. A quittance, in which Giselbert is said to have "compounded" (*composuisse*) for adultery with the same woman, is said to do him no good, since the quittance said that at the time he was single but now is married.[410]

We will see in Chapter 10 that the Brussels court would order amends when adultery was shown in cases of separation. We have already seen that adultery is occasionally discovered (and ordered amended) in spousals litigation. We have, however, noted that straight prosecutions for adultery are quite rare in the Brussels register. This is the only one in the sample, and an examination of the entire register reveals that it is the only such prosecution of a layman.[411] We speculated earlier that routine cases of adultery were heard in lower-level courts within the Brussels jurisdiction.[412] This case suggests another possibility, that aggrieved husbands, at least occasionally, brought actions against adulterers and then settled with them without any sentence being entered in the register.

410 *Frederix c Sprengher* (22.vi.53), no. 506, T&C no. 1049; *Officie c Sprengher* (1.xii.53), no. 551.

411 Disc. T&C no. 1050.

412 See n. 411, disc. T&C no. 1051.

What made this case different was that Giselbert confessed to the *fama* of adultery, which, in turn, led Platea to admit Arnold to proof of the *fama*, which, in turn, led to a sentence appearing in the register. The promotor intervened, and Giselbert confessed, thinking that his quittance would save him from having to make amends. It did not, however, because the quittance referred to a single, not a double, adultery. Whether this means that Giselbert committed adultery with Quenegonde at least twice, once when he was single and once when he was married, as the wording of the sentence seems to suggest, or whether, in fact, the quittance was misworded, we cannot tell. Nor can we tell whether the quittance was for a settlement with Arnold or with the promotor. It would be odd, however, for a court that tended to impose amends for almost every possible offence revealed to allow a private settlement to preclude a prosecution, and so it seems more likely that the composition was with the promotor.

CONCLUSION

We began this long chapter asking a series of questions that were suggested by the statistical differences between the sentences at Brussels and those at Cambrai. Does the content of the sentences tell us anything about why there were so many more office spousals cases at Brussels and why there were so many more spousals cases involving sexual intercourse? On the basis of the statistics, we could not be sure that it was the conscious policy of the court to pursue such cases, though there were some indications that it was, such as the virtual absence at Brussels of cases involving sexual offenses alone, a category of case that seems to have been left to the lower ecclesiastical courts or to the secular courts. An examination of the sentences themselves, however, and the fact-patterns that they reveal suggest that it is highly likely that what we are looking at is a conscious policy, particularly of Platea. Both he and Rodolphi continued the practice that had begun at Cambrai of discouraging office cases of divorce from the bond by setting the standard of proof high. From the beginning of the register, there are virtually no cases of clerical sexual offenses, and the sexual offenses of lay people that are punished are those that are revealed in the course of other types of litigation. Separation cases, an occasional case of divorce from the bond, and cases about marital property are brought in the Brussels court, but they are brought by the parties, not by the promotors. The overwhelming focus of the prosecutorial effort at Brussels is on spousals cases, particularly spousals cases where potential presumptive marriages are at stake, and within that category, spousals cases where two potential presumptive marriages are at stake.

What the sentences, particularly those of Platea, reveal is that the concern with such cases was not misplaced. A large number of probably young women had been deflowered under circumstances where they now said that they expected marriage. In many cases they could not prove the promises, but the court had some sympathy with their plight, awarding them, in some instances, a dowry for deflowering, and in many instances giving them something, such as a share of the costs. After 1454, Platea rarely imposed the full range of *leges* that it was possible to impose on someone who alleged clandestine promises but failed to prove them. He did, however, become more and more concerned about frivolous allegations, and he may have considered changing the standard of proof in cases where clandestine promises were opposed to public ones.

With the advantage of hindsight, we may see that the policy of pursuing presumptive marriages in situations where at least initially, because of the promotor, the person who wanted to allege such a marriage did not have to pay the costs of pursuit, brought out of the woodwork not only a number of presumptive marriages, but perhaps even more women who had been deceived and women who imagined that they had been promised marriage. The policy may also have produced a reaction in three-party cases. Faced with the prospect of a challenge to their planned marriages, some couples may have deliberately consummated their espousals in order to raise the stakes and, in the situation where there was no intercourse following the first putative espousals, ensure that they would get married, despite the fines that they would have to pay for their behavior. In one Cambrai case not in the sample, this was clearly done in defiance of the women's parents; in another case, that was probably the situation.[413] In how many more cases this was the underlying situation we cannot tell.

Since the people who ended up in court were so obviously interacting with what the court was doing, it is difficult to draw conclusions about the social behavior of those who did not end up in court. We are certainly looking at a biased sample of fifteenth-century society in Cambrai diocese. The Brussels non-deflowering dowry cases and some of the Cambrai instance cases show us segments of society that we would not expect to have existed from the sordid tales of illicit intercourse and betrayal that we read about in the office and office/instance spousals cases. Some link between these two worlds is provided by the cases of dowry for deflowering, where the wronged woman is given some compensation that can, at least, be compared with that of the wealthier litigants' dowry in cases not involving deflowering, and which, if we can judge from the fact that relatively few cases of dowry for deflowering were contested, seems to have been conceded by many of the deflowerers.

Again, with all caution because of our dependence on the perceptions of four very different judges, it would seem that both Rodolphi and Platea, but particularly Platea, thought that the world at which he was looking was out of control when it came to marriage. Not only is there the sheer quantity of cases of illicit intercourse that one, or in some cases both, of the parties thought would lead to marriage, but there are also a strikingly large number of cases in the Brussels register where abduction, or 'mutual abduction' is mentioned. Platea and Rodolphi seem to have been the only judges of the four who fairly regularly imposed amends on women who went off and promised marriage

413 *Office c Gillaert et Meersche* (n. 103), T&C no. 1052; *Office c Vekemans, Scuermans et Brughman* (n. 103), T&C no. 1052.

or had sexual intercourse, or both, without the consent of their parents.[414] Now there are plenty of sexual offenses in the Cambrai registers, too; indeed, there are probably more of them because of the practice of the Cambrai court of pursuing certain more routine adultery and fornication cases. Of the four judges, Nicolaï is the one who indulges in the highest levels of rhetoric about sexual offenses, particularly about violations of what seem to us to be arcane rules about incest. With all of these qualifications, however, the world of the Cambrai registers is one in which marriage practices are more in control than they are in the world of the Brussels register. Whether the impression that one gets from the registers also reflects the reality is hard to know on this evidence, but it is possible that it did.

[414] Listed T&C no. 1053.

10

Divorce *a mensa et thoro* and *salvo iure thori* (Separation)

THE COURT OF YORK

We begin with a case that does not seem at first glance to be very promising.[1] All that survives are four membranes of depositions of six witnesses, who were examined in the consistory court of York, two of them on 21 February, two on 22 February, and two on 30 March 1349.[2] The roll is damaged, and some of the testimony has to be reconstructed. Fortunately, the testimony is quite consistent, and we can be reasonably confident that what is missing in one witness's testimony followed closely what is present in that of others.

The story that the witnesses tell is chilling. They testify that one Richard Scot of Newcastle upon Tyne boasted in various pubs[3] that he had committed adultery with at least three, probably six, and perhaps seven different named women and that he had children by at least three, probably four, and perhaps five of them,[4] which children he had supported and recognized[5] as his own. They also testify, somewhat confusedly, that Richard had been cited, perhaps more than once, before the official of the archdeacon of Northumberland in the church of St John in Newcastle where he had confessed his adulteries and was condemned to do penance. They further testify that on one occasion – though they are quite vague about the date – Richard had beaten his wife, Marjorie (Margery) Devoine, with a stick about her head and shoulders and had drawn blood. When a doctor came to tend to Marjorie, Richard told the doctor to get out of his house; otherwise, he said, he would break the doctor's

[1] Portions of the first section of this chapter were originally given as a paper at the International Congress of Medieval Canon Law, Syracuse, NY, 15 August 1996.

[2] Transcribed in App. e10.1 "*Richard Scot of Newcastle upon Tyne c Marjorie de Devoine of Newcastle upon Tyne* (1349)" (see T&C no. 1175), from CP.E.257. References below to "T1," "T2," etc. are to the different witnesses.

[3] See App. e10.1: T1 (*in diversis tabernis*), T2 (*infra tabernam Johannis de* [. . .]).

[4] Details T&C no. 1056.

[5] *aluit et agnovit* (T3–T6), *aluit et recognovit* (T1).

arms and legs.[6] One of the witnesses also testifies to another occasion on which Richard admitted in the presence of Marjorie and others both that he had beaten Marjorie and that he had committed adultery with the named women.[7] As a result of these events, the witnesses say, Marjorie left Richard. Indeed, one seems to testify that she is no longer his wife.[8] All the witnesses also testify, formulaically, that these things are either "notorious and manifest in the town of Newcastle"[9] or that there is *communis*, or *publica*, *fama* about them.[10]

We may approach this document in three different ways, each of which I will caricature, and each of which I will argue is incomplete and, because incomplete, false to the evidence that we have before us. The first approach is that of a traditional historian of legal doctrine. For such a person, the interest of this case lies in what it tells us about the grounds for separation from bed and board, *divortium a mensa et thoro*. The grounds for separation from bed and board remained quite debatable throughout the classical period of canon law.[11] Raymond of Peñafort's *Summa de matrimonio*, which may be taken as representing mainstream opinion even for the fourteenth century, lists only adultery, which Raymond calls fornication, as a cause for separation from bed and board.[12] Use of the word "fornication," the word used in the "except" clauses in the Vulgate edition of Matthew's Gospel,[13] rather than "adultery," allows Raymond to expand the grounds somewhat. The grounds include sodomy, committed, as the gloss attributed to John of Freiburg makes clear, either with the complaining spouse or another, and also spiritual fornication, heresy, or conversion to Judaism or paganism. Nowhere, however, does Raymond mention cruelty, even extreme physical cruelty, as a ground for an action of separation from bed and board.

He does, however, mention cruelty as a defense to the action for restoration of conjugal rights.[14] "A man seeking restoration," he says, "should not be restored [if] his cruelty is so great that adequate security cannot be provided to the fearful woman, or [if] he is pursuing his wife with capital hate."[15] While similar views on the topic can be derived from other canonists,[16] it has been supposed that it was not until Panormitanus, a full 75 years after our case, that a mainstream canonist held that cruelty was a sufficient ground for an action

[6] T2; T1, T3, T5, and T6 testify more vaguely to the threats to the doctor, whom T4 calls "Master John."
[7] T2.
[8] *tunc uxorem* (T2), implying that she is not now.
[9] T&C no. 1057.
[10] *fama communis* (T1, T2 [twice], T4 [twice], T5, T6 [thrice]), *publica vox et fama* (T1, T3, T4).
[11] See, generally, Esmein, *Mariage*, 2:106–13; Brundage, *Law, Sex*, 371–2, 455, 510–11.
[12] Raymond of Peñafort, *Summa de matrimonio* 4.22, pp. 574–5. For the work, see Ch 1, at n. 3.
[13] Mt 5:32, 19:9.
[14] Raymond of Peñafort, *Summa de matrimonio* 4.19, p. 568.
[15] *Id.*, citing X 2.13.8, X 2.13.13 *in fine*.
[16] Ref. T&C no. 1058.

of separation from bed and board, and that proposition did not become the *communis opinio* until the sixteenth century.[17]

This account of the doctrinal developments relies heavily on Adhémar Esmein, who refers to the canon *Si qua mulier* that Raymond of Peñafort placed in the *Decretals* (X 4.19.1). *Si qua mulier* was, Esmein implies, the source of the exception of cruelty in a case of restitution of conjugal rights and ultimately, for Panormitanus in the fifteenth century, the basis of an affirmative action of separation on the ground of cruelty. In his edition of Esmein in 1935, Jean Dauvillier pointed out that both Alexander III and Gregory IX had allowed separation in the situation where one spouse was threatening the life of the other, and that Bernard of Pavia and Innocent IV had both stated that separation could be granted on this ground, but that the doctrine was then suppressed between Innocent and Panormitanus.[18] Raymond in his *Summa*, however, relies not on *Si qua mulier* for the exception of cruelty but on two other texts, on one of which Panormitanus also relies for his statement that cruelty is the basis of an affirmative action for separation.[19] It seems unlikely that Panormitanus reinvented the affirmative action for separation on the ground of cruelty after it had been suppressed for 175 years. This suspicion is reinforced by the fact that discussion of *Si qua mulier* prior to Panormitanus hints, though it does not quite say, that an affirmative action might be available.[20] The story is almost certainly more complicated than the one that Esmein and Dauvillier tell. As we will see, we have evidence of an action for separation on the ground of cruelty in the court of York at the end of the fourteenth century, and as we have just seen, hints of it can be found in the canonists before Panormitanus. It is thus by no means clear that practice in separation cases was far ahead of the doctrine of the canonists. It may be more likely that what happened was a more subtle interplay between doctrine and practice.

In the light of this history, our case is a frustrating one for the doctrinal historian. Since Marjorie seems to have alleged both Richard's adultery and his cruelty, we cannot tell whether the latter would have been, by itself, a sufficient ground for separation. In short, we cannot tell whether the York court was anticipating by 75 years the doctrine that is thought to have been first announced by Panormitanus. We can, however, make use of the information that our doctrinal history has provided us to begin a probabilistic reconstruction of some of what is missing from our record. If we assume that the York court took the law as Raymond states it, then the underlying action in *Scot c Devoine* must have been an action for restoration of conjugal rights. Mainstream opinion regarded both cruelty and notorious adultery as defenses to an action for restoration, and mainstream opinion regarded adultery as a ground

[17] Esmein, *Mariage* 2:110–12.

[18] Lit. T&C no. 1059.

[19] See n. 15. Panormitanus, *Commentaria in* X 4.13.1, fol. 57ra, no. 4, cites X 2.13.13 but not X 2.13.8.

[20] Lit. T&C no. 1060.

for separation but did not so regard cruelty. Hence, if the mainstream was being followed, then what we are looking at is Marjorie's defense to an action for restoration (with the possibility that she may also have counterclaimed for separation). Since we lack the libel, we cannot be sure, and it is, of course, possible that the York court had anticipated the development ascribed to Panormitanus. Nonetheless, in the absence of firm evidence to the contrary, it is probably safer to assume that the York court was following mainstream opinion.[21]

A second approach to this material is that of an incautious social historian. For such a person this document is of some interest. What we have here is six ordinary medieval men testifying about the married life of an ordinary couple in the very north of England in the mid-fourteenth century. The story they tell is not pretty. We all know that patriarchal societies have a double standard when it comes to adultery. Here, Richard Scot committed adultery with at least three different women and boasted about it. If Marjorie had even been suspected of adultery, Richard would have killed her. In fact, he almost did, and that brings us to a second point: Patriarchal societies operate by the systematic oppression of women. One of the ways in which this is achieved is through wife beating. Not only did Richard Scot beat his wife but one of the witnesses also tells us that when he was charged with wife beating in the court of the archdeacon of Northumberland, he said that he had the right to beat his wife.[22]

This account of the incautious social historian's view of the case is even more obviously a caricature than is my account of the doctrinal historian's. (Perhaps that is because I am more sympathetic to doctrinal history than I am to incautious social history.) There are, however, serious problems with using our case as evidence for the propositions just advanced in the name of the incautious social historian. In the first place, if the witnesses are to be believed (and whether they are is an issue to which we will have to return), Richard Scot boasted of having committed adultery with at least three women and of fathering children by at least the same number of them. Richard's boast is, no doubt, an indication that his views about the shamefulness of adultery were quite different from those of St Raymond of Peñafort. But it really tells us little about whether Richard espoused a double standard. For all we are told here, he may have been a believer in free love. Richard's behavior with regard to Marjorie is more telling. Again, if the witnesses are to be believed, he beat her at least once, and he also claimed in court that he had a right to do this. We do not know, however, how the archdeacon's court reacted to this claim,[23] and we do know that he was punished for his admitted adulteries. To extrapolate from one case, even if we accept it as true, to a whole society is, I would suggest, unwarranted.

A third approach to this material is that of an institutional historian. For such a person there is much about this case that is puzzling. Newcastle upon

[21] Disc. T&C no. 1061.
[22] *dixit se licenciam habere verberandi uxorem suam* (T3).
[23] Disc. T&C no. 1062.

Tyne is in the diocese of Durham, not that of York, and the consistory court of York normally heard cases from the diocese of Durham only on appeal from the consistory court of the bishop of Durham. The witnesses tell us that there were proceedings in the court of the archdeacon of Northumberland, but these proceedings seem to have been *ex officio*, not the instance proceedings that would have given rise to this type of deposition, and no appeal is mentioned.[24] The absence of the surrounding records, of course, makes it possible that there was an appeal from the consistory of Durham that the witnesses do not mention, but it is also possible that in the disruption of the years of the Black Death, Marjorie and Richard were somehow able to bring their case directly to the court of York, avoiding both the lower courts that might have claimed first-instance jurisdiction.[25]

The institutional historian will also note two other features of this case. First, not only do we have no indication of proceedings in the lower court but we also lack the surrounding documents that are frequently found in these case files. We lack the libel or appeal, the exceptions that were usually taken to this initial document, the articles and interrogatories for Marjorie's witnesses.[26] We also lack any indication of Richard's side of the story.

Second, cases that raise issues of separation from bed and board are rare in the surviving records of the York consistory court. Of the 86 marriage cases among the cause papers that survive from the York consistory in the fourteenth century, only 1 is a separation action (if we assume that *Scott c Devoine* is a defense to a restitution action).[27] In 1395, Marjorie, wife of Thomas Nesfeld of York, sued her husband for separation *a mensa et thoro* on the ground of cruelty.[28] (This is the first clear indication that we have that one could sue for separation in the York court on the ground of cruelty alone.) The witnesses on both sides testified that Thomas beat Marjorie. Thomas's witnesses, on the other hand, justified his action on the ground that Marjorie had left his house without his permission. Thomas offered security for his good behavior in the future and received a favorable sentence from both the commissary general of the court and a special commissary to whom the official of the court had committed the case on appeal. The case was appealed once more, this time to the Apostolic See, but it seems unlikely that this appeal was ever pursued. In addition to this case and *Scot c Devoine*, there is one case in which a woman may have raised issues concerning separation in her defense to a restoration action by her husband. Again, the sentence went for the husband, and this time *apostoli* were denied for the attempted appeal to the papal court.[29] In a complicated case in which the basic action is one for divorce on the ground of precontract,

[24] Disc. T&C no. 1063.
[25] Disc. T&C no. 1064.
[26] Disc. T&C no. 1065.
[27] Disc. T&C no. 1066.
[28] Ch 4, at n. 262.
[29] *Hadilsay c Smalwod* (Ch 4, n. 260); lit. T&C no. 1067.

a woman defends on the ground of cruelty, successfully it would seem, against her husband's cross-petition for restoration *pendente lite*.[30] Issues of cruelty are raised in a petition for alimony and court costs in a three-party marriage-and-divorce case, and an action for restoration of conjugal rights probably had a cross-petition for separation on the ground of adultery, though this is not evidenced in the surviving cause papers.[31]

These cases are typical of English separation cases. There are very few of them, in comparison with marriage formation cases or even with divorce cases based on the invalidity of the marriage, and they are rarely successful. The English attitude toward separation is strict: You made your bed; now lie in it, with whomever you made it.[32] As a result, there are very few separation cases. The depositions in *Scot c Devoine*, then, indicate what a strong case the plaintiff must have in order to obtain a favorable sentence.[33]

If we combine the insights of the doctrinal historian, the social historian, and the institutional historian, we can get some more out of our tantalizing record. The institutional historian, perhaps with some help from the social historian, will tell us that we are looking at the depositions of witnesses on one side of a case, produced by a woman who hoped to win her case, and who had six men who were willing to come a long distance under trying circumstances to support her.[34] Her case was not an easy one to win. The court rarely granted separations and rarely allowed an action for restoration of conjugal rights to fail. Borrowing from the insights of the doctrinal historian, we know that in order to obtain a separation, Marjorie was, in all likelihood, going to have to prove that Richard had committed adultery; in order to defeat an action for restoration of conjugal rights, she was, in all likelihood, going to have to prove either adultery or extreme cruelty and that Richard's cruelty toward her was incorrigible. We do not know whether she succeeded, but we do know that the case was in a court about 70 miles from her hometown, under circumstances where local inquiry would have been difficult, and that the procedure employed seems to have been quite unusual.

Let us add to this an element on the social side. Marjorie was not poor. While the court of York heard at first instance some cases involving quite ordinary people, cases on appeal usually seem to have been brought by people of some substance. Totally apart from the question of court costs, the cost of travel and of the travel of witnesses[35] posed a considerable barrier to those of modest means trying to bring their cases more than a few miles from home. That Marjorie and Richard were people of some substance is indicated also by occasional hints in the witnesses' depositions. The beating is alleged to have occurred in

[30] *Huntyngton c Munkton* (Ch 4, at nn. 215–18).

[31] *Normanby c Fentrice and Broun* (Ch 4, at nn. 195–9); *Colvyle c Darell* (Ch 4, at n. 251).

[32] Helmholz, *Marriage Litigation*, 100–107.

[33] Helmholz, *ibid.*, offers a more qualified assessment. Pedersen, *Marriage Disputes*, 135–6, concurs with the judgment offered here.

[34] Disc. T&C no. 1068.

[35] T1, T3, T5 and T6 suggest that they are to receive *viatica* for their testimony.

Richard's hall (*aula*); one of his confessions is alleged to have occurred at the gate of his manse (*ad portam mansi*); Richard seems to have had no trouble coming up with the money to settle the claims of the mothers of his illegitimate children, and the witnesses are specifically asked if they are tenants (*tenentes*) of Marjorie.[36] All of these phrases could be formulaic or reflective of a reality not quite as grand as they sound, but taken together with the fact that Marjorie seems to operating quite comfortably miles from home, they suggest that she was not poor.

In these circumstances it is inconceivable that Marjorie did not get professional help in presenting her case to the court. (Here, again, the institutional comes to the fore.) Some advocate or proctor (or perhaps both) heard Marjorie's story and asked himself, "How can we convince this court to do something that it rarely does?" The answer, obviously, is that we have to show an extreme case. Does this mean, necessarily, that there never was an adultery (much less five), that there never was a beating (much less a doctor driven out of the house)? I do not think that we can go this far on this record. In other cases where the witnesses directly contradict each other, we may suspect outright lies.[37] Here, what we may have is a shading of the truth, a heightening of the story for dramatic purposes.

There is a stock figure in modern British popular culture known as a 'Geordie'. He comes from the north of England; he is macho and muscular, a great drinker and womanizer, violent, and stupid. The witnesses' description of Richard Scot fits the type perfectly, perhaps too perfectly. We have no record of any defense, and Scot may have been a person of some stature. (Of course, modern sociological research tells us that at least today neither adultery nor wife beating is confined to any one social class.)[38] What we do know is that somehow Marjorie managed to get her case to the court of York where her witnesses tell a compelling story of a wild man living in the north, a man whose very name suggests the alien and hated Scots. We have no idea whether Marjorie's strategy worked. We should, however, be cautious in accepting her witnesses at face value, and we should have no doubt that what we are looking at here is a strategy. The fact that Marjorie used such a strategy suggests, at least to me, much about the law and about social attitudes in the court of York in the mid-fourteenth century. Totally apart from whether anything like this ever happened to Marjorie, the fact that she chose to frame her case in these terms is evidence of what the York court thought was both legally and socially possible. Whether other courts were operating with the same law and the same attitudes one case, of course, will not tell us.

We may expand our English sample, though it is difficult to do so. There are, for example, no separation cases recorded in the eight years of litigation reported in the Ely act book. (There is one case of spousal abuse, but as we have

36 Ref. T&C no. 1069.
37 See Donahue, "Legal Historian," 21–32.
38 Lit. T&C no. 1070.

seen, that case does not raise issues of separation.)[39] There are three cases in the fifteenth-century York cause papers that raise issues of separation. They tell us a bit more but not much. In *Joan widow of John Ireby of Rounton c Robert Lonesdale of York*, Joan sued for divorce *a mensa et thoro* on the ground of cruelty.[40] Despite extensive testimony about physical violence, a sentence for the husband by the commissary general is affirmed by a special commissary of the official, with no reported result on a further appeal to the official. The depositions are quite detailed, and they recount stories of senseless acts of violence. A number of witnesses testify that Robert struck Joan with a burning torch a couple of months previously and damaged her eye and cheek, so much, according to one, that the skin of her cheek hung down. He did this, they say, because she served him dinner on a new pewter vessel because the servants had neglected to clean the old ones. When pressed, however, the witnesses say that they did not actually see Robert do this but heard about it from the servants, and some say that they saw the wound. A number of witnesses testify that Joan left Robert because he threatened to harm her if she did not bring back a dog that she had released from a chain. Once more, however, the testimony is hearsay. The only testimony about an event that a witness actually saw is that Robert hit Joan with a stick and "broke her head" when she presented him with a bill for her maintenance while she was unmarried. This testimony, however, is singular; no one else testifies to it.[41]

While one can see how under the prevailing rules of evidence a court might have found Joan's case unproven, one does have to wonder why this testimony did not provoke more sympathy for Joan. We should recall, however, that the result in this case is not to force Joan to live with Robert. He did not ask for restitution of conjugal rights, and it is not awarded. What Joan does not get is a judicial separation of goods, and this seems clearly to be a principal object of the suit because the articles seek, and the witnesses supply, extensive testimony about the value of the goods that she brought into the marriage (variously estimated at 40 pounds or 40 marks). These Robert has retained, at least at the time of the testimony. It is less clear what happened to her land (valued at 11 or 12 marks per annum). It is possible, though no one quite says so, that she has gotten that back by the time the case is over. If we recall the uncertainty of the law as to whether a separation should be granted on the ground of cruelty alone and the failure of Joan's witnesses to come up with firm proof of the cruelty, it is possible that the couple reached some financial settlement that allowed the court to leave on the record an unfavorable judgment about the basic suit. The possibility that something like this happened is enhanced by the fact that more than eight months pass between the final deposition and the rendering of the sentence.[42]

39 *Office c Fysshere* (Ch 4, at n. 247).

40 (1409–10), CP.F.371. This case was formerly misclassed in the sixteenth-century cause papers (CP.G.33).

41 Text and lit. T&C no. 1071.

42 It is also possible that John defended the case in the intervening period, but the sentence mentions no process other than what we have.

Cecily Wyvell of York fares better in her action against her husband, Henry Venables, donzel.[43] Cecily probably married Henry at a fairly young age. Some of her witnesses are only in their 20s, and Cecily's mother lived with the couple, at least at the beginning of their marriage, 13 years previously. She introduces five witnesses, who testify variously to Henry's adultery and cruelty.

Henry's defense to Cecily's libel puts their respective personalities into issue. She alleges that he was cruel and violent; he counters that he is "a respectable man, meek, sober, pious, affable, quiet, peaceful and humble."[44] Cecily's witnesses are at pains to counter this description. Henry, they say, is "severe, unruly and terrifying" while Cecily is "a decent woman, humble, and kindly," or Henry is "out of his mind and a madman," or Henry is "severe, a wild man, an adulterer, and terrifying," while Cecily is "a decent woman, humble, cautious, and kindly."[45]

When it comes to adultery and specific instances of the cruelty, the witnesses divide. Two of them, from Newcastle on Tyne, testify to Henry's adulterous relationship with a woman named Mabota, who lives in a place they call 'Westchester'.[46] Henry, they say, openly took Mabota as his concubine and said that "no bishop would separate them while he was alive." One witness testifies that Mabota has three children by Henry whom Henry has acknowledged as his.[47]

The York witnesses, though they know about the adulterous relationship, focus on Henry's cruelty to Cecily while they where living in their house in Jubbergate (where Cecily still lives). The story that they tell is, once more, chilling. Two witnesses report that 10 years earlier, Henry threw Cecily on the floor for no reason and struck her with his fist in the eye, so that the eye came out its socket and lay on her cheek. She would have lost the sight in the eye had not her mother put it back in its socket. They also report that he beat her with a stick called a 'warder'. One witness testified that Cecily was so crazed by fear on one these occasions that she would have jumped out of a high window into the Ouse had her mother and the servants not prevented her.[48]

Henry's defense to all of this is that the adultery was condoned and that the cruelty did not happen. Since he presents no evidence, it is not surprising that the judgment goes against him. It seems that he has not been living with Cecily for some time. Their last child (of three) was born seven years previously, and no one reports any encounter between them more recent than that. Although a number of witnesses report that Cecily feared to live with Henry, it does not seem that she was the one who moved out. That raises the question of why Henry bothered to defend the case at all.

Perhaps the dynamics of litigation can explain his behavior. Even if Henry was ready to terminate the relationship when Cecily filed her suit, he probably

[43] (1410), CP.F.56. See Ch 4, at nn. 118–20, for a case that may involve the same woman.
[44] T&C no. 1072.
[45] T&C no. 1073.
[46] Disc. T&C no. 1074.
[47] One of the York witnesses also testifies to this.
[48] T&C no. 1075.

would not have wanted to concede all that she charged if admitting it would affect his reputation and perhaps the financial settlement that he would have to give her. Faced with the charges, he hires a proctor and says "contest the case." The rest is up to the proctor, who answers Cecily's libel virtually word for word. The object is to include every possible defense that might emerge in the testimony. Once the plaintiff's testimony is in, then Henry has another decision to make. The testimony is devastating. Can he produce plausible witnesses to a plausible defense? It will cost him money to do so. Maybe now it is just better to let the judgment go against him. His proctor and/or advocate will tell him what kind of standard he has to meet if he is going to have even a chance of winning. They may even ask him "Are you sure, Harry, that you want this woman back?"

Whether any of this happened in quite the way that the witnesses said it did is more difficult to determine. The picture the witnesses draw of Henry is remarkably like that which Marjorie Devoine's witnesses draw of Richard Scot. There is a similarity in Henry's boasting about his mistress, about the fact that the adultery takes place far to the north, in the gruesome details about the physical violence. The story of the eye, which is particularly hard to believe (not that it could not have happened but that Cecily did not lose the sight of the eye as result of the injury), may even, as a recent commentator has pointed out, be suggested by the legend of St Lucy.[49]

The record in *Agnes Benson of York c Peter Benson of the same*, like that in *Scot c Devoine*, is deficient.[50] Hence, we do not know whether the positions and articles and the depositions that we have are from Agnes's case for divorce *a mensa et thoro* or from her defense to an action of restitution. The witnesses, a husband and wife, testify to the Bensons' marriage six years previously and then to an event that took place in the witnesses' house about a year later. As they were sitting down to dinner, Peter Benson told Agnes's son by a previous marriage to get away from the table. Agnes protested: "It is not fitting for you to make a fuss about where he is standing because you have given him little or nothing."[51] At this point, Peter drew a knife and would have killed or grievously wounded Agnes had not the host and his daughter prevented him. Agnes did not return to the house where she and Peter were living and has feared to do so ever since.

The two witnesses provide different details (the second witness describes Peter's angry words on more than one occasion, including an outburst in which he calls Agnes a "false whore"), but their basic testimony is consistent. It also seems more credible than some of the testimony that we have been seeing in separation cases. Whether this means that the York court by the middle of the fifteenth century was prepared to grant a separation on the basis of one instance of aggravated cruelty is hard to tell. We have no sentence in the case.

[49] Lit. T&C no. 1076.

[50] (1448), CP.F.235.

[51] T&C no. 1077.

Once in 1390 and once in 1409, women had brought separation actions on the grounds of cruelty alone without alleging adultery. That suggests that the court had passed the barrier of insisting that an affirmative action of separation had to be based, at least in part, on adultery. But both of these women ultimately lost their cases. What this case tells us is that by 1448, at least as a defense to a restitution action, the professionals of the court were not telling people that they had no chance of succeeding unless they presented extreme, and probably exaggerated, evidence of cruelty.[52]

The cause papers do not quite exhaust what we know about how the York consistory court treated separation actions.[53] The fragmentary act books of the court from the 1370s reveal a few actions that either resulted in separation or might have resulted in separation.[54] None of these actions is likely to have produced cause papers, and so the absence of such actions from any of the surviving cause papers is to be expected. Because the evidence of these entries is difficult to interpret, we must examine a few of them:

The entry in the case of *Robert de Moreby spurrier and Constance his wife*, reads in its entirety:[55]

> Again, on the same day [20 February 1371], there appeared before the lord official Robert de Moreby, spurrier, and Constance his wife on account of the various disagreements and discords that had arisen between them and on account of the danger of death of Constance [inferred from] the threats of death often made by Robert to Constance. The official, with the consent of Robert, granted them license to live apart, and Robert swore on the holy gospels of God that he would thereafter do no bodily harm to his said wife nor have it done, and concerning their common goods they put themselves on the judgment and arbitration of Sir William de Chester and William Grene, mercer of York.

This is a consensual separation of the kind that, as we shall see shortly, we find in the French ecclesiastical courts, including a separation of goods, which is committed to arbiters. The fact that this record is totally routine suggests that such cases were not unusual in the York consistory in the 1370s. Since this is a consensual separation, we cannot be sure that there was spousal abuse. If you wanted to get a separation and this is what you had to say, this is what you said. What lies behind this we can only guess on the basis of the record. The couple may already have been living apart and were cited for it by the dean of Christianity of York, but the fact that they have enough wealth that they need to have arbiters separate their goods suggests that in their case, just moving out of the house was not sufficient. There is no evidence that the consistory court proceeded against them *ex officio* (either for living apart or for marital discord, both of which could result in *ex offico* citations). Rather, this is a case of noncontentious jurisdiction, what the French call *juridiction gracieuse*. The

[52] Lit. T&C no. 1078.
[53] Another possible example T&C no. 1079.
[54] Lit. T&C no. 1080.
[55] (1371), M2(1)b, fol. 2r, T&C no. 1081.

York official seems to have exercised a fairly wide noncontentious jurisdiction, including allowing his court to serve as a registry of recognizances of ordinary contracts.

The case of *Joan daughter of William Matheuson and Robert de Potterflete*[56] is less clear because the final disposition is missing and the interim ruling is hard to make out:

Again on 18 March [1374], there appeared before the lord official sitting as for tribunal Joan daughter of William Matheuson and Robert de Potterflete, and Joan proposed orally that Robert took her as wife and conceived five children by her, but she, having been sworn, alleged that for fear of death she did not dare cohabit with him. She (?they) took the oath of calumny, etc. They were given the next Tuesday *to learn how the official would treat them about this.*[57] Again, Robert confessed that since Lent last past he had carnally known Elena de la Chaumbre.

Although the language has more suggestions of a contentious matter, this case is probably also proceeding consensually. Clearly the official is not going to rule on the spot just because Joan says she fears for her life. He makes her swear, and then he makes her, perhaps both of them, take the oath of calumny. Perhaps the official was concerned about the children, though there is little other evidence of such concern in other separation cases. The fact that Robert's confession of adultery comes at the end of the entry suggests that he, too, was trying to get the separation. Perhaps he was more willing to confess this ground than that Joan had reason to fear for her life.

The range of possible rulings that the court could make was wide. *John de Kellinglay and Cecily his wife* is typical of one possibility:[58]

Oath of John Kellinglay about treating his wife: Again, on the same day [31 October 1374], there appeared personally before the commissary general of the lord official of the court of York sitting as for tribunal John Kellinglay and Cecily his wife, which John swore on the holy gospels of God, which he touched physically, that from that day forward [he would treat] Cecily his wife decently and honestly in bed and board and in all other matters concerning the conjugal pact, and that he would not beat or strike her in an aggravated fashion[59] with any instrument nor with his hand or foot nor beat her in an unseemly fashion or chastise in great matters or small under pain of 12 whippings around the market of Pontefract and under pain of going on two Sundays before the procession of the cathedral church of St Peter of York in the penitential mode with a candle of one pound of wax in his hand if it should happen that he should fail in these requirements or in any one of them. Subsequently, moreover, Cecily similarly took an oath that she from that day forward would obey John her husband and submit [to him] humbly as she is bound, subject to the penalty.

[56] (1374), M2(1)c, fol 15r, T&C no. 1082.

[57] Italicized text is conjectural.

[58] (1374), M2(1)c, fol. 21r, T&C no. 1083.

[59] *atrociter* probably derived from the Roman-law concept of *atrox iniuria*.

The record does not say that John was charged with *atrox iniuria*, though we can hardly imagine that some such charge did not precede this. There is no reference to the couple having been cited to appear before the commissary general or his official. It is possible that there was no office proceeding prior to this, and that the rector of Pontefract sent them to York and told them to do this. It is even possible that the case began as a separation action and the commissary general talked them into doing this. One can certainly imagine a wrangle before the judge (or before the rector) in which she said "he beat me," and he said "she was insubordinate and needed correcting," and the authority figure said: "Both of you swear not to do it, and we won't try to sort out who was at fault previously." So far as we can tell, neither of them has to do any penance for past behavior, though that may have been handled locally. In short, what lies behind this case is probably similar to what lay behind the *Nesfield* case, except that the parties in this case seem to have been willing to accept the court's solution without first going through the expense of introducing proof in a separation action.

The case of *Richard ?Macloyne and Alice his wife* shows us a possible intermediate solution, between granting a separation and forcing the couple to return to marital life subject to a security for future behavior. The couple had taken oaths similar to those taken by John and Cecily Kellinglay, but the entry continues:[60]

> And Richard and Alice unanimously consented to live separately and apart, and they immediately asked the lord official [to grant them] this. But the lord official said expressly that he did not want to grant them license to live apart but he would well allow [it] for a time until peace and concord might better be restored between them.

These cases afford a glimpse into what has been called the court's role "as a rather heavy-handed marriage counselor."[61] There are other examples, principally from lower-level ecclesiastical courts.[62] There was almost certainly more of it, both because the survival rate of records from lower-level ecclesiastical courts has not been good and because the line here between what gets worked out in court and what gets worked out in other settings, such as neighborly or pastoral counseling, is quite porous. Granted, however, that spousal abuse seems to be a widespread phenomenon and marriages that end up in discord a virtually universal phenomenon, it is surprising that we do not see more records of English church courts dealing with it. It is, for example, unclear that the court of York continued to play the role in cases of marital disharmony that it seems to have been playing in the 1370s. There is one case of consensual separation and property division, with an accompanying appointment of arbitrators, in

[60] (11.xii.1374), M2(1)c, fol. 22v, T&C no 1084.
[61] Lit. T&C no. 1085.
[62] *Ibid.*

the act book for 1420.[63] A recent, careful survey of the fifteenth-century act books has failed to disclose any others, and this despite the fact that the act books continue to reflect other types of noncontentious jurisdiction, such as recording recognizances.[64] If such cases exist in these books they are certainly not common.

SEPARATION AT PARIS, CAMBRAI, AND BRUSSELS

The situation on the Continent was quite different, or perhaps it would be better to say that the situtation was quite different in the 'Franco-Belgian region',[65] the area of northern France and modern Belgium that we have studied.

Paris

As we have seen, between November of 1384 and September of 1387, the Paris consistory court heard 102 separation cases, 25 percent of the total (410) number of marriage cases. These separation cases are further subdivided into 15 (15%) cases of separation *a thoro*, 72 (71%) cases of separation of goods, and 15 (15%) where the type of separation cannot be determined.[66] In addition, there were 5 criminal actions of adultery, 1 of which also involved a separation (and all of which could have), 8 criminal cases of wife beating, 3 of which also involved separations (and all of which could have), and 1 criminal case in which a man was ordered to take back his wife (an informal separation that in this case does not seem to have succeeded).[67]

Gender ratios are difficult to calculate in instance separation cases because in a number of them, there does not seem to be much of a contest.[68] Taking all the evidence that we have of who was the moving party (including who ultimately paid the fee), it would seem that men brought more actions for separation *a thoro* than did women (8/13 cases in which the gender of the plaintiff can be determined, 62%), and women dominated in the cases where separation of goods was sought (59/64 cases in which the gender of the plaintiff can be determined, 84%).

Not only were a number of separation cases heard; a number of separations were granted. Of the 72 plaintiffs who sought separation of goods, 46 (64%) obtained it, and separation of goods was granted in 3 of the criminal cases of wife beating. Of the 15 plaintiffs who sought separation *a thoro*, 5 (33%) were granted it (sometimes with separation of goods), and separation *a thoro* was

[63] *Wilkynson and Wilkynson* (1420), Cons.AB 1, fols. 177r–177v, quoted in Helmholz, *Marriage Litigation*, 103 at n. 106.

[64] Personal communication from Prof. David Smith.

[65] For this phrase, see Ch 12, n. 1.

[66] See Table 7.3. As in Ch 7, references are to *Registre de Paris*, with an additional number indicating the position of the entry on the column.

[67] Further possible examples T&C no. 1086.

[68] See at nn. 114–19.

granted in 1 of the criminal cases of adultery. One more plaintiff was probably successful in an action for separation *a thoro*, and one more may have been. A separation, probably *a thoro*, was probably granted in one of the actions of uncertain type, and in another a separation of uncertain type was probably granted.

Both the difference in the success rates in the two types of separation cases and the difference in the proportion of the two types of cases are statistically significant, and both differences point in the same direction.[69] Separation *a thoro* was much harder to get than separation of goods. In marked contrast to other types of cases, the sentences in separation cases and the motivations for them are normally given.[70] The sentences make it quite clear why it was easier to get a separation of goods than it was to get a separation *a thoro*. As we shall see, separations of goods could be granted for a broad range of reasons, while the party seeking to obtain a separation *a thoro* had to prove that the defendant had committed adultery. Two cases suggest that the defendant could answer this charge with a defense of *in pari delicto* (i.e., that the plaintiff had also committed adultery).[71] No case says that a condonation defense was available, but it may have been.[72]

The difference between a separation *a thoro* and a separation of goods was that in the latter, the obligation to render the conjugal debt remained, at least in theory. This feature is expressed in a phrase that occurs in about half the sentences of separation of goods (22/46), *salvo iure thori*. We may doubt whether this legal difference made a practical difference in most cases. Couples who obtained a separation of goods because of the cruelty, usually of the man, clearly did not have an obligation of co-residence, and the relaxation of this obligation probably applied to couples who had obtained such a separation for other reasons as well. The legal difference, however, may have made a practical difference in some cases. Jeanne Ferrebouc, who had already obtained a separation of goods from her husband Jean, litigated for more than two years by long-form procedure in order to obtain a separation *a thoro*. As with all long-form cases, no sentence survives, but she probably obtained her separation *a thoro*.[73]

We have seen that there was some doubt in the writings of the academic lawyers whether a separation could be granted for cruelty when there was no evidence of adultery.[74] The Paris court seems to have resolved this doubt by granting a separation in such situations, but only a separation of goods, *salvo iure thori*. So far as I have been able to determine, this type of separation is not discussed in the academic writers, but because it was not discussed there was no

[69] Success rate: $z = 2.31$, significant at .98; types of case: $z = 9.79$, significant beyond .99.

[70] For the one case where it is not given, see at n. 99.

[71] Ref. and disc. T&C no. 1087.

[72] It was available as a matter of the common law of the church. Tancred, *Summa de matrimonio* 33, p. 89, citing C.32 q.1 cc. 1–3; C.9.9.11.

[73] Disc. T&C no. 1088.

[74] See at nn. 11–20.

statement that it was unavailable. A court that granted such a separation would not have the support of the academic writers, but it would not be going contrary to what they said either.[75] Whether the development of this type of separation (which was quite widespread in the northern French courts) ultimately led to the acceptance by the academic writers of separations on grounds other than adultery we cannot, in the present state of our knowledge, tell. It is certainly possible, however, that it did.

Separations of goods were, moreover, available from the Paris court for reasons other than cruelty. The sentence of 13 March 1385, separating Jeanne and Pierre Auberti, is typical: "Today they were separated so far as goods are concerned, saving the right of bed, and this because of the mismanagement (*malum regimen*) of the husband and dissipation of goods and the cruelty of the husband, etc., and each of them is content concerning the goods that are common between them."[76] The sentence is typical, but it is not a formula. Each separation sentence is somewhat different, giving us some confidence that it has been designed to fit the facts of the case. Sometimes the emphasis is on the inability of the parties to live together in peace: "They were separated so far as goods are concerned on account of the enmity, discord, rancor, and hate that has arisen between them, lest worse arise out of it, and this with the consent of the couple."[77] Sometimes the emphasis is on the inability of the man to manage the community property: "We separated [them] because of the mismanagement of the man, etc., and because he incurred many obligations to many people without his wife's knowledge and to her disadvantage."[78] Whatever the cause of the separation, community property is frequently mentioned. The parties may consent to a division of the community that has already taken place. (This seems to have been the situation in the *Auberti* case, quoted earlier.)[79] Or the parties may be sworn to make a division themselves: "They swore to make a good division."[80] Or a commissary may be given to make the division for them.[81]

The pattern of grounds for granting a separation of goods that we just outlined on the basis of sentences from the early months of 1385 maintains itself throughout the remainder of the register. Seventeen of the sentences of separation of goods mention cruelty (*sevitia* or *sevitia et austeritas*) of the man as a motivation for the sentence. To these probably should be added the three cases that mention "harshness" (*austeritas*) without adding cruelty, though harshness may be less strong.[82] Seven of these sentences also mention mismanagement of

[75] Disc. T&C no. 1089.
[76] (13.iii.85), col. 76/3, T&C no. 1090.
[77] *Beurgny c Beurgny* (31.iii.85), col. 91/1, T&C no. 1091, with another example.
[78] *Gontier c Gontier* (20.iii.85), col. 82/3, T&C no. 1092, with another example.
[79] Cf. *Perrieres c Perrieres* (n. 78), T&C no. 1093.
[80] *Thiphaine c Thiphaine* (n. 77), T&C no. 1094.
[81] E.g., *Puteo c Puteo* (21.ii.85), col. 61/5.
[82] Examples T&C no. 1095.

property (*dissipatio bonorum, malum regimen*).[83] To these probably should be added the unique case that mentions harshness without cruelty and adds "foolishness" (*fatuitias*),[84] and the two cases that mention harshness without cruelty and add more standard language of mismanagement (*malum regimen et dissipatio bonorum*).[85]

Nine of the sentences of separation of goods mention mismanagement of property without mentioning cruelty or harshness. All of these mention *malum regimen*; four add *dissipatio bonorum*, and one adds a specific charge of mismanagement.[86] Two of the 'pure' cases of *malum regimen* specify that as a result of the sentence, neither spouse will be liable on the contracts of the other, a result that presumably followed in all such cases; hence, mention of it may indicate that the husband's incurrence of inappropriate obligations was the ground of the mismanagement charge.[87]

Nineteen of the sentences are grounded on the inability of the parties to live together in peace. The standard words for this are "enmities, rancors, and hatreds" (*inimicite, rancores, et odia*), either singly or in combination. Two of the sentences couple one or more of these words with cruelty (*sevitia*), one adds "discords" (*discordie*) to the combination, and one adds "beatings" (*verberationes*).[88]

Some light is cast on what is involved in these cases by the inhibitions and injunctions that sometimes accompany them. Such orders are found in 24 of the 72 separation cases (33%). They can appear at the beginning of the case, with the sentence of separation, or after the sentence of separation. In 13 of the cases in which they appear there is no sentence of separation, and in a number of such cases it is clear that the inhibition was intended to substitute for a sentence of separation. The inhibitions are of two general types: (1) that the husband is not to beat (or ill-treat) the wife "beyond the conjugal manner" (*ultra modum coniugalem*) and (2) that the husband is not to dissipate or sell or remove the community property. A penal sum, normally of 20 or 40 *livres*, and a threat of excommunication are usually attached to the first of these but not to the second.

Four of the sentences motivated by the mutual hatred of the couple contain inhibitions of type one.[89] Although we cannot exclude the possibility that such inhibitions were present in other such cases and the clerk failed to note them, the fact that these inhibitions are relatively unusual suggests that in these cases, there may have been particular reason to fear that the man would seek out his separated wife and do physical harm to her. That this is so is also suggested by

[83] Examples and disc. T&C no. 1096.
[84] *Kerautret c Kerautret* (n. 82).
[85] *Messaiger c Messaiger and Bruneau c Bruneau* (n. 82).
[86] Examples and disc. T&C no. 1097.
[87] *Perrieres c Perrieres* (n. 78); *Chardon c Chardon* (5.xii.85), col. 231/2.
[88] Examples T&C no. 1098.
[89] Examples and disc. T&C no. 1099.

the fact that one of these cases is the only one that adds *verberationes* to the standard formulae of *odia et rancores*.[90]

In six of the cases in which a sentence motivated by the cruelty of the husband is granted, there is also an inhibition of type one. In five of the cases the inhibition is given at a preliminary stage of the proceedings; in one it is contained in the sentence of separation in what may have been a one-session case.[91] That this case was one in which there was particular reason to fear that the man would seek out his separated wife and do physical harm to her is suggested by the fact that four of the cases that have preliminary inhibitions of type one do not repeat the inhibition in the sentence, but one does.[92] Presumably in the other cases, there were reasons for believing that the wife might be in danger of a beating while she was still living with her husband but not after she had been separated from him.

The wording of inhibitions of type one tends to be quite formulaic, but they are frequently combined with inhibitions of type two that are far less formulaic, and hence give us some confidence that they have been crafted to fit what the judge perceives to be the situation of the parties. In one case, for example, the judge adds to a type one inhibition an inhibition against the man that he not alienate any of the community property and against the woman that she "not say injurious words to the man or provoke him to anger."[93] In another such case, the husband is ordered not to dissipate the community property and is warned that if he does so there will be a separation of goods granted, and the wife is ordered "under similar penalties" (?both the monetary penalty attached to the type one inhibition and the threat of separation) that she obey her husband.[94]

Only one case that has an inhibition of any sort and that results in a sentence of separation has no inhibition of type one. In May of 1386, Jeanette Chevrier was ordered, on penalty of excommunication, to obey her husband and render him the conjugal debt in a safe place. The reason for this unusual order with its unusual wording is clear enough from the description of Simon Chevrier; he was a leper.[95] One of the advocates of the court is to report back to the court on his findings about the charge of cruelty that Jeanette made against Simon with a view to obtaining a separation of goods. The case was heard four more times, an indication that the court was having difficulties with it. In one entry, the court sets a date for the parties to hear its determination whether they could be separated in goods because of the leprosy, and both the man and woman are ordered not to withdraw or dissipate the community property. But when the separation is finally ordered, it is not ordered on the ground of the leprosy

[90] *Boudart c Boudart* (n. 88).
[91] *Barrote c Clerici* (n. 71); for the five others see n. 92.
[92] Listed T&C no. 1100.
[93] *Pastour c Pastour* (n. 92), T&C no. 1101.
[94] *Messaiger c Messaiger* (n. 67), T&C no. 1102.
[95] *Chevrier c Chevrier morbo lepre infectum* (7–28.v.86), refs. in TCas.

but on that of the man's cruelty, and the case is set down for another day for the man to swear (about what it does not say) and for the choosing of a safe place where the couple can cohabit for purpose of rendering the debt.[96] In the final entry nothing is said about the safe place. The man swears to make a good division for the woman, and the case is set down for making the division and for providing for the children. Although the case was supposed to return, it did not. A commissary was given to make the division, and he may have succeeded in having the parties do it without the necessity of returning to the court.

The problem of what to do when one of two spouses becomes leprous was not new in the fourteenth century. Two decretals of Alexander III, both of which were placed in the *Liber extra*, dealt with the problem. In the first, Alexander holds that the archbishop of Canterbury and his suffragans should urge, "with careful exhortations (*sollicitis exhortationibus*)," husbands to follow their leprous wives and wives to follow their leprous husbands into exclusion and minister to them with conjugal affection.[97] If they cannot be persuaded to do this, they should be enjoined to keep continent and excommunicated if they do not. Another decretal to an uncertain bishop, but probably of a considerably earlier date, repeats the injunction that leprosy is not a ground for separation, emphasizes that lepers have the right to marry, and insists that the healthy spouse render the debt to the leprous one.[98] If we have the chronological order of these decretals right, we may suggest that Alexander came to realize the pastoral impracticability of his earlier position. But both decretals were *lex vigens*, so far as the court of Paris was concerned, and the question was how they affected the relatively new institution of separation of goods.

The court had, in fact, dealt with another case of a leprous spouse just a month before the *Chevrier* case.[99] In the first entry in the case, Pierre and Marie Abbatisvilla are granted a separation of goods. No motivation is stated, and nothing in the entry indicates what the problem is. This is the only separation in the entire act book for which the motivation is not stated. The following week, tutors (including the husband) are assigned to the couple's children, and here the wife is expressly said to be infected with leprosy.

It would seem that the difference between *Chevrier* and *Abbatisvilla* is that the former case was contested and the latter was not. If Pierre and Marie could agree, they would be quietly separated and no motivation stated. Only the routine granting of tutors allows us to determine their tragic situation. Simon Chevrier contested the separation. The court considered granting it on the ground of leprosy, but ultimately decided that it had enough to hold, perhaps with a bit of a stretch, that he had been guilty of cruelty. The formal order insisted that Jeanette render him the debt "in a safe place." Ultimately, however, so far as the record allows us to tell, no safe place was chosen.

[96] *Id.*, col. 310/5, T&C no. 1103.
[97] X 4.8.1.
[98] X 4.8.2.
[99] *Abbatisvilla et Abbatisvilla* (6.iv.86, 13.iv.86), col. 288/5, 292/3.

One other inhibition case does not have an inhibition of type one. It is a case where the husband swears and promises to treat his wife "amicably, as a husband ought to treat his wife, and the wife swears to obey him." The cryptic entry then suggests that the same was enjoined on them under penalty of excommunication.[100] There is no sentence of separation in this case, and it seems clear that this agreement, probably fostered by the court, was a substitute for such a sentence. That seems even clearer in the sole entry in another case:[101] "[JB] and [JB] appearing promised under penalty of excommunication and 40 *livres*, viz., the man not to beat or maltreat his wife beyond the conjugal manner and the wife to obey the same her husband under the same penalty. And the man willed and consented that if he should beat the same his wife beyond this manner, they would be separated, etc." A similar final inhibition focuses more on the property aspects of the couple's relationship:[102]

> In a case of separation the plaintiff [wife] proposed cruelty and 'dilapidation' of goods, etc., and the defendant countered with the harshness and disobedience of the woman, etc. At length the man was inhibited that he not beat his wife under penalty of excommunication and 100 *livres* or mistreat her, and that he not dissipate the common goods between them or incur obligations himself to the prejudice of the wife, and that he bring back to the community anything that had been taken out by him, etc., and that he swear that he would do so. And the woman vice versa, and it was enjoined on the same woman under similar penalty that she obey her husband, etc.

Notice both the size of the penal sum and the fact that a woman can be accused of "harshness" but apparently not of cruelty.

In another case, a similar injunction was issued (including the large penal sum), but this was not the end of the case. Eight months later the couple obtained a separation on the ground of the husband's cruelty.[103] It certainly looks as if the couple attempted a reconciliation, perhaps under court pressure, but that it did not succeed. There are two other cases where the inhibition was clearly intended to be the end of the case and, so far as we can tell, was. In one it is ordered:[104] "Concerning [CS], plaintiff in a case of separation, against [GS] today the parties were inhibited, the husband under penalty of excommunication and 100 marks of silver that he not beat or ill-treat his said wife without warrant (*indebite*) nor dissipate or alienate the common goods between them, and the woman was similarly inhibited that she not alienate or carry off any of the common goods between them, and she was enjoined to obey her said husband, thus they departed *sine die*." In the other, a clerk is ordered to treat his wife with marital affection and in the conjugal manner and not to beat her "cruelly or enormously."[105]

100 *Pontancier c Pontancier* (24.xii.86), col. 406/5, T&C no. 1104.
101 *Borde c Borde* (7.xii.85), col. 232/4, T&C no. 1105.
102 *Trubert c Trubert* (11.v.86), col. 304/4, T&C no. 1106.
103 Details T&C no. 1107.
104 *Senescalli c Senescalli* (11.x.86), col. 376/7, T&C no. 1108.
105 *Potelier c Potelier* (14.xii.85), col. 235/6, T&C no. 1109.

In other cases, it is more difficult to tell whether the inhibition was intended to be the final order, but so far as I can determine, it was the final order. In three cases an order is sent to an advocate of the court to come back with an "information" on the charges and countercharges of the couple (sometimes a day is set for this to happen), and the court issues an interim inhibition, always including one of type one and sometimes including other elements as well, and that is the last that we hear of the case.[106] Two of these cases involve petitions for restitution by the man, and in one of them the petition is granted and the order of type one is given before the charges and countercharges are heard.[107] In two other cases restitution is ordered, in one without any grounds for separation being stated and in the other both before and after they have been stated.[108] Another case, at the libel stage, ends with an order that the husband take back his wife and not beat her.[109] Two other cases have inhibitions that may have been sufficient to persuade the parties not to come back.[110] There is not much indication that the Paris court was following the doctrines prescribed in Tancred about possessory, as opposed to petitory, actions, but these cases provide some indication that it was.

We have already seen that the granting of a separation *a thoro* was by no means automatic. What the cases just discussed show is that it was not automatic in separations of goods either. It certainly looks as if in some cases the court either persuaded the parties to attempt to reconcile or insisted that they so attempt. Contested cases, as we have seen, produced commissions to court officers "to return an information to be made."[111] When a judgment of separation says that the judge was "sufficiently informed," he is probably referring to this procedure, even though there is no entry that records the referral.[112] Even where the sentence seems to have been granted simply on the statements of the parties, the sentence will often add that the matter "was established for us."[113] This must mean, at a minimum, that the court believed the statements of the parties.

The fact remains, however, that almost two-thirds of the parties who sought a separation of goods got it. This was particularly true where the nominal defendant did not contest the case. Indeed, in some cases, it is difficult to tell who is the plaintiff and who the defendant, a characteristic most notable in the cases where the ground of the sentence is that the parties are quarreling.[114] Six cases mention that the separation is given with the consent of or by the will of

[106] Examples T&C no. 1110.
[107] *Cuillere c Cuillere* (n. 106); *Sampson c Sampson* (n. 106) (petition granted).
[108] Listed T&C no. 1111.
[109] *Rogerii c Rogerii* (10.x.86), col. 370/2, T&C no. 1112.
[110] Listed T&C no. 1113.
[111] Examples T&C no. 1114.
[112] *Sufficienter informati*: examples T&C no. 1115.
[113] Examples T&C no. 1116.
[114] Examples T&C no. 1117.

the parties.[115] At least in some cases, it would seem that if the man was willing to admit his wife's charges, a decree of separation of goods would be granted by consent.[116] Whether the late medieval northern French courts were granting separations of goods on the basis of consent is controverted in the literature.[117] We will return to the issue after looking at the Cambrai separation cases. For now, we might note that after mentioning consent (and nothing else) several times in judgments in 1385, the Paris official seems to have backed away from that proposition and to have insisted on saying that he had some proof of the grounds for separation other than the consent of the parties.[118] It seems clear that consent alone was not a sufficient ground. The issue was how the acceptable grounds were to be proved. One may legitimately doubt, however, how far the Paris court was, as a practical matter, from separation of goods by mutual consent.[119]

Cambrai and Brussels

Our sample of Cambrai straight marriage instance cases revealed 34 cases of separation, approximately one-quarter (27%) of the marriage instance cases. Applying this proportion to the total number of sentences, we estimate that they represent about 5 percent of the sentences.[120] All but one of the sentences are definitive, and in all the definitive sentences a separation is granted.[121]

In addition to these cases there are 14 cases in our sample of marriage cases in which a couple is charged *ex officio* with unauthorized separation. In all but two of them, one or both are also charged with adultery. In all of these cases the couple are fined, but in 12 of them they also obtain a separation. To these should be added the one instance case of separation for adultery that has strong office elements, and in which a separation was ultimately granted. These 15 office cases represent an estimated 6 percent of the marriage cases, or slightly more than 4 percent of the total number of sentences.[122]

The nature of the Cambrai records does not allow us to see cases that were brought but were abandoned short of a sentence of some sort, but granted the plaintiffs' success rate, it seems highly unlikely that there were many such cases.[123] Nor do we find, as we do at Paris, inhibitions to couples to live together where no sentence of separation was granted. (One sentence of separation refers to, and orders the couple to make amends for the violation of, such an

115 Listed and disc. T&C no. 1118.
116 *Croix c Croix* and *Bruneau c Bruneau* (n. 113), almost say that, except that one adds the phrase *et quia alias constat* and the other *per confessionem viri et alias*.
117 Lit. T&C no. 1119.
118 See cases cited in n. 115.
119 See Lévy, "Officialité de Paris," 1279.
120 Disc. and lit. T&C no. 1120.
121 Disc. T&C no. 1121.
122 15/247 marriage cases in the two samples; 6% times 70%.
123 Disc. T&C no. 1122.

inhibition, which had previously been ordered.)[124] If we concluded that it was much easier to get a separation at Paris than at York or Ely, it looks as if it was even easier at Cambrai.

The number of separation cases dealt with by the two officials whose sentences are recorded in our records was approximately proportional to the number of sentences that each of them rendered.[125] The same is not true, however, of types of separation cases. Oudard Divitis (1438–9) heard 6 of the 15 criminal separation cases in the sample (40%) and only 4 of the instance separation cases (12%).[126] That Divitis had a somewhat different attitude toward instance separation cases may also be indicated by the fact that his sentences in such cases are much skimpier than those of his successor Grégoire Nicolaï, though this difference may be due to the fact that they used different scribes.

These differences suggest that we may be looking at a range of possible variations in practice within the courts of one diocese. With this in mind, I examined all of the separation sentences in the Brussels court book, making use of the index to the book. The reader will recall that the chronological range of this book starts later than that of the Cambrai book and ends later (1448–59 vs 1438–53). It, too, represents the work of two officials but of only one scribe. (This fact allows us to discount the possibility that the variations in the Cambrai sentences are the result of scribal peculiarities.) The search produced 82 cases, somewhat more than 5 percent of the total number of cases that are represented in the book.[127] This suggests that the Brussels court heard proportionally fewer separation cases than did the Cambrai court, and one possible reason for this difference is that the Brussels court heard only six criminal cases that involved separation (and one that was mixed criminal and civil). The ratio of instance separation cases at Brussels to the total number of sentences approximates that of Cambrai (roughly 5%), while the proportion of criminal cases is much lower (less than .05% vs approximately 4%).

Jan Rodolphi *alias* Flamingi, the official of Brussels through September of 1452, accounts for 402 sentences in the book; the remaining 1,188 were issued while Jan de Platea *alias* de Lira (Lier) was official. Rodolphi was thus responsible for 25 percent of the sentences. He was also responsible for more than his share of separation sentences (37%, 30/82).[128] Platea rendered proportionally more separations in criminal cases than did Rodolphi, but the number of criminal sentences for both of them is so small that little can be made of this fact.

We thus have a remarkable series of differences that seem to be peculiar to the judges, as can be seen in Table 10.1.[129] With due caution (because of size

124 *Office c Tiérasse et Tiérasse* (18.xi.52), no. 1373, disc. T&C no. 1123.
125 Details T&C no. 1124.
126 Disc. T&C no. 1125.
127 Disc. and lit. T&C no. 1126.
128 This number assigns to Rodolphi two cases that were begun while he was official but not completed until after he left office.
129 For problems with the table, see disc. T&C no. 1127.

TABLE 10.1. *Separation Sentences in the Cambrai and Brussels Registers (1438–1459) by Judge*

Judge	Criminal	%	Civil	%	Total	% Total	% Sentences	%Total Sentences
Divitis	24.5	73	9.1	27	33.6	24	19	12
Nicolaï	36.6	35	67.9	65	104.5	76	81	9
Rodolphi	1.0	5	21.0	95	22.0	27	25	5
Platea	5.0	8	54.0	92	59.0	73	75	5

Notes: 'Criminal' and 'Civil' give the number of criminal and civil separation sentences rendered by each official (extrapolated from the sample in the case of Divitis and Nicolaï, actual count in the case of Rodolphi and Platea) and the following percentages the proportion of each type of sentence to the total separation sentences that each judge rendered; 'Total' is the total number of separation sentences rendered by each judge; '% Total' gives the proportion of separation sentences to the total number of separation sentences rendered by the two judges in each court; '% Sentences' gives the proportion of total sentences rendered by the two judges in each court; '%Total Sentences' gives the proportion of separation sentences to the total number of sentences rendered by each judge.
Source: Registres de Cambrai; Liber van Brussel.

of the samples in some of the cells), this table suggests, as we have already noted, that there was a quite dramatic difference between the Cambrai and the Brussels courts in the number of separation cases heard in the criminal process, and that Divitis heard a substantially greater proportion of criminal separation cases than did his successor. The table may also point to a change over time. In the 1440s and 1450s, there was less of a tendency to hear separation cases in the criminal mode. So far as the proportion of separation sentences to all types of sentences is concerned, Divitis rendered a somewhat greater proportion and Nicolaï a somewhat smaller, whereas Rodolphi and Platea rendered roughly the same proportion.

These differences may be peculiar to the four judges involved, but to the extent that they illustrate chronological trends, they are both contrary to and in accordance with some broader trends in northern French marriage litigation that we will discuss in Chapter 12. In northern French courts in the fifteenth century, I will argue, criminal process tended to dominate the civil in marriage litigation, and the civil tended to disappear. To the extent that we are looking at a decline in criminal process in separation cases, that decline was contrary to the overall trend in marriage litigation. Once separation actions became an almost exclusively civil matter, however, they seem to have followed the trend in that their numbers, both absolutely and proportionally, tended to decline.

As was the case at Cambrai, plaintiffs in separation cases at Brussels had a high success rate. Of the 75 instance cases, 70 result in judgments of separation, as do 5 of the 6 office cases.[130] The one office case that does not result in such a

[130] Disc. T&C no. 1128.

judgment has a judgment dissolving the marriage on the ground of consanguinity.[131] Of the five instance cases that do not result in such sentences, one is evidenced only by an interlocutory sentence admitting the libel.[132] A separation may have been granted in this case (there is evidence that other separation sentences were not recorded),[133] but we cannot be sure. Another of the five sentences is a confirmation of an agreement of reconciliation of a couple who had separated without the judgment of the church.[134] The remaining three were brought as actions by the husband for restoration of conjugal rights. In two, restoration is ordered, subject to a *cautio* given by the husband in one case that he not alienate his wife's goods and in the other that he not mistreat her.[135] In the third, the last entry is an interlocutory sentence ordering the wife to live apart from her husband "with an upright and respectable woman in Brussels."[136] The first two cases show that it was possible to lose an action for separation in Cambrai diocese, at least where the separation was alleged as counterclaim in an action for restoration of conjugal rights, and they raise the suspicion that in many of the cases in which the separation was granted, neither of the parties was trying very hard to prevent it. This is a topic to which we must return.

Although it is not always possible to tell who is plaintiff and who is defendant in separation cases in Cambrai and Brussels,[137] where we can tell, it is female plaintiffs who predominate. Our sample of Cambrai instance separation cases reveals 25 female plaintiffs as opposed to 8 male (76% female). The actual count of Brussels instance separation cases reveals 46 female plaintiffs and 20 male (70%).[138]

Compared to the Paris sentences of separation, the Cambrai and Brussels sentences have two striking differences. In the first place, so far as we can tell, all of them are separations *a mensa et thoro*, or, as the Cambrai formula has it, *divorcium quoad thorum et mutuam servitutem*. Almost all of the Cambrai and Brussels separation sentences contain this formula (or at least *divorcium quoad thorum*), so that we suspect that in the few in which it is not present, the scribe simply neglected to put it in. None of the Cambrai and Brussels separation sentences, so far as I am aware, contains the formula *salvo iure thori*. The second difference is that in place of the careful delineation in the Paris book of the grounds for the judgment of separation, Cambrai and Brussels feature only two, adultery and/or the maddeningly vague *morum discrepantia*.

131 *Office c Gheerts en Bertels* (14.v.51), no. 270.
132 *Kerchove c Soutleuwe* (10.x.52), no. 405.
133 See n. 130.
134 *Heckene en Malscaerts* (3.ix.56), no. 1015, disc. T&C no. 1129.
135 *Keynoghe c Zoetens* (16.iv.51), no. 260; *Gouwen c Uls* (23.i.56), no. 924; text and lit. T&C no. 1130.
136 *Perre c Meys* (10.i.55 to 7.ii.55) (T&C no. 1131), refs. in TCas.
137 See, e.g., paragraph following n. 174.
138 Disc. T&C no. 1132.

Discrepantia is a not very common classical Latin word, meaning "discord, dissimilarity, discrepancy."[139] None of the standard dictionaries reports any peculiarly medieval usages of the word. *Mos*, of course, is a very common classical Latin word, with a wide semantic field. In the plural it can mean "manners, morals, character," in either the good or the bad sense, and it is probably in that meaning that it is to be taken here. So far as I am aware, the use of *morum discrepantia* as a technical legal term is confined to the Cambrai and Brussels courts.[140]

In order to get some sense of what the phrase means in our separation sentences, we must look at the contents of those sentences more closely. We have already seen that there were some differences in the types and quantity of separation sentences that our four judges rendered, and differences are also to be noted in the ways that they worded their sentences.

As we have already noted, Oudard Divitis renders skimpy instance sentences of separation, and there are relatively few of them. He never uses the term *morum discrepantia*. His first recorded instance separation sentence establishes his pattern: "We tolerate in patience that [CV] plaintiff and [HN] defendant, who are married – lest worse result therefrom – remain separated from each other until, with God's guidance, they determine to reconcile with each other, and we dispose of their goods in lawful form, dividing the costs between them and for [good] reason, issuing a definitive sentence in this writing."[141] It will be noted that this is not the language of a sentence given as of right; it is, rather, language of dispensation. Particularly telling in this regard are the phrases *in patientia tolleramus* and *ne deterius inde contingat*, phrases that had been used in dispensations since at least the twelfth century.[142]

This core of the sentence, with its dispensatory language, its emphasis on the temporary nature of the separation, sometimes with the dividing of costs, almost always with the formulaic separation of goods, and frequently with the addition that the couple are to live chastely (*caste vivendo*), is found in virtually all the Brussels/Cambrai separation sentences over the succeeding 20 years. Minor variants occur in the wording. Sometimes the word for "separated" is *segregati* as here; sometimes it is *separati*. "They will" (*voluerint*) and/or "they can" (*potuerint*) is frequently substituted for "they determine" (*duxerint*). Sometimes, as here, the court "disposes" (*disponimus*, *disponentes*) of the couple's goods; sometimes, it "ordains" concerning them (*ordinamus*, *ordinantes*);[143] sometimes it does both. If there is any significance in these variants, it is now lost; we suspect that they are simply artful variations of the basic formula.

139 Lewis and Short, s.v.

140 Anne Lefebvre's more extensive search for a somewhat later period did not discover any. *Officialités*, 179–206, esp. 201–4.

141 *Verhommelen c Verneyen* (10.i.39), no. 111, T&C no. 1133.

142 Ref. T&C no. 1134.

143 One is reminded of the 'ordination' of a vicarage in England, where the bishop approved the financial arrangements for compensating the vicar.

Minor wording variations like these aside, Divitis's sentences stick closely to this basic formula. In the case just quoted, the couple were fined for having lived apart without a judgment of separation, and both of them, apparently, for having committed adultery.[144] In another case in the sample, it is stated expressly that no fines were imposed, but the sentence is virtually the same, with the addition of the *caste vivendo* formula and the omission of an indication of who was plaintiff and who was defendant.[145] This omission raises the possibility that the couple jointly asked for the separation. Another sentence also omits an indication of who was plaintiff and who defendant, but we know that there was a plaintiff and a defendant in this case because the notes of the fines tell us that plaintiff and defendant were fined for living separately, but only the defendant was fined for her adultery.[146] The last instance sentence has a fine only for living apart, but the plaintiff wife and the defendant husband are identified as such.[147]

There are six criminal cases of unauthorized separation in the sample of Divitis's sentences. In all but one of them, one of the couple had also committed adultery. Divitis granted separations in four of the cases; he did not grant separations in one of the adultery cases and in the one case that did not involve adultery.[148] Before we conclude that Divitis refused to grant a separation in these latter cases, however, we should consider the possibility that he was not asked to grant one. In the case where no adultery was mentioned, the couple were back in court six months later, when the wife obtained an instance judgment of separation in the standard form and the man was fined for adultery.[149]

Three of the four sentences of separation that Divitis granted in criminal cases are phrased in the same form that he employs in the instance cases, tacked on to the end of a criminal sentence for unauthorized separation and adultery.[150] The fourth such sentence in the sample is quite different: "The divorce, nonetheless, sought by [MJ] on account of the sin against the law of his marriage committed and confessed by this [JP] we celebrate, and ordain concerning their goods in lawful form, issuing a definitive sentence in this writing."[151] This is, of course, language of right rather than of dispensation, and from a legal point of view it is more correct than the other sentences. Jean du Piet had committed adultery; Marie le Jolie had not, at least so far as had been shown. Marie was entitled to a judgment of separation; it was not a matter of the grace of the court. But the same was also true of the three sentences of separation that Divitis granted in the other criminal separation cases; only one of the spouses was known to have committed adultery. It is possible that the difference lies in the fact that

[144] *Verhommelen c Verneyen* (n. 141), disc. T&C no. 1135.
[145] *Gobert et Appelterre* (12.v.39), no. 222.
[146] *Eede c Vrijes* (24.i.39), no. 127.
[147] *Provost c Provost* (24.iii.39), no. 185.
[148] Examples and disc. T&C no. 1136.
[149] *Tannaisse c Petit* (6.iii.39), no. 158.
[150] Listed T&C no. 1137.
[151] *Office c Piet et Jolie* (15.x.38), no. 46, T&C no. 1138.

Marie had asked for the separation and Jean had not, whereas in the other cases, both spouses had asked for the separation. It is also possible, however, that the granting of a separation by way of dispensation in situations where it was not clear that the law allowed it had become so common in the Cambrai court that it led to ignoring the fact that there were some situations in which it was a matter of right.

The instance separation sentences of Grégoire Nicolaï are more substantial than those of Divitis. In all 29 sentences in the sample, Nicolaï begins by reciting the procedural steps that had led to his sentence. Despite the amount of verbiage that doing this adds, the process described need not have amounted to much. There was a libel or petition by the plaintiff. More often just the latter is mentioned, suggesting something quite informal and probably oral. The defendant replied. Then the parties offered "oaths, assertions, and confessions" (*sacramentis, assertionibus, et confessionibus*). Sometimes we hear of "allegations" and/or "conclusions." Rarely do we get an indication that any proof beyond the sworn statements of the parties was offered or taken.[152] The suspicion that in many cases there was little or no contest is heightened by the fact that in many of the sentences, it is expressly stated that the separation is granted with the consent of the defendant.

Unlike Divitis, Nicolaï normally gives an explicit ground for his instance separation sentences. In 15 of them (52%), it is the adultery of the defendant. In 13 of these cases, Nicolaï also mentions the consent of the defendant and grants the separation, making use of the language of dispensation that Divitis had employed: "on account of the sin of the same defendant and his express consent intervening in this, we admit the divorce sought by the plaintiff, tolerating in patience that the same parties, living chastely, remain separated until, with God's guidance, they can and will be reconciled with each other," and so on.[153] One of the two sentences in such cases that does not mention the consent of the defendant is otherwise the same as the sentence just given.[154] We suspect that in this case, the scribe forgot to include the mention of consent. The other sentence is different: "on account of the sin of [?the same defendant], the merits of the case, moreover, having been duly considered, and lest, if it were done otherwise, worse might come of it, we tolerate in patience," and so on.[155] As we will see, the clarification of the meaning of the phrase *ne deterius inde contingat* appears in other sentences of Nicolaï. The express mention that Nicolaï has weighed the merits of the case suggests that the defendant did not consent, and that Nicolaï must here make the further determination that leaving the parties together is likely to have bad results. This is, again, inconsistent with the law as we understand it. If the defendant had committed adultery and the plaintiff had not, she was entitled to a separation as a matter of right.

152 Disc. T&C no. 1139.

153 *Lanchsone c Blanchart* (20.iii.43), no. 443, T&C no. 1140.

154 *Val c Pontbays* (2.iv.46), no. 904.

155 *Sandemoin c Fiesve* (22.vi.43), no. 487, T&C no. 1141.

Nicolaï's early separation sentences in cases where adultery had not been shown are grounded on the consent of the parties and the fear that if the separation is not granted, worse will come of it: "on account of the consent of both of these parties intervening in this and lest, if it were done otherwise, worse might come of it, we tolerate in patience," and so on.[156] One can well imagine how this wording might have made Nicolaï uncomfortable because it seems to make the judgment of separation depend on the consent of the parties and not on the judgment of the church that cause for such a separation had been found.[157]

It is probably for this reason that Nicolaï began to experiment with saying something more: "on account of incompatibility of the couple who are presently contending with each other and the repugnancy of their *mores* – lest, if it were done otherwise, worse might happen – by the common consent of the same parties, we tolerate in patience," and so on, "ordaining concerning their goods in the form of law or in that form with which each side shall be reasonably satisfied," and so on.[158] What was needed was something other than the consent of the parties to support the proposition that if they were not separated, something worse (than a separation) would happen. It was found in the very squabble that was taking place before the court. Anyone who has watched a couple screaming at each other in a modern divorce court has, we might suggest, some sense of what Nicolaï is talking about. And we can certainly imagine him saying to himself, "If I don't let this couple separate they are going to start throwing things at each other (if they haven't done so already), and someone is going to get hurt." One can even sense more hope than expectation in his assertion that when it came to the division of goods, they would behave reasonably.

Twenty-two months later Nicolaï tried another formula "on account of the discrepancy (*discrepatio*) of the *mores* of the couple – whence truly not little danger could arise from their daily cohabitation – we tolerate in patience that the same parties – as they consent on both sides – living chastely may remain separate," and so on.[159] *Discrepatio* is a rather uncommon classical Latin word that means "discrepancy" or "dispute." Perhaps someone told Nicolaï that this was not quite the word he wanted; perhaps he realized it himself. Eight months later he reworded the formula: "on account of the discord of *mores* (*morum discrepantia*) of the couple, and lest, if it were done otherwise, worse might come of it, there intervening the consent of both of the parties, in patience – as the plaintiff asks – we tolerate," and so on.[160] This formula became fixed.

156 *Sciethase c Bayvouts* (9.ii.43), no. 430, T&C no. 1142. Cf. *Sombeke c Wesembeke* (25.viii.42), no. 303.

157 Disc. T&C no. 1143.

158 *Cupere c Craeys* (15.xii.42), no. 397, T&C no. 1144. We depart here from the sample to examine all of Nicolaï's separation cases containing the phrases *morum incompatibilitas* or *discrepantia*, as indexed in the edition.

159 *Cantignarde c Tondeur* (3.x.44), no. 541, T&C no. 1145.

160 *Feluys c Herinc* (28.vi.45), no. 729, T&C no. 1146.

Nicolaï used it, with slight variations, in 20 more recorded sentences, and it was adopted by the Brussels officials when the officiality was founded late in 1448.[161] It took some time, however, for this phrase to become the dominant one. "Incompatibility of *mores*" (*morum incompatibilitas*) appears in three sentences around the time when Nicolaï first used the phrase *morum discrepantia*, and it is used in one case that appears somewhat later in his registers.[162]

Once the formula employing *morum discrepantia* was adopted, Nicolaï's sentences become even less informative than they were when he was experimenting with it. All but 2 of the 21 sentences that contain the formula also mention the consent of the parties, and those two, which were rendered a day apart, probably omit the mention of consent because the scribe forgot to include it.[163] The formula is used in two office cases brought for separation without the judgment of the church, but these cases are otherwise indistinguishable from the instance ones in which the couple is fined for unlawful separation, except that we cannot tell which spouse took the lead in asking for the separation.[164] Four are rendered in cases (one office, three instance) where the fines tell us that adultery was also involved. In one such case, both spouses had committed adultery, and so we might imagine that neither of them was entitled to a separation for adultery, but in the other three, only one of the couple is fined for adultery.[165] Only two cases elaborate on the meaning of *morum discrepantia*. In one, we are told that the wife of a man who was seeking restoration of conjugal rights – and the woman had previously been ordered by the court to return to her husband – alleged that because of the husband's "cruelty and harshness" she did not dare return to him, even if he gave surety. The official granted her a judgment of separation "on account of the cruelty and harshness of the man previously alleged and the discord of *mores* of this couple."[166] In the other case, the "harshness of the man" is simply added to *morum discrepantia* as a ground for the sentence.[167]

The Brussels sentences in separation cases add something, but not much, to our knowledge. As we have noted, there are 75 instance cases involving separation, of which 70 have sentences of separation. Of these 45 (64%) are grounded in the adultery of one of the parties, although 20 (29% of total separations granted) also add *morum discrepantia*.[168] Twenty of them (again, 29%) are grounded in *morum discrepantia* alone. Hence, more than half of the sentences use the phrase *morum discrepantia*. The remaining five sentences of

[161] See *Registres de Cambrai*, s.v. *discrepantia morum*; *Liber van Brussel*, s.v. *Scheiding van tafel en bed*, *onverenigbaarheid van karakter*.

[162] Listed T&C no. 1147.

[163] Listed T&C no. 1148.

[164] Listed with disc. of fines in instance cases T&C no. 1149.

[165] Listed T&C no. 1150.

[166] *Brodel c Hardouchin* (21.x.45), no. 803, T&C no. 1151.

[167] *Wérye c Roussiel* (10.vi.46), no. 939.

[168] And one adds leprosy: *Tyriaens c Huens* (27.x.57), no. 1234, T&C no. 1152.

separation do not give a ground, either because it is simply absent or because the sentence confirms one previously given.

We noted that Rodolphi gave proportionally approximately the same number of separation sentences as did Platea. The proportion of separation sentences that he gave for *morum discrepantia*, however, was considerably less than the proportion of such sentences that Platea gave. Only 3 of Rodolphi's 20 instance sentences of separation are for *morum discrepantia* (15%), whereas 17 of Platea's 50 instance separation sentences were solely grounded on *morum discrepantia* (34%) and an additional 20 (40%) were grounded on both adultery and *morum discrepantia*. This difference in proportions is not surprising if we recall that Rodolphi's tenure overlaps with that of Nicolaï at Cambrai (1448–52) and that Nicolaï himself had begun to experiment with granting separations on the basis of *morum discrepantia* only three years before Rodolphi took office.

That Rodolphi was cautious about granting sentences of separation on the basis of *morum discrepantia* can also be seen in the wording of the sentences themselves. Like Nicolaï and Divitis before him, he uses the basic language of dispensation: "We tolerate in patience that the parties, living chastely, stand and remain apart from each other, until they wish to reconcile themselves," followed by a formal separation of goods.[169] Where Rodolphi's separation sentences differ from those of Divitis and Nicolaï is that in addition to the formulaic "lest worse come of it," he gives the reasons why one might think that worse would come of it as part of what we would call his "findings of fact": "Having seen propositions and allegations, assertions and confessions of the couple on both sides and particularly their age and *morum discrepantia* and continual serious dissensions, and also the discords, quarrels and dangers of [their] children and friends, with other things that could justly move our spirit, and lest worse come out from it, having invoked the name of Christ, we say, discern, and declare that the divorce from bed that the couple on both sides have asked for ought to be admitted and is admitted, tolerating in patience," and so on.[170] Two of Rodolphi's instance separation sentences follow this form.[171] The third is quite different: "Having paid attention to the allegations of [TJ], layman, and [MB], a married couple, notably their *morum discrepantia* and also the disgraceful beating and wounding that this [TJ] did to the person of [MB] his wife with a knife and a stick, with the other things that are to be attended to and supplied by law, the name of Christ having been invoked, lest worse come of it, we tolerate in patience," and so on.[172]

Rodolphi also renders sentences of separation in three of the five cases where we cannot tell the grounds for the separation. One of these had previously been heard by the dean of Christianity of Brussels, but the procedure in the officiality

[169] *Houschels c Guidderomme* (13.xi.50), no. 217, T&C no. 1153.
[170] *Voghelere en Scocx* (23.i.50), no. 127, T&C no. 1154.
[171] *Voghelere en Scocx* (n. 170); *Meskens en Huekers* (10.iii.50), no. 143, disc. T&C no. 1155.
[172] *Jambotial en Brakevere* (26.v.52), no. 377, T&C no. 1156.

suggests that this is not an appeal but a relitigation of the case, with a libel, a reconventional libel (counterclaim), and witnesses produced by the *actrix*, the *acta* held before the dean being introduced by way of proof. If we are reading the somewhat cryptic sentence correctly, Rodolphi denied the petition in the reconventional libel (which probably asked for restoration of conjugal rights), declared that the wife was not to be compelled to return to her husband, confirmed the sentence of the dean (which probably granted a separation), and ordered relaxed an *arrestum* (probably some sort of interlocutory order concerning property) that had been issued against the woman on the security of a *cambium* of a hundred *florins* and other movable goods.[173] The other two cases grant the separation "on account of the causes alleged by [the *actrix*] and confessed by the *reus*" or "for certain reasonable causes designated in the *acta* of this case or derivable from the same."[174]

In only two of the six cases in which Rodolphi grants a separation without any mention of adultery is there any indication of who was plaintiff and who defendant. The other four expressly say that the divorce was sought by both the man and the woman. In one of the cases where the woman is called *actrix*, the defendant confessed all. Only in the case that was before the dean of Brussels is there any indication that the man resisted the granting of the sentence, and it is at least possible that the cause of that resistance was more a concern over financial matters than any genuine desire to continue the marital relationship.

The two sentences that vaguely mention "causes" suggest that Rodolphi was prepared to grant a separation for reasons other than adultery or *morum discrepantia*, but he was unable or unwilling to specify in a sentence precisely what these might be.[175] The three granted on the ground of *morum discrepantia* do tell us something about the contents of that phrase. The third sentence is for physical cruelty, or, as we would say, spousal abuse. It is perhaps not by chance that the consent of the parties is not mentioned in this sentence. If this is what was going on, the official is going to separate them, so long as they tell him what is going on.[176] The other two sentences mention the age of the parties and describe wrangles between them; they may refer to a somewhat different sort of problem: cases not of what we would call spousal abuse but, rather, what we would call a 'dysfunctional family'. This possibility is heightened in the case that tells us that children and the relatives are also involved in the wrangling.[177]

Platea's separation sentences grounded in *morum discrepantia* are more routine; they remind us of Nicolaï's later sentences. All 20 of the sentences granted for both adultery and *morum discrepantia* are his, suggesting again that once the court had hit upon the phrase it tended to dominate, even in areas that had traditionally been based on other grounds. There are also indications

173 *Brabantia c Zelleke* (11.vi.51), no. 280.
174 *Houschels c Guidderomme* (n. 169); *Heckene en Malscaerts* (n. 134), T&C no. 1157.
175 See n. 174 ; disc. T&C no. 1158.
176 At n. 172.
177 N. 171.

that Platea, like Rodolphi, distinguished between spousal abuse and the 'dysfunctional family' as grounds for separation. Four of his sentences mention the cruelty of the husband. In two, it may have been particularly serious because it is given first and somewhat elaborated: "On account of the cruelty and harshness of the defendant confessed before us by this defendant plainly and on account of the *morum discrepantia* of this couple," and so on, and "On account of the cruelty of [HD] against [AV] perpetrated many times and confessed, and on account of the *morum discrepantia* of the defendants [*sic*]," and so on.[178]

But if 4 of Platea's separation sentences that do not mention adultery mention the cruelty of the husband, 16 do not. Unlike Rodolphi's sentences grounded in *morum discrepantia*, Platea's early sentences on the same ground all mention the consent of the parties, and two mention the consent of their relatives.[179] In the meantime, Platea has begun to add *morum discrepantia* to sentences of separation based on adultery, but he does so with a slightly different formula: "on account of the *morum discrepantia* of the same [couple] who are unwilling mutually to accept each other (*propter morum eorundem discrepantiam sese adinvicem admittere nolentium*)."[180] I am not sure what this means; the most obvious meaning is that the *morum discrepantia* is that the couple does not want to live together.[181] Over the course of some 15 months, Platea experimented with this phrase in cases involving adultery; he then began to apply it to cases in which adultery was not involved.[182] And the phrase remained the normal accompaniment of *morum discrepantia*, whether by itself or in addition to adultery, for the rest of the book.

After the introduction of the phrase *sese adinvicem admittere nolentium*, mention of the consent of the parties tends to drop out. Consent of the parties is mentioned without *sese adinvicem admittere nolentium* in one case that postdates the appearance of *sese adinvicem admittere nolentium* in a separation sentence that did not involve adultery.[183] It appears in one non-adultery sentence where the other phrase does appear.[184] It seems, however, that consent and *sese adinvicem admittere nolentium* were regarded as alternatives. Logically, they are not quite alternatives, if we take *sese adinvicem admittere* to refer to living together. The whole point of the separation of goods sentences at Paris was that the couple did not have to reside together, but the obligation to render the debt continued, at least in theory. Cambrai separation sentences did relieve the couple of the obligation to render the debt, and with this in mind, we might wonder if *sese adinvicem admittere nolentium* is a euphemism for the couple's refusal to have sexual intercourse with each other. That would fit quite well with the fact that the phrase first appears in cases that involve adultery ("After

178 Listed with other examples T&C no. 1159.
179 Listed T&C no. 1160.
180 Listed T&C no. 1161.
181 This would, at a minimum, deny that the innocent party had condoned the adultery.
182 *Wouters c Mustsaerts* (20.vi.55), no. 806; *Vekene c Thuyne* (n. 178).
183 *Broecke c Oudermoelen* (n. 179).
184 *Gabriels c Zande* (18.ii.57), no. 1119.

he/she did that, I'm certainly not going to bed with him/her"). It would also fit with the one, probably two, cases that specifically mention that the couple are beyond the age where one could expect sexual activity.[185] The way that this factor is coupled with *ne forte deterius inde contingat* in these sentences suggests that Platea has balanced the possible harm to which keeping the couple together might lead against the likelihood that they will not *caste vivere* and has found the latter possibility improbable. The same inference might be derived from the one sentence that substitutes the verb "join" (*adiungere*) for *admittere*, and perhaps from the one that adds "suffer" (*compati*) and the one that substitutes the *compati* for *admittere*.[186]

But what is the harm to be feared if the couple are forced to stay together? Except for the cases in which Platea mentions cruelty, he tells us little. In eight cases the adjective "peacefully" (*pacifice*) is added to *sese adinvicem admittere nolentium*, once more conjuring up the image of a couple throwing things at one another, or at least constantly quarreling.[187] Other variations tell us less, and some cases may be no more than artful or mistaken variations of the formula.[188]

In his last separation sentence in the book, Platea tells us more: "We declare that a divorce from bed and mutual servitude between the couple is to be celebrated and we celebrate [it], on account of their *morum discrepantia*, *sese adinvicem compati nolentium*, and especially because of the adultery perpetrated and committed by the defendant with [EH], and on account of the dangers that could quite likely occur between the couple, [and we] wishing, so far as it is within us, to avoid them [the dangers] and to make available for the couple quiet and peace."[189] This case may have been unusual. The plaintiff is called *domicella*, the highest indication of status that we normally get in the Cambrai and Brussels records. It was also, quite unusually, a contested case. The defendant resisted the charge of adultery; the plaintiff produced witnesses; documentary evidence was introduced (perhaps of the defendant's conviction for adultery in another case); exceptions to witnesses were introduced, and more testimony taken (though this does not seem to have ultimately been made a part of the record). The record was sufficiently complicated that Platea mentions that he took counsel with the *iurisperiti*, a formula not found in his more routine separation cases. The greater amount of documentation could have made Platea more confident of his judgment that he was doing the right thing, a confidence that he chose to express in his sentence.

On balance, however, I am inclined to think that this sentence articulates Platea's processes of thought in other cases where he says less. In order to support this proposition, we must confront an issue that has been raised in the

[185] *Oeghe c Breecpots* (19.xi.56), no. 1059; cf. *Vischmans c Meys* (24.vii.56), no. 998; both T&C no. 1162.

[186] Listed T&C no. 1163.

[187] Listed T&C no. 1164.

[188] Disc. T&C no. 1165.

[189] *Ofhuys c Platea* (27.xi.59), no. 1584, T&C no. 1166.

literature: To what extent could instance separations be obtained in the Cambrai and Brussels courts in the mid-fifteenth century simply because the couple wanted them?[190] There can be no doubt that a number of Cambrai and Brussels separation sentences mention the consent of the couple, and a few seem to ground the judgment, at least in part, on their consent. The number of such cases becomes even larger if we add to it those sentences of Platea that express the converse of the couple's consent to separation: *sese adinvicem admittere nolentium*. To this evidence should also be added the fact that a strikingly large number of the Brussels separation sentences also confirm a document separating the goods of the couple, a document frequently drawn up as the result of arbitration or appearance before a notary or before the *scabini* of a particular town.[191] This is quite different from the Paris practice in which the court first adjudged the separation of goods and then proceeded to have the couple actually make the separation, either by themselves or under the supervision of a court officer. This evidence, combined with the dramatically high proportion of grants of separation, certainly suggests that a fifteenth-century couple in the Cambrai diocese who had decided to separate and had the money to pay the fees did not have great difficulty getting the court to confirm their decision.

The question, however, is whether all that the couple had to do was to come into court and consent to a judgment of separation or whether they had to tell the judge why it was that they were "unwilling mutually to accept each other." I am inclined to think that at least in theory, Platea thought that he had to make an independent judgment that if they were not separated "worse would come of it." The fact is that of the 28 sentences that contain the formula *sese adinvicem admittere nolentium*, all but two contain the additional phrase *ne forte deterius inde contingat*. Of the two exceptions, one is a case in which the husband was found guilty of public adultery[192] and the other is the sentence quoted earlier that spells out in more detail the reasons for believing that "worse would come of it."

Thus, the history of both Nicolaï's and Platea's separation sentences suggests that having come perilously close to, perhaps going over the line of, granting separation sentences on the basis of consent, both men pulled back and worded their sentences in a way that suggested their independent judgment that it was better if the couple separated. Neither man, of course, was familiar with modern psychological theories of marital breakdown, and both were willing to assign fault (cruelty, adultery) where fault could be found. The fact is, however, that both men were willing to grant separations for what we might call 'irretrievable marital breakdown', and Platea's last sentence shows some compassion for a couple who were in such a situation, even though the cause of the breakdown may well have been the couple themselves. Platea's thinking on this topic is

190 See literature cited in n. 117.

191 See *Liber van Brussel*, s.v., *schieding van tafel en bed*, *goederenregeling* (collecting 34 examples).

192 *Thonijs c Jacopts* (n. 187) (which does add *pacifice*).

particularly striking when we recall that he first hit upon, and continued to use, the formula *propter eorundem morum discrepantiam sese adinvicem admittere nolentium ne forte deterius inde contingat* in cases where the quite traditional ground of adultery would have sufficed. Perhaps he had come to the conclusion that adultery is not always exclusively the fault of the adulterer.

Oudard Divitis's sentences of separation in criminal cases of unauthorized separation have been discussed. It remains to say a word about those of Nicolaï, Rodolphi and Platea. Seven such sentences appear in the sample of Nicolaï's surviving separation sentences, and we estimated that they represent about 20 percent of those that he rendered.[193] All of the cases also involve the adultery of one or both of the couple, although in one case this fact is mentioned only in the list of fines.[194] In all cases the couple are fined for the unlawful separation and for the adultery.[195] The pattern of the sentences is quite clear. Where only one of the couple has committed adultery, the court grants a separation in standard form, on account of the adultery, at the petition of the innocent party and with the consent of the guilty party.[196] In one of the cases where both had committed adultery, the same formula is used (the man petitions), but Nicolaï adds the formula "lest, if it were done otherwise, worse might come of it."[197] In the other case where both had committed adultery, he is vaguer, stating that the separation is granted at the petition of the woman, "on account of the reasons alleged by the *rea* at the end of this, and noting that the *reus* confessed them," with the addition of the *ne deterius* formula.[198] In the one case in which adultery is not mentioned in the sentence, though it is in the list of amends, the grounds for the sentence of separation are also different: "Noting their *morum discrepantia* – this is the ground [of the sentence] – their consent also intervening in this, lest perchance, if it were done otherwise, worse might come of it, we tolerate in patience," and so on.[199] In the cases where both had committed adultery, the additional language is probably necessary to overcome the standard doctrine that a spouse *in pari delicto* was not entitled to a judgment of separation. In the other case, the sentence reveals none of the standard grounds for separation, although the fines indicate that adultery was involved.

Jan Rodolphi renders sentence in only one unauthorized separation case in the sample, itself a quite unusual case. The couple had solemnized a marriage and lived together without making an inquiry into their suspected consanguinity. Then, they had separated without the judgment of the church. Rodolphi fines them for both offenses (it is hard to escape the feeling that there are

193 See Table 10.1.

194 *Office c Tiérasse et Tiérasse* (n. 124).

195 In *Office c Wyet et Paiebien* (13.vii.42), no. 280, the judge imposes a quite dramatic corporal penance on the woman for bigamy.

196 E.g., *Office c Laerbeken et Elst* (19.iii.46), no. 891, T&C no. 1167.

197 *Corwere c Gruters* (26.x.42), no. 371, disc. T&C no. 1168.

198 *Office c Poulle et Poulle* (7.x.52), no. 1352, T&C no. 1169.

199 *Office c Tiérasse et Tiérasse* (n. 124), T&C no. 1170.

elements here of "Catch 22") and dissolves the marriage for a consanguinity now proven.[200]

Jan de Platea renders sentence in only six unauthorized separation cases (an actual count). All involve adultery. Despite this fact, all but one also ground the separation in *morum discrepantia*. The one exception involves not only adultery but also attempted bigamy.[201] The remaining five all include the phrase *sese adinvicem admittere nolentium*, with or without *pacifice*, and all but one add *ne forte deterius inde contingat*.[202]

Thus, except for Divitis, the sentence patterns of our four judges in criminal cases involving unauthorized separation follow, as a general matter, the pattern that we have seen in their instance separation cases. It remains to ask why it is that there are so many fewer criminal unauthorized separation cases at Brussels than there are at Cambrai. It is, of course, possible that fewer couples in the Flemish-speaking areas of Cambrai diocese separated without the judgment of the church than did those in the French-speaking areas, but that seems unlikely. The Brussels sentence book does seem to be less concerned about recording fines in instance cases than are the Cambrai sentence books, and it is possible that other record-keeping devices were being used for some types of routine criminal cases. On balance, however, it seems most likely that what we are looking at is chronological development. Divitis heard a disproportionately large number of criminal unauthorized separation cases and disproportionately fewer instance ones. Nicolaï greatly expanded the proportion of instance separation sentences, but kept up the pressure in the criminal area as well. His slightly later contemporary, Rodolphi, may have decided to confine routine separation litigation to the civil side only, because his only criminal unauthorized separation sentence is in a case that presented a number of other issues. Platea returned to using the criminal mode occasionally but not nearly so much as Nicolaï had. The few such criminal cases that he heard were probably particularly egregious examples or ones in which the promotor insisted on proceeding for unauthorized separation as well as adultery. As on the civil side, and despite the qualifications about the civil side that have been suggested, the overall trend in the Cambrai diocese in the mid-fifteenth century seems to have been to leave separation as a matter in the control of the couple themselves.

CONCLUSION

We have seen in this chapter that the courts of Paris and of the diocese of Cambrai had developed a substantial jurisprudence about marital separations, in Paris by the end of the fourteenth century and in Cambrai by the

200 *Officie c Gheerts en Bertels* (14.v.51), no. 270.

201 *Officie c Speelman en Strijken* (17.v.54), no. 616.

202 Listed T&C no. 1171.

mid-fifteenth.[203] That the Franco-Belgian courts had such an extensive separation jurisdiction has been noted by others, and examples of it have been noted over a quite wide geographical area and well into the sixteenth century.[204] By contrast, York and Ely, despite their extensive documentation, do not have anything comparable in the area of separation. What we have found for York and Ely may be generalized for the English courts in the later Middle Ages and into the sixteenth century. We must be careful here, as elsewhere, not to exaggerate the differences. There are English cases, like the Franco-Belgian ones, that proceed more by the consent of the parties than by the strict insistence on the law; we noted such cases in fourteenth-century York, and there is at least one case in the fifteenth century in which arbiters were chosen to make a separation of goods.[205] The fact remains, however, that separation of goods is not a usual category of case in the English church courts, and in no English court are separation cases ever a substantial portion of the marriage jurisdiction.

Clearly enough, as noted, some of the English cases that seem at first blush to be about marriage formation are, in fact, separation cases or, rather, divorce cases. Parties whose marriages have broken down sue for annulment on the basis of a prior informal *de presenti* marriage, conveniently forgotten at the time of the current marriage and conveniently remembered when that marriage broke down.[206] Possibly the presence of such suits in the English records and their relative absence in the Franco-Belgian ones explains why there are so many more separation suits in the Franco-Belgian records.[207] Denied the collusive suit that the English used because of the strict Franco-Belgian doctrine about *de presenti* marriages, the Franco-Belgian litigants, we might argue, used the more honest and more straightforward separation action.

Like the argument made in Chaper 7 about the difference between *de presenti and de futuro* marriage litigation in the two countries, this argument depends on there being massive amounts of perjury, this time in the English courts alone.[208] Such perjury did exist. We have seen quite clear evidence of it in some cases, and in many more cases we suspected it. It seems highly unlikely, however, that the proportion of English couples who obtained a collusive divorce is comparable to the proportion of Franco-Belgian couples who obtained a judicial separation. Hence, even if we add to the paltry number of English separation cases all the divorce cases in which we suspect collusion, we still do not have anything

[203] The arguments presented here were first developed in Donahue, "English and French Marriage Cases."

[204] Lefebvre-Teillard, *Officialités*, 179–206. Indeed, well into the eighteenth century in the case of Cambrai. See Ch 12, n.46. For a discussison of recent work with separation cases from the next diocese to the west of Cambrai in our period, see App. e10.2: "The Tournai Separation Cases" (see T&C no. 1176).

[205] Helmholz, *Marriage Litigation*, 100–107, esp. 103.

[206] *Ingoly c Middleton, Easingwold and Wright* is a striking example, but we have seen others about which we had strong suspicions. See Helmholz, *Marriage Litigation*, at 64–5.

[207] Disc. T&C no. 1172.

[208] Chapter 7, at n. 343.

like the proportion of couples who were separated by the Franco-Belgian courts (and to these we also have to add those Franco-Belgian couples who successfully obtained an annulment).[209]

If lying does not fully account for it, there must be something else to explain the difference in the proportions of English and Franco-Belgian separation cases. Although it is possible that marriages were more stable in England than they were in the Franco-Belgian region, it seems more likely that fewer separations appear on the English court records not because fewer marriages in England broke down but because fewer cases of marital breakdown came to court. In short, our suspicion is that the English separated themselves and never went to court about it.

Such separations would have to have been voluntary if they were not judicially sanctioned. If a husband or wife simply moved out on the other and could have been reached by the process of the court, he or she could have been sued for restoration of conjugal rights. Such cases are not common in the English records, but they do exist.[210] Such a couple would also have had to avoid prosecution, and prosecutions are recorded against married couples who did not live together.[211] In this regard, the fact that the prosecution in English church courts was less well organized than that in the Franco-Belgian church courts may have allowed more cases of this variety to go unnoticed or to be tacitly accepted by the parish communities that bore the responsibility for criminal prosecutions in the church courts.

There is one other major difference between the legal system of England and those in the Franco-Belgian region that may help to explain this dissimilarity. There was a substantial difference in the systems of marital property. Here we must generalize. What I will say next represents a distillation of the rules of the English common law, a law that applied to most freehold land and to some types of disputes about chattels. In the case of Franco-Belgian region, I will outline what might be called the lowest common denominator of those customs for which we have evidence that antedates the official redaction of the customs in the sixteenth century.

So far as marital property is concerned, the aphorism that "at English common law husband and wife were one and that one was the husband" may be amusing but it is misleading. The fundamental characteristic of the common law of marital property by the time of *Bracton* (1230s) was not the unity of husband and wife but their separation. The husband had his lands, the wife hers. The husband's heirs succeeded to his lands, the wife's heirs to hers, and as a general rule neither husband nor wife had the power of testamentary disposition over land. True, the husband's lands were subject to the wife's dower – her right to a life estate, normally in one-third of those lands, if he predeceased her – and the wife's lands were subject to the husband's right to take the rents

[209] Disc. T&C no. 1173.
[210] See, e.g., at nn. 29–31.
[211] Butler, *Language of Abuse*, 350–9, collects a number of examples.

and profits during the marriage and to his right to a life estate in the whole if she predeceased him and if a child were born of the marriage. Each party had to join in a conveyance if the land was to be sold free of that party's interest, but the husband could convey his interest both in his land and in that of his wife without her consent.[212]

These were the rules for land; in the case of personal property we can be considerably less certain. It would seem that during the marriage, the husband had the power to manage and to alienate both his chattels and those of his wife, a fact that led some courts to suggest that he "owned" his wife's chattels. If he predeceased his wife, she was apparently entitled to whatever was left of her chattels and to one-third of his. If she predeceased him, he may have been entitled only to a third of what was left of her chattels.[213]

If the fundamental characteristic of marital property in England was separation despite the marriage and if the fundamental division was between land and chattels, in Franco-Belgian customary law the concept of separate property coexisted with that of a community of property because of the marriage, and the fundamental divisions were among family land (*propres* or *héritages*), acquired land (*acquêts* or *conquêts*), and movables (*meubles*). The husband's family land was his separate property, or perhaps it might be better to say the separate property of his family, because the husband's power to alienate it was tightly controlled in the interest of his heirs. The husband's family land was also subject to a dower interest in his wife, generally a life estate of one-half, which further impeded his power to alienate it. The wife's family land was subject to the same limitations with respect to her heirs, but the husband had no dower interest in it. The acquests, on the other hand, were – I use the term with some hesitation – community property of husband and wife. The usual pattern called for their equal division upon the death of one spouse between the spouse's heirs and the surviving spouse. Each spouse's half was subject to his or her testamentary disposition, and in some areas the husband's sale or gift of acquests required the wife's consent. The rules about movables were as uncertain as those in England about personal property. Suffice it to say that the husband had extensive powers of management and control over them, but the wife's right of succession to all or part of them was leading some writers to conceive of them as being community property as well.[214]

There is some controversy as to how far back we can trace community property in the Franco-Belgian region. I am inclined to see it in the thirteenth century.[215] There is more of a consensus that it can be found in the fourteenth century, and that will suffice for our purposes here since the first Franco-Belgian records with which we are dealing come from quite late in that century.

212 Donahue, "What Causes," 64–5, and sources cited.

213 Lit. and disc. T&C no. 1174.

214 Donahue, "What Causes," at 66–7.

215 *Ibid.* at 67–9. I am encouraged in this statement by Godding, *Droit privé*, secs. 474–80, pp. 265–70.

It is a characteristic, then, of English marital property patterns that husband and wife hold their property separately and of the Franco-Belgian region that there is community property. May this fact be used to explain the differences that we see in the separation cases? This is the point at which the difference in the property systems in the two countries becomes telling: A couple that voluntarily separated in England did not have the difficulty of dissolving a community of goods because, by and large, no such community existed. In the Franco-Belgian region, however, because of the community of goods between husband and wife, a judicial pronouncement was necessary to achieve what could be done in England voluntarily and with a minimum of fuss.

The intervention of the court was required in the Franco-Belgian region not only because of the greater difficulty of dividing commingled property but also because the dissolution of the community dissolved the liability of the community for debts of the community, and creditors had to be notified of this fact and their claims settled. Further, dissolution of the community added to the list of grounds for separation: In addition to cruelty and adultery, bad management or "foolishness" became a ground, at least for separation of goods.[216]

In summary, we are not saying that the separation rate in either country was as high in the late Middle Ages as it is today. The economic forces that held marriage together in the Middle Ages and shorter life spans saw to it that it was not. What we are saying is that the evidence is consistent with the proposition that the separation rates in England and the Franco-Belgian region were roughly the same in the later Middle Ages and that the marked difference that we see in the number of separation cases in the two countries can be explained by the difference in marital property systems in the two countries. We offered both negative and positive arguments: A separate property system, such as that in England, makes separation without judicial intervention easier, and a community property system, such as that of the Franco-Belgian region, necessitates judicial intervention and the invention of new grounds for separation. Although we had some doubts about the negative argument, the positive argument had considerable force, and the combination of the two seemed compelling.

216 *Malum regimen*: *Clodoaldo et Clodoaldo* (n. 115), *Auberti c Auberti* (n. 76), *Perrieres c Perrieres* (n. 78), *Gontier c Gontier* (n. 78); *fatuitas*: *Kerautret c Keraútret* (n. 82).

11

Social Practice, Formal Rule, and the Medieval Canon Law of Incest

THE RULES AND THEIR APPLICATION

Our examination in some depth of marriage litigation in five medieval church courts has revealed relatively few cases that dealt with the complicated rules, outlined in Chapter 1, about the marriage of relatives.[1] This finding may be surprising to some readers. A view popularized by F. W. Maitland in a footnote (but which had roots going back to the Reformation) holds that the medieval incest rules were so complicated and so extensive that all medieval marriages were dissoluble as a practical matter, because virtually any couple could get a divorce by showing some hitherto unsuspected relationship between them.[2] This view was founded on more than speculation. Medieval history offers a number of examples of highly visible divorces granted or sought on the ground of incest: Robert the Pious and Bertha of Burgundy in the eleventh century, Eleanor of Aquitaine and Louis VII of France in the twelfth, Philip Augustus and Ingeborg of Denmark in the thirteenth.[3]

Even before the analyses presented in this book, research had cast considerable doubt upon this view. What research had shown was the danger of writing legal history from *causes célèbres*. The visible is not necessarily the usual; high politics affects both the law and its application in ways that make it difficult, if not impossible, to draw conclusions about the normal from the spectacular. What this research showed, then, was that the rules incapacitating those who were too closely related from marrying each other were of considerably less practical importance than had once been thought.[4]

[1] Portions of the first two sections of this chapter first appeared in Donahue, "Monastic Judge." Lit. T&C no. 1177.

[2] Pollock and Maitland, *History of English Law*, 2:385–7, 393 n. 5; Helmholz, *Marriage Litigation*, 77–87; see Donahue, "Policy," 252–3, and sources cited.

[3] Lit. T&C no. 1178.

[4] For a summary of the research referred to, see at nn. 9–12.

More recent work on the social import of the medieval incest rules does not seek to return to the view that all medieval marriages were practically dissoluble because of the existence of a complicated and extensive notion of incest. Rather, it seeks to argue that because of the church's enforcement of the incest rules, the family in the West developed in a way quite different from what would have happened had the rules not been there. Georges Duby, for example, argues that the nascent lineages of aristocratic France were checked, though not destroyed, because of the requirement that they had to marry their children out of the group with which they already had close kinship ties.[5] Jack Goody, in a provocative and far-ranging study, argues that the weakness of family ties in the West, in marked contrast to the strength of such ties in almost every other part of the world, is the result of the church's inexorable pressure against inheritance strategies designed to strengthen the family.[6] In Goody's view, the enforcement of the rules requiring exogamous marriage is perhaps the most striking manifestation of this pressure.

A legal historian should not attempt to have the final say about such arguments. Duby's view depends on years of careful work on the growth of aristocratic families in France from the ninth through the twelfth centuries. Although the legal historian may wonder whether the men of these families ever had a 'model' of marriage – to use Duby's term – in quite the same way that the canonists had a model of marriage, ultimately the legal historian must defer to Duby's assessment of the social forces that are likely to have been at work in such families. Similarly, Goody's view depends on a lifetime of work in the comparative anthropology of the family and of family property. Although the legal historian may question, for example, whether Roman legal sources suggest quite the preference for first-cousin marriage that Goody thinks that the Romans had, ultimately the legal historian must defer to Goody's assessment that the Western family after the fall of Rome differs markedly from the patterns found in most of the rest of the world, and that Christianity is probably as good a place as any to look for an explanation of this difference.[7]

The legal historian can, however, make a contribution to such arguments by offering suggestions as to the meaning, sources, perhaps even the motivation of the bodies of written law that form a key element in these arguments. The legal historian may also offer a caution that until one knows how these bodies of written law were applied, one is unlikely to get very far in assessing their social effect. Whether having a body of court records to go with the written law is a sufficient condition for assessing the social effect of a body of law is a difficult question that we cannot fully treat here, but we can offer the initial proposition that a body of written law alone, like a *cause célèbre* alone, is as likely to be misleading as illuminating.

[5] Duby, *Chevalier, femme et prêtre*; *id.*, *Medieval Marriage*.

[6] Goody, *Development of Marriage and Family*; cf. Goody, *Oriental, Ancient and Primitive*.

[7] See most recently, Symposium, "Legal Systems and Family Systems," especially Saller, "European Family History and Roman Law."

Unfortunately, for the key periods for both Goody's and Duby's arguments – the early Middle Ages and the twelfth century, respectively – there are no runs of court records. Indeed, there are no church courts, at least not in the modern sense of the word 'court', a separate institution staffed by professionals that resolves disputes or prosecutes crimes.[8] Such institutions were just beginning to develop at the end of the twelfth century, and in most areas they were not firmly established until the middle of the thirteenth century. This fact alone should make us cautious about accepting any argument, such as Goody's and Duby's, that posits a strong effect of the church's law on an unwilling society. If the church lacked an effective enforcement mechanism, then the rules that we find in the collections of canon law are more likely to have been either reflections of what society in some sense already believed and was doing or expressions of an ideal that would have an effect only if society accepted it.

Lacking any court records in the periods in which the influence is said to have taken place, we may proceed in two ways: (1) We may look at the body of rules themselves and try to discern what those who promulgated them may have been trying to do, or (2) we may look at the court records from a later period and try to reason back from what seems to have been happening in this later period to what may have happened when the rules were first promulgated. Both arguments are complicated. We will deal only with the second here.

The pioneering work of Michael Sheehan and Richard Helmholz showed, at least for England, that the number of marriage cases that raised issues about incest paled in comparison with the number of cases that raised issues about the exchange of either present or future consent.[9] That work is confirmed in Chapters 2 through 6 of this book.[10] Anne Lefebvre and Beatrice Gottlieb surveyed the surviving records from late medieval France.[11] That work is confirmed in Chapters 7, 8, and 9 of this book. Rudolf Weigand, Klaus Lindner, Christina Deutsch, and Christian Schwab have worked on Germany.[12] An international group on ecclesiastical court records produced reports on the surviving records of Austria, Belgium, England, France, Hungary, the Netherlands, and Switzerland and has made some preliminary soundings in Germany, Spain, and Italy.[13] Most recently, a group of Italian scholars have begun to explore the ecclesiastical court records in that country.[14] While the patterns of these records and of their survival vary markedly from country to country, and considerably more work in situ needs to be done, the conclusions about incest cases that Helmholz and Sheehan arrived at on the basis of a relatively small sample of English cases have held up remarkably well: Incest cases do not comprise a large portion of

[8] See, e.g., Helmholz, *Canon Law and Ecclesiastical Jurisdiction*, 139–42, and sources cited.

[9] Sheehan, "Formation"; Helmholz, *Marriage Litigation*. See Ch 1, at n. 29.

[10] See also Donahue, "Policy"; Donahue, "Monastic Judge"; Donahue, "English and French Marriage Cases."

[11] Lefebvre-Teillard, *Officialités*; cf. Gottlieb, *Getting Married*.

[12] Lit. at T&C 1179.

[13] Donahue, ed., *Records 1*, 2.

[14] See Ch 12, at nn. 75–83.

the marriage business of the medieval church courts. There are some such cases. There are instance cases in which one party is seeking a divorce or seeking to resist a claim to enforce a marriage on the ground that the parties are too closely related, and there are office cases in which the judge on his own motion orders a divorce or prohibits the marriage of a couple found to be too closely related. The number of such cases, however, pales in comparison with the number of instance cases in which one party is seeking to enforce a marriage legitimately – as he or she alleges – entered into or to obtain a separation on the ground of adultery or cruelty, or in comparison with the number of office prosecutions of fornication or adultery.

Arguments from silence are always risky, but since we are forced to argue from the relative silence of our records, let us try to see where this silence leads us. First, the search has now been extended widely enough and has covered enough different types and levels of courts that we are probably safe in arguing that the records are not there. Second, with a bit more hesitancy, we can probably argue that the records never were there, that is, that the sample is wide enough and the circumstances of its survival peculiar enough that we are probably looking at a relatively unbiased sample of what once was. The sample *is* biased toward the end of the Middle Ages, but that is probably a bias in the underlying population: More records were kept at the end of the period than at the beginning, and hence more have survived. Third, not only were relatively few cases of incest recorded but there were also relatively few such cases. This step may seem obvious, but it is dependent on the fact that many of the records we have seem to record all business that came before the court in a given period.

Hence, we conclude that medieval church courts from the thirteenth through the fifteenth centuries heard relatively few cases involving incest. What are we to make of this fact? In the first place, we can probably reject once and for all the suggestion that all medieval marriages were *de facto* dissoluble because of the incest rules. This is not to say that we do not have evidence of some people using the church courts to get out of marriages that had proven to be intolerable. We do have such evidence, and the means used to do it varied from place to place. In England, the most common means seems to have been by corrupt use of witnesses to a prior marriage.[15] In the Franco-Belgian region, the practice, at least in some dioceses, of granting separations for relatively light reasons seems to have provided an outlet for some people.[16] This is not to suggest that medieval marriages were as dissoluble as marriages are today, but simply that they were not *de facto* as indissoluble as they were *de iure*.

While there were ways to dissolve a marriage that had proven intolerable other than by using the incest rules, we must report that the use of one of the

[15] *Ingoly c Middleton, Easingwold and Wright* is a striking example, but we have seen others about which we had strong suspicions. See Helmholz, *Marriage Litigation*, 64–5.

[16] Donahue, "English and French Marriage Cases," 352–3, and sources cited; Lefebvre-Teillard, *Officialités*, 191–2, 201–4; Ch 10.

incest rules looks suspicious. In both England and the Franco-Belgian region, we occasionally find a divorce being granted on the ground of affinity by illicit intercourse.[17] Normally the relationship is very close: One of the spouses is alleged to have had prior sexual relations with the other's sibling or first cousin. Any time a legal proposition is dependent on the testimony of one of the parties and of their close relatives, one has reason to suspect perjury – a proposition that medieval judges knew as well as modern ones. On the other hand, literary tradition suggests that we should be wary of disbelieving all these stories. Perhaps in a world of arranged or partially arranged marriages, some people ended up by marrying the wrong sibling. We probably cannot go much further than this on the evidence, other than to say that even if all the cases of affinity by illicit intercourse are founded on perjured testimony, they still do not add up to *de facto* dissolubility because of the incest rules. There are only a few such cases, and as we shall see, the courts were chary of accepting such allegations.[18]

The fact that we have relatively few incest cases in the church courts does not, of course, tell us that the rules about incest had no social effect. Synodal legislation throughout the Middle Ages, and particularly in the high Middle Ages, stressed that people were to be told what the rules were, and considerable effort was made to get couples who were contemplating marriage to have banns promulgated in the church.[19] Promulgation of banns was conceived of as a device for ensuring that marriages within the prohibited degrees did not take place. But marriages that took place without the promulgation of banns were valid, and the court records suggest that such marriages were quite common, at least in some periods and in some places. In England throughout the Middle Ages, the typical marriage case involved at least one, sometimes two, unsolemnized marriages.[20] Yet the number of these cases that raise issues of incest is relatively small. That, in turn, suggests either that the courts were ignoring the incest rules or that people, by and large, were following them, or some combination of the two. We may now turn to an extraordinary group of cases that suggests both that the courts were, in some cases, ignoring the rules and that people were, in many cases, following them.

RICHARD DE CLYVE AND THE CANON LAW OF INCEST

Richard de Clyve was a monk of Christ Church Canterbury, the cathedral priory. He was probably professed as a monk of Canterbury in 1286; in 1288 he was a student at Paris writing to the prior of Canterbury about a shipment of French wine that was about to spoil.[21] In December of 1292, he was appointed

[17] For examples, both successful and unsuccessful, see at nn. 39, 42–7, 54, 58, 64, 70, 74–5, 78, 80, 83–4, 139–49, 158–63, 169–71.

[18] *Ibid.*

[19] See Sheehan, "Marriage Theory and Practice"; Diebold, "Application en France"; Donahue, "English and French Marriage Cases," 345, and sources cited.

[20] See Ch 3, at nn. 37–40; Ch 6, at nn. 23–4.

[21] Ref. T&C no. 1180.

by the prior and convent of Canterbury as commissary of the diocesan court of Canterbury, *sede vacante*, the vacancy being that between the death of Archbishop Pecham and the accession of Archbishop Winchelsey in 1294.[22] Richard served as commissary of the diocesan court again during the vacancy following Winchelsey's death in 1313.[23] He probably died in 1326.[24] He thus had a long and full life, 40 years as a professed monk, and to make the chronology plausible we must assume that he was in his 20s when he was appointed judge of the diocesan court in 1292.

Throughout his life Richard was associated with legal affairs. He served as the prior and convent's lawyer when he was not serving as a judge during vacancies.[25] In order to become a good canon lawyer in the late thirteenth century one had to study canon law at a university. The letters from Paris in the late 1280s suggest that Richard was there because the priory had sent him there to study canon law. Thus, when Richard became commissary of the diocesan court in 1292, he was young and right out of law school.

It was an experience to test the mettle of a man considerably his senior. Immediately upon Richard's taking office, Richard de Feringes, archdeacon of Canterbury, announced that he would not accept the jurisdiction of the prior and convent, appealed to Rome, and caused a minor schism within the diocese.[26] Many clergy sided with the archdeacon, and as a result, Richard de Clyve's most routine official acts became difficult, if not impossible, because clergy of the diocese refused to obey him.[27]

Richard de Clyve responded as the prior and convent of Canterbury had responded in previous jurisdictional disputes.[28] He exercised his jurisdiction to the fullest, excommunicating those who resisted his authority. He kept careful records of his actions. Because the authority of the prior and convent during vacancies was never again seriously disputed, these records remain the fullest that we have for the Canterbury diocesan court for any of the medieval vacancies.[29]

Because of the circumstances of Richard's tenure in office, we must be cautious about regarding anything that happened during this vacancy as typical. Further, there is evidence that Richard was involved in the retention of his records, and he may well have chosen atypical cases to retain.[30] The fact is, however, that more than a third of the marriage cases that survive from Richard's tenure involve incest, the highest percentage I know of from any medieval ecclesiastical court.

[22] Churchill, *Canterbury Administration*, 2:13; disc. T&C no. 1181.
[23] Ref. and disc. T&C no. 1182.
[24] Searle, "List," 177.
[25] Ref. T&C no. 1183.
[26] See Woodcock, *Medieval Ecclesiastical Courts*, 16–18.
[27] *Ibid.*
[28] See *Select Canterbury Cases*, introd. 12–14, 16, 26–7.
[29] Disc. T&C no. 1184.
[30] Disc. T&C no. 1185.

Of course, it is possible that other courts in this period were hearing as many incest cases. Thirteenth-century church court records are quite rare, and what we have tends to come from higher-level courts.[31] Further, two of Richard de Clyve's incest cases were continuations of cases brought before his predecessor.[32] The evidence, however, suggests that the number of incest cases in this group of records is unusually high. Fresh out of law school with no experience as a judge, and his life, except for a period of study in Paris, having probably been spent in the cloister, Richard was put in a situation in which he was called upon to exercise his jurisdiction to the fullest. He conducted extensive visitations of many parishes in the diocese and excommunicated those who tried to prevent him from doing so. He excommunicated rectors, vicars, and rural deans who refused to obey his mandates to conduct inquisitions into the vacancy of benefices.[33] In short, Richard's attempt to ferret out incest in the diocese may be viewed as part and parcel of his campaign to enforce the law to its fullest.

Richard de Clyve was not stupid, however, and he learned on the job. Of the 18 incest cases that survive from his brief tenure in office, 13 contain his sentences, and from the beginning they show that he knew the rules, knew how to ask the right questions, and knew how to calculate the degrees.[34] They also show that at first he did not encounter much resistance to his campaign against incest. The witnesses were willing to testify; they told what seem to be plausible stories, and Richard decreed some divorces and enjoined penance on the incestuous parties.[35] As the vacancy progressed, however, the cases changed subtly. The witnesses became less certain; some of them, we may suspect, conveniently forgot things they knew quite well.[36]

There is more explicit evidence that Richard encountered resistance to his campaign against incest: In one early case, he ordered the dissolution of a marriage and decreed that the woman be whipped around the parish church for having married within the prohibited degrees. A royal clerk who knew the woman and apparently also knew Richard wrote Richard and politely suggested that the sentence was too severe, that he should allow the woman to commute the penance by paying a fine. The case was appealed, and thus Richard did not have the opportunity to change the ruling as a result of the letter. The fact that he kept the letter, however, suggests that he thought it significant.[37]

Evidence that Richard began to withdraw from his campaign against incest abounds: In one case, Richard began to write a sentence decreeing dissolution of a marriage on the ground of affinity by illicit intercourse in the first degree.[38]

[31] E.g., *Select Canterbury Cases*.

[32] App. e11.1, "Richard de Clyve's Incest Cases" (see T&C no. 1261), nos. 1, 3; disc. T&C no. 1186.

[33] Woodcock, *Medieval Ecclesiastical Courts*, 16–18.

[34] E.g., App. e11.1, nos. 4, 6; disc. T&C no. 1187.

[35] E.g., *id.*, nos. 1, 3, 4, 6, 11.

[36] E.g., *id.*, nos. 5, 13, 16, 17; lit. T&C no. 1188.

[37] *Id.*, no. 3.

[38] *Id.*, no. 10.

He crossed it out and held that the relationship had not been proven. In another case, the proof of spiritual affinity (*confraternitas*) seems quite clear, but Richard decreed, again, that the relationship had not been proven.[39]

Richard did not abandon the campaign, however. He continued to pursue incest cases throughout the vacancy.[40] But his method of dealing with them changed. In four of the later cases, Richard asked a question that he had not asked before: "Will there be scandal in the community if this marriage is allowed to stand?" Sometimes the witnesses said there would be, and where they did, he gave sentence against the marriage; sometimes they said there would not be, and where they did, his sentences favored the marriage.[41]

There is also evidence that Richard had doubts about one aspect of the law of incest from the very beginning: Of the 18 cases, 7 raise an issue of affinity *per copulam illicitam*.[42] These cases arose in a number of ways. Sometimes one of the parties sought a divorce in an instance case, or objected to a marriage-enforcement action, on the ground of the affinity; in one case the matter seems to have arisen out of objections raised to banns, and in another the matter arose at visitation.[43] In none of these cases does Richard sustain the objection. In the two earliest cases, no sentence has survived.[44] In four of the later cases, he sustained the challenged marriage.[45] In one, an inferior judge had ruled against the divorce; the case was appealed to the official of the provincial court on the ground that the inferior judge had no jurisdiction, and no further sentence is recorded.[46] In the last two cases, Richard not only sustained the marriage but enjoined penance on the person who had alleged the illicit intercourse.[47] It is hard to escape the conclusion that Richard had determined that the dangers of corrupt allegations of affinity *per copulam illicitam* outweighed the dangers to the souls of those who were married within such an affinity and that absent some extraordinary showing, he was simply not going to enforce the law on affinity *per copulam illicitam*.

What does all this tell us about the social effect of the incest rules in the Middle Ages? Obviously, the evidence is annoyingly skimpy. It is rare that we can see as clearly as we can in Richard's case the intersection of law and society through the medium of a very human judge who seems to have been trying to do the right thing. But if the story of Richard de Clyve and the incest rules tells us anything, it is that the medieval canonical legal system could not operate for long without the cooperation of a large number of participants. If the witnesses are going to lie, if the whole community is going to resist the application of

[39] *Id.*, no. 13; lit. T&C no. 1189.
[40] E.g., *id.*, nos. 11, 12.
[41] *Id.*, nos. 9, 13, 15 (not specifically scandal but many questions about *fama*), 18.
[42] *Id.*, nos. 2, 7, 8, 10, 14, 16, 17.
[43] References T&C no. 1190.
[44] App. e11.1, nos. 2, 7; disc. T&C no. 1191.
[45] *Id.*, nos. 8, 10, 16, 17.
[46] *Id.*, no. 14; disc. T&C no. 1192.
[47] *Id.*, nos. 16, 17; disc. T&C no. 1193.

the law, a court, particularly a court largely dependent on moral suasion rather than on force, is not going to be able to apply the law.[48] Judges, even if they are professed monks, are also members of the wider community, and they are going to share the community's values. They may well seek to apply their discretion to bring their judgments more in conformity with the community's norms, at least with the norms of that segment of the community who will testify, who will tell them what will cause scandal and what will not. The judges' friends will tell them when they have gone too far, and they will begin to wonder whether the law that they learned in Paris can be applied literally in Kent.

But if Richard de Clyve could not have done what he did without some cooperation from the community, the fact is that he got cooperation in many cases. At least by the end of the thirteenth century, many ordinary men and women in Kent thought that incest was scandalous in degrees far more extensive than we would today.[49] Perhaps it is significant that both cases in which the witnesses testify that there will be scandal are cases of consanguinity, one involving third cousins and the other first cousins twice removed; whereas both cases in which the witnesses testify that there will not be scandal are cases of affinity, one of spiritual affinity and the other involving a marriage to a first cousin twice removed of the former husband of the bride.[50]

Clearly there is evidence here that society in late thirteenth-century Kent did not accept all of the church's extensive rules on prohibited marriages. In one sense, Maitland was right.[51] The law had engaged in a flight of fancy that had departed from what could be justified on either social or moral grounds. The law had to be modified. It was modified formally in the Fourth Lateran Council, and it was modified informally by judges like Richard de Clyve who refused to apply it. But even as modified, it ended up being quite different from what most societies, including our own, would regard as appropriate. All of this would suggest, if it does not quite prove, that the medieval rules about incest did not go so much against the societal grain as recent commentators would suggest that they did.

INCEST CASES AT YORK, ELY, AND PARIS

York

What do the analyses that we have undertaken in this book add to our knowledge of this topic? We have said that application or attempted application of the incest rules at York, Ely and Paris was quite rare, but it did exist. In

[48] Force was available. See, e.g., *id.*, no. 1. But the process by which it was obtained was complicated. See Logan, *Excommunication*.

[49] E.g., App. e11.1, nos. 9 (fourth degree consanguinity) and 15 (second and fourth degree consanguinity).

[50] *Id.*, nos. 13, 18.

[51] See at n. 2.

the York cause papers, the issue is raised 16 times in 178 cases, or roughly 9 percent of the cases; 6 of these cases are divorce cases, and in the remaining 10 the issue is raised as a defense to a marriage-enforcement action.[52] Of the 9 fourteenth-century cases, only 3 have sentences at any level; this is striking, considering how many York marriage cases do have sentences. In both marriage-enforcement cases that have sentences, the defense of incest (consanguinity in the fourth degree in one case, affinity by illicit intercourse with the degree not stated in the other) fails, but in the consanguinity case, we suspected that it might succeed ultimately because the witnesses on appeal look remarkably solid.[53] In the affinity case, the sentence below looks solid (no result on appeal is recorded); the judge expressly finds that the intercourse was proven but the relationship was not.[54] In the divorce case, the relationship (affinity in the fourth degree with the defendant's former wife) is conceded. The question is whether the *actrix* consented after a dispensation was obtained, and the special commissary of the official apparently holds that she did not.[55]

The fourteenth-century cases that do not have recorded sentences are decidedly a mixed bag. In one, a couple appeals before judgment from a lower-court judge who is proceeding against them *ex officio* for divorce on the ground of affinity by illicit intercourse; in another, a man is seeking a divorce from his wife on the ground that she had had intercourse with his first cousin more than 12 years previously.[56] In one of the four marriage-enforcement actions, the affinity claim (unspecified consanguinity between the *actor* and the *rea*'s former husband) is but one of a number of reasons offered to block the claimed marriage.[57] In another, the claim of affinity by illicit intercourse with the *reus*'s second cousin is more central, but the witnesses also suggest that the *reus* was forced into the marriage.[58] In the third, the witnesses about consanguinity (fourth or fifth degree) look remarkably weak.[59] In the fourth, it looks as if the *actrix* is not going to get her dower because she was consanguine (second cousin once removed) with her deceased husband.[60]

Of the seven fifteenth-century cases, five have sentences from at least one level of court. Two divorces are granted for consanguinity (third or fourth degree; fourth degree), and one for spiritual fraternity (the husband's mother was the wife's godmother at confirmation). The case of consanguinity in the fourth degree looks solid. The commissary general did the examining himself; the witnesses (one of whom described himself as being 100) traced the relationship

[52] Table 3.3.
[53] *Doncaster c Doncaster* (Ch 4, at nn. 253–4).
[54] *Godewyn c Roser* (Ch 4, at n. 78).
[55] *Nutle c Wode* (Ch 4, at n. 244).
[56] *Office c Baker and Barker* (Ch 4, at n. 243); *Helay c Evotson* (Ch 4, at n. 245).
[57] *Hopton c Brome* (Ch 4, at n. 47).
[58] *Acclum c Carthorp* (Ch 4, at nn. 75–7).
[59] *Blakden c Butre* (Ch 4, at nn. 116–17).
[60] *Hiliard c Hiliard* (Ch 4, at nn. 264–8).

clearly.[61] The other consanguinity case is more problematical. The relationship is conceded (hence the uncertainty as to precisely what it was). The issue is a dispensation. A dispensation pretty clearly existed, but apparently it was insufficient, and so the woman gets her divorce.[62] The case of spiritual fraternity is the most problematical of all. While the process by which the lower court granted the divorce looks solid, the relationship was conceded in the lower court; we see the case in York because the couple's son is bringing a collateral attack on the divorce on the ground that it was obtained by collusion in order to deprive him of his inheritance.[63] Two defenses to marriage-enforcement actions, one based on affinity by illicit intercourse with the *rea*'s second cousin, the other on spiritual fraternity (the mother of the *rea* is the *actor*'s godmother), fail. In the first case, there seems to be no doubt about the intercourse, but the depositions as to the relationship of the woman to the *rea* are contradictory.[64] In the other case, the defense is soundly defeated by the production of a papal dispensation.[65] In both the cases that have no sentence, it is clear that the defense of incest (in both cases consanguinity in the second and third degrees) to a marriage-enforcement action is secondary to a more important defense, absence in one case, force in the other.[66]

Clearly, when compared to the other issues that are raised in the York actions, the law of incest comes fairly far down on the list of what is at stake. Where it is raised, the courts seem to be requiring quite a high standard of proof, certainly to dissolve a marriage and probably also to defeat a marriage-enforcement action.[67] There is evidence of people getting trapped in a complicated body of law that seems, from a modern point of view, to have little justification, as there is some evidence of people manipulating that law to achieve purposes quite unrelated to it. While there are far too few cases of this type to make statistical statements about them, such cases seem to have a disproportionate number of litigants from the highest social echelon that we normally see in the court of York. But however much we might sympathize with the widow who probably lost her dower because her husband was her second cousin once removed,[68] and with the man whose wife was able to divorce him because he seems to have gotten an ineffective dispensation, and however much we might wonder whether the couple who got the divorce for spiritual fraternity were really trying to cut off their heir, these people were not dealing with a body of law with which most York litigants were concerned.

[61] *Kyghley c Younge* (1462), CP.F.202. See Ch 2, n. 43.

[62] *Schirburn c Schirburn* (1451–2), CP.F.187.

[63] *Ask c Ask and Conyers* (1476), CP.F.258.

[64] *Chew c Cosyn* (Ch 5, at n. 178).

[65] *Wistow c Cowper* (Ch 5, at nn. 191–3). It was suggested in Ch 5 (before n. 198) that this was the result that both litigants wanted.

[66] *Baxter c Newton* (Ch 5, n. 20); *Talbot c Townley* (Ch 5, at nn. 89–95).

[67] Disc. T&C no. 1194.

[68] See discussion, Ch 4, at nn. 272–6.

Ely

As we have noted, there are somewhat more cases at Ely that raise issues of incest than there are at York. As Table 6.4 shows, 16 percent of the Ely cases (14/88) in which the defense to a marriage-enforcement action or the claim for a divorce action is known, as opposed to 10 percent of the York cases (17/178), raise the issue.[69] A brief review of these cases, all but one of which have been dealt with previously, suggests both why there is this difference and what the significance of incest was in the matrimonial litigation at Ely in the late fourteenth century.

One divorce is granted at the instance of the parties on the basis of affinity by illicit intercourse, the man having had intercourse prior to his marriage with his wife's second cousin. The action is confessed by all three persons concerned, and five witnesses support their claims. Collusion is not the inevitable conclusion that one can draw from this record, but it could be.[70] In the only other instance divorce action in this group, the woman's basic claim is her husband's impotence. He disappears and thus cannot be examined by the matrons, and so she proceeds to produce four witnesses to fourth-degree consanguinity, and the court pronounces a divorce on this ground. There can be little doubt that the husband was impotent, just as there can little doubt that the consanguinity was an afterthought. The court may have winked at these witnesses.[71]

Issues of incest are also raised in office cases in the Ely register, a type of case that we see little of in the York cause papers.[72] Unlike the Cambrai cases that will be examined, however, all the Ely cases seem to have been brought at the very beginning of the marriage, or at the very beginning of its public phase. A couple cited for clandestine contract of marriage confess to a *de presenti* marriage followed by intercourse. The boy's father alleges consanguinity and produces witnesses to that effect. The couple apparently have no answer to the charges, and their marriage is dissolved for consanguinity in the third and fourth degrees.[73] Another case begins with a similar citation after an urban dean inhibited the solemnization of marriage (even though no one had objected to banns) on the ground of affinity by illicit intercourse. Once more the parties confess to a *de presenti* marriage plus *copula*. The woman who was the man's prior sexual partner attempts to prove (with considerable help from the court) that she is related to the *rea* and fails. She is ordered to do penance, and the couple is ordered to solemnize.[74] In a third case, the initial citation is for illegal solemnization. The couple's marriage seems pretty clearly to be impeded by affinity by illicit intercourse in the third degree. They obtain a papal dispensation,

[69] Disc. T&C no. 1195.
[70] *Marion c Umphrey* (Ch 6, at nn. 101–2).
[71] *Pyncote c Maddyngle* (Ch 6, at nn. 182–3).
[72] Disc. T&C no. 1196.
[73] *Office c Symond and Page* (Ch 6, at n. 229).
[74] *Office c Barbour and Whitheved* (Ch 6, at nn. 215–17).

but this is held to be inadequate. The case seems to involve a substantial amount of local politics.[75]

In other cases, brought at least initially *ex officio*, we can be less sure that the divorce of an actual marriage was at stake, though it likely was, given the prevalence of informal *de presenti* marriages in Ely diocese.[76] In one case, a vicar is cited *ex officio* for having refused to solemnize a marriage. His response is that five parishioners had reclaimed against the banns on the ground of consanguinity (the degree is never stated). Four of them appear and testify, and the court ultimately holds that the contract, if there was one, is void for consanguinity.[77] In another case, a reclamation of banns alleges affinity by illicit intercourse. The couple both confess that the man had previously had intercourse with one Matilda, but they say that they do not know whether Matilda is related to the *rea*. Witnesses are produced. The record does not say who produced the witnesses, but it does say that the *rea* is dismissed from the *reus*'s suit.[78] It seems clear that the marriage was not allowed to go forward, perhaps contrary to the desires of the couple, perhaps contrary to just that of the man. In another case, a man who has the same surname as the *reus* and a woman are cited *ex officio* to show cause why they reclaimed against a couple's banns. In addition to unrelated accusations of the impediment of crime, they allege that the couple's marriage is impeded by affinity by illicit intercourse or by public honesty, because another man, a consanguine of the prospective husband, had intercourse with the prospective wife or, at least, contracted to marry her. Five witnesses are produced, but then the reclaimants are contumacious. The case is still proceeding when the register ends, but it seems unlikely that anything will come of it.[79] In the last office case on a reclamation, no citation is mentioned; the couple simply appears. The *reus*, if he should be called that, proposes that his marriage is impeded by affinity because of the *rea*'s intercourse with a relative of his ("within the fourth degree" is all that is specified) and her precontract with another man. The *rea* excepts that the alleged precontract was impeded both by the fact that the man had a living wife and by her spiritual comaternity with the man. Without hearing the full story of the previous marriage, the official rules against the current marriage on the basis of the affinity by illicit intercourse.[80]

The instance cases in which the issue of incest is raised are all ones in which the issue seems to be an afterthought. One that is not discussed in Chapter 6 is typical. In a competitor case, the *reus* excepts to the first *actrix* on the basis of precontract with the second. The first *actrix* replicates that

[75] *Office c Slory and Feltewell* (Ch 6, at nn. 191–7).
[76] Lit. T&C no. 1197.
[77] *Office c Bourn (vicar)* (Ch 6, at n. 228).
[78] *Page c Chapman* (Ch 6, at n. 49).
[79] *Office and Andren and Edyng c Andren and Solsa* (Ch 6, at n. 218).
[80] *Borewell c Bileye* (Ch 6, at nn. 152–6).

the *reus* and the second *actrix* are consanguine. Although two witnesses are produced to this effect, the official orders the second *actrix* and the *reus* to solemnize, holding that no consanguinity is proven. In an unusual move, the first *actrix*'s proctor accepts the decision.[81] In an interlocking competitor case, the *rea* in the first case proposes that the marriage claimed by the *actor* cannot stand because it was induced by fear, because they are consanguine, and because she was (?) previously married to the *reus* in the other case. She wins on all three points, and one wonders how much of a role the consanguinity played.[82]

The final two cases are quite unusual. In one, the official apparently gives a couple a dispensation "under the table" for affinity by illicit intercourse probably in a quite remote degree, but in the meantime, the woman has formed a relationship with another man, who sues and ultimately succeeds in having the first marriage held invalid and his sustained.[83] The other begins as a quite standard competitor case, which the *reus* successfully defends on the ground of his precontract with the second *actrix*. He is then cited for failure to solemnize with the second *actrix* and defends this action on the ground of affinity by illicit intercourse (his own, in a degree not specified). The case is still proceeding when the register ends. If this claim is not the product of a subsequent discovery, it is the product of a highly manipulative strategy.[84]

The reason why there are more cases that raise issues of incest at Ely than at York seems clear. Seven of the Ely cases begin with one or another form of office citation, a type of case that is reflected in only one of those at York.[85] The Ely office cases, begun on reclamation of banns, suggest a range of motivations lying behind the reclamations. In only two cases is there a suggestion of community opposition to the marriage because of the potential incest. Such opposition seems likely in the case of the vicar who was faced with five parishioners reclaiming against a couple's banns on the ground of consanguinity, less likely but at least possible in the case of affinity by illicit intercourse attested by witnesses who are not identified as supporting any particular party.[86] All the rest of the cases have quite definite 'movers': the father of the man, a woman who was the man's prior sexual partner, a clergyman opposed to a local faction, a man with the same surname as the *reus*, and in one case, it would seem, the would-be husband himself.[87] When these cases are coupled with the two instance divorce cases, in one of which we suspected collusion and in the other of which the incest claim is clearly raised after the

[81] *Teweslond and Watteson c Kembthed* (21.vii.79 to 24.xi.79), fol. 119r–124r.

[82] *Pope and Dreu c Dreu and Newton* (Ch 6, at n. 122). There is some doubt whether the Dreu-Newton marriage was previous.

[83] *Gobat and Pertesen c Bygot* (Ch 6, at n. 89); disc. T&C no. 1198.

[84] *Blofeld and Reder c Lile* (Ch 6, at nn. 176–7).

[85] *Office c Baker and Barker* (Ch 4, at n. 243).

[86] *Office c Bourn (vicar)* (at n. 77); *Page c Chapman* (at n. 78); disc. T&C no. 1199.

[87] Listed T&C no. 1200.

actrix encountered difficulties in proving her basic claim of impotence, and are also coupled with the instance cases in which the incest claim seems to be an afterthought, we are probably correct in concluding that for the most part, incest in late fourteenth-century Ely was not a matter of great social concern but a complicated body of rules that could be used strategically or tactically to achieve ends quite different from those suggested by the rules themselves.[88] That this should be the case is not surprising considering that the degrees involved, in those cases in which they are mentioned, are quite remote and, by this time, dispensable for those who had the persistence and the money to obtain a dispensation.

Once more, Maitland was, in some sense, right. The law of incest could be used manipulatively and was so being used at Ely in the late fourteenth century. By and large, however, it was not being used to dissolve long-standing marriages entered into by couples unsuspecting of the relationship. Where it did play a role was in marriage-formation cases. Its role there was not nearly so important as the role played by precontract or by factual disputes about the existence of the contract. It appears more often in marriage-enforcement cases than any defense other than precontract or denial, but those other defenses combined appear more often than it does.[89] We return once more to the extensiveness of the degrees that are mentioned. From what we can tell from the litigation, it would seem that the men and women of Ely diocese in the late fourteenth century were well aware that they could get into trouble by contracting marriage or having sexual relations with close relatives. Where they opened themselves to trouble was when they engaged in the same behavior with somewhat more remote relatives. That at least at some levels of society they did so out of ignorance is suggested by the case of affinity by illicit intercourse in which the couple quite frankly concede the intercourse and admit that they do not know whether the third party is related to them or not.[90]

Paris

The story of the canon law of incest in the Paris register can be quickly told. There is only one case involving it, a dissolution of *sponsalia* on the ground that the former wife of the man (who was probably seeking the dissolution) was the second cousin once removed of his current fiancée.[91] The remoteness of this relationship, coupled with the total absence in the Paris register of other cases involving these rules, suggests either that sophisticated Parisians of the late fourteenth century knew the rules and behaved accordingly or that the Paris court was not particularly concerned about them. Perhaps some combination of the two is the most likely conclusion.

[88] See at nn. 70–1, 81–4.
[89] See Table 6.4.
[90] *Page c Chapman* (at n. 78).
[91] *Rivers c Contesse* (Ch 7, at n. 135).

INCEST CASES AT CAMBRAI AND BRUSSELS

Introduction and Prosecution of Sexual Offenses Involving Incest at Cambrai

Cambrai and Brussels are quite a different story from Paris.[92] Divorce cases, cases involving the dissolution of *sponsalia*, and cases involving the dissolution of presumptive marriages all produce violations or claimed violations of the incest rules. There are 19 such cases in the Cambrai sample (19/207, 9%) and 15 in the Brussels sample (15/157, 10%).[93] This is close to the percentages at York (9%), somewhat less than what we found at Ely (16%). To this number should be added for Cambrai (there are no comparable cases in the sample for Brussels) the number of adultery and fornication cases that involve allegations of incest (16/36, 44%; see Table 8.7). While the comparison here is between somewhat dissimilar institutions (as we have seen, neither Brussels nor York and Ely regularly handled straight cases of adultery or fornication), the fact is that 14 percent of the cases in the larger Cambrai sample involved issues of incest (35/258), the second highest number in our five courts.

It is characteristic of prosecutions of adultery and fornication at Cambrai (whether incest is involved or not) that the sentences make a sharp distinction between a finding that the offense had been committed and a finding that the *reus* had 'incautious conversation' with the *rea* so that *fama* of the sexual relationship arose. 'Incautious conversation', like solicitation of a sexual relationship that did not happen, was subject to amends, and hence virtually all of those prosecuted were convicted of something, but the sentences carefully distinguish among offenses, and they also carefully distinguish between offenses that were found and those about which only *fama* was found.[94]

The same pattern is followed where incest is also alleged. In 11 cases (9 adultery and 2 fornication), a potentially incestuous degree of relationship between the couple is conceded, but there is only *fama* that they had intercourse.[95] In 3 cases (2 adultery and 1 fornication), the intercourse is found but the relationship is known only by *fama*.[96] In 1 case (adultery) both the intercourse and the relationship are known only by *fama*.[97] In only 1 case (fornication) is incest found, and this only for the woman (apparently she confessed); the man seems to be held only for allowing *fama* of the intercourse to arise.[98] In the cases where intercourse is found but the relationship is known

[92] This section was written before I had examined Vleeschouwers-van Melkebeek, "Incestuous Marriages." Her conclusions differ somewhat from mine and are best discussed in App. e11.2, "Recent Work on Incest Cases at Cambrai and Brussels" (see T&C no. 1262).

[93] Disc. T&C no. 1201.

[94] Details T&C no. 1202.

[95] Listed T&C no. 1203.

[96] Listed T&C no. 1204.

[97] *Office c Hughe* (1) (2.vii.46), no. 953.

[98] *Office c Walop et Rueden* (14.iii.39), no. 171, T&C no. 1205.

only by *fama*, the level of rhetoric, and probably the amends, are increased because the couple went ahead and had intercourse anyway despite the *fama*.[99]

The relationships are in many cases quite close: first degree affinity (wife's mother; the woman whom his brother had previously, or was defamed to have previously, known; wife's daughter; previous sexual partner's father; previous sexual partner's daughter), and second degree consanguinity (*consanguinea germana*, probably first cousin; *nepos*, probably nephew).[100] One can certainly imagine how scandal could have arisen about 'incautious conversation' between such people. There are two cases of spiritual affinity, probably both with godmothers, though the ambiguous term *commater* is used (one of them is also the putative first cousin).[101] In other cases the relationship is vaguer: "in some degree, as he confesses, consanguine"; "affine, while he lived, within the fourth degree"; "consanguine, as the *reus* asserts, in a remote degree, not describing it otherwise"; "in the fourth degree"; "consanguinity between him and [the woman's former husband] in a prohibited degree, and hence affinity between him and [her]"; "his consanguine and also affine"; "his consanguine."[102] While such accusations could have arisen as the result of genuine scandal, one suspects that the promotor had something to do with stirring them up. In one case, we know that the charges were raised by "a certain partner in adultery of the *reus*."[103]

The fact is, however, that only one of these charges of incest was proven, and that, apparently, because the *rea* (but not the *reus*) confessed. We do not know what the amends were for 'incautious conversation', but it is hard to imagine that they were high. They were probably higher for illicit intercourse knowing of the *fama* of a relationship; at least the intercourse was proven or confessed in such cases, but there are relatively few such cases. If the promotors of Cambrai were engaged in a campaign to ferret out illicit incest, they were remarkably unsuccessful in proving it. This is a theme to which we will return when we examine the cases in which marriage formation or dissolution was involved.

There is one more striking characteristic about the Cambrai adultery and fornication cases, whether or not incest was involved. There are very few women defendants. Discussion of possible explanations for this phenomenon is best left to the margin,[104] but one deserves mention here: In some cases, the promotor may have agreed not to prosecute the woman in return for her testifying against the man. This option might have seemed particularly attractive to the promotor in situations in which the woman did not have the money to pay his costs or

99 *Office c Porte et Hennique* (n. 96) is a particularly good example.
100 Listed T&C no. 1206.
101 Listed and disc. T&C no. 1207.
102 Listed and disc. T&C no. 1208.
103 *Office c Quintart* (n. 94), T&C no. 1209.
104 Disc. T&C no. 1210.

the amends. We do not know in how many cases this would have been so, but some of these women seem to have been quite poor.[105]

Prescinding from adultery and fornication prosecutions at Cambrai and returning to types of cases that are comparable to those heard in our other courts, the relatively high proportion of incest claims in such cases did not produce a correspondingly high proportion of cases in which the claim of incest was sustained. At Brussels, the claim of incest was successful in only five cases (5/15, 33%); at Cambrai it succeeded in a higher proportion of cases (8/19, 42%). The Cambrai number is, however, skewed by the fact that the incest claim prevailed in five of seven actions for dissolution of *sponsalia*, where, as we will see, the court was willing to rule on the basis of *fama*. In the case of divorce either of existing or presumptive marriages, the court finds incest in only 3 of 12 cases (25%).[106] What is interesting about all of these cases is how the four different judges reacted to them over the course of their tenures. Exploring the range of those reactions may, in turn, allow us to infer something about social attitudes in the diocese of Cambrai in this period.

Divorce from the Bond – Cambrai

Table 8.7 indicates that there are 12 cases of divorce from the bond in our Cambrai sample, strikingly all office cases, 9 of which involve incest.[107] Strikingly, too, the promotor succeeds in dissolving the marriages in only 2 cases (17% success rate). Of the incest cases there are 8 where the impediment is described as one of affinity: 5 by illicit intercourse, 1 by licit, and 2 in which the nature of the affinity is not further described. There is also 1 case of an alleged impediment of consanguinity.

We begin with the two cases in which marriages were dissolved. In February of 1439, Divitis dissolved the marriage of Amand de Sceppere and Marguerite Clercs.[108] Amand was a widower who had previously been married to Marguerite Ghiselins, who, Divitis finds, was related to Marguerite within the fourth degree of consanguinity. Three banns were proclaimed on the espousals of Amand and Marguerite in the church of Schorisse.[109] Knowing that there was *fama communis* about the affinity, the couple went to Ghent (a relatively short boat ride up the Scheldt) in the diocese of Tournai and solemnized their marriage there in the parish of Sint-Michaël. Divitis pronounced this marriage "null or at least invalid" (*nullum aut saltem invalidum*), ordered them to make amends, pay the costs of the promotor, and furnish two pounds of wax for the chapel of the officiality. He also gave them license to marry others.

[105] This is suggested by *Office c Pont* (n. 94), in which the man solicited the woman with the promise of two bushels of grain.
[106] Our samples may be understating here; see App. e11.2.
[107] Disc. T&C no. 1211.
[108] *Office c Sceppere et Clercs* (21.ii.39), no. 150, T&C no. 1212.
[109] Now a part of Maarkedal, prov. Oost-Vlaanderen, about 2 miles southeast of Oudenaarde.

In September of 1442, Nicolaï dissolved the marriage of Hugues Brohon and Jeanne Destrées.[110] Jeanne had been the concubine of the uncle of Hugues, Mathieu, who was probably a priest.[111] They had even had a male child, who was now dead. Knowing that "they could not join with each other in marriage nor cohabit in the flesh without the penalty of incest, ... they sought to contract incestuous nuptials with each other and for this purpose sought out a foreign city, to wit, Laon, where truthful notice of these premises could not be had."[112] They contracted *sponsalia* in the hand of the priest and the face of the church of Saint-Pierre-le-Vieux, and when the *curé* refused to solemnize the marriage because they did not have dimissory letters from their *curé* or bishop, they had the incestuous marriage solemnized in a priory and by an alleged religious of the order of the Knights Hospitallers.

The level of rhetoric of this sentence has already been considerably higher than that of the previous sentence, but at this point Nicolaï goes, in the colloquial phrase, 'over the top':[113]

[P]roceeding from bad to worse, they presumed to defile themselves often and very often with the incestuous mingling and cohabitation in the flesh that they had planned under the guise [of marriage], in and through these [acts] damnably committing incest, essaying, to the extent that they were able, illegal, wicked marriage, a mockery of the sacrament of marriage, and busied themselves with the guise of their sin.

For this reason, they were condemned to make amends "corresponding to such enormities" and pay the costs of the promotor:[114]

[We] determine and announce that between them, the affinity standing in the way, effective marriage could or can neither be contracted nor subsist, and that whatever was attempted in this matter was and is void, null, and vainly, though *de facto*, presumed. We quash, annul, and dissolve this very thing [marriage] insofar as it has proceeded *de facto*.

[We] inhibit them, therefore, and each of them that they not presume to cohabit further with each other under type or color of marriage, to stay with each other, or even to have other conversation with each other from which even suspicion of further incestuous cohabitation could or ought to find an excuse, under penalty of excommunication and prison at the pleasure of the most reverend our lord of Cambrai, if – may it not happen! – they do so to the contrary.

What accounts for the difference between these two cases, not only of the level of rhetoric but also of result (dissolution, a fairly mild injunction to make amends, coupled with license to marry others, as opposed to dissolution, a ringing injunction to make amends, a strong injunction for the future, and no license mentioned)? To a certain extent it is a difference in style between the two judges. Divitis rarely raises the level of rhetoric; Nicolaï does so fairly

110 *Office c Brohon et Destrées* (10.ix.42), no. 321.
111 Lit. T&C no. 1213.
112 *Office c Brohon et Destrées* (n. 110), T&C no. 1214.
113 *Ibid.*, T&C no. 1215.
114 *Ibid.*, T&C no. 1216.

frequently. Behind this we may suspect a difference in personalities and perhaps in attitudes toward sin and sinners.

Both couples, it should be noted, had defied the authority of the church by going to another diocese and getting their marriages solemnized. This was regarded as a serious offense, even in more relaxed England.[115] There are, however, reasons for thinking that Hugues and Jeanne would have been regarded as more serious offenders than Amand and Marguerite. In the case of Hugues and Jeanne, the affinity was very close. Second-degree affinity may not have been dispensable as a regular matter; it certainly was not easy to obtain such a dispensation. All we know about the relationship between Amand and Marguerite was that is was within the fourth degree. Marguerite could have been as distantly related to Amand's former wife as third cousin. Fourth- and third-degree affinity (third and second cousins) was dispensable; it was just that this couple did not obtain the dispensation. No mention is made of Amand and Marguerite's failure to obtain dimissory letters, and it is even possible that the *curé* of Schorisse gave them this advice: "You can't get married here because of the rumors about Marguerite's relationship with your former wife, but take a boat up the Scheldt to Ghent, and my friend the pastor of Sint-Michaël will marry you." Not only did Hugues and Jeanne go to another diocese; they did not even go to the closest one (which would have been Noyon, if we assume that they were living in Cambrai), and they ultimately did not even get married in a parish church because the *curé* in Laon refused to marry them without dimissory letters. Their marriage was solemnized before a "supposed" (*assertum*) Knight Hospitaller.

To this we might add the difference in the way in which the affinity arose – legally irrelevant but perhaps not irrelevant in explaining the attitudes of the two judges. Jeanne had been Mathieu's concubine, and Mathieu may have been a priest. Amand, by contrast, had been lawfully married to his former wife, who, unfortunately, turned out to be related to a woman he now wanted to marry. Amand and Marguerite seem like a respectable, slightly older couple, who got caught in the snares of medieval incest law. Hugues and Jeanne, by contrast, seem like low-life types, and the marriage may even have been put together as a cover for Mathieu's continuing relationship with Jeanne.

The remaining cases show the great reluctance of both judges to dissolve a public marriage unless the proof of the impediment was clear. The only other sentence by Divitis in this group begins with a ringing declaration that the marriage of Gilles Sadonne and Catherine vander Keere, contracted solemnly and followed by cohabitation, is valid, notwithstanding what the promotor has proposed. Divitis then proceeds to order the couple to make amends, Gilles because he proceeded to contract marriage with Catherine knowing that there was *fama* that his son had previously had sexual relations with her, and Catherine because she had abandoned Gilles without judgment of the church and formed an adulterous relationship with another man. (The sentence also notes

115 See Ch 6, at nn. 189–219.

that Gilles had failed to reclaim Catherine, though it is unclear whether he was fined for this.)[116]

The sentence is well within the law. Clearly, Gilles (it is interesting that nothing is said of Catherine here) should not have proceeded to solemnize his marriage with Catherine until it was determined whether the *fama* was true. It was also clear that Catherine should not have left Gilles without judgment of the church after the public marriage, though here, knowledge of the incestuousness of the relationship might have provided an excuse. Of course, even if Catherine was justified in leaving Gilles, she should not have formed an adulterous relationship with another man. Whether Gilles was obligated to take steps to get Catherine back is a matter of more doubt, but then again, it is not clear that he was fined for that. Divitis may have mentioned his failure to do so in order to emphasize the difference between his situation before the marriage and after.

As is usual with Divitis's cryptic sentences, there is much that we would like to know that we do not know. We know that no witnesses were heard in the case (apparently the promotor could not produce the son in court, or the son would not have testified in the promotor's favor). Catherine probably firmly denied that she had sexual relations with the son, and perhaps she also testified that she had not known of the *fama*. (That seems hard to believe, but she may have said it.) That would have excused her from having gone ahead with the marriage to Gilles but would, at the same time, have deprived her of any excuse for leaving him. That makes it look as if her reason for leaving him was in order to take up with another man.

It is possible that the story was more complicated. Gilles and Catherine may both have known about the rumor. Indeed, it may have been true. They got married anyway. Then they had qualms of conscience and decided to separate. This would explain why Gilles made no effort to get her back. It would also explain why she took up with another man. They did not count on the promotor's insistence on keeping up appearances, however. When the case came to court, either Catherine could not bring herself to admit the truth of allegations or she did admit it, but Divitis would not upset a public marriage on the basis of the confession of one of the parties alone and the promotor had no other proof. We should keep this last possibility in mind as we look at Nicolaï's remaining sentences.

These sentences reverse the order of Divitis's last sentence; first, the couple are ordered to make amends, sometimes in quite strong language; then they are told that their marriage can stand. The following sentence is typical:[117]

> [N]eglecting and notwithstanding the *fama* that was at work about their mutual affinity – which well could have impeded their contracting marriage – not bothering with and not waiting for, indeed, not asking for a declaration from a competent judge about it, despite the fact that nothing stood in their way [of their doing this], they presumed to contract

[116] *Office c Sadonne et Keere* (17.i.39), no. 120, T&C no. 1217.
[117] *Office c Oems et Cloets* (23.i.45), no. 630, T&C no. 1218.

matrimonial agreements and then marriage, to solemnize and to consummate with sexual intercourse, in and through the foregoing, showing themselves to be deliberately ignorant ['seekers after ignorance'].

The last phrase, *affectatores ignorantie*, appears to be a technical phrase for deliberately not pursuing a matter that ought to have been pursued.[118] For this the couple is condemned to make amends, pay the promotor's costs, and furnish half a pound of wax apiece for the chapel of the officiality:[119]

[W]e nevertheless decree and declare that the marriage contracted, as previously described, by and between these defendants, solemnized, and consummated by sexual intercourse [is] valid, efficacious, and to remain in effect so long as they both live.

More serious offenses call for a higher level of rhetoric and, presumably, higher fines. In *Office c Thomas vanden Huffle et Catherine Seghers*,[120] not only did the couple know of the *fama* of the consanguinity between Catherine and a woman with whom Thomas had confessed he had illicit sexual relations, but Thomas had also bribed the woman to withdraw her opposition to their banns. This couple showed themselves to "be 'seekers after ignorance'" and also of "incestuous marriages."[121] But the bottom line is the same: The marriage is to remain firm, "since no impediment sufficient to dissolve it is apparent."[122] In *Office c Pierre van Beerseele et Élisabeth Smets*,[123] the couple had deliberately not had the banns proclaimed in Bergilers, whence Élisabeth came, because they knew that if they did, her relationship to a woman with whom Pierre had previously committed adultery would be made known. This made them "seekers after incestuous marriages," but was not sufficient to dissolve their solemnized and consummated marriage, "since it is not clear that there is enough about the alleged impediment to give us the confidence to dissolve a marriage that has already been contracted."[124] In *Office c Josse Brumère et Élisabeth de Calant*,[125] the couple had contracted clandestinely, had clandestinely consummated the contract, and had had the marriage solemnized in another diocese without obtaining letters dimissory, the last apparently because Josse had had illicit sexual relations with Élisabeth's sister (of which Élisabeth was aware). There is a long list of things for which they are to make amends, but the marriage is allowed to stand, "since it is apparent that there is no impediment, at least not one sufficient to dissolve [an existing marriage], notwithstanding what has been alleged to the contrary."[126]

118 See Ch 9, n. 297. The phrase is probably derived from *Cum inihibitio*, Ch 1, n. 77, and appears frequently in sentences of Nicolaï, e.g., at nn. 121, 124; *Registres de Cambrai*, s.v. *affectator*.
119 *Office c Oems et Cloets* (n. 117), T&C no. 1219.
120 *Office c Huffle et Seghers* (6.iii.45), no. 660.
121 *Ibid.*, T&C no. 1220.
122 *Ibid.*, T&C no. 1221.
123 *Office c Beerseele et Smets* (4.xii.45), no. 840.
124 *Ibid.*, T&C no. 1222.
125 *Office c Brumère et Calant* (6.v.46), no. 1131.
126 *Ibid.*, T&C no. 1223.

All of these cases are subsequent to *Office c Brohon et Destrées* and to *Office c Tiestaert, Hove et Beckere*, the case discussed in Chapter 9 in which Nicolaï displays heightened concern about *affinitas per copulam illicitam*.[127] They suggest that he experienced a change of heart and moved from enforcing the law in this area in all its rigor to allowing as much as the law would allow, and perhaps more. *Office c Brumère et Calant* is the easiest result to explain in terms of the existing law. In this case, Nicolaï finds that the affinity (by illicit intercourse with the *rea*'s sister) arose after the *rei* had converted their clandestine promises of marriage into a presumptive marriage by having intercourse. Granted that finding (the factual basis for which we cannot tell, though we do know that witnesses were heard and that the contract that gave rise to the presumptive marriage took place "many years ago" [*iam pluribus annis effluxis*]), the law was clear. Preexisting affinity was a diriment impediment to marriage, but affinity that arose after the marriage was not grounds for its dissolution.[128]

Office c Huffle et Seghers and *Office c Beerseele et Smets* are harder to explain. In both cases, the affinity was preexisting, the man confessed the intercourse, and the relationship (second degree in the first case, third degree in the second) was proven.[129] Yet in both cases Nicolaï found that the impediment had not been sufficiently proved (*minime constet* in the first; *non liqueat*, in a particularly tortured phrase, in the second).[130] The only legal explanation that I can give for these holdings is the one suggested previously: Nicolaï had decided that he would not dissolve a marriage on the basis of the confession of the parties alone, at least not a confession to affinity by illicit intercourse. Whether he would have insisted on two unbiased witnesses to the act of intercourse itself, we cannot tell. But the law of proof might have allowed him to go that far.

Once we have seen that an unusually high standard of proof is being demanded in these two cases, we must reconsider what is happening in the other cases where the sentence is less clear about what was established but the marriage is sustained. Divitis may also have demanded a high standard of proof. His one sentence in the sample favorable to the marriage, *Office c Sadonne et Keere*, is open to this interpretation, as is Nicolaï's sentence in *Office c Oems et Cloets*.[131] Indeed, the pattern that emerges from these sentences suggests that both the judgments and the rhetoric in *Office c Brohon et Destrées* and *Office c Tiestaert, Hove et Beckere* are what is hard to explain. Something about these cases, or these defendants, touched a raw nerve in Nicolaï, who, we must remember, was at this time relatively new on the job. It could have

127 See at nn. 110–14; Ch 9, at nn. 293–302.
128 Lit. T&C no. 1224.
129 T&C no. 1225.
130 Nn. 122, 124.
131 At nn. 116, 117.

been simply that the defendants were young, of relatively low station, and particularly unconcerned about conforming their sexual behavior to the rules.

The promotors got the word. After *Office c Brumère et Calant*, I have found only two more cases in the Cambrai registers, both in the sample, in which affinity is raised as a possible ground of dissolution of an existing marriage. In one, Nicolaï refuses to dissolve a long-term marriage on the basis of a *fama* of affinity of an unspecified type, though he does fine the parties for having married despite the *fama*, and he does mention that he conducted an *ex officio* investigation into the truth of the *fama*.[132] In the other, Nicolaï allows a clandestine presumptive marriage to stand, ordering the couple to make amends for having entered into such a marriage and having entered into it despite the *fama* of an, again, unspecified affinity. He orders the couple to solemnize, specifically holding that *fama* alone is not enough to impede an existing marriage.[133]

The one case of consanguinity is very much in the pattern of the cases of affinity. The couple are fined for solemnizing their marriage knowing of the *fama* of their consanguinity; they are therefore "deliberately ignorant," but the marriage is to be sustained, "since no impediment sufficient to dissolve [an existing marriage] is apparent."[134]

Divorce from the Bond – Brussels

We have already seen that Nicolaï at Cambrai was, it would seem, trying to discourage the promotors from bringing cases for divorce from the bond by demanding a high standard of proof. Certainly, such cases decline over the course of his tenure. The same practice seems to have been followed in Brussels. There is only one office divorce case in the sample, and although the divorce was granted, the unusual nature of the case suggests that it was exceptional. The couple in question were to make amends for having had their marriage solemnized knowing of the *fama* of their consanguinity and without obtaining any judgment about it. They then "stood for a time in the same house, board, and bed," and, in an extraordinarily awkward phrase, "they many times presumed to attempt to use force concerning the carnal act between each other."[135] Whatever this phrase means, it suggests that they did not succeed in having intercourse. They then separated without the judgment of the church. Since that time the man has sinned with many single women against the law of his marriage, and the woman has taken up with two married men by one of whom she has had children. Whatever this couple's difficulty was with having intercourse with each other, they did not seem to have had any difficulty with others. After this series of amends, Rodolphi dissolves the marriage on the ground that "it is

132 *Office c Johenniau et Chavaliere* (T&C no. 1218), T&C no. 1226.
133 *Office c Raes et Piperzele* (31.x.49), no. 1220, T&C no. 1227.
134 *Office c Heymans et Nath* (18.xii.45), no. 850, T&C no. 1228.
135 Disc. T&C no. 1229.

clearly apparent from the depositions of the witnesses that they are connected to each other in the fourth degree of consanguinity."[136]

This couple would probably have come to the attention of the promotor even if there had been no issue about consanguinity, and Rodolphi was clearly multiplying the amends (something that he had a tendency to do in other cases). This marriage had not been consummated and could, in this period, have been dissolved by the pope. Older law recognized (whether correctly or not we need not decide) that couples could be incapable of having intercourse with each other, even if they could have it with other people. On a human level, this marriage did not look as if it had any promise of success. Rodolphi had at hand a valid reason to dissolve it, and he did.

The other divorce case in the sample is an instance case in which the woman raises a defense of third-degree affinity to a suit by her husband for restoration of conjugal rights. Platea at first orders her to return to her husband, but not to have intercourse with him. She appeals to Rome, but the appeal is declared frivolous. Platea denies *apostoli* and says that he is prepared to hear the divorce claim. He then allows her to live separately from her husband during the pendency of the case, and that is the last we hear of it.[137]

Dissolution of Presumptive Marriages – Cambrai

In three cases in the Cambrai sample, a presumptive marriage seems to be conceded – indeed, it seems to be desired by the parties – and the issue is whether it must be dissolved because of incest. In one of the cases, it is clear that the promotor is trying to get the marriage dissolved despite the wishes of the parties. In the other cases, the role of the promotor is more ambiguous.

The clearest case is the earliest. Divitis finds that the couple had contracted clandestinely and that the man had deflowered the woman and procreated many children by her. He orders them to solemnize their marriage, notwithstanding the impediment of consanguinity alleged by the promotor. He also orders them to make amends and pay two pounds of wax to the chapel of the court.[138]

The promotor introduced witnesses, but they clearly did not prove the consanguinity. We cannot tell whether the couple had failed to solemnize their marriage because they feared that the possible consanguinity would stand in their way (a fact that is mentioned in some of the succeeding cases) or whether this was simply a couple who chose to marry informally. In either case, the promotor's proceeding against them seems to have resulted in regularizing their situation, one that had been going on for some time, as the reference to *plures proles* indicates.

The next two cases are similar. In both cases the *rei* contracted publicly; in both cases, it would seem, the publicity brought to light a possible affinity

136 *Officie c Gheerts en Bertels* (Ch 9, n. 357), T&C no. 1230.
137 *Perre c Meys* (Ch 9, n. 357).
138 *Office c Pevenage et Stapcoemans* (24.i.39), no. 126.

between them. In one case it was an *affinitas per copulam illicitam* of the *rea* with a blood relative of the man; in the other case the precise nature of the affinity is not stated, but it was probably *affinitas per copulam illicitam*. In both cases, the couple knew of the *fama* of the *affinitas*. Notwithstanding this, in both cases the couple consummated their relationship, converting the promises into a *matrimonium presumptum*, if such a marriage were valid, and in both cases, they attempted to go further publicly, in one case by having the second banns proclaimed, in the other case, apparently, by attempting to have the marriage solemnized. In both cases, the couples were fined for consummating their marriage before solemnization (one case specifically mentions the excommunication that they incurred under the synodal statutes for doing this) and for proceeding while knowing of the *fama* of the relationship (in one case the couple had intercourse while the case was *sub iudice*), and were ordered to pay the costs of the promotor. The ultimate results of the two cases are quite different, however. In one case, Nicolaï orders the couple to solemnize their presumptive marriage on the ground that "*fama* alone cannot destroy a marriage that is already contracted." In the other case, Nicolaï orders the couple under a penalty of excommunication and 20 *florins* not to cohabit or have sexual intercourse, to pay the costs of the promotor, and to pay a pound of wax each to the chapel of the court.[139]

The sentence that declares that *fama* alone cannot destroy a marriage that is already contracted states a correct principle of law. No proof is mentioned other than the oaths, replies, and confessions of the parties. The woman apparently did not admit the intercourse with the man's relative (less likely, but possible, is that she admitted the intercourse but that there was no firm evidence of the relationship of the two men). In the other case, witnesses were introduced, though the sentence does not say by whom. It is possible, then, that the difference in result in the two cases can be accounted for by the fact that in the second case the affinity was proven and in the first case it was not. While that is possible, it does not seem likely. It seems more likely that it was not proven in the second case either. The second sentence does not find that the affinity existed; the couple are not fined for having committed incest, and the presumptive marriage is not declared null. All three issues would have to have been addressed had the affinity been proven.

We must search elsewhere to account for the difference in the two results. There are a number of differences in the facts. In the first case the couple had had intercourse; indeed, the *rea* had been deflowered, before they contracted and at a time when only the *rea* knew about the *fama* of the affinity. The *reus* only found out about it after the first bann.[140] Hence, it is possible that the man consummated the marriage before he knew of the *fama*, though the sentence does not say this. Even if he did, it is hard to see how that could account for the difference in the two sentences.

139 Listed T&C no. 1231.
140 Disc. T&C no. 1232.

What happened in the second case is clearer. The couple both knew of the *fama* of the affinity. They nonetheless proceeded publicly to espouse each other, "and would have proceeded further to solemnize their pretended marriage had the *curé* of the place not manifested the impediment on account of the *fama*."[141] The couple then went off and began to cohabit (the same language is used that is used in concubinage cases), consummating the marriage and converting it, to the extent that they could, into a presumptive marriage. They also procreated "many children."[142] Thus, while the first couple defied the authority of the church by continuing a sexual relationship that had begun before the promises of marriage (thus transforming the relationship into a presumptive marriage), this couple seems to have defied it even more because it looks as if they deliberately went out and consummated the marriage in order to create a presumptive marriage and planned to live together without the blessing of the church. Hence, despite the fact that the level of rhetoric is not quite so high in the second sentence as it is in the first, the official may in fact have thought the second couple's offense more serious, and hence he put them in a quite dreadful situation: They do not have license to marry others; indeed, they may be married to each other but they cannot cohabit nor can they have intercourse, and as is frequently the case, nothing is said about what is going to happen to the children.

I know of no canonical authority for this order.[143] That it was not appealed probably tells us that the couple could not afford an appeal. Even if it was authorized, it was certainly not required; it was unwise, a bad piece of judicial craftsmanship, and inhumane besides. The chronological order of these cases is, in fact, the opposite of the order in which we have been describing them. Since such cases were probably quite rare, one hopes that as he matured, Nicolaï came to realize that the best way to treat such cases was to punish the couple severely but to allow the marriage to go ahead.

Dissolution of Presumptive Marriages – Brussels

As we have seen, nine cases in the sample raise issues about the dissolution of alleged presumptive marriages, five straight office and four office/instance. Six of them involve the rules about incest. It is not always clear in these cases who is arguing for what, and it is best to begin with those in which dissolution is ordered.

The first such case, and the only case decided by Rodolphi, involves a couple who had lived in a concubinage relationship "for many years." They then got engaged. The sentence does not say that the engagement was public, but it probably was because the first cousin of the *reus* opposed the marriage on the ground that he had had sexual relations with the *rea*. The couple then once more

141 T&C no. 1233.
142 *Office c Blekere et Clements* (T&C no. 1231): *plures invicem proles procreando.*
143 Disc. T&C no. 1234.

had sexual relations. The couple are to make amends for their concubinage and for having sexual relations after the opposition. Their espousals are dissolved, and they are ordered under a penalty of 20 *saluts*[144] not to have sexual relations, to cohabit, or to deal with each other in such a way that a suspicion that they were having sexual relations could arise.[145]

The case bears a marked resemblance to *Office c Blekere et Clements*.[146] There is, however, a major difference. Rodolphi specifically annuls the espousals (which would, in fact, have been a presumptive marriage had it not been for the impediment). The couple are thus free to marry others, though he does not say that. Hence, although he does not say so, he must have found that the *affinitas per copulam illicitam* existed. Willem Godevaerts, the first cousin, alleged that it existed, but it takes more than one witness to make a full proof. Other witnesses are mentioned (produced by whom the sentence does not say), and we have the usual responses, confessions, and assertions of the parties. If the *rea* had confessed the intercourse, however, the sentence probably would have said that. The other witnesses may have testified to *fama*; they may even have testified to the intercourse or to circumstances that would have given rise to an inference of intercourse. It is unlikely that they actually saw it, though they may have said that they did.

That brings us back to the concubinage relationship. There was probably a reason why this was concubinage and not marriage, and that reason normally was that there were class differences between the man and the woman that made marriage socially unacceptable. Eventually, the *reus* decided to do the right thing by the *rea*, but when he announced his engagement, his family swung into action and broke it up. While this is not the only possible background to this case, it is a plausible one, and if this is right, the promotor and the court supported the family.

The other case in which a presumptive marriage is dissolved for *affinitas per copulam illicitam* may be the work of the promotor alone, though someone must have told him the story. Jan van Crane and Barbara Bastijns were found to have had publicly contracted espousals and to have had intercourse before and after their espousals. Jan Marien was found to have deflowered Barbara before the espousals, and he was "connected to [Crane] in the fourth degree of consanguinity." In strong language, Platea nullifies the presumptive marriage and orders Crane and Barbara to make amends for "presuming to contract an incestuous engagement (*affidationem*) of this sort and to transform it into presumptive marriage, thus committing incest" and Marien and Barbara to make amends for deflowering and *stuprum*.[147]

There seems little doubt that Platea thought that Crane and Barbara were aware of her prior relationship with Marien. (Otherwise, it would not have

144 Disc. T&C no. 1235.
145 *Office c Bouchoute en Triestrams* (28.ix.50), no. 200, T&C no. 1236.
146 See at n. 139, and text following.
147 *Officie c Crane, Bastijns en Marien* (13.v.57), no. 1150, T&C no. 1237.

been presumptive of them "to contract an incestuous engagement of this sort.") That, in turn, suggests that the relationship between the Crane and Marien was closer than the fourth degree of consanguinity.[148] The only other difficulty with this case is the first description of the relationship between Marien and Barbara: "affinity arising from the sowing of the seed of [Marien] with Barbara."[149] That could mean that they did not complete sexual intercourse, and if they did not, there was no affinity. Considering the order to make amends, however, this phrase is probably just Platea's graphic way of describing sexual intercourse, part and parcel of the heightened rhetoric of the entire sentence.

In four cases in the sample, Platea orders the presumptive marriage solemnized notwithstanding the allegations that the relationship is potentially incestuous. The language with which Platea rejects the impediment tends to be quite dismissive. Let us look at some examples.

(1) "Notwithstanding the *fama*, such as it is, of the consanguinity which is said to [literally, if the text is to be believed, "ought to"] exist between the engaged couple, but which was not proven."[150] In this case, the promotor was probably alleging the impediment because he produces the witnesses, but it is possible that he was put up to it by outsiders who were trying to impede the marriage. If they were, the couple's consummation of their public espousals raised the stakes because, as we have seen, *fama* could impede the solemnization of espousals, but not of presumptive marriage.

(2) "Notwithstanding the spiritual relationship alleged by the promotor but not proven." Here, there is evidence that the couple actively resisted the charge because they are the ones who produced the witnesses. The case ends with a strange note that the promotor's action against the *reus* for deflowering is saved for the promotor.[151] While it is possible that the promotor could prosecute such an action, even though the couple are to marry, there is no other case in the sample or in any of the other Brussels cases that I have examined where such an action is contemplated. It seems more likely that the deflowering action involved another woman. (This is a pattern that we will see more clearly when we come to the three-party cases.)

(3) "Notwithstanding a vague and uncertain *fama* about an asserted consanguinity which it is [also] asserted does not subsist between the [*rei*] and [which] proceeds from no certain source, which we consider frivolous and inapt."[152] The espousals in this case were public, and the "vague and uncertain *fama*" may have proceeded from the local rumor mill. It is not even clear that the promotor supported it once he had alleged it because the witnesses in this case

[148] Reference and disc. T&C no. 1238.
[149] See n. 147.
[150] *Officie c Voert en Katherina Ols* (7.ix.54), no. 680, T&C no. 1239.
[151] *Officie c Beckere en Leneren* (1.vii.55), no. 810, T&C no. 1240.
[152] *Officie c Gansbeke en Permentiers* (26.vi.56), no. 981, T&C no. 1241.

are vaguely said to have been produced "on the articles," and not specifically by the promotor.[153]

(4) "Notwithstanding the opposition of Katherina concerning and about a consanguinity that she alleges binds her with the *rea*, but not proven by her or verified by the promotor, which we consider frivolous and not in derogation of the clandestine marriage."[154] Katherina was a married woman with whom the *reus* was found to have committed adultery. Her motivations for trying to impede his marriage seem, despite the passage of centuries, both obvious and reprehensible. It is, however, quite remarkable that neither she nor the other *rea*, who had been deflowered and had entered into a presumptive marriage with the *reus*, is specifically ordered to make amends. This may be a scribal error; the wording of the amends suggests that there is more to come, which is simply not there.[155]

These four sentences proceed in chronological order and suggest Platea's growing impatience with unproven allegations of violations of the incest prohibitions. That makes his judgment in *Officie c Crane, Bastijns en Marien* all the more remarkable, for the case is dated between the third and fourth sentences in the examples.[156] It is possible that Platea was annoyed when such allegations were not proven but harsh when they were, but by this time Platea was an experienced enough judge to know that in many situations, one has to proceed in cases that one is not sure of proving in order to catch all possible instances that turn out to be provable. That in turn suggests that Platea was telling the promotors (and third parties who were trying to upset marriages) to proceed only in the obvious cases, and it allows us to suspect that *Office c Crane, Bastijns en Marien* was an obvious case.

Dissolution of Sponsalia – Cambrai

Seven cases in the Cambrai sample of dissolution of *sponsalia* involve incest. In five of the seven, the promotor succeeds in dissolving the *sponsalia* of a couple who, so far as we can tell, are seeking to maintain them. In the first case the couple are successful; Divitis, after hearing the depositions of witnesses, holds that the couple are to proceed with the solemnization of their marriage, notwithstanding the impediment of affinity (in what degree is not said) alleged by the promotor. *Leges* are specifically not imposed, but the couple are to pay the promotor's costs.[157] In the other case in which the couple are successful, the *reus* does not get off so lightly. He knew the rumors that he was consanguine

153 *Ibid., nec non testium super articulis huiusmodi productorum, receptorum, iuratorum, et examintorum depositionbus sive attesationibus.*

154 *Officie c Chienlens, Houmolen en Michaelis* (3.xii.56), no. 1072, T&C no. 1242.

155 *Ibid.*, T&C no. 1243.

156 N. 147.

157 *Office c Base et Honters* (Ch VIII, n. 75).

with the *rea* and is fined for having proceeded to enter into *sponsalia* with her without waiting for the decree of a competent judge. The *rea* is absolved of all articles but is ordered to share in the promotor's costs with the *reus*. Nicolaï, after hearing the depositions of witnesses for the promotor, holds the *sponsalia* valid and orders the couple to solemnize.[158]

The five cases in which the promotor was successful give us, by negative inference, some idea of what the promotor's evidence in the previous cases failed to show, so that the *sponsalia* were allowed to stand. Four of the cases involve *affinitas per copulam illicitam* in very close degrees. In one of them, after hearing testimony of witnesses, Nicolaï holds that the *reus* is to make amends because

knowing and not able to ignore that at another time he had carnally known [EB], the lawful sister of [LB] *rea*, he presumed to enter into espousals, insofar as was possible, *de facto* with the same [LB] *rea*, two banns having been proclaimed in the face of the church, and he would have proceeded further to contracting and, in a manner of speaking, solemnizing the marriage and to incestuous mingling with the *rea* under the color of such marriage that would have then been present, had the impediment of this sort of affinity not been made public from another source, thereby most grievously failing and breaking the law.[159]

The *rea* is absolved of the articles of the promotor (apparently she knew nothing about it) but shares in paying the promotor's costs. Nothing is said about dissolving the *sponsalia* or license to marry others. That both results follows is clear enough, though perhaps the official did not want to mention the second. In another such case, also after hearing testimony of witnesses, Nicolaï holds that the *reus* is to make amends because

after sexual intercourse had with Laurence de Lasne named in the articles, who, as *fama* has it, can be deemed the aunt of the *rea*, notwithstanding the *fama* that insists on the opinion that there is affinity between him and the *rea*, he presumed to contract *sponsalia* with the same, the *rea*, three banns being proclaimed about it, under cover of which he would have taken care to proceed further to the solemnization of the marriage, had the impediment not come to the notice of the *curé*, thereby failing and breaking the law.[160]

Once more the *rea* is absolved of all charges (and the *reus* is absolved of the rest of the promotor's charges). Both share in paying the promotor's costs, their *sponsalia* are dissolved, and both are given license to marry others.

The results in these two cases are the same (though we might imagine that the fines for the *reus* in the first were stiffer), but the rhetoric is considerably stronger in the first than in the second. We hear nothing in the second of banns "insofar as was possible" (*utcumque*), solemnization "in a manner of speaking" (*talem qualem*), or "most grievous" breaches of the moral and criminal law (*per premissa gravissime delinquendo et excedendo*). Most notably, in the second

[158] *Office c Cailliel et Planque* (28.iv.53), no. 1430; disc. T&C no. 1244.
[159] *Office c Girete et Bossche* (26.i.43), no. 411, T&C no. 1245.
[160] *Office c Borquerie et Frarinne* (9.vii.42), no. 291, T&C no. 1246.

case Nicolaï does not conjure up a lurid picture of an incestuous sexual union under the color of a non-marriage. While some of these differences could have been the product of the moment (or of the scribe), there was a substantial difference between these two cases. There was no clear proof that Laurence de Lasne was the aunt of Égidie, the *rea*; there was just *fama* that she was. This is clear not only from Nicolaï's awkward description of the relationship (*quam, fama volente, poterat* [EF] *corree materteram reputare*),[161] but also because he dissolves the *sponsalia* "because *fama* impedes them" (*cum fama impediat*). In the first case, there was no doubt about the relationship and that the *reus* knew about it (*sciens et ignorare non valens se alias cum quadam* [EB], [LB] *corree sororem legitimam carnaliter cognovisse*).

The third case is, on its facts, someplace in between. The *fama* was that the *reus* had had sexual relations with the *rea*'s daughter, now deceased. That the dead girl was the *rea*'s daughter seems clear enough both from the wording of the sentence and the nature of the relationship; the question was whether the *reus* had had intercourse with her. Apparently he denied it, and the witnesses could not prove it. So far as Nicolaï is concerned, that makes no difference: "*Fama* of this sort impedes the contract of marriage between the *reus* and *rea*, and rightly ought to impede it."[162] Their *sponsalia* were entered into *de facto* because they could not be entered into *de iure*. Once more the couple pays the promotor's costs and the *rea* is absolved of the charges of the promotor; nothing is said of license to marry others. The rhetoric is not particularly strong, and hence there is no suggestion that Nicolaï thought that the *reus* was lying when he denied, as he must have, that he had had intercourse with the daughter. Apparently, however, the denial was not enough to overcome the *fama*. Perhaps an *ex officio* oath would have been enough, but offering that was in the discretion of the official; Nicolaï chose not to exercise his discretion.

The fourth case of *affinitas per copulam illicitam* is quite different. In a previous and unrecorded sentence, the court had ordered the *reus* to solemnize his marriage with the *rea*. Now the *reus* confesses that prior to the *sponsalia*, he had had sexual intercourse with the *rea*'s mother. Nicolaï reverses his previous sentence, dissolves the *sponsalia*, orders the *reus* fined for adultery with the mother and for entering into the *sponsalia* conscious of the impediment, and orders the *reus* to pay both the promotor's costs and those of the *rea*. The *rea* is absolved from the charges of the promotor; she was, Nicolaï says explicitly, deceived by the deed of the *reus*, and she, but not the *reus*, is expressly given license to marry another. Nicolaï did not render this sentence on the basis of the *reus*'s confession alone. The promotor produced witnesses, and the *rea* produced counter-witnesses. Whether Nicolaï believed the *reus*'s confession is hard to tell. As we have seen, he was quite capable of fining someone for an offense which he confessed, even when the court was convinced that the offense had not happened. What the witnesses did convince the court of, however,

161 Disc. T&C no. 1247.
162 *Office c Oiseleur et Grumulle* (22.ix.42), no. 330, T&C no. 1248.

was that there was *fama* that the *reus* had had intercourse with the mother, and Nicolaï says that had it known of this *fama* at the time, he would not have issued its sentence and that the knowledge of its existence is sufficient to warrant reversing the sentence.[163] Whether the *reus* concocted the story of the intercourse with the mother and also concocted the *fama* we cannot tell on this record, but it is not inconceivable. He certainly did not want to marry the *rea*, and he succeeded in that objective.

The last case involves spiritual affinity. If I am reading the recital of the procedure correctly, there was no dispute about the facts;[164] the question was whether what the *reus* did at the baptism of two of the *rea*'s children was sufficient to make him their spiritual father. Nicolaï holds that it was. He was present with others at the baptisms as a godfather; they observed all the solemnities that godfathers are wont to observe. The couple is fined for having proceeded to contract *sponsalia* when that bond and the *fama* of it existed, and for having had one bann, "insofar as was possible," proclaimed on it.[165] Their *sponsalia* are dissolved, and they are ordered to pay the promotor's costs. Nicolaï's attitude toward them is hard to discern. He does accuse them of having "rashly gone against both canonical and civil sanctions."[166] What civil sanctions he is talking about is unclear,[167] and he may have felt it necessary to justify a prohibition that the couple, and perhaps the wider society, thought unjustified.[168]

Dissolution of Sponsalia – Brussels

The seven straight-office dissolution cases in the Brussels sample are of a quite different nature from the instance or mixed dissolution cases. Six of them are grounded in consanguinity or affinity, one in the impediment of vow. Dissolution is ordered in one of the consanguinity cases. In all the others the promotor fails.

The promotor's failure is particularly dramatic in the four sentences of Rodolphi's in the sample. In none of them are the costs of the promotor charged to the parties. (Like the other officials in Cambrai diocese, Rodolphi normally charged the promotor's costs to the parties even when the promotor's case failed of proof.) Three of the cases involve affinity by illicit intercourse. In the first, the *rea* is allowed to purge herself 'three-handed' of the *fama* that she had intercourse with the *reus*'s brother.[169] In the second, the official defers the oath to the *rea* that she did not have intercourse with the *reus*'s brother, now deceased. Rodolphi specifically finds on the basis of testimony of other witnesses that the

[163] *Office c Bohier et Fèvre* (14.v.46), no. 922, T&C no. 1249.
[164] *Office c Monchiaux et Maquet* (24.ix.42), no. 340, T&C no. 1250.
[165] *Ibid.*, T&C no. 1251.
[166] *Ibid.*, T&C no. 1252.
[167] Nicolaï probably has in mind C.5.4.26.2 (Justinian, 530), which prohibits the marriage of godfather and goddaughter.
[168] See at nn. 49–50.
[169] *Officie c Bugghenhout en Huneghem* (22.xi.48), no. 11, T&C no. 1253.

fama of such intercourse alleged by two named witnesses was "invented out of hate and spite."[170] In the third, there seems to be no question that the *reus* had had intercourse with a third party (and had had two children by her), but the witnesses are specifically found not to have proven that this woman was a consanguine of the *rea* or even that there was *fama* that she was.[171] In the fourth case, Rodolphi simply finds that the allegation of consanguinity between the *rei* was "frivolous and invalid."[172]

Granted the promotors' notable lack of success with such cases during Rodolphi's term of office, it is unsurprising that Platea heard relatively few such cases and that in all of them, he found that there was enough to the promotors' charges to warrant imposition of costs on the parties. In the first case, he finds that there was *fama* that the woman had taken a vow of chastity when she was sick. She is to make amends for having proceeded with her espousals notwithstanding that *fama*. (The wording of the sentence makes clear that she should have obtained a judgment of the church to "purge" the *fama*.) Platea nonetheless finds that there is no true proof that the oath was taken.[173] In the second case, the espousals are dissolved for what is said to be fourth-degree consanguinity between the parties.[174] In the third case, the espousals are allowed to proceed. Platea finds that the *reus* attempted intercourse with a fourth-degree consanguine of the first *rea*, but that the woman had resisted, and no intercourse actually took place. (They both are to make amends for the attempted intercourse.)[175]

None of these cases involves the heightened rhetoric that we find in some of Nicolaï's sentences involving incest. In the case of the vow, we are almost certainly dealing (potentially) with a simple vow and, hence, an impedient rather than a diriment impediment to marriage. Witnesses were heard; they did not prove the vow. The woman apparently did not admit it. Perhaps she should not marry, but the external forum will not insist on it. (This attitude should be contrasted with the cases in which Nicolaï is willing to allow *fama* of consanguinity or affinity to impede espousals; Platea is here following the similar holdings of Rodolphi in cases of affinity by illicit intercourse.) In the case of the putative affinity, Platea allows the oaths of the parties (no witnesses were heard) to clear the marriage of potential invalidity (though the impediment was eminently dispensable). Hence, the only case that does not reflect a relatively relaxed attitude toward the complexities of the medieval law of impediments is the one in which, if we are to believe the sentence, *sponsalia* in the fourth degree of consanguinity are dissolved. I am not sure that we have to believe the statement of the degree.[176] Even if we do believe it, there is telling explanation on the

170 *Officie c Brunen en Roelants* (25.x.49), no. 110, T&C no. 1254.
171 *Officie c Hemelrike en Verlijsbetten* (10.ix.51), no. 310, T&C no. 1255.
172 *Officie c Goffaert en Defier* (28.i.52), no. 343, T&C no. 1256.
173 *Officie c Alboeme en Arents* (12.x.54), no. 701, T&C no. 1257.
174 *Officie c Ghelde en Herts* (25.ii.57), no. 1120, T&C no. 1258.
175 *Officie c Beckere, Houte en Rode* (1.vii.58), no. 1332, T&C no. 1259.
176 Disc. and lit. T&C no. 1260.

face of the record for why the sentence came down as it did. The couple are to make amends because "they presumed to enter into such incestuous promises without the consent of their relatives, by contracting clandestinely."[177] In the other two cases the espousals were public, and there is no suggestion that the relatives opposed them. We might even suggest that in the aberrant case, the relatives who opposed the marriage had a considerable amount to do with producing the witnesses who testified that the couple were third cousins.

CONCLUSION

We may conclude briefly. Social attitudes toward the incest rules in Cambrai diocese are harder to discern than they were at Canterbury because we lack depositions. On the basis of the what got prosecuted we may suspect, as we did in the case of Ely, that at least as far as marriage was concerned, a large number of residents of the diocese, if not all, knew that they could not marry close relatives, either consanguines or affines, and did not seek to do so. The remoter degrees were more problematical and seemed to have caused more trouble. The residents also knew that they were not supposed to have sexual relations with close relatives, though they sometimes did so. The Cambrai cases of sexual offenses, however, show that many more people were accused of having done so than were actually convicted of having done so. Finally, they knew that they were not supposed to marry or have sexual relations with close relatives of those with whom they had had sexual relations, though, once more, there are instances of violations, or attempted violations, of the rule. While all of our courts are concerned about *fama*, those in Cambrai diocese seem particularly so, and particularly concerned that *fama* of a potentially incestuous relationship be purged by a judicial proceeding before the couple married. Some couples, by contrast, seem to have quite deliberately taken advantage of the higher standard of proof required to dissolve a marriage by consummating their *sponsalia* when they were faced with an accusation that their marriage was barred by an incest impediment. Some got their marriages solemnized in other dioceses, but in this they were no different from couples at Ely.

So far as the effect of the incest rules on already formed marriages is concerned, the conclusion that we reached on the basis of a more impressionistic study of the surviving evidence has survived remarkably well. All or most or even a great proportion of late medieval marriages were not *de facto* dissoluble because of the complicated law of incest.[178] Some, a relatively small number, did get dissolved on these grounds. Far more important, though again not so important as other grounds, was the use of these rules in conjunction with cases about marriage formation. In the process, some marriages that concededly had been formed, though most of them relatively recently and quite informally, did

[177] *Officie c Ghelde en Herts* (n. 174).

[178] See at nn. 9–13. An earlier version of this passage is quoted in d'Avray, *Medieval Marriage*, 114–15.

get dissolved. Cambrai and Brussels, which, it has been argued, are exceptions to the rule, do not seem on closer comparative analysis to be that exceptional.[179] If we carefully distinguish, on the one hand, between what the promotor was trying to prove and what the official was willing to accept, and, on the other, between those marriages that had concededly been formed, particularly those that had so far as we can tell been in existence for some time, and those that were simply in the process of formation, then the number of marriages that had actually been formed and that the official held invalid was really quite small. We should also recall that recent work with the records of the papal penitentiary would suggest that by the period of the Cambrai/Brussels records, many of the relatively few couples whose marriages were blocked could obtain a dispensation for, it would seem, quite modest costs.[180] Knowledge of the availability of such dispensations may have made couples who were aware of an impediment in the more remote degrees less reluctant to proceed to marriage despite the impediment.

A cynic might suggest that what we are seeing at Cambrai and Brussels is simply a device to raise revenue, both for the court and for the papacy. Someone less cynical might suggest that what we are witnessing is a heightened concern, shared by both the promotors and the officials, that marriage in Cambrai diocese, and particularly in its northern half, was, in some sense, out of control. Both characteristics of the ecclesiastical courts in Cambrai diocese are also to be found in the other types of cases that we have examined. What those characteristics might mean when we compare the Cambrai/Brussels records with those of the other courts that we have examined is the topic of the next chapter.

[179] See App. e11.2.
[180] See Ch 4, n. 267.

12

Broader Comparisons

THE DIFFERENCE BETWEEN ENGLISH AND FRANCO-BELGIAN MEDIEVAL MARRIAGE CASES

The time has come to see how far we can generalize the conclusions that we came to on the basis of our study of five courts and to take a glimpse at others' work with the rest of Western Europe. This section[1] suggests, with some hesitancy, that the patterns we have seen in the five courts can be generalized to England and to what we have called the 'Franco-Belgian' region.[2]

Tanneur et Doulsot and *Dolling c Smith* Generalized

More than 220 years after *Dolling c Smith*,[3] Colin Tanneur and Perette Doulsot of Villers in Champagne were cited to appear before the court of the official of the bishop of Châlons-sur-Marne to answer charges by the promotor that they had clandestinely exchanged promises to marry.[4] While the judge was interrogating Perette under oath about this charge, she confessed that a month before, Colin had come to her father's house at night and had talked with her about a marriage contract. After much talk, Colin had sworn by the faith of his

[1] The arguments developed in the first three subsections of this section were first presented in Donahue, "English and French Marriage Cases." Lit. T&C no. 1263.

[2] I apologize for the awkward phrase 'Franco-Belgian'. Belgium did not exist in this period, and the borders of France were not where they are today. But to call Cambrai diocese 'France' in this period is just wrong, and some of our evidence comes from Flanders, the relations of which to France were tenuous. As we will see later in this chapter, there are reasons to believe that the situation in southern France was different from northern, and so references to 'Franco-Belgian' are, in the case of France, references to the region known as the *pays de droit coutumier*, the region of customary law.

[3] Ch 2, text at nn. 1–7.

[4] (4.i.1494); see App. e12.1, "*Office c Colin Tanneur et Perette fille de Jehannot Doulsot de Villers-en-Argonne*" (see T&C no. 1292), and discussion in Gottlieb, *Getting Married*, 201–2.

body that he would take her to wife and that he would never have anyone else as wife except her, and she promised the same. After this they exchanged tokens of their affection. Since Perette admitted that no one had been present when all this had happened, it was open to Colin to deny the charges, and the case would have failed for want of proof. Colin, however, did not deny the charges but admitted that the events had taken place as described. The couple were fined a pound of wax each "for the clandestinity" and ordered to solemnize their marriage within a week.

There are many differences between *Dolling c Smith* and *Office c Tanneur et Doulsot*. The most important from the point of view of the parties is that William Smith firmly did not want to marry Alice Dolling and took his case all the way to the court of Canterbury to ensure that he did not have to do so. By contrast, Colin Tanneur seems to have needed only the nudge provided by the court appearance to get him to the altar. (It is possible, of course, that there was opposition to the marriage that does not appear on the record.) The difference, however, between Franco-Belgian and English marriage cases does not lie in this direction. As we have seen, there were many bitterly contested Franco-Belgian marriage cases, just as there were many English ones that were hardly contested at all.

There are, however, a number of other differences between these two cases that seem to be generally characteristic of marriage litigation in England and in the Franco-Belgian region in the later Middle Ages. First, the English case was an instance case. It was brought by Alice Dolling, and the remedies she sought were for herself alone. The French case was a criminal case, an office case. It was brought by a court officer, a prosecutor (promotor), and the parties were ordered to pay a fine and the promotor's costs, as well as to solemnize the marriage. Now there are marriage cases brought *ex officio* in the English records just as there are instance marriage cases in the Franco-Belgian. But the striking thing about the Franco-Belgian records for many jurisdictions is that the office mode in marriage cases seems to dominate the instance, particularly when we reach the fifteenth century. Our best Franco-Belgian records for the later Middle Ages are from Cambrai and Brussels, the Paris archdeacon's court, and the bishops' courts of Châlons-sur-Marne and Troyes.[5] As we have seen, there are instance cases in the records of Cambrai and Brussels, though particularly in the latter, the trend is definitely toward the office form.[6] In the Paris archdeacon's court and the bishops' courts of Châlons and Troyes, the great bulk, indeed perhaps all, of the marriage cases, other than separation cases, are office cases. By contrast, there are a large number of instance cases in England to balance the office cases. The English office cases, moreover, show no evidence of an organized prosecution, of a court officer charged with bringing office cases before the

[5] See Ch 8; Donahue, ed., *Records 1*, 96–8, 107–9, 110–12.

[6] The change in style in the office cases in Cambrai that occurred relatively early in the period is indicative. See above, Ch 8, at nn. 9–11.

court. Because a far greater proportion of Franco-Belgian marriage cases are office cases, the judge plays a much more active role in Franco-Belgian marriage cases than he does in England, at least in instance cases.

There is a second difference between these two cases that is characteristic of marriage cases in the two regions. The dispute in *Dolling c Smith* was about an alleged marriage formed by words of the present tense, in the terminology of the classical rules, *sponsalia per verba de presenti*; the dispute in *Office c Tanneur et Doulsot* was about a promise of marriage, *sponsalia per verba de futuro*. Now there are disputes about marriages by words of the future tense in the English records, but they almost always involve allegations that the words were followed by intercourse. As we have seen, such cases also exist in the Franco-Belgian records, but there are also a great many Franco-Belgian *de futuro* cases that do not involve allegations of intercourse but simply seek judicial enforcement of a promise of marriage. Cases seeking to enforce a simple promise to marry are very rare in the English records, just as cases seeking to enforce a *de presenti* marriage are very rare in the Franco-Belgian records.

Before we proceed to explore the reasons for these differences, it is well to sound a note of caution. There are some remarkable elements of unity in what we see in marriage litigation in the two areas. Hardly a sentence of a church court in either country throughout the long period from Alexander to the council of Trent can be shown to violate the classical rules. (The most notable possible exception to this statement is the expansion in the Franco-Belgian region, but not in England, of the grounds for granting a separation.) The common academic training of the principal officers of the church courts in both countries and the availability of appeal, in some cases going all the way to the papacy, ensured a basic uniformity of application of the law. What was different was not the rules that were applied but the kinds of claims that were made before the courts, and the way in which the courts processed them.

I have asserted that the differences found in the two cases are characteristic of marriage cases generally in the two regions. In order to determine what the possible reasons for these differences might be, we must compare more precisely. The pattern of survival of the records in the two regions makes direct comparison difficult. It was not by chance that 220 years separated our two illustrative cases. Thirteenth-century records from church courts in the Franco-Belgian region are rare. By and large, it is not until after the Hundred Years' War that we begin to get runs of records in the Franco-Belgian region from which we can derive usable statistical material. The English records are fuller and earlier, but they are by no means complete. Nonetheless, it is possible – somewhat impressionistically here – to confirm that our two cases are, indeed, 'modal' cases.

As we move forward from the latter part of the thirteenth century, the English cases continue to show the same pattern as *Dolling c Smith*.[7] Cases seeking to establish that a marriage has in fact taken place are by far the most common

[7] E.g., Helmholz, *Marriage Litigation*; Sheehan, "Formation."

form of marriage litigation. Within that large group, allegations of a *de presenti* marriage that in one way or another lacked the normal solemnity or ceremony are the most common source of litigation. Now, as R. H. Helmholz and others have noted, the number and proportion of this type of case, and indeed of marriage cases generally, seem to decline in the English records toward the end of the fifteenth century.[8] Other types of cases seem to occupy more of the courts' time, and within the marriage cases the number and proportion of annulment and separation cases seem to be on the increase. But the *de presenti* informal marriage case remains an important topic of litigation in the English church courts throughout the Middle Ages and beyond.[9]

The Franco-Belgian pattern is more complicated, perhaps because the surviving records give us only tantalizing glimpses. Nonetheless, the contrast with England is striking. In the Franco-Belgian region there are very few *de presenti* marriage cases for the whole of the Middle Ages. There are also comparatively few instance marriage cases (with the notable exception of the register of the official of the bishop of Paris discussed in Chapter 7). A substantial majority of the cases, both instance and office, concern *de futuro* espousals, some followed by intercourse, some concerning the enforcement of the promise itself.[10] The other major topic of litigation about marriage is separation cases, of which, as we saw in Chapter 10, there are far fewer in England.

We are dealing here with patterns of litigation, not with absolutes. The question is not whether one could allege a *de presenti* marriage in an instance case before a Franco-Belgian court in the fifteenth century. The evidence suggests that one could. The typical pattern of litigation, however, excludes such cases. There are practically none in the largely instance cases before the official of Paris in the late fourteenth century. There are a few, but very few, in the largely office cases at Cambrai and Brussels in the middle of the fifteenth century. I have found none, once more, in the largely office cases in the episcopal courts of Châlons-sur-Marne and Troyes and in the court of the Paris archdeacon in the latter part of the fifteenth century. The number of such cases also seems to have declined in England, but it declined in comparison with what it had been previously; it never approached the level that the Franco-Belgian records show.

These differences have been known for some time. There is one more that has appeared in the course of this book, although I hesitate to put it forward too firmly because all the surviving records from the two regions have not been subjected to the numerical analysis that we did for the five courts with which we have dealt in this book. If, however, we assume that York, Ely, Paris, Cambrai, and Brussels are typical, plaintiffs seeking to establish a marriage in the English courts had a much higher success rate than did either plaintiffs or promotors in the Franco-Belgian courts. As to separation and divorce, particularly the former,

[8] Helmholz, *Marriage Litigation*, 166–8. I cast doubts on this proposition in App. e3.2, n. 6, but we can take it here as probable.

[9] E.g., Houlbrooke, *Church Courts*, 56–67; cf. *id.*, *English Family*, 68–73.

[10] Lit. T&C no. 1264.

there are so few cases in the English courts that one cannot speak of a statistical success rate, but the few cases that there are do suggest that it was much more difficult to get a separation in England than it was in the Franco-Belgian region. Hence, success rates in spousals litigation in the Franco-Belgian region are low, those in separation litigation high; it is certainly the opposite in England so far as spousals litigation is concerned and seems to be the opposite in England so far as separation litigation is concerned. Once more, if the somewhat lower success rates in spousals litigation at York in the fifteenth century can be generalized, the English seem to have been moving in the Franco-Belgian direction in that century, but as with cases of *de presenti* marriage, the movement in this direction comes no place near to reaching equivalent results.

As often happens with historical phenomena, the particular is easier to explain than the general. We have a better idea of why the Franco-Belgian region might have showed these characteristics than we do why the English might have begun to move in the Franco-Belgian direction in the fifteenth century. We have already discussed the differences between English synodal legislation and that of the Franco-Belgian region on the topic of clandestine marriage.[11] In the Franco-Belgian region, but not in England, informal marriage without any aggravating factors was, in many places, punished by automatic excommunication. In some dioceses, including Châlons and Cambrai, penalties could be imposed for failure to publicize promises of marriage (*verba de futuro*) and for failure to proceed to solemnization of the promised marriage within a fixed period. This local legislation might have had an effect on the types of cases brought before the Franco-Belgian courts, but it is unlikely that it had so great an effect that it alone could have produced the striking differences that we find in the records of cases in the two regions. Even if it did, that simply puts the social question at one remove: Why did the society of the Franco-Belgian region in the later Middle Ages create legal institutions so different from those in England?[12]

The differences, then, that we have to explain are six: (1) In many Franco-Belgian dioceses participants in *de presenti* informal marriages were punished by automatic excommunication, whereas in England they were not. (2) In some Franco-Belgian dioceses penalties could be imposed on those who exchanged informal promises of marriage, whereas in England they could not. (3) More people in England litigated about *de presenti* informal marriages than did people in the Franco-Belgian region. (4) In the Franco-Belgian region, but not in England, church courts regularly enforced promises to marry unaccompanied by intercourse. (5) Enforcement of the marriage rules was largely an office matter in the Franco-Belgian region; it was much less so in England. (6) Less certain but probable on the basis of what we have seen is the difficulty of getting a Franco-Belgian court to hold for the existence of a marriage and its willingness to separate one, while the converse pattern seems to prevail in England.

[11] Ch 1, text and nn. 80–8; cf. Ch 8, at nn. 18–26.
[12] See Ch 7, text following n. 343.

Behind all of this is a long-term trend in both countries toward fewer cases of *de presenti* informal marriage and to less willingness to enforce an informal marriage, however contracted. We have suggested further that the differences between the English and Franco-Belgian records are not just differences in litigation patterns and legal institutions; they reflect differences in how the English and Franco-Belgians got married.[13] More people in England engaged in *de presenti* informal marriage than in the Franco-Belgian region; more people in the Franco-Belgian region made contracts to marry than in England. Why should there be these differences? Is there any way to explain all of these phenomena at once? Are they in any way connected?

What Does the Property Difference Explain?

An obvious place to look for an explanation of these differences is in the rules concerning marital property and succession to property in the two regions. In Chapter 10 we outlined the differences in marital property between the two areas and suggested that they might account, at least in part, for the greater number of separation cases that we see in the Franco-Belgian courts. Here, we must add to that discussion the rules about inheritance, operating at the same broad level of generality: the rules of the English common law and the 'lowest common denominator' of the Franco-Belgian customs.

As is well known, the inheritance pattern of the English common law derives from the inheritance pattern for military tenures. By the mid-thirteenth century, it applied to virtually all freehold tenures, whether military or not. Land descended to the next of kin of the deceased, direct descendants if there were any, with representation. Males were preferred over females, the eldest male over younger males. If there were only females within a given class, they took equally as coparceners.[14]

As is also well known, the basic inheritance pattern in Franco-Belgian customary law did not derive from the inheritance pattern for military tenures. By the time of the early *coutumiers* (late thirteenth to early fourteenth centuries), military tenures were treated separately and had an inheritance pattern not unlike that under the English common law, but the general pattern of inheritance differed markedly from that of England. The basic principle of inheritance in the Franco-Belgian customary law was equality among heirs; hence, the inheritance was partible far more frequently than it was in England. It was also a basic principle in many regions that endowed children would be excluded from the inheritance. The combination of the two principles produced in some regions a rule that endowed children had to return their endowments to the common fund so that the division among heirs could be equal. In other regions, preferred children had the option of putting their advancements in the common fund if they wished to share in the paternal inheritance. In still other

13 Lit. T&C no. 1265.

14 See Baker, *Introduction* (4th ed.) 265–8.

regions, the deceased could by testament, perhaps even by antemortem gift, overcome the presumption of equality and prefer one child over another. These patterns of rules tended to arrange themselves geographically, as Jean Yver has elegantly demonstrated.[15]

It is a characteristic, then, of English marital property patterns that husband and wife hold their property separately and of English inheritance patterns at all levels of society that one child takes his parent's property to the exclusion of his siblings. In the Franco-Belgian region, on the other hand, the tendency is to community property between spouses and to partible inheritance among children.

Can we go further than we did in Chapter 10 and explain the differences not only in number and types of separation cases in the two regions on the basis of the differences between the property systems but also in the number and types of marriage-formation cases? Such an explanation might proceed along the following lines: The Franco-Belgians, we might argue, were more concerned with their children's marriages than were the English because under most Franco-Belgian inheritance customs, all of their children stood to inherit their property. In England, only the marriage of the heir needed to be arranged, whereas in the Franco-Belgian region the marriages of all children needed to be arranged because almost all children were heirs. Hence, we see more litigation in the Franco-Belgian region about marriage contracts because they were more common. We also see more concern with informal marriages – punishing them with automatic excommunication – but fewer informal marriages, in fact, because more marriages were arranged.[16]

The argument is based on a series of assumptions that it may be well to make explicit. In the first place, the argument assumes, as we did in outlining the classical rules of canon law on the formation of marriage, that the question of who is going to control marriage choice was of crucial concern in medieval society, both in England and France. For this chapter, this must remain an assumption, for setting out the evidence for it would take us too far afield. Fortunately, we may refer to a large body of recent literature that supports the assumption in different ways.[17]

Second, the argument takes no account of regional, class, and chronological variations, and thus seems to assume that the phenomenon and its explanation were constant within each country across place, class, and time. There is certainly no *a priori* reason for this to be true, and we will, as we proceed, attempt to introduce a chronological dimension. If, however, our generalizations about the English and Franco-Belgian property systems and about what the English and the Franco-Belgian court records show are valid as generalizations, an attempt to correlate the variance in the two phenomena ought to be legitimate, unless there is some systematic regional or class bias in either the dependent

[15] Yver, *Égalité entre héritiers*.
[16] Lit. T&C no. 1266.
[17] Ref. T&C no. 1267.

or the independent variable. There may be such biases, but it is plausible to assume that the biases cancel each other out. It is probable, for example, that the poor are systematically underrepresented in the church court records, but then again their inheritance customs are systematically underrepresented in our generalizations about the rules in the two regions. We may thus continue with our argument if we keep in mind that some segments of the population in both regions are probably not being accounted for.

Third, the argument assumes that among the groups struggling for control of marriage choice, parents (taken in the broad sense of senior members of a family, members of a family who exercise authority) are the most concerned, other than the marriage partners themselves. This cannot simply be assumed for medieval society. We know that lords were also concerned about the marriage choice of their vassals and serfs and that for different reasons the church was concerned with marriage choice. Nonetheless, we may, for purposes of the argument, leave the interests of lords and the church to one side. It is easier to do so in the case of the church because we are treating the church as the dependent variable. We are assuming that the concerns of the church are the same in the two regions, and we are trying to explain differences in church institutions by looking outside the church to social forces independent of it that shaped its behavior.

Lords are not so easily dismissed. They were certainly a force independent of the church throughout the Middle Ages, and their concern with the marriage choice of those subject to them was real. While we cannot ignore lords' concerns, we may, for purposes of this argument, combine their concerns with those of parents. We can do this because lords' concern about marriage choice was a concern about property and was exercised through property. In general, lords were not concerned with the marriage choice of the landless; they were concerned with the marriage choice of those who held land of them, be it by servile or free tenure, and of those who would inherit land that was held of them. Lords, then, like parents, had some present control over property and were concerned with its devolution to the next generation, children proposing to marry. Lords were not always concerned because not all property was held of a lord (movable property was not, at least for free people, and some land was not), but where it was so held, lords' concerns combined with parents' and in many cases were exercised through the parents. For the argument to work, lords' concerns about marriage need not have been directed to the same ends as parents'; they just had to have been about the same thing and to have been exercised in the same way.

Fourth, the argument seems to assume that parents' concerns with the marriage choice of their children was coterminous with their concerns about the passage of property to their children. This seems the most questionable assumption of all, for in every society of which I am aware, parents have been concerned about more than the property aspects of their children's marriages. In our own society, a host of concerns about the personal qualities of our children's proposed marriage partners bedevil us as parents; it is hard to imagine that some of these concerns did not trouble medieval parents as well. Further, in medieval society more than in our own, marriage was a vehicle for forming alliances among families. Property was, of course, important in this regard, but so was politics, be it the politics of the relations among kingdoms or lordships or the politics of the relations among guilds and guild members or the politics of the relations among peasant villagers. (Political considerations about marriage were also, of course, of concern to lords.)

We can, however, save our argument if we modify the fourth assumption. If property is one of the concerns that parents have about the marriage choices of their children, the argument will still work if we can also assume that their other concerns about the marriage choices of their children are of roughly equal force in both England and the Franco-Belgian region. There are many reasons why parents or lords might want to control marriage choice, but as to most of them, there is no reason for believing that there should be any systematic difference between England and the Franco-Belgian region. In the case of property, however, certainly one of the concerns that parents and lords have about marriage choice, there is a difference between the two regions, and the argument just outlined offers an explanation for why the Franco-Belgians should have been more concerned about the marriage choice of more people than the English were. Recalling that the difference we are seeking to explain is one of degree and not of kind, a difference of degree heightened, in all probability, by the differences in the institutions in which we see it manifested, can we say that the difference in property systems between England and the Franco-Belgian region 'explains' the differences in marriage cases that we see?

We have noted that there is a difference between English and Franco-Belgian marriage cases, a difference that suggests a difference in how the English and Franco-Belgians got married, certainly a difference in how they litigated about marriage formation. We have also noted that the crucial issue about marriage formation seems to be the question of who is to control marriage choice, and that the way that Franco-Belgian institutions were structured seems to have given more control to people other than the marriage partners. What gives the property explanation of these differences its force is the fact that throughout the Middle Ages and at all levels of society, possession of property was, if not a prerequisite, at least highly desirable before a couple embarked on a marriage. Children whose parents were still living rarely had much property before they married.[18] This fact gave parents both the power and the responsibility to arrange their children's marriages. From this point of view, there is nothing puzzling about the evidence of arranged marriages that we see in the Franco-Belgian records; what is puzzling is the evidence of unarranged marriages that we see in the English records. The property argument seeks to explain these unarranged English marriages by suggesting that the English impartible inheritance system created a large class of propertyless children who got married despite the fact that they had no property or prospects for property, and whose marriages were,

[18] Disc. T&C no. 1268.

therefore, informal and unarranged. On the other hand, the argument suggests, far more marriages in the Franco-Belgian region were arranged because far more children would come into property under the Franco-Belgian system of partible inheritance. The Franco-Belgians were, however, more concerned that unarranged marriages be prevented because the Franco-Belgian system of partible inheritance deprived Franco-Belgian families of the power that an English property holder could exercise over the marriage choice of his children, all but one of whom would take nothing if they married against his will.

As soon as we spell out the argument this way, its problematic quality becomes apparent. In the first place, the attitude ascribed to English parents toward the marriages of children who did not stand to inherit is inconsistent. On the one hand, we are asked to believe that the English did not care about the marriages of such children because such children did not stand to inherit. On the other hand, we are asked to believe that they did care about the marriages of such children, but the property system ensured that they could adequately control the marriages of such children because such children did not stand to inherit. The English did not need any other means to control these marriages; such children were totally dependent on them. Both attitudes may have coexisted; English parents' attitudes may have been inconsistent, or some parents may have had one attitude and others the other. But the coexistence of these inconsistent attitudes requires an explanation not given by the argument.

The problems with the argument, however, are deeper than this. The argument takes the succession rules as fixed and explains the attitude of parents toward their children's marriages as a result of them. But we cannot assume that the succession rules were fixed. In both regions, with some exceptions, the succession rules could be changed by voluntary action of the property holders.[19] Franco-Belgian parents did not have to accept their children's choice of spouse; they could disinherit them if they married contrary to their wishes.[20] English parents did not have to disinherit their younger sons and daughters, but they could provide for such children during their lifetimes, thus partially disinheriting the heir. It was open, then, to English parents to express their disapproval of their children's marriage choices by failing to provide for them if they were younger children or by providing for others if the errant child were the heir.[21] The fact that both property systems could be changed voluntarily meant that parents in both regions could put pressure on their children not to marry against their wishes. The type of threats that they could make differed in each region because of the differences in the underlying property systems, but the threats could have led to the same result. In neither country could parents completely control the marriages of their children. Canon law saw to it that they could not. But the secular property law in both regions gave them a card which they could and did play. The interesting thing is that they seem to

[19] Disc. T&C no. 1269.
[20] Ref. T&C no. 1270.
[21] Lit. T&C no. 1271.

have succeeded in the Franco-Belgian region but not in England, and why that should have been the case is not explained by our property 'explanation'.

If we shift the focus of the argument from the rules about succession to the rules about marital property, we encounter similar problems. We might argue that Franco-Belgian parents were more concerned than English parents about the marriages of their children because their children's spouses stood to share in their property under the Franco-Belgian system of community property, whereas they did not under the English system of separate property. That argument, however, oversimplifies the marital property systems of the two regions. Community property in the Franco-Belgian region was largely confined to movables and acquests; normally it did not extend to the patrimony that the child stood to inherit. The English system of dower and curtesy made it possible for an English spouse to share in his or her spouse's patrimony even though it was separate property. Further, both systems were subject to change. On the one hand, ways were devised in England to circumvent dower and curtesy. On the other hand, couples in England could approximate the results under the Franco-Belgian system of community property by acquiring property in their joint names. To what extent Franco-Belgian couples could approximate the results under the English separate property system is less well known, but we know that in a later age, notarial practice in many areas allowed for partial or even total separation of the community.[22]

There is a final problem with attributing explanatory force to the property rules. Not only does the argument assume that the property patterns could not be changed voluntarily in individual cases, but it also assumes that there were fixed property rules, like those outlined earlier, before the rules and practices about marriage came to be fixed. The argument thus assumes that the property rules have priority in time. As I have attempted to show elsewhere,[23] the differences between the English and Franco-Belgian marital property systems were developing in the thirteenth century, at a time when the differences in marriage practices may also have been emerging or may even have already been in place. Recent work with inheritance practices in the Franco-Belgian region also suggests that the situation before the thirteenth century was highly fluid.[24] One can, of course, find material going all the way back to Carolingian times that reflects practices or states norms that look like what one will find in the early *coutumiers*. The *coutumiers* were not created out of nothing. What one does not find, however, is judicial or intellectual institutions that allow customary norms to harden into rules that prove resistant to change. Although our evidence about when the Franco-Belgian marriage practices came to diverge from the English is thin before the end of the fourteenth century, the evidence from that period does not suggest that the divergence was new at the time. Indeed, one of our differences, the imposition of automatic excommunication for clandestine

22 See Donahue, "What Causes," 68–9; disc. T&C no. 1272.
23 Donahue, "What Causes."
24 E.g., Tabuteau, *Transfers of Property*; White, *Custom, Kinship, and Gifts to Saints*.

marriage, seems to date from the early thirteenth century, at least in some dioceses.[25] In this state of our knowledge, it makes no more sense to say that the property rules explain the marriage practices than it does to say that the marriage practices explain the property rules.[26]

An Overarching Social Difference?

What we need, then, is some overarching explanation on which both the marriage practices and the property rules can be seen as dependent. The overarching explanation that I offer is both complicated and fuzzy, but it seems right now to be the most plausible: The difference we are trying to explain is a small one heightened by the litigation pattern. Many Franco-Belgian marriages were probably indistinguishable from many English ones.[27] But the difference that produced the difference in results, I would like to suggest, is fundamental, in the sense that it goes to the very core of how people understood themselves. The legal differences are dependent on it. However strong the sense of family and of community was in England, it was weaker than it was in the Franco-Belgian region. The English, with their separate ownership system of marital property, with their winner-take-all inheritance system, with their abundant evidence of do-it-yourself marriages, with their strict attitude toward judicial separation, but with their apparent do-it-yourself system of separation, are, for the Middle Ages, an unusually individualistic people. The Franco-Belgians, with their community property, with their shared inheritance system, with their carefully planned marriages, their reluctance to hold that a marriage, particularly an informal marriage, existed, with their system of judicial separation that brought more cases before the courts but judged them by broader standards, are more communitarian. We are dealing here, we might suggest, with a cultural phenomenon that developed independently over the course of centuries and of which both the property system and the marriage cases are an expression.

Like the property argument offered previously, this argument needs to be spelled out and qualified. The individualism of the separate ownership system of English marital property has to be qualified by the great power of the husband to manage his wife's property while the marriage lasted and by the expectancy that each spouse had in the other's land. The individualism of the English impartible inheritance system has to be qualified by the fact that the present holder of landed wealth had responsibilities to past and future generations in the management of that wealth, responsibilities that could, in some circumstances, be legally enforced.[28] The evidence of English do-it-yourself marriage comes

25 See Ch 1, at nn. 84–7.

26 Disc. T&C no. 1273.

27 I take this to be, for a somewhat later period, a principal point of Pillorget, *Tige et rameau*.

28 We refer particularly here to entailed estates and feoffments to uses. It should be noted, however, that English law tended to give the power to alienate to present holders even of land subject to these arrangements.

largely from court cases, and it may be that a disproportionate number of do-it-yourself marriages ended up in court. Despite these qualifications, however, and despite the fact that great variations could be achieved in the property system by private action, the core systems, the default systems, of succession and marital property in England seem to focus much more on the individual property holder than do the core or default systems reflected in the *coutumiers*. The fact that the default system of succession in England concentrated wealth in the hands of one person meant that in many families, the children who did not inherit were left to seek their fortunes, to a greater or lesser extent, on their own. Similarly, however aberrant the do-it-yourself marriages that we see in the English church court records may be, the records of all those *de presenti* informal marriages are there, and there are few, if any, like them in the Franco-Belgian region. Similarly, there are many more records of judicial separation in the Franco-Belgian region than there are in England.

The communitarianism of the Franco-Belgian marital property system also has to be qualified by the great power of the husband to manage the community while the marriage lasted. The communitarianism of the Franco-Belgian inheritance system needs to be qualified by the power of the current property holder in many of the customs to prefer one child over another by endowment or testament or both. The evidence of arranged marriages in the church court records needs to be qualified by the fact that many of the *de futuro* marriages in the Franco-Belgian records seem to be informal and made without much concern for family consent (consider, for example, *Tanneur et Doulsot*). Despite these qualifications, however, the core or default system of property in the Franco-Belgian region remains more communitarian than the English. One simply does not find many, if any, English wives seeking separation from their husbands for incurring obligations *ipsa inscia et absque eius [uxoris] proficuo*.[29] The basic principle of inheritance remains *égalité entre héritiers*. The canonic system of marriage is modified, at every turn it would seem, so that concerns other than those of the marriage partners are considered.

The distinction between individualism and communitarianism that we are seeking to make does not correspond exactly to the traditional distinctions in family types – joint versus stem, horizontal versus vertical, kin group versus lineage, extended versus nuclear – nor does it necessarily tell us much about authority within the family. Obviously, concern for the individual is more likely in situations where family ties are less extended and where authority within the family is weak. Too much depends, however, on the strength of the kinship ties and how the authority is exercised for there to be an exact correspondence between our dichotomy and any of the broader types of family or of authority.

Similarly, the correspondence between more individualistic and more communitarian attitudes, on the one hand, and impartible and partible inheritance, on the other, is not exact. It happens in this case that the workings of the

[29] *Gontier c Gontier* (Ch 10, n. 78).

Franco-Belgian partible inheritance system suggest a more communitarian attitude toward the family and that the workings of English impartible inheritance suggest a more individualistic attitude. Much of the evidence for this, however, is found at a level of detail below the generalization about types of inheritance systems, particularly in the different powers to alienate that the present holder of property had in each region. One can certainly imagine how a partible inheritance system might result from quite individualistic attitudes and be quite individualistic in its operations, just as one can imagine how an impartible inheritance system might be quite communitarian. Generalization is made more difficult by the fact that communitarian impulses were clearly also at work in England, as were individualistic ones in the Franco-Belgian region. When the two regions are compared, however, the English property and marriage-formation systems seem more individualistic than the Franco-Belgian.

Can we go any further? Can we offer an explanation for why the English might be more individualistic than the Franco-Belgians, the Franco-Belgians more communitarian than the English? In a previous essay,[30] in attempting to explain why the Franco-Belgians developed community property and the English did not, I suggested that after one took into account the technical legal explanations for the differences between the two regions and explanations based on the differences in the relative power and interests of lords and families, there remained an unexplained residue of variance that could only be accounted for by what I called the "anthropological" explanation, a difference in attitudes toward the family, reflecting, perhaps, an historical difference in family type or structure. This difference in attitude was independent of any economic differences, for the two regions were remarkably similar economically, particularly in the thirteenth century when the difference in marital property systems seems to have emerged.

The evidence for differences on this "anthropological" level is admittedly thin.[31] We can point to the survival in the Franco-Belgian region of notions of familial community and to the treatment of marriages as partnerships (*compagnie*), ideas for which there is little or no evidence in England. We can also point to the facts that the *laudatio parentum* does not seem so prevalent or extensive in England as it is in the Franco-Belgian region in the eleventh and twelfth centuries and that England never developed a *retrait lignagier*.

Beyond these bits of evidence, what gives the suggested explanation its power is that if this difference between the two cultures existed, it could explain much that is otherwise difficult to explain. It could explain not only the difference in marital property systems but also the difference in inheritance systems and marriage practices as well. Let us offer, then, an account of the changes in marriage practices across time, changes for which the evidence is more solid, and underlying which may be this basic difference in attitude toward the family:

30 Donahue, "What Causes."

31 Some of it is recited in Donahue, "What Causes," at 84–7. For England, see, most controversially, Macfarlane, *Origins of English Individualism*.

The notion that marriage choice should be personal to the marriage partners is an odd one in European society of the twelfth century when the classical rules of canon law on marriage formation were fixed, but it may be even odder in the society of the fifteenth. Although the society of the twelfth century knew a considerable amount of hierarchical structure, the society of the fifteenth knew more. This concern with authority is manifested not only in government but also within the family. One need not fully accept Lawrence Stone's suggestion of a shift from open lineage families in the Middle Ages to restricted patriarchal families in the Renaissance to accept the idea that there seems to have been considerably more concern with authority within the family in the later Middle Ages than in the earlier.[32] Now it has been suggested that as the vertical distance in a society increases, as class lines and structures of authority become more evident, the legal system will tend to move from a dispute-resolution mode to a law-enforcement mode.[33] In the context in which we are dealing, instance cases will give way to office. If at the same time control within the family is becoming more of an issue, we would expect to see greater willingness by the elements of the society that are in control to support family control over the marriage choice of their children.[34] This long-term trend toward greater hierarchy within society, more exercise of control by the upper elements of society over the lower, and more control by parents over children occurred in both England and the Franco-Belgian region. But if marriage litigation is any evidence, it happened sooner in the Franco-Belgian region than it did in England, and the shift was more complete.

In the present state of our knowledge, all that we can say is that such a shift in concern about authority within the family could have operated on preexisting differences in attitudes toward the family in such a way as to produce the phenomena that we have observed. The long-term trend in both regions away from cases of *de presenti* informal marriage could indicate that in both the Franco-Belgian region and England, parents were having greater success in controlling the marriage choice of their children.[35] But in the Franco-Belgian region, family authority was stronger. It may have been stronger for a long time, perhaps even since before the formation of the rules about marriage of the classical canon law. As it turned out, by the late fourteenth century, more parents were able to persuade their children to make promises of marriage at a relatively young age, and the church courts were willing to enforce such promises by criminal sanctions. Of course, the contract need not have been made by the parents, but the focus on the contract stage made it easier for parents.[36] For the young persons who escaped from the network of parental authority and made

[32] Stone, *Family, Sex and Marriage in England*, 4–9.

[33] Black, *Behavior of Law*, 29–30.

[34] Lit. T&C no. 1274.

[35] It probably also indicates a greater awareness in both countries of the proper forms, but that explanation is not inconsistent with this.

[36] Lit. T&C no. 1275.

an informal *de presenti* marriage, excommunication followed, at least in some dioceses, and as a result of the excommunication, access to the church courts to enforce the marriage was difficult. The church courts in the Franco-Belgian region, therefore, became more of a law-enforcement mechanism and less of the dispute-resolution mechanism that they were in England. They were, to use the jargon, co-opted by parents in their struggle against their children, and in the Franco-Belgian region more than in England, the original vision of the classical rules of canon law on the formation of marriage, if we have it right, was obscured.

The co-optation was, however, as are all co-optations, a willing one. We have seen that churchmen throughout the Middle Ages were concerned that people observe the proper ecclesiastical forms for marriage. This concern goes back at least as far as the twelfth century and was embodied in the canons of the Fourth Lateran Council in 1215. As late as the latter part of the fourteenth century, however, as Sheehan perceptively noted, societal recognition of a marriage, even if the ecclesiastical forms had not been followed, was an important element in proving a marriage.[37] By contrast, the impression that one gets from the Franco-Belgian registers of the latter part of the fifteenth century was that the court personnel regarded unsolemnized marriages as deeply flawed, if not quite invalid. Social acceptance of a couple as married made no difference to the court, if the marriage was not solemnized. There may, then, have been a subtle shift in the attitudes of churchmen, a shift that might account for their willingness to be co-opted by the lay elders of the society and, of course, ultimately for the adoption of the decree *Tametsi* by the council of Trent.[38]

Qualifications Based on Our Five Courts

Although I cannot resist the temptation to generalize, as I have in the preceding sections of this chapter, much of what has been done in this book points in somewhat different directions. If one stands at a fairly large distance away from the cases, the patterns that are described in the preceding sections seem to emerge. I do not wish to withdraw from the proposition that quite distinct patterns of litigation are characteristic of England, on the one hand, and what we have called 'the Franco-Belgian region', on the other. These differences call for the types of explanations just offered.

While our five courts can be made to fit into the overall pattern, there is much about them that should make us uncomfortable with letting the matter rest there. York and Ely are more like each other than they are like Paris, Cambrai, and Brussels (and vice versa); the characteristics that they share with each other seem to be characteristic of many, if not all, late medieval English church courts, and the same can be said of Paris, Cambrai, and Brussels and what is known of other Franco-Belgian courts in roughly the same period. And yet,

[37] Sheehan, "Formation," 60–1; disc. T&C no. 1276.
[38] Lit. T&C no. 1277.

the differences between York and Ely are substantial, and those between Paris, on the one hand, and Cambrai and Brussels, on the other, are even more substantial. The detailed study of these five courts that we have attempted reveals institutional differences among the courts that do not correspond to the differences between England and the Franco-Belgian region that we have emphasized in this and, to a certain extent, in preceding chapters. It has also revealed differences within what we find in each court, differences that may reflect social differences within the geographical areas that were subject to the courts' jurisdiction, or – and this is the point we will emphasize – among the types of people who came before the court. A word about some of those differences is in order.

Cambrai and Brussels have, as we have seen, a disproportionate number of marriage cases, all out of proportion to what we find at York, Ely, and Paris. Had the Cambrai and Brussels courts dealt exclusively or virtually exclusively with such cases, we would have to conclude that we are dealing with a jurisdictional peculiarity of the region. Other kinds of disputes were heard in the other kinds of courts. Some such explanation probably accounts for some of the difference that we see. It almost certainly accounts for some of the differences that we see in the types of cases heard at Brussels, as opposed to those heard at Cambrai. We know that there were other courts in York province and in Ely and Paris dioceses that heard marriage cases; we were less sure about Cambrai and Brussels. We also suspected that there were certain kinds of cases being heard by the Cambrai and Brussels courts that were not being recorded in the sentence books (notably, matters that could be regarded as 'gracious acts' and perhaps certain kinds of routine criminal cases). Properly discounting for all of these differences, however, does not seem fully to account for the fact that the Cambrai court heard proportionally twice as many marriage cases as did that at York and almost three times as many as did that at Ely and Paris, and the proportions at Brussels were similar.[39]

Assuming that this disproportion is real, that is, that overall, across jurisdictions there were proportionally more marriage cases in the Cambrai diocese in the mid-fifteenth century than there were in Ely or Paris dioceses in the late fourteenth century or in York diocese (the number of extra-diocesan cases being small enough that we can ignore them) throughout the fourteenth and fifteenth centuries, what might account for it? When we consider how much more active the promotor was at Cambrai and Brussels than he was at Paris, at least before the official of that court, the far greater proportion of cases that were brought by the Cambrai and Brussels promotors than were brought *ex officio* at Ely, and the virtual absence of office cases at York, one should probably look to prosecutorial efforts for a first line of explanation. The promotors at Cambrai and Brussels, as we have seen, pursued marriage cases (and cases of sexual offenses) to the virtual exclusion of other kinds of cases. All the non-marriage cases in our samples were instance cases. It is possible that the behavior of the promotors

[39] Tables 8.1 and 8.2, and accompanying text.

tells us nothing about the underlying social reality. The proportion of marriages that needed to be fixed and of serious sexual offenses to the population was the same in all five places in the periods in question, but active promotors pursuing such cases brought to light more than the parties themselves or their communities would have chosen to bring to light. One might even associate this clerical behavior with an increasing sense of the need for reform in the mid-fifteenth century, a sense that was ultimately to lead to a substantial Calvinist reform movement in the same region in the sixteenth century.

Before we proceed too far down this road, however, we should recall what was learned in Chapters 8, 9, and 11 about the relationship between the promotor and the parties in marriage litigation at Cambrai and Brussels. Sometimes it was possible to proceed against the will of both parties, but more often than not, the promotor was being helped by someone. There are many cases where we know that he was being helped by one of the parties and a number where we know that another member of the community had brought the matter to the promotor's attention. There are also some cases (what we called 'straight' office cases) where we cannot tell that the promotor was being helped by one of the parties, though we suspected that he was in some of them. The existence of the promotor, the rigorism that we can see in some of the judges, and the financial incentives that the promotor and the court had to pursue cases all contributed to raising the proportion of cases involving marriage and serious sexual offenses, and, as we have seen, the promotor frequently was not successful. He would not have been able to do what he did, however, without the cooperation either of the parties or other members of the community.

Granted the number of possible explanations for the large proportion of marriage cases, it would be foolish to argue that that proportion alone shows that there were more marriages that needed to be fixed and more serious sexual offenses in the diocese of Cambrai in the mid-fifteenth century than there were in our other areas. The sentences suggest, however, that some, perhaps all, of the judges thought that there was something seriously wrong with marriage in the diocese in this period, that the institution was, in some sense, spinning out of control. The rhetoric, at least, of many of the sentences suggests an urgency that is not found in the sentences of York and Ely. (There are too few sentences at Paris to make a comparison.) There are also three other characteristics of the Cambrai and Brussels cases that suggest a somewhat different kind of dispute and a somewhat different set of problems: Cambrai and Brussels are characterized by a strikingly high percentage of cases in which a presumptive marriage is alleged, a strikingly high percentage of cases involving three parties, and a strikingly high percentage of cases involving both. The proportions of these types of cases are particularly high at Brussels.

Of the Cambrai cases, 27 percent involve presumptive marriage; 52 percent of the Brussels cases do. Of the Cambrai cases, 23 percent involve three parties; 39 percent of the Brussels cases do. Of the Cambrai cases, 8 percent involve three parties and presumptive marriage; 31 percent of the Brussels cases do. Comparison with York and Ely so far as presumptive marriage is concerned is

TABLE 12.1. *Types of Marriage Cases – Troyes and Châlons (1455–1499)*

Type of Case	No.	%
1: Fornication	110	20
2: Informal and overlong engagement	83	15
3: Seduction and man's breach of promise	69	13
4: Informal engagement and woman's breach of promise	52	10
5: Male single adultery	44	8
6: Informal engagement and man's breach of promise	29	5
7: Double adultery	28	5
8: Seduction and man's breach of promise (denied)	26	5
9: Termination of an informal engagement	23	4
10: Termination of a formal engagement	19	3
11: Overlong formal engagement	14	3
12: Formal engagement and woman's breach of promise	14	3
13: Presumptive marriage	11	2
14: Bigamy	11	2
15: Formal engagement contested by informal fiancé	10	2
TOTAL	543	100

Source: Gottlieb, "The Meaning of Clandestine Marriage," 57–66.

a bit misleading since so many cases there involve *de presenti* marriage, which, if proven, needs no proof of intercourse (though sometimes that also is proven). Be that as it may, only 9 percent of the Ely cases involve presumptive marriage and only 8 percent of the York cases; 32 percent of the Ely and 23 percent of the York cases involve three parties, but none involves presumptive marriage. Of the Paris cases, 14 percent involve presumptive marriage, and for all practical purposes, there are no three-party cases.[40]

Statistical analysis of the type attempted here has not been done with the other Franco-Belgian records from the fifteenth century, but Beatrice Gottlieb did do some statistical analysis of the records of Troyes and Châlons-sur-Marne. She did not calculate the percentage of marriage cases as opposed to other types of cases. (She does say that it is high, an impression that I can confirm from my own examination of the records without being able to confirm that it is as high as it is at Brussels/Cambrai. Both courts seem to have been the sole ecclesiastical court for their area, and so heard a number of cases of clerical discipline, swearing, minor cases of blasphemy, and assaults by and against clerics, a jurisdiction, in short, similar to that of the archdeacons in England.) Gottlieb drew a sample of 800 marriage cases from 1455 to 1495 (of which 257 either did not fall into any of her categories or did not reveal enough information). Her typology of cases is somewhat different from ours (Table 12.1),[41] but can quite easily be converted into one compatible with ours (Table 12.2).

40 See Table 8.7 for the basic figures for Cambrai and Brussels. For the comparisons, see Table 6.3 (York, Ely) and Table 7.3 (Paris).

41 The typology is best explored in Gottlieb, *Getting Married*, 193–232, but the numbers come from Gottlieb, "Clandestine Marriage," 57–66.

TABLE 12.2. *Types of Marriage Cases – Troyes and Châlons (1455–1499) – Revised*

Type of Case	No.	%
Sexual offenses w/o implication of marriage	182	34
De futuro, two-party	233	43
De futuro plus *copula*, two-party	106	20
Three-party	22	4
TOTAL	543	100

Notes: If we leave out the routine sexual offenses, the proportions are 65%, 29%, and 6%, respectively.
Source: Table 12.1.

Even if we exclude the routine sexual offenses from the calculation, the proportion of three-party cases is dramatically lower at Troyes and Châlons than at both Cambrai and Brussels, and the proportion of marriage cases in which a presumptive marriage is potentially involved is dramatically lower than that at Brussels, though it is similar to that at Cambrai. The Troyes and Châlons cases make a particularly good comparison set, because we can remove some of the possible variables. Both courts had active promotors, as did the courts at Cambrai and Brussels; the cases bear similar if somewhat later dates, and Châlons diocese (in the province of Rheims) had similar, though not quite the same, synodal legislation, while that of Troyes (in the province of Sens) was also quite similar.[42] Perhaps most important is Gottlieb's more impressionistic finding. Marriage was not "out of control" in Champagne in the late fifteenth century, although, as has been true in many societies, some young women got into trouble.[43]

This is probably not enough on which to base the conclusion that something quite different was happening with regard to marriage in the diocese of Cambrai, and particularly in its northern half in the mid-fifteenth century, quite different from what was happening in other dioceses in the same region at the same time, but it is enough on which to base a conclusion that further investigation is called for. Myriam Greilsammer has argued that the later Middle Ages in Flanders and Brabant witnessed considerable tension between young people, particularly young women, who wanted to marry on their own and their families who wanted to control their marriages.[44] She points to the synodal legislation of Cambrai, which, as we have already noted, pushes the concern with clandestinity back to exchange of *verba de futuro*. There seems to have been a considerable amount of secular legislation in both provinces on the topic of rape, legislation that broadened the definition of the offence in such a way that the penalties imposed on those who abducted women against their will could

[42] Refs. and disc. T&C no. 1278.
[43] Gottlieb, *Getting Married*, 270–89.
[44] Greilsammer, "Rapts de séduction." She repeats the argument, with some modification in *id.*, *Envers du tableau*, 55–85.

also be applied to consensual abductions, particularly of women below the age of 25. Such legislation, of course, existed elsewhere. We have seen it, for example, in England. The greater quantity of such legislation in Flanders and Brabant might be explained by the multiplicity of jurisdictions there. Further complexities are introduced by the fact that Greilsammer was able to find relatively few examples of secular enforcement of such legislation, but there are some examples, and she is probably right that private settlements "in the shadow of the law" may well have occurred. We have found a number of abduction cases in our church court records (which Greilsammer excluded from her search).[45] There is not enough here to conclude that tensions over marriage choice were particularly high in Flanders and Brabant, but they may have been.[46]

Some of the peculiarities of the Cambrai and Brussels cases are shared by Ely. Ely is the only other court of our five that has a substantial number of office cases. The proportion of three-party cases at Ely is higher than that at Cambrai and somewhat, but not much, less than that at Brussels (32% vs 23% vs 39%). Of the Ely marriage cases, 16 percent involved issues of incest; Cambrai is second with 14 percent.

The institutional explanation for some of these similarities seems relatively straightforward. The Ely court was attempting to enforce the law of its own motion in addition to providing a forum for dispute resolution. That was an even more noticeable characteristic of the Cambrai and Brussels courts. That fact certainly accounts for the greater number of office cases in these courts. All five courts had other courts within their jurisdictional areas that also had office jurisdiction (the archbishop's exchequer court, archidiaconal, urban decanal, and peculiar courts at York; archidiaconal courts at Ely and Paris; decanal courts at Cambrai and Brussels). What differed was the amount of jurisdiction over *ex officio* matters that was conceded to these courts. At York and Paris, it was enough that office cases are very rare in the classes of records that survive, while at Ely, Cambrai, and Brussels, both the nature of the jurisdiction and the nature of the surviving records allow us to see more office cases.

Behind the institutional, however, lies the social. Paris was a very large city that produced enough instance business to occupy the official of a busy court virtually full time. York was nothing like the size of Paris, but it was the ecclesiastical capital of a province that produced enough instance and appellate business to occupy the consistory court virtually full time. Both the Paris and the York courts dealt with some quite ordinary people. The bulk of the litigants in Paris, however, seem to have been of roughly the same social class as the litigants at York who came from the city of York and some of the larger towns, men and women whose families contained members who at York enjoyed the freedom of the city or who at Paris would be described as *bourgeois*. Such people are also to be found at Ely, Cambrai, and Brussels. (There seem to be somewhat more of them at Cambrai than at Brussels, and the reason is hard

[45] The cases are gathered with references to discussions of them in Ch 9, n. 414.

[46] Disc. T&C no. 1279.

to fathom because the amount of urbanization in the two halves of the diocese was roughly the same.)[47]

Rural people are virtually, if not entirely, absent from the Paris register. There are large numbers of them in the York cause papers, ranging all the way from the substantially landed (virtually everyone who calls himself a knight or a donzel in the York records gives himself a rural place of residence) to the substantial peasants, who probably were roughly equivalent in terms of income to the lesser urban craftsmen. The upper range of the landed is almost absent from the Ely act book, and the social range of the court may penetrate a bit lower into rural society. Hence, while there is substantial social overlap in the litigants at York and Ely, the urban is better represented at York, as are the upper ranges of society.

It is hard to determine just who the litigants are at Cambrai and Brussels. Places of origin are recorded only sporadically; clues as to social status are quite rare.[48] We tend to think of the area covered by the diocese of Cambrai as being quite urban in the later Middle Ages. It certainly had a number of vital urban areas. The diocese, however, also covered a wide swath of territory, some of which was quite rural. These rural areas seem to be overrepresented in the Cambrai and Brussels sentence books. There are, of course, litigants from Cambrai, Valenciennes, Mons, Brussels, Mechelen, and Antwerp, just as we would expect, but not so many as we would expect. There are probably as many rural litigants in the Cambrai and Brussels sentence books as there are in the York cause papers (where, as we have seen, the ratio was approximately 62/38).[49] The ratio may be a bit lower than the 70/30 rural/urban ratio that we calculated for Ely (principally because of the rather large number of towns in the diocese that are smaller than the ones just named but which still should probably qualify as urban, e.g., Binche).[50] An analysis of the admittedly spotty placenames in the Cambrai register suggested that 60 percent, perhaps more, of the parties came from rural areas.[51]

The Cambrai and Brussels registers thus have something in common with the Ely registers that differentiates them certainly from Paris and, to some extent, from York: many rural litigants.[52] The relatively few indications of status that we get in the Cambrai and Brussels registers does not allow us to calculate social class in the way we did for York and Ely, but save for an occasional person who emphasizes his or her status, there is nothing to suggest that the people who appeared before the Cambrai and Brussels courts exceeded the status of substantial farmers or urban craftsmen that are the modal litigants at Ely and York. The dominance of the office mode of proceeding in these courts

[47] Disc. T&C no. 1280.

[48] Disc. T&C no. 1281.

[49] Derived from Table e3.App.6.

[50] See Table 6.8 and Ch 6, at n. 260.

[51] See Tables 8.10 and 8.11 and accompanying text.

[52] The difference from York lies not so much in the rural–urban split as in the fact that a number of rural litigants at York were of relatively high social status.

means that the litigants could have been of even lower status. They did not need to come up with a court fee to get the case going, and virtually no one seems to have been represented by a proctor or advocate.

Prosecutions of people more rural than urban, some of whom may be of lower status than the modal litigants at Ely, could be reaching a class of people of whom we have seen very little. It is possible that what we find in the Cambrai and Brussels courts are representatives of a rural *demi-monde*, people who did not know about the rules or, if they did, did not care about them. Such people are found before ecclesiastical courts in England, too, both rural, like the commissary court of Hereford, or urban, like the commissary court of London.[53] Those courts did a large business in routine sexual offenses. They rarely get involved in marital matters. It is possible that the promotors of Cambrai and Brussels started asking such people to whom they were married, if anyone, and began to get quite startling answers, hence the rather large number of people who are arguably married to two people, the rather large number of arguably presumptive marriages, and the number of potential violations of the incest rules.

The problem with this suggestion is that it flies in the face of a great deal that we know about peasant marriage in the later Middle Ages, which, admittedly, is not nearly so much as we would like to know. The standard accounts of peasant marriage in the Middle Ages (which are heavily biased toward English sources) suggest that peasant marriages were at least as tightly controlled as urban ones, if not more so. We should remember, however, that only a tiny fraction of marriages came before the courts, even ones as busy as those of Cambrai and Brussels. We saw, in the court of Ely, people who clearly did not know the rules; we saw perhaps more who did know them and were trying to evade them. The confessions recorded in the records of Troyes and Châlons give us a number of examples of both.[54] Whether the fact that we see what seem to be more cases of potential bigamy, presumptive marriage, and violation of the incest rules at Cambrai and Brussels is the result of the fact that the promotors in those jurisdictions were more vigorously pursuing such cases, or because there were in fact more such cases, is not something that we can tell on the basis of the records we have. We should recall, however, that the promotors have a quite low success rate in establishing the more serious offenses. Many more presumptive marriages, for example, were charged than were proved. That fact would, of course, suggest that the problem was more in the minds of the judges and promotors than it was in reality, but what actually happened and what can be proven in court are not necessarily the same thing.

Gottlieb did not calculate a success rate for Troyes and Châlons, but she has a large number of examples of couples who do not seem to need more than a single appearance in court to set matters right.[55] Such cases also exist at Cambrai and

[53] See Donahue, ed., *Records 2*, 170–1 (Hereford); Wunderli, *London Church Courts*, 81–102.

[54] Gottlieb, *Getting Married*, 233–51.

[55] *Ibid.*, passim.

Brussels, but there seem to be more cases, particularly at Brussels, in which at least one of the couple is resisting and refuses to confess. One would not want to suggest on the basis of this evidence alone that resistance to ecclesiastical jurisdiction was stronger in the area covered by the Brussels court than it was in that covered by the Cambrai court, and that in turn was stronger than it was in southern Champagne (Troyes and Châlons), but it is at least possible. To go further would take us down a road that leads to the debates about the origins of the Reformation in Belgium, and we would never return.

What we can say is that in comparison with the court at Ely, the courts at Cambrai and Brussels pursued what they perceived to be instances of "out-of-bounds" behavior more vigorously.[56] In this regard, the two courts do fit into the broad pattern of difference between England and the Franco-Belgian region that we have outlined. We must leave open the question of whether the reason the Cambrai and Brussels courts did so is that there was more such behavior to pursue, but the records are open to that possibility.

There is one more substantial difference between Ely, on the one hand, and Cambrai and Brussels, on the other. In Cambrai diocese, plaintiffs, both men and women, have a much lower success rate in establishing a marriage, and women who are the primary movers in cases of presumptive marriage have a much lower success rate than do women who are trying to establish either a presumptive marriage or a *de presenti* one at Ely. Ely shares this characteristic of a high plaintiffs' success rate with York. A relatively low plaintiffs' success rate in establishing a marriage also seems to be characteristic of Paris, but the nature of the litigation there (and of the surviving records) is sufficiently different that this comparison is dangerous. Since we do not have comparable figures for other English or Franco-Belgian courts, it is probably safer not to generalize. What we can say is that it is likely that more disappointed and deceived women left the Cambrai and Brussels courts than left those at York and Ely. This is perhaps enough to base a suggestion that the women involved in the Cambrai and Brussels courts were more naïve, perhaps younger. This is not enough to demonstrate that Cambrai and Brussels illustrate the truth of the reformers' charge that the rules of the classical canon law were being used as means for seduction, but it is consistent with that charge. The men of Cambrai diocese who appear before these courts are, for the most part, a singularly unattractive lot.

Let us now turn briefly to the similarities that we have found between York and Paris, similarities that York and Paris share with each other and not with Ely, on the one hand, and Cambrai and Brussels, on the other. We have suggested that York and Paris are dealing with litigants of somewhat higher average social standing than are the courts at Ely, Cambrai, and Brussels. One of the ways in which we can demonstrate this is that virtually all the cases from York and Paris are instance cases. By and large, the parties hire their own lawyers and conduct their own litigation, and the court serves as a referee. We also suggested that

[56] Disc. T&C no. 1282.

there are more urban litigants at Paris and York than there are at Ely, Cambrai, and Brussels, though we could not quite prove this because of the uncertainties about the origin of many the Cambrai and Brussels litigants.

These similarities allow us to isolate an urban segment of the York cases and compare it with Paris. Here the similarities cease. While I argued that there was not so much difference between urban and rural marriages in late medieval Yorkshire as some have argued, there is no question that a considerable number of the urban marriages were self-arranged by parties who were mature and that a number of them seem to have been self-arranged by parties who were in service, in their late teens, perhaps early 20s, and who planned to solemnize their marriage after they left service. Self-arrangement is totally inconsistent with virtually everything that we see in the Paris records. Not only that, but there are indications, though admittedly only indications, of a substantial gender-age gap, the men being quite a bit older than the women, and of the women being quite young, perhaps even in their early to middle teens. There is no evidence in the Paris records of life-cycle servanthood, considerable evidence of it at York (and some at Ely). While it is possible that we are dealing with people of higher status at Paris than we are at York, there are no indications of it. What little evidence we have suggests that except for the very few who claim nobility, they are the same types of people whom we find litigating at York.

The difference in what seems to be the underlying marriage pattern at Paris does not dictate that the litigation will be almost exclusively about *verba de futuro*, but it is consistent with it. The same may be said of the instance cases at Cambrai, which fit the Paris pattern quite well, and are probably the product of urban marriages or of attempted marriages, similar to those at Paris, but in smaller cities.

What is difficult to explain on this basis is why the same litigation pattern, the almost exclusive focus on *verba de futuro*, is also found in the rural areas of Cambrai diocese, where there seems to be much more self-arranging of marriages, and in the Troyes and Châlons records where the same pattern seems to prevail. (Of course, there is evidence in all three areas of parents or relatives in the background, just as there is at York and Ely; what we do not find in these non-urban cases is the exclusive dominance of the arranged marriage.) It is here that we must fall back on the social-structural explanation that I offered earlier in this section because there seems to be no other way to explain it.

WHERE DO WE GO FROM HERE?

If the argument of the preceding section is even half correct, we would expect to find substantial variations in the litigation patterns about marriage in the church courts based on the underlying social characteristics of the institution of marriage and the family in the region from which the litigation comes. The law was the same throughout Western Europe. The common training of the personnel of the courts saw to it that, by and large, it was applied. We must be careful to take into account local legal variations, such as the greater criminalization of the Franco-Belgian courts or possible effects of the synodal legislation about clandestine marriage, but our analysis of the effects of these variations suggests that it was not sufficient to prevent underlying social forces from being seen in the varying patterns of litigation and, indeed, that these local legal variations were themselves the product of the same underlying forces.

With this in mind, let us look very briefly at what lies outside of the English and Franco-Belgian records that have been our principal focus. We have said little in this book about the German records. They are not so extensive as those in the Franco-Belgian region or in England, but we have fairly good representative records from central and southern Germany from the fourteenth and fifteenth centuries.[57] They have been examined, and some excellent pioneering work has been done with marriage cases in them.[58] What needs to be done with these records is to subject them to the kind of analysis that we have used on the records of the five courts examined in this book. We need to know about how the marriage cases fit into the overall pattern of litigation generally in these courts. We need more precise quantitative and impressionistic evaluations of these cases, some of which has already begun, before we can be confident that all the similarities and differences between these records and those in England and the Franco-Belgian region have been identified.[59]

In the present state of our knowledge, however, it seems fair to say that the German records are more like those in England than they are like those in the Franco-Belgian region. The focus of litigation is on marriage formation, not on its separation or dissolution. Informal *de presenti* marriages are very much in evidence. Klaus Lindner suggests that the pejorative German term for clandestine marriage, *Winkelehe* (literally, "marriage in a [dark] corner"), was not used for all informal marriages, but only for those which were later discovered to have been formed despite a diriment impediment.[60]

If the marriage litigation in the records of the German ecclesiastical courts requires further analysis, what needs to be explained about marriage litigation in the ecclesiastical courts of the Mediterranean world is what seems to be its relative absence. A few examples from southern France may serve to illustrate. The annoyingly incomplete but fascinating records from the small mountainous jurisdiction of Mende give us one *de presenti* and one *de futuro* marriage case from around 1270 and two *de presenti* marriage cases from around 1340.[61] The number of cases recorded in the two books has not been counted, but it runs into the hundreds. Similarly incomplete sets of records from the official of the bishop of Elne at Perpignan from the years 1413 and 1414 give two *de presenti*

[57] Donahue, ed., *Records 1*, 40–7, 117–22.
[58] See literature cited in Ch 11, n. 12.
[59] Indeed, there are a great many more records in England and the Franco-Belgian region that require this analysis.
[60] Deutsch, *Ehegerichtsbarkeit*, 269–80, questions this finding on the basis of the Regensburg records, but notes that informal marriages were tolerated by the court, so long as a priest was eventually notified.
[61] Ref. T&C no. 1283.

marriage cases and one interlocutory sentence against a runaway wife to return to her husband.[62] Six large process books from the last years of the fourteenth century and the first years of the fifteenth century survive from the court of the official of the bishop of Marseilles.[63] These do not record every case that came before the court but gather together, for reasons that are not completely clear, the entire *processus* in selected cases. Only one of these books seems to contain any marriage cases, and there are only three of them – two in which a *de presenti* marriage is alleged and one in which a woman is seeking to be separated from her current husband on the ground that her former husband, who was presumed dead, is really alive.[64] There survives from the court of the officiality of the bishop of Carpentras a series of more than a hundred registers, both civil and criminal, running from 1427 to 1563 and beyond.[65] An examination of the first 10 years of these registers discloses only one marriage case, a case of dissolution of a marriage for consanguinity.[66]

Although the sample is very small, these cases do not suggest that there was any bias against litigating about a *de presenti* marriage in southern France. Perhaps more important, however, is how few marriage cases they reveal. Only in Perpignan could marriage litigation have been a substantial part of the court's business, and so little survives from Perpignan that we cannot tell that it was.

A relatively unsystematic search in Spain and Italy in the late 1980s revealed even fewer marriage cases. A few were discovered in the surviving records of the court of the bishop of Montalcino and in those of the archbishop of Siena.[67] Similarly, a few were discovered in the surviving records of the court of the bishop of Pamplona.[68]

Four months of the notarial register of the court book of the archbishop of Pisa in 1230 have been published.[69] It contains 9 matrimonial matters out of 59 entries (15%). There are too few entries to subject the individual entries to any statistical analysis, but taken as a group, the cases seem to reveal a somewhat different legal world. There are three two-party contested spousals cases, one of which employs an early version of the "formula libel," another of which alleges *sponsalia* plus *copula* and is defended on the ground of prior bond, and the third of which (only the depositions survive) may have been defended on the ground of vow.[70] None has a recorded result. There are two sentences in three-party cases, both of which raise issues of prior bond. In one the prior bond

[62] A.D. Pyrénées-Orientales, G145*bis*, fols. 7r, 8r (runaway wife), 9r.
[63] Donahue, ed., *Records 1*, 67–9.
[64] A.D. Bouches-du-Rhône, 5 G 775, fols. 167r–168v (1408), 231r–236v (1409), 240r–243v (1410) (separation).
[65] Donahue, ed., *Records 1*, 74–5.
[66] A.D. Vaucluse, GIII^{bis} 81–87 (1427–37). To my shame, the notes that contained the specific reference to the case have gone missing.
[67] Donahue, ed., *Records 1*, 159–62.
[68] *Id.*, 187–8.
[69] *Imbreviaturbuch*.
[70] Listed T&C no. 1284.

is sustained; in the other it is held void on the ground of force.[71] There are two routine, and so far as the record shows uncontested, renunciations by female orphans of the marriage contracted for them, in one case by her tutors and in the other by her mother.[72] In an uncontested case, a woman obtains dissolution of her *sponsalia* on the ground of nonage.[73] In the final case, the archbishop orders a wife to return to her husband despite the husband's adultery, upon the latter's posting surety.[74] The wording of the sentence suggests that the archbishop was acting as an arbitrator in this case. One final marriage case is found in the surviving acts of the archbishop independent of the register; in 1241, the archbishop dissolved a marriage on the ground of impotence. These records suggest, though they certainly do not prove, that while Italian ecclesiastical courts did hear marriage cases in this period, they heard relatively few of them compared to other types of cases, and that the issues that were raised emerged out of a marital system in which the choice of young people, particularly young women, about marriage was for the most part highly controlled.

Recently, considerable attention has been devoted to Italian episcopal archives, and the work suggests that earlier surveys considerably understated the quantity of records of marriage cases that may be found in that country. Indeed, it seems highly unlikely, on *a priori* grounds, that there were no marital disputes in southern Europe in the high and later Middle Ages, and the recent research would suggest that such was not the case.[75] It is also possible that some of the jurisdiction that we find in ecclesiastical courts in northern Europe was exercised by secular courts in southern Europe.[76]

The work with Italian episcopal archives is all quite recent (and is still ongoing) and, to my shame, it did not come to my attention until it was too late to incorporate it fully in this book. Let us focus here, briefly, on the study that, to date, comes closest to the kind of study undertaken in this book, Cecilia Cristellon's dissertation on marriage litigation in the court of the patriarch of Venice from 1420 to 1545. Cristellon's statistical analysis of the cases stops in the year 1500, though she has a number of suggestive remarks about the later period.[77] Table 12.3 shows her basic division of the types of cases.

The table divides the 706 cases into five categories: suits to establish a marriage (*matrimonio*), suits to enforce promises to marry (*sponsali*), suits to declare a marriage null (*nullità*), suits to separate an already married couple from bed and board (*separazione*), and suits that cannot be fit into one of the previous categories but which seem to deal with 'marriage matters' broadly

[71] Listed T&C no. 1285.

[72] *Mugiolachi* (20.v.1230), no. 15, pp. 101–2; *Lame* (24.v.1230), no. 17, p. 102.

[73] *Vico c Truffe* (16.viii.1230), no. 47, pp. 133–4.

[74] *Vitalis c Consilii* (12.v.1230), no. 9, pp. 96–7, disc. T&C no. 1286.

[75] Lit. T&C no. 1287.

[76] Dean, "Fathers and Daughters," offers considerable evidence that it was.

[77] For an updated version of Cristellon's statistics and those from a number of other Italian tribunals, see Seidel Menchi, ed., *Tribunali del matrimonio*, which arrived on my desk as I was reading the proofs of this book.

TABLE 12.3. *Types of Marriage Cases – Venice (1420–1500)*

Type of Case	FP	MP	%FP	Uncertain	Total Cases	% Total Cases	%Mm Cases
Marriage	125	145	46		270	38	51
Betrothal	6	4	60		10	1	2
Divorce	85	47	64	1	133	19	25
Separation	46	72	39		118	17	22
Unclassified	75	85	47	15	175	25	
TOTAL	345	361	49		706	100	100

Source: Cristellon, *Charitas versus eros*, 103–4.

TABLE 12.4. *Types of Marriage Cases – York (1300–1499), Ely (1374–1381)*

	York 1300–1499					Ely 1374–1381				
Type of Case	FP	MP	%FP	TOT	%TOT	FP	MP	%FP	TOT	%TOT
Marriage (Mm)	85	54	61	139	68	33	17	66	50	57
Betrothal	26	1	96	27	13	8	0	100	8	9
Mm or betrothal						13	10	57	23	26
Divorce	17	14	55	31	15	2	4	33	6	7
Separation	7	0	100	7	3	0	0		0	0
TOTAL	135	69	66	204	100	56	31	64	87	100

Source: Tables 3.5, 3.6, 6.5.

conceived (*non classificabili*). All the cases are instance cases, and in most of them the gender of the plaintiff can be identified. The first column of percentages gives the female/male gender ratio. The second column of percentages gives the proportion of each type of case to the total number of cases; the third column of percentages ("%Mm Cases") gives the proportion of each type of case to the total number of cases that have been identified as falling into one of the four categories defined as "Marriage"; that is to say, it excludes the cases in the "Unclassified" category. The bottom lines indicate that cases to establish a marriage make up about half of the classified cases, about a quarter seek to invalidate a marriage, about a quarter seek to separate the parties, and cases that seek to enforce promises of marriage are only a tiny fraction.

Tables 12.4 and 12.5 rearrange the statistics developed in previous chapters in order to make them comparable to Cristellon's categories. I had to struggle to create a category in Table 12.4 of litigation concerning promises to marry. Ultimately, all the cases in which a *de futuro* promise was alleged or in which an abjuration *sub pena nubendi* was alleged were included under "Betrothal," but in virtually all the former cases and in all the latter, the plaintiff also alleged that the parties had had sexual intercourse. Hence, if we wanted to, we could exclude the category of "Betrothal" entirely. These are almost all

TABLE 12.5. *Types of Marriage Cases – Paris (1384–1387), Cambrai (1438–1453), Brussels (1448–1459)*

	Paris 1384–1387							Cambrai 1438–1453							Brussels 1448–1459						
Type of Case	FP	MP	%FP	Unc	TCas	%TCas	%MCas	FP	MP	%FP	Unc	TCas	%TCas	%MCas	FP	MP	%FP	Unc	TCas	%TCas	%MCas
Marriage	46	15	75	3	64	16	17	31	0	100	25	56	22	27	52	13	80	16	81	52	60
Betrothal (No *cop*)	48	115	29	27	190	46	52	20	43	32	36	99	38	47	8	12	40	13	33	21	25
Divorce	3	1	75	6	10	2	3	0	0	0	12	12	5	6	0	0	0	2	2	1	1
Separation	62	15	81	25	102	25	28	21	9	70	13	43	17	20	11	7	61	0	18	11	13
Other	9	10	47	25	44	11	0	4	1	80	44	49	19	0	7	4	64	12	23	15	0
TOTAL	168	156	52	86	410	100	100	76	37	67	146	259	100	100	78	36	68	43	157	100	100

Notes: For an explanation of the categories, see the text accompanying Table 12.3.
Source: Tables 7.4, 8.8, 8.9.

cases in which it is alleged that a marriage has been formed. That is roughly 85 percent of the cases at York, 93 percent at Ely, where we had to create a third category of marriage-formation cases to accommodate those that employed the 'formula' libel. The high percentage of marriage-formation cases means that that the proportion of divorce cases (15% at York, 7% at Ely) is also far lower than it is at Venice, and, in comparison with Venice, separation cases hardly exist. The proportion of female plaintiffs is somewhat higher at York and Ely than it is at Venice: roughly, two-thirds versus one-half. Finally, the York and Ely cases (like the Cambrai/Brussels cases considered in Table 12.5) contain a substantial number of marriage-formation cases in which three or more parties are involved. I do not know whether the same is true of the Venetian cases, though Cristellon reports that a number of them involve allegations of prior bond. At Ely there are some *ex officio* cases mixed in with the straight-instance cases, but it is always possible to tell who the moving party is, and that party has been categorized as 'plaintiff'.

The situation in the Franco-Belgian region is, as we have seen, quite different. Table 12.5 shows that in the Paris register, over half the marriage cases that fall within Cristellon's categories (52%) are cases that seek enforcement of a promise of marriage, where the couple have not had sexual intercourse. These cases are overwhelmingly brought by men (71%). About 17 percent of the cases here classified as "Marriage," overwhelmingly brought by women (75%), allege promises of marriage followed by intercourse. Most of the rest of the cases (28%) are separation cases. There are very few *ex officio* cases in the Paris register, though there are some. The number of cases in which the gender of the plaintiff is listed as uncertain is the result of the fact that a number of couples had agreed on a result by the time they got to court.

At Cambrai and Brussels (where, as before, the numbers are based on samples), as at Paris, there are virtually no cases in which a marriage is alleged to have been formed by the exchange of *de presenti* consent. As at Paris, the cases called "Marriage" are cases in which promises of marriage followed by intercourse are alleged. There is a difference in the proportions of the two types of cases. At Cambrai almost half of the cases (47%) allege promises of marriage unaccompanied by intercourse, whereas cases of marriage formed by promises of marriage followed by intercourse represent at least a quarter of the cases (27%). At Brussels the proportions are more than reversed: 60 percent of the cases allege promises of marriage followed by intercourse, whereas only a quarter of the cases allege promises of marriage unaccompanied by intercourse. *Ex officio* prosecution accounts for many of the cases at both Cambrai and Brussels, more at Brussels (where there are relatively few instance cases that are not separation cases). Where the moving party can be identified, he or she is listed as plaintiff, but the number of uncertain plaintiffs is the result of the fact that we cannot always determine who is the moving party.

When we compare the Venetian records to the five courts that we have studied (Tables 12.3 to 12.5), a number of surprising features emerge. One might expect that if Italian marriage cases could be found, they would look much more like what we find in Paris, and to a lesser extent at Cambrai and Brussels, than they would look like what we find at York and Ely. As we have noted, the register of the Pisan episcopal court from the thirteenth century contains very few marriage cases, and those few seem to be concerned mostly with the enforcement of promises to marry, not with marriages allegedly formed by *de presenti* consent. The studies of Italian marriage patterns by the late David Herlihy and others have shown not only by inference from statistics but also by qualitative evidence that Italian marriage in the later Middle Ages, at least among the urban middle class and above – the type of people who tended to use the ecclesiastical courts in instance suits – was tightly controlled by the seniors of the family. Young women did not have much opportunity to engage in the informal exchanges that are so much the subject of litigation in England, and which appear at least occasionally in some areas in the Franco-Belgian region. When marriage contracts were made, they were formal contracts made by notaries, and hence less likely to be a matter of dispute.[78]

If this was, in fact, the marriage pattern in Venice, then the low number of cases in the Venetian courts involving promises to marry unaccompanied by intercourse is just what we would expect. What needs to be explained is why there are so many such cases at Paris. The explanation offered in Chapter 7 was that these cases were not disputes in the normal sense of the term. The parties, at least the men, wanted a formal record that they had not contracted marriage, probably so that they could contract marriage with someone else (or at least try to). The same thing may be happening at Cambrai and Brussels in the cases that do not allege intercourse, though that is less easy to see on the record that we have.

That leaves, then, a difference that may not turn out to be a difference once we burrow more deeply into the Venetian records, but which right now seems to be a difference. Virtually no one at Paris, Cambrai, or Brussels alleges a *de presenti* marriage. A great many people at Venice seem to do so, or at least seem to be arguing that a marriage has been formed though not consummated, rather than simply that promises of marriage have been made. That was not the case in thirteenth-century Pisa. It is possible that we are looking at a change in marriage practice that is informed, if not motivated, by the fact that by the fifteenth century, Italians became aware that unconsummated *de presenti* marriages were no longer indissoluble.[79] The suggestion seems at least worth making.

There is, of course, one respect in which the Venetian records are more like the Franco-Belgian ones than they are like the English. The English records have very few separation cases. In both the Franco-Belgian and the Venetian records, separation cases are a substantial part of the jurisdiction. It was argued that the substantial presence of separation cases in the Franco-Belgian records and their virtual absence from the English records may be accounted for, though

[78] See n. 82.

[79] Disc. T&C no. 1288.

TABLE 12.6. *Grounds for Divorce – Venice (1420–1500)*

	MP	FP	Total	%
Prior bond	36	48	84	71
Nonage[a]	0	15	15	13
Affinity or consanguinity[b]	3	6	9	8
Impotence	0	5	5	4
Orders	2	2	4	3
Servile condition	0	1	1	1
SUBTOTAL	41	77	118	100
Uncertain[c]			15	
TOTAL			133	

Notes: See T&C no. 1289.
Source: Cristellon, *Charitas versus eros*, 108–11.

perhaps not fully accounted for, by the difference in marital property systems in the two countries. A formal record of separation and an actual separation of goods are virtually required in a community property system; they are much less of a necessity in a system where the spouses have separate property. In this regard, the dotal system of Venice, though certainly not the same as community property, is more like a community property system than it is like a separate property system. The untangling of the dowry, like the untangling of the community property, is more likely to require that separating couples obtain a formal judgment of separation.

There is one more oddity about the Venetian records: the high proportion of divorce cases in comparison with all the other northern European courts. Here we need to ask what the grounds are that are being claimed for the annulments. Cristellon provides the data that gives us a start (Table 12.6).

Whatever else is happening here, it is clear from the table that the Venetians were not making extensive use of the law of incest to dissolve marriages. That a relatively high proportion of cases should involve nonage is consistent with the marriage pattern that probably prevailed in Venice. The question is what we are to make of the high proportion (71%) of the cases that involve the impediment of prior bond. More study of the Venetian records is clearly called for. It is possible, as suggested in some of the cases of prior bond in England, that the allegations are corrupt. It is also possible, however, and perhaps more likely on an *a priori* basis, that what we are looking at here is the equivalent of the three-party marriage-formation case that we saw in England, Cambrai, and Brussels.[80] As noted many times in this book, the legal issue raised by a case of divorce on the ground of prior bond is the same as that in a marriage-formation case defended on that ground. It is simply a question of who sued first. Only a more careful examination of the records would tell whether these cases involve

[80] In a personal communication, Dr. Cristellon tells me that a number of the "Marriage" cases involve third parties. She did not, however, break these cases out separately in her statistics.

long-term, or relatively long-term, marriages that are sought to be dissolved on the ground of prior bond as opposed to marriages that are in the formation stage.

Obviously, we are only beginning to analyze these newly discovered Italian records. Cristellon found 270 Venetian marriage-formation cases over the course of 80 years. Let us assume that that was all there were (though there do seem to be some gaps in the records). There are 64 such cases at Paris over the course of 3 years. If we extrapolate that number over 80 years we get 1,680 cases. Similarly, Cristellon found 720 cases at Venice dealing with 'marriage matters'. The equivalent number for Paris over 3 years is 410. If we extrapolate that number over 80 years we get 10,933 cases. Venice did not have the population of Paris, but it was not too far different, and if extrapolation is permissible, Paris had more than 6 times the number of marriage formation cases and 15 times the number of marriage cases generally. The present state of our knowledge still suggests, then, that there was less marriage litigation in the Mediterranean world than in northern Europe, and if that is the case, there must be some explanation.

I offer an explanation with considerable diffidence. There is much that we do not know, and generalizations over wide ranges of time and region are dangerous. Nonetheless, the pattern of marriage in southern Europe seems to be quite different from that of northern Europe. At least in the cities, women marry young and men marry late, producing a notable gender-age disparity.[81] The default legal system of marital property and marital prestations is also quite different in southern Europe, and while the differences in the default systems tend to blur in practice, there remains what appears to be a substantial difference in the actual property systems as well. Southern Europeans are people of dowry, whereas northern Europeans are people of dower or of community property (or both). Could it be that these differences account for the substantial number of litigated marriage cases that we see in the records of the northern ecclesiastical courts and their comparatively small number, at least as so far discovered, in the records of the southern European ecclesiastical courts? It seems hard to believe that there is not some connection between the two phenomena, though what that connection is is not immediately apparent.

Focusing more on the demographic pattern than on the property pattern (though the two are related), what we see in southern Europe is a marriage pattern like that which seems to have prevailed, at least among certain people, in Paris. In Paris, that suggested marriage pattern produced litigation about marriage formation that really was not litigation. People went to court to get a declaration that a *de futuro* contract of marriage did not exist, and they knew that that was the result they were going to get. A marriage pattern like this one, coupled with a strong notarial tradition such as existed in southern Europe, may have produced a situation in which those who had contracted to marry knew that they had done so because they had the notarial record to

[81] Lit. T&C no. 1290.

prove it.[82] While such contracts may not have complied with the formalities that the church was encouraging for marriage, they produced fewer situations in which the existence of an informal marriage might be a matter of dispute. Hence, there was less litigation about marriage formation.

Pursuing this idea would lead us to conclude that if parents (and elders) were more successful in the Franco-Belgian region than they were in England in controlling marriage choice, they were even more successful in southern Europe. They were not, of course, completely successful. *Romeo and Juliet* is, after all, an Italian story. They were sufficiently successful, however, that we do not see anything like the amount of litigation about marriage formation in southern Europe that we see in northern Europe.

I must again emphasize how tentative this suggestion is. It may or may not be correct, though it fits the evidence now before us. I hope, however, that it serves to stimulate more work in the court and notarial records of southern European that deal with this topic, work that seems to be proceeding as we write.[83]

I must also emphasize the significance of this work, particularly that with Germany and Italy, because older work with the former and recent work with both may require that the argument of this book be revisited. While the evidence is by no means all in, it looks as if the litigation pattern in those areas was more like England than it was like that in the Franco-Belgian region. If that proves to be right, then my argument, based as it is on positing an exceptional English individualism – something about which I am already quite uncomfortable – is going to need some recasting. Once more, if the recent work proves to be right, the English pattern is more like the norm and the Franco-Belgian more like the exception, and we need an explanation not for English exceptionalism but for Franco-Belgian exceptionalism. That is going to take some work, but that is, I think, where we are right now.

[82] Disc. T&C no. 1291.

[83] See works cited in n. 75.

Epilogue and Conclusion

By the sixteenth century, Alexander's rules about the formation of marriage were in trouble. There was, to begin with, the difficulty of proof of informal marriages, something that we saw in *Dolling c Smith* and in dozens of cases like it. Partially in response to this problem, the Fourth Lateran Council in 1215 had required couples to have banns of marriage proclaimed publicly before they married, but the council had not invalidated marriages that simply complied with Alexander's rules. Secondly, Alexander's rules encountered opposition in those portions of society where marital property was important. In particular, the Roman lawyers kept alive the tradition that parental consent was necessary for the validity of a marriage, and the Roman rules on dowry and customary rules about community property affected – adversely, it would seem, to women in particular – the equality that seems to lie at the root of Alexander's rules.[1]

It would seem that the French proved particularly resistant to Alexander's rules. There was nothing that the French could do about the law of the universal church that said that informal marriages were valid, but, as we have seen, French local councils throughout the Middle Ages proclaimed that those who married without the usual ecclesiastical solemnities were automatically excommunicated. The reformers were quick to attack Alexander's rules. For both Luther and Calvin they violated the fundamental principle of the authority of fathers in managing the affairs of their families, including the authority to determine whom their children would marry.[2] When the council of Trent came to consider marriage in 1563, an intense debate ensued.[3] The delegates from France had been instructed to press for two changes in the law: No marriage was to be valid unless publicly solemnized in the church after promulgation of banns, and no marriage of a son or daughter subject to paternal power was

[1] See Donahue, "Case of the Man Who Fell into the Tiber."
[2] Lit. at T&C no. 1293.
[3] Esmein, *Mariage*, 2:161–215, 483–9, tells the story fully with copious references to the *acta* of the council. See also Jedin, *Konzil von Trient*, 4.2:96–121, references at 277–81.

to be valid without parental consent. The Italians, however, argued that the validity of nonsolemnized marriages was a matter of doctrine, like the Trinity, that could not be changed. To change the rules, they also argued, would be to concede too much to the reformers. The result, the council's decree *Tametsi*, was a compromise. It had four important elements:

First, Alexander's rules were confirmed and anathemas proclaimed against those who held that they had been invalid.

Second, Alexander's rules were changed for the future. Marriages not solemnized before the parish priest and at least two witnesses were thereafter declared to be invalid.[4]

Third, marriages of minors without parental consent were condemned, but were expressly declared to be valid. Indeed, the parish priest was authorized to dispense with the promulgation of banns if he feared that force might be applied to the couple.

Fourth, because the general promulgation of these rules in countries that were no longer Catholic would have led to the invalidation of Protestant marriages, at least in the eyes of the church, the Tridentine rules were declared to take effect only when they were promulgated in the parish.

The French were furious.[5] They refused to promulgate *Tametsi* in their country, and the Tridentine rules, it can be argued, did not come into effect in France until early in the twentieth century.[6] They promulgated instead their own ordinance, the *ordonnance* of Blois of 1579, similar to Trent but stricter:[7]

First, the promulgation of banns was made a condition of the validity of the marriage. A priest who married a child in the power of its parents without parental consent was to be held guilty of misprision of rape.

Second, those who suborned the consent of the child in power were to be punished capitally for rape, the consent of the child being irrelevant.

The *ordonnance* raised more problems than it solved. First, the sanctions were draconian, and draconian sanctions have a tendency not to be enforced. I know of one case where the capital sanction was imposed, but such punishments were certainly not common.[8] Second, by refusing to promulgate the decrees of the council, the French, in fact, left Alexander's rules in effect. The possibility was raised of canonically valid marriages that were not valid secularly. Third, the statute was unclear as to just what conditions were necessary for validity. It needed to be amended in 1639 by another *ordonnance* that required parental consent as a condition of the validity of the proclamation of the banns.[9]

The decrees of the council of Trent were not promulgated in England either. The monarch was, by this time, a Protestant. The English church continued

[4] The parish priest was also to proclaim the banns and keep a marriage register, but these were not made elements of validity.

[5] Lit. T&C no. 1294.

[6] Disc. and lit. T&C no. 1295.

[7] Ordonnance de Blois (1579), arts. 40–1, in *Recueil des grandes ordonnances*, 173–4.

[8] Diefendorf, *Paris City Councillors*, 165–6.

[9] *Id.*, 167.

to condemn informal marriages, as had the medieval church, but it did not invalidate them. Indeed, it might not have had the power to do so under the new Erastian arrangement. In 1753, 190 years after the decree *Tametsi*, parliament, in Lord Hardwicke's Act, finally invalidated, in most cases, informal marriages not performed by an authorized church of England clergyman.[10] The sanctions of the act are much less severe than those of the *ordonnance* of Blois. It is hard not to see in the contrast between both the timing and the contents of the *ordonnance* of Blois, on the one hand, and Lord Hardwicke's Act, on the other, a fundamentally different attitude toward marriage, at least among those who had the power to make statutes.

In those areas in which the decree *Tametsi* was promulgated, it had, of course, the immediate effect of invalidating *de presenti* marriages that were not performed in the presence of the parish priest (the specification of that particular priest turned out to be a problem) and at least two witnesses. It had another effect that is less often noted. The second branch of Alexander's rules, the formation of a marriage by consent *de futuro* followed by sexual intercourse, also disappeared. While this does not follow ineluctably from the words of the decree, the practical difficulties of completing this form of contract in the presence of the parish priest and two witnesses achieved this effect. Hence, two of the major sources of matrimonial litigation that we have studied in this book – marriages alleged to have been formed by informal exchange of present consent and marriages alleged to have been formed by exchanges of future consent followed by intercourse – disappeared from those courts that were situated in areas in which the decree was promulgated. More in the state of our current knowledge we cannot say. A comparative study of post-Tridentine marriage litigation in England, France, and one of those areas in which the Tridentine decrees were promulgated would be enlightening.

Writing in the 1740s, Charles de Secondat, baron de Montesquieu, addresses the theme of the consent of fathers to the marriage of their children:[11]

The consent of fathers is founded on their authority, that is, on the right of property. It is also founded on their love, on their reason, and on the uncertainty of that of their children, whom youth confines in a state of ignorance and passion in a state of ebriety.

In the small republics, or singular institutions already mentioned, they might have laws which gave to magistrates that right of inspection over the marriages of the children of citizens which nature had already given to fathers. The love of the public might there equal or surpass all other love. Thus Plato would have marriages regulated by the magistrates: this the Lacedaemonian magistrates performed.

But in common institutions, fathers have the disposal of their children in marriage: their prudence in this respect is always supposed to be superior to that of a stranger. Nature gives to fathers a desire of procuring successors to their children, when they have

10 Details in Outhwaite, *Clandestine Marriage*, 75–144.

11 Montesquieu, *Spirit of Laws*, 440–2. This discussion is derived from my historical introduction (Donahue, "Comparative Law") to the *Oxford Handbook of Comparative Law*.

almost lost the desire of enjoyment themselves. In the several degrees of progeniture, they see themselves insensibly advancing to a kind of immortality. But what must be done, if oppression and avarice arise to such a height as to usurp all the authority of fathers? Let us hear what Thomas Gage says in regard to the conduct of the Spaniards in the West Indies.[12] . . . [Gage's account describes the Spanish as forcing the Indians to marry at a young age in order to increase the amount of tribute that the Spanish receive.] Thus in an action which ought to be the most free, the Indians are the greatest slaves.

In England the law is frequently abused by the daughters marrying according to their own fancy without consulting their parents. This custom is, I am apt to imagine, more tolerated there than anywhere else from a consideration that as the laws have not established a monastic celibacy, the daughters have no other state to choose but that of marriage, and this they cannot refuse. In France, on the contrary, young women have always the resource of celibacy; and therefore the law which ordains that they shall wait for the consent of their fathers may be more agreeable. In this light the custom of Italy and Spain must be less rational; convents are there established, and yet they may marry without the consent of their fathers.

Montesquieu begins with some general assumptions about the way in which paternal power is organized the world over and about how fathers and children behave and are disposed the world over. From this he derives the proposition that the laws will require that fathers consent to the marriage of their children. He then notes that there are exceptions in "small republics" and "singular institutions," a phrase that he uses for institutions that are rarely found. In Sparta and in the Platonic Republic, magistrates chose the marriage partners of the citizenry. Perhaps that might be justified in a tightly knit community where "the love of the public might there equal or surpass all other love." But the "common institution" is that fathers control the marriage of their children, a provision that Montesquieu attributes both to the greater prudence of fathers and to a natural desire of fathers to see themselves continued in their offspring. Montesquieu regards it as an abuse that a colonizing power took over the marriage choices of a subservient population in order to increase its revenue: "in an action which ought to be the most free, the Indians are the greatest slaves." He does not consider the possibility that a parental consent requirement might also be inconsistent with liberty of marriage. He then notices that in England children frequently marry without parental consent. His observation is acute and, in comparison with France in his period, he may well be right. He then suggests that the reason for the difference is that English women do not have the alternative of going to the convent, as French women do. His explanation then causes him puzzlement because he also thinks that Spanish and Italian women frequently marry without parental consent, and they, like French women, have the option of going to the convent.

This is not Montesquieu at his best. He has jumped too quickly to an assumption about a common institution without the empirical survey of institutions that we sometimes find in his work. His analysis of the motivations of fathers

[12] Citing Thomas Gage, *New Survey of the West Indies*, 3rd ed.

smacks of natural-law analysis without the rigor that the best of the natural-law thinkers have. (He seems to suggest that the desire of fathers to see the prosperity of their offspring is somehow biological rather than rational.) His comparison of England and France is made without careful consideration of the difference in laws between the two countries. (France in his period, at least arguably, did require parental consent for the civil validity of a marriage; England did not.) His proposed explanation for the difference between England and France fails in its own terms when he considers Spain and Italy, and he does not pause to consider whether his generalization about practice in Spain and Italy may be mistaken (as it may well be).

All of this should not, however, obscure the fact that Montesquieu employs something very close to, if it is not the same thing as, modern comparative method. He posits a virtually universal requirement for parental consent. If that is right, then the explanation for it must be virtually universal, perhaps something biological: the lack of prudence of the young, their passion, the desire of fathers to see their line succeed. There are exceptions. They must be explained. Small, tightly knit communities may share a commonality of values and purposes that will lead them to entrust such decisions to the magistracy. Colonial powers may repress subject peoples. Montesquieu then moves from the law to its evasion or violation. He sees a difference among countries and seeks, though he fails, to explain that difference on the basis of religious differences.

Despite the modernity of his method, Montesquieu's vision of this topic is not ours, at least not ours in the West. Convinced as we are that marriage should be based on the choice of the couple, and confronted with many societies in which that is, by and large, the case, what for us needs explaining is why that should not be the case in a particular society. What Montesquieu may be telling us is that from an historical point of view, what needs to be explained is Alexander's rules and England's seeming acceptance of them.

This book has gone on far too long, and it is certainly time to conclude. Fortunately we can do so briefly, because the conclusions that I draw from this story are not formal conclusions; they are more like themes that run across the centuries:

First, a commonplace: Marriage and the family are social institutions as well as legal ones, and the power of the law to affect them is limited. The marriage litigation that I have studied reasonably systematically, that from the later Middle Ages, suggests that ordinary people will manipulate the system at every turn. The way that they manipulate it may tell us something about the underlying social forces. To put this point more bluntly, marriage in England and in what we have called 'the Franco-Belgian region' in the later Middle Ages was a quite different institution, and these differences are reflected in the kinds of cases that were brought. The difference in social institutions can be seen most clearly in the marriage-formation cases, but they can also be seen in the separation cases if we are willing to push the explanation one step back and ask why the marital property systems differed.

Second, when it comes to marriage law, women's voices do get heard. The law, at least in this area, gave them formal equality, and they were aware of that fact. Whether on balance they got anything approaching a fair shake over the course of centuries is a much more difficult question to answer. We were, however, able to confirm that the courts, at least in some times and places, were sympathetic to what we called the story of the woman wronged.[13] Where the records allow us to hear women's voices, they suggest that women's recourse to the law may have been inversely related to their real power and status in society. To put it another way, women rarely used the legal system to oppress others (though they did so occasionally), and when they had recourse to the legal system, it is some indication that they were being oppressed by others. The high proportion of female plaintiffs in the court of York and that of Ely in the fourteenth century is certainly evidence of female agency (as is the number of office/instance cases in which a woman joined with the promotor at Cambrai and Brussels in the fifteenth century), but the decline of the proportion of female plaintiffs in York in the fifteenth and their low proportion in Paris litigation in the late fourteenth century may indicate that the women in the populations that were using those courts had less to complain about.

Third is the great power of a simple religious idea: "What God has joined, let not man divide." From this follows not only the extraordinary reluctance of Western law to allow divorce, but also, more broadly, ecclesiastical jurisdiction over marriage. When secularization came, the religious elements in the law were not, at least not immediately, forgotten. The peace of Augsburg of 1555, with its notion that religion was contained within the boundaries of states, curiously reinforced this unification of church and state in this particular area. Whether the jurisdiction remained with the church or was handed over to the state, both church and state expected that the religious ideas of the dominant religion about marriage would be reinforced by the state.

Fourth, whether it is simply ironic or whether it is an extraordinary intersection point across centuries, the modern idea of marriage based on romantic love received a powerful legal stimulus from a celibate pope of the twelfth century. His ideas were almost overpowered in the sixteenth century, but, ultimately, it is Alexander's ideas about the formation of marriage and not those of the drafters of the *ordonnance* of Blois that came to prevail in the West. So far as what happened when Alexander's rules were formally in effect is concerned, I suspect that he would have been amazed, and not a little distressed, by what some people did with his rules. In the cases that are genuinely about the formation of marriage, the English look as if they are more in tune with what Alexander seems to have been trying to do, but I suspect that he would have been far more approving of what the French did with separation cases.

Fifth, there is considerable evidence, particularly from the later Middle Ages, that Alexander's rules were being used to produce results of which the religious authorities could hardly have approved, which were contrary to the customs

[13] See, e.g., Ch 4, following n. 110; Ch 9, conclusion.

and expectations of ordinary lay people, and which produced a neuralgic reaction in many who exercised secular power. Modern scholarship has tended to blame Alexander for these results. I am inclined to blame him, too, but I would suggest that his naïveté was a more sophisticated naïveté than that which is usually attributed to him. It is not that Alexander created rules out of religious principles without regard to their likely practical effect. Alexander's decretals suggest that he was an eminently practical man. He was also a very good judge, as were many of the bishops on whom he relied as judges delegate. What Alexander did not foresee was what would happen when the processing of a very few cases, involving people of quite high status, by men at the top of their profession, became the routine processing of hundreds of cases by men who were just ordinary judges. He failed, in short, to foresee that the judges of the later Middle Ages would not be anything like as good at judging as he had been.[14]

Sixth, be that as it may, the system was, in some quite real sense, not working in the later Middle Ages. The question remains as to why it took until 1563 to change it. Part of the answer to that question, of course, is bound up in the question of why it took the Reformation to produce the council of Trent when so many were aware from, at least, the fourteenth century of the need for church reform. I would suggest, however, that there is something peculiar to marriage law that made reform difficult. Alexander's rules were deeply embedded in the twelfth-century theology of marriage. The theology of marriage changed in the thirteenth century, changed in a way that would probably have made a solemnity requirement (what Trent ultimately adopted) easier to reconcile with the theology. But the canonists and the theologians parted company academically sometime early in the thirteenth century. They ceased reading and reacting to each other's work. Canonic commentary on marriage in the later Middle Ages continues to recite twelfth-century marriage theology, and shows little or no awareness of the achievements of Thomas Aquinas, Bonaventure, and Duns Scotus in this area. If the lesson that one draws is that it is a mistake to hand over a religious legal system to lawyers, so be it. But that is a topic for another book.

[14] Some were very good. John Newton at Ely certainly stands out. Here we may see a problem in what the medieval church rewarded. Richard Scrope became archbishop of York, and John Newton, so far as we can tell, never even got a prebend.

Bibliography and Abbreviations

Primary Sources

Les actes de la province écclésiastique de Reims, ed. Th. Gousset, 4 vols. (Rheims 1842–4)

A.D. Aube = Archives départementales de l'Aube: G 4170 (case register; see *Registre de Troyes*)

A.D. Bouches-du-Rhône = Archives départementales des Bouches-du-Rhône: 5 G 775 (process register)

A.D. Lozère = Mende, Archives départementales de la Lozère: G. 963; G943 (case registers)

A.D. Marne = Châlons-sur-Marne, Archives départementales de la Marne: G 922 (case register)

A.D. Pyrénées-Orientales = Perpignan, Archives départementales des Pyrénées-Orientales: G145*bis* (case register)

A.D. Vaucluse = Avignon, Archives départementales du Vaucluse: GIII^{bis} 81–7 (case registers)

Ancienne discipline du diocèse de Troyes jusqu'en 1788, ed. Charles Lalore, 3 vols. (Troyes 1882)

L'ancienne procédure ecclésiastique dans le nord de la France, ed. Édouard Fournier, Société d'études de la province de Cambrai, Recueil, 33 (Lille 1931)

Augsburger Offizialatsregister (1348–1352); see Secondary Literature under "Schwab"

Bernard of Pavia *(Bernardus papiensis), Summa de matrimonio, in id., Summa decretalium*, ed. Theodor Laspeyres (Regensburg 1860), 287–306

Bracton = Bracton on the Laws and Customs of England, ed. George Woodbine, trans. S. E. Thorne, 4 vols. (Cambridge, MA 1968–77)

C. (followed by book, title, and *lex* numbers) = *Codex Iustinianus;* see below under *Corpus Iuris Civilis*

C. (followed by *Causa* number), q. (followed by *quaestio* number), c (followed by chapter number) = *Decretum Gratiani,* in *Corpus Iuris Canonici* 1

Die Canones-Sammlungen zwischen Gratian und Bernhard von Pavia, ed. Emil Friedberg (Liepzig 1897)

Cartularium Abbathiae de Whiteby, ed. J. C. Atkinson, 2 vols., Surtees Society, 69, 72 (Durham 1879, 1881)

CCA = Canterbury, Cathedral Archives: ChAnt = Chartae Antiquae, ChCh = Christ Church Letters, Eastry = Eastry Letters, ESR = Ecclesiastical Suit Roll, SVSB = Sede Vacante Scrapbook. Also Sede Vacante Visitation Rolls; Literary MS. D.8.

CCR (followed by date) = *Calendar of Close Rolls (1272–1485)*, 45 vols. (London 1892–1954)

CFR (followed by date) = *Calendar of the Fine Rolls (1272–1509)*, 22 vols. (London 1911–62)

CIPM (followed by date) = *Calendar of Inquisitions Post Mortem [Henry VII]*, 3 vols. (London 1898–1955)

"Collectio Claustroneoburgensis" = Ferdinand Schönsteiner, "Die Collectio Claustroneoburgensis," *Jahrbuch des Stiftes Klosterneuburg*, 2 (1900) 1–154

"Collectio Wigorniensis" = Hans-Eberhard Lohmann, "Die Collectio Wigorniensis," *Zeitschrift der Savigny-Stiftung für Rechtsgeschichte (Kanonistische Abteilung)*, 53 (22) (1933) 36–187

Compotus sigilliferi curie Tornacensis (1429–1481), ed. Monique Vleeschouwers-van Melkebeek, 3 vols. (Brussels 1995)

Cons.AB (followed a number); see below under "York"

Corpus Iuris Canonici, ed. Emil Friedberg, 2 vols. (Leipzig 1879, repr. Graz 1959). For the ordinary gloss (cited by 'v°' followed by the *lemma*) I have used the Venice edition of 1572.

Corpus Iuris Civilis. References are to the "Berlin stereotype edition," ed. Teodor Mommsen, Rudolf Schöll, and Wilhelm Kroll, *Corpus Juris Civilis*, 3 vols., 1, 12th ed. (Berlin 1911); 2, 9th ed. (Berlin 1915); 3, 3rd ed. (Berlin 1904), all many times reprinted. For the ordinary gloss (cited by 'v°' followed by the *lemma*), I have used *Corpus juris civilis iustinianei cum commentariis*, 6 vols (Lyon: Cardon, 1604).

Councils and Synods I: A.D. 871–1204, ed. Dorothy Whitelock, Martin Brett, and C. N. L. Brooke, 2 vols. (Oxford 1981)

Councils and Synods II: A.D. 1205–1313, ed. F. M. Powicke and C. R. Cheney, 2 vols. (Oxford 1964).

CP (followed by a letter and a number), see below under "York"

CPL (followed by date) = *Calendar of Entries in the Papal Registers Relating to Great Britain and Ireland, 3: Letters: 1342–1362*, ed. W. Bliss and C. Johnson (London 1897)

CPPet = *Calendar of Entries in the Papal Registers Relating to Great Britain and Ireland, 1: Petitions, 1342–1419*, ed. W. H. Bliss, (London 1896)

CPR (followed by date) = *Calendar of Patent Rolls (1216–1509)*, 54 vols. (London 1893–1916)

CUL, DMA, D2/1 = Cambridge University Library, Department of Manuscripts and Archives, D2/1 (Act book of the Ely consistory court, see also Stentz, *Calendar*)

D (followed by title, fragment, and section numbers) = *Digesta seu Pandectae*; see under *Corpus Iuris Civilis*

Decrees of the Ecumenical Councils, ed. Giuseppe Alberigo, trans. Norman P. Tanner, 2 vols. (London 1990)

Decretales ineditae saeculi XII: From the Papers of the Late Walther Holtzmann, ed. Stanley Chodorow and Charles Duggan, Monumenta iuris canonici, Series B, Corpus collectionum, 4 (Vatican City 1982)

Hereford County Record Office, Court Books–Acts of Office–Box 1–Book 1–1442–43

Honorius, *Quaestiones de matrimonio*, ed. B. Grimm, *Die Ehelehre des Magister Honorius: ein Beitrag zur Ehelehre der anglo-normannischen Schule*, Studia Gratiana 24 (Roma 1989)

Hostiensis (Henricus de Segusio), *Lectura in Decretales* (*In primum* [etc.] *librum decretalium commentaria*) (Venice: Iuntas, 1581).

Summa aurea in titulos decretalium (Venice: Iacobus Vitalis, 1574)

Hugh of St Victor, *De sacramentis Christiane fidei*, in PL 176:173–616, trans. Roy J. Deferrari, *Hugh of Saint Victor on the Sacraments of the Christian Faith* (Cambridge, MA 1951)

Das Imbreviaturbuch des erzbischöflichen Gerichtsnotars Hubaldus aus Pisa, Mai bis August 1230, ed. Gero Dolezalek, Forschungen zur neueren Privatrechtsgeschichte, 13 (Cologne 1969)

Johannes Andreae, *In* (*primum* [etc.]) *librum decretalium novella commentaria* (Venice: Franciscus Franciscius, 1581)

Kanonistische Ergänzungen zur Italia Pontificia, ed. Walther Holtzmann, *Quellen und Forschungen*, 37 (1957) 55–102, 38 (1958) 67–175, and separately (Tübingen 1959)

Liber senteciarum van de Officialiteit van Brussel, 1448–1459, ed. Cyriel Vleeschouwers and Monique van Melkebeek, Verzameling van de oude rechtspraak in België, 7th ser., 2 vols. (Brussels 1982–3)

Literae Cantuarienses, ed. J. B. Sheppard, Rolls Series, 85, vol. 1 (London 1887)

Lower Ecclesiastical Jurisdiction in Late-Medieval England: The Courts of the Dean and Chapter of Lincoln, 1336–1349, and the Deanery of Wisbech, 1458–1484, ed. L. R. Poos, Records of Social and Economic History, n.s. 32 (London 2001)

Martin Luther, *Sämmtliche Werke*, ed. Ernst Ludwig Enders and Johann Conrad Irmischer, 2d ed., 67 vols. (Frankfurt am Main 1832–81)

William Lyndwood, *Provinciale seu Constitutiones Angliae* (Oxford: H. Hall, 1679; repr. Franborough 1968)

M2(1)b, M2(1)c; see below under "York"

J. D. Mansi, ed., *Sacrorum conciliorum nova et amplissima collectio*, 31 vols. (Lucca 1759–98)

Robertus Maranta, *Speculum aureum* (Venice: Haeredes Bonelli, 1574)

E. Martène and U. Durand, ed., *Veterum scriptorum . . . collectio nova* (Paris 1724–33)

Charles de Secondat, baron de Montesquieu, *The Spirit of Laws*, trans. Thomas Nugent, 2d ed. (London 1752)

Panormitanus (Niccolò de' Tudeschi), *Commentaria in* (*primum* [etc.]) *decretalium librum* (Lyon: Senetonii Fratres, 1547)

The Paston Letters A.D. 1422–1509, ed. James Gairdiner, 6 vols. (Westminster 1904, repr. New York 1965)

"Pedigree of Colville," in William Brown, "Ingleby Arncliffe," *Yorkshire Archaeological Journal*, 16 (1901) 121–226 (ap. II, 210–11)

Peter Abelard (Petrus Abelardus), *Epitome theologiae christianae*, title, c. 31: *De coniugii sacramento et quod non confert aliquod donum, sicut coetera faciunt*, in PL 178:1745

Peter the Chanter = Petrus Cantor, *Summa de sacramentis et animae consiliis*, ed. Jean Albert Dugauquier, 3 vols. in 5, Analecta mediaevalia namurcensia, 4, 7, 11, 16, 21 (Louvain 1954–)

Petrus de Ancharano, *In quinque libros decretalium commentaria* (Bologna: Societas typographiae Bononie, 1580)

PL = *Patrologia latina*, ed. Jacques-Paul Migne, 221 vols. (Paris 1844–64)

Quinque Compilationes Antiquae, ed. Emil Friedberg (Leipzig 1882)

Raymond of Peñafort (Raimundus de Pennaforte), *Summa de poenitentia et matrimonio cum glossis Johannis de Friburgo* (Rome: Ioannes Tallini, 1603; repr. Farnborough 1967) (used in preference to the ed. Xaverius Ochoa and Aloisius Diez in Universa Bibliotheca iuris 1 C [Rome 1978])

Recueil des grandes ordonnances, édits, et déclarations des rois de France... depuis 1536 jusques 1681 inclusivement, ed. Jean A. H. M. B. Pichon (Toulouse 1786)

Register of the Freemen of the City of York. 1:1272–1558, ed. Francis Collins, Surtees Society, 96 (Durham 1897)

Registre de l'Officialité épiscopale de Troyes 1389–1396, ed. Jean Breban, Thèse de Doctorat d'État en droit (typescript) (Paris 1954)

Registre des causes civiles de l'Officialité épiscopale de Paris, 1384–1387, ed. Joseph Petit, Collection de documents inédits sur l'histoire de France (Paris 1919)

Registres de Sentences de l'Officialité de Cambrai (1438–1453), ed. Cyriel Vleeschouwers and Monique van Melkebeek, Recueil de l'ancienne jurisprudence de la Belgique, 7th ser., 2 vols. (Brussels 1998)

Registrum Roberti Winchelsey, ed. Rose Graham, vol. 2, Canterbury and York Society, 52 (Oxford 1956)

Reg Melton 2 = *The Register of William Melton, archbishop of York 1317–1340*, ed. David Robinson, vol. 2, Canterbury and York Society, 72 (Torquay 1978)

Repertorium poenitentiariae Germanicum, ed. Ludwig Schmugge, et al., 7 vols. to date (Tübingen 1998–)

Tomás Sánchez, *Disputationum de sancto matrimonii sacramento tomi tres* (Antwerp: apud haeredes Martini Nuti & Ioannem Meursium, 1626)

Select Cases from the Ecclesiastical Courts of the Province of Canterbury, c. 1200–1301, ed. Norma Adams and Charles Donahue, Publications of the Selden Society, 95 (London 1981)

Select Cases on Defamation to 1600, ed. R. H. Helmholz, Publications of the Selden Society, 101 (London 1985)

Heinrich Singer, *Neue Beiträge über Dekretalensammlungen vor und nach Bernhard von Pavia*, Sitzungsberichte der kaiserlichen Akademie, phil.-hist. Klasse, 171.1 (Vienna 1913)

"Some Early Civic Wills of York [part 4]," ed. Robert B. Cook, *Associated Architectural Societies Reports and Papers*, 33 (1915) 161–77

Statuta antiquissima Dioecesis Cameracensis, ed. Edmond H. J. Reusens, Analectes pour servir à l'histoire écclesiastique de la Belgique, 2d section, fasc. 6 (Leuven 1903)

The Statutes of the Realm, 11 vols. in 12 (London 1810–28; repr. Buffalo 1993)

Les statuts synodaux français du xiiie siècle. I: Les statuts de Paris et le synodal de l'Ouest (xiiie siècle), ed. Odette Pontal, Collection de documents inédits sur l'histoire de France, sér. in 8°, 9 (Paris 1971); *II: Les statuts de 1230 à 1260*, ed. id., *id.*, 15 (*id.* 1983); *III: Les statuts synodaux de la seconde moitié du xiiie siècle*, ed. Joseph Avril, *id.*, 19 (*id.* 1988); *IV: Les statuts synodaux de l'ancienne province de Reims (Cambrai, Arras, Noyon, Soissons et Tournai)*, ed. *id.*, *id.*, 23 (*id.* 1988); *V: Les statuts synodaux des anciennes provinces de Bordeaux, Auch, Sens et Rouen (fin XIIIe siècle)*, ed. *id.*, *id.*, 28bis (*id.* 2001)

M. J. Stentz, *A Calendar and Study of a Consistory Court Record from the Diocese of Ely*, Ph.D. diss., University of Toronto (Ottawa 1991)

Summa 'Elegantius in iure divino' seu Coloniensis, ed. Gérard Fransen and Stephan Kuttner, Monumenta iuris canonici. Series A, Corpus glossatorum, v. 1, t. 1–4 (New York, Vatican City 1969–90)

Tancred of Bologna (Tancredus bononiensis), *Ordo iudiciarius*, ed. Friedrich C. Bergmann, in *Pilii, Tancredi, Gratie, Libri de iudiciorum ordine* (Göttingen 1842, repr. Aalen 1965), 87–316

Summa de matrimonio, ed. Agathon Wunderlich (Göttingen 1841)

Testamenta Eboracensia, ed. James Raine, [Sr], James Raine, Jr and John W. Clay, 6 vols., Surtees Society, 4, 30, 45, 53, 79, 106 (Durham 1836, 1855, 1865, 1869, 1884, 1902)

Thomas Aquinas, *The "Summa Theologica" of St. Thomas Aquinas*, 22 vols. (London 1920–5)

VI (followed by book, title, and chapter numbers) = *Liber sextus decretalium*, in *Corpus Iuris Canonici* 2

Vacarius, *Summa de matrimonio*, ed. F. W. Maitland, "Magistri Vacarii Summa de Matrimonio," *Law Quarterly Review*, 13 (1897), 133–42, 270–87

Richard Whitford, *A Werke for Householders* (London: Robert Redman, 1537) (STC [2d ed.] 25425)

WH (with a number) see Works of Reference

David Wilkins, *Concilia Magnae Britanniae et Hiberniae*, 4 vols. (London: R. Gosling, 1737)

X (followed by book, title, and chapter numbers) = *Decretales Gregorii Noni*, in *Corpus Iuris Canonici* II.

Year Books of Richard II: 6 Richard II 1382–1383, ed. Samuel E. Thorne, et al., Ames Foundation, Year Books of Richard II, 2 (Cambridge, MA 1996)

York, Borthwick Institute (YBI), Cause Papers (CP), E series (fourteenth century); F series (fifteenth century); G series (sixteenth century). Numbers following a slash are not in use by the archive and have been added simply for convenience.

Consistory Court Act Books (Cons.AB)

York, York Minster Archives and Library, M2(1)b and M2(1)c (fragmentary act books of the consistory court from the 1370s)

Works of Reference

Charles Donahue, Jr., ed., *The Records of the Medieval Ecclesiastical Courts. 1: The Continent; 2: England*, Comparative Studies in Continental and Anglo-American Legal History, 6–7 (Berlin 1989, 1994)

DuCange = Charles du Fresne, sire DuCange, *Glossarium mediae et infimae latinitatis*, 10 vols. (Niort 1885)

Eilert Ekwall, *The Concise Oxford Dictionary of English Place-names*, 4th ed. (Oxford 1960)

Konrad Eubel, *Hierarchia catholica medii aevi*, 3 vols. (Münster 1898–1910)

Historical Manuscripts Commission, *Report on Manuscripts in Various Collections*, vol. 1 (London 1901)

Index of Dean and Chapter Wills = Francis Collins, *Index of Wills, Etc., from the Dean and Chapter's Court at York,* A.D. *1321 to 1636*, Yorkshire Archaeological Soc'y Record Series, 38 (York 1907)

Index of York Registry Wills = *id.*, *Index of Wills in the York Registry, 1389 to 1514*, Yorkshire Archeological Soc'y Record Series, 6 (York 1889)
Charlton T. Lewis and Charles Short, *A Latin Dictionary* (Oxford 1879)
J. F. Niermeyer, *Mediae Latinitatis Lexicon Minus* (Leiden 1976)
OED = *The Oxford English Dictionary*, ed. J. Simpson and E. Weiner, 2d ed., 20 vols. (Oxford 1989)
The Place-names of Cheshire, ed. J. McN. Dodgson, 5 vols., English Place-Name Society, 44–8, 54, 74 (Cambridge 1970–97)
The Place-names of the North Riding of Yorkshire, ed. A. H. Smith, English Place-Name Society, 5 (Cambridge 1928)
The Place-names of the West Riding of Yorkshire, ed. A. H. Smith, 8 vols., English Place-Name Society, 30–7 (Cambridge 1961–3)
P. H. Reaney, *A Dictionary of British Surnames*, 2d ed. (London 1976)
Répertoire des statuts synodaux des diocèses de l'ancienne France, ed. André Artonne, Louis Guizard, and Odette Pontal, Documents, Études et Répertoires publiés par l'Institut de Recherche et d'Histoire des Textes, 8 (Paris 1963)
David M. Smith, *The Court of York, 1400–1499*, Borthwick Texts and Calendars, 29 (York 2003)
Ecclesiastical Cause Papers at York: The Court of York, 1301–1399, *id.*, 14 (York 1988)
A Guide to the Archive Collections in the Borthwick Institute of Historical Research, *id.*, 1 (York 1973)
A Supplementary Guide to the Archive Collections in the Borthwick Institute of Historical Research, *id.*, 7 (York 1980)
Peter Spufford, *Handbook of Medieval Exchange* (London 1986)
Victor Watts, *A Dictionary of County Durham Place-Names*, English Place-Name Society Popular Series, 3 (Nottingham 2002)
WH (with a number) = Walther Holzmann's list of decretals of the twelfth century accompanied by his still-unpublished notes. The typescript is held at the Institute of Medieval Canon Law in Munich, and portions of it have recently been made available online: http://www.kuttner-institute.jura.uni-muenchen.de/index_e.htm.

Secondary Literature

Philippe Ariès, *L'enfant et la vie familiale sous l'Ancien Regime* (nouv. éd.; Paris 1973)
André Armengaud, *La famille et l'enfant en France et en Angleterre du XVIe au XVIIIe siècle: aspects démographiques*, Regards sur l'histoire, 24 (Paris 1975)
Margaret Aston, *Thomas Arundel: A Study of Church Life in the Reign of Richard II* (Oxford 1967)
J. H. Baker, *An Introduction to English Legal History*, 4th ed. (London 2002)
H. S. Bennett, *Life on the English Manor 1150–1400* (Cambridge 1937, repr. Gloucester 1987)
Judith M. Bennett, *Women in the Medieval English Countryside: Gender and Household in Brigstock Before the Plague* (New York 1987)
Donald Black, *The Behavior of Law* (New York 1976)
Lloyd Bonfield, "Marriage Settlements and the 'Rise of the Great Estates'," *Economic History Review*, 32 (1979) 483–93
Paul A. Brand, Paul R. Hyams, Rosamond Faith, and Eleanor M. Searle, "Debate: Seigneurial Control of Women's Marriage," *Past and Present*, 99 (1983) 123–60.
Christopher Brooke, *The Medieval Idea of Marriage* (Oxford 1989)

M. E. Bruguière, "Canon Law and Royal Weddings, Theory and Practice: The French Example," in *Proceedings of the Eighth International Congress of Medieval Canon Law*, Stanley Chodorow, ed., Monumenta Iuris Canonici, C:9 (Vatican City 1992), 473–96

Gene Bruker, *Giovanni and Lusanna: Love and Marriage in Renaissance Florence* (Berkeley, CA 1986)

James A. Brundage, *Law, Sex and Christian Society in Medieval Europe* (Chicago 1987)

Medieval Canon Law (London 1995)

Sex, Law, and Marriage in the Middle Ages, Variorum Reprints, CS397 (Aldershot 1993)

"Widows and Remarriage: Moral Conflicts and Their Resolution in Classical Canon Law," in *Wife and Widow*, 17–31

K. F. Burns, *The Administrative System of the Ecclesiastical Courts in the Diocese and Province of York: Part I, The Medieval Courts* (1962) (unpublished typescript on file at the Borthwick Institute)

Sara M. Butler, *The Language of Abuse: Marital Violence in Later Medieval England*, Ph.D. diss., University of Dalhousie (2001)

Irene J. Churchill, *Canterbury Administration*, 2 vols. (London 1933)

Cecilia Cristellon, *Charitas versus eros: Il matrimonio, la Chiesa e i suoi giudici nella Venezia del Rinascimento (1420–1545)*, Ph.D. thesis, European University Institute (2005)

John Dart, *The History and Antiquities of the Cathedral Church of Canterbury* (London 1726)

David Dasef, *The Lawyers of the York Curia, 1400–1435*, B.Phil. diss., University of York (1976)

Jean Dauvillier, *Le mariage dans le droit classique de l'Église* (Paris 1933)

D. L. d'Avray, "Marriage Ceremonies and the Church After 1215," in *Marriage in Italy*, 107–15

Medieval Marriage: Symbolism and Society (Oxford 2005)

Medieval Marriage Sermons: Mass Communication in a Culture Without Print (Oxford 2001)

Trevor Dean, "Fathers and Daughters: Marriage Laws and Marriage Disputes in Bologna and Italy, 1200–1500," in *Marriage in Italy*, 85–106

Michiel Decaluwe, "De zelfschieding in de zuidelijke Nederlanden in de vijftiende eeuw," *Pro Memorie: Bijdragen tot de rechtsgeschiedenis der Nederlanden*, 3 (2001) 32–48

Louis de Naurois, "Matrimonium gaudet favore iuris," *Revue de droit canonique*, 29 (1979) 54–73

Christina Deutsch, *Ehegerichtsbarkeit im Bistum Regensburg (1480–1538)*, Forschungen zur kirchlichen Rechtsgeschichte und zum Krchenrecht, 29 (Cologne 2005)

Étienne Diebold, "L'Application en France du canon 51 du IVe concile du Latran d'après les anciens statuts synodaux," *L'Année Canonique*, 2 (1953) 187–95

Barbara B. Diefendorf, *Paris City Councillors in the Sixteenth Century: The Politics of Patrimony* (Princeton, NJ 1983)

Charles Donahue, Jr., "The Canon Law on the Formation of Marriage and Social Practice in the Later Middle Ages," *Journal of Family History* (Summer 1983) 144–58

"The Case of the Man Who Fell into the Tiber: The Roman Law of Marriage at the Time of the Glossators," *American Journal of Legal History*, 22 (1978) 1–53

"'Clandestine' Marriage in the Later Middle Ages: A Reply," *Law and History Review*, 10 (1992) 315–22

"Comparative Law Before the Code Napoléon," in *The Oxford Handbook of Comparative Law*, Reinhard Zimmermann and Mathias Reimann, eds. (Oxford 2006), 1–32

"The Dating of Alexander the Third's Marriage Decretals: Dauvillier Revisited After Fifty Years," *Zeitschrift für Rechtsgeschichte (Kanonistische Abteilung)*, 99 (68) (1982) 70–124

"English and French Marriage Cases in the Later Middle Ages: Might the Differences Be Explained by Differences in the Property Systems?" in *Marriage, Property and Succession*, Lloyd Bonfield, ed., Comparative Studies in Continental and Anglo-American Legal History, 10 (Berlin 1992), 339–66

"Female Plaintiffs in Marriage Cases in the Court of York in the Later Middle Ages: What Can We Learn from the Numbers," in *Wife and Widow*, 183–213

"Ius in the Subjective Sense in Roman Law," in *A Ennio Cortese*, Italo Birocchi et al., eds. (Roma 2001), 1:506–35

"Institutional History from Archival History," in *The Weightier Matters of the Law*, John Witte and Frank S. Alexander, eds., Essays on Law and Religion, 51 (Atlanta 1988), 33–55

"A Legal Historian Looks at the Case Method," *Northern Kentucky Law Review*, 19 (1991) 17–47

"Lyndwood's Gloss *propriarum uxorum*," in *Europäisches Rechtsdenken in Geschichte und Gegenwart: Festschrift für Helmut Coing zum 70. Geburtstag*, Norbert Horn, ed. (Munich 1982), 1:19–37

"The Monastic Judge: Social Practice, Formal Rule and the Medieval Canon Law of Incest," in *De Iure Canonico Medii Aevi: Festschrift für Rudolf Weigand*, Peter Laundau and Martin Petzolt, eds., Studia Gratiania, 27 (Rome 1996), 49–69

"The Policy of Alexander the Third's Consent Theory of Marriage," in *Proceedings of the Fourth International Congress of Medieval Canon Law*, Stephan Kuttner, ed., Monumenta Iuris Canonici, C:5 (Vatican City 1976), 251–81.

"Proof by Witnesses in the Church Courts of Medieval England: An Imperfect Reception of the Learned Law," in *On the Laws and Customs of England: Essays in Honor of Samuel E. Thorne*, Morris Arnold, Thomas Green, Sally Scully, and Stephen White, eds. (Chapel Hill 1981), 127–58

"Roman Canon Law in the Medieval English Church: Stubbs vs Maitland Re-examined after 75 Years in the Light of Some Records from the Church Courts," *Michigan Law Review*, 72 (1974) 647–716

"Was There a Change in Marriage Law in the late Middle Ages?," *Revista Internazionale di Diritto Commune*, 6 (1995) 49–80

"What Causes Fundamental Legal Ideas? Marital Property in England and France in the Thirteenth Century," *Michigan Law Review*, 78 (1979) 59–88

Charles Donahue, Jr., and Jeanne Gordus, "A Case from Archbishop Stratford's Audience Act Book and Some Comments on the Book and its Value," *Bulletin of Medieval Canon Law*, n.s. 2 (1972) 45–59

Decima Douie, *Archbishop Pecham* (Oxford 1952)

Georges Duby, *Le Chevalier, la femme et le prêtre: le mariage dans la France féodale* (Paris 1981), trans. B. Bray, *The Knight, the Lady and the Priest: The Making of Modern Marriage in Medieval France* (London 1984)

"Dans la France du Nord-ouest au XIIe siècle: Les 'Jeunes' dans la société aristocratique'," *Annales E. S. C.*, 19 (1964) 835–46

"Lignage, noblesse, et chevalerie au XIIe siècle dans la région mâconnaise," *Annales E. S. C.*, 27 (1972) 803–23

Mâle Moyen Age: de l'amour et autres essais (Paris 1988)

Medieval Marriage: Two Models from Twelfth-Century France, trans. E. Forster, The Johns Hopkins Simposia in Comparative History, 11 (Baltimore 1978)

Christopher Dyer, *Standards of Living in the Later Middle Ages: Social Change in England c. 1200–1520* (Cambridge 1989)

Edward Edwards, *Memoirs of Libraries*, 2 vols. (London 1859)

Emlyn Eisenach, *Husbands, Wives, and Concubines: Marriage, Family, and Social Order in Sixteenth-century Verona*, Sixteenth Century Essays & Studies, 69 (Kirksville, MO 2004)

Friedrich Engels, *Ursprung der Familie, des Privateigentums und des Staats* (Hottingen-Zürich 1884), trans. as *The Origin of the Family, Private Property and the State* (Harmondsworth 1985)

Adhémar Esmein, *Le mariage en droit canonique*, 2d ed., 2 vols., rev. Robert Génestal and Jean Dauvillier (Paris 1929–35)

Anna Ferrante, et al., *Measuring the Extent of Domestic Violence* (Sydney 1996)

Andrew J. Finch, "Parental Authority and the Problem of Clandestine Marriage in the Later Middle Ages," *Law and History Review*, 8 (1990) 189–204

"*Repulsa uxore sua:* Marital Difficulties and Separation in the Later Middle Ages," *Continuity and Change*, 8 (1993) 11–38

Joseph Freisen, *Geschichte des canonischen Eherechts: bis zum Verfall der Glossenliteratur*, 2d ed. (Paderborn 1893, repr. Aalen 1963)

Jean Gaudemet, *Le mariage en Occident: les moeurs et le droit* (Paris 1987)

Sociétés et mariage (Strasbourg 1980)

Philippe Godding, *Le droit privé dans les Pays-Bas méridionaux du 12e au 18e siècle*, Mémoires de l'Académie royale de Belgique, Classe de lettres, sér. 2 in 4°, vol. 14, fasc. 1 (Brussels 1987)

P. J. P. Goldberg, "Marriage, Migration, Servanthood and Life-Cycle in Yorkshire Towns of the Later Middle Ages: Some York Cause Paper Evidence," *Continuity and Change*, 1 (1986) 141–69

Women, Work, and Life Cycle in a Medieval Economy: Women in York and Yorkshire c. 1300–1520 (Oxford 1992)

Jack Goody, *The Development of Marriage and the Family in Europe* (Cambridge 1984)

The Oriental, The Ancient and the Primitive: Systems of Marriage and the Family in the Pre-industrial Societies of Eurasia (Cambridge 1990)

Beatrice Gottlieb, *Getting Married in Pre-Reformation Europe: The Doctrine of Clandestine Marriage and Court Cases in Fifteenth Century Champagne*, Ph.D. diss., Columbia University (Ann Arbor, MI 1974)

"The Meaning of Clandestine Marriage," in *Family and Sexuality in French History*, Robert Wheaton and Tamara K. Hareven, eds. (Philadelphia 1980), 49–83

Thomas A. Green, *Verdict According to Conscience: Perspectives on the English Criminal Trial Jury, 1200–1800* (Chicago 1985)

Myriam Greilsammer, *L'envers du tableau: mariage et maternité en Flandre médiévale* (Paris 1990)

"Rapts de séduction et rapts violents en Flandre et en Brabant à la fin du moyen-âge," *Tijdschrift voor Rechtsgeschiedenis*, 56 (1988) 49–84

Barbara Hanawalt, *The Ties That Bound: Peasant Families in Medieval England* (New York 1986)

John Hatcher, *Plague, Population and the English Economy, 1348–1550* (London 1977)
R. H. Helmholz, *The Canon Law and Ecclesiastical Jurisdiction from 597 to the 1640's*, The Oxford History of the Laws of England, 1 (Oxford 2004)
Canon Law and the Law of England (London 1987).
Marriage Litigation in Medieval England, Cambridge Studies in English Legal History (Cambridge 1974, repr. Holmes Beach 1986)
David Herlihy, *Medieval Households* (Cambridge, MA 1985)
Women, Family and Society in Medieval Europe: Historical Essays, 1978–1991 (Providence 1994)
David Herlihy and Christine Klapisch-Zuber, *Les Toscans et leurs familles: une étude du "catasto" florentin de 1427* (Paris 1978)
W. S. Holdsworth, *A History of English Law*, 17 vols., various eds. (London 1903–77, repr. 1982)
George C. Homans, *English Villagers of the Thirteenth Century* (Cambridge 1941, repr. New York 1960, 1970)
Ralph Houlbrooke, *Church Courts and the People During the English Reformation, 1520–1570* (Oxford 1979)
The English Family, 1450–1700 (London 1984)
George E. Howard, *A History of Matrimonial Institutions*, 3 vols. (Chicago 1904, repr. Littleton 1994)
Jana Jasinski, et al., *Partner Violence: A Comprehensive Review of 20 Years of Research* (Thousand Oaks, CA 1998)
Hubert Jedin, *Geschichte des Konzils von Trient*, 4 vols. in 5 (Freiburg 1951–75)
James Patrick King, *The Canonical Procedure in Separation Cases: A Historical Synopsis and a Commentary*, Canon Law Studies, 325 (Washington, DC 1952)
Julius Kirshner, "*Maritus lucretur dotem uxoris sue premortue* in Late Medieval Florence," *Zeitschrift für Rechtsgeschichte* (*Kanonistische Abteilung*), 108 (77) (1991) 111–55
David Knowles and R. Hadcock, *Medieval Religious Houses, England and Wales*, 2d ed. (London 1971)
Mia Korpiola, *Between Betrothal and Bedding: The Making of Marriage in Sweden, ca. 1200–1610*, Ph.D. thesis, University of Helsinki (Saarijävi 2004)
Rudolf Köstler, *Die Väterliche Ehebewilligung*, Kirchenrechtliche Abhandlungen, 51 (Stuttgart 1908)
Stephan Kuttner, "*Ecclesia de occultis non iudicat*," in *Acta Congressus Iuridici Internationalis Romae 1934* (Rome 1935), 3:225–46
Peter Landau, "Hadrians Dekretale 'Dignum est' und die Eheschliessung Unfreier in der Diskussion von Kanonisten und Theologen des 12. und 13. Jahrhunderts," *Studia Gratiana*, 12 (= Collectanca Stephan Kuttner, 2) (1967), 513–53
Anne Lefebvre-Teillard, *Les officialités à la veille du concile de Trente*, Bibliothèque d'histoire du droit et droit romain, 19 (Paris 1973)
"Règle et réalité dans le droit matrimonial à la fin du Moyen-âge," *Revue de Droit Canonique*, 30 (1980) 41–54
"Règle et réalité: Les nullités de mariage à la fin du Moyen-âge," *Revue de Droit Canonique*, 32 (1982) 145–55
"Une nouvelle venue dans l'histoire du droit canonique," in *Proceedings of the Sixth International Congress of Medieval Canon Law*, Stephan Kuttner and Kenneth Pennington, eds., Monumenta Iuris Canonici, C:7 (Vatican City 1985), 647–57
John Le Neve, *Fasti Ecclesiae Anglicanae, 1300–1541*, rev. ed., 12 vols. (London 1962–7)

Jean-Philippe Lévy, *La hiérarchie des preuves dans le droit savant du moyen-age*, Annales de l'Université de Lyon, série 3, droit, fascicule 5 (Paris 1939)

"L'officialité de Paris et les questions familiales à la fin du XIVe siècle," in *Études de droit canonique dédiées à Gabriel le Bras* (Paris 1965), 2:1265–94

Klaus Lindner, *Courtship and the Courts: Marriage and Law in Southern Germany, 1350–1550*, D. Theol. diss., Harvard University Divinity School (1988)

Filippo Liotta, *La continenza dei clerichi* (Milan 1971)

F. D. Logan, *Excommunication and the Secular Arm in Medieval England: A Study in Legal Procedure from the Thirteenth to the Sixteenth Century*, Pontifical Institute of Mediaeval Studies, Studies and Texts, 15 (Toronto 1968)

The Medieval Court of Arches, Canterbury and York Society, 95 (Woodbridge, Suff. 2005)

Runaway Religious in Medieval England, c 1240–1540 (Cambridge 1996)

Alain Lottin et al., *La désunion du couple sous l'ancien régime: L'example du nord* (Villeneuve-d'Ascq 1975)

Joseph H. Lynch, *Godparents and Kinship in Early Medieval Europe* (Princeton, NJ 1986).

Alan Macfarlane, *Marriage and Love in England: Modes of Reproduction, 1300–1840* (Oxford 1986)

The Origins of English Individualism: The Family, Property, and Social Transition (Cambridge 1978)

F. W. Maitland, "The Deacon and the Jewess," *Law Quarterly Review*, 3 (1886) 153–65, in *id., Roman Canon Law in the Church of England* (London 1898, repr. New York 1968), 158–79

Marriage in Italy, 1300–1650, Trevor Dean and K. J. P. Lowe, eds. (Cambridge 1997)

Victor Martin, *Le Gallicanism et réforme catholique: Essai historique sur l'introduction en France des décrets du concile de Trente (1563–1615)* (Paris 1919, repr. Geneva 1975)

Connor McCarthy, *Marriage in Medieval England: Law, Literature and Practice* (Woodbridge 2004)

Christine Meek, "Women, the Church and the Law: Matrimonial Litigation in Lucca under Bishop Nicolao Guinigi (1394–1435)," in *Chattel, Servant or Citizen: Women's Status in Church, State and Society*, Mary O'Dowd and Sabine Wichert, eds., The Institute of Irish Studies, The Queen's University, Belfast, Historical Studies, 19 (Belfast 1995), 82–90

René Metz, *La femme et l'enfant dans le droit canonique médiéval*, Variorum Reprints, CS222 (London 1985)

E. Miller, "Medieval York," in *A History of Yorkshire: The City of York*, P. M. Tillott, ed., The Victoria History of the Counties of England (London 1961)

S. F. C. Milsom, *Historical Foundations of the Common Law*, 2d ed. (London 1981)

Olin H. Moore, *The Legend of Romeo and Juliet*, Ohio State University Contributions in Languages and Literature, 13 (Columbus 1950)

Roland Mousnier, *La famille, l'enfant et l'éducation en France et en Grande-Bretagne du XVIe au XVIIIe siècle*, Les cours de Sorbonne, 2d fasc. (Paris [1975])

Paul Ourliac and Jehan de Malafosse, *Histoire du droit privé*, 3 vols. (Paris 1961–8)

R. B. Outhwaite, *Clandestine Marriage in England, 1500–1850* (London 1995)

Dorothy M. Owen, "White Annays and Others," in *Medieval Women*, Derek Baker, ed. (Oxford 1978), 331–46

Steven Ozment, *When Fathers Ruled: Family Life in Reformation Europe* (Cambridge, MA 1983)

Frederik Pedersen, *Marriage Disputes in Medieval England* (London 2000)
Romeo and Juliet of Stonegate: Marriage Litigation and the Ecclesiastical Courts in York in the Fourteenth Century, Ph.D. diss., University of Toronto (1992)
"Romeo and Juliet of Stonegate": A Medieval Marriage in Crisis, York Borthwick Institute, Borthwick Paper, 87 (York 1995)
René Pillorget, *La tige et le rameau: familles françaises et anglaises, XVIe-XVIIIe siècle* (Paris 1979)
Henri Platelle, "Épreuves et nouveaux départs (XIVe–XVe siècles)," in *Les Diocèses de Cambrai et de Lille*, Pierre Pierrard, ed., Histoire des diocèses de France, n.s. 8 (Paris 1978), 64–93
Frederick Pollock and F. W. Maitland, *The History of English Law Before the Time of Edward I*, 2d ed. reissue (Cambridge 1968)
Léon Pommeray, *L'officialité archidiaconale de Paris aux xve–xvie siècles*, thèse pour le doctorat en droit, Université de Paris (Paris 1933)
L. R. Poos, "The Heavy-Handed Marriage Counsellor: Regulating Marriage in Some Later-Medieval English Local Ecclesiastical-Court Jurisdictions," *American Journal of Legal History*, 39 (1995) 291–309
J. B. Post, "Sir Thomas West and the Statute of Rapes, 1382," *Bulletin of the Institute of Historical Research*, 53 (1980) 24–30
George L. Priest and Benjamin Klein, "The Selection of Disputes for Litigation," *Journal of Legal Studies*, 13 (1984) 1–55
J. S. Purvis, *The Archives of York Diocesan Registry*, St Anthony's Hall Publications, 2 (York 1952)
Geneviève Ribordy, *Faire les nopces: le mariage de la noblesse française, 1375–1475*, Studies and Texts, 146 (Toronto 2004)
Joel T. Rosenthal, "Fifteenth-Century Widows and Widowhood: Bereavement, Reintegration, and Life Choices," in *Wife and Widow*, 33–58
Antonia Sahaydachny, *De coniugio seruorum: A Study of the Legal Debate About the Marriage of Unfree Persons Among Decretists and Decretalists from* A.D. *1140–1215*, Ph.D. diss., Columbia University (1994)
Richard Saller, "European Family History and Roman Law," *Continuity and Change*, 6 (1991) 335–46
Jean Scammell, "Freedom and Marriage in Medieval England," *Economic History Review*, ser. 2, 27 (1974) 523–37
"Wife-rents and Merchet," *Economic History Review*, 29 (1976) 487–90
Christian Schwab, *Augsburger Offizialatsregister (1348–1352): Ein Dokument geistlicher Diözesangerichtsbarkeit: Edition und Untersuchung*, Forschungen zur kirchlichen Rechtsgeschichte und zum Kirchenrecht, 25 (Cologne 2001)
Eleanor M. Searle, "Freedom and Marriage in Medieval England: An Alternative Hypothesis," *Economic History Review*, 29 (1976) 482–6
"Seigneurial Control of Women's Marriage: The Antecedents and Function of Merchet in Medieval England," *Past and Present*, 82 (1979) 3–43
William G. Searle, "List of Deans, Priors and Monks of Christ Church Monastery," in *Christ Church Canterbury*, ed. *id.*, Cambridge Antiquarian Society Octavo Series, 34 (Cambridge 1902)
Silvana Seidel Menchi and Diego Quaglioni, eds., *Coniugi nemici: La separazione in Italia dal XII al XVIII secolo*, I processi matrimoniali degli archivi ecclesiastici italiani, 1; Annali dell'Istituto storico italo-germanico in Trento, Quaderni, 53 (Bologna 2000)

Matrimoni in Dubbio: Unioni controverse e nozze clandestine in Italia dal XIV al XVIII, id., 2; *id.*, 57 (Bologna 2001)

Trasgressioni: seduzione, concubinato, adulterio, bigamia (*XIV–XVIII secolo*), *id.*, 3; *id.*, 64 (Bologna 2004)

I tribunali del matrimonio (*secoli XV–XVIII*), *id.*, 4; *id.*, 68 (Bologna 2006)

Michael M. Sheehan, "Choice of Marriage Partner in the Middle Ages: The Development and Mode of Application of a Theory of Marriage," *Studies in Medieval and Renaissance History*, n.s. 1 (1978) 3–33; in *id., Marriage, Family, and Law*, 87–117.

"The Formation and Stability of Marriage in Fourteenth-Century England: Evidence of an Ely Register", *Mediaeval Studies*, 33 (1971) 228–63, in *id., Marriage, Family, and Law*, 38–76 (page references are to the latter)

"Marriage and Family in English Conciliar and Synodal Legislation," in *Essays in Honour of Anton Charles Pegis*, J. Reginald O'Donnell, ed. (Toronto 1974), 205–14; in Sheehan, *Marriage, Family, and Law*, 77–86

Marriage, Family, and Law in Medieval Europe: Collected Studies, James K. Farge, ed. (Toronto 1996)

"Marriage Theory and Practice in the Conciliar Legislation and Diocesan Statutes of Medieval England," *Mediaeval Studies*, 40 (1978) 408–60; in *id., Marriage, Family, and Law*, 118–76

Charles E. Smith, *Papal Enforcement of Some Medieval Marriage Laws* (Baton Rouge, LA 1940)

Richard M. Smith, "Geographical Diversity in the Resort to Marriage in Late Medieval Europe: Work, Reputation, and Unmarried Females in the Household Formation Systems of Northern and Southern Europe," in *Woman Is a Worthy Wight: Women in English Society c 1200–1500*, P. J. P. Goldberg, ed. (Wolfeboro Falls, NH 1992), repr. as *Women in Medieval English Society* (Stroud, Gloucs. 1997), 16–59

"Marriage Processes in the English Past," in *The World We Have Gained: Histories of Population and Social Structure*, Lloyd Bonfield, Richard M. Smith, and Keith Wrightson, eds. (Oxford 1986), 43–99

"Some Issues Concerning Families and Their Property in Rural England 1250–1800," in *Land, Kinship and Life-Cycle, id.*, ed., Cambridge Studies in Population, Economy and Society in Past Time, 1 (Cambridge 1984), 1–86

Peter Spufford, *Money and Its Use in Europe* (Cambridge 1988)

Doris Mary Stenton, *The English Woman in History* (London 1957)

Lawrence Stone, *The Family, Sex and Marriage in England, 1500–1800* (New York 1977)

Symposium, "Legal Systems and Family Systems: Jack Goody Revisited," *Continuity and Change*, 6 (1991) 293–374

Emily Z. Tabuteau, *Transfers of Property in Eleventh-Century Norman Law* (Chapel Hill, NC 1988)

Joan Thirsk, "The European Debate on Customs of Inheritance, 1500–1700," in *Family and Inheritance*, Jack Goody, Joan Thirsk, and E. P. Thompson, eds. (Cambridge 1976), 177–91

Juliette Turlan, "Recherches sur le mariage dans la pratique coutumière (XIIe–XVIe s.)," *Revue historique de droit français et étranger*, 35 (1957) 477–528

Richard Vaughan, *Philip the Good*, 2d ed. (Woodbridge 2002).

Monique Vleeschouwers-van Melkebeek, "Aperçu typologique des principales sortes de registres produits par l'officialité de Tournai au moyen âge, avec notes sur le registre de sentences de Bruxelles (1448–1459)," in *Bronnen voor de Geschiedenis van de Instellingen in België: Handelingen van het colloquium te Brussel, 15.–18.IV.1975*, Hugo de Schepper, ed. (Brussels 1977), 423–42

"Aspects du lien matrimonial dans le *Liber sentenciarum* de Bruxelles," *Tijdschrift voor Rechtsgeschiedenis*, 53 (1985) 43–97

"Eendrachtelic commen ende vriendelic vereffent: Boedelverdelingen voor de schepenen van de Keure van Gent tussen echtparen gescheiden van tafel en bed 1439–1450," *Handelingen van de Koninklijke Commissie voor de uitgave der Oude Wetten en Verordeningen van België*, 47 (forthcoming)

"Incestuous Marriages: Formal Rules and Social Practice in the Southern Burgundian Netherlands," in *Love, Marriage, and Family Ties in the Later Middle Ages*, Isabel Davis, Miriam Müller, and Sarah Rees Jones, eds., International Medieval Research, 11 (Turnhout 2003), 77–95

"Marital Breakdown Before the Consistory Courts of Brussels, Cambrai and Tournai: Judicial Separation *a mensa et thoro*," *Tijdschrift voor Rechtsgeschiedenis*, 72 (2004) 81–9

"Self-Divorce in Fifteenth-Century Flanders: The Consistory Court Accounts of the Diocese of Tournai, *Tijdschrift voor Rechtsgeschiedenis*, 68 (2000) 83–98

Sue Sheridan Walker, "Feudal Constraint and Free Consent in the Making of Marriages in Medieval England: Widows in the King's Gift," in Canadian Historical Association, *Historical Papers 1979* (Ottawa 1979), 97–110

Rudolf Weigand, *Die bedingte Eheschliessung im kanonischen Recht*, 2 vols., Münchener theologische Studien, Kanonistische Abteilung, 16, 39 (Munich 1969, 1980)

Glossen zum Dekret Gratians: Studien zu den frühen Glossen und Glossenkompositionen, Studia Gratiana, 25–6 (Roma 1991)

Liebe und Ehe im Mittelalter, Bibliotheca eruditorum, 7 (Goldbach 1993)

"Die Rechtsprechung des Regensburger Gerichts in Ehesachen unter besonderer Berücksichtung der bedingten Eheschliessung nach Gerichtsbüchern aus dem Ende des 15. Jahrhunderts," *Archiv für katholisches Kirchenrecht*, 107 (1968) 403–63, in *id., Liebe und Ehe*, 245*–305*

"Zur mittelalterlichen kirchlichen Ehegerichtsbarkeit," *Zeitschrift der Savigny-Stiftung für Rechtsgeschichte* (*Kanonistische Abteilung*), 98 (66) (1981) 213–47, in *id., Liebe und Ehe*, 307*–341*

Stephen White, *Custom, Kinship, and Gifts to Saints: The* Laudatio Parentum *in Western France, 1050–1150* (Chapel Hill, NC 1988)

Wife and Widow in Medieval England, Sue Sheridan Walker, ed. (Ann Arbor, MI 1993)

John Witte, *From Sacrament to Contract: Marriage, Religion, and Law in the Western Tradition* (Louisville, KY 1997)

Sybil Wolfram, *In-laws and Outlaws: Kinship and Marriage in England* (New York 1987)

Brian Woodcock, *Medieval Ecclesiastical Courts of the Diocese of Canterbury* (London 1952)

Richard M. Wunderli, *London Church Courts and Society on the Eve of the Reformation*, Speculum Anniversary Monographs, 7 (Cambridge, MA 1981)

Jean Yver, *Égalité entre héritiers et exclusion des enfants dotés* (Paris 1966)

Subject Index

This is a subject index of the printed text (not the footnotes or T&C). Persons and places are indexed selectively (names of judges and registrars, for example, but not parties to cases). A fuller index of persons and places and a table of authorities will be found in the e-book. Only the names of cases that are used as modal cases throughout the book (e.g., *Dolling c Smith*) are indexed here. A complete list of case names will be found in the e-book. Each of the five courts that are featured in this book has three main entries: The first gathers general entries about the court and its processes; the second, entries about legal aspects of the marriage cases heard by the court, and the third, entries about the social aspects of those cases. The general entries under 'marriage' follow a similar pattern and gather entries that deal with more than one court. Individual topics in these entries (e.g., 'crime, impediment of') are listed separately with cross-references. Cross-references internal to the main entry are in small caps. Cross-references are truncated to save space (hence, a cross-reference to 'general, business *under* York' will be found under 'York, consistory court of, in general, business of'. Main entries are quite strictly arranged by nouns (hence, 'presumptive marriage' is under 'marriage, presumptive'). The topic of witnesses and their depositions is indexed highly selectively. Witnesses are found in virtually all the English cases. They are not found in some of the Continental cases, but they are found sufficiently frequently that the best way to find them is to read through the chapters that concern those cases.